TRANSCENDENCE OF LOSS OVER THE LIFE SPAN

TRANSCENDENCE OF LOSS OVER THE LIFE SPAN

Patricia Weenolsen

Psychology Board of Studies
University of California
Santa Cruz, California

● **HEMISPHERE PUBLISHING CORPORATION**
A member of the Taylor & Francis Group

New York   Washington   Philadelphia   London

TRANSCENDENCE OF LOSS OVER THE LIFE SPAN

1 2 3 4 5 6 7 8 9 0   B C B C   8 9 8

This book was set in Times Roman by WorldComp. The editors were Linda A. Dziobek and Mary Prescott.

BookCrafters, Inc. was printer and binder.

Cover design by Sharon DePass.

Library of Congress Cataloging in Publication Data

Weenolsen, Patricia.
   Transcendence of loss over the life span/by Patricia Weenolsen.
    p.   cm.
   Bibliography: p.
   Includes index.
   1. Loss (Psychology). 2. Developmental psychology. 3. Meaning (Psychology). 4. Death—Psychological aspects. 5. Women—Psychology. I. Title.
   [DNLM: 1. Attitude to Death. 2. Life Change Events. 3. Women—Psychology. BF637.L53 W397t]
B575.D35W44 1988

ISBN 0-89116-736-6 (cloth)
ISBN 0-89116-582-7 (paper)

For those who, all unknowing, taught me pain
Without which so many others could not have taught me love.
Especially

> *Constance DuBois, psychologist*
> *Rosemary Thomas, poet*

For those who taught me growth—creating and letting go

> *My daughters Pamela, Valerie, Melissa, and Jennifer*
> *Anne Elizabeth*

And for him who taught me

> *M. Brewster Smith, professor*

Contents

Preface

At the window stands 6-year-old Marjorie in her pink tutu and dancing shoes, waiting for her father to return. But he was killed in an industrial accident a year ago under strange circumstances, and now another man has moved into the house, a man who kisses and touches her and makes her promise not to tell. Perhaps her dad will come to rescue her the way he used to when they played the game of "monster." So she keeps her vigil at the window, never leaving the house, not even to go to school. She no longer dances.

When Vera's alcoholic husband walked out on her, after she had devoted 30 years to him, she had a nervous breakdown. Still in love with him, even though he was now with someone else, she managed to pick up the pieces of her life and return to school and a business career. Now at 67 a severe eye disease threatens her with total blindness.

Janet's sudden losses of those dear to her—her parents when they divorced and placed her in a foster home, her 8-year-old son to leukemia, her 15-year-old a suicide, her husband who fell in love with her sister, a double loss—these have brought her to the brink of suicide, and she still experiences occasional fugue states. Her career and a richly rewarding love affair help her cope. But as we sit in her living room with the rain pattering on the roof, she hears her dead children moving about the house.

How are we to comfort Marjorie, now grown to womanhood but still with the little girl inside her, keeping vigil? What can we say to Vera to ease the loss of sight that threatens all she has recovered? If we encourage Janet in work and love, will the ghosts of her children eventually be laid to rest?

What can be the meaning of a life filled with loss and ending in death? This is the central problem of human existence. It has haunted humankind probably since we first became capable of the foreknowledge of death that distinguishes us from animals. Humans have defended against loss and death with philosophy, religion, love, and psychology. These are ways of making sense of the senseless. It makes no sense that we should be born, grow to beauty and skill, love and be loved, bring talent to fruition, only to be cut down in myriad ways. There must be a reason, if we could only find it. Either we are not cut down, that is, we do not really die, or we die for a purpose that, once understood, relieves us of a tragic sense. But will we ever know that purpose?

Many questions about loss pervade our thoughts. What *is* it that is lost when a child dies, a job is terminated, a debt is past due, or even when the biopsy is negative, the teenager graduates, the family is gathered for the holiday feast? We speak of having lost our self-respect, for example, when we are laid off, but in addition to this and salary what else is it that we lose? Does loss originate from outside ourselves or from within? Can we differentiate losses into types and, if so, are there different ways of overcoming them? Are some losses more typical of a certain age and stage than others? Do we ever completely transcend our losses, minor or major, or is there a sense in which we never get over them? Why is it that positive life events may actually be as stressful, implying loss, as negative events? Why do we seem to overreact to some minor losses and take more serious ones in stride, shake a fist at the bus speeding past us and shrug at a missed job opportunity? Why do we "cry with joy"—is it joy, really? Why is it that we can only describe the depth and extent of our love for one another in terms of its absence—"I'd give my life for you"—the ultimate loss? What is a blessing in disguise—a loss that brings with it the transcendence of some greater loss? Are there personality traits that we can cultivate to protect ourselves from loss—like being aggressive, nurturing others, deferring to others, or putting things in order—and *how* do these protect us? Are there patterns of loss in our lives—repetitions of the same losses, as well as the same ways of transcending them, over and over? When and how do these patterns start? Are we aware of them and can we turn this awareness to our advantage? Perhaps most important, how can we use answers to the forgoing questions to counsel others in overcoming loss, re-creating their lives and their selves, and becoming all that they can be, both for their own sakes and for the betterment of our community and world?

Seeking answers to these and other questions, and after a pilot study, I took the life histories of 48 women aged 25 to 67. I decided to investigate women in this first study partly because, as a woman, I am naturally interested in our experience but also because the field of life span development has a long history of either ignoring women or trying to apply male findings and theories to them, sometimes with appalling results. In recent years this situation has improved, and a number of fine studies have begun to elucidate the ways in which women's experiences converge with those of men and the ways in which they diverge. (These studies are reviewed in Chapter 1.)

The 48 women in my sample were equally distributed among three groups: married and employed, married and unemployed, and unmarried and employed. The women were randomly selected from an area in central California, although many had moved from another state or country. (See Chapter 1 for more details of the methods used.)

Studies of men, such as those of Levinson (1978) and Vaillant (1977), include such important constructs as the life structure and its revision, the dream, mentoring, various polarities, and the development of defense mechanisms. No doubt these constructs will be found to have valuable if variable applications for women as well, some of which will be similar to those for men and some different. The same must be true of the constructs in this book; those of loss, transcendence, loss and transcendence (L/T) life themes, and metaphorical systems should be of great value in describing the male experience. Indeed, this book includes materials from traditional studies of men as well as my own pilot work, counseling, and collegial experiences, and my next L/T research project will be a study of loss and transcendence in men. The theoretical constructs pertain to humans rather than men or women, but they must be studied in different populations. The results of my research, in the context of the traditional discipline of life span human development, suggest a new life span developmental paradigm based on the above constructs.

In this book I set forth the L/T paradigm, which spans a number of fields: psychology (development, thanatology, personality, and clinical), sociology, anthropology, biology, literature, and the arts. Where the paradigm connects with previous work, I provide brief literature reviews. Then I delineate the major L/T theoretical constructs as well as my empirical findings. In most chapters I include the life histories of a number of my interviewees, along with theoretical analyses within the L/T framework; these analyses reveal patterns of loss and transcendence in our lives and the impact they have on self-creation. The chapters conclude with elucidation and discussion of further theoretical as well as clinical applications.

Chapter 1 defines loss, transcendence, and other terms of the paradigm. It then describes the methods of study, including the sample, the interview form, other instruments used, and the procedures.

Chapter 2 explores the issue of loss, not only through death but also through experiences such as betrayal by loved ones, abuse, occupational incompetence, and ill health. Classifications of loss are suggested along a number of dimensions that emerge from the histories of Inez, Lorellen, Gwen, and Tess. An obvious loss has many ramifications of which we may not be aware, but which are the true sources of our feelings of bereavement. The metaphorical relationship of loss to death and its impact on the destruction and re-creation of the life and the self are set forth.

Chapter 3 deals with transcendence, or the myriad ways in which we overcome loss and re-create our lives and our selves in a more or less meaningful manner. There are three basic modes of transcendence, and there are degrees of transcendence as well; there are also stages in the loss and transcendence process that are analogous to stages of bereavement and recovery. The histories of Marjorie, Faith, Sue, and Della illustrate various modes of transcending losses.

In the first, second, and third chapters I begin to show how an individual pattern of loss and transcendence emerges in each life history. In Chapter 4 I explore this L/T life theme further with illustrations from the lives of Ronnie, Judith, and Kendall. An L/T life theme has an "expanded" version, which includes the major events and relationships contributing to the theme, and a "core" version, which summarizes in a few words the loss pattern versus the transcendence pattern. The histories show the great variety and uniqueness of the themes, the extent to which each person creates his or her own theme, the roots of the themes, their metaphorical relationship to life and death, and the degree of awareness or consciousness in people of their own themes.

As I have indicated, the L/T life themes are patterns of loss and transcendence over individual life cycles. When we examine them, we find that many minor losses in word, deed, or incident represent a few key losses in the individual's mind and that the key losses represent the death of the self. There is thus in each person's psyche a metaphorical relationship between death and individual losses. The same is true of transcendence and life. Thus, each individual has within his or her self a network of thoughts, events, relationships, feelings, responses, and behaviors that represent major losses and ultimate death. Other experiences represent the major transcendences and ultimate life, immortality, or rebirth. In this "metaphorical system" no event, relationship, or word stands merely for itself; rather it represents other events, relationships, or words and, ultimately, life or death. In Chapter 5 I trace the metaphorical systems in the life histories of Crista, Kara, and Annette and show how they operate.

We usually think of the self as a given. It *feels* immutable and whole. But the life histories teach that the self is in a continuous process of creation, birth, or emergence over the life span. Further, the histories reveal that there are types (and possibly stages) of the self; that the self may be less than it can be, unemerged or relatively unborn; that it can be submerged and living through another, alternative self; that it can be split rather than whole; and that it can emerge relatively integrated. Chapter 6 shows the relationship of the L/T life theme and the metaphorical system to the creation of the self, its origins, development, destruction, or enhancement. The lives of Lexie, Babs, and Sibyl help us to see how this happens.

Life and self meaning may be defined as a sense of purpose or a feeling of coherence; the purpose may be divine or human; the coherence is created by the individual. Chapter 7 delineates how meaning is created through the transcendence of loss. Four different types of life meaning emerge. The meaning of "meaning" and "meaninglessness" and the possible stages of the development of meaning are suggested in the lives of Patty, Alice, and Nora. One process of life meaning creation is the life review.

Certain losses and their symbolic equivalence to death can be traced from birth through infancy, childhood, adolescence, young adulthood, middle age, senescence, and dying. Certain modes of transcendence are appropriate to specific losses but are also typical of specific ages or stages. Chapter 8, the heart of the book, involves a reconceptualization of life span human development, employing traditional interpretations and empirical data, but within the L/T paradigm. It traces the development of a meaningful self and life through the transcendence of losses across the life span. The chapter concludes with the case history of Ursula, a truly remarkable woman in her fifties. A school dropout at eight, survivor of a number of abusive husbands, menial worker to support her children, Ursula longed throughout her life for an education to become a writer; then at 50 she discovered that her problem had been dyslexia, took classes to remedy this, and even won a local short story-writing contest!

At this point I begin to set forth wider applications of the L/T paradigm. Chapter 9 describes loss and transcendence in dyadic relationships (focusing on the problem of sexual jealousy), families, groups, and generations. Material from the lives of all the interviewees is synthesized to present a clear view, but the lives of Heather, Paula, and Melanie are highlighted.

Chapter 10 lays the foundation for a reconceptualization of personality, emotion, and psychopathology within the L/T paradigm. The histories of Vera, Frances, and Jaclyn assist us in our understanding of how pathologies develop, as well as how certain personality characteristics, emotions, and pathologies promote survival.

Chapter 11 begins a reinterpretation of society and culture in terms of loss and transcendence, with illustrations from the lives of Tori and Harriet.

Chapter 12, the concluding chapter, draws together major strands of the book, suggesting the roles of time and death in the creation of meaning. That time and death are foundational in our understanding of metaphorical systems, self-creation, and other L/T constructs is illustrated by the lives of Elaine and Em. This chapter evaluates the significance of the L/T paradigm for understanding and counseling others and for living our own lives.

We each experience life within the framework of the rules of interpretation that we have created. Adler called this framework the "spectacles" through which we see our world (Ansbacher & Ansbacher, 1959). Like the more tangible ones, these spectacles have prescription lenses, no two of which are exactly the same; and they tend to change for the individual as well as he grows older. If you lose your job tomorrow, you may interpret the loss as an opportunity to forge a new career from the hobby you have always

loved, a challenge, scary but exciting, that you think you can meet successfully because you have met such challenges well in the past. If your friend
loses his job, he may interpret it as another in a long series of rejections,
occupational and personal. The two interpretations of job loss (even presum-
ing similar financial assets and family responsibilities) may be dramatically
different, because from the interaction of different selves with different life
circumstances have emerged different rules or frameworks for interpreting
new experiences.

Natural scientists and social scientists wear Adlerian spectacles as
well. We seek to interpret the life experience through sets of rules devised
from observations of many individuals, ourselves included. The spectacles
through which the social scientist makes sense of life data are the theories
or paradigms of the time; they offer the most economical explanations
for the most data and they are "truth" for a while, until the times, the
culture, and the data change, making old paradigms obsolete and giving
rise to the new, as Kuhn has articulated (1962). Marris (1975) called these
paradigms the "fundamental metaphors" through which life data are interpreted.

Thus both individuals and scientists have spectacles or fundamental metaphors or paradigms by which they explain experience and make it meaningful. The paradigm set forth in this book, stated most economically, is that
individuals create meaningful lives and selves through the transcendence of
loss; that the creation of meaning through the transcendence of loss pervades
not only the life of the individual throughout the span of her development but
also her relationships to significant others as well as to groups, communities,
and generations; that personality and psychopathology can be reconceptual-
ized and illuminated within this framework; that the creation of meaning
through the transcendence of loss is a central function of both society and
culture; and that this entire process can be systematized on both a microscopic and a macroscopic level. This paradigm is of help in describing,
interpreting, explaining, and to some extent predicting life data, including
some data that were hitherto puzzling. The hope is that this fundamental
metaphor illuminates the human condition in new, revealing, consoling, and
revitalizing ways.

This work lays the foundation of a new theoretical framework for the
interpretation of human experience over the life span. It reconceptualizes
human experience in terms of loss and transcendence and demonstrates the
dialectic between loss and transcendence in terms of types, stages, processes, patterns, and themes. Although heavily dependent on the explications
of behaviorist, psychoanalytic, cognitive, and other major theoretical positions, the L/T paradigm is basically a humanistic-existential approach.

But it is humanistic existentialist with a difference. My training has been
in traditional psychological methods—random sampling, generalization, statistical analysis. I see the methods of the humanistic existentialists as the soft

underbelly of the school. The quantitative tells us what is out there, the qualitative tells us what it means. Both are valuable. Neither can be omitted when we are investigating the major life and death issues. I use both.

It is my hope that this book will be of value to psychologists, psychiatrists, educators, counselors, physicians, philosophers, social scientists, researchers, social workers, those in the helping professions, and all students of the human condition, whether they are formal undergraduate or graduate students or intelligent laypersons.

Most conscientious contemporary writers struggle with the use of gender-fair language, aware that human persons—their existence, dignity, and worth—are created by either recognizing them or ignoring them. The use of "she or he" is easy, and I use it especially when I want to be sure that both genders are understood. But repeated usage of "himself or herself" in a paragraph is cumbersome, distracting, and aesthetically displeasing, as is the messy mix of plural pronouns with singular nouns (i.e., a person feels attracted to others because they . . .). Simply referring to "individuals" guts the text of the humanity that this book seeks to vitalize. My solution is an increasingly popular and helpful one. I try to alternate male and female pronouns in large sections of prose, generally ignoring stereotypes. The exception is that, when I am already referring to a female, as in an account of motherhood, I choose a male child to avoid pronoun confusion, and when discussing fatherhood I speak of a female child.

In order to protect the identities of the interviewees, names and geographic allusions were changed; details that might be identifying were disguised, omitted, or made more general; a few occupations were replaced by similar but less readily identifiable ones; numbers and sexes of children and siblings were often changed, especially when they did not seem crucial to the history; and a few important incidents had to be omitted or generalized.

In these pages you will meet many brave women who have transcended or are transcending many losses. At some point you may want to go back and reread the story of the one for whom betrayal was a major issue. Or you may want to check all of those for whom rape or unemployment had a strong impact. There are two aids for you to do this. First, if you are looking for a specific case history that had certain characteristics like betrayal and healing (but you do not remember the interviewee's name), you can turn to the table of Loss and Transcendence Life Themes in Chapter 4. Second, if you are concerned with a specific issue, such as fantasy, marriage, loneliness, children, or religion, you may find it in the index, where I have also attempted to list the names of those interviewees for whom the topic has been a major issue. Some issues, like love, were of such major importance to virtually all the interviewees that I did not attempt to list them.

My gratitude to the interviewees is profound. They have opened to all of us their homes, their lives, and their selves, revealing the principles on which this work is based. I pass their insights and perceptions on to others in the hope and expectation that they will help us all in the challenging projects of living, teaching, understanding, healing, and guiding.

My editors, Kathleen Roach and Ron Wilder (acquisitions), Dr. Hannelore Wass (series editor), Linda A. Dziobek (production), and Mary Prescott (copy), have guided the book to its completion with extraordinary dedication and warm, cheerful wit to lighten darker days. I thank John Pickering, former editorial director of the Pennsylvania State University Press, who introduced me to Hemisphere.

Any contribution this work may make is a gift from the Psychology Department of the University of California at Santa Cruz as well as that entire institution. Drs. Elliot Aronson, Frank Barron, Craig Haney, David Harrington, Pavel Machotka, Wendy Martyna, Barry McLaughlin, Ted Sarbin, and Ms. Judy Tessier each encouraged various facets of the work's inception and inspired me by their own examples. The institution itself supported me financially, intellectually, emotionally, and spiritually for 5 years on a road not usually taken. For me, the University of California at Santa Cruz has made all the difference.

Splendid research assistants also contributed to this work, especially Gordon Gilbreath, Joni Lesser, Bruce Ruttenberg, and Genevieve Yandell. There are many who have shaped my development as a psychologist, including Drs. Rhoda Lindner and Ralph Hupka at California State University, Long Beach, and Drs. Mihalyi Csikszentmihalyi and Robert Kahn at the University of Chicago. Many, many colleagues and friends have inspired me with their courage, strength, and integrity, sustaining me both personally and professionally. Among them are Dr. Patricia Sullivan and Mr. Frank Mihm, as well as the undergraduate and graduate students who for some years have joined with me in various communities called "classes," where ideas generate, spark, and ignite.

Humbly I follow in the footsteps of some of the great thinkers of our time, who have so influenced me that I believe I write from them without knowing and therefore without citing. Foremost among these are Ernest Becker, R. D. Laing, Irving Yalom, Franz Kafka, G. A. Kelly, Jules Henry, Jean Piaget, Otto Rank, Alfred Adler, Karen Horney, and, of course, Sigmund Freud.

Finally, this work bears the imprints of many. However, both in the field of psychology and in the landscape of my life, Dr. M. Brewster Smith towers as mentor, guide, supporter, and friend.

Patricia Weenolsen

TRANSCENDENCE
OF LOSS
OVER THE LIFE SPAN

1

Methods of Study: A Beginning

In a life filled with loss and ending in death, how do we find the courage to go on? Make sense of the senseless? Create meaning from the meaningless? How is it that, for some people, losses are blessings in disguise, whereas for others they result in suicide? How can a series of losses that would stagger you and me leave some individuals stronger and more optimistic? How can a loss that you and I might take in stride be perceived as calamitous by someone else? And why do similar losses seem to befall the same person over and over?

It was to investigate the relationship of loss and life meaning that I began my study. But I was also motivated by another factor. As a life span developmental psychologist, I had noted how few, limited, and incomplete our life span theories were (i.e., Erikson, 1950; Vaillant, 1977; Levinson, 1978; Freud, 1953, reprinted 1985; Piaget, 1952, 1974); further, there was little mention of the humanistic-existential issues of meaning, loss, and death— the issues that I perceive as central to human development. Surely, these issues are manifested in our lives in different ways at different ages and under different social circumstances? Although the *meaning* of meaning is different for the 2-year-old, the 40-year-old, and the 70-year-old, its creation is still a central developmental task.

DEFINITIONS

My study began with difficulty. I had to define loss, and I had to define its opposite, whatever that was. I'd lived long enough to know that what is loss

1

to me might be gain to you. Let me jump ahead and borrow an example from one of this study's life histories. You and I would probably agree that your stolen wallet represents a loss. It had money in it; the credit cards must be replaced, which will necessitate a loss of time, and also boredom, which is a loss of stimulation. The wallet may have been given to you by a friend, so it carries some of that friendship with it, and in that sense you *feel* (quite irrationally) that your friendship has been violated. It may have contained pictures of loved ones, business cards, a pass to an art movie house, or a prediction from a fortune cookie. All of these are aspects of who you are; when they are taken from you, something of your *self* is taken as well. But, to one of my interviewees, 40-year-old Marjorie, her wallet was one of a number of things she'd lost in a small span of time. These "losses" represented to her signs that inauthentic aspects of her identity were dropping away, that she was letting go of the "garbage" in her life so that she could be free to become her better self. She responded by voluntarily giving up or "losing" other aspects of who she was, including her name. (See Marjorie's complete history in Chapter 3, "Transcendence.")

It was immediately apparent that I could not be the one to define the nature and extent of loss, except in very general terms. I could say that a loss is anything that took away from (killed) some aspect of an individual's life and/or self. That could be anything from a missed bus (or a stolen wallet) to the death of a loved one. My interviewees would have to be the ones to define loss specifically; loss would be what was loss to them, although undoubtedly there would be events, such as the death of a loved one, that would constitute loss for most people.

What was the reverse of loss? It wasn't simply gain. When one copes with a loss, or when a loss is merely threatened, one is not left unchanged. A biopsy may be negative, but the individual is no longer the same. Piaget's (1952) notions of assimilation and accommodation were helpful here. If a pebble is tossed into a lake, its influence is not simply at the point of impact. A loss and how it is met influence the entire life and self, minusculely, moderately, or greatly (a continuum). The word "transcendence" seemed to embody the notion I had in mind. When a loss is overcome, the life and self are consequently re-created. If the transcendence is great, the individual experiences the mystical sense of going beyond self commonly associated with the word "transcendence." But, in my view, transcendence also is a continuum, and we can go beyond who we are at any one moment, however slightly. A series of these "going beyonds" is development.

There was one other problem with the notion of transcendence, however, and that was the problem of projecting personal values on what constitutes it. For example, one interviewee's entire family has a marvelous time with alcohol; the experience is often transcendence (over daily losses) to them but would certainly give pause to someone who has suffered from the devastation of an alcoholic relative. Here again the interviewees would have to define what was transcendence for them.

The same was true of the word "meaning." The interviewees defined the word, as well as what was meaningful for them.

Thus, I define loss as anything that destroys some aspect of an individual's life and/or self and transcendence as the overcoming of loss and the re-creation of self and/or life. I define life as the external aspect of the individual, similar to Levinson's (1978) concept of "life structure," the individual's events and relationships; the self is the internal aspect (also structured), both process (I) and role manifestations (me's); one's life and one's self (obviously overlapping) constitute one's identity. (See Chapter 6, "The Self," for an elucidation of these concepts.)

With these definitions in mind, I derived "focused questions" on the model suggested by Sellitz, Jahoda, Deutsch, and Cook (1959) for "formulative studies." These were my guiding ideas or expectations, which I now reframe as proposals as follows: (1) Life is meaningful to the extent that we transcend loss; it is the transcendence of loss that makes life meaningful, because the life and self are re-created, reborn, resurrected. (2) Because life and self are the two aspects of our identity, a meaningful life results in a meaningful self and vice versa. (3) Life meaning is *created*, not *found* (in contradiction to the belief of Frankl, 1963). (4) Life span development is the continuous transcendence of loss; it occurs on a continuum, depending on the magnitude and measure of each loss and each transcendence. (5) Loss and transcendence result in a restructuring of one's life and one's self to a greater or lesser degree. (6) Individual lives can be described, explained, interpreted, and to some extent predicted in terms of the histories of individual loss and transcendence. (7) To the extent that loss and transcendence occur as part of systematic and predictable socialization, data on human growth and development can be systematized through understanding the loss, transcendence, and meaning involved. (8) Loss is metaphorical of death, and transcendence is metaphorical of life, rebirth, resurrection, or immortality. This is important because it means that we are in a continual life-and-death struggle. Each moment of our lives is filled with a loss or a transcendence of some kind, in a dynamic equilibrium analogous to Piaget's (1952) concept. That you are reading this at the moment means that you are probably not playing volleyball on a sunny beach in the Bahamas; you choose to re-create your self in *this* way, rather than another. (9) Findings with regard to the above proposals may be influenced by age and by marital and employment status; for example, more loss may be reported by married, or unemployed, or older individuals. (10) If we are indeed in a continuing metaphorical struggle between life and death, much can be explained that was heretofore mysterious in terms of emotions, relationships, personality, psychopathology, society, and culture. (11) Findings with regard to these proposals will therefore have implications for mental health professionals, who may help their clients to understand the "real" issues in a manifested problem in terms of life, death, and meaning, either actual or metaphorical.

From these central proposals, and from any relevant literature, I generated a number of subproposals, again derived from groups of focused questions (Sellitz et al., 1959), for different parts of the study. To prevent confusion, I will report these in the appropriate chapters. However, to give one example, in the area of loss and transcendence (L/T) life themes, I generated the following proposals: (1) Each of the life histories would exhibit a pattern of repeated losses and modes of transcendence, the L/T life theme. (2) There might be a number of subthemes, but there would be a single dominant theme, to which the subthemes would be related. (3) The individual would be aware of his or her themes. (4) The themes would originate either in childhood experiences or in adult ways of conceptualizing one's life.

It will be noted that there are many proposals; these form the constructs of the L/T theoretical paradigm.

LIFE SPAN STUDIES OF WOMEN—INFLUENCES ON IDENTITY DEVELOPMENT

Loss and transcendence occur in major relationships and events—in work, marriage, and parenthood, for example. It is through loss and transcendence in these events and relationships that identity develops. The role of women in our society has changed dramatically over the past 30 years. Huston-Stein and Higgins-Trenk (1978) pointed out that these changing roles have led to age *and* cohort differences in role choices—differences of considerable magnitude. The 30-year-old woman in 1950 had different attitudes toward employment and motherhood from the 30-year-old woman of today. The 50-year-old woman today has changed in her attitudes, partly because of her age but also partly because of historical changes. These differences are also a function of differences in employment and home experiences. Whereas the male has always expected that employment would be central to his life, the female may have started her life employed in a low-status job, stopped to have children, gone out to work as a result of economic pressures or divorce, postponed motherhood for a career, or balanced employment, wifehood, and motherhood in multiple roles that may be quite stressful (Baruch, Barnett, & Rivers, 1983); she may expect to work outside the home when her children are grown as well.

Thus, in studying the influences of loss and transcendence on identity creation, it seemed sensible to consider women with *various* trajectories at *various* ages, for example, to interview employed women of 20, 30, 40, 50, and 60, unemployed women of these ages, those who are married and those who are not. Ideally, one would further divide into groups with children and groups without, but here the design would be too complex for the small sample.

Current theories of human development have been taken to task eloquently for their inadequacy to the feminine perspective (Gilligan, 1977, 1979, 1982; Rossi, 1980; Belenky et al., 1986). Baruch et al. (1983) further believe that these theories largely ignore outside world events. Gilligan (1979) sees the theories of Freud, Erikson, Piaget, and Kohlberg as trying to "fashion women out of a masculine cloth" (p. 432) and perceiving women as deviant from the norm, which is masculine. According to this norm, healthy development consists of progression from attachment to autonomy, that is, of increasing individuation; the woman, who values affiliation, intimacy, and relating to others, often at the sacrifice of other aspects of her development, is at once conforming to societal (and masculine) expectations and demonstrating inferior development! She is then devalued for conforming to these expectations and devalued for any deviance from them (see Chesler, 1972). The expectations are coded in words like "nurturance," "responsibility," "caring," "warmth," and "helping." Outside employment for a woman may be sanctioned to a greater extent when it is part of her overall role as "nurturer."

But is there something inherently superior in autonomy and career over intimacy and caring? Rossi (1980) and Gilligan (1977, 1979, 1982) both point out that studies of men, such as those of Vaillant (1977) and Levinson (1978), show men themselves valuing intimacy more highly in their middle years, whereas women may move toward greater autonomy and assertiveness, partly because of economic pressures (see Cytrynbaum et al., 1980; Chiriboga & Thurnher, 1975). Men, after having spent the years from birth to 35 in relationships valued mainly as instrumental to career, success, and identity, may move toward affiliation. Are the men moving backward? Or is the implicit moral judgment that one path is superior to another unjustified? And to what extent is such development inborn, and to what extent imposed by the culture? It seems that, to the extent that it is imposed by the culture, the culture must be held accountable for any behavior it chooses to label as deviant!

Gilligan (1977) suggests that the masculine and feminine stereotypes "reflect a conception of adulthood that is out of balance, favoring the separateness of the individual self over its connection to others, and leaning more toward an autonomous life or work, than toward the interdependence of love and care" (p. 482).

An even more basic question, in my view, is whether or not separation and individuation are *de facto* at odds with intimacy. Does differentiation from the other necessarily mean one must be less related? Or is the capacity for intimacy heightened by individuation, there being so much more "other" to whom one can relate? Intimacy with one less individuated is more like intimacy with oneself, not necessarily a superior state. As we shall see, much of loss and transcendence is about separation and individuation, and the isolation that these can bring, versus unity with others that may result in a metaphorical return to the womb (see Yalom, 1981; Rank, 1929, reprinted 1973; Menaker, 1982).

The call of feminists and humanists is toward a life span theoretical approach broad enough to embrace the development of both genders with equal truth. (Another solution, of course, would be a separate developmental paradigm for each gender.) Rossi (1980) argues that the midlife search for self may be a cohort phenomenon rather than a developmental one, as current studies have concentrated on the cohorts born between the early 1920s and the early 1930s (our discipline is young!). Rather than being faced with issues of growing older and a sense of mortality, these study subjects may be caught in a cohort-particular "life cycle squeeze" born of large families as a postwar phenomenon, economic problems, the necessity for women to work, and higher educational expectations for their children.

Economic pressures, increased incidence of divorce, and the search for fulfillment urged on individuals by the human potential movement of the 1960s have all contributed to a dramatic increase in women's employment (Barnett & Baruch, 1978). In their excellent analysis of the sources of competence in women, Barnett and Baruch (1978) cite the conflicting literature on the effects of a woman's employment on her happiness, marriage, and children, but summarize the effects as being generally positive. "We do believe that it is very difficult for anyone restricted solely to the domestic sphere to develop a sense of competence, given the realities of our society" (p. 149). Women who remain inside the home are expected to develop vicariously, placing the development of others before their own, and the authors seem to intimate a possible difference in self-development that might be reflected in the life histories and themes of the present study. On the other hand, it is equally possible that, for some women, helping others to develop assists their own development and is not a sacrifice—that one may lose oneself to find oneself.

Scarf (1980) would disagree that this is a possibility. She interprets the preponderance of depressive syndromes in women as being the result of biological factors that make attachment a greater necessity for women than for men. Overlying these biological factors is the reality that women are defined in worth by the men in their lives. When society sets up losses for women, such as what Sontag (1972) terms "the humiliating process of sexual disqualification" as a woman ages, a woman is defined as worth less, and ultimately worthless, and the attachment bonds are disrupted, resulting in depression. Nolen-Hoeksma (1986), on the other hand, attributes the higher incidence of depression in women to a tendency to focus more intensely than men on their feelings (and so possibly their losses).

Baruch, Barnett, and Rivers (1983) cite evidence that work is central to a woman's sense of mastery, which, along with pleasure, they have found essential to her life satisfaction. Rubin (1979) also investigated "women of a certain age" (a translation from the French phrase for the older woman which implies that she is too old to tell her age but also that a kind of gallant mystique surrounds her, a sexual maturity comparable to vintage wine). Like Baruch et al., Rubin considers employment outside the home as more satisfying. In her interviews with women between the ages of 35 and 64, she found that the "empty nest" period was one of emergence, excitement, and anticipation as women returned to the work they had left many years before. During these women's years at home, their abilities and talents had not been taken seriously and, for many, the time out to raise their children had been a period of vocational, intellectual, and artistic "silence" (Olsen, 1978). The women emerge like butterflies, sexier than they have ever been (while their husbands grow less interested), fearful of failure, but still anxious to take last chances. Rubin finds in women a sense of loss if they give up their work, succumbing to marital, family, and community pressures, and a sense of guilt if they continue their work—another double bind!

But there is a mystery here. If an individual's identity is partly determined by his or her occupation, a woman may trade her identity as somebody's wife and somebody else's mother for a new identity as somebody's secretary, teacher, or physician; family may be exchanged for company, school, or hospital. Why is the sense of worth increased? Only because she is paid? Women are still owned and defined by their role relationships to someone else, as are men. The answer may lie in the value society sets on motherhood and wifehood as compared with the value it sets on occupations outside the home. Lip service is given to the value of motherhood and wifehood in lieu of pay, mainly by men.

The issue of life span development in different marital and employment statuses for women is ultimately one of comparative losses to self, the overcoming of these, and the re-creation of self. As Baruch et al. (1983) point out, there is no one pattern, no one "lifeprint." The L/T paradigm may shed some light on the process.

SAMPLE

After a 5-woman pilot study, 48 women, aged 25–67, were randomly sampled by telephone, using the local directory. The area covered by the directory was Santa Cruz and its vicinity, a central California coastal community with a high proportion of college students and retirees, at the outer edge of a large metropolitan area. Three marital-employment groups were investigated: married-employed (ME), married-unemployed (MU), and unmarried-employed (UE). All the women were white, with the exception of one who was East Indian.

Female respondents were asked if they would be willing to participate in a 3-hour interview on how women view their lives. If they agreed, preliminary information on age and marital-employment status was obtained and checked against an age by marital-employment grid to see if there was an opening. If there was, an appointment was made. The interviewees were not paid.

With regard to age, a decision was made to distribute the ages represented as evenly as possible over a section of the life span. To ensure this evenness, I decided to sample a limited number of women in each 5-year period so that

I would not end up with too many women at one end of the age spectrum. The final sample comprised 48 women, 6 in each of the following eight 5-year age groups: 25–29, 30–34, 35–39, 40–44, 45–49, 50–54, 55–59, and 60–64 (including one 67-year-old). In all, across age groups, there were 16 ME, 16 MU, and 16 UE. Further, of the six interviewees in each age group, two were ME, two were MU, and two were UE. The purpose of this distribution obviously was not to analyze such small cells but rather to ensure even age, occupational, and marital representation and to be able to easily collapse these cells for various analyses. For example, the 25–44 age group could be compared with the 45–64 age group along various dimensions without having a hidden weight of 30-year-old unmarried and employed persons; or MU, ME, and UE groups could be compared and contrasted.

Resource limitations prohibited interviewing women over a wider age span, which would have required a larger number of interviewees, just as they militated against interviewing both men and women in this particular study. However, the theoretical framework should apply across genders and ages, with some qualitative variations (e.g., the meaning of "meaning" to the young, or the losses incurred by men, or the whole range of male issues). I did not interview individuals in the fourth logical cell, those who are unmarried and unemployed, whose omission I also regret. I chose to eliminate this group, rather than one of the others, because I felt that unmarried, unemployed individuals might be less typical of the population as a whole.

Obviously, there are many limitations on the generalizability of the sample to the U.S. population. California is not the United States (despite some rumors to the contrary), and a college and retirement coastal community is not even California. The sample is too small not only for generalization but also for tests of magnitude of effects. However, the sample is legitimate for an exploratory study of a new theoretical approach, such as this (Sellitz et al., 1959), and is similar in size to Levinson's sample of 40 men (1978). Random sampling is never really random, as has often been noted. Many individuals refuse to take part. Others may not be listed in the telephone directory because they are new in town, on the run from creditors, famous, schizoid (not mutually exclusive conditions), cannot afford phones, prefer to be unlisted, etc.

Table 1 shows the age, marital status, employment status, religion, and socioeconomic status of the interviewees. For a more detailed description of the sample, see Appendix A.

I had not planned to code the frequency of child abuse and alcoholism, but the incidence was so salient and the experience reported to be so stressful that I decided to do so. Forty-four percent reported alcoholism as affecting their lives—for instance, fathers, mothers, siblings, more distant relatives, husbands, or children killed or injured by drunk drivers. This can be compared with expert estimates of the impact of alcoholism. Royce (1981) observed: "If each alcoholic affects the lives of 4 or 5 others—spouse, children, employer, employee, innocent victim of accident or other, then our 8.8 million alcoholics have an impact on 35–40 million others, for a total of about 50 million citizens" (p. 29). It appears that the rates for my interviewees may be a bit high, although they reported effects on many more than four or five lives.

A similar percentage—42 percent—reported physical abuse or violence as affecting their lives. Physical violence or abuse was defined as childhood punishment that did injury (not simply spanking); rape or molestation; and being knocked down, beaten, or thrown by the husband. In a discussion of the prevalence rates of child sexual abuse alone, Finkelhor (1986) points out that for females they range from 6 to 62 percent. This range can be attributed to the restrictiveness of definitions in some studies, the age range surveyed, the specificity of questions asked, whether questionnaires were self-administered or face to face, etc. However, when one studies Finkelhor's tables it becomes apparent that an estimate of one in three or four females being abused by age 18 is not unreasonable. This is confirmed by the Santa Clara County Child Abuse and Treatment Program (1980) and by Bass and Thornton (1983). A similar prevalence will appear in my interviewees' histories. That the addition of physical abuse brings the prevalence to 42 percent indicates that my sample is probably about average on this dimension.

INSTRUMENTS

The major instrument employed for this study was the L/T Life History, Form B (Appendix C). It was constructed along the conceptual framework described above and is detailed to a greater extent throughout the book. The L/T Life History was supplemented, insofar as events are concerned, by the Social Readjustment Rating Scale (Holmes & Masuda, 1974; Holmes & Rahe, 1967). Finally, the Myers-Briggs Type Indicator (Myers, 1962, 1977), a brief inventory of personality attributes, suggested by Jungian theory, was employed to determine the possible relationship of loss and transcendence to personality. A brief description and rationale of each instrument follows.

Loss and Transcendence Life History

The L/T Life History (see Weenolsen, 1977, 1981) includes a decade-by-decade life history and evaluation and questions about important people and events; losses and how they were handled; attitudes toward motherhood and occupation; decisions, regrets, hopes, disappointments, responsibility, and control; attitudes toward death and dying; support networks; feelings about age, gender, and health; paranormal experiences, secrets, and fantasies; and life review, life theme, and life meaning. The Templer Death Anxiety Scale (Templer, 1970; Templer & Ruff, 1971) was embedded to examine the relationship of loss to death anxiety. Several questions from the Shneidman *You*

TABLE 1 The sample[a]

Name	Age	Marital status	Employment status	Religion[b]	SES[c]
Lorellen	33	M	U	O	2
Crista	41	M	U	P	3
Marjorie	40	U	E	O	2
Lexie	30	M	U	P	2
Kara	31	U	E	N	2
Melanie	26	M	E	P	2
Nadine	64	M	U	P	2
Heather	36	M	E	C	2
Patty	32	M	E	N	2
Paula	28	U	E	J	2
Della	39	M	U	O	2
Robin	25	U	E	C	2
Theo	38	U	E	O	2
Ronnie	51	M	E	C	2
Gwen	55	U	E	O	3
Irene	53	M	U	P	3
Annette	65	M	U	P	1
Britt	38	M	E	C	3
Inez	40	U	E	P	3
Sissy	60	M	E	P	3
Denise	32	M	E	N	2
Kendall	33	U	E	J	1
Sibyl	61	M	E	O	3
Charyn	27	U	E	P	2
Frances	40	M	E	P	1
Sue	35	U	E	P	2
Winnie	25	M	U	P	2
Babs	44	M	E	P	2
Yves	45	M	E	P	2
Harriet	60	M	E	N	3
Opal	55	U	E	P	2
Greer	47	U	E	P	2
Faith	55	M	E	C	3
Nora	59	M	U	C	1
Vicki	42	M	U	P	2
Tess	25	M	U	P	1
Judith	50	M	E	P	3
Willa	46	M	U	P	3

Finally, in the assessment experience of the researcher, it seems to offer a very good thumbnail sketch or summary of what is revealed by other, much longer measures. It yields measures of several major aspects of personality: extraversion-introversion, thinking-feeling, sensing-intuition, and judging-perception. From combinations of these, 16 personality types may be derived, and they will be reported and evaluated in case histories, where pertinent.

Procedure

Employing the L/T Life History with the Templer and Shneidman questions embedded, the SRRS, and the MBTI, a pilot group of five interviews was conducted. From the results of these interviews, changes were made in the L/T Life History toward increased structure and in the SRRS toward a clearer format. Because time tended to exceed the 3-hour limit, I decided to ask interviewees to complete the SRRS and mail it in stamped addressed envelopes that were provided. In the main study, 39 of 48 interviewees returned the SRRS.

Interviewees were procured using random sampling of the local telephone directory. I conducted the interviews at the interviewee's home, my home, or the university offices, at the choice of the interviewee. I taped each interview and also took it down by hand, to increase the accuracy of the subsequent transcription.

HOW THE HISTORIES WERE ANALYZED

It is my firm conviction that data of studies such as this should be analyzed both quantitatively and qualitatively. The quantitative analysis tells what is out there; the qualitative analysis tells what it means. Without numerical data as a substrate, qualitative analysis can degenerate into mere unsubstantiated opinion, prone to the whim of any Adlerian pair of spectacles focused upon it. On the other hand, restriction to quantitative analysis can also restrict the questions that are asked and eliminate some of the most important ones.

Descriptions and results of both quantitative and qualitative analyses appear throughout this work. The protocols were rated on L/T life themes, or patterns of recurring loss and transcendence in individual lives; a description of this method appears in Chapter 4, "Loss and Transcendence Life Themes."

Undergraduate research assistants performed other rating tasks. For example, they rated the protocols on loss and transcendence orientation. These loss and transcendence ratings were based on the interviewee's account, not on the raters' judgment of how much loss or transcendence was involved. One woman's protocol might include a long monologue on her car breaking down, her dissatisfaction with how her relatives treat her, shopping problems, and so forth; this would be rated as high loss-oriented because negativity pervades the entire interview, even though the rater might not consider these losses very traumatic when compared with the death of a child, for example. Another interviewee might have sustained losses that were objectively more traumatic, such as the loss of a job, and not be rated as high loss if she did not seem to dwell on it, if it did not seem to represent a network of losses for her, or if she moved from a discussion of this loss to an account of how she transcended it. Thus, the rater was not in the position of having to weigh objectively the impact of the various losses, because *it was the reported impact on the interviewee, not how such a loss would affect the rater*, that was being assessed. The SRRS assisted with this assessment. Typically, one pole was very easy to rate and the second was more difficult. For example, it might be easy to say that this woman had endured a great deal of loss or that woman was highly transcendent, but the transcendence status of the first woman and the loss status of the second were more difficult to judge.

Other ratings were performed to place the protocol on a loss-transcendence dimension and to categorize it as to loss-transcendence stage. Solid reliability ratings in the .80's were achieved using all four methods of rating the protocols on loss and transcendence. For a description of these ratings and also of the interrater reliability studies, see Appendix B.

APPROACH TO THE LIFE HISTORIES

In recounting a life history, many choices must be made. The brief accounts in this book are distillations from histories that average 25,000 words each (plus the L/T Life History form and the other measures described above). Although I have had to *select* what to include and exclude, my selection is based mainly on the major events and relationships as reported by the interviewees. These events are considered major according to (1) their reported impact on the interviewees and (2) the amount of space and time devoted to them. For example, at age 40, Inez says little about her childhood, whereas Tess, at 25, says much, partly because she is so much nearer to it. (See Chapter 2, "Loss.") It is how the interviewees *construe* the facts, rather than the actual truth or falsity of the facts, that is important, because these constructions reflect how they feel they have lived and who they believe they are (see Kelly, 1955). Thus, this personal narrative approach emphasizes the life history as seen by the individual rather than a strictly objective account (Datan, Rodehzaver & Hughes, 1987).

There is a Catch-22 here. Does the paradigm arise from the data, or do the data arise from the paradigm? A psychoanalyst would show how the same facts of the case fit the psychoanalytic paradigm (Rat Man can be interpreted existentially!). A behaviorist would see these histories in terms of stimulus, response, and reinforcement and the other concepts of that school. These interpretations will assist us as well, but in the main we will see how the facts fit the existential (and humanistic) L/T paradigm, and how this paradigm assists us to describe, explain, and interpret the human experience in new and illuminating ways.

I tell the histories straightforwardly first, with almost no commentary. At the end of the history, I begin to point out the L/T life theme, stages, orientation, and any helpful evidence from the personality and life events inventories. Last, I give a brief theoretical analysis of the case within the L/T framework, with perspectives on clinical interventions.

For each chapter I have selected histories that best fit the concept being discussed and also illustrate a variety of aspects and issues. This selection was often *very* difficult. There were many histories that illustrated or elaborated on concepts of loss, for example. Aspects of *all* the histories have been related throughout the book, but only about half have been told. Had I more room, I would have told all—no history was without its despair, drama, dreams, and joys. All have much to teach about the transcendence of loss over the life span.

2

Loss

Although loss and death pervade our lives, there has been surprisingly little systematization or classification of these concepts. Perhaps our defense mechanisms have protected us from the study of loss as well as they often protect us from its experience! In this chapter I set forth a general classification of loss along a number of different dimensions. I define, describe, explain, and interpret a sample of losses from the almost infinite variety extant. The lived experiences of loss in four case histories illustrate this classification. I discuss various clinical perspectives on loss as they appear in the histories and conclude with a taxonomy of loss that should assist clinicians in their therapeutic endeavors.

DEFINITION OF LOSS

I define loss as anything that destroys some aspect, whether macroscopic or microscopic, of life and self. Loss is not change, but change incorporates both loss and its overcoming. Because there is change in our lives from moment to moment, there is loss as well, although we often do not recognize the loss until it reaches a certain threshold of significance. We do not notice the first leaf just beginning to yellow, but at some point enough leaves are yellow, red, russet, and falling for us to become aware of and acknowledge the change of season.

NATURE OF LOSS

We cannot speak simply of "loss" or "gain" because such terminology implies a mechanistic view of the individual as one who can be added to or subtracted from without affecting the whole, to whom an experience happens with no change in the rest of the life or self. Piaget (1952) saw that with every new piece of knowledge the entire cognitive structure is revised, because of changes in the relationships of the various parts to each other and to the whole. When a small stone is thrown into a lake, the waters ripple in ever-widening concentric circles. So it is with great and small events and their impact on our lives and selves.

Loss results in the death of one aspect of life and self and the consequent re-creation of other aspects. In the histories we shall see over and over how the interviewees feel they are being destroyed and re-created. The goal of the individual is to live more and more fully, to expand the self with ever more vitality and richness. At any one point in our lives, we are either expanding or shrinking, moving more toward life or toward death on a life-death continuum.

MAJOR VERSUS MINOR LOSS

We think of loss in terms of material objects or in terms of relationships. The death of a loved parent, spouse, or child is obviously a great loss. The theft of a purse, misplacement of an engagement ring, or destruction of the family photograph album in a fire are occasions of frustration, anxiety, or grief. Although there is considerable agreement that the loss of a child in a hit-and-run accident is a major one and the loss of an earring is relatively minor, two issues emerge from the histories. First, a seemingly minor loss, such as the theft of Marjorie's wallet, may be major to Marjorie because of what it represents to her, an aspect of her identity that is falling away. Second, it is obvious that the major-minor distinction is not dichotomous but rather on a continuum. The deaths of loved ones brought more anguish to some than to others, because of their meaning and how they were transcended.

The major losses that emerged from the life histories were the deaths of husbands and children; separation from loved others; losses of "self" or identity, communication, health, jobs, educational opportunities, or money; losses of children to handicap, adoption, or disapproved life styles; losses of time, trust, tradition, control, independence, freedom, security, status, or kindness; losses of competence, predictability, hopes, ideals, illusions, or self-confidence (very frequently reported). Other losses included abuse, alcoholism, criticism, environment, disillusionment, self-submergence, feelings of fragmentation, psychopathology, rape, abortion, accidents, instability, suicide attempts, both conventionality and unconventionality, family conflicts, perversion, sin, distance from others, frequent residential moves, bitterness, sarcasm, manipulation, negativity, domination, injustice, and handicap. In addition, there were all the losses that came with transcendence, of which more will be said later. Many of these losses will be explicated in the life histories.

In addition to these major life events with their heavy burden, even minor life events, the many small deaths of life, involve a loss that must be overcome in some way. Small incidents are often termed "meaningless"; actually, they are not, as from a multiplication of their number much of the life and self are forged. In fact, every event of our lives, from the minutest incident to the greatest experience, from a plucked blade of grass or a missed bus to the departure of a loved one on an inevitable journey, involves change, great or small. And every change involves some form of loss that must be overcome in some manner and that results in a re-creation of life and self, massive or minuscule.

Small losses affect us because they are metaphors of larger loss. When the car breaks down, it represents a loss of freedom, continuity, time, a boss's good temper perhaps, and even our own invulnerability.

PRIMARY VERSUS SECONDARY LOSS

There are losses that are secondary to the primary losses mentioned above. For example, an illness is a loss of good health but also of all the activities associated with good health—being able to play tennis, do the marketing, or even dress. Layoff from a job brings a whole train of additional losses in its wake, not only the loss of income but also losses of collegial companionship, health insurance, hope of accomplishment, self-esteem, novelty of daily events, a different environment, a sense of purpose, a structure for our time and for our lives, the activity that distracts us from our own mortality, the dreams our income might have purchased, perhaps a more tranquil family and home, faith in the future, and the gift of being able to give to children, friends, and charity.

These secondary or derivative losses are often more painful than the primary losses, but individuals are often unaware of them. Counselors, psychiatrists, and psychologists, however, trained in a specific loss such as unemployment, understand the anguish of secondary losses and must direct therapy toward their relief, and then the client believes he is working through the primary loss. Frequently there is much confusion between the primary and secondary aspects of a relationship or a job.

ACTUAL VERSUS THREATENED LOSS

The losses mentioned above were all sustained by at least one interviewee. However, perhaps the most frequent loss experienced was that of threat. (For a discussion of threat appraisal, see Lazarus, 1966.) A common misperception seems to be that, if an event is threatened but does not come to pass, no loss is involved. The individual wonders, "Everything is going to be okay. So why don't I feel better?" Of course, there are many losses, of safety, distraction, self-concept, feeling of invulnerability, etc. A biopsy may be negative, but the self is not the same afterward. There has been a death of some aspect of one's life and one's self.

INTERNAL VERSUS EXTERNAL LOSS

Losses may be "external," such as the loss of a material possession, a relationship, or an achievement, or "internal," such as loss of self-esteem. However, each external loss involves an internal one, some loss to the concept of the self as possessing that material object, and loss of the meaning it had for the self—for instance, of being loved (and lovable) or of being successful (and capable of success). Loss may also involve loss from the ideal, both from the *societal ideal* as set forth by our parents, our peers, and our institutions and from the *self-ideal*, or the picture we have of ourselves as conforming to the societal ideal. Thus, no loss is ever exclusively external or internal, exclusively a loss to life or a loss to self.

CHOSEN VERSUS IMPOSED LOSS

We tend to think of loss as something imposed on us, as when a car hits our child. But some losses may be chosen because they are ways of transcending other losses—the loss of weight, for example. As M. Brewster Smith has observed (personal communication, 1979), loss may also include "the outgrown, the forsaken, the self-renounced"; that is, loss is not necessarily what has been taken from us against our will but may be what we have given up in order to minimize or avoid other forms of loss. In this case, loss may be accompanied by satisfaction or euphoria rather than unhappiness. But even voluntary loss results in an inevitable restructuring of the life and self.

The chosen-versus-imposed polarity is more ambiguous than it appears at the outset. First, many losses that appear to be externally imposed have elements of choice in them. We will see that Tess *chose* the jobs from which she was subsequently laid off. Was this choice deliberate at some level? Second, a loss may be externally imposed, but we can *choose* our response to it, as humanists and existentialists have emphasized (May, Angel, & Ellenberger, 1958; Fromm, 1967; Yalom, 1981). One interviewee, Faith, had all kinds of obstacles to the development of her artistic talent; she chose responses that would transcend these obstacles (see Chapter 3, "Transcendence"). Jaclyn chooses indecision and vegetation as responses to her environment (see Chapter 10, on personality and psychopathology).

DIRECT VERSUS INDIRECT LOSS

A loss may happen directly to us, or indirectly through another person. That which hurts the child very often anguishes the parent, whether it is a bone marrow transplant or being beaten up at school. In this sense, the more we love, the more we open ourselves to loss. But love is a form of transcendence, pervading the other forms, as we shall see, and it is in a dialectical relationship with loss. Often it is true that the less we lose, the less we transcend!

TIMING OF LOSS

Time is the dimension on which we measure the various types of loss and their effects (in line with the formulation of Neugarten, 1968). These types of loss include:

1. *On-time* loss, or the age by stage developmental losses. These include such normative life events as starting school, graduating, looking for work, getting married, having a baby. They are life events that are *expected* at a certain time, but the losses associated with them often come as a surprise—losses of friends, freedom, structure, predictability, etc. They may have a less devastating impact on the individual than other types of loss because their transcendence may be rehearsed and have sociocultural supports. (A full account of on-time, life span losses and their transcendence appears in Chapter 8, on individual development.)
2. *Off-time* loss includes losses that are inevitable but are commonly associated with a certain stage in life and occur at an earlier or later stage, such as the loss of a daughter to leukemia in her adolescence, or of a parent in childhood or beyond middle age, or of a job just short of pension eligibility. Off-time losses tend to be more destructive than on-time ones, as evidenced by the research of Parkes (1972) showing that the rate of death among young women significantly increases following untimely bereavement. I believe that one reason for the traumatic effect of off-time losses is that they compel us to question the predictability of on-time losses.
3. *Time-irrelevant* loss, which may be common or uncommon but is nevertheless unexpected, such as accident, natural disaster, economic recession, abortion, rape, or onset of a rare disease. Many such losses are time-irrelevant in that they may or may not occur at any time during a person's life and they have little or no specificity for a particular developmental period.

Very often, a life event is expected at a certain age but does not happen. The student does not graduate, the young man is rejected by several women and does not marry at 23, the young woman tries to build a career in her early twenties but is fired from job after job (see Tess's story later in this chapter). A double loss is involved here. The individual is not "on time" with the expected life event, is "off time," late, and knows it. She loses both the life events and the expectation of them. But she also loses the experience in transcending on-time losses, experience that would help her later. Tess does not learn to deal with the many problems in a job, with a boss, co-workers, and customers, to increase her competence. One can lose a job at any time throughout life, and in that sense job losses are time-irrelevant. But one expects to have a job at the outset, so the loss is a loss of being on time, making it off time as well as time-irrelevant—there are elements of all three types of loss in such a situation.

On-time, off-time, and time-irrelevant losses all ultimately lead to a revision of how the individual measures and conceives of future time and the length and quality of his or her life. (See Chapter 12, "Time and Death.")

MEANING OF LOSS

The meaning of loss differs according to the developmental stage in which it occurs. For example, to a 22-year-old woman the (off-time) loss of a breast may mean restriction of (on-time) mating possibilities; to a 70-year-old woman it may mean another in a constellation of losses moving her toward (on-time) death. Other losses are far less obvious but include the day-by-day, minute-by-minute losses implicit in some forms of socialization, as seen in education, for example. (See Chapter 8, "Individual Development.") To Lorellen, rape and abortion represented the loss of her babies and what they meant to her, continued evolution. We will see that the individual develops an entire network of repeated losses that symbolize not only each other but also death. (See Chapter 5, "Metaphorical Systems.")

THE METAPHORICAL LIFE-AND-DEATH STRUGGLE

The ultimate loss is, of course, the loss of life and therefore the loss of self, or death (see Weenolsen, 1986b). Death is the ultimate meaninglessness because it cannot be overcome and leads to no re-creation. Both insignificant and major losses foreshadow the ultimate. If we can somehow create meaningfulness by transcending the smaller losses, or deaths of life and self, we may be able to create some meaningfulness from the ultimate loss. In other words, loss and death are metaphorically related, loss being a smaller death of self and life. Analogously, the overcoming of loss and subsequent creation of meaning is metaphorically related to the overcoming of death by the creation of ultimate meaningfulness or immortality or rebirth. Each loss we endure is a metaphor of death that diminishes the meaning of life, and each transcendence of loss enriches the meaning of life. In death, therefore, it is the loss of meaning that we fear.

Because our lives are a dialectic between loss and overcoming, we are in a continuous metaphorical life-and-death struggle. Self and life meaningfulness are created by overcoming loss in some fashion to a greater or lesser degree and consequently reinterpreting and re-creating life and self. It is through the transcendence of loss that we create a life and self that are more or less meaningful, because loss and transcendence are metaphors of death and continuing.

Smaller losses require similar although less extensive re-creation and may be mourned. We will see numerous examples of this in the life histories to follow. The *Book of common prayer* (p. 332) reminds us: "In the midst of life we are in death," not simply because the seeds of our physical decline are already sown within us but also, as I interpret it, because we are continuously experiencing the smaller deaths of life. Death is not simply something that happens to us at the end of life. We are always ending and beginning, dying and experiencing rebirth, either gradually or traumatically.

THE FUNDAMENTAL ILLUSION

The fundamental illusion is that there is no death metaphorically and therefore actually. Endings always seem to take people by surprise. They believe that their intentions to be faithful, or to continue on some path, constitute a guarantee, all that is needed. They think that their feelings, negative or positive, will never change.

The fundamental illusion is that there will be no loss requiring transcendence. The fundamental illusion is that changelessness is possible. We see this in interview after interview, especially in the loss-oriented, to such a degree that this fundamental illusion and its betrayal may be the factor most salient in the experience of loss. Paula expects "total love and devotion" that will last forever (Chapter 9). Lorellen believes that the beautiful, safe-appearing locale will remain that way from moment to moment—even though others have not—so that rape could never intrude. For many interviewees, it is the *shock* of the unexpected, of divorce and death, that is traumatic, not simply the incident. Shock in those who experience off-time loss events, such as the woman who is widowed at 30, is to be expected. But many are shocked at events that are on time or time-irrelevant. Disappointments of motherhood arise because the children change, moving farther and farther from the ideal.

This fundamental illusion cuts both ways: not only can positive conditions not change, marriage, children, and health; but also negative conditions cannot change, restrictions, dangers, maltreatment, and betrayal. Those we loved have restricted, abused, and betrayed us in the past, so others will in the future. Believing that what is negative cannot change—a kind of "negative faith"—blocks positive possibilities. Some defend themselves against loss by trying to "expect the worst, and you'll never be disappointed"; their expectation is that they can predict the shape of change, which is simply a corollary to the fundamental illusion—the belief that loss is predictable, not only its event but also its feelings, its impact.

The most disastrous consequence of the fundamental illusion is the inability to let go—of people, past events, prized possessions, self-concepts, and the shape and form of things and relationships. (See Chapter 12, "Time and Death.")

In some sense, all losses involve the loss of illusion, in that the relationship, possession, or achievement did not endure, as we felt it would; it is difficult to conceive of a scratch on the cabinet we have so lovingly refinished, or to imagine just what form the deterioration of an externally committed relationship will take. There are many other manifestations of the fundamental illusion: the world will always be fair; our hard work will be rewarded accordingly; good will triumph; we have always won wars, so we will win this one.

LIFE HISTORIES

An analysis of the L/T life histories will provide illustrations of the above concepts, suggest others, and expand our understanding of the nature and process of loss. The following four histories are loss oriented; they stress the losses endured and say little about overcoming and re-creation. This was the choice of the interviewees, and we do not make judgments as to whether there actually is more loss in these lives than in those recounted in the chapter on transcendence, for example. The losses are as the interviewees experienced them, not as we would experience them.

While quite successful in her career, Inez has endured losses in her personal relationships, both at work and in love, spanning a period of over 20 years. Her losses have been mainly direct, on time, or off time, and externally imposed when we do not consider her responses. Betrayed by men both as lovers and as career supervisors, Inez will need to learn to trust again. We will see the main roots of repeated loss in her teenage years and the roots of transcendence at the age of 3.

Inez

". . . and he was with somebody else."

Inez is a very beautiful physician on the staff of a large hospital in a major city. In her early forties, she appears younger.

Inez grew up in an East Indian country as part of an extended family. Her mother successfully combined motherhood and a traditionally female career where "she always seemed to find herself." Her father loved detail work and was "broad and expansive, artistic and compassionate." Their marriage was a stable one, although Inez spent many of her years in a boarding school. Her grandfather was authoritarian, her grandmother organized and a woman who "could have happily run anybody's life in the house [laughter]." Her aunt also was rigid, authoritarian, but loving.

Inez had a number of diarrheal illnesses as a child, for which she was hospitalized and from which she nearly died. She particularly remembers "a lady doctor who used to look after me, and one day when she was crossing the road she was run over by a car and died, and I know I really fretted for her a lot." Another thing she remembers was "coming off the anesthesia before they were through with the surgery, and it was horrible. I could remember it for years and years and years. You can feel everything that's happening, and they're just holding you down."

When asked if she feels she changed much during her childhood, Inez attests to a belief: "I don't think you change, I think you evolve . . . so I have problems with the semantics."

Inez describes her adolescence as fairly good, with the one exception of an authority battle between her grandmother and herself. "When you're in college, after having made your own decisions all your life, to suddenly go home and be forced into being a little child is very difficult. . . . She didn't like me being in charge of myself, and I didn't like her being in charge of myself [laughs]."

Asked when she decided to become a physician, Inez responds, "When I was three and I got sick. I had two loves, medicine and biology, and I always thought I could be a doctor, and for all my hobbies I could do biological things, like catch butterflies and study birds."

While in medical school, Inez fell in love with a man who proposed to her through her parents. They were together in a nonsexual relationship for about 7 years. His parents were pressuring her to marry, but she wanted to finish medical school first. They were also pressuring for a dowry, "which meant money, and I felt that my profession was a dowry, and I wasn't going to ask my parents for anything. . . . Here I was able to earn a living."

Her fiancé was "extremely brilliant, extremely talented. We had a lot in common . . . he was older . . . and he was my best friend. We studied a lot together, practically all our dating time was studying. . . . If he had an exam he'd say, 'bone up on such and such a topic,' and I would make notes on it, even though I didn't quite understand it. I'm pretty good at outlining, picking up what's important, and I would have it for him and go over it with him. . . . And we shared a lot of hobbies. We did a lot of hiking. . . . I think my main motivation for finishing med school was so I could get married to him. I was really in love with him."

But there were problems between them. "He got very very jealous, because I was gregarious and would speak to people, spend time with them. I remember once I was invited to dinner by one of the boys in class, and I accepted, and he got furious at me, and I said: 'Look, I have my whole life to spend with you, and I want to do that, and he only asked me for one evening because he wants to talk to me, and that's the least I can do for him. I'll come back after dinner.' So he was very possessive and jealous."

Her best friend was much more the "traditional woman. And I was like a radical. She seemed to be very quiet, she would never speak in front of men. If I had an opinion, I'd give it . . . so she seemed to represent more the femininity that he wanted, whereas I was more of an equal. And he began getting very possessive, forbidding me to have anything to do with my cousins, not letting me sit next to people who were not women, and on one occasion . . . it was at night, and on my way home I was walking through a lot of back lanes, and he beat me up 'cause he was so jealous and so angry, so that made me very frightened. But at that time I kept thinking, he's so ridiculous, when he marries me he'll know I'm a virgin."

During this time he was secretly dating her best friend. "She never once told me that she was going out with my boyfriend. She's very close and secretive. Obviously it wasn't a good friendship. She had asked him not to tell me either, and one night I had to go downstairs [in the dormitory] to mail a letter, it was almost midnight, and I heard his voice, and they were talking, and I didn't think anything about it . . . so I just went back to my room. . . . I was so naive and so full of trust. And then I began thinking something has changed. What am I missing? And so I started really getting depressed."

She finally confronted him, thinking all the while that the problem was with his parents, and he told her he was marrying her best friend. She barely passed her exams. The whole experience was "very traumatic." He had to justify his breakup with her to his relatives, so he gave as his excuse that Inez was promiscuous, ruining her reputation and making her unmarriageable in her community. Inez handled this by working hard, but also lost weight and got an ulcer. Later he tried to win her back, but as this did not include a proposal of marriage, she did not go for it (he didn't end up marrying her girlfriend, either). Inez had been part of a triangle without even realizing it.

In her twenties, during a rotation on pediatrics that she loved, Inez decided that she wanted to be a pediatric surgeon. In order to get away from her unhappy past, she came to the United States, but found that it was difficult for women to get into surgery. "I feel that I'm in a system that has a lot of economic inequities," as well as sexual ones. "Pediatricians are about the lowest paid doctors, and we're specialists."

For Inez, the thirties were "traumatic because when you change countries, you change centuries." She had to restart as an intern and encountered a great deal of prejudice. "I worked for a boss who was very unsympathetic and a bully. . . . He liked men to be very docile and women to be very aggressive in his sense of aggressiveness. He had no place for a woman who could be soft or gentle and get things done. I mean, there wasn't that category in his mind. And he bullied me in front of all the students." He asked her the most common form of a disease, and when she responded with the most common form in *her* country, he ridiculed her. But she came from a culture where elders were revered, so she accepted the abuse and always showed politeness. She was also accustomed to cooperation rather than the competition she found in the United States.

A fellow resident helped Inez with her problems; they began dating, but the expectation of sex came as a shock to her, and he raped her. Even more traumatic was the fact that he lied to her about living with another woman. For the next few years he promised to marry her, and she was once again part of a romantic triangle. She got pregnant by him, and he promised that they'd have a baby later but insisted that she get an abortion. This was against her religion, but she did it. Part of her reason was knowing that she could not return home pregnant or with a child and that the chief who ridiculed her would kick her out.

She moved to another country to finish her residency, and this boyfriend, like her first one, tried to get her back to no avail. There was still another man "who was charismatic. He ran after me. And the same thing happened with him. Oh, yes, he was going to marry me, but there was one condition; he wouldn't marry me unless he had sex with me. By this time I had a very low self-image." She was afraid people thought she was a whore and considers that their relationship constituted mental rape, because he had at least a dozen other women on the side and finally told her he was marrying a previous girlfriend.

At last Inez met another man, a returning college student, with whom she had an enjoyable courtship and whom she married. But, for reasons she still cannot fathom, he suddenly stopped talking to her. He visited her family abroad and came back in culture shock, telling her he didn't want to stay married, that he needed his own space. "And I walked into the bedroom once, and he was with somebody else. . . . He told me he'd been living with her for four months." He would have left sooner, but Inez was fired from her job for reasons "99% due to racism" and he stayed with her a little longer. Meanwhile, she was pregnant but lost the baby because of all the stress. "I always say I lost my pregnancy, my husband and my job all at the same time." She picked up scab jobs to tide them over, while she tried to get him to go to counseling, feeling "rejected sexually" because her husband was involved with 20-year-olds. "And you think you are seen as a body, and I'm a body *and* a mind, and he's just negated that part of me, which I find is the most important part. . . . My body's just the place my mind lives in. Now I see he didn't reject me, he just hasn't come to terms with himself." He promised to let her know before he divorced her, but one day she went to work and her hospital colleagues expressed their sympathy. They'd read about it in the local paper!

Inez is helped by a network of friends, most important of whom is her former mother-in-law, with whom she has a close friendship. They know the same songs, pick the same television programs, and have the same tastes and thoughts. Her friends warn her that if she keeps hanging around her mother-in-law she'll never find anyone else, but the bars her friends suggest aren't for her.

Inez sees both good and bad in her recent development. She feels that in the United States she has had to adjust to a more industrial, mechanical view of the individual, that she is not important. On the other hand, "I finally learned that basically I was a caring person. . . . The reason I had gotten into these situations was part naiveté, and just the fact that it wasn't my culture. It wouldn't happen to you in [my country]"—a curious bit of reasoning, as her first triangular relationship with its elements of betrayal happened in her country. Attributing her troubles to the alien culture perhaps mitigates her responsibility.

More recently, Inez's losses have escalated. A close relative was lost to death, and a friend, with whom she and her mother-in-law had a kind of strange but happy family, committed suicide. A big section of her family disowned her because she is now a divorced woman. She is gradually getting over the guilt. "For a long time I went through a lot of guilt, thinking: 'Oh, if I'd only cooked more dinners, maybe if I'd kept the house neater'," her husband would have stayed. But "if I'd done everything right, then he'd have found other reasons to leave. 'Cause when you want to leave that badly, you leave. And I just can't afford to feel guilty about this any more. And it's been hard, very hard, because when I see him I still have that love for him. And our conversation is so flippant and light and without content that it hurts."

Inez reveals her metaphorical system quite openly when, speaking of the fact that she would be tempted to get involved with someone like her husband again, she says, "I have to realize that meeting the same kind of person doesn't mean I'm meeting him again." And yet, might she not respond to him in similar ways, possibly eliciting similar behavior and seeing similar behavior where none existed? Or is there a certain kind of person who promises and betrays, to whom she is attracted?

She does believe in Karma: "I don't think you can go through life hurting people and never have any of that come back to you." She feels that it is technology that makes one afraid of death in our society and that women are partly responsible for the sexism and racism.

Her way of handling these recent losses has been to get "depressed, practically suicidal, because I felt so worthless. I had counseling, did a lot of reading, and because my finances were so terrible I had to put in a few extra hours of work. I don't think work has ever been an escape, but at least there was a time when I wasn't thinking only of myself." Indeed, her best experiences have been saving the lives of critically ill babies in the nursery. She tells of recently running into the mother of a baby whose life she saved, and whom everyone else thought would not live. The baby is flourishing— this is a high point for her.

Betrayal, broken promises, jealousy, humiliation in front of others, and some problems with authority figures pervade Inez's life and history. These are transcended to some extent by the satisfactions she gains in being a physician. Her expanded L/T theme, therefore, would be betrayal by others, especially men in triangular relationships, but also by friends, career supervisor, rapists, different cultural values; transcended by service in the form of healing others. The core theme is betrayal versus healing.

On her Social Readjustment Rating Scale, Inez tended to rate everything as moderately or extremely stressful. Nothing was rated below 40, and many events were rated at 80, 90, or 100 (an error in following instructions). This illustrates the extent to which some individuals may simply perceive everything as more stressful than other individuals do, either chronically or because they are in a difficult life period. Chronic perception may be due to an especially hard life or to lifelong depression; it may be a personality trait. Inez's loss-oriented protocol is rated as demonstrating high loss, low transcendence. (See Appendix B for an explanation of the ratings.) She is seen as being in the grieving stage of the L/T process. (See Chapter 3, "Transcendence," for L/T stages.)

Theoretical analysis

The story of Inez is pervaded by broken promises and betrayal. There is a pattern of triangular relationships, the first of which occurred when she was in medical school and her best friend was dating her fiancé over an extended period. Her career supervisor bullied and shamed her in front of her colleagues (betraying her ignorance and culture?). A fellow resident helped her with her problems and raped her while he was living with another woman. The next lover "mentally" raped her; he said he was going to marry her and make her a mother, while in reality he was dating a dozen other women at the same time. Her husband betrayed her with younger women. Part of her family has disowned her because of divorce—a kind of betrayal.

The betrayal goes well beyond the sexual sphere; there often seems to be an element of cruelty, perhaps even sadism. Her medical school boyfriend spread the rumor that she was promiscuous—apparently to save himself rather than to injure her. Her best friend never told her; indeed, there is often lying in her history, and over extended periods. The medical chief's ridicule seems cruel through Inez's eyes. Her first American boyfriend insisted on abortion, promising later children. Her husband slept with his girlfriend in her bed and divorced her without warning her first as he had promised; the notice appeared in the papers. He did postpone the divorce so that she could get over the loss of her job.

Broken promises also run through Inez's history as part of the betrayal motif—divorce notification, marriage, another child. Jealousy is frequent as well, and when an individual is jealous, it is because she or he fears betrayal (sexual jealousy is discussed at length in Chapter 9, on relationships). There is some difficulty in relating to authority figures (the grandmother, the medical chief), and some of the quarrels with her men friends seem to have been over issues concerning dominance and submission (the proper role for females?). Her ex-husband, of a lower socioeconomic status than herself (which she claims did not matter), treated her as a body without a mind. She assisted her first fiancé in preparing for his exams, a peculiar inversion of her superiority or a channeling of it into an acceptable outlet. Some men resented her independence, so revenge may have been a motive. Women's issues are never far from the surface.

Finally, there is a thread of public humiliation and loss of esteem throughout Inez's history. There is the proper way for a woman to behave, and there is her way. The public, the community, the family (hers and others) are very much a "third person" in her relationships, almost a Greek chorus, whose judgment and re-creation of her self can be swayed by others: her fiancé could tell them she was promiscuous and they believed; others could tell them she was divorced, and they disowned; the medical chief could tell her colleagues she was incompetent, and that became their judgment to some extent; her ex-husband could publicize their divorce without her knowledge—her colleagues would inform her. Neither her own culture nor the alien one is hospitable. They are rife with sexism and/or racism, prejudice against who and what she is. Her warm relationship with her mother-in-law is metaphorically the final acceptance by her first fiancé's family.

Inez handles her losses with counseling, reading, and extra work but also with depression, suicidal feelings, and illness, further causing loss to her self. A behavioristic psychologist might see her childhood experiences with illness as positive reinforcement or reward for this method of handling loss; illness resulted in good childhood experiences of hospital and medical care the second and third times. When one is in psychic pain, one can convert into the physical to be cured, the psychodynamic psychologist would add. Thus one can transcend psychic loss by metaphorizing it, and Inez has had reinforcement for this process. This may be the root of her choice of her major transcendence method, which is the healing of pain in others. When Inez heals others, she re-creates a self who heals rather than one who experiences injury. In healing others, she experiences healing, and this heals her self as well.

But more important, she may be creating new losses as metaphors of the old, so that the healing of new losses will become the healing of the old. One must ask why she persisted in trust; one must ask if she heard promises where only suggestions existed.

Underlying the issues of betrayal, promises, and jealousy is the issue of trust. Erikson (1950) believed that trust versus mistrust is the first psychosocial crisis the infant must negotiate from birth to the age of 1. At this age the infant must depend on others for his life; how the others care for him, whether in a loving and predictable manner or unkindly and capriciously, will determine whether he develops into someone who is basically trusting (of others with his life in the L/T view) or who cannot trust, who in the worst case may even become paranoid. Nor can the human successfully negotiate succeeding stages if this first one is not well resolved. To this conceptualization may be added the basic personality dispositions with which the child is born (e.g., see the New York Longitudinal Study of Thomas & Chess, 1977); I would also emphasize the importance of survival, the creation of self or its destruction, the metaphorical system and its roots.

From Inez's history we have no indication of the quality of her infancy. What knowledge we have of her caretakers seems to be positive. They were authoritarian and loving. The first instance of betrayal in her story occurs when she is in her late teens and early twenties. Yet illness may be thought of as betrayal by the body that the caretaker preserves—the body cannot be trusted, it lets us down—and she was ill quite often at an early age. Further, it was not the omnipotence of the parents that saved her but rather that of the physicians. They had the omnipotence her parents had, and later they also betrayed her. Authority and power are issues for Inez—she has become her own parent as the powerful one who saves children. She cannot be betrayed again.

Social learning psychologists might explain Inez's desire to be a physician as a modeling response; others in her family were in medicine. Although this probably contributed to her decision, it does not stand alone without the behaviorist, psychodynamic, and L/T explanations.

Ultimately, if I make a promise to you, it is not simply a statement of a certain act I will perform in the future. It is a statement that I will help you to create your self, to become more alive, more of your self than you now are, that I will make of you a wife and all that implies, make of you a mother, make of you a physician. Just as threat also constitutes loss, promise constitutes transcendence—you begin to become who you will be. Then, if I break my promise, that growing part of you is killed off like the new branch of a plant. You react with shock, yearning, and grieving—the first stage of the L/T process.

Betrayal is a metaphor of death; it is death in perhaps one of its worst forms. We know that the death of a child is possibly the most difficult loss to bear. Betrayal is the death of the child in us, that which is just coming into being, the new and potential, the hope, the bud. Betrayal invalidates the personal myth, the vital experience; it says you did not experience your life the way you thought you did. And the betrayals of Inez were long. When Inez's fiancé betrayed her, he told her that all she thought she was—loved by him, loved by her best friend, respected by his family and their community—did not exist and never had. When asked if there is anything without which life would be meaningless to her, Inez replies (with many of us), "Love." Inez is repeatedly being told not only that she is not loved but that when she thought she was, she was not. Inez had begun growing in a certain direction where she thought love was, and death was there instead. This happened numerous times. Part of her was killed off, and the myth had to be revised extensively. We see this revision in her life history. Betrayal kills—this is the meaning of Jesus' betrayal by Judas; it is betrayal unto death. Lovelessness is meaninglessness and no integration is possible.

Inez's metaphorical system must include metaphors of betrayals, jealousy, trust, promise. Her world view, how she sees people and interprets their actions, must be in these terms. "I have to see that meeting the same *kind* of person doesn't mean I'm meeting *him* again." Can she experience any man without reference to those who have gone before? Why does she persist in trusting the untrustworthy? Does she seek out the untrustworthy, or does she create them? I believe she is still trying to create the untrustworthy as people whom she can trust, a manifestation of the fundamental illusion. She is still trying to become trusting. Medicine does this. Her patients must trust her with their lives, and when they do she can trust her self with their lives as well as her own. If she was not trusting, considering her history, she would be extremely paranoid; and indeed this form of repeating losses to overcome them may be a defense against paranoia, just as paranoia would be a defense against repeating these losses! (Some therapists might not believe her story at face value and might simply label her paranoid.) The L/T clinician would need to help her work this through, building trust in herself by making her medically trustworthy, so that parents trust her to save their children. When she fails, the trust issue must be recognized.

Finally, death is the figure to whom one must submit. In overcoming death every day, Inez does not submit, does not betray, and keeps the promises of parents to their children and of children to their parents—the promises of life.

The second life history is that of Lorellen, a woman who underwent a number of time-irrelevant traumas, direct and externally imposed, although some were chosen. Her greatest fear is of indirect loss; the baby she carries may be endangered. She seeks to overcome and re-create through spiritual healing and expansion.

Lorellen

> *"And I believe that through prayer you get in touch with a divine part of yourself and energy in the universe. I do have a spiritual nature, but I don't believe in any dogma."*

The above sentences of Lorellen's life history suggest the balance between high loss and high transcendence through spirituality that characterizes her life and our assessment of it. A dark, petite woman in her early thirties, married and unemployed, pregnant with the first child she was to keep, she sat with me in front of a blazing fire, her hands conveying to me the intensity of her various experiences.

Her parents were the opposite of each other in many ways, her mother a "stable" woman who worked hard both in the home and out of it, while her father was more rebellious, bohemian, and unconventional. "Nature was his god, and his home was where he liked to worship." One of her happiest memories was going to the country with her father several times (an adventure in travel that she attempted to reproduce as a young adult, with disastrous results). Her other major early memory was of injuring herself.

"I was about two. I put my hand in an electric heater, and I burnt my little finger and my ring finger. As I grew up, I didn't get much medical care for that. The tissue in my fingers didn't grow, but the bones did. So my fingers were curved. Later on, when I was sixteen, I had plastic surgery that took skin from the side of my abdomen and put it into my fingers so that they could be straight. I feel in some subtle way that it affects me as a person. On an energy level I feel that these are possibly cuts in my energy. According to polarity, these two fingers are water and earth. Water controls reproduction, and earth is elimination. . . . I've had this problem with my pregnancy, and it just seems that this might be related."

Their home burned to the ground, her parents were divorced, she also accidentally caused injury to another, the guilt for which remained with her. Her father started going downhill, drinking and becoming careless about his personal habits. This was during her adolescence, a time when she struggled to be popular, and she felt a serious lack of counseling and guidance in sexual matters from her mother.

Unconventionality characterized Lorellen's friends, as it had her father, especially her best friend, who was a kind of arty beatnik. Lorellen began experimenting with sex. She had not formed life goals yet. She painted and dreamed of love, became politically active and agnostic.

Lorellen's twenties began with a serious love affair, love-ins, peace marches, and drugs.

"The first time for that was like being in a jeweled city. It was at night, and the street lights looked like strings of pearls along the road. Someone was playing the piano, and at the same time I was watching someone pour wine. It seemed to me that the wine being poured out was like the music being poured out. There was like—like all is one somehow."

This quotation expresses well the nature not only of her consciousness expansion with drugs but also of her expansion through other experiences.

Lorellen's breakup with her boyfriend was followed by a series of unhappy relationships, communes, friends busted for drugs, material possessions ripped off, activism, and a lot of physical violence, including several rapes and abortions, each of which "undermined my health, both physical and emotional." Two of the rapes took place on beaches—one in Hawaii, the other in the Caribbean—as she sought solitude for growth and consciousness expansion. In both cases her assailant appeared "from nowhere." Indeed "I remember that the twenties were very unhappy for me. These experiences, the loss of love and being raped, kept piling tragedy on tragedy. I'm amazed that I didn't crack up earlier than I did." But during this time, she was also moving toward a profession in the holistic health field and greater spiritual awareness, as well as longing for more stability in her life.

She met her present husband, who "wasn't everything I'd been looking for, but he was someone." He was stable, supportive, wanted children, and is a good person. She had, in the meantime, developed a successful career doing body work and counseling with women.

When I interviewed Lorellen, she was pregnant. Because of her spiritual beliefs, she feared that the various traumas sustained by her body, particularly the abortions, might have disrupted her energy fields and might pose a health threat to the baby; there was already a threat of complications, which worried her. To Lorellen, pregnancy was metaphorical of more than the evolution of one human. By affecting one person deeply, she feels she will influence the evolution of the culture.

Lorellen wants to have her baby, love and be loved, write a book about her professional work, thereby alleviating the pain around her, and continue her spiritual evolution. For her, the meaning of life is "evolution—personal, social and spiritual." It is love that makes life worth living, and since she has had so much loss of love, one can see that she must struggle to create that meaning. Death for her is "an ascending into light—sort of a diffuse energy, but with positive feelings. I don't see it as annihilation." At the end of her life "I would like to be an authority, and somebody who is really looked up to in terms of how to live, how to be healed—to heal the planet, to heal the individual lives."

As to Lorellen's L/T life theme, on the one hand is the loss of love, the house where she was raised, the unity of her parents, her father as he had been, her lovers, her own physical integrity, aborted infants, and ideals. Much of the loss was through sudden violence done to her person—rapes, abortions, and abusive lovers who beat and strangled her. On the other hand is transcendence, expressed in her travel to beautiful places, her increasing search for spiritual evolution, and her attempts to bring this to women through holistic mind and body work, teaching that the body is indeed the temple of the soul. Ironically, it was in her travels, searching for consciousness expansion, that much of the physical violence was sustained; in her account, there seems to have been a battle between expansion and violence. She expresses the fear that the violence done to her may have taken too heavy a toll. Her energy fields may be permanently damaged; the greatest expression of love (for her) may be denied; her baby may not survive. While her life history was highly loss oriented, her spiritual practices and convictions, through love of nature, holistic healing, and philosophy, were very strong—whether strong enough to finally overcome, one cannot tell.

The L/T theme, then, is one of loss of stable love through physical violence (rapes, abortions, beatings) versus transcendence through natural beauty, physical and spiritual evolution, healing, and beliefs. The core theme is injury from physical violence versus spiritual evolution through healing. Both poles of this theme are associated with the conflict between the dominant culture and the counterculture, which has been the backdrop of her life, beginning with her father and mother. Lorellen sees her theme in quite a similar manner. She says, "I see it as a lot of tragedy. I want to reprogram my life so that I'm being fulfilled."

She seems to be deliberately reaching for stability, a compromise between the two poles of her L/T theme. She has married a man with whom she can build a stable life—"by the time I met him, I was at the end of my rope." She fell in love with her head, not her heart. Stability is the operant word here, in reaction to all her losses and in recognition that the transcendent spiritual has perhaps not been enough. It is a compromise; one senses that she is bruised and needs to recoup. Is the damage permanent? Can it be overcome? She believes she can "create a positive life," but she isn't sure. She is clearly acting in the context of or in reaction to the losses that have gone before.

A secondary theme, then, might be the gypsy or bohemian life (her father, friends, and counterculture) versus the stable life (her mother) in which she is now engaged, but this theme seems to be embedded in the first one. The two aspects of herself are her mother and father, perhaps roots of conflict. The theme is further expressed in her sentence completions. She says: I have lost "my heart," and life is like a "coevolution."

Lorellen's Myers-Briggs Type Indicator (Myers, 1962, 1977) confirms her sociability and responsiveness to other people's feelings. As one might expect, she rated her idiosyncratic or time-irrelevant life events, particularly the rapes and abortions, as far more stressful than the more normative, on-time ones (such as love affairs and marriage). Her methods of transcendence would be classified as *general*, mainly, with the striving toward stability and reprogramming seen as a *situational* effort. (See Chapter 2, "Transcendence.") Interestingly, she sees her life theme in terms of the loss pole—tragedy—while she sees her life meaning in terms of the transcendence pole—spiritual development.

Lorellen is in the searching (second) stage of the loss and transcendence process, moving toward replacing (the third stage) much loss with the stability of husband, baby, house, family, holistic healing, a book, and creativity. Much may depend on the survival and health of her baby, because this means so much to her metaphorically, and there is still a great deal of integration to be done. Gradually, her concept of self may alter in this direction as well. She is re-creating her self by re-creating her life.

Theoretical analysis

In summary, Lorellen reports an unusual number of major traumatic loss events with many instances of violence resulting in physical injury. According to her metaphorical system, physical injury results in, and therefore represents, spiritual injury. Traces of physical injury remain and may threaten additional harm to her unborn child, whose loss would block her own spiritual evolution. There is thus a continuum of physical to spiritual ingrained in how she perceives the world, her spectacles.

Lorellen's L/T life theme seems to be rooted in the stability-unconventionality dichotomy between her mother and father. Thus her mother and father were aspects of herself in conflict with each other. The father in her leads her to unconventionality, travel, disaster (rapes and abortions), and consciousness expansion. The mother in her is leading her to salvation through stability with its possible accompanying constriction. It is a Laingian split (Laing, 1976) that has brought her often to the edge. At present she says of her father, "I don't wish to disown him," and indeed that would be to disown that aspect of herself. Yet she cannot tolerate what he has become, "sloppy . . . dirty . . . his hair is filthy . . . alcoholic"—what she might become.

As we will see in a later chapter, the infant cannot distinguish between self and other. The infant *is* the parent, and this is the real source of identification, rather than the later introjection of parental values as Freud believed (1923, reprinted 1961). Separation and individuation take place but the child is always partly parent, and the split between parents, which may be small or great, as in Lorellen's case, will be reflected as fragmentation in the adult child to a lesser or greater degree. Lorellen's story shows the conflict between these two aspects embodied.

Lorellen cannot refer to one rape without comparing it to the others, or to one abortion or to her pregnancy without referring to the damage abortion has done, as well as other physical damage she has sustained. Thus, the losses that Lorellen has endured are metaphorical of each other—their event, her responses, their significance to her. There is an entire unique metaphorical system here. (See Chapter 5, "Metaphorical Systems," for an explication of this concept.)

Losses have not been fully transcended, which is perhaps the reason for their recurrence. This issue is addressed more fully in the chapter on L/T life themes, but it may be suggested here that if the first rape was not worked through, enduring it again (metaphorically) and again was a way of reexperiencing it in order to work it through. This brings us to the issue of responsibility, which will be discussed later; suffice it to say that even if Lorellen bears some responsibility for her *reactions* to rape, the rapists are entirely responsible for *committing* rape.

Lorellen's life losses had led her to "the end of my rope" when she met her husband and embarked on her present course of stability. These losses may still lead to the destruction of her child, who represents physical and spiritual evolution. Loss as destruction and a form of death and transcendence as birth and immortality are thus metaphorically related in her history.

Finally, it is important to point out that Lorellen's father, an aspect of herself, is losing his life through alcoholism. Many of Lorellen's glorious highs have been similarly on drugs. He negates her experience, and perhaps it is this which is intolerable to her.

Clinically, if Lorellen gives birth to a healthy child, she may tend to blame herself for each subsequent illness or other problem the child has. She will be attributing the vicissitudes of life to the conflict she has not yet resolved. She must guard against this. If the child is dead, Lorellen's cure may lie in finding other ways of giving birth metaphorically, perhaps through assisting others or through one of the arts.

Lorellen tells her life so that it makes sense to her and to us. This is the meaning it has for her. These are the incidents she raises to salience to make a coherent story or myth, and these are the interpretations she gives to those incidents. We have no way of knowing what did not fit and was thus left out; we can only guess that the omitted is also thematic.

Our third loss-oriented life history is that of Gwen, a woman who endured an extraordinary amount of major time-irrelevant, externally imposed, direct and indirect loss.

Gwen

"God, I just wanted someone to give me a touch."

Gwen is a solidly built widow in her mid-fifties. As she leads us through her house, my assistant and I note that there are keys in the locks of all the doors. Gwen reviews her unusual life with a kind of clipped wit.

Gwen's mother was 16 when she married. "I'm not sure she's ever grown," with a laugh. Her mother was "childish, self-centered" with a "cruel streak if she didn't get her way," which she showed by "beating me. Constantly telling you how ugly you were, and how stupid you were. And yet, now that I'm older and talk to her, I realize that a lot of it couldn't be helped. I was terrified of her for years. I'd absolutely panic. She used to dump me wherever she could dump me. . . . And I was always the oddball. Wherever I was dumped people knew I was just dumped. And you always got to be told." In fact, Gwen insisted on taking the surname of another, kindlier relative because she did not want to be part of her parents' lives.

As for her father, he "never meant to be cruel. He was neat. I wish he'd had a little more backbone. But he was very kind to people, very gregarious, very open, a hard worker." Gwen recollects many of these kindnesses. Her parents owned a rooming house in New York City. One night a woman came banging on their door, crying "I've killed him! I've killed him!" "And my father went downstairs and I trotted after him. This woman was living with this guy, which in those days was terrible. He was a monster. She'd finally shoved a knife in his chest. He was lying on the floor . . . saying to my father 'help me.' And my father said: 'I'm not going to help you unless you say *you* did it, you bastard'." The man finally agreed, and her father called the police and put the man's hands on the knife to substitute his fingerprints for the woman's.

Other instances of her father's kindness occurred when the welfare people came around to check on the boarders. "The poor people—I think they got about $10. You weren't allowed to have a radio; that was a sign of affluence. And if you couldn't cook in your room, I think you got an extra $2 or $2.50 a month. My father used to allow them to cook. These were old converted brownstones, and they had the old gas lights. He knew about the time of the month that they would come to check, so we'd keep the front door locked. My father had the gift of gab. So when they'd come—and they were mostly harridans that had those jobs—my father'd be keeping them at the front door. 'Oh, you look lovely, lassie. I bet this job is terrible on you.' Meantime, I'd get the nod and go running through the house telling people to hide their stoves. And they'd be allowed to get that extra $2.50 per month to be able to eat." It seems reasonable to speculate that both the examples of kindness on her father's part and her own ability to be effective in implementing them had a healthy impact on Gwen's growth and helped to strengthen her sense of self—much needed for the traumas she was to endure.

One other instance of caring and kindness shows the character of Gwen's father. "One particular room had eight or nine old ladies. And they were terrified of thunder and lightning. Now, my father would make believe, when the thunderstorm came, that the light wasn't working in the hall. All that had happened was that he had unscrewed the bulb. And he'd get up there and fiddle with that light for half an hour, forty minutes, kidding around with them, telling them how pretty they were, how he'd missed them, until the storm was over. Then he'd tighten the bulb up and it would be fixed. But he never ever said this was what he was doing."

Gwen's mother was as cruel as her father was kind, and her father was weak in his relationship to her. Her mother beat Gwen unmercifully. "You'd go to school black and blue, and I'd lie. I'd say I got into a fight or whatever. I didn't want anybody to know. Because I was ashamed. Because I didn't know anybody else who acted that way. . . . It was confusing because there wasn't anybody to talk to. And the few times that I did confide in someone, it went right back to my mother, and I got a double beating. And things got a lot tougher than that. Like 11 o'clock at night I'd be told: 'Get out. We don't want you around.' I never had to knock on a door that wouldn't open. . . . Nobody ever made me go into a long explanation. I'd just stand there, and they'd say: 'Come in.' I don't often think about these things any more."

"God, I just wanted someone to give me a touch," she says of her childhood. So she "tried to hide away from life" until she was about eight, when she began asserting herself and became a brat. However, she particularly remembers the kindness of the Jews in another neighborhood. "I was the only shiksa in about 44 blocks. I got tremendous kindness from the Jewish people. So I felt Jewish, and I acted Jewish because I felt that way. I got in with these Irish Catholic kids, and they almost made hamburger meat out of me."

The rooming house into which they had moved brought her face to face with many stark realities. "In those days, people lived in rooms that were no wider than from that wall to here, and lived out their whole lives in it. They got like $10 a month. There were no centers, or any place for them to go. They'd use the public toilet down the hall. And I always remember—it affected me and my mother a lot, which is now why I tolerate her more than I would normally—you would see a whole person's life—they would die in these rooming houses. You would call the Health Department. They'd come with green plastic bags, and zip the body into it. And they'd take a brown paper bag and take out the few little things they had. I can remember—that's an emotional thing [tears], just seeing their whole life go into a paper bag." Gwen clearly cares about the issue of human worth in these childhood experiences, and they remain with her today.

One of the places Gwen's mother dumped her was with a married couple whom she loved very much until her early teens, when the man "began tickling me in weird ways. I knew something was wrong, but I couldn't tell what. In those days you weren't as smart as the kids today. So I finally went to my mother, and my mother went to the wife. Of course I got called all kinds of names, like liar. It was pretty traumatic for me, because I didn't understand."

A related traumatic incident took place in Gwen's mid-teens. Her parents had separated, her mother didn't want her, and Gwen was working and living in a furnished room, when her mother insisted that she go to a physician for an examination. "Then he gave me a pelvic exam which just terrified me, because I really knew nothing. I heard him pick up the phone, and he was angry. He said: 'Damn it, this girl IS a virgin.' And I realized what she had told him. I could have died. I hadn't even kissed a boy yet, much less messed around. I was just mortified. God, the stories she would tell people about my father and I. Oh yes, she told people my father and I were having relationships together. . . . It's just that she has a very wicked heart." Gwen feels that her mother's problems started in her own childhood, because Gwen's grandmother has told of being threatened with a knife by Gwen's mother and being terrified.

Gwen met her first husband, who was in military service, while she was working in her mid-teens. She became pregnant and had very little food to eat, "a can of soup a day." His parents, who were European, had been writing her lovely letters and, thinking that at last she would have a family, she went to Europe, only to find that they resented her. When just a toddler, her second child was hit by a car and underwent a tremendous personality change. After much difficulty, in which her mother played a part, Gwen and her children were able to return to the United States.

A major problem with Gwen's first marriage was the penuriousness of her husband. Gwen had to sneak $5.00 from her own pay to buy a child a pair of shoes. She and her husband broke up when she was about 30. The reason? "My fault. I grew and he didn't." She grew because of the identity both he and her job gave her. "He was devastated. He always wanted a mummy to clean and cook. . . . I still feel guilty." She could no longer stand him physically.

After the divorce, Gwen "ran into" a man who had been "stealing" her parking place at her apartment house, and he became her second husband. They were very much in love, although he was considerably older. He seems to have been the opposite of her father: macho, commanding respect, very much in charge. With her first husband still trying to win her back and using their children to influence her, Gwen had her second husband's child. Shortly before this, however, "I tried to commit suicide" because of the pressure exerted by her husband and ex-husband, "both pulling and pushing, until I just couldn't take it any more." She came close to dying. "I was over the top and saw the body. I saw them tying the string on my toe. I heard the nurse saying: 'That was a young one, wasn't she?' And then a voice said: 'It's your choice. Do you want to go back, or do you want to stay?' I remember thinking: 'Do I want to stay?' And it was so funny, because I felt: 'Should I go, or should I stay?' I thought: 'I'll go back.' And with that the pain came."

Her first son by her second marriage was also hit by a car during toddlerhood, and he died of his injuries. At this point Gwen found herself able to walk away from the "guilt trips" her mother and first husband were "laying on" her.

Her second husband raised her self-esteem, telling her how intelligent she was. Gwen contrasts him with her first husband, of whom she says, "He gave me a sense of identity, a feeling of being wanted . . . for the first time in my life I enjoyed going home." But "he was demanding. He didn't consider me a whole person. I was just a female. . . . My mother used to look at me and say: 'What are you thinking in that rotten head of yours?' [My first husband] looked at me and said: 'What are you thinking in your head?' And so I really was convinced there was something nuts wrong with me. And it was so neat when I met [my second husband]. He knew what I was thinking before I thought it. I didn't even have to complete the thought. He knew it. And I thought: 'I'm not weird.' It was just like a whole freedom. It was great!"

Gwen had finished high school in her twenties, and her second husband encouraged her to go to college in her thirties. By this time, though, he had become seriously ill. His sister had died of a genetically transmitted disease. Gwen often wonders whether this was what her husband really had and whether it might affect her two youngest children. However, she believes that negative thoughts bring illness and tries to avoid them.

As Gwen finished college, in her forties, her husband was going downhill. "Being able to have someone who I was so thrilled with, and that I could look up to as a man—seeing someone that you really love go downhill. Seeing him standing at a telephone sobbing, saying: 'I don't know how to use a telephone.' Or waking up in the middle of the night and him not there, and looking all over for him, and finding him out in the pouring rain on the back porch, looking through the railing, and not knowing how to come back upstairs. Or he'd turn on the water and just stand there; he didn't know how to turn it off, and flooded the house." Nor would he take his medication, for fear of becoming impotent and losing Gwen.

Meanwhile, Gwen's children were leaving home. She now feels aloof from most of them, although close to two who stood by during her husband's illness and death. When she finally had to put him in a nursing home, she felt very guilty. In discussing her reasons for this, she says, "I want to die; I guess most people do," but not in a nursing home.

Two weeks after her husband died, Gwen had a "visitation" from him. "I didn't know what time he had died. He came and told me it was so many minutes after six. He came to me—his spirit. I saw him, I felt him, and I spoke to him. And I wasn't a bit afraid." She describes him as a light that appeared to her, touched her on the shoulder, and woke her up. "And he said: 'What you told me about after death helped, honey'." (She had been reading to him about death to comfort him.) He then told her where to find something she had been looking for, and she found it.

Gwen's only other similar experience had taken place after her little boy died. A little girl, who later died of bone cancer, had seen the automobile accident. Gwen had been troubled that the child should have to see this in addition to her own illness. Several months later Gwen was driving to another city, but something odd happened. "I couldn't drive home. I got in the car, and kept driving and driving, and all I kept seeing were the [city lights]. I kept thinking, this is ridiculous. I can't get home. And with that, on the radio, the singer began singing 'Hold my hand, I'm a stranger in Paradise.' The whole car turned so cold that I was shivering. And then my son—I didn't see him, but he was there: 'Mother, she held my hand—she was the last hand that was held out to me as I left to go to the other side, and I was there for her'."

During the period of her husband's severe illness and her children's leaving home, Gwen obtained teaching credentials and began to teach. She loves the children but hates "the crap teachers are taking." Her house burned to the ground because of an accident (someone hit a gas main). She also was in an automobile accident and was told she would never walk again. She was desperate because she needed to teach school to support her ill husband. "I remember one day I was in bed, and I said, 'Oh, God, just let me walk.' And I was really low. I heard a voice say: 'Get up and walk.' And I said: 'I can't.' And this voice said [it again]. So I got up and took my first steps. I didn't run around the room—I made maybe two or three, but I did. I remember I called to [my husband]: 'Look!' He didn't know whether I had fallen on my face or what. And somehow I began to grow in a way I never had before."

Even so, she is still not very religious because she has always had an aversion to being part of a group where everyone must think alike.

At present, in her fifties, Gwen is a widow, and feels keenly the rejection by men because of her age. She is dating a man with whom she can share sexually, but not mentally, and says, "I would like to find a mate, married or unmarried. I don't need someone to give me a home; I've got a home. I don't need a job; I've got a job. I don't need somebody to support me. I don't need somebody to rear my children. I want to share. And frankly, I'm old-fashioned enough that I want some sort of commitment. . . . For years you're responsible for children and family, and suddenly you still have all these things left to give, and there's no one there to give to. . . . I feel like I'm ugly, and I feel like I'm old. I sure get lonesome."

Her mother also is still a problem. "And I feel like a rat. Because I keep thinking, be bigger than that—overlook it. . . . Oh, I had her down last weekend, but I really don't like her. I'm ashamed of myself that I don't like her. It isn't that I don't like her from the past. I don't like her now. She's demanding. She wants to be waited on hand and foot. . . . 'My hair is dirty,' she said. And I said 'wash it.' She said, 'I've never washed my own hair'."

If Gwen could come back as anything she wanted, she'd come back as "a man, tall, dark hair, curly, long legs. And my girlfriend said she's coming back as a male next time, and she's going to service all the lonely fifty-year-old women. Men have it made. They're in command. They get respect. They don't have to earn it."

Compared to the 47 other women in this research, Gwen seems to have had an unusual amount of bad luck. But when asked if she thinks so, she says she does not. "I think my mother was a little unusual [laughs]. But other than that, no. As a whole, no."

In reviewing Gwen's history, one is struck by the unusual number of losses resulting from accidents and physical injury to herself and her loved ones. These are balanced by the instances of her father's kindness, her love for her second husband, her successful completion of her education in middle age, her fairly satisfying career as a teacher, her wit and "gutsiness," and especially her psychic experiences. The L/T theme of inordinate, sudden, often accidental and capricious loss is exemplified by her mother's cruel physical abuse all through her childhood, her memories of death in the rooming house, the beatings by other children, attempted murder, the molestation by the relative, the pelvic examination, one child hit by a car who survived and another child who did not, the threat of a genetic disease to two other children, the destruction of her house, her own automobile accident, and the long illnesses and death of her beloved second husband. Capricious or accidental loss is transcended by humor, by fulfilling work as a teacher, and especially by an unusual number of psychic experiences—the visitations of her second husband and son, her own out-of-body experience at the time of her suicide attempt, and her miraculous cure after her accident. The core theme is capricious or accidental loss versus psychic experiences (also capricious), or body versus spirit (body is vulnerable, spirit protects and magically undoes).

The protocol on the whole is loss oriented. At one point Gwen says, "you never get over your losses," and the yearning and searching for love is the most salient current aspect. Although we know that her second husband was most beloved, it is his illness that she speaks of most, not what they did together. Gwen would be seen as currently searching, trying to find a replacement; indeed, her entire protocol seems focused on search, which is probably what saved her, considering her extraordinary loss history. Another person might have been destroyed, psychologically or physically, might never have gone beyond shock, numbness, yearning. Something in Gwen seems to have gotten her beyond her mother, the neighborhood, the lack of education.

Theoretical analysis

Gwen's case is an unusual example of major losses that are external in nature, imposed from without, and perhaps balanced between direct and indirect. It is difficult in her history to find an example of loss that is chosen or imposed from within by virtue of her personality, although to the extent that there were losses involved in returning to school, for instance, instead of doing something else, we know that there were chosen losses and/or losses imposed from within.

In many of the histories it is reasonable to ask if, and to what extent, an individual bears any responsibility for apparently accidental losses. For example, did Lorellen somehow put herself in situations where she was vulnerable to rape? We have speculated that the second and third instances might have been ways of working through the first rape, or all might have been modes of self-destruction (bearing in mind that the rapist bears full responsibility for his act), of moving toward death on the continuum; metaphorically, she raped herself, committed suicide—she was another person afterward. In this sense, incurring loss may be a method of transcending it.

With Gwen it is more difficult to attribute responsibility. Perhaps she incited some of her mother's abuse, and the death lessons of the rooming house and her father's kindnesses were the two aspects on which she chose to focus. It is much harder to see even minimal responsibility in the automobile accidents of two children, both hit by other drivers. Did she not watch them closely enough? How many mothers have had their attention lapse with no more suffering than an anxious search for the wandering toddler? What responsibility can be attributed to her for a truck hitting a gas main and blowing up her house—that she somehow knew she was selecting a house susceptible to such an accident? Much of the existential concept of responsibility seems more far-fetched in Gwen's history of loss than it does in other histories, although it is common to say that even if we are not responsible for our losses, we are responsible for our responses to them or "response-able."

In Gwen we see an individual for whom death and disaster and the beatings that threaten them have been capricious from childhood on. There is no reason for the ways in which death strikes, no way to anticipate or be prepared. The sum of a person's life, its meaning and substance, can be stuffed into a paper bag. This is the "worth" of a human being, she tells us with tears. Death destroys what is good and seems to be without meaning or explanation.

It is no wonder, then, that at times the meaningless or unexplained is overcome by the unexplained and the inexplicable, that is, by psychic experiences. If the body must endure physical violence, then the mind or spirit or psychic may overcome. In this sense we see her theme as physical versus spiritual. The body is too vulnerable; the spirit protects or magically undoes. The psychic gives death meaning by making it not the end.

Traditional clinical psychology would label Gwen's psychic experiences as episodes of dissociation, or dissociative reactions, brought on by life crises that threaten to destroy the ego; dissociation protects it. The split is also reflected in Gwen's language. She begins reciting a painful incident with "I" and switches to "you," perhaps to distance herself from it. Elements of hallucination would be seen in the experiences of hearing her son's voice, not being able to get home, hearing the song on the radio, seeing her husband after his death (a common bereavement reaction). In addition, her use of psychic experience or the magical undoing of loss would be seen as regression to childhood defense mechanisms, employed because more mature mechanisms such as altruism, humor, sublimation, and anticipation are not adequate to the task. (See Vaillant, 1977.)

What would be missed in this analysis is that it is not simply the integrity of the self but the life or death of the self that is at stake. As Piaget (1952a) pointed out, the child must learn object permanence, usually by about 18 months. Just because something has disappeared does not mean it no longer exists; on the contrary, the child learns to expect the reappearance of the mother or the rattle. What Piaget did not point out was that the child must then learn the opposite, that some things disappear forever; they die. In order to overcome death of a pet, for example, the child counts on what Piaget terms the "magical" reappearance, just as mother and rattle reappeared. It is quite possible that Gwen used this mechanism when she was being beaten. I am reminded of another child of five who, while being beaten, used to call to her imaginary friend to come to take the punishment that was rightfully hers—it was the friend who had done the naughty deed. (That the friend disappeared when beatings were in progress eventually broke them up!) The mechanism is common in cases of multiple personality.

This psychological analysis is not meant to deny the possible "reality" or validity of psychic experiences. It is simply to show that the reductionism of traditional psychology seems to eliminate the death aspect so consistently that one cannot but wonder if it is intentional and/or defensive. Even if psychic experiences are "real" or valid, the use rather than rejection of them, or even their occurrence, is still consistent with the L/T psychological paradigm, whereas it is eliminated by traditional psychology.

Tess's losses are direct and off time and most seem to her to be imposed from without, although to us they may seem to be imposed from within. She feels that she has no control over job or relationship loss.

Tess

"I wanted someone to love . . . something no one could take away from me."

Tess is an attractive brunette in her mid-twenties. Her little son plays quietly in another corner of the living room.

Tess's mother had several children by a previous marriage. She had been deserted when the youngest was less than a year old. Tess was the only child of both her parents and the baby of the family, unexpected, welcomed, and worried over because there was little food. Her siblings were jealous because she was the only blood relative of her father. She got a lot of attention from everyone, however. "I was always on stage, being the youngest child, a cute little girl."

Tess's mother was an alcoholic as long as Tess can remember. She worked hard both as a mother and on an assembly line, although she loved mathematics, and Tess regrets that she was unable to do more with it. Her mother did teach her good values, such as not to steal, and Tess could always cry on her shoulder, but her memories of her mother are largely negative, such as being spanked with a belt that left welts on her back. Her father was angry with her mother for the spanking, and Tess took that as a victory, particularly because she was permitted to go to an amusement park. "She'd get drunk and she'd drag me out of bed to do the dishes. She was really erratic about stuff like that." Another time her mother said, "You're so lazy you're not worth the milk you drink." But she'd also tell her how pretty she was. "So now that I'm an adult I think, Oh well, I'm pretty, I can get whatever I want. . . . But when things get really important . . . I don't have a lot of confidence in myself, even though I know I'm a good person inside. It's still sort of like at the base of my brain, like the Chinese water torture, and it's just impossible to get rid of. I've tried and tried for years."

Tess's father also had a violent temper. When he got a certain look in his eyes, all the children would flee. Tess says he is affectionate and is the one who taught her how to love. But the prospect of his anger made her tense and afraid that she was "going to get zapped, even when it wasn't my fault."

Tess had been an outgoing child until a move in elementary school changed her. "Perhaps I didn't know the rules of being with other children. I had a hard time with teachers—they hated me. I was a real daydreamer. And I got teased a lot. I always felt like I was sort of the underdog . . . I was made a scapegoat . . . and the kids really picked up on that." One teacher even made up a story in which Tess didn't go to a party because she was too engrossed in doing something else. And he would hit the children "right over the head with a big fat book . . . I got real depressed. And mother was really worried about me. I didn't have any feeling of self worth at all. I went from adored little child, adored little sister to underdog of the class. . . . And I came from a poorer background, new kid in the school." She did make one friend whom she still sees, but she was termed "an obnoxious child" and was mainly interested in reading and writing. She couldn't cope with the other children in school; she had no armor to deal with their harsh remarks. "I'm mad at my mom for not giving me the armor, and not teaching me how to fight back." But her mother told her she was incredibly sensitive to everything and that made her beautiful.

When Tess became a teenager she and her mother clashed even more bitterly. "The older I got, the less fair she became. . . . It made me so mad I just wanted to kill her for this total dominant thing. . . . I was not able to voice my opinions in any way, grind my teeth or anything like that. . . . I am the most outspoken of all the children, especially to her. And I'd scream and yell at her, I'd cuss her [laughs], I'd carry on, cry." Later Tess was able to handle her mother just by telling her she would do as she pleased, because her mother was always trying to manipulate her and she had learned that alcoholics "run all the other people in their lives."

For Tess in high school "the biggest thing in my whole life was being the prettiest girl, and the most friendly and the most popular. . . . I had to be in the group and have nice clothes, because again I thought that was the way to acceptance," just as she had discovered that being brainy and doing well stood her in better stead than daydreaming. She was shy and insecure, so she forced herself to take classes in subjects like dance and athletics. "I remember daydreaming in the outfield. I don't know what I was thinking of all those times. I was always thinking about princes and princesses, dreaming up stories in fantasyland, just because it was more interesting [laughs]." One day the ball rolled right past her, and the captain nearly brought her to tears.

Tess wanted to be a professional ballet dancer and started taking ballet lessons at 13. But she worked so hard she couldn't do it, her ballet teacher thought she was a "spoiled brat" and she ended up in tears, refusing to do things. If she thought she could not do something, she would make a joke of it, everyone would laugh, and the teacher would be furious. "She should have seen I needed more encouragement." Tess feels that her mother was jealous of her ambition, often made disparaging remarks, and didn't think she was capable. "I needed someone to back me." She was singled out for special singing honors in high school because of her hard work, rather than talent, but "Mom never came to those performances. I was crushed by that.

I thought this was the most important thing in my life. . . . Her excuses were 'I'm too tired, I can't do it, I work late'!" Tess decided to sing for herself instead of someone else, and she is eloquent about the beauty of singing in harmony with others. "The music is inside of you, outside of you, you're caught in the wave."

Tess's first important sexual relationship was with a VIP senior when she was a freshman in high school. They went together for 2 years, mainly so that she could move up in social standing; "you really get your place then in the whole system of things." She did not enjoy sex until years later. She went to bed for love and thinks of herself as having been a prude until she was in her mid-teens. "I really wanted to be held. And I knew that they would not like me if I said no."

After Tess and her first boyfriend broke up (he was too possessive and his mother disapproved), she fell in love with John, who was to be her second husband. At first they were just high school friends, engaging in activities together. He wasn't particularly handsome, as he is today, but he was popular. They went together until the end of high school. Tess wanted to marry, but he was going away to college and felt the relationship was through. As it happened, he "ended up getting busted for marijuana in some redneck town . . . came back and floundered around . . . went to work where his father was working."

The split with John hit Tess hard, and she went through a bad stage of going to bars. "I was really a good dancer, like Saturday Night Fever. I knew I could be envied because I looked nice, and I wore my clothes nicely. . . . I was also going out and screwing anything that was available." Her father caught on to this but called her a "tramp" instead of trying to talk to her and find out what was wrong, not realizing she was really looking for love. She feels that she learned a great deal about herself during this period, however.

At this point Tess began a destructive relationship, "the worst thing that ever happened in my life." She was practically living with the man involved, cooking, doing everything to win his approval. But he'd tell her, "You can't do this. You're dumb." Sexually he rejected her night after night, because he drank and probably because he had other girls. "More than anything I didn't want him to leave me. . . . I would have done anything to keep that from happening." Finally they broke up, and she found someone else who "used me a lot. . . . This seems like a pattern in my life. I go from one man to another. I haven't spent a whole lot of time on my own."

Tess's work history has been characterized by a series of traumatic experiences that have left her with profound feelings of incompetence. Just after high school she took a job at a fast-food restaurant, but quit it when she found out it wasn't "classy." She was still living at home. Her next job was in a restaurant working as a waitress. "I've been fired from about six jobs. . . . I get bad vibes, and I get unsure, and I start to panic, and then everything goes wrong. I can't do one thing right after that. . . . I just start dropping things." She had heard someone was going to be laid off and assumed it was herself. She started to make errors in addition, and she ended up being fired, even though she hadn't been the original one targeted. This experience was traumatic, and she describes it in detail: "I had one employer that was a real tense sort of person . . . and he'd shout at everybody. . . . I was just close to tears and so tense all the time. And they couldn't understand why I kept on making mistakes"; this was in an office job. She believes her tense reaction to anger began with being around her father. At another job she did very well but was working about 15 hours a day and "came this close to a nervous breakdown," so she took a pregnancy leave.

After her series of bad relationships with men and during these work crises, Tess was drinking heavily. She met a man who began to turn her around. He asked her, "Why is it that you need a playmate all the time? Can't you ever do anything by yourself?" "And that's when I started to realize that there was someone here besides just this face and this body that was important." Tess felt that he was such a neat person and so deep that he wouldn't really be interested in her, so "I blew the whole thing." He had just gotten out of a 2-year stint in jail after being busted for marijuana, and he didn't want to get tied down, so Tess tried to make him jealous, which she now recognizes "was pretty childish. I wish I hadn't reacted that way. He probably could have pulled me out of the whole thing."

Instead she fell in love with the brother of the man who'd left her (and who was living with another woman while Tess sent him money). They would go out and drown their sorrows in drink. He was "extremely sensitive. Because he had so many weaknesses himself he could really be in tune with other people's weaknesses. He really understood, and I think that's what attracted me to him. He was a good talker, too, I guess because of the drugs. This time when I first moved in with him, I didn't even know what heroin was, the furthest I'd ever gone was smoking pot [laughs]." They lived together, she got pregnant with their son, and they married. "The whole family was a snitch, was on alcohol, drugs, stole from each other, etc. . . . I didn't think that stealing was funny, or okay, or humorous." They had connections within the judicial system, so in exchange for leniency they'd supply the names of their sources. They were always on the run. "I slept with a shotgun under my bed." She says of her first husband that he "was a good person . . . deep down inside, but he was so incredibly weak." Later, after Tess and her first husband broke up, he died of an overdose.

Tess really wanted a baby, even though she knew she might have to raise him alone. "I wanted someone to love . . . something nobody could take away from me." Now she says her son accepts her as she is, and she doesn't have to play adult games with him. She went on welfare to support them both, a move largely condemned by her older siblings.

When she and her first husband split up, John reentered her life "and sort of picked up the pieces." They have a lot more in common than she and her first husband did, but John isn't as "compassionate" or "sensitive." During the interview she made a number of allusions to the possible temporariness of the marriage. "This relationship that I have right now is probably the most independent relationship I've ever had. . . . I'm still my own self and not completely tied to my husband. . . . If I were to split up with John, I don't think I'd [go from one man to another]. . . . I'm starting to emerge as my own person a bit more. . . . I'd love to grow old with him. I love him so much, but so many different things happen in a lifetime. . . ." She feels that although he loves her, he can't help her with her insecurities because he can't deal with his own. He's been putting the pressure on her to get a job, and she's terrified of another rejection. He wants to go back to school and retrain.

After having been fired from many jobs, Tess returned to junior college and took a course in business education. This was disappointing. She was a straight A student, pushing herself to exhaustion and causing enmity among the students because she would "speak out" about her previous business experiences. But when she got a clerical job in the business world, it was quite different from the classroom.

Tess's mother died about 2 weeks before the interview took place. At the end "She was lonely a lot. . . . Her home was like her fortress but also prison." She could hardly find her way around town, only went out after dark, and was disoriented. The family had only recently decided to seek the help of Alcoholics Anonymous for the families of alcoholics. Meanwhile, they had been concerned because the mother had lost so much weight, consumed mainly sweets, had an enlarged liver, and contracted every virus going around. When the mother got sick again, it was Tess who cared for her. "One day my dad called up and he said that she had diarrhea so bad that she couldn't make it to the bathroom. It was really tough for me to go over there, and I had to treat my mother like a baby, put her in the bathtub and bathe her. And when she was in the hospital I did a lot of the things that the nurses did, and I thought it would be hard on me. At first I had nightmares because of the catheter, but it helped me in the long run. . . . I was able to massage her back, and things that the nurses wouldn't normally do. So now that she's gone I'm really glad I did that because we sort of made up for all the things that happened when I was a child, and all the things I went through because of her alcoholism. My older sister has the same problem, she's still carrying it around, all the guilt . . . and I was able those last days to get rid of it, because that physical contact, and that reversal of positions—she was the weak one needing something, and I was able to help her. It sort of made up for all those years." Tess was with her almost up to the end, but the suffering upset her, she wished her mother could die in peace without all the tubes, and she regrets not having been there the last few minutes. She thinks that you can learn something from things that are "terrifying" and this makes them less so.

Tess reflects back on her life thus far. "I'm probably more secure in myself. It seems like my adult life has been really difficult. I think I've learned a lot from just the fact that it has been difficult." On the job she feels that she has tried to use the pretty girl image because it has worked in the past, rather than showing her intelligence first, and then she is infuriated when they think she doesn't know anything. She wishes she had more purpose in life. She was educated to do secretarial work because she didn't know what else to do and had to make money, but it bores her. The education itself was much more interesting.

Tess has sought counseling several times, most recently after she was fired from her last job because she was not doing enough work (she was involved with her wedding, and the job was boring). The counselors have been encouraging her. She has a line on another job, one for which she is probably overqualified, but that would translate into less pressure on her; however, she is scared to go, wonders if I will drive her and drop her there on my way, what the interview will be like, thinks she might just pick up an application. "I'm afraid of the interview. . . . If I don't feel completely capable of working myself, how can I convince someone else?" She says that she doesn't know if she's "competent" or not, and in talking about this she stumbles frequently over the word. "And it's such an ugly word." The issue of the fact that her husband works at a job he doesn't like, supporting her and her son, while she stays home is "tearing our marriage apart," so it's important for both of them to find work they like, although she resents having to work *and* take care of the home. She thinks she'd really like some form of psychology as a career, because people are in so much pain and she feels she could help.

Tess sees herself as "in a mirror, and it's a little bit distorted. But when something happens, like I get fired from my job, there are so many self-doubts that it gets to be like the mirrors that you see at the amusement park, or maybe like looking in a pond, and somebody drops a pebble, and I'm pushing and pulling trying to get myself in focus."

For her life theme, Tess sees herself as involved with people and "reaching out . . . my hands, and they keep on getting slapped and I have to keep on pulling them in . . . but it's getting a little better. Each time I get them slapped they open again a little more quickly instead of keeping withdrawn." She sees herself as both a winner and a loser—she can get to the core of people very soon, but she lets "other people's judgment of me affect me profoundly."

Tess's life history is characterized by feelings of lack of competence and self-confidence, manifested in major losses in work and relationships. This is transcended by a son as someone who loves and accepts her unquestioningly and also by drugs, alcohol, and fantasy, including fairy tales. Only her face and body are accepted, never her whole self. She, as body, goes from one man to another and is abused. The core L/T theme seems to be incompetent, unemerged self versus general transcendence—drugs, alcohol, unquestioning acceptance, and fantasy. (Unquestioning acceptance *is* fantasy.)

Tess's life history is undoubtedly very loss oriented. She begins almost every answer to a question with a negative statement; if she is asked how something was, she responds with how it was not. In the loss and transcendence process she is rated as high loss, low transcendence in the yearning and grieving stage, because even searching is difficult for her.

Theoretical analysis

Throughout my interview with Tess, I had the sense of someone struggling to be born. Indeed, the words "the unborn" and "the unemerged" kept echoing in my mind as I listened to her. There is *birth*, the *event* that takes place at a certain moment on a certain day, but there is also *birth*, the *process*, the birth of the self, which may take many years and may never be complete. In a sense, we are always in the process of giving birth to ourselves. This is how I felt it was with Tess.

Much of Tess's account was in terms of things that had never happened, encouragement never received, armor never provided, compassion never given, and so forth. Others are to blame for how she is, what she does and does not do. She is incomplete. Her mother told her she was stupid and not worth "the milk you drink," not worth a mother's milk, nourishment or nurture, not worth living. Her father told her that she was a tramp, teachers that she was obnoxious, bosses that she was incompetent, boyfriends that she was worthless. Who Tess is, is what she is not. This defines her. And that is what she became—someone who is not. We tend to act in accordance with how others perceive us (Rosenthal & Jacobson, 1968), and we tend to create ourselves in the image others have of us. Tess may think that she never realized she had certain positive attributes, but indeed she never had them, only the potential for them.

And so Tess is defined in terms of lack—with one exception. She was always told that she was pretty, that she could have anything she wanted because of her looks, even love. Until the ballet debacle in her teens, she gained approval by employing her looks in performance; she was always "on stage." There is one curious aspect of this. She *is* quite pretty and has a good figure, but she really is not above average. Her references to her prettiness seem to exceed the facts. She may have been a very pretty child and may still see the pretty child in her mirror. Or, being told over and over, she may have taken it for objective fact.

Rogers (1961) observed the importance of being loved unconditionally in childhood in order to actualize one's potential, which is to become fully one's self. It appears that Tess was loved selectively, for looks alone, and learned to love only the aspect of herself that she had been taught was lovable, external appearance. Freud (1930, reprinted 1961) believed that love and work were the two things one must be able to do well in order to be happy and healthy, and Erikson (1950) averred that in the age period from 6 to 12 the basic psychosocial task is the development of a whole set of competencies important to our culture, particularly in school. This was the age at which

Tess experienced the move that was so traumatic for her, during which she had so much difficulty with teachers and peers, became "obnoxious," and daydreamed. Now she *feels* incompetent and this *makes* her so, in spite of her obvious brightness. The judgments of others have been internalized. As for love, most of her experiences, based once again on her looks, have been disasters; only her son (a charming, well-behaved little tyke) accepts her unconditionally, and one wonders how things will be as he grows older. The areas of work and love are areas of profound loss for Tess, and these are the ways in which her self is incomplete.

Life losses are most often thought of as losses of things once possessed, but they can also be losses of the things never possessed. Then what one never had is idealized, and the discrepancy is greater and perhaps even more keenly felt. Further, one becomes the one who never has or never was and is only what one was not. Possibilities become impossible. Alternative futures become alternative pasts and are foreclosed. Something has died that never lived—stillborn.

Tess's transcendence modes are mainly *general* (rather than *situational* or *dispositional*) to the point of abuse or self-destruction. She has had considerable experience with drugs and many of the major people in her life have been involved; she even lived off the proceeds; one of her husbands died of an overdose. Her mother died of alcoholism, her husband works in a distillery, and she also has been a chronic abuser of alcohol. In addition to drugs and alcohol, she has indulged in fantasy to the point where it has interfered with reality—in school and on the athletic field. Her fantasies used to be of fairy princes and princesses; now they are of herself as entertainer. In none of these is there effective transcendence.

Again, there is one major exception! When her mother was dying, she cared for her and was thereby able to overcome much of the negativity of the relationship, to convert guilt and anger into love and caring, making something good of something bad, a powerful lesson that has not been lost on her. This form of transcendence is situational; what she does not say about that experience, but what comes through in her detailed account, is that she had to have been very *competent* in the care she gave her mother to relieve her pain (and the mother's pain was to some purpose, therefore, an issue with which we shall deal in Chapter 12, "Time and Death"). A few more incidents like this one, of being *compelled* to competence, might really turn Tess around! Her son seems well cared for, but she takes no apparent pride in this.

Tess uses the metaphor of the mirror to describe how she sees herself and her life. The metaphor is extremely apt. First, it was her looks which were of value while she was growing up, which won her love and approval. Clothes were important; she envied a friend whose mother loved her and cared about the clothes she wore—love and clothes or appearance are repeatedly equated. Second, the mirror, the pool, and the reflection are aspects of the myth of Narcissus, who fell in love with his reflection and from whose name the word "narcissistic" is derived. It is often said that women in our society are trained to be narcissistic, and this is certainly true of Tess. A psychoanalyst would see Tess as narcissistic, as not having grown far enough to love others, as having endured severe narcissistic wounds. Even her love of her son is a reflective love; she loves him because he accepts her. Third, as Mead (1934) saw, the mirror can reflect the self as seen by others and thereby create the self. Cooley (1902) referred to the "looking glass self." The self knows who it is only by holding itself up to the reflections others give back. Society is the mirror. When Tess defines the way in which she is a loser, she says, "I let other people's judgment affect me profoundly." And more, she let other people's judgment create her—insofar as she is created. But this creation is, as I have indicated, largely in terms of negatives, of not being.

When Tess cared for her dying mother, she experienced a role reversal. She was mothering her mother as she herself would have been mothered. In this sense she was metaphorically mothering herself and restarted the birthing process. A clinician might lead her to other experiences of competence to help her to complete it.

CONCLUSIONS: LEVELS OF LOSS

The life histories teach a number of lessons about loss. The classifications suggested in the first part of this chapter assist us in an approach to the study of loss. Off-time and time-irrelevant losses seem to be more difficult for the interviewees than on-time loss. Losses that are imposed from within—for example, Tess's feelings of incompetence or lack of worth originally derived from her mother, an aspect of her inner self—seem especially difficult to deal with, because there is not a basic sense of ontological security (Laing, 1976), centering, and strength from which to develop. The core of the self is damaged. Losses secondary to the primary ones often are not taken into account by the individual; one of the clinician's main tasks is to recognize them, bring them to the surface, and assist the client in dealing with them. This is analogous to solving a problem by breaking it into smaller ones. It is also apparent that the life histories are stories of struggles to survive, Gwen's and Tess's more directly, perhaps, but Lorellen's and Inez's in terms of who they believe they are and need to be.

These histories show us that loss occurs on five levels. First, as we have seen, there is the level of the specific loss incident, or the primary loss. A medical chief ridicules a resident in front of others. A woman undergoes an abortion. A son dies of leukemia. A young girl is fired from a number of jobs.

Second, there is the level of associated or secondary losses, which follow directly and with some immediacy in the wake of the primary loss. Embarrassment in front of colleagues and lack of self-confidence can lead to different medical judgments, and one may not be called on to perform certain tasks.

Infertility or scarring may result from abortion. A husband and wife fight and lose each other while their son is dying. The young girl, out of work, must go on welfare, enduring the contempt of her relatives and losing her friends. These are, of course, just a few of the many secondary losses associated with the primary ones.

Third, there are the more remote, abstract, or holistic losses to the life and self. Such losses are those of alternative or planned-for futures, possibilities, dreams—life as it might have been. The physician is now vulnerable to self-doubt and may fail. The aborted mother has lost a dream of her child. The roles of mother and father are no longer available when the son dies; even if there are other children, the roles are drastically altered; and the plans for the child's future are gone. The unemployed young girl must provide her young son with one future rather than another.

Fourth are the losses to the self or self-concept. How the self is defined must undergo revision. Something has been cut from the self as a whole, leaving behind only a part-self. The physician may be neither healer nor lovable. The pregnant woman may not be a mother. The parents of the dead child are guilty forever. The young girl is incompetent and lacks the ability to survive.

Finally, there are the metaphorical losses, or the idiosyncratic meaning that a loss has for the individual because of his or her metaphorical system. For Inez, the chief's ridicule was another form of betrayal by a male. Lorellen's abortion meant destruction of precious energy for evolution and possibly of future children. The death of a son for Gwen was not final but made the other side known to her. Being fired further defined who Tess was by defining who she was not, blocking her birth or emergence as a full self.

These, then, are the five levels of loss: primary, secondary, holistic, self-conceptual, and metaphorical. They are levels of each of the myriad losses we all sustain. Awareness of them helps us to understand better why loss affects us so deeply. In addition, it helps us to take steps to remedy the losses on each level, rather than dealing with loss on the primary level alone. You lose your job. You get another just as good. Why does the emptiness and pain persist? The answer probably lies on the other levels, where the loss has not been transcended by replacement or integration. A clinician will recognize and assist with these. Or, you lose your job, and you do not get another right away. Why aren't you as miserable as you should be? You have probably transcended the losses on the other levels to some extent. For example, you are becoming someone you would rather be.

The life histories also help to answer the question, Can we say that one loss is worse than another? For instance, can we judge Gwen's loss of a child to be worse than Inez's loss of her fiancé to her best friend? By "worse" we might mean that the loss is more painful or more destructive to the life and self. The answer is that we can make judgments when the differences between losses are obvious. A foreclosure on a mortgage is obviously a greater loss than a $10 parking ticket in all but the most unusual cases (where the metaphorical level is salient). But because the metaphorical, holistic, and self-conceptual levels of loss largely determine its severity, and these are much more idiosyncratic than the primary or even secondary losses, judgment becomes difficult. We can accept a consensus, such as the scales of stressful life events developed by Holmes and Rahe (1967) (see also Holmes & Masuda, 1974), but we must be careful in applying it to individuals. To understand ourselves, we must understand our losses on all levels. A loss history is thus of great value to the clinician.

Finally, the life histories show that we can never completely "get over" a major loss in the sense that all its effects are negated, that it is "forgotten." Our losses become part of who we are, as precious to us as other aspects of our selves, and so does the transcendence of those losses. This fact illuminates the phenomenon of pathological grief (see Chapters 10 and 12).

This chapter has focused on some of the major dimensions of loss. But it does not really end. Succeeding chapters, while exploring related topics in the L/T paradigm, will shed light on additional aspects of this most profound of human experiences.

3

Transcendence

Life and death form a continuum on which we are always moving in one direction or another, always becoming more alive or more inert. We may think of life events and our responses to them as preponderantly vital or lethal. We are, at any moment, either expanding or shrinking, compared to who we were before. As we shrink, life becomes meaningless, but as we expand and become more alive, life is meaningful, because death is the ultimate meaninglessness and life the ultimate transcendence (although we shall see later how death can be transcendence as well). Stagnation is an illusion. Growing and dying are a single dynamic process, loss and transcendence, the one dependent on the other. As we transcend we are deathless for a while, metaphorically overcoming death itself, enjoying the illusion that because we are not yet destroyed, we never can be.

Transcendence is a two-step process. First, loss is overcome in some fashion. Second, aspects of life and self are re-created as a result of the loss and overcoming. When an important relationship departs from our lives, it leaves a gaping hole that must be filled somehow, just as a vacuum must be filled. The self becomes one who has endured this loss, who has overcome it, and who now restructures life and self in a different way.

Transcendence has its metaphorical equivalent in immortality, rebirth, or resurrection, rather than death. For example, material gain involves gain in the abstract as well—in prestige, power, control, possibility, hope, illusions— all overcoming previous limitations.

Of course, it can be argued that *succumbing* is a form of overcoming, just as flight is a form of fight. (We can make the attacker feel guilty, give him no object on which to vent his rage, etc.) We cannot lose what we have given up, and the life and self are certainly re-created. We may elect to sustain specific losses so as not to endure more overwhelming ones; for example, a young woman may decide not to apply for jobs so that she will not be rejected. Succumbing has a way of perpetuating the myth of who we are metaphorically—the young woman will not become one who has been rejected over and over.

Lorellen transcends her losses partly through her beliefs in the evolution of the physical into the spiritual and the importance of expanded consciousness as well as through a new emphasis on stability. When she concentrated on immortality, she came closer to dying; now she is surviving by stressing physical security, baby, husband, and culture. Until recently, much of her transcendence was general and dispositional (drugs, counterculture, nature, travel, beliefs), but she is now making an effort at situational transcendence as well. Marriage, motherhood, and career may provide the balance she needs, while generating their own losses. Finally, Lorellen may even find expanded consciousness in restriction!

There are three major modes of transcendence, or groups of ways in which we overcome and re-create. They are situational, dispositional, and general. In this chapter I shall define each briefly and then discuss each in more depth. A delineation of the *loss and transcendence process* is followed by illustration with the histories of Marjorie, Faith, Della, and Sue.

DEFINITIONS

The first, external, mode of transcending involves dealing with the specific situation in a *situational* fashion. For example, the loss of a loved one is transcended by the ritual of funeral or memorial service, the caring of friends and relatives, sitting shibah, the temporary ease of sedatives perhaps, the release of grief in sorrowing. The loss eventually may be overcome to the degree that these external activities are effective—the letting go, the giving up, the detaching necessary and preliminary to the re-creation of life and self.

The second, *dispositional*, mode of transcendence is mainly internal and comprises the mechanisms of defense outlined by Freud (1926, reprinted 1959) as well as personality traits that may be defensive. A man who has lost his wife may anger easily, cursing doctors and God, finding solace in tears, withdrawing so as not to be pitied. In psychological terms he is aggressive, displacing his anger onto the doctors, emotionally labile, intolerant of succorance or affiliation. He may use other defenses such as intellectualization, projection, reaction formation, denial, isolation, or dissociation. For example, he may deny that his wife is dead or may have feelings of unreality. Although these modes of transcendence have external behavioral manifestations, they are mainly going on inside him.

The third mode of transcendence is neither specifically appropriate to the loss situation nor in specific reaction to it. This more *general* form of transcendence is often used to minimize the effect of everyday losses or to escape, although it may be employed predominantly in times of crisis. General transcendence includes meditation, athletics, travel, religious experience, the arts, occultism, sex, games, drugs, movies and television, and alcohol. Csikszentmihalyi (1975a) alludes to these as *flow activities*, "because one tends to lose one's sense of time when one is so engaged, and one forgets one's problems." Love and work may be general, situational, or dispositional transcendence modes, as we shall see.

The word "transcendence" is often used to describe a mystical feeling of rising above and beyond constraints, a sense of the ineffable, a flood of joy, or a peak experience, and indeed the transcendence of loss is often accompanied by such feelings. It is probable that the greater the threatened or actual loss, the higher the potential feeling of transcendence. Small losses completely transcended or large losses only marginally transcended would not bring about this feeling to as great a degree. This concept explains the apparent paradox that we must experience great sorrow in order to experience great joy, that the depth of love can be gauged, heightened, and expressed only by reference to its eventual or possible loss. The feeling of transcendence is quite common in such general transcendence activities as religious practice (which overcomes the loss of self, life, and God and metaphorically bestows the ability to fly over mortality as well as other omnipotences) and art (which overcomes the loss of perfection and resultant guilt). (This is discussed at length in Chapter 11, on society and culture.)

TYPES OF TRANSCENDENCE

Situational

In situational transcendence, we deal directly with the life event as it occurs. A woman is attacked; she may stand and fight, retreat, go through a prescribed ritual, reason with the attacker, write a nasty letter, sue, blame someone else, offer to fix the problem, and so forth. In this case, overcoming hostility, or the metaphorical threat of death, may entail inflicting death on someone else. Many of us are faced with "kill or be killed" situations at work and in destructive relationships, as well as on more literal battlefields. The case histories illustrate the role of situational transcendence in individual lives.

Inez does not seem to have had much recourse to situational transcendence of her losses. She had been taught to respect her elders and said nothing to the chief of medicine when he abused her. She did complain to a friend, who later raped her. Situationally powerless in love and work, she became ill, developed an ulcer; problems about which she could do nothing "ate away" at her inside. Inez seems not to be able to kill metaphorically, even if her life depends on it. This is the problem of the victim. She has transcended through healing, first by being healed herself as a child and then by healing children professionally—rehealing the child in her. She also reads and finds comfort in religion, particularly the concept of Karma: those who betray her betray themselves. There is less general transcendence in her life than in the lives of the other women; she hopes for more creative activity eventually. She is also finding comfort in the friendship and support of others, especially women. Metaphorically, when she heals others she heals her own losses as well, and she can become a healer rather than one who is betrayed, active rather than passive. Healing bestows life on others. It will be noted that this transcendence is metaphorically situational in that she overcomes the losses of others, but it becomes a form of general transcendence as well in that she escapes her own losses. In her other life situations adequate transcendence is more difficult. Dispositionally, she becomes ill and depressed, succumbing rather than overcoming, and re-creating her self in this form.

Our other interviewees showed more situational transcendence. Lorellen tried to start a family, write a book, and did do body work and counseling. But these enterprises may not enhance her life and self because so much of her has been killed already. Gwen goes to dances in search of a mate, risking the small deaths of rejection for the life-giving potential of a significant relationship. Tess attempts situational transcendence when she applies for jobs, tries to work, goes on welfare. For her, situational transcendence is most difficult.

Dispositional

The second mode of dealing with loss is dispositional, referring to internal activity rather than external behavior. The person who deals with a problem situationally is certainly explaining his actions to himself; and the person who deals with a problem internally, with thought and feelings, may externalize some of that process, such as explaining it to another. But most acts of transcendence are predominantly dispositional or situational.

One example of dispositional transcendence is the defense mechanism. A man is told that his wife has died in an airplane accident. He responds, "Oh, no, are you sure it's her, it can't be, she was here only a minute ago, I think I hear her upstairs," using the defense of denial. A woman wants to return to school and earn her degree, but it will mean leaving the children with sitters more often, and the house will be messier than it has been for the past 10 years. Instead of saying it's something she wants to do, she rationalizes: "The children will benefit from the money I'll earn and from having a mother who knows more," giving an acceptable reason for what some see as an unacceptable course of action. (Indeed, if one's actions ever need justifying, one need only think up some way in which a child might benefit!) During final exam week, a student learns that her boyfriend has been jailed for marijuana. She says to herself, "I can't deal with this now or I'll flunk my exams. I'll deal with it the day after tomorrow," suppressing her fears. A co-worker is always telling his colleague how tired she looks, probably projecting his own weariness onto her, because facing it might slow him down.

These and other defense mechanisms are ways of changing a situation by reinterpreting it, denying it, deliberately putting it out of mind, or even radically distorting it. They are all attempts to avoid losing what one has already lost—wife, comfortable conscience, energy, the relationship with a boyfriend—that is, aspects of who one is.

Freud (1923, reprinted 1961; 1926, reprinted 1959) believed that defense mechanisms protect the ego from id attack, but I believe they protect the self from death in its many forms. However, if the ego is overcome by impulses from the id, the self may die socially, in suicide, in other forms of pathology, or it may kill.

Vaillant (1977) recognized four categories of defense mechanisms: immature, neurotic, psychotic, and mature. One may reinterpret the mature mechanisms within the L/T framework as follows. The mature mechanisms are humor (the release of the desire to kill in biting, mordant laughter), suppression (killing death by hiding it or smothering it), altruism (overcoming the death of another; only God overcomes death, so one becomes Him), and sublimation (creating new life out of dead matter).

Most individuals have certain defense mechanisms that they use habitually, rather than suiting the mechanism to the situation. These habitual defense mechanisms become personality traits. On the other hand, many personality traits are also defensive; they are stable ways of thinking, behaving, and feeling regardless of the situation. A person who is very orderly and scheduled defends against chaos, falling into the abyss; the artist, however, who may glory in disorder, is defending against human restriction, limitation, the Procrustean bed that binds and imprisons in mortality. Personality defenses against death are myriad (as we shall see in Chapter 10, on an L/T reconceptualization of personality, emotion, and psychopathology).

When either defense mechanisms or personality traits become inappropriate to an unacceptable degree, they are labeled psychopathological. Socking the school principal for not giving you a raise is inappropriate and can get you jailed; socking the enemy on the battlefield may save your life and earn you a medal. Meekly submitting to your daughter's demand for the car keys is probably inappropriate; submitting to your God is not. Socking the boss and submitting to a child's demand are thought of as abnormal or even signs of pathology because they are inappropriate to the setting and situation. But now I'll tell you that the boss has been tormenting you for 3 years, and your daughter is in remission with leukemia, and does your behavior seem pathological?

General

The third mode of transcendence is not external behavior specifically geared to the loss situation, such as the funeral ritual for a death, nor is it an internal readjustment of the situation, or a cross-situational personality trait. The third mode, general transcendence, rather than altering the situation by external activities or internal processes, alters the self that experiences the situation. Further, it alters the experiencing self across situations, major or minor. This alteration of the experiencing self is accomplished by such activities as drinking, fantasizing, drug ingestion, meditation, religious experience, dancing, jogging, watching movies or television, painting, listening to music, traveling, and other "leisure" activities during which one loses awareness of time passing (Csikszentmihalyi, 1975a). Because time is the measure of life, when life is unbounded, no endings are possible. These activities are often termed forms of escape, but escape from what? From life's problems, its losses, the awareness of death. We are not losing when we are not aware of losing or when, on the contrary, we are having one of Maslow's peak experiences, as many who engage in religious, athletic, and creative activities will attest. We go beyond our selves instead. (Chapter 11, on the societal and cultural manifestations of loss and transcendence, explores general transcendence in greater depth.)

All of us engage in transcending the losses of life in some of these general ways, but some do it to such an extent that transcendence becomes loss; this is the case with alcoholics, a number of whom appear in our case histories. Addiction to anything—drugs, work, running, love—can become psychopathology; the self is stiff, rigid, with impermeable boundaries, making growth difficult. Awareness of self is lost, and the self becomes one who loses awareness. If a tree falls in the Amazon forest with no one around to hear it, does it make a noise? If the self is unaware of itself, does it exist?

Thus, the three modes of transcendence are situational (on-situation or situation-specific), dispositional (off-situation or across situations), and general (situation-irrelevant) transcendence. These three modes are ways of facing loss, threatened or actual, interpreting its meaning and consequences, dealing with it in some fashion, preventing it, foiling it—in short, overcoming it so that life and self can continue, no matter how changed. From this derives not only new life and new self but also meaning, part of which is the sense of continuity (uninterrupted time, metaphorically not dying).

DEGREES OF TRANSCENDENCE

We tend to think of the transcendence of loss as an act that has been completed. However, there are degrees of transcendence.

First, there is *incomplete* transcendence. Only part of the problem has been resolved, and the rest remains. Or the individual is in the process of transcending loss. Dolores is being sexually discriminated against at work.

Her fellow co-worker is having an affair with the boss, and he in return is giving her job perks, raises, and a promotion that should go to Dolores. She complains to the boss and then to his supervisor. Her boss simply goes underground with the favoritism, making a show of impartiality to avoid a lawsuit. Dolores's life at work is now an easier one, but there are still losses, partially or incompletely transcended.

Second, there is inappropriate or *maladaptive* transcendence. The transcendence is not appropriate to the loss and causes more loss than it transcends. Dolores tells her boss off, giving him the perfect opportunity to fire this troublemaker. Or she quits without having found another job, without much money in the bank, or a plan for law school. She has certainly transcended the sexual discrimination problem; no further acts will occur on that job. But she is now jobless, scared, anxious about money, and possibly regretting her rashness.

At this point, she may turn things around. She may always have wanted to start her own business, go into another field, or go back to school. The Chinese symbol for "crisis" is "danger and opportunity." She may not have wanted to face her desire for something else; in fact, she may unconsciously have made the worst of her predicament instead of the best, trauma substituting for the courage to make a change. She may discover leisure, music, other people; or she may take her small savings and backpack through Europe—a priceless experience healing hurt and giving her a new perspective. We might term this *neotranscendence*.

Pathological transcendence, an extension of the maladaptive type, may range from mild to moderate to severe. Most of us "cut off the nose to spite the face" occasionally, the satisfaction we derive seeming worth it. The neurotic consistently engages in transcendence that provokes somewhat more loss than it overcomes. The phobic approaches a bridge and, rather than cross it, goes 200 miles and 4 hours out of his way or forgoes it entirely. The more severely disturbed finds transcendence either in loss to herself or in causing loss to others. Suicide overcomes all problems with work, lovers, and family, re-creates the self as dead and as a myth among those left behind. (For further discussion, see the section on psychopathology in Chapter 10.)

Completed transcendence is the degree of transcendence we will find to a considerable extent in the cases of Marjorie, Faith, Della, and Sue. However, completed transcendence is also a misnomer. Dolores might continue to pursue her sex discrimination problem on the job, file a grievance with the Equal Employment Opportunity Commission, call in various women's groups, begin individual and class action lawsuits (on contingency fees), and 4 years later settle out of court for a reasonable sum. The problem is ended, and she is re-created as the person who won; she is no longer someone who *is* discriminated against, but she is still someone who *was*!

Serious losses are never completely transcended; the loss remains in memory, a part of the self. We never completely get over the death of a child.

The child lives on inside us, and we help ourselves by helping others with the same problem.

THE PROCESS OF LOSS AND TRANSCENDENCE

Integration with the literature from the field of death and dying leads to a possible phase-stage formulation for the process of loss and transcendence, one which I have empirically verified.

The loss and transcendence process comprises the two phases of mourning and resolution, which in turn comprise four stages; the first two stages are the mourning phase, and the second two are the resolution phase. The four stages are

1. *Grieving*, which often begins with shock or numbness and is followed by yearning. The yearning is the desire for that which is lost and for the replacement of what was valued in the lost; sometimes this is accompanied by hopelessness, no replacement seems possible, and the individual does not progress to the next stage or his progress is delayed.
2. *Searching*, or the attempt to find the replacement for the lost; sometimes the individual keeps searching, but no replacement is perceived as worthy and he does not progress to the next stage.
3. *Replacement*, or the finding of the substitute(s) for the lost, approximating its value on all levels of loss as nearly as possible (not exceeding it, because that would devalue the lost); sometimes the replacement is accepted but the loss of the original is still keenly felt, particularly with regard to specific attributes or activities, which hinders progress to the final stage.
4. *Integration*, or the incorporation into the self of the story the individual tells himself about what the loss meant, how it was incurred, his guilt or helplessness to avoid it, how he dealt with it, and its ultimate meaning to him in terms of how the self is changed or restructured as a result of that loss and transcendence. Preliminary attempts at integration are demonstrated in the recounting of experiences over and over after a loss, particularly a death or disaster, as Moos (1976) has observed. This recounting begins in the grieving stage but is characterized by minute changes as the rationale of behavior and meaning is constructed and the individual progresses through search and replacement. Through the various integrations the story becomes a myth of life, self, and meaning. The myth of self is the story of how the individual creates meaning through the transcendence of loss and then interprets and re-creates his life in accordance with that meaning. It is the pair of spectacles through which he sees himself, largely fiction, and like all fiction subject to dispute, exposure, or startling revelation. This myth is what is revealed in the life history of the individual.

We can think of these L/T process stages in two ways, microscopically and macroscopically.

Microscopically, these are the L/T process stages that an individual goes through with every life event, grieving, searching, replacing, and integrating, although, when the events are at the minor end of the life event continuum, the process may be much speeded and the individual is doubtless unaware of it. It follows that, at any one time, an individual may be in the replacing stage with a material loss, for example, in the searching stage with a relationship loss, and so forth, although at the time only one or two of these is likely to be salient in consciousness. Further, if the relationship loss is a heavy one, it is likely to contaminate the material loss on the holistic and metaphorical levels, thereby delaying the transcendence of the material loss as well.

Macroscopically, the individual is oriented toward either loss or transcendence at any one period in time and also over large blocks of life; he is oriented toward grieving or searching, replacing or integrating. This is another way of saying that he is in an *overall* stage of L/T process. If he is oriented toward transcendence, the replacing stage, he is doing much replacing in many areas of life and recounts that life in terms of replacement—*sees* it in these terms as a coherent whole. The history is predominantly lost or predominantly transcendent.

The L/T stages are sequential but not irreversible (as are Piaget's cognitive stages, 1952). An individual might progress from grieving to searching and then return to grieving but would not skip to full integration. The reversion is simply accounted for by a new loss, probably perceptual, on abstract, self-conceptual, or metaphorical loss levels. In fact, we see this pattern of going back and forth quite frequently in the histories. The individual goes from grieving to searching, back to grieving, more quickly through searching and to replacing, back to searching, and so on forward; progress is more like a horizontal fever chart than a straight line. Conceivably, an individual who is lost now might be, or might have been, transcendent at another period of life. We find this easier to believe with some than with others. It is hard to see Nora (Chapter 7, "Life Meaning") as transcendent ever, but Lorellen is moving in that direction and may have been when she was in her teens. It is hard to see Faith (this chapter) as lost for very long, because of her marvelous ability to reconceptualize events in a positive manner.

Loss and transcendence constitute a single unified process. Loss and transcendence are in a dynamic equilibrium with one another, as are assimilation and accommodation (Piaget, 1952). One is not possible without the other, although sometimes we will find that what we think is loss is actually transcendence—the "blessing in disguise."

LIFE HISTORIES

We now turn our attention to four life histories that exhibit a transcendence orientation to a greater or lesser degree, in order to explore the concept of transcendence in more depth. The first story is Marjorie's. We met Marjorie in the Introduction to this book, the 6-year-old standing by the window, watching for her dead father's return.

Marjorie

"I'm not comfortable feeling powerless."

One of the qualities that moved me in virtually all the life histories I gathered was the courage shown by the women in the face of serious travail. Nowhere is this more evident than in Marjorie's story. Marjorie is titian-haired, in her early forties, and has the body of a dancer.

"The most important incident, that seems like a reference point, is my father's death when I was six." There was some question about a possible suicidal aspect of the accident that took her father's life, which was never resolved. This death generated a series of traumas that changed the course of Marjorie's life. She had been a dancer, but when her father died, she stopped and became afraid to leave the house. As she describes the impact of her father's death:

"I got real fearful. . . . I think that I was afraid that I'd come home and everybody'd be gone. I had to stay home to make sure that everybody didn't leave. I can remember that fear being there from age six until twelve. Whenever my mom left . . . I would maintain [a] vigil. . . . I think that there are different ways of looking at fear. One is to do something to counter it, which is to leave before you're left, and reject before you're rejected. And there's been some of that pattern of . . . taking charge of my life so that no one else could. . . . And then I wouldn't be at risk of being hurt again." In the light of the rest of her history, Marjorie's observation of a pattern around the issue of control seems a perceptive and accurate one. But not only did Marjorie become more fearful. Her mother, although deeply affected by the death, got a job and eventually remarried, so Marjorie felt she lost her mother as well as her father. However, it is characteristic of Marjorie to see loss as opportunity for growth. "The less I got [of my mother], the more I was able to get or create for myself."

Another trauma generated by the death of Marjorie's father was that of her stepfather's molestation of both herself and her younger sister over an extended period. He indicated to Marjorie that, if she cooperated, he would leave her sister alone, and, of course, he was telling the same to her sister. Marjorie's sister left home, but Marjorie was in conflict over the situation for years "because I really both needed him and didn't need him at the same time. And I did love him." After her sister left, "I didn't have any validation, I didn't have anybody at home left that I could team up with and get some support. On a purely unconscious level, I'm sure I just split. I was sure that I needed to do this for my own survival." Marjorie's sister told their mother, but she didn't believe it, which is a classical reaction in situations of this kind, as Machotka (1967) has pointed out. "She just went to sleep over the whole thing." Her mother became an alcoholic. While Marjorie was passionately involved with her stepfather, he became involved with other very young girls as well.

During her adolescence, Marjorie worked and had a number of close friends, both male and female. She then decided to study nursing: "I don't know why I went into nursing. It certainly wasn't something I always wanted to do," but she'd had some other relatives in the medical field who impressed her. "Somehow it felt right. I can remember having really strange dreams about nursing before I went into it, just from stories [I'd heard]. They were dreams of dark corridors and very, very sick people—certainly not happy, and certainly not positive. I didn't have any of the administering to the sick and needy, and they're getting well. It was none of that. It was sort of creepy. I wasn't sure I liked nursing the first few years I was in it. It was a real struggle sometimes."

While in nursing school, Marjorie suffered a serious bout of depression, which a man, who was later to be her husband, helped her through. For this depression and subsequent anger she underwent psychotherapy, during which she confronted her family:

"There was confrontation with my stepfather, telling him exactly what I thought, with the support of a therapist being there. And I told my mother how I felt. I told him that I was very angry with him, and that he hurt me, and that he was sick. I can't remember—I just remember the anger. I remember sitting in a therapy room and just screaming at him. Basically his response was a denial, and making everybody else wrong . . . or there were extenuating circumstances, or it wasn't the way I thought it was. He was very facile with words, and he could really paint an interesting picture. But I felt very supported by this therapist. And my mother was very passive through it all, of course. 'Dear, dear, what is going on? My goodness, poor Marjorie. . . .' My sister . . . began therapy at that time . . . she was dealing with similar issues over my stepfather."

Marjorie's depression progressed to a breakdown. "A young man proposed to me, and I realized that I couldn't make love with him. The conflict came up over a sexual confrontation. I had to acknowledge that I was a grown woman and a sexual being. I was just confronted with all this unfinished business inside. It was revulsion. I just felt revulsed by it. I did not feel sexually attracted . . . and I had not made love with anyone up to that time. . . . I did a suicide attempt, and that was it. It was either shit or get off the pot [laughs]." "And there was this tremendous movement after, in terms of therapy."

Marjorie married, had several children, and went into holistic nursing, about which she is very enthusiastic. She and her husband found they had different values. She was tolerant, impulsive, and spontaneous, whereas he was a long-term planner. She describes him as more practical, judgmental, thinking, introverted perhaps. A crisis occurred when she became ill and had to face the poverty of the marriage, and they divorced.

"I think in marrying I thought I was going to re-create the home, the family, the love, the support that I hadn't had during my adolescence." This is a recurring theme in the life histories as a whole, the idea of creating the home one never had.

Her regret is that she did not get out of the marriage sooner because she was fearful and did not believe in herself, also a recurring theme in the histories. Another regret is that she has not had more long-term relationships; through this intimacy she believes one develops. After her divorce she created a number of important relationships, however.

"My whole world down here is a relationship [laughs], in a large sense of the word. I am a person who relates. I am a woman who has created intimacy a lot in my life. I have a wide variety of friends. There's a lot of sides to me. I have a higher tolerance for intimacy" with her men friends, women friends, and her children. This ability for intimacy is one of the transcendent aspects of Marjorie.

Marjorie again refers to control in characterizing her children; the balance between being involved and letting go is a very delicate one.

Not long ago, she decided to let go in a larger fashion. She left job and family and took a long journey, during which she began meditation as a spiritual practice. "It was a clearing out and a cleaning out time. . . . It confronted me with a lot of the things that I think my active life keeps me from looking at, like my self-concept, self-worth, who I think I am in relationship to all the things I do. . . . There is less garbage in my life right now . . . I don't take on people's stuff in the same way I have in the past. . . . I would say my own spiritual evolution has been the most dramatic during my thirties."

She says further, "There is a part of me that makes changes before I know I'm making them." Where these changes are leading are the long-term relationships she is working toward, an expression of her creative needs in some field such as dancing, which she left when her father died, and a feeling that she is "evolving into something that will continually be of service." She characterizes her work as "definitely a best experience," as well as love and traveling.

Recently, she has gone through an unusual series of material losses, of possessions that meant a great deal to her and connected her with the past. "I just think that some things are going to drop away. I am not sure what they are, but some of it may be outer identity, such as my name . . . that sense of self as I have known it in relation to outer things may be changing. I feel less attachment to my outer world than I have before." Thus, in the face of losses beyond her control, Marjorie controls them by almost willing them as expressions of spiritual development. "I don't fully understand it all, but I know it's happening," a spiritual development that is almost a tide on which she is being borne, in which outer things drop away.

The theme of control repeats itself in how she sees environment as influencing her life. "I would say that living in an earthquake zone influences our lives. And on a larger scale we are on a self-destructive bent with the world. It's made me . . . really try to see ways I can influence my small world for the better," take control of the uncontrollable, which began with her father's death. "I'm not comfortable feeling powerless."

To direct questions on control, Marjorie answers that she has a lot of control in her life, and when asked in what ways she has not, she returns to her childhood. "As a child, and then as a young adult who was still behaving like a child, my attitude was one still of feeling like I was a little victim." The theme of control is repeated by the impact of a relative's death on her life. "I realized that it was me who was in charge of my life, and there was really only so much time that could be spent on this earth."

The loss of relationship as a form of death is expressed in Marjorie's dream: "A lot of times I have had very key dreams that have helped me. I have lived through my dreams. A dream comes, and then something in my outer world changes. This is . . . a strange dream that happened just before I left my husband. He came to me in a garage and his face was painted as the Greek tragedy, as the masks of the theater" (which she had left at the age of 6 when her father died, and to which she contemplates a return). "It was half black and half white, half smiling and half sad. He came to me in the garage like a work space. It was like how we said goodbye. The next scene showed that he was dead. He was in a coffin, only he wasn't dead. Everyone came around to say goodbye, and when I came . . . I kissed him goodbye, and he rose up from the coffin, and he showed me that he wasn't really dead. To me that dream just said I'm really saying goodbye to a part of my life and that relationship is really dead and gone." There is also something of magical, 6-year-old thinking in this dream—a kiss will waken the dead, as she might have thought it would waken her father. The metaphorical relationship between her father's death and the death of her marriage is suggested here, as well as, perhaps, the hope for resurrection. Marjorie has also had a number of psychic experiences, including out-of-body experiences and the return of her father in youthful form when she was young.

Marjorie sees several themes to her life. One is that it is important that things make sense to her. Another is "undoing in a way what I felt happened when I was a child, in terms of loss, and in terms of change, and in terms of unclearness . . . [as well as] having an ongoing relation with my children . . . ongoingness in that it's real, which means that there is also space to fall out of love with each other." In terms of life conflict, "there has been a self-destructive core to me which is just now dropping away, real self-rejecting," which may be the identity she is exchanging.

She sees life meaning as giving each person the "necessary experiences in terms of growth and self-awareness and consciousness so that we can ultimately unify into a kind of cosmic whole. . . . At different stages of our lives we have to deal with developing an identity, developing a sense of selfhood, and then dropping the sense of that individuality." As a nurse she has worked with schizophrenics who never developed that sense of "separation from the rest of the world. . . . You have to develop it to drop it away." Separation, or emergence, must come before unity, selfhood before selflessness or transcendence of self into the cosmic.

We have traced in Marjorie's history a theme of loss of control over traumatic events versus letting go. Her father's death (which she rated as most stressful) seems to be the pivotal point at which she first became a victim, which carried through her adolescence as a victim of her stepfather and through her twenties as a "tyrannized" victim of her husband (we must remember that there is mythologizing going on, that she would have described her husband differently when they were married, and that he would have described the situation differently). Marjorie transcends loss through therapy, letting go of her relationships and of consciousness through meditation and of possessions as forms of identity. She describes her guru as an idealized father figure; in a sense, he may be teaching her to let her father go. Her father may have committed suicide (the question will always remain). One could look on suicide as a way of gaining control by letting go. In this sense, Marjorie may be identifying with and emulating her father. Her history also makes clear the impact of the loss of what we never had, particularly father, home, and marriage. Marjorie is grounded in intimate relationships that seem to aid her spiritual evolution. In the L/T paradigm she seems to fall most clearly in the integrating stage; she is re-creating herself, but with very firm grounding in the experiences and relationships of her life. She was rated as transcendence oriented. She is managing to unite the L/T poles by controlling through letting go. The core theme is loss of control versus control through voluntary loss. In transcending through letting go, even of aspects of her identity, she is clearly re-creating a self who *can* let go.

Theoretical analysis

Marjorie's is a protocol that I feel would have been more loss oriented had I interviewed her earlier in her life. She has had much loss, and its effects have been ongoing rather than discrete. Her father's death affected her entire life; there was not simply a death, a mourning, and a going beyond. One of the effects was a stepfather who sexually abused her and her sister (was there jealousy between them?), leaving her confused because she loved him, needed him and didn't need him, and undoubtedly identified him with her father. It is quite possible, therefore, that somewhere in her unconscious her father died because of their metaphorical relationship. In other words, time, cause, and effect have no meaning in the unconscious. The fact that her father died before her relationship with her stepfather, and not as a result of their metaphorical relationship, is beside the point. This was probably a reason why the loss could not be worked through; the relationship with her father was ongoing and lethal. To the extent that she identified with him, it would destroy her.

Another possible reason why the death could not be worked through was that, in spite of all the devotion she felt flowing toward her father and from him, at some point it must have been illusory—he did make the decision to leave them all. How much could he have loved them? How much could he have loved her, the person she was, actress and dancer, which she subsequently gave up? He may have been seriously ill and this may have motivated his suicide, but the lack of knowledge, the unresolved nature of his death, has been damaging.

Sexual adjustment was difficult for Marjorie, as it is for many abused women. [It is estimated that one in three or four females and one in five to ten males are sexually abused by the age of 18 (Bass & Thornton, 1983; Finkelhor, 1986).] The reasons for the difficulties were the complex family dynamics typical of the incestuous family. These included conflict over her relationship with her stepfather and possibly metaphorically her biological father, possible jealousy between sisters, feelings of mistrust and betrayal, guilt toward her mother, and especially the invalidation of her mother, who refused to be part of the triangle and somehow attributed the entire situation to something in Marjorie, perhaps in fear of losing the man she loved—again. She was not protecting her daughter; her husband was of more value. The love she thought existed between herself and her second husband did not, in Marjorie's eyes, exist—and what did that say of the first relationship, voluntarily left by her father? Of what worth could Marjorie be under all these circumstances, left by her father and then her mother, her stepfather, and her sister? Sexual adjustment was also difficult because the sexual relationship threatens loss of control and yields power to the other, and too much control over death and sex (the small death) had been lost by Marjorie already.

Marjorie coped in a number of ways. She gave up dance and the theater and with these much of the identity that had been abandoned. She stood in fearful vigil at her window, lest the rest of her life go away or not return. Indeed, much of this period was spent in fear. When her stepfather sexually abused her, she was in too much conflict to know what she needed and what she did not; perhaps she was paying a price for his fatherliness, undoing death. In late adolescence, mental illness in the form of severe depression and sexual maladjustment plagued her. Psychotherapy helped her situationally in that she could now communicate her anger to her mother and stepfather, although their responses were denial and evasiveness. She married a man who could be seen as controlling—of time, of order, of schedules, and thus of chaos, which is (temporarily) defeated by time, order, and schedules. In control lay safety and life; death is chaotic, not organized. Marjorie developed ways of controlling so that metaphorically her father could never kill himself and abandon her again. She leaves a relationship before she is left—by husband, lover, and daughter. She controls her consciousness through meditation—it might leave her in breakdown. She lets go physically, emotionally, and spiritually—she is now letting go of who she is (lest she leave herself). She has chosen an occupation in which she specializes in preventive medicine—keeping death away before it gains a foothold. She even left her job temporarily (and was capable of doing it) although she loves it, to take a long journey, clear out and clean out the garbage. She still regrets the acting and dancing—who she might have been—but I wonder if such a life might not have been too threateningly disorganized for her, being someone else, a kind of splitting, more of which she did not need.

Perhaps one of Marjorie's main modes of transcendence is "undoing . . . what I felt happened when I was a child." The losses were not immediately transcendable in adequate or satisfactory fashion, but later through therapy, intimate relationships with children and friends, work, and meditation; she has been able not to undo, but to overcome and re-create. Undoing, by the way, is an (immature) defense mechanism (Vaillant, 1977). In other words, the situational transcendence was weak in the first 20 years of her life, and therapeutizing of the situations was helpful. Since then, this mode has strengthened, as has general transcendence. The improvement seems to have been quite dramatic, so how could one expect that she is what she once was?

Marjorie is transcending by giving up and losing. The extreme of this way of transcending could be becoming stripped until there is no more to lose. Die and one cannot be killed—by father or stepfather.

For Marjorie, she is in the process of developing a new self, a new identity, which seems to be not only a product of the metaphorical transcendence of earlier situations but also now a cause; a benign circle seems to be in effect. Her guru gave her a new name, although she is not ready to use it regularly—not ready for complete rebirth. She has given up the dream of another father for the children; they are now too old. Aspects of her identity are dropping away; there is a new freedom to become who she is, no longer held back by who she was, no longer helpless victim. The creation of a meaningful identity (life and self) through the transcendence of loss is nowhere more evident than in Marjorie's story.

Faith's is a different path to transcendence. At 55 years of age, she tells an inspirational story of overcoming obstacles by turning them into strengths and re-creating her life and self in the process.

Faith

On menopause: "I always figured that maybe God decided that I needed to spend the rest of my life being an artist, and not being a mother [laughter], so he took care of things for me."

Faith is married and is devoted to her profession as an artist. Of her parents, Faith says that they had enormous potential, which they did not fulfill. "My mother was a very intelligent woman, but I never felt she did much with her intelligence. I guess that whole generation was that way, they basically devoted their whole lives to their children. What it did to me quite often was make me feel guilty. . . . Not that [motherhood] isn't a wonderful vocation, but so often she would not do something she wanted to, and basically kind of blame it on the fact that she had to stay home and take care of the kids or her husband, my dad. What it did was made me vow when I grew up that I wouldn't do that to my own kids, so that I would let them feel that I was a separate person on my own besides being a mother."

Faith's father was a musician who never accomplished much, primarily because her mother was jealous of the time music might take away from their marriage. "I guess that also led me to make sure that my husband reached his full potential. . . . Some of the best memories I have of my childhood are Mom playing the piano and Dad singing, nights like that. Somewhere along the line she just kind of stopped doing it, and he stopped singing, so it all went down the drain, which is really too bad. . . . My youngest daughter has inherited that voice, she's got a gorgeous voice, and I keep trying to get her to do something with it, because I see nothing happened with my dad's voice." She hears her daughter's voice in the context of her father's and feels threatened by a metaphorical repetition of loss. Thus, blocked artistic talent seems characteristic of a number of members of Faith's family, again a loss repeated. Unfortunately, she also sees the same sort of inhibiting relationship that existed between her parents in the relationship between one of her daughters and her husband.

Aside from this, however, Faith feels that the marriage of her parents was a good one, as were their influences on her. Her mother guided her positively about sex and marriage (one of the few mothers in the sample to do so) and through her own lack of actualized potential made Faith feel it was "necessary to develop myself." Faith's only family concern was that her parents seemed to favor her brothers over herself.

In the first years of school, Faith developed minor childhood illnesses that kept her out a lot, so that she was not promoted to the highest track, and "that just burned me up. . . . I decided I would show them, so by midyear they had to promote me into the high grade, and that sort of gave me an incentive to always be on the top in my class in school." Loss motivates her to achieve, rather than crushing her. At about age 6, when Faith was in the hospital, a particularly important incident occurred. Her parents brought her "an adult-level how-to-draw book, which was the biggest thrill of my whole youth, because that's my first recollection that somebody else besides myself knew I was born to be an artist. . . . By fourth grade I was doing adult-level portraits."

When asked about the source of her artistic interest and talent, Faith responds, "I think basically it's an inherited talent. I inherited primarily from my dad's mother, whom I never met. She died when my dad was a baby, but she did an absolutely incredible" piece of statuary with a religious theme. "I could sense from that work of art, not because of the subject matter, but because of something communicated . . . that's beyond verbal communication, that's deeper than that—I almost felt like I knew my grandmother, even though I had never met her, and I always felt that really great art was basically an expression of the god spirit within you." She recalls with regret a time when a brother had done something wrong and her father forced him to kneel in front of the statue and say three Hail Marys'; she felt this was a perversion of the art. That statue has always been very important to Faith, and now her father, who is very old, is thinking of giving it to someone else in the family, because Faith no longer uses the family name. This breaks her heart because she has such a deep feeling for it.

In her adolescence, Faith had a girlfriend whose mother worked in the library and, knowing how Faith loved art, allowed her into special art collections in spite of her youth. "It got to the point that the librarians knew me so well, the minute I walked in the door they gave me the key to the art room. And you couldn't take most of those books out, but I used to sit there and look at the books, and I was just so inspired by them."

Others also encouraged Faith in art, including the guidance teacher in high school, to whom she brought her drawings and who encouraged her to go to Pratt Institute of Art in New York. However, "my folks decided I wasn't going to be a starving artist in a garret in New York, so they didn't feel they could support me through college and my brothers too, and so of course, in the old way of things . . . I agreed that my brothers needed the education. But it wound up that neither of them was interested in going to college," so none of them went. "So they sent me to business school. I hated it. Although at this point in my life I'm glad I had that education, because being an artist is, as far as I'm concerned, a business in itself. You've got to do the accounting and all that secretarial work." Thus Faith finds a way to justify an educational setback.

Faith's first serious love affair was with the scion of a famous family, whom she met when she was a senior in high school and decided not to like. "He had to be a spoiled brat. And I think he sort of sensed it, and it wound up that I did fall very much in love with him [laughter], and he was drafted right out of high school, and he was shot down over Germany and killed. In fact, I knew it happened before it was even in the paper, because it was one of those ESP things. I saw exactly how he died. I saw the plane go down in flames . . . he was a tail gunner, and in my dreams I was screaming at him to get out of the plane, and the plane went down in flames over a hill, and that's exactly how it happened."

Faith has had a number of paranormal experiences such as this one. "We sort of are that kind of family. The day my brother got killed in an automobile accident, my mother was sitting watching television with my dad, and all of a sudden on the screen she saw my brother's face. They were watching a golf tournament or baseball or something, and he waved to her and smiled as if to say: 'I'm okay, Mom.' And about an hour after that she got the phone call that he'd been killed—World War II."

Some time after the tragic affair with her first love, Faith became involved in a whirlwind courtship with someone else, whom she did not marry for two reasons. One was that "all he really wanted to do was come home, get a job and get married, and to me school and an education were so important that I couldn't see marrying someone that didn't think it was as important as I felt it was. . . . The other thing was that he was talking one day about the kind of house he wanted—to have a buzzer system in the garage so that when he wanted me he could push a buzzer and I would—and this was before women's lib and all that [laughter], but I hit the ceiling. Why, I'm going to come at your beck and call! . . . You have to have a few love affairs, and you find out what is good or not so good about the relationship. . . . I gradually got to a point where I knew exactly what I wanted other than attraction."

In her twenties, Faith married her present husband. This came about through her mother's arrangement to have Faith stand in as a godmother at a christening ceremony; her husband-to-be was the godfather. "I still get the chills when I think about it, but walking down the aisle with that child in my arms I had déjà vu that some day I would be doing this with his child. It was a weird experience." Pictures were taken, of course, and when her husband-to-be took them back to his barracks, he was teased so much about his "wife and baby" that he made a date with Faith and went to see her paintings. "He was so impressed by my paintings." They fell in love and married.

They lived in a tiny apartment and worked her husband through college. "After a year, the woman who lived downstairs, a crotchety old woman about 94 years old, who had whale oil lamps in her apartment because she didn't believe in this confounded electricity," was not getting her milk delivered by the milkman. Faith's husband noticed one day that their milk had come and not hers, so Faith told him to leave one of their quarts for the old lady. "Well, it wound up she accused us of taking her good milk and replacing with our ordinary milk." They bought a house.

Some time later they had children and traveled around the country, because her husband was recalled into the service and had to go through additional military training. Faith raised babies and took art classes.

When Faith's husband finally got out of the armed forces and became a professional, they moved to the west. Faith tried to join an art association but was rejected; she was told, " 'You're not putting enough of yourself into your work,' which at the time I couldn't understand, because I thought I was putting all of myself into my work [laughter], and I really didn't understand it until I went into the abstract, and then I understood what she was talking about, that there was another whole dimension to painting other than trying to capture the realistic impression of something." This rejection was difficult for Faith to take.

Soon afterward, her husband's work necessitated their traveling to a city in the midwest "which seemed like the end of the world to me, but again, harkening back to my childhood where my mom had prevented my dad from doing things. . . . How could you prevent a man from doing something as wonderful as that? I talked him into it, and I thought, I'll put my art career in neutral and go back. . . . Well, it wound up being the best thing for my career that could have happened, because the year after we went there, he decided that since they give big bonuses, and since I had done so much for him, he wanted to send me on a trip to Europe! . . . So I was looking through my art magazines, and I saw this ad for college art studies abroad . . . here I had five little kids, and I said: 'Who the heck wants to go on just a tour?' He took the magazine, read it, sent for the information . . . without telling me, and got it all squared away that I would take that six weeks in Paris. He says the kids took care of him for the six weeks." A woman, who was supposed to care for the children as soon as they came home from school, took to calling the oldest to find out how things were going and coming several hours late. "If I had known that, I just would have flown home on the next plane."

At the art institute in Paris, Faith met a major art mentor, whom she would have met at art school had she gone. "I always feel I went through the history of art in my career. I started out very realistically and gradually progressed to more of a sense of color . . . that other people couldn't even see." The experience in Paris was an intense one, which she describes in great length. "By the end of the third week suddenly it was all coming together. . . . He said he felt I had learned the most of anybody in the whole class. Because I was ready for him."

On her return to the midwest, Faith found her paintings increasingly in demand by executives at the company for which her husband worked. Some of them told an art exhibitor about Faith, and the exhibitor held a showing of her works, which were critically acclaimed in the local newspapers. Once again her husband's work brought them back to the west, where Faith won a prize for her art, now innovative, at the art association that had earlier refused her membership! "So that was a big milestone for me, because it had hurt those years back when I wasn't accepted."

Faith's husband has continued his emotional, monetary, and active support of her art, even allowing her needed solitude in a second house, which is a kind of retreat, where she spends about 2 weeks a month. "He lets me come up here, and one of the reasons we have the place is 'cause he's well aware that an artist needs time by herself, that you can't create in the midst of a bunch of confusion, and every once in awhile I just need to get away from things." In exploring the reasons for her husband's responsiveness, she says, "He always says he doesn't have any creative talent, which is a bunch of baloney. Anybody that can [do what he does professionally] has a lot of creative talent [laughs]. He said one of the things he always wanted to be underneath was an artist, so that's why he's so responsive to what I do. He doesn't understand what I do, but he respects what I'm doing." However, an artistic talent was discovered in her husband late in life. Their daughter, also an artist, had some of her work destroyed at a college she attended. "So she dropped out . . . she wound up, she and her dog, and her guitar, hitchhiking across the country." Her guitar was ripped off, and she was so brokenhearted that her father made her a new one. "He had never done anything like this before. He had done a little chip carving. So I went to the library and got out a book on how to make guitars, and he started. So he's made guitars, violins, dulcimers."

Meanwhile, another of their children ended up living with a lover. "It was very difficult for us, against our principles, but it isn't against most of the kids' principles these days [laughter]. And then they wanted to get married on the top [of a mountain] in a darn service and all of this hippie kind of ceremony, but it wound up being beautiful, 'cause they had done the whole thing themselves."

When asked about menopause, Faith asserts its ease: "I always figured that maybe God decided that I needed to spend the rest of my life being an artist, and not being a mother [laughter], so he took care of things for me." After this she took a degree in art at a major university, not because she had to, but because she had always wanted it.

After the children left the house, "I suddenly found so much more time to devote to my art career, but I also wound up getting trapped into—well, it wasn't a trap, it was a good experience for me, but I wound up being president of an art association for a couple of years, and on the board of directors for a museum. . . . And then all of a sudden I pulled myself up short and realized that I was faced with making the choice of spending all my time doing that stuff or doing my own art work, and I felt that my art work was more important and backed off on all of that, and basically devoted my time to art."

Faith has now expanded her art activities to include writing and presentations of slide shows. Of her first such experience, she says, "I was scared to death when I went over to give it before the director of the museum, but he was so impressed with it, he said: 'Yes, come back and give it to the docents,' and then I did it . . . for the public." Faith's husband gave her a "retrospective" party not long ago, to which they invited everyone to bring the paintings they had bought from Faith. "As everybody was leaving they would say: 'We really love all your work, but we think we have the best one' [laughs]."

Faith became allergic to some of her art materials and had to switch over to a different medium, which greatly upset her. Then she had an accident in which she broke her wrist, which compelled her to handle the materials in an entirely different fashion from what had ever been done before and led to her own original and idiosyncratic contribution to the field—another in her series of blessings in disguise. "I realized I was making some of the more important statements in my life." She was greatly helped through this period by other mentors as well as her husband.

Asked about the processes involved in her work, Faith responds, "I really was expressing the way I work, which is to not have anything preconceived, but to throw my logical brain into neutral for awhile, and I work with my subconscious emotional brain, and from that I switch back to my logical brain, and I correct the construction. In my paintings I came to that by trying to paint [a major symphony], and that took me a whole year to accomplish. The hardest part was to express that chorale, you know, that last movement, and what I wound up doing was finding out that instead of just the organic flow that I have in these paintings, I had to do some constructive stuff, because [the musician] is so structured."

Faith is not afraid of death, because her mother had a "life after life" experience and conveyed it to her daughter. She'd like her epitaph to be "I'm going to go up there and paint a sunset." She sees a pattern in her life: "I see, as an overview, things happening that somehow are meant to happen, like the right teacher coming along at the right time." Meaning in life for Faith is "doing something worthwhile for others in a service or philosophical way"; the latter is how she sees her painting. She sees herself as *making* meaning but admits this would be most difficult without her husband.

Faith is rated highly transcendent, integration stage. She has had high losses, but she has overcome them, re-creating life and self as well as meaningfulness. Some of the losses she has overcome have been those of others, particularly of artistic potential. She does not seem to linger in yearning or searching fashion over her losses. An obstacle arises, and her approach is replacement and integration. Love, work, and friendship are well integrated in her life, and although the children have been somewhat disappointing, she does not linger over that but rather finds something positive about their differences.

Faith's theme may be seen as overcoming a series of obstacles to artistic development; both the obstacles and the means of overcoming them have been well timed, and she has been assisted by a succession of mentors, foremost among whom is her husband. The obstacles as losses have been the unactualized potential in those around her, her own lack of education, family responsibilities, critical rejection, allergy and accidents, her first love affair, which ended in a tragic death, and the loss of her grandmother's artwork, which is a metaphorical loss to her; she is still grieving over this. Not only does she see uncanny timing in her life, as if aspects were preplanned or guided in some fashion, but also she exists on different levels of consciousness, both in relation to her art and in her paranormal experiences. Indeed, her life reads like a series of stories on how losses are turned into triumphs. Core theme: Obstacles versus destined mentors with felicitous timing.

This protocol illustrates the ease with which a life history could be seen simply as a manifestation of one personality characteristic, achievement motivation. Certainly, Faith has been highly motivated to achieve from early childhood, and she sees others in these terms. But a great deal of the protocol (much more than can be reproduced here) is taken up with concern for the art itself, which seems to be the overriding passion, through which all losses, overcomings, relationships, and re-creations are interwoven.

Theoretical analysis

The orientation of this history is toward transcendence. It is not that there is a lack of loss; objectively, there seem to have been as many losses as in some of the loss-oriented histories. But the focus is on the transcendent aspects.

Loss is dealt with in a number of ways. First, there is a tendency to see the loss as a blessing in disguise or as having a good outcome. The move to the midwest for her husband's job seemed as if it would be disastrous to Faith's career, but it turned out to be exactly the opposite. That her parents compelled her to take business courses instead of art courses (reported in a number of histories) was a source of anguish and frustration, but it paid off later when art became a business, and she took the art courses on her own. The crotchety paranoid woman who caused Faith and her husband so much trouble was also a cause of their buying a house. Early menopause, which is threatening to some women, gave her the rest of her life to be an artist instead of a mother. The children leaving also gave her more time for art, instead of empty-nest regrets. Breaking her wrist lead to a breakthrough—a new technique. Her daughter's guitar was stolen, but the result was her husband's actualized latent talent.

Second, and related to the above reinterpretations of loss, are the curious reversals through which loss is considered to be for the better, not simply because of longer-range results, but because it motivates. Her mother's unactualized potential was an influence for the better because it was an example of how not to be; it showed her that it was "necessary to develop myself." Similarly, her illness and being kept back made her so angry that she excelled where others might have been crushed, as happened to Kendall (see Chapter 4, on L/T life themes). Her love affairs had endings but, with the exception of the tragic death of one lover, they showed her what she wanted in a man.

Third, and related to the above two transcendence modes, is the sense she has of timing that played so great a part in her life. Timing led her to walk down the aisle as a godparent with the man who was to become her husband (although a network of good relationships with her mother, her mother's friends, etc. played an important part). Timing led her to study art with one of the great figures in the art world when she was ready, rather than prematurely. Good timing seems to have been an aspect of some of the losses seen as blessings as well. The timing seems providential; part of a grand design is implicit. Off-time and time-irrelevant losses become on time, in her view.

Fourth, losses as metaphors of other losses seem to have had lessons to teach, rather than to need further working through. The lack of fulfilled potential in her parents is one, although she frets that the same may happen to her children. She will not block her husband's development as she feels her mother blocked her father's (and her daughter may be blocking *her* husband's). While losses are metaphors of other losses (and triumphs of other triumphs), providing spectacles through which to see the world, they teach. Sometimes the triumphs are many years later, as when she was admitted to the art association and became president, after having been rejected previously.

Fifth, although the psychic is not salient in her history, she states that it runs in the family, and one gathers there are many more instances, particularly experienced by her mother. This seems connected with the notion of a grand design and helps to overcome the loss by giving it meaning—death is not the end, and neither is loss. (See Chapter 7, "Life Meaning.")

The sixth and final transcendence method seen in Faith's protocol is that even when there is a loss, there is a gain immediately afterward that, while not necessarily connected, seems to transcend the loss. A high school art teacher was horrible, but a friend got her access to rare art books. She had to go to the hospital for an operation when she was a child, her first night away from home, but her parents brought her an art book that turned out to be a milestone in her life.

One of the things we note about Faith's losses is that none of them seems ongoing for a period of years, as were Vera's abuse by her husband (see Chapter 10), Gwen's abuse by her mother, and Inez's betrayal by her first love and best friend. Faith's losses were difficult—the death of her first love, the rejection by the art society—but they were relatively quick. Another thing to note is the emphasis she places on *not* repeating losses. As we have noted, many of her losses seem to be more like obstacles, because she does not let them become permanent by either dwelling on them or by allowing them to stop her.

The major exception is the artwork that symbolizes so much of her life, and which she may not inherit. This may be connected with a subtheme in Faith's history that seems almost buried in her protocol. While she was growing up, her mother always averred that Faith's brother Tim was her father's favorite, and her father said brother Tom was her mother's favorite. She felt left out. Whose favorite was she? (She later says she understands that, since she was the only girl, that secured her position.) When the question of education came up, they all agreed that, with limited finances, her brothers should attend college (as it turned out, they didn't want to). Faith excuses this by saying that in those days education was considered more important for males because they had to get jobs and support families. Now a brother may be given the artwork because Faith's married name is not the family name and the work was that of her father's mother. One cannot help wondering why the father, whose artistic talent went unactualized, is not bestowing the artwork on the logical member of the family to receive it. The wound is quite raw, Faith's eyes tear, but here again she has tried a number of coping methods in her attempts at transcendence: she wrote a letter giving up claim to it, but her husband would not let her mail it; she offered to have the work appraised and pay the cost into the estate, and so forth.

Turning to the issue of balance among modes of transcendence, we do find it. That Faith can give a coherent positive view of her life may be taken as evidence of dispositional transcendence. Although we were not with her at the time her actual losses were occurring, she leaves no doubt that they were painful. Her situational transcendence modes are very strong. Perhaps she is fortunate that her work involves general transcendence (and perhaps any line of work can, for the right person); however, this calls for much situational transcendence as well, business skills, and art problems to be solved. Art is psychoanalytically considered to be sublimation, one of the mature defense mechanisms (Vaillant, 1977), so there may be a dispositional aspect as well. The question arises of whether art, like the general transcendence modes of alcohol, drugs, and TV, can become addictive; probably anything can. In Faith's case, although there seems to be some obsessing on her work, she has proved that she can break with it when she must, although this is painful.

Not only is the mature defense mechanism of sublimation in evidence but also altruism in herself and her husband—they do so much for each other. However, she doesn't see it as sacrifice; indeed, she doesn't believe in sacrifice, because it makes others feel guilty (a rationalization of her artistic endeavors). She sees her art as in the service of others. She has also been able to postpone, suppress, and anticipate—to put her art away for a while; and to compromise, apparently, and attend the wedding of which she disapproved, even to find it beautiful.

Finally, Faith and her husband have helped create each other, he insisting on the best art supplies for her, arranging a retrospective, agreeing to her solitude; she helping him to discover his own artistic talent and subordinating her art to his career development when necessary.

We turn now to Della's history. A sense of divine plan helps Della to transcend life losses.

Della

"I felt I was becoming the person I was destined to be."

Della is a fresh-faced, matronly woman, appearing much younger than her late thirties. Her religion, Latter-day Saints (LDS; Mormon), is of primary importance to her. Two adorable, curly-headed girls slip through the living room during the interview, kiss their mother, and head to the kitchen for juice and cookies.

Both Della's mother and father were loving parents; however, they divorced when she was 10. Her father was an alcoholic, was unfaithful, and never paid alimony or support, even though ordered to by the court, which left them scrimping on her mother's salary as a secretary. Della admires her mother for not turning her against her father, as she might have done under the circumstances. Raised in the midwest, Della was an only child, associating mainly with adults and pursuing solitary activities like playing with paper dolls. She does not see herself as having changed during childhood. "I just became what I was at the beginning." She feels her mother's influence was positive, because she was compassionate and kind. Her father gave her feelings of inquisitiveness about life and "even in a strange way . . . the beginnings of my foundation in the church that I belong to now."

In adolescence Della was fortunate to have a group of girlfriends who had the same ideals, even though they had different religious backgrounds, so she did not get into the trouble she sees many adolescents in today. The group also ran the class, trading offices. Up to that time she had been shy, but she began to risk extending herself to others. Also in adolescence there was more freedom for parties and movies. However, she was not popular with boys, was unhappy with how she looked, and says "I think you don't know who you are" during this period. The physical and emotional changes are difficult because "they don't get together" for a while. At considerable financial sacrifice, her mother sent her to charm school, which helped.

College (a predominantly LDS institution) was a great experience. She lived in the dorms, where she went from being an only child to having a group of "sisters." "That experience of four years of college may have been the biggest difference in my life. It began to maybe clarify or maybe crystallize the values that I had been taught all along but didn't know that they were important to me. As I mentioned, I'm LDS, and my father was too, but not active. My mother was not baptized into our church until she was middle-aged, so there hadn't been very regular church attendance or formal religious teaching even though the principles existed in what my mother was teaching me. Finally, everything seemed to fall into place. I can see a purpose for life. I felt I had a real testimony [to] what life was about. . . . I really have a feeling that we came here to this earth from an existence before. I'm not sure what that was like, but we came here with several purposes in mind. One was to gain a physical body. One was to face challenges, make decisions and choices, to become whatever the best self is that you can be. I think also to raise a family. LDS seemed to fit and feel right with me." She also began to know her relatives better, and they all proudly attended her college graduation. In high school she had thought the sole two Mormon boys were dull and assumed all Mormons were like that, but in college she discovered that it had just been those two boys.

In her twenties Della began teaching, an occupation she had at first rejected. Her years of teaching she describes as frustrating, with many discipline problems, but rewarding as well. However, she would not return to teaching today, because the violence, drugs, and lack of respect are frightening. Also, the pay is poor. As she was growing up, she had felt she didn't like children very well, but she did like them when she taught them. When her children are grown she may return to psychology or even go to law school, because she loves learning.

Della met her future husband, also a Mormon and newly returned from his mission abroad. "He seemed to kinda glow" was her first impression. They dated for several years, during which he tended to make the decisions. Although she thought this was "cute and masculine," it was a difficult situation for her, and she believed it would modify over time. He was not sure that marriage was the right thing for them, so she decided to take advantage of an opportunity to go abroad on a fellowship to study. "So I went. . . . I was determined . . . not to wait the rest of my life for him." At first she was overwhelmed at the prospect of going so far from home, but she loved every minute of it. When she returned, he decided they should be married. "It was what we term a temple marriage. Most marriages . . . just within our church are termed 'marriages for time.' . . . The ceremony ends with 'death do you part.' Being married in the temple . . . there's a sealing . . . that enables you, if you continue faithful and valiant . . . after this life" to sustain both the marriage and the family. This is a marriage for eternity. What determines the type of marriage? "Generally it's a matter of worthiness. It's determined by an interview with your bishop." Individuals must have followed certain steps in order to be worthy. "For some couples, moral cleanliness is a problem"; they must not have had sexual relations. They are asked if they are tithing 10 percent of their earnings and "can sustain" or believe in the president of the church as a prophet.

Della describes her husband as honest, moral, intelligent, reliable, and a good father to their children. The first year of adjustment was extremely difficult for her. Living with a man was different from living with a group of girls, and she thinks it would have helped to have had a father in the home. The lack of her former independence with money and so forth was painful. She did not work because her husband's military career took them to different places, but she enjoyed keeping house, being with other young wives, and becoming part of her husband's career, a unit with him.

"About that time we became really wanting to have a family and finding that I was not getting pregnant. . . . We began to go to an infertility clinic. I think that's maybe where some difficulty started. That experience seemed to take a lot of romance out of the marriage for me. Because you become a clinical object, you know, go home and perform, come back and we'll analyze what happened. Anyway, we did not have children."

Della feels that during her thirties she was "becoming the person I was destined to be." They decided on adoption. "That was a real high in my life. It was a big decision. . . . You kinda wonder what is intended, if anything is intended by not being able to give birth to children. . . . The social services agency of our church made us feel good about the whole procedure, about the girls who gave birth to these babies. . . . In all of our counseling they wanted to be sure that we didn't feel that these are bad girls or anything like this. We came away with positive feelings that this was a girl who is in a circumstance, that this is an alternative . . . she's made this choice of placing the baby up for adoption. That's not a pleasant thing for her, you know, to give birth when you're not married." One day they received a phone call that a baby had been born in another city. They flew there, where they were told a little bit of her background. "Then they said they'd like us to take the baby into the other room and just to spend a few minutes with her and just kinda feel of her little spirit . . . I don't know if you'd say getting the vibrations. . . . We took her into a room and had a prayer together, my husband and I. I remember looking at that little face. She just seemed to look right through me as though she had known me maybe before. . . . It was a terrific feeling. We decided she was ours."

On the way to adopting their second child, they had a traumatic experience. "We got a call one day again about a baby. Oh, I was so excited. I thought this is going to be the same fantastic experience again, and I can hardly wait. . . . This was a little boy. . . . I walked into the room expecting to have just that excitement again, and something was different. I couldn't even pick him up [tears]. And my husband was really surprised at my reaction, and I was, too. I remember telling him 'I don't know why it is, but I can't. I don't have that same feeling. I don't feel that this is our baby.' And it was an awful feeling because we wanted a baby, a second one." At the social worker's sympathetic suggestion, they spent the night there. "It was a lot of soul searching . . . and a lot of praying together, and trying to find out what was occurring. We went back the next morning and said we couldn't take him." Her husband thought it might be because it was a boy, but she was certain it was not. Some months later when another call came "I was really terrified, because I thought, which experience is it going to be? In my prayers, I tried to find out in communicating with the Lord what He intends for me. . . . I was really scared, not wanting to go into the room. . . . But when we went in, it was terrific, it was like the first time again." Since then she's tried to "sort out what was happening. I still don't know. The only thing I can think of is that somehow these two particular little spirits, these little girls, were the ones that were intended for me."

About her family, Della says, "I feel happier raising these little girls, being a wife and mother, than doing anything else that I can think of. Everything is exciting to me, each new phase of their life." She feels you risk a lot having children. "You open yourself for a lot of pain, but more joy than you'd find anywhere else." The pain occurs when she must put the children's needs ahead of her own, not being able to go to the movies or the theater when they're sick, the restriction of choice. The joys are in their kisses, teaching them: "I can teach them about flying a plane. . . . They draw things from me that I haven't realized were even me."

Della and her husband went through some serious financial difficulties. After the service her husband started a business, which went bankrupt. "I wish my husband's career had been easier for him." It was an "awful experience. . . . I think that was an occasion that showed me a strength that my husband had. We just were determined to see it through, and he didn't throw up his hands and cry, and say what are we going to do. . . . We're managing to do what we can." The problems arose through friction between her husband and a business partner. "I think probably that's been the source of most of the problems within our marriage, financial difficulties that we incur. . . . In some ways it brought us closer together. In some ways it put some distance between us because . . . I personally would have moved quicker into things than my husband."

When asked about her most important possession, tears come to Della's eyes as she responds, "my testimony of Jesus Christ." When asked why the tears, she says, "Because it's my most private, personal. I know, that surprised me, too," she laughs. She denies feeling that there is a sorrow connected with it. Recently she has experienced a role reversal with her mother, who is now ill and needs mothering from her daughter. She recounts the sudden death of a friend's teenage son after a very brief bout with cancer. She hopes her epitaph reads: "She was a fortunate person. She did the best she could." If she could teach people a lesson, it would be "that there's a purpose for you being here, and that you are a child of your Heavenly Father." One of her church activities is to go to the mortuary to "dress one of our sisters for burial. That's part of my responsibility. The first time I did this is was a frightening experience. . . . When someone has gone through the temple, there is a particular burial clothing that you put on them. . . . It's not a pleasant experience handling the body, but . . . I've tried each time, with some preparation of prayer, to realize . . . that this is a loving thing that you're doing for that person. By doing that there's not the morbid fear of handling the body."

Although Della believes that much psychic experience is a hoax and some may even be in the spirit of the devil, "if the Lord wants you to have that particular experience [of seeing into the future], you could. I can't imagine why the necessity would be there." However, she believes that the president of her church is the prophet, with spiritual gifts, and he "can see things." A relative had an experience in which his dead father told him to move just as a mortar shell exploded where he had been. It would have killed him.

Della believes that life meaning is "obtaining a body, using the free agency that you have to make choices, achieving the potential that you have, and recognizing whatever talents you have. . . . The meaning of life maybe would be becoming like our Father in Heaven." She feels that the women's movement asks the right questions but is moving in an unhealthy direction. "It's important for people to discover what their potential is and to live up to that. But I don't think you do that all by yourself, and I feel that's what the thrust of the women's movement is, that you become this person without the rest of society. For me personally, the greatest periods of growth in my life have come with ups and downs, of challenges . . . . For instance, with raising the children you have to put something of yourself aside, but it draws more from you."

Della's protocol, although not heavy with loss, does include some, such as the divorce of her parents, her own childlessness, financial problems, and the nonadoption of a child. Money for Della seems to mean simply the wherewithal for living. Her losses are transcended by a view of them as intended within God's divine plan and by dedication to that plan, submitting to the will of God. We can abstract from the losses a common thread, lifelessness due to misfortune, which in turn is perceived as intended. Core theme: Lifelessness through misfortune versus divine plan.

Della's protocol is rated as transcendence oriented, low loss, high transcendence.

Theoretical analysis

Much of Della's metaphorical system is the religion of which she is a member and through which she transcends loss. Her religion teaches situational and dispositional transcendence as well. It teaches that even losses like infertility and the infant she did not adopt may be intended by God, part of his divine plan. Thus her religion provides a meaning to life by providing a purpose for the losses that might make it meaningless. Her religion also provides transcendence of the ultimate loss, which is death, by immortality for those who remain faithful and valiant and have the other moral qualities sanctioned by the church. Transcendence of death in this church is especially effective because some of it is carried out in this life—the sealing of the marriage within the temple, for example. In this sense, eternity is begun within this life, without waiting for death. We can see that the metaphorical system is extensive: not only does it provide purpose but it is also the context of major and minor life events; marriage and adoption; her attitudes toward unwed mothers, the psychic, and the women's movement; her daily church-related activities and scripture reading; and also change—"I just became what I was at the beginning."

Della experiences her self as "becoming the person I was destined to be." There is a self already, and the work of life is to grow in this rather than to create self. One wonders if who she was had to be submerged to some extent during the first year of marriage, when her husband was taking charge, and if this was good or bad for her. She speaks of difficult adjustment and yet of becoming part of her husband's career, a unit with him, obviously on his terms. Her personality test shows characteristics of which we have only vague hints in the history: skeptical, critical, independent, stubborn—possible factors in the difficult adjustment (she tells us independence was a factor) and her attitude toward her husband's financial problems. Is she required to repress a part of her self? Is this the price of the transcendence her religion gives her? Repression of part of self is not necessarily evil. Perhaps it is part of the divine plan that faults be repressed so that better qualities may develop. A different self is created. In addition, she experiences her children as expanding her self, creating her in a way, calling up things in her she didn't know were part of her, or exercising unused, undeveloped parts of her self.

Della transcends generally through her religion and also through very effective rationalization. When she's stuck home with sick kids, prevented from doing what she wants to do, she turns it around by building the relationship. When caring for the dead body of her "sister," an unpleasant duty, she thinks of it as an act of love and it becomes easier. Her religion has taught her dispositional as well as situational transcendence, how to perceive and metamorphose. Even her father's virtual desertion (he had been unfaithful for many years and contributed no support) is converted into something good, the foundation of her faith; not being much of a father, he gave her a heavenly one instead.

The lack of money from men as a means to survival may be a subtheme of this protocol; her father did not support, and her husband is having a difficult time doing so. They are in debt. She is becoming her mother, mothering her, but also raising children under financial deprivation. (Financial deprivation is echoed in other parts of the protocol as well.) She does not tell us the cause of their infertility. I'll go out on a limb and say that I feel that, if she were the cause, she would have referred to it, especially the long, often painful procedures and attempts. Therefore, a subtheme may be male weakness, which cannot support, earn a living, procreate. This may be why she could not accept a son. It would also make her open to an all-powerful male figure, her Heavenly Father. By identifying her husband with God, His virtues, she can make him potent enough to promote their survival.

There are tears when Della speaks of her most precious possession, "my testimony of Jesus Christ." She doesn't know where the tears come from. Are they tears of joy? They do not feel like tears of loss, and surely this faith is powerful and redeeming. They may be tears of association with the losses that are transcended by faith. We are reminded of the joy in the transfiguration of saints, the transports of the mystics, and perhaps many of us have felt such "pure joy," bringing tears to our eyes. These are not the tears of the mother of the bride or the graduating student, in which there is much loss. (See Chapter 8, "Individual Development.") These are the tears of pure life, overcoming all limitations and death. Limitation and death are lost, and so the self also dies, and "pure joy," like orgasm, is death experienced.

Our final case study in transcendence is the remarkable story of Sue. Some will argue about whether Sue's renunciation is ultimately transcendence or loss.

Sue

"It's very difficult to figure out exactly what kind of love you have for somebody."

Sue is a petite blonde in her mid-thirties, the manager of a fast-food restaurant. Her story is at once inspiring and puzzling.

Sue was raised in a secure, stable home. Her parents were both teachers. Her mother was "the best" and "miraculous" and stayed home to raise her during her early childhood. Her father was loving, preoccupied with his job, but always willing to make this up to her. "I think my parents are the best. I feel like I *need* to feel that way"; it's important to respect them. But they were "motivated by love . . . any complaints that I might have seem real unimportant . . . They've become friends. They're my counselors, still."

Although she was an only child, many relatives gave support in times of difficulty, such as death. Her maternal grandmother in particular gave lots of love and communicated her own spiritual faith. At first Sue and her family lived in a tiny house on their own property while they were building a large one; when they eventually moved into it, she remembers the "overwhelming" sense of largeness, but the move was not traumatic. Because her parents were teachers there were many summer outings, on which she brought her friends.

Sue's best friend grew up in her neighborhood. Sue says, "We went to college together and do keep in touch. [She was] quite different than I am. I sometimes think in a marriage relationship we would have been a good complement to each other [laughs]. Even though we're both of the same sex . . . she was very socially oriented and extroverted, while I feel like I was a little bit more introverted, and she was verbal, while I was a listener, but our similarities, too, were that we were both only children, we both had very similar parents."

Sue's husband-to-be also grew up in her neighborhood. They played together during childhood and dated in adolescence. "Bill was very self-determined, had his own ideas about things to the point of being stubborn. . . . He sets his sights and goals high, and he achieves until he reaches them, and that was even real obvious when he was a child. . . . He was sensitive to the way somebody would feel . . . he cared about other people." He recognized the needs of others, had good friends, was loyal, loved the outdoors and animals, kept in good physical condition, and "could do just about anything." She says she shouldn't speak of him as if he were past, as he still retains these qualities. By the time they were seniors in high school, they felt as though they had a commitment to each other. Sue felt they would marry, but that scared Bill because his parents had been through a messy divorce.

Meanwhile, Sue knew she wanted to go to college and emulate her mother by teaching, marrying, having children. Her father favored teachers' training as insurance. When Bill and Sue went to college they decided, at his suggestion, to try dating for a while, then got back together again and began a sexual relationship, which, while enjoyable, made them feel guilty. Her parents, although they disapproved, never brought it up or discussed it, seeming to feel it was all right if she wasn't struggling with it.

Of her adolescence Sue says, "I wish that I had struggled through adolescent traumas a little bit more, rather than facing them when I was twenty-seven or twenty-nine. Even though I did struggle against some of my parents' values, there wasn't a big upheaval during that time, and having it happen later, I missed the guidance," from parents and counselors. She was an adult going through adolescence.

In college she was also very involved with her studies; she earned enough credits to graduate, but did not, "that was odd," because she was pregnant. She and Bill had split up again, and he did not know of her pregnancy. She went through 3 months of anguish. "Abortion was not an alternative . . . it wasn't legal," and it was against her values. Her parents were supportive, but she felt badly about their embarrassment as they explained to their friends. They considered the possibility of adoption and rejected it. Then, unaware of the situation, Bill came back into her life. "By his choice, he came back and said he had missed me, and two weeks later I told him I was pregnant, and that I'd not made a decision what to do, and he said: 'I think that we should get married.' I think we've always been in love," but having grown up so close to each other "it's very difficult to figure out exactly what kind of love you have for somebody. . . . We've been great brothers and sisters, we've been lovers, we've been a lot of things, but how much do we know about each other? Now, looking back, I realize everybody starts out with those kinds of doubts [laughs]," even though they haven't grown up together.

Shortly after their marriage they had an accident in which a young woman was killed, a traumatic event, the result of which was that "we focused again on how temporary we are," and they decided to move in with her parents. Their son was born, and things went fairly well because her parents were gone quite a bit, so they had some privacy. Sue says that it was probably a hardship for Bill, although she doesn't know how he felt. He was working and going to school. Her mother helped tremendously, and Sue was pleased with how close the baby became to his grandparents. "One of the most exciting things . . . was I taught him to swim when he was six months old, and that was an incredible joy . . . bringing my father extremely close to him at a very early age, because my dad was an avid swimmer, and I can still remember him bringing his friends to the back yard, and saying: 'You have to see this,' and here he's swimming for all he's worth from one side of the pool to the other—just incredible!"

Sue returned to college, finished her degree, and got a job teaching part-time. But her relationship with Bill was "going in so many different directions. . . . It would have been very beneficial to us to have been building that more at that early time, rather than falling into some set patterns that were difficult to break later, such as not being able to communicate with each other. [Laughs] We didn't have time, and then we sort of forgot how." Their son was four when they moved to another city and purchased a small house and·a small business for Bill, which kept him busy all day into the evening. They hardly saw each other. They usually had housemates, and she found herself being closer to them. "He would come home still being in that same space. It was a difficult time for him then to relate to somebody, where I'd been with the children all day and needed an adult to talk to. [Laughs] I'm sure I talked his ear off, and he was coming out of his silence, I must have driven him nuts. . . . So there was always somebody else in the household, which often I'm sure substituted my need to outlet. . . . I didn't feel Bill was receptive, but they were often more available, and sometimes I feel like those two housemates knew more about me than Bill did. . . . We had a pattern of noncommunication set up, and we didn't quite succeed in breaking it down."

The business was not profitable enough. Bill sold it and found a job a considerable distance from where they lived. At first he commuted; then he stayed nearer his job several nights a week. They developed two sets of friends, who were dissimilar. "I mean, it was very separate, it was not a marriage." Their housing became more and more separate, and they "both simultaneously became sexually involved with other people . . . close friends." Bill bought a house in another city, and Sue resolved to take their son to him there and then decide what to do. "I got scareder and scareder that our marriage was not very good. . . . I wanted to see a counselor, but that was an ego blow to Bill. . . . I'd always been very dependent on his decisions." Thus Sue was afraid to make a go of the marriage and afraid to get out of it. She's always needed someone close, and she realized Bill was not that person now.

So she brought their son, now seven, to live with his dad, while she took off for distant places. "A lot of places I thought I wanted to see, but they were really pretty empty. Even friendships, because I had changed so drastically. . . . I wasn't the person they knew, and we didn't have much in common. I had always given the sense of—now whether this was really inside of me I don't know—calm and peacefulness about my life." But, like an adolescent, she was ill at ease with "who I was, what I was doing, where I was going, if I was going anywhere, if I wanted to go anywhere." She wasn't even a good listener any more and had difficulty in relating to others, because she didn't have much to give. When asked how she came to be this way, she responds that it was "disillusionment with marriage" and surprise at her involvement with another man, a very important relationship that developed from mutual need.

When Sue looks back on her twenties, she feels that the major problem was lack of communication. "With all the information that I had about . . . how important communication was, and yet it always being a very subtle part of my life . . . I wish I'd tuned into the need for it . . . with my husband, with my parents, too. Just not taking the time . . . I sort of lost that for awhile, and . . . forgot to talk to people; it became superficial. I'd never been very much involved in petty small talk, and that was about all I did during that time, just: 'How was your day?' Not really caring about the answer." She feels she got that way by being overinvolved and trying to accomplish her goals all at the same time. She could have postponed her teaching credential, although she's glad to have it.

She decided to let her son live with her husband for a year. She had a great deal of conflict about this, but she realized that her husband needed the boy because of his own difficulties in being a child of divorced parents and going back and forth between them. He didn't want this for his son. Also, "I realized that I had some serious finding to do of myself," too heavy for their son to handle, and so it would be "more healthful . . . for our child if he had the constancy of his dad." However, she wanted to support her son by being available, so she got a waitressing job in their town. Bill was now living with someone who loved their son very much, a "wonderful girl . . . and they seemed to have a good, solid relationship that I probably envied at the time, although I saw how we'd fallen away from having that possibility, and felt like there were too many memories for us to develop that, so I didn't end the year in terms of thinking: 'Well, if she wasn't there, I'd have that.' And also I felt like that was very healthy for our son. He'd been without male and female roles in the household. . . . It was tearful and traumatic, and yet I felt like she was a good mother figure at the time, and I was a good, supportive person. I would always be my son's mother, but I wasn't a very good mother figure [laughs] without having a relationship with a husband."

Apparently, Sue struggled with her role without too much success, trying to make it a good situation for her son, "feeling like maybe I was an older sister," feeling that she was giving up her motherhood. A friend of hers from another city found her changed from her old positive self to someone who "obviously wasn't healthy" and invited her to the other city for a respite.

Sue went, found a teaching job, and was helped by the couple with whom she lived. Bill started divorce proceedings but didn't follow through. Meanwhile, he broke up with his girlfriend and "felt very confused, wondered about our relationship again." She realized that her commitment lay with Bill, and she began to hope it could be worked out. However, she felt, and still feels, his tendency to hold back on their involvement, for fear of being hurt. She was doing better, largely because she found substitute children in her job and also because of her friends, who gave her emotional "strength and shared their spiritual values. . . . My focus was on Christ, and the rest of my life would follow that. . . . And loud and clear kept coming through: 'Your primary focus is your son. He's a gift to you, and you need to be looking out for his well-being before somebody else's.' But, boy, was I scared! For a year I hadn't had the role." She went for a routine physical examination; a growth was found, fortunately benign, but she sent for her son. She likens this to the accident in which the young girl was killed—it changed her perspective. Although she feels that God is in control of how long one lives, and therefore there is no worry about this, it helped her feel that her "son needed to know how much I felt like that was a privilege," being a mom. So her son came to live with her. She was also close friends with a woman who was dying at the time, someone "incredibly powerful and dynamic," who "made me feel more solid about what I thought, that human relationships are important, [but] a relationship with God is even more important."

After a while, Sue realized that the bond between her husband and her son was gradually being eroded by distance and that this bond was extremely important to both. "We definitely needed to get closer to his dad, because that was a relationship I wanted him to have, though our differences kept us from living in the same household." They both finished the school year and moved back to the town where his father was. She lived in a camper, part of the time with her son, and did odd jobs to make ends meet. She's been unable to get a teaching job, so she became a fast-food restaurant manager instead and does volunteer teaching on the side. Her son now lives with her in a house and is 13 years old.

On being asked if she's involved with an important man now, she responds with a laugh, "just my husband." Did they get back together? "No, we haven't. My commitment is still with my husband, and we don't have a sexual relationship. We are very supportive of each other. I realize that he has sexual relationships with other people, although I don't think there's anybody in particular. It's like a real slow process of either me realizing that that commitment may not be for life, and that's okay, but right now that's how I view it, and possibly for him to get over realizing that even being in pain, as I mentioned before, is not as bad as not allowing yourself to feel love."

Her 2-year celibacy was difficult at first but is not any longer. She has gotten over "looking at other people's situations and wishing them for myself. . . . Christ has promised me that he will fulfill all things as long as I turn them to him." She feels lonely when there's no one with whom to share a particular incident. The celibacy "just sort of happened, and I would like to believe that the commitment I have to Bill is the reason. . . . I'm not sure he's aware of it, but I'm pretty sure he knows I don't date."

Currently she's taking a course in sign language because "I've always [been drawn] to deaf people, and occasionally I've been confronted with not being able to communicate with them, and it was just something I have admired other people being able to do."

Sue believes that being "an encourager to people and wanting to listen" is a recurring life theme for her, as well as the patience which others have recognized. Life would be meaningless without God. "I've even questioned whether or not I could do without my son . . . just in pursuing how much of a commitment I was making to God, if God should make that decision that I would be without my son . . . through death . . . seeing if I really have given everything up for Christ. . . . I'm not sure how I'd react. But because I believe that He wants our ultimate good, He would only do that if He thought that was best."

When we seek patterns of recurring loss and transcendence in Sue's history, we are struck by the number and variety of ways in which communication plays an important role. Both of her parents and she herself have made communication their profession. Sue characterizes herself as a listener, who encourages—that is, the passive participant in communication—but she is also a teacher. Communication may have been a rather selective process in her natal family; certain things, such as her sexual activity, were not discussed. She feels that lack of communication, or poor communication, was the major source of her problems with her husband; she did not know how he felt about important issues, like living with her parents; he came home from work too tired to talk, in another space, whereas she needed adult talk after a day with children and probably talked too much; in her twenties she engaged in small talk rather than taking the time for the kind of communication that would build relationships. There was poorer communication with her parents as well. She has always been drawn to those who cannot hear communication and is learning the language to reach them. She communicates with God via prayer, and responses come to her in the form of realization; for example, her son is a gift and he needs to know it.

Thus, we see that communication is a source of transcendence and lack of communication a source of loss for Sue. Because communication is the means by which close relationships are established, and these (including God) are more important to Sue than anything else, we can understand its importance. She transcends through teaching, friendships, her bond with God. It is what people say or do not say to her that is preeminent, not what they do, how they are, or what they have.

Beyond this, there seems to be quite a bit of idealization, with commitment to what is idealized (parents, son, husband, God, friends). The ideal is, of course, unattainable. The core L/T theme, then, is communication as mediator for idealized relationships, both lost and preserved.

Sue's personality profile shows her to be quite introverted, relying on feelings more than thinking, with a balance between sensing and intuition as well as between judging and perceiving. On the Social Readjustment Rating Scale she tends to rate experiences she has had as less stressful than experiences she has not had, with the exception of the marital separation. This is consistent with one who idealizes and possibly denies. This protocol is rated as high loss, high transcendence and as somewhat more transcendence oriented than loss oriented.

Theoretical analysis

The several aspects to consider in Sue's history are the ways in which death informs her of her life priorities, the possible roots of the L/T life theme and the metaphorical system it represents, the role of idealization and commitment in her life, and finally what communication means. At first, these aspects may seem somewhat diffuse and unrelated, but they are not.

Several times in her history, threatened or actual death gives Sue a new perspective on her life and influences her in an important decision. When she and her husband were accidentally involved in the death of a young girl, "we focused on how temporary we are" and decided to return to live with her parents, because as new parents themselves, they would need that kind of support. An elderly woman friend of hers who was dying made her feel more confident in her growing conviction that her mutuality with God was even more important than her mutuality with humans. A benign growth made her send for her son. She tests her religious faith against the worst possible eventuality—if her son died. In each instance, the possible or actual death motivates the transcendence of loss. Sue lives much of her life within the context of ultimate things.

The roots of Sue's L/T life theme—communication as mediator of idealized relationships, lost versus preserved—are difficult to discover. Paradoxically, parents whose profession was communication may have blocked some communication of disagreement-provoking thoughts at home; however, Sue gives us such an idealized picture that we learn only incidentally that lack of communication about her sexual activity, and also her own lack, distanced her from her parents in adulthood. Another possibly idealized relationship—that with Bill—began in childhood; still another, her relationship with God, seems to have begun at her grandmother's knee, although certainly her parents had conservative traditional values consonant with Christianity. Dependence, perhaps, on parents, best friend, husband, and God may have begun in childhood; in this sense, she seems to be solidly rooted in the past, with a few strong and thick roots, rather than many-rooted like some of our other interviewees.

Finally, we might look into the phenomenon of idealization itself, by which negative communication is denied or repressed, probably because it would destroy the thing idealized, make of it something less. Idealization, then, may protect both the idealized and the idealizer from negative impulses too threatening to deal with. Sue says she *needs* to feel her parents are the best, and then explains this by the value of respecting (honoring) one's parents (following the Commandments), as if this were somehow superimposed on a different reality. As a parent herself, she is uncertain of her role; perhaps she is a sister, she is not enough of herself yet, she goes in and out of parenthood. So idealization may be the following of Commandments. Similar idealization and obedience to Commandments may preserve Sue's status in her son's eyes, relieving her of blame for her variable enactment of the role of mother. If she honors her own parents, her child may honor her, and metaphorically she is her son, honoring herself.

In some ways communication and idealization may be antithetical. Idealization seeks to veil the truth; communication seeks to reveal it, to put people truly in touch with each other (or to appear to do so). An existential interpretation of what communication accomplishes might view each human being as irretrievably alone, never able to know another truly and completely, but succeeding in knowing another to some degree by effort at honest communication. However, there are problems. I do not know myself completely; I may unwittingly conceal part of myself from myself and/or from the other; I could never totally reveal how I am at every second, or who I am. Since I am always changing, *am* I, ever? Ultimately, then, I am alone. However, I will always try to moderate this aloneness because when I am one with anything—dyad, group, or community—I am part of something larger than myself, and that partness survives my own demise in both actuality and impact. This will be discussed more fully in Chapter 6, "The Self," and Chapter 9, "Loss and Transcendence in Relationships."

Communication transcends the loss of oneness or unity with another; idealization may accomplish unity by not communicating anything that would disrupt it—an illusion of unity—but the sacrifice is that of true closeness. Ultimately, the idealizer is more alone, and in this sense perhaps Sue did need to be communicating more, idealizing less, to achieve the close relationship for which she yearned.

The puzzle of Sue for me is the relationship with her husband. She seems to me to be committed to a dream. Their history together is one of his straining away from the relationship and then wanting it back. This began in high school and continued in their marriage and after—almost 20 years! She excuses him and blames herself. She sacrifices teaching so that her husband can be with their son; she says he would never make the long trip. Or is she sacrificing to be near her husband—he dating others, she celibate, she committed to one who is not committed to her, and all within the context of high religious values and faith? Ultimately, is she defending herself against close relationships by this commitment or is she a very highly transcendent individual? By making her relationship with God most important, Sue seems to distance herself; indeed, proximity versus distance might be a subtheme of her history, a coming together and a drawing apart, perhaps protectively. Communication with others took place in a communal household for a while, but it is now communing with God.

When we look to types of transcendence in Sue, we see a balance to some degree, with general transcendence in religion predominating but situational transcendence as seen in her occupation quite strong, in her personal

relationships more questionable. Dispositional transcendence has been dependence, denial, rationalization, altruism, and suppression, as well as substitution and sublimation (her volunteer work with children when she could
not teach, her teaching of other children when she did not have her son with
her). When she says she hit adolescence about 10 years late, she may be
right.

Sue's story is an example of renunciatory loss which is a form of transcendence. While we all give up certain things for other things, for Sue,
renunciation becomes a test. By renouncing husband, son, marriage, teaching,
she cannot lose them, because ultimately they all remain in God.

CONCLUSIONS: LEVELS OF TRANSCENDENCE

We have examined four of the more transcendence-oriented life histories in
some depth. What observations can we make across histories, and what
conclusions can we draw from them on the nature of transcendence?

First, obviously there are levels on which transcendence takes place, just
as there are levels on which loss takes place. These are the levels of primary
transcendence, secondary, holistic, self-conceptual, and metaphorical. Loss
and transcendence are in dialectical relationship, part of the same process.

Second, in the transcendence-oriented life histories, we do indeed see
more of a balance among the three types of transcendence than in the loss-
oriented histories, where one form of transcendence seems to predominate,
or even be abused, and there is little of one or two of the others. The implication
of this for counseling is that it is important to see that individuals with problems
are not only situationally competent, not only employing mature defense
mechanisms, or not only generally transcendent.

Third, we saw that the transcendence pole of the L/T life theme seems
to have roots in childhood and to be traceable through life, although it undergoes expansion or contraction depending on life's circumstances and the
individual's response to them.

Fourth, it must be noted that none of these protocols is a very low-loss
protocol—even Della has had her share. This raises the question of whether
there can be high transcendence without high loss. A number of protocols
were rated high transcendence, low loss, with very low loss indeed. Typically,
these women were not risk-takers; they prized stability and security, accomplished good works in the community, and did not reach the peaks manifested
by Della, Marjorie, Faith, and Sue. Transcendence is thus dependent on loss,
the definition of transcendence includes the concept of loss, and loss and
transcendence are one process. As I have said, the stages of this process are
grieving (numbness and yearning), searching, replacement, and integration.
We can see how Marjorie, Faith, Della, and Sue replace and integrate, but
we see some grieving and searching as well. They move back and forth, from
one stage to another on the continuum, as their lives unfold.

A related issue is whether there is an optimal level of loss resulting in an optimal level of transcendence. The relation of loss to transcendence may be curvilinear. The higher the loss, the higher the transcendence, up to a certain point, at which loss, quantitatively and qualitatively, may be too great. However, although this formulation makes sense, we know from our cases that individuals develop metaphorical systems (see Chapter 5), which are more or less loss or transcendence oriented, and these systems are only loosely related to the facts and highly dependent on the individual. Many in Sue's place, for example, would have chosen to keep both son and job in the far-away city, cut the ties with husband, and develop a new network of friends, resulting in a new primary relationship or marriage. That is the rule; Sue is the exception. But Sue's metaphorical system, which coincides with her values to quite a large extent—God, loyalty, commitment, love, communication— leads her to perceive her life and self as she does and consequently to act as she does.

These life histories, as well as those from the previous and succeeding chapters, illustrate the wealth and variety of ways in which people transcend. No chapter could encompass all, although an entire book on transcendence might begin to do justice to the topic (and Chapter 11, on cultural and societal manifestations, explores general transcendence in more depth). These individuals are overcoming loss and re-creating their unique selves, and they are doing this through daily choices that derive from how they see their lives and world, their metaphorical systems, what signifies death to them and what signifies life. Their choices are determined by what is meaningful, what would make sense in the context of their systems. Daily, they triumph over the metaphors of death and give birth to themselves.

4

Loss and Transcendence Life Themes

As we saw in the previous chapters, individual patterns of repeated loss and patterns of repeated transcendence are manifested in the life histories. I have termed these L/T life themes (see Weenolsen, 1978, 1985b, 1986a, 1986d), although it is clear that the life theme is also a self-theme in this paradigm. The notion of life themes has been suggested by a number of other psychologists as well as biographers and novelists.

This chapter begins with a brief review of what others have had to say about life themes, followed by a recapitulation of the methods employed to determine L/T life themes. The histories of Ronnie, Judith, and Kendall are helpful in elucidating this process, and a table of all the expanded and core L/T life themes in the study gives an idea of their nature and variability. In the last section of this chapter I discuss issues in L/T life themes such as their number, uniqueness, and variety, their etiology, the extent to which individuals are aware of their themes, event salience in the cognitive organization of themes, consistency of themes from one life period to another, phenomenological reasons for repeated loss events, themes recurring *across* protocols, and finally the L/T life theme in the therapeutic setting.

LITERATURE ON LIFE THEMES

A number of psychologists have observed an underlying pattern, collection of elements, theme, or group of themes in the accounts individuals give of their lives. In 1962 Gordon Allport observed "the possibility that a life may be understood almost completely by tracing only a few major themes or intentions" (p. 416). He called these themes "central motifs" and cited Floyd Allport (1937) as proposing the term "teleonomic trends" for life hypotheses held by the individual that can be seen as ordering his or her daily activities. However, he cautioned that the appearance of such a theme or hypothesis may be superimposed by the interviewer rather than implicit in the life of the interviewee. Further, he asked how *conscious* the interviewee is of the theme. Allport agreed with William James (1890) that there may be more "dominant trends" than simply one or two. He further suggested the use of direct methods and projective methods as checks on the eliciting of any life themes.

In 1938 Murray described "an underlying reaction system" or "unity-thema"; these are needs that have their roots in specific childhood experiences, "gratifying or traumatic." It seems plausible that the theme observed in responses to the Thematic Apperception Test might be the same as, or strongly related to, the life themes suggested above.

The Adlerian concept of "life style" as the "spectacles" through which the individual views or cognitively organizes his or her life seems relevant to the concept of theme and is often demonstrated in the clinical situation (Ansbacher & Ansbacher, 1959). Although Adler conceived this organization or "cognitive map" in terms of inferiority versus superiority, of trying to create "significance within the social structure," it need not be restricted to this concept. As Mosak (1979) described it, the "life style" includes "the long-range goals of the individual, the conditions . . . requisite . . . for security." It is largely nonconscious and "fictional," a personal mythology that may be observed by a therapist in the patient's "life-style summary," in which "basic mistakes," or the confusion of myth with reality, are evident. The spectacles may be working to the patient's detriment, and she or he may need a new prescription.

In his provocative discussion of affect, Tomkins (1978) cites "the phenomenon of connecting one affect-laden scene with another affect-laden scene," a process that he terms "psychological magnification" (p. 211). He does not believe this process occurs with all experiences; some scenes are transient and are not experienced as connected with other scenes, and others are "recurrent, habitual scenes"; he gives the example of shaving every morning. If all life consisted of these two types of scenes without psychological magnification, it would be dull and impoverished. However, the connection of one affect-laden scene with another is a different process. "Through memory, thought and imagination, scenes experienced before can be co-assembled with scenes presently experienced, together with scenes which are anticipated in future. The present moment is embedded in the intersect between the past and the future in a central assembly" (p. 217). Tomkins calls this whole series of scenes the "plot of life," comprising nuclear scenes and scripts. "These nuclear scenes and scripts are relatively few in number for any individual, but are composed of very large numbers of families of such scenes" (p. 229).

These recurring affect-laden scenes, psychologically magnified because there are differences among them that form a story, may indeed be viewed as thematic in that they center around recurring issues, conflicts, regrets, decisions, and commitments.

Psychoanalytic clinicians (cf. Dewald, 1972) have observed the "organizing fantasy" of their patients; a traumatic childhood event or relationship that has gone unresolved has been projected onto adult individuals, relationships, and situations; the process of psychoanalysis assists the patient in the transference, regression, working through, and eventual giving up of the infantile longings with subsequent healthy functioning.

The existential concept of a "life project" around which the individual's choices, commitments, goals, and decisions all pivot might also be construed as the embodiment of a life theme (Sartre, 1969). The knowledge of death, of limited time, is the crucible in which the life project is conducted and authenticity sought. A related concept is Buhler and Massarik's (1968) developmental delineation of goal setting, which gives purpose and meaning to the individual's life. May (1977), Boss (1957), Binswanger (1958), and other existential clinicians have analyzed their clients and written their case histories within this type of framework.

The life theme has also been defined as "an affective and cognitive representation of existential problems which a person wishes to resolve" (Csikszentmihalyi & Beattie, 1979, p. 45). Thirty professional and blue-collar men were interviewed, and important or traumatic childhood events were found which provided the subsequent theme; this became "the basis for an individual's fundamental interpretation of reality and way of coping with that reality," (p. 45), a concept of theme closest to the Adlerian "life style." A single theme was emphasized, consciousness of theme was suggested, and there was no check on the possible "imposition" of themes by the researchers.

In the course of interviewing members of three-generation families for a research project (Csikszentmihalyi & Rochberg-Halton, 1981), Weenolsen (1978) found that interviewees seemed to return to the same conflict, decision, or commitment in many of their answers, no matter what the questions; in fact, the questions were often slightly rephrased, or tenuous connections were made by the interviewee, so that she or he could discuss this central conflict or decision because it seemed more relevant. From these conflicts, decisions, or commitments, the interpretation and evaluation of all subsequent behavior seemed to radiate. The conflict, decision, or commitment seemed to form a "continental divide" in the life of the interviewee from which all subsequent decisions, interpretations, and evaluations flowed.

"For many, the crucial decision was not like others, which could have been relegated to the past. Other choices had been made over the course of the lifetime—choices of college, mate, home, etc. Once made, these choices were finished. But the vacillation around that one key decision remained, to be frequently reaffirmed. These individuals had left behind part of themselves still standing at the crossroads, wondering about the road not taken. That road had been romanticized. The landscape never changed; time, that had turned the leaves to autumn on the chosen road, stood still on the road not taken. This choice had formed a life theme, in that all that had happened since seemed to interpret it, and be interpreted by it" (Weenolsen, 1978, p. 1).

Weenolsen saw these themes as "discontinuous" or "continuous" (antecedent to the loss-oriented versus transcendence-oriented distinction), depending on whether the crucial choice still seemed a matter of conflict or life had proceeded relatively smoothly since. The use of time pervaded these themes; time was something to be captured in photos or possessions or given to the children, not wasted on drinking. Different members of the same family, including different generations, demonstrated the same or similar themes (first suggested by Hess & Handel, 1959), such as alienation in one family, commitment to family continuity in another, all manifested consistently in relationships, work, and environment even though the initiating decision or conflict for each individual was obviously different. Although the possibility that the interviewer was superimposing life themes was not addressed, the fact that the research was originally for a purpose different from that of eliciting life themes suggested that the themes might exist in the interviewees' lives rather than simply in the interviewer's mind.

Garraty (1957) pointed out that biographers have long sought and found simple themes unifying the lives of their subjects. The popular biographies of Emil Ludwig are prime examples; he found in Goethe a tension between genius and daimon, in Bismarck a conflict between pride and ambition. André Maurois saw the lives of his subjects in terms of metaphors, the symbol of water recurring in Shelley's life and work, the symbols of rain and peacocks in Disraeli's.

Finally, a psychobiographical study of Arthur Koestler (Weenolsen & Barron, 1979) yielded a central theme in both his life and his work: that man is doomed to an unresolvable conflict between his existence as an individual and his existence as a part of society, a conflict between whole and subpart. In later years, this seems to have been partly resolved by the union of physical with psychic phenomena, the reality basis of the psychic (Koestler, 1972).

In Chapter 1, I proposed that there would be a pattern of repeated losses and transcendences, with one theme dominant over possible subthemes; that individuals would be aware of their themes; and that these themes would originate either in childhood or as adult ways of conceptualizing experience.

METHODS

The L/T life theme is a pattern of recurring losses and transcendences that are very similar or related to each other; this pattern appears in the life history as set forth by the interviewee, although no loss is *exactly* the same as another. The death of a child is different from the death of a parent, and the death of one child is different from the death of another child. The patterns are based on actual events in the lives of the individuals, but they are also ways of viewing those lives, interpreting them, and organizing a coherent life history or mythology. In other words, the individual "sees" his or her life in terms of these major events and their impact, past, present, and future. Further, the elements of the L/T life theme determine values, choices, commitments, goals, and decisions, which in turn perpetuate the theme!

The L/T life theme has an "expanded" or "extended" version and a core version. The expanded version includes the major loss and transcendence events, relationships, decisions, commitments, regrets, and so forth as related by the interviewee. The core version is a bipolar summary. Thus, the expanded version *supports* the core.

The L/T life theme is determined by listing the major life events and relationships as recounted in the life history, noting repetitions, amount of attention given by the interviewee to the experience, and significance accorded by the interviewee. This is similar to Freud's notion of the abstractions of unity, as observed by Holland (1985). How the interviewee reconstructs his or her life was given more importance than whether, or how, the actual events occurred. Then I looked for common denominators or patterns in the list. For example, Nora's protocol was filled with accounts of how her mother, husband, son, daughter, and neighbors had mistreated her. The underlying loss for her was seen as loss of potential love through mistreatment, cruelty, or inconsiderateness of others, and her own reactions of bitterness and resentment. There was little transcendence in this protocol, except for a number of references to wanting to travel, take to the road, go to Europe "in order to see how others survive," as well as a few reminiscences of singular acts of kindness in others. I interpreted this as transcendence through leaving (mainly by car), or "turning away" from bitter relationships to fantasy (about travel and remembered kindness). Core theme: Bitter relationships versus getting away. The polar theme was thus supported by the specific major events of the life; Nora's expanded theme supported her core theme.

Were the themes inherent in the life histories, or were they (unintentionally) imposed by the researcher, against which G. Allport (1962) cautioned? A reliability and validity check indicated that the themes seemed to emerge from the protocols. (See Appendix B.)

Now let us examine the stories of Ronnie, Judith, and Kendall to illustrate some of the major issues of the L/T life themes concept.

LIFE HISTORIES

Ronnie

"I would like to have lived during the time of Chopin, Balzac. It's such a romantic period. . . . I would have to be wealthier, or I

wouldn't have enjoyed it. It would have been like going to recitals,
listening to Chopin's music for the first time. Maybe having an affair
with Balzac, or at least being written about . . . living in Paris."

Now in her fifties, married and employed, Ronnie's earliest memory is
a happy one, a move with her large family from the city to the country near
her grandparents, where there were trees to climb, creeks to fish, and wild-
flowers. Here she recalls happy family gatherings.

Although Ronnie's father took her and her siblings on many enjoyable
camping trips, he was domineering and violent. He refused to allow his
children to listen to classical music, forced them into lessons they didn't want,
and forbade them lessons they did want. Ronnie's incipient musical interests
were frustrated. He also hit her mother and the children. "We were hit many
times. We were knocked down. . . . [He would get] angry at us . . . usually
for strange things, now that I look back. I remember my sister getting a terrible
spanking because she fell down and cut her elbow badly, to the point where
it needed stitches, which meant a doctor's bill. I think that is what angered
my father, because he was a penny-pincher. . . . We seldom saw doctors.
Any time we got into trouble like that (through carelessness, the way he looked
at it), we were punished. I was punished severely when I was about eleven,
because I went against his wishes and played with a neighbor who happened
to be [of a different religion]."

Ronnie's relationship with her "very passive" mother was much better,
but she resented her mother for not fending off her father's violence. Her
mother also never taught her anything about sex or menstruation. However,
when her father's health forced an early retirement, her mother took a job to
pay the bills; from this job she had to walk home several miles late at night
in the dark, which scared her. "That is what I really love about my mother.
. . . It took guts to do that . . . she was frightened . . . walking home late
at night in the dark, with wilderness on both sides, no street lights. . . . She
had a flashlight. Terribly exhausted, too, after being a waitress. That's a long
way to walk after a whole day of waitressing."

Ronnie's teenage years were characterized by rootlessness. After her
father became disabled, he also became restless, and they moved frequently,
which made her unhappy because she had to leave her friends. Her parents
were divorced when she was a teenager, partly because of their fights over
his attending community dances without her mother. She says she was happy
about the divorce and wished it had happened earlier—a recurring comment
among interviewees who were children of divorced parents. Ronnie's mother
remarried.

In high school Ronnie had fun dating in a group. She met her husband-
to-be there. He made a pass at her, which she repelled, but from this he
learned to behave himself, and they became engaged, though she was not
"madly in love. I had been so thoroughly turned off by sex in my childhood

days in [the midwest]. It was never talked about. It was something that was snickered about. And it was definitely dirty. And the Sunday school class that my parents sent us to every Sunday to get us out of the house was a turnoff, because the teacher just taught us how dirty our bodies were, you only touch when you really have to, you only look when you really have to. So with that, and not having any open discussions within the family. . . . My husband had to teach me just about everything about sex."

College was ridiculed by her father and his relatives and was out of the question, even though Ronnie had a profession in mind which she yearned to take up and which required further training.

Ronnie was married at 20. What impressed her most about her husband was that he was intelligent, attending college, and "really liked women"; she had wondered if men did, perhaps as a result of the relationship between her mother and father as well as her early training.

Ronnie stayed home to raise her children, which she enjoyed—it made her less self-centered—although she was frail and always tired. Her mother-in-law was a domineering woman who disapproved of Ronnie and feigned illness to get her way. "I wish I had had a different mother-in-law. She caused friction between [my husband] and me. She wanted us to get a divorce. . . . None of her daughters-in-law was acceptable. When she was my house, I heard how terrible the other daughters-in-law were. . . . We all would match notes, and we knew we would never be able to please her, but it was unnerving when she would go to someone else's house and say: 'Well, [Ronnie and her husband] will be getting a divorce soon.' When her father-in-law was ill he wanted to die at home, but her mother-in-law wouldn't have him, so he died alone at the hospital. She had instilled guilt feelings in the children, so they would never confront her with her cruelties. Meanwhile, Ronnie's father had remarried, and his wife became Ronnie's close friend—"sweet, happy-go-lucky, scatter-brained but hardworking"; and her father treated his second wife the same way he'd treated the first.

Ronnie underwent a traumatic experience when her stepfather made a pass at her. "He tried to put his hand under my sweater, and kiss me in a very unfatherly manner. That hurt me. . . . I'll never understand why he did that, because he was close to my mother." After that "I was afraid to get too close to him. I mean, there was no more kissing him hello and goodbye, and hugging like I would a father. . . . And then another thing happened. I was home alone, and the husband of our best friend came by, and he tried to get fresh with me, too, and I had to push him away. I was upset about that for weeks."

Ronnie, her husband, and her children moved into a house near relatives. Ronnie's children were sweet; she had never had any trouble with them. But they went through a profound change under the influence of their relatives' child. Ronnie fought with them over this issue and tried to keep her children away.

Another move put them in a neighborhood where several children were "absolutely unbelievably mean to the other kids in the neighborhood." So she tried to keep her own children in the backyard. As for her own feelings about the neighborhood, "I felt uncomfortable for the first six months. They stared at me and the clothes I wore, and I thought they were so terribly casual. They were small in their views. It was almost like [the midwest] all over again [laughs], so I stayed home a lot . . . and I enjoyed it immensely just staying home and baking" and walking. Her father and stepfather lived in the area, and she was close to her stepmother, but the couple separated, divorced, and moved away. After this, her father's health deteriorated. Ronnie also was influenced by a local minister. She found herself teaching catechism, which she detested, because "I didn't believe what I was teaching. . . . I couldn't tell them about Adam and Eve with a straight face [laughs]."

At about this time an opportunity arose to go to Europe with a friend, and her husband gave her permission for the trip. "It was an education to see whole different cultures . . . it was completely beautiful. . . . I had friends who [said]: 'Your husband's going to let you go alone without him?' Even the men thought he was crazy to let me go." (You had to ask his permission?) "Oh, yes, I would never have gone. I would now [laughs]."

In their new neighborhood, a woman, after expending considerable effort, finally succeeded in seducing Ronnie's husband. Ronnie found out about it after a long time and was very hurt. "She was an absolutely gorgeous thing, perfect figure, perfect face, and she strutted around the neighborhood in her tight pants. . . . They were bright red, and they showed everything. . . . She didn't see much of her husband. . . . We wondered whose husband she was after. . . . She would call my husband up" to help her with some problem in the house. While Ronnie suspected the affair, her husband denied it and she believed him, but when she finally found out it was true, it had been going on for some time.

Meanwhile, one of her children, who had been highly gifted and professionally trained in music, gave up that career, which was like the one her father had frustrated in her as a child, and this disappointed Ronnie very much. Her daughter, having broken with the values of her mother and being prone to severe depression, attempted suicide. Ronnie evinced disappointment in all her children.

Ronnie returned to work in her forties under sweatshop conditions, in a store where women were exploited. "The women were expected to take care of customers, do their own inventory and ordering, and at the same time, if they were short of checkers, you had to stop all these things and go out there and check out the customers, but at the same time you had only a certain number of days to get in this inventory. There was an awful lot of pressure, and if you would confront these little assistant managers with it . . . they would never pay overtime, you had to clock out . . . and then come and do it, but a lot of women . . . were afraid. They were divorced, they had to work. But I fought with those assistant managers every day . . . and I got away with it."

Ronnie switched to another occupation where she can work her own hours, be her own boss, where every day is different, and she loves it. In the course of this work she met a man with whom she almost had an affair. He was a charmer, a "game player, but at the same time I thought he was serious."

Meanwhile, her husband had to have surgery, for which her mother-in-law blamed Ronnie, saying the illness was the result of all the rich foods she cooked. "So I let her have it. . . . That settled our relationship. She no longer gets letters from me, or flowers sent to her on Mother's Day, because her son would never think to do it, it was always the wife. . . . We severed our relationship." Her husband took a while to recuperate and became jealous of her male clients during this process.

At present, the relationship between Ronnie and her husband seems to be a standoff. She knows about his year-long affair with the neighbor in tight pants; he is upset about her near affair. "So this is where my husband and I have been having some very verbal, honest, forthright communications lately." He demanded that the game player "stop seeing my wife," and Ronnie's reaction was, "How can you make an abrupt end of the beginning affair with this man when you had this long affair?" He said, "I've always loved you." Ronnie says, "I have been unhappy because of his choice . . . because I dislike her so much, and really he doesn't like her either. . . . He had our affair much hotter than it was. . . . It hadn't gone that far." Ronnie observes that she has changed a lot in her forties, particularly in being much less inhibited about sex and in feeling attractive. "I wish I had more of an affair with that man," she says, but in another part of the interview she wishes she had not gotten involved with him. The ambivalence exists because both loss and transcendence, particularly the re-creation of self as being uninhibited sexually, have been embodied in the same relationship.

When asked about fantasies, Ronnie responds with an incident she remembers from her childhood in the midwest. "One day I was walking home from school with this little boy who walked me home every day. He asked me to pull my panties down, and I wouldn't do it. I ran away. I cried to my mother. I told her what Jimmy'd asked me to do. She didn't add anything to it. She didn't scold him, [or] say there was nothing wrong with it. She said nothing. So my fantasy is that I am this little girl, and this little boy asks me to take my panties off, and I do it, and we actually enjoy exploring each other. This was something that was denied me as a child, and I think that was unfair, so I fantasize about it." She senses her own refusal and the norms on which it is based as a victimization, and yet this return to childhood sex is, perhaps, safer than what she might do now as an adult.

Ronnie's Social Readjustment Rating Scale was remarkable only in that many of the less normatively stressful life events were scored quite highly and vice versa; that is, Ronnie's was not a normative view. With regard to life meaning, Ronnie says, "Learn to cope, accept disappointments and joy in the good things." This seems quite close to her transcendence pole, that is, overcoming loss by active coping. Ronnie sees a pattern of "giving myself to my children, and now giving myself to me more than I used to."

Ronnie's expanded life theme is loss through victimization by other people's negative actions (father, stepfather, mother-in-law, neighbors, seducer of husband, children), transcended by active shaping of life in career and relationships, physically and sexually. Experimenting with assertiveness pays off. Core theme: Victimization versus assertiveness. Her protocol is loss oriented, in the searching stage, particularly for a solution to her marital problems; she seems to be moving toward the replacing stage. She is rated as high loss, low transcendence.

Theoretical analysis

One of the major questions about life themes is whether there is a single theme or several themes or even six or eight. Ronnie's case illustrates the presence of a major theme plus several subthemes that may contribute to the major theme or may only be tenuously connected with it. These subthemes should be acknowledged rather than ignored, in order to gain a less distorted, more rounded view of the person as a whole. However, Ronnie's case is typical in that one theme predominates.

Ronnie's father was domineering, violent, a penny-pincher, punishing, and possibly unfaithful (he and his wife fought over his dancing with others), and in addition he frustrated Ronnie's musical interests. Her mother was passive and self-sacrificing, treated badly by her husband, and feared sexual attack at night on her way home from work. In high school, Ronnie's husband-to-be made a pass at her, which she repulsed. Her relatives ridiculed college (those who went were "putting on airs"), so her career aspirations were aborted. Her mother-in-law tried to promote a divorce between Ronnie and her husband, dominating all her children with "feigned illness"—a passive mode. Ronnie's stepfather made a pass at her, as did the husband of one of their best friends. Her children were badly influenced by relatives and neighborhood children. A neighbor seduced her husband, and their affair lasted over a year, her husband denying it initially. Her children's lives are beyond her control and disappointing. One is suicidal, and another gave up musical gifts—both extremes of passivity. On the job, Ronnie found "sweatshop," exploitative conditions, which she was able to fight, in contrast to her fellow employees. A "charmer" nearly seduced her, a "game player" who left her with very mixed feelings, partly because he lied a great deal. She sees a pattern of giving herself to her children and is now in the process of meeting her own needs. The underlying pattern of loss is one of passivity, of being victimized by others either directly or indirectly (her seductive neighbor, kids who are bad influences, etc.).

Ronnie demonstrates transcendence by sacrificing herself and being passive within the family, keeping her children in the backyard (passively, hiding out), sticking up for her rights with the "little managers" at the store where she worked, choosing a career in midlife where she could be independent and successful, trying to fulfill her love of music vicariously through her children, repelling "passes," breaking off with her mother-in-law after years of abuse, confronting her husband about their relationship, helping her children with their difficulties and communicating with them, breaking up with a potential lover, and keeping herself attractive by working out at a spa. In earlier life she transcended passively; her role model for this was her mother and, considering the violence of her father and the times, passivity was probably the better part of valor. In adulthood, particularly in middle age, Ronnie has moved toward situational transcendence—handling situations by manipulating them physically, verbally, and actively—and her skills in transcendence are increasing. She is not the victim she was.

The major reason for her growth in situational transcendence seems to be the freeing of heretofore repressed, but very healthy, sexuality. This forms a subtheme. It runs through part, but not all, of the major theme above. Sexuality was dirty, something to snicker at, and not really discussed in her family or community when Ronnie was growing up. A little boy asked Ronnie to pull down her pants and she fled to her mother, but she now rehearses a different outcome in fantasy, resenting as victimization her lost opportunity. Ronnie felt turned off to sex as an adolescent and young adult, enduring a number of "passes" that upset her. However, during the middle years, interest in and enjoyment of sex seem to have grown. Perhaps now she has more permission. Her relationship with her husband is more satisfying for both, although he explains his affair with the neighbor by saying he wants sex every night, Ronnie doesn't, and so he uses the neighbor to fill in. Ronnie keeps herself attractive to men in her line of work by exercising to stay well muscled and well toned (which she is). One of these men has attempted an affair with her, and about this she has mixed feelings. She feels less inhibited. She would like to have lived in Balzac's time, to have had an affair with him in Paris, and been "written about." Her growing derepression of sexuality seems to have been a motivating force in a number of her more transcendent decisions and actions, an experiment in assertiveness that has paid off in her feeling desirable, sexy, of worth, not to be victimized. Sexuality, then, repressed and developing, seems to be an important subtheme; through it she has been a victim but is also emerging.

Another possible subtheme is her interest in music, a form of general transcendence. This was frustrated in childhood, but she found a vicarious outlet for it in her son's abilities and activities, unfortunately brought to only limited fruition. When asked what makes her sad, she replied, "Mozart sometimes makes me sad. Mozart's second movements are very emotional, and I've read some things about his life, and he was badly treated by the church, and people took advantage of him. He died young." Here again, however,

Mozart was a victim and died young. Victimization seems to be equated with death, and, in overcoming victimization, Ronnie overcomes death metaphorically. The historical period she would have lived in was the time of Chopin and Balzac, attending recitals, having an affair. If she could return as anything she pleased, it would be as a "great pianist."

We first encounter an aspect of Ronnie's L/T life theme in her frustrated musical interest and her account of how she and her mother were victimized during her childhood. It seems reasonable to conclude that her passivity, which in the extreme is death, began at that time. As we will see in Chapter 10, on personality, aggression is a way of taking life from another for oneself, and this was Ronnie's experience of the first important man in her life. Her mother modeled giving up her life for others but also actively working for them, as Ronnie has done. Her father's way led to ill health, in both his marriages, and Ronnie is critical of his behavior, seeing ill health as the consequence. More than anything, in discussing her possible love affair, she seems to fear exploitation. The emergence of Ronnie's active, more successful transcendence is probably due to a combination of her father's weakening powers of violence, her mother's activity at work (which she was compelled to do after her husband became ill), her own sexuality, success resulting from her tentative assertiveness, and a personality predisposition toward more activity. While her mother gave life, her father took it, metaphorically, and this duality of giving and taking life must be a strong part of Ronnie's makeup.

Ronnie sees much of the world through the victimization-assertiveness dichotomy, defending against attack, metaphorically saving her own life. Victims like Mozart die. She resented her mother for not defending her, and she has practiced defense, trying to defend her children as well, bringing her music to fruition in her son. In a sense, the children will "inherit" aspects of the L/T life themes of their parents, as we shall see.

Ronnie has told us her story in only a few hours and selected the incidents that were most meaningful. She recounts her story through her own spectacles or metaphorical system; that is, she selects or omits, elaborates on or passes quickly over the major events and people. One may well imagine that her mother, father, husband, and children would have different tales to tell, that discrepancies might even be large. The story is Ronnie's myth, out of which she creates her life. One not attuned to victimization, for example, might be less assertive and select different incidents from which the fabric of his life is woven. Thus, it is what her story conveys, rather than the actual facts or events, that is important to us.

One final question: Is there a sense in which the abused appear to be vulnerable, thereby inviting further abuse, exploitation, and victimization? Victimization is, after all, a denial of responsibility. It is saying, "I am not to blame. This was done to me. I didn't do it to myself." And yet, perhaps one does, to some extent, trained in manner by past exploitation. Perhaps one almost wears a sign saying, "I have been victimized—I am a victim—therefore, I am here to be preyed upon." Victim is part of one's identity, and to lose one's identity is scary. One might, like Ronnie, work through the victimization with practice. And certainly, being nonresponsible gives one permission to engage in forbidden, often sexual, acts.

The next history shows us an interesting admixture of major L/T life theme and minor themes.

Judith

"I like the challenge of something different and exciting, and not knowing what's going to happen another hour from now."

Fifty-year-old Judith lives with her husband and assorted pets in a beautiful house overlooking the ocean. Her dog wheezes noisily, a condition due to allergy of some years' duration—nothing serious, she believes. Judith had difficulty answering the questions because she had not thought much about her past. She "snaps" her answers.

Her mother was strict; she would hit first and ask questions later, but her mother did "roll with the punches." Her father was easygoing. As a child, Judith was sick a lot, and feels that this was why her mother was "overprotective." Her mother was dominated by her father's decisions. She had younger siblings who were unplanned, "a shock." Judith changed her evaluation of her mother's influence from "in between" to "for the better" because both her parents were "nice people."

Judith had always wanted to be a nurse, she thinks because of her own need for ear and throat operations. With regard to her childhood hospital experiences, she says: "I was scared, probably of the unknown." She has very happy memories of her nursing training.

"I'm recalling something very funny. When we were student nurses, we wore the blue and white striped uniforms, the pinafores; everybody looked good, tall and short, fat and skinny. But the day you finished, you became able to put the white uniform on. . . . It was a tradition that you get ripped out of your uniform. And these interns knew when all the student nurses were finishing. . . . And I was standing there at 8:00 in the morning, ready to go off duty. And one came in one door, and one came in the other, and there wasn't a thing you could do about it [laughs]. These two men are now probably very sedate surgeons." Suddenness and surprise give pleasure.

One of the few losses that Judith sustained was of a boyfriend in nursing school, who dropped her abruptly. One night, he said: "I don't want to see you anymore," and she never found out why. To recuperate, she visited a friend in another area and quite by accident joined the program that was to educate her in her lifelong specialty, that of nurse anesthetist.

After nursing school, Judith and a few girlfriends shared an apartment in a town where there were many available single men, and they all dated extensively. It was here that she joined the armed forces and met her future husband, who lived some distance from the town and was to be transferred west. People would ask them, "How long does it take to get there?" They'd reply, "one fifth," which meant "it would take one fifth of whiskey for the whole bunch of them to drive [from there to town] to what they called their little pad at the beach. Not very rough, but fast living, lots of parties. I just didn't want any part of that. But then I did call him for a date. . . . Well, he had to marry me because I'd given up my apartment, quit my job, and half of my possessions had already been shipped [west]." She and her husband had to pull strings to get her out of one branch of the military service so she could join him in another.

There followed a long period of travel with the armed services. Her husband was rarely home, and she depended on other military wives for support. After many years of trying to have a child, they adopted one through the "gray market," because military families were not thought stable enough by adoption agencies. She gives an account of how they got the baby.

"We were in [a western state] at the time, and the delivery was in [another state], and there was an airplane strike, and the mother could not get out of the hospital until the baby was picked up. . . . So the commanding officer of the base was nice enough to write up a set of orders" for her husband to fly on a military plane to the state where the baby was. "So here he was, armed with diapers and a bottle and the baby clothes, and [his relatives] went to the hospital with him, and they picked up this three-day-old baby, which he put in the car bed and took on a bus to the air base, and put her in the hospital there until his flight [home]. We have pictures of him coming off that ten-hour flight with a brand new baby. She was sound asleep, but he was a wreck [laugh] 'cause he'd never changed any diapers or given bottles. That was quite an experience."

Judith's husband was sent overseas, and she was happy raising their daughter, an easy child. "The wives all play bridge, and they go to these crazy luncheons. They have to have an opportunity to dress up in a hat and gloves. . . . I was fairly active in the wives organization." Judith says that they did not actually decide not to have a second child; it just happened that way, and now she regrets it. "We didn't really talk about it."

When a temporary job for a nurse anesthetist opened up at just the right time, someone called Judith, she took the job, and she has now had it for many years. The retirement of her husband proved to be a temporary problem. "There was just a little bit too much togetherness. . . . I told him I'd married him for better or worse, but not for lunch . . ." so he got another job.

At this point, Judith observes, "Your tape is going to be quite interesting with the dog snoring" (that's what she called its wheezes), "and the cat meowing."

Judith finds her job in obstetrical anesthesia, particularly resuscitating babies, satisfying. "It's a challenge, and every patient's different, and every situation's different." She belongs to a team of nurse anesthetists and anesthesiologists who have been working together for years. "We're all growing old disgracefully together [laughs]." She maintains that there is no jealousy in this group.

Judith enjoyed her travels, with the exception of one town. "It was the end of the world as far as I was concerned. It was before anything was built up then. It was inconvenient. In order to even go to the grocery store, it was miles away, and the weather was hot." However, she enjoyed all her moving around. "Love it. How else do you get to clear out your garage? [laughs]."

A pregnancy scare in Judith's forties turned out to be a tumor for which an operation was scheduled. She told the physician, 'Make sure I'm the first one on that schedule, because if you leave me any longer than that, I'm not going to have it done.' I'm frightened [of the] anesthesia. You know so much about it. . . . I found out later all the other doctors thought I had a malignancy. That thought never entered my mind." (What do you envision happening during anesthesia?) "Just the idea of not being able to control myself. . . . I was afraid of not waking up, dying." Fortunately, the tumor was benign.

Judith and her husband bought a house on the ocean and had a fishing boat for a while, until the price of gasoline went too high. This move proved problematic for their daughter, who considered the area "Siberia, and just hated leaving all her friends. . . . The first summer here . . . I could tell you the Greyhound bus schedules, meeting all her friends." As for her relationship with her daughter, "there were times when she thought we were too dumb to come in out of the rain. All teenagers think their parents are one step above morons. We've gotten a lot smarter since she's gotten older." Her daughter now lives by herself and suffers asthma attacks. "It's not that she's not managing well; she's just not managing [laughs]." Judith isn't happy with how her daughter has turned out. "We were disappointed, but it's her life. She's had several jobs. . . . She moved in with a friend. We do not approve of the fact that she's living with him. I'm still older generation. But we've had to accept it. If we hadn't accepted it, we would have lost her, too. He's not what we would have picked for her. He has difficulty holding a job, he doesn't have much of a goal in life, what he wants to do, but it could be worse. They're not into drugs." (Does she have a goal?) "No, and that's sort of disappointing to us. It would have been absolutely no problem financially to send her to any school she wanted. Maybe that's why she didn't want to go."

There is a sense in which Judith seems to avoid trouble by not knowing about it. "If you don't know you're supposed to have a midlife crisis, you don't have one." And "I didn't know I was supposed to be afraid of my mother-in-law," so she was not, as were her sisters-in-law.

At a number of points in the protocol, Judith mentions how well timed or how luckily events happen to her. "Actually, they called and asked me if I'd like to come back to work. They hit me at just the right time. I was getting bored." This seems related to her enjoyment of novelty. "I like the challenge of something different and exciting, and not knowing what's going to happen another hour from now. Not routine."

She is concerned about age-appropriate behavior; she disapproves of letting older women into student nursing programs, because they will work only 10 or 15 years. She talks about having had accidents while engaged in activities typical of younger people and how embarrassing it was to have to tell how they had happened.

When queried about her dog's illness: "Well, she gets a little rattling in her chest. I listen to her chest, and if it sounds juicy, I give her one pill, and if it doesn't, I give her something else. She's on medication. She's had it three years. A lot of it is fake. She knows she gets attention"—a neat trick in a sleeping dog! Since this chest rattling had been called snoring before, it suggests that there is some denial going on. However, she also refers to the fact that she knows her parents will die some day, she is thinking of readying herself for this by taking a course in death and dying, and she is unsure how she will handle this crisis.

Judith's overall theme seems to be concerned with a tension between unpredictability and stability, with both losses and transcendences on this dimension. Her mother hit first, asked questions later, her siblings were "unplanned," her fiancé jilted her with no explanation; her lack of ability to get pregnant and her uterine tumor both surprise her; the nonadoption of a second child simply happened; if you don't predict something, it doesn't happen. On the transcendence side, she loves the unpredictability of traveling and moving; the fun of the ritual uniform strip; her work as nurse anesthetist, because each patient is different; the way their daughter entered their lives. At times unpredictability is related to conventionality, age-appropriate behavior, but it can get boring, at which point she floats with the next happy accident. Judith sees her theme as, "I enjoy being a wanderer." A related theme is one of breathing: her daughter has trouble with it; so does her dog; it is her job to facilitate it. Breathing is the most predictable thing a body does if life survives. Core theme: Major unpredictabilities transcended by minor ones.

Some of the interviewees seemed to have a personal metaphor. Judith's is that of fishing on the ocean. The water, like life, bears her where it will, and she loves it (she notes that her astrological sign is Pisces), but she enjoys the luck of the fisherperson; whatever chances to hook her line is hers. She snared her husband with a series of lucky happenings. Her advice is, "Don't try to make trouble for yourself." Don't rock the boat. Don't make waves. She is seen as low loss, high transcendence, and integrating.

Theoretical analysis

Judith's protocol demonstrates high transcendence and low loss. But how can there be high transcendence of low loss? The answer lies partly in the levels and types of loss and transcendence and partly in whose loss is being transcended. As a nurse, Judith transcends the losses of others, which she does well. She gives life to others by giving them breath to ease their pain, by assisting at their birth.

The losses that Judith reports in her history are being ill, hit, jilted, infertile, and having a tumor removed. Judith does not dwell on these at length, for the most part; when she does, she details how she coped. The losses could have been serious and long term, but she transcends situationally. She gets over them. What she is not aware of, of course, is the various levels of loss. Although the incident levels may be low, the levels of abstract or holistic loss as well as of metaphorical loss are high. She befriends both unpredictability and death. Make of these a friend, and they cannot be your enemy.

Judith's transcendence is dispositional as well as situational. She uses denial effectively. Her dog's chest rattling is snoring and also faking. That her tumor might be malignant never occurred to her. Her negative evaluation of her mother is changed to a gentler one—converted by rationalization. She believes in not causing trouble for yourself, and this includes how you think. General transcendence is also evident in her travel dreams and activities, how she talks of nature, floating on the water. She gives life to infants and is harsh on older people's behavior if it is inappropriate to their age, such as 50-year-olds training for a new career when they have only a few years left to bring that training to fruition. Yet she does not think of the implications for herself. She also is 50.

Whereas Judith is highly transcendent through coping skills, losses she can handle, denial, rationalization, and pleasure in the moment, there is another way in which she does not seem transcendent. She has had no "peak experiences" and is the only interviewee to report this. She does not feel she has made a contribution; however, she hopes she has done no harm. There is a feeling here of holding one's breath, staying on an even keel, floating, not rocking the boat. The price of no lows is no highs; a placid sea does not dip, but neither does it rise. Leaving to fate such decisions as not having a second child, going back to work, residential moves is a way of floating and eluding responsibility, not making a wrong choice.

Judith's history is filled with nonmajor incidents of unpredictability as a way of life, in which she seems to take delight (the many moves, the stripping of the new nurse, calls to return to work, etc.). There is much stability overall. There is predictability in the unpredictabilities, which makes them safe. Minor losses and transcendences are metaphorical of larger ones, and the smaller unpredictabilities are metaphorical of the larger. By transcending the smaller, she metaphorically transcends the larger. Indeed, she holds fast to stability by not making the major decisions—to return to work, adopt another baby, and so forth. These seem to be made for her, almost by default.

Can death hit a moving target?

Kendall

"I was always in detention."

Now an attractive brunette divorcee in her early thirties, Kendall lives in a charming studio apartment furnished in rattan, wicker, Indian spreads, incense holders, and plants.

Kendall was born and raised in England by Jewish immigrant parents. Her parents owned a small grocery store, and her mother was a busy housekeeper, trying to appear successful; she was also naive, private, prudish, and singularly uncommunicative about the "facts of life." "I've never seen my parents naked. My mother told me that seeing a man naked was ugly, like close your eyes and think of England. . . . It sometimes amazes me that my sister and I were ever born. . . . My sister and I were totally naive until it was, in my case, too late. Like I came home pregnant."

Her mother also had a strong sense of superiority, which she expressed in her rearing of the children. "Up until the age of twenty, twenty-one my sister and I were not allowed to wear blue jeans . . . only common people wore blue jeans. . . . She always has this thing about common people. Like chewing gum or eating fish and chips wrapped in newspaper on the street. It's taboo. You don't do that. What's so wrong about chewing gum walking down the street, I don't know." Her father is "very English. Very insular in his emotions. Not tactile at all." He was dominated by her mother but was also supportive in a crisis.

The relationship between her mother and her father was a reasonably good one but a source of endless amazement to Kendall and her sister. "It's like they have these little routines, their little chats down like, anything interesting in the paper dear, do you want a cup of tea, dear? Oh, I don't know, dear, are you making a cup of tea? Okay, if you're making one, I mean it'll just keep going on like this. I just go up the wall. . . . They're like a little double act. My sister and I . . . couldn't take any more of this day-to-day trivia soap opera stuff. . . . They just have this little planned out life . . . I mean, they preordained it for themselves. Like they have it all planned what has to happen and when it has to happen, and how it will happen, and then it happens. Then we talk about it for six months."

Kendall and her sister didn't get along when they were younger but became buddies in their teens.

Kendall's family favorite was her Aunt Anne, a loving and compassionate woman who visited the sick. "She used to make us dolls and take us for picnics and go to the movies. And do a lot of those things that we didn't do with our mother. Then she died of lung cancer when I was about nine or ten, I guess. That was sad, watching her wither away. . . . Toward the end they wouldn't even let us go and see her, because she was so diseased, and not too pleasant to see. She was a lovely woman as I remember her." Kendall recalls how she found out about her aunt's death, one of the traumatic events of Kendall's life. "I was in bed, and my mother came up and knocked on the bedroom door and she said: 'You'll be pleased to hear that Auntie Anne passed away in her sleep in the night.' I said: 'Oh,' and she closed the door and left, and I remember crying about that." (Why did she say that you'd be pleased to know?) "Because we knew the agony that she was in. I mean, she'd cough up this frothy—it was ugly to watch. We'd get sent out of the room, obviously I wouldn't want anyone to see me doing that if I was that ill. Then they would be pumping her with morphine and whatever they'd use to give people to stop the pain, and all that. She knew how she looked, and she knew it was only a matter of time before she slipped away and she finally did. It was a long, agonized death . . . she was skin and bones, gaunt. There was this whole thing of, like, putting on a brave front, you know. When the warm days come, and when I get over this. Of course, everyone knew, but nobody would say. Everybody kept up this false pretense that everything would be all right. The only way everything would be all right would be if she was literally put out of her misery, and the suffering." (Was she?) "It's possible, I don't know, but that woman, I mean, if there's going to be any mercy killing, they should have done it a long time before they—I mean, before they finally gave her an extra large dose of whatever."

Much of the rest of Kendall's childhood was spent in athletics, which she loved enough to want to become a physical education teacher. She was also a top student. "I was in the St. John's Ambulance Brigade. It was like a nursing brigade of little beings all in our little uniforms, practicing slings and such." However, her mother was too concerned with appearances and not with educating and nurturing. Further, "My parents had such expectations in terms of marrying a nice Jewish boy . . . and bringing on the grandchildren . . . there's no way I could possibly fulfill all those things . . . they would make it known that we would like you to be going down this road. . . . It was like constantly I would feel that they were being disappointed by whatever I did."

During Kendall's early adolescence, she herself became seriously ill. "My adolescence I think I was pretty much on my own 'cause I was real sick, and I was in the hospital for long periods of time. Nobody was telling me what was going on, and I thought I was dying. . . . I kinda shut up and withdrew. That was like eleven to thirteen. . . . I was sick, nobody knew what was wrong with me, or if they did, nobody was telling me. It wasn't until like the whole thing was like over, they finally started telling me what was going on. The doctors would send me out of the room and talk to my mother. She wouldn't tell me, because she probably didn't understand. . . . I had a blood disorder. I would be smothered in bruises. I had a lack of platelets, which is part of the blood clotting system. . . . It looked like my parents beat me black and blue. . . . If I cut my finger it would take two or three hours for it to stop bleeding. . . . I had a spleen removed. That solved the problem. But they were doing bone marrow tests, which were one of the leukemia tests they do. I'd go off to the library and get out the family doctor books, and of course you convince yourself that you've got every disease under the sun. . . . So it was pretty frightening." When Kendall asked what was wrong, they told her they didn't know, but she thought they just weren't telling her. "I was growing like a big mushroom in my head. . . . I was on cortisone tablets for long periods of time. I was this huge swelly faced monster. I went back to school, and they thought I was a new girl. Nobody recognized me. That was a pretty lonesome time."

Unfortunately, when Kendall got back to school, even though she'd missed many months during her 2-year illness, they would not let her stop a grade, because she was older, so her schoolwork slipped badly. "I hadn't had the basic groundwork in some of the languages, Greek, Latin, French. Science, physics, and chemistry were pretty bleak, too. So for awhile I made big efforts to catch up. But it became an insurmountable task. I was plodding away. Then I discovered what boys were, and that seemed much more fun. Better than homework and all this classical stuff. . . . That was pretty confining. We all had to be young ladies, wear our hats straight and be proper. . . . The more developed you were, the more likely you were to get a boyfriend. . . . I was a tomboy, I guess. I would stand back in awe, and watch my friends have boyfriends. I didn't have a boyfriend or like anyone who was vaguely interested in me until I was about fifteen—George—we used to take my dog for walks and hold hands and kiss in the park. It was very innocent, but it used to make my heart flip. So I suddenly felt this is very nice."

It was at this time Kendall and her sister became close. "My sister took me to a jazz club, and I met beatniks, and I thought how terribly interesting and exciting! All these long-haired, unwashed people with ban-the-bomb badges, stomping around to traditional jazz." They were forbidden to go to this club, so they sneaked off and lied for each other. They weren't allowed to date, either, which made them objects of ridicule at school. Occasionally, they'd get caught and be grounded for a month or two, with no pocket money. Although Kendall did not have a special boyfriend, when she was 16 "I think there were about three virgins left in my class at school. I mean, everybody knew who was still a virgin, and who wasn't. I was just *dying* . . . not to be one of the last to go. So I finally found a man who—a man, he was a boy, too [laughs]—he was equally curious, so we consummated our curiosity. That was funny [laughs]. Oh, is that it? Okay, at least we got that one over with."

His parents were pretty open-minded about the relationship, but her parents had no idea. "My mother would have had a complete fit if she'd known. I still think she would like to think both my sister and I are virgins. It's like she wouldn't even acknowledge the fact that I had a child at this point."

During her mid-teens, Kendall's sister was mysteriously packed off to Europe to live with her grandparents for 2 years. They have never figured this out and still speculate about the cause of this separation.

When Kendall was in her senior year of high school, she was expelled for witchcraft and dabbling in black magic. The way this came about was that she invited her friends over for a party with a Ouija board, a mother found out and complained, and Kendall was out. Her father protested, to no avail. "The headmistress summons me to her office. Made me fall into a tearful, quivering heap," and also told her she would not give her a recommendation to go to teacher training college. This was a blow, because Kendall had her heart set on becoming a physical education teacher, but without the letter she could not. Kendall believes her father thinks there was another underlying reason for her expulsion. "Well, I was pretty rebellious. I mean, you had to wear your beret so that the badge of the school showed at all times. At that time bouffant hairdos were all the rage. So we'd all back comb and tease our hair, and put our hats back on our head, and anchor them with sixteen hairpins. You'd get kept behind after school and detention for that. You could get kept in detention for having a ladder, a run, in your stockings. If your shoes weren't shined, you'd get stuck for three quarters of an hour detention. If you'd talk back to a teacher, you'd get stuck for detention. I was always in detention. 'Cause I hate wearing nylons, my nylons would always have runs and holes, and I'd have to go in there and sit and sew them up for three quarters of an hour. Sit in silence 'cause I got caught talking in assembly. The woman was a retired brigadier from the army. She ran the school like that."

Unable to pursue the career of her choice, Kendall went to college instead and spent 2 years "dawdling" in home economics.

One summer Kendall fell in love with a law student who delivered bread to the coffee shop where she worked as a waitress. "He would deliver the buns and loaves of bread and cakes and stuff. Very romantic. He did deliver the buns [laughs], that's for sure." They loved each other, and a few weeks after he returned to law school Kendall realized she was pregnant. "I didn't tell anybody I was pregnant, until I was seven months gone, by which time it was becoming a bit of a strain. . . . I was thinking of all these reasons I wasn't pregnant, and why I wasn't getting my period. I completely tried to block it out that this had happened, because I didn't want to have to deal with it. I attempted various things like taking large quantities of quinine pills and a hot gin bath, riding a bicycle for miles and miles, running up and down cliff faces. . . . I just blocked that I was pregnant. Until my mother said I didn't look well. She thought I ought to go to the doctor. Then I said, 'Well, as a matter of fact, I think I'm about seven months pregnant,' at which point she broke down. 'Oh, my god, what's your father going to say?'" At this point her mother was going down the stairs, just as her father was coming up, and she informed him, "Your daughter's pregnant," at which he started crying: "We never thought you or your sister were virgins, but we thought with your education you would have heard about contraceptives." Kendall finally faced up to the fact that she was going to have the baby and, after much conflict, decided that the best thing for the child would be to give him up for adoption. She selected the parents through an adoption agency. Her parents never acknowledged that the baby was born. "Every year I write and say, did you realize last Tuesday . . . Charles was twelve. They never write back and acknowledge, yes, we were thinking about him, or we were thinking about you, and wondering how you were faring. They'd never ask me. They'd never. So now I make a point every year on his birthday. Letting them know." Kendall also informed her mother's best friend of the baby's birth; her mother had never told her.

The delivery of the baby was also a traumatic event. "I had no notion what was going to happen to me. My mother never prepared me in that way, though I did ask her. I never went to any classes, breathing or pushing or coaching or any of that stuff that they do these days. It was still a lot of stigma certainly around where I grew up, about being pregnant and not being married." Kendall also felt the stigma at the hospital. "The nurses were such bitches." Her father had taken her to the hospital and the nurses "shoved me in this room, gave me an enema, I'd never had one of those before. It frightened me to death. And gave me a warm bath, and said: 'We're real busy tonight. There's the buzzer. Don't press it unless it's necessary.' So there I was pumping and heaving, groaning and getting on with it, and the waters broke. I thought, Oh my god! I didn't even know what it was, I thought I was peeing myself and my bladder had burst, or something." The nurse came in and cleaned her up, and again admonished her not to press the buzzer. "I'm thinking, I'm real sorry I'm having this baby, you know. So she went off, and I thought, right you motherfuckers, I ain't pressing this button until it's nearly all over, or I'm a goner, or whatever. So . . . I just carried on until I knew his head was out, and then I pressed the buzzer. She said: 'What is it now?' I said: 'I think he's being born.' She said: 'How do you know it's a he, and how do you know it's being born?' I said: 'Take a look.' And then she looked, and then she started panicking, and then she started wheeling in oxygen, and the doctors were running in and out. I said: 'Get all that stuff out of here, let me watch my baby be born.' So I did, and that was just wonderful. . . . It was like I felt I'd done it. I felt a sense of achievement, I had produced this child without somebody with forceps or giving me an episiotomy."

Kendall cared for her baby for a couple of weeks in the hospital and then visited him in a foster home until he was adopted. Afterward, she went on a "promiscuous binge," because she was angry at having had the baby and having had to give him up. Then "I got a job as a sales demonstrator. I traveled the country with my little suitcase, selling . . . living in hotels . . . out of suitcases. That was a pretty isolated existence. Being in strange towns. Not knowing anyone. Eating on my own. Being on my own. Then there'd be all these weird traveling salesmen coming and banging on your door at midnight. Coming to my room for a drink. Say, go away, leave me alone. Like, I went from a real promiscuous binge to being celibate and withdrawn, isolated." She landed in the hospital with an infection. "My father came to the hospital and said: 'This is not the life for you, off to secretarial school with you, my girl!' [Laughs] So off I went to typing and shorthand." Kendall has been doing secretarial work ever since.

At this point she met Arthur, with whom she lived for several years. He was "not very nice . . . real selfish. He'd cheat a lot. He'd tell lies. He'd exaggerate. He was a spoiled rich boy. . . . I wanted a boyfriend, I think. It was important to me to have some sort of substantial relationship, which I'd never had. Everybody that I'd grown up with were married and pushing toddlers around at twenty or twenty-two. If you hadn't done that, you were an old maid already. It's that kind of small town [laughs]."

Another traumatic incident occurred when her sister was raped, became pregnant, and had to have an abortion. This was a couple of years after Kendall herself had had her son, when she was about 21. It was a tough issue to deal with. "She resented me, because I had gotten pregnant and had a child. . . . I tried to help her as much as I could. . . . Two years went, and she wouldn't go out with any men. The first man she slept with she got pregnant again and [had] another abortion. She fell apart and made me swear that I would not tell my parents. . . . She started having strange dreams, and a lot of problems in terms of coping. She tried to commit suicide a couple of times, and finally she made the all-out effort, and I found her just in time and got her to the hospital. She said she'd never forgive me for having saved her and stuff. Anyway, we worked our way through that, and she saw a psychiatrist. We . . . shared a lot about growing up. I mean, this is where a lot of my perceptions of my childhood have changed . . . and I suddenly realized that there's all this stuff that had been going on that we'd never talked about. . . . But it all suddenly became real focalized when she tried to die, and that made us become real close. . . . She's now happily married. . . . She has a nice husband who cares about her a lot." They won't be having children, because her husband had a vasectomy in order to avoid fathering a child with Tay-Sachs disease, which runs in his family. Kendall says that while her sister was going through her ordeals of rape, pregnancies, abortions, and suicide attempts, Kendall herself was "going crazy, too. I was on Valiums and Libriums and sleepers and uppers. I mean, all on prescription, but that's the way a lot of doctors deal with it."

With a student, Kendall came to the United States in her mid-twenties and decided to stay. To avoid deportation she married the student, who was more of a friend than a lover. "We stayed married for two years, 'cause I had a friend that was an immigration lawyer, and he told me that, to be on the safe side, I ought to stay married for two years. So we did that, and then I went and got the do-it-yourself divorce book, and did that. Now we're divorced, and I am allowed to be here." She likes it here because the climate is better for her health.

In addition, Kendall confides other important incidents since she moved here. "This is all confidential, right? [Laughs] I've had affairs with two women in my thirties, which have both been really warm and special. . . . I don't see it as the whole gay sexual thing . . . so I am basically heterosexual. . . . I don't know if I'm bisexual, I just happen to have two good women friends that I feel close to. . . . Something I've learned in my late twenties, early thirties, is the specialness of women friends. . . . I did operate on that every other woman was a threat to me or my man. . . . [Women] are more open and honest. There's still a lot of game-playing goes on, on both sides. . . . I got to spend a whole weekend with a bunch of women that were in their sixties, and we had such a blast with daughters and friends of their daughters. . . . Another thing growing up thinking, this is what mums do, this is what grannies do . . . and they don't! . . . I'm beginning to stop boxing people, you know, like categorizing, this is how you should be at this age." She also took psychedelic drugs for the first time in her thirties and found them surprisingly enlightening. "I've smoked pot for years, but I think most people have."

Until a few weeks before the interview, Kendall had had a secretarial job and was also a shop steward for the union. She had worked at the job for a couple of years with increasing responsibility, for which she finally decided she should have some recognition and compensation, something more than just her boss's praise. However, the personnel department turned down her bid for a raise. Kendall's response was, "Bye, I'm not sitting here doing all this stuff for nothing." She says she'd been a shop steward for the clerical workers, battling for better conditions, and this was the last straw. Now she's feeling pressured financially and looking for work. "I'd like to do some lobbying work, some political-type stuff. I mean, I've been doing that sort of stuff for quite a while." Or she'd like to work for the union. "At last clerical women are beginning to organize. I think that could be exciting, getting in on doing work to help, because when clerical work was done by men, it was always highly paid. As soon as it became a predominantly female profession, shoo! Forget the pay, ladies!"

Kendall is optimistic about her future. "Other women I talked to [think the] thirties are pretty exciting. In terms of, like, peaks, and deciding what you want to do with your life. You stop playing around. There's more focus to your energy rather than [scattering] all over the place. . . . It's like a gathering, like a harvesting." However, "I wish I had met Mr. Right [laughs]. Someone to love. I would like to have a nice relationship with a man. It's been a long time. I get fed up with being on my own, sometimes."

Kendall keeps a journal of her experiences and also foretells the future with the tarot and the I Ching. She doesn't know why these work, but they do. Her current relationship with her family is a passable one. They made a big fuss over her sister's twenty-first birthday, with a dinner party, a gold bracelet, and some other gifts. "It was understood because of what I had done to the family that there would be no such event for me. However, on my twenty-first birthday they did give me a beautiful gold bracelet and within, like, two or three months it was gone. I think it was stolen off my arm in the tube going to work one day. . . . I regretted it because, for some reason, it was like a token that they really did care enough."

As for her attitudes toward death, she recalls an incident that happened only a few weeks ago. "I went to a funeral that was such a happy occasion . . . inspiring . . . positive. . . . He's a psychic. . . . This good friend of his gave the address, saying we should all be so happy that he's gone. He communicated with me this morning. It was at the Chapel of the Four Seasons, and it was light. It was like a big greenhouse, and there were trees and plants. It was like he's walking in the garden with the Lord . . . like you're born and you die, and then you go, and it's better. . . . I've always felt this is not the total thing. . . . I have a friend who nearly died and came back, and related these kind of experiences that they've had. Like being without their body, and seeing it. . . . You feel sad that you'll never see them again, or talk to them, or whatever, but there's no reason to suppose that that's the total end to everything."

The major losses that Kendall sustained were the restrictions of her parents; the death of her Aunt Anne, who was the nurturing mother to her; her own ill health and a loss of security in living when she was in her early teens; her sister's wholeness and sanity for a while; her expulsion from school and with this the hope for further training in the profession she had chosen; her son to adoption; her relationship with men; and most recently her job. Transcendence has been through the birth of her son, which she describes as a peak experience, despite the hardships of the actual birth process; her close relationships with her sister and with other women; the tarot, I Ching, Ouija, and other psychic activities and beliefs; her political activism as shop steward and her hope to increase this. Running through all these activities is a flare for the unusual, the unconventional, which both punishes and rewards. Thus, her extended theme is: The unconventional leads to many losses, problems with parents, aunt's death, her own rare disease, schools, illegitimate child, thwarted career ambition, lack of substantial relationship, and loss of truth through the false-ness and pretentions of others, transcended by ironic sense of humor and unconventional activism, behavior, and beliefs. Core theme: Loss and tran-scendence through unconventionality.

Theoretical analysis

One of the most important early influences on young Kendall was her beloved Aunt Anne. This aunt was a mother substitute, treating Kendall and her sister like the daughters she did not have, taking them on picnics and to museums, educating them, and enriching their lives. In some ways Aunt Anne seems to have been a conventionally good woman, doing charity and visiting the sick. She died a horrible, lingering death when Kendall was about 10. Kendall may have identified with her aunt and thus felt that part of herself had died as well. The lesson may have been that good works and conventional behavior are punished. There may have been some anger that her Aunt Anne died and her mother survived. Certainly, the way her mother informed her of the death sounds unfeeling and even cruel.

Many children experience the death of a mother or mother substitute and are not necessarily traumatized. It takes another serious, similar incident to set up the pattern, and in Kendall's case that incident was not long in coming. Kendall developed a rare blood disorder. Like her aunt's, this disease was lingering. Kendall must have felt she was following in her aunt's footsteps, dying again, especially as no one told her anything—a repeat of the circumstances of Aunt Anne's death.

Kendall's parents, particularly her mother, were inordinately strict, prudish, experienced by Kendall as limiting life, especially physical life, or anything related to one of the self's most important and vital aspects, the body. Then Kendall's body was further assaulted by her aunt's illness and death, followed by her own illness and imagined death. These incidents formed a fertile breeding ground for breaking out of boundaries and limitations, or for unconventionality, which characterized Kendall's later development. It will be observed that even Kendall's illness was an "unconventional" one. Her mother was so overly conventional as to be unconventional in her adopted culture; Kendall and her sister were "mother's girls" at school. It is possible that Kendall lived hard as a way of staving off restriction and death.

It is interesting to note the suggestion of vindictiveness in the birth of her son. Her mother can't bear the thought that her children are no longer virgins, but every year Kendall reminds her of the birthday of her only grandchild, ironic in that she yearns for grandchildren. Ever concerned with what people might think, Kendall's mother never told her best friend about Kendall's giving birth and hustled her away instead. But Kendall took it on herself to tell the friend, thereby further shaming her mother. Indeed, the pregnancy and birth seem to have been used as a weapon. Kendall nearly lost her sister to suicide, her companion and aide in her wild life style, her alter ego in many ways.

A subtheme running through Kendall's history is that of problematic embodiment, or difficulties with the physical aspect of life. Her mother never explained sexuality. The body was bad. In spite of her athletic talent and activity, she was prevented from physically sublimating in teaching it to others. Sexuality has brought her loss and transcendence, death and birth. The birth was a difficult experience. Her physicality has been precarious. It is for all of us, of course, but she had to learn this at an early age. Sex with men seems to have brought her little joy; with women it has increased intimacy.

The male-female dichotomy is particularly pronounced in Kendall's history. Over and over she refers back to her mother's inadequacy, her stifling of the physical. The sister, on the other hand, saved her, and then she in turn saved her sister. Together they have worked through their childhood in an almost therapeutic fashion. The women lovers have continued bolstering self-esteem in Kendall. The men have been distant or only temporarily supportive like her father—sex playmates, more objects than human, or louses.

Kendall's sister seems to have carried on the good work begun by Aunt Anne; indeed, Kendall and her sister have given each other the substitute mothering they needed. They are a loyal couple. Kendall often refers questions about herself to her sister's experience. This is the phenomenon of "alternate lives," or living not only one's own life but the life of another as well. It is particularly a phenomenon of sisters or best friends. Life is perceived and experienced through another's eyes as well as one's own. The normal boundaries or limits between self and other do not quite apply—self is also one's sister. Sometimes one escapes one's own life almost entirely by living the sibling's life, as was true of Sissy, another of my interviewees. In Kendall's case, I think her sister's influence was a strongly positive one.

One last subtheme in Kendall's history is the truth-falsehood dichotomy. At an early age Kendall learned that appearances were what counted, not truth. Her mother virtually trained her in this, so her lies about her whereabouts in her teens, when she and her sister covered for each other, were consistent with her upbringing (undoubtedly unintentional on the mother's part). The truth-falsehood dichotomy is the relationship of appearance to reality, which is taught to the child from infancy through the interpretation of the child's experiences. The incoming data from the senses are defined: this is a cookie, that is Daddy; cookie is to eat, Daddy is to smile and wave and grab a finger. When the child is then trained to deny reality, it can erode trust in his or her own perceptions and experience and put a vulnerable child in a schizophrenic double bind. Something is what it is and is not at the same time, both real and not real. Kendall learned to turn this on her mother as a weapon, lying to her, doing the unacceptable, telling her mother's best friend the "truth." As it was unacceptable, her mother had had an unacceptable child and was therefore an unacceptable mother. Thus Kendall developed a healthy contempt for false pretenses, even using them to stay in this country; her marriage of convenience was, after all, a pretense. Kendall had to survive by knowing the difference. She had learned from the premature death of her Aunt Anne, and her own near premature death as well, to cling to the real and physical, or that which is not, nonbeing, may lay claim to you.

Table 1 sets forth the L/T life themes developed from all the life histories in this study, including the pilot effort. In this table the extended theme is described first, followed by the core theme.

TABLE 1   Fifty-three loss and transcendence life themes
(The following people are listed in the order in which they were interviewed.)

Lorellen. Loss of stable love through physical violence (rapes, abortions, beatings, etc.) versus transcendence through natural beauty, physical and spiritual evolution, healing and beliefs; both poles are associated with the conflict between the dominant culture and the counterculture. Core theme: Injury from physical violence versus spiritual evolution through healing.

Crista. Concern with environment, particularly visual, expressed in lifelong conflict between country and city living, which are metaphorically related to death and life; what keeps her in the country is the necessity to be helpful, rooted in childhood, when she was reared to help and submerge her own interests in those of others; if she did not, the threat was family violence, breakup, and death. Responsibility for others brings its own rewards but is at the expense of her own identity emergence, of which the environment is an expression. Core: Country versus city, as expression of self-submergence through helping versus emergence.

Marjorie. Loss of control over traumatic events (death of her father, long molestation by stepfather, etc.) versus letting go in order to gain control—letting go of relationships, consciousness through meditation, and possessions as forms of identity; she was a *victim* of loss events, particularly the death of her father. Core: Loss of control versus control through voluntary loss.

Lexie. Splitting of self (or identity) expressed in split of parents, split between career and motherhood, from her body, with society, in the conflict between being and doing, between forms of womanhood, between light and dark forces, reality and pretense; this splitting results in recurrent loss of identity. It is transcended by fantasy and by transient satisfactions from both sides of splits. Core: Self versus self, or split self.

Kara. Loss of freedom through restrictions imposed by religion, family, monogamous relationships, work, and the possibility of children, versus independence, freedom from control. She "parachutes" out of any situation that restricts her, enjoys the view, and takes control. Core: Restriction versus freedom.

Melanie. Family amid groups of families, marriage as part of group marriage; work with groups, family, town, and world as community, and the importance of communication among these networks, versus loss of significant relationships. Core: Loss of community versus transcendence by community.

Nadine. Importance of security in home, husband, job, child, and body (health); willingness to accept confinement, even when it's constricting, for sake of security, versus exhilaration in physical freedom, mainly dance and swimming. A major expression is disappointment in child, attempt at "rigid" upbringing of "free spirit." Core: Security in rigidity and confinement versus free body and spirit.

Heather. Dependence due to sense of vulnerability or lack of safety, based on violence in society—the Kennedy assassination, local family murders, husband's warnings, versus independence expressed by love of horses, riding, work, attempts at liberation from restrictive husband. Core: Safety in dependence and restriction (mediated by societal violence) versus liberation.

Patty. Losses through multiple family deaths in short period of time; losses also through insanity, pretenses, surfaces, appearances connected with these deaths; transcendence through birth and work with children. Pretense is inauthentic, a form of death by not being one's self. Core: Death versus birth.

TABLE 1   Fifty-three loss and transcendence life themes (*Continued*)

Paula. Loss through training in incompetence at survival tasks, so that emergence
into individuation is traumatic, resulting in inability to leave overwhelmingly competent home; this is transcended through succession of metaphorical families, competence in art, representing emotional investment and personal development. Repeated
loss of men loved, to other women, based on unrealistic expectations, which also
pervade her metaphorical families. Core: Self-mergence versus self-
emergence.

Della. Losses through lifelessness—parental divorce, childlessness, financial problems
(loss of wherewithal to live), nonadoption of a child—all are intended within God's
divine plan; they are transcended by dedication to that plan, submitting to the will
of God. Core: Lifelessness through misfortune versus divine plan.

Robin. Loss through being done to, being confined and restricted, and being passive
in the face of this, versus independence through taking action. Core: Passive versus
active.

Theo. Loss through overreaction to separation, environment falling apart, transcended
by service to communal activity, counterculture, theater, and by "crying a river of
tears, which nourishes me." Core: Splintering versus temporary cohesion.

Ronnie. Loss through victimization by negative actions of other people (father, stepfather, mother-in-law, neighbors, seducer of husband, children), transcended by
active shaping of life, in career, and, relationships, physically and sexually. Experimenting with assertiveness pays off. Core: Victimization versus assertiveness.

Gwen. Inordinate, sudden, often accidental, and capricious life losses through cruel,
physically abusing mother, memories of death in the rooming house, beatings by
other children, attempted murder, the molestation by a relative, accidents of two
children (one died), the destruction of her house, threat of genetic disease to two
other children, long illness and death of beloved husband, and her own auto accident;
transcended by humor, fulfilling work as teacher, and especially many psychic
experiences, including visitations by her dead second husband and son, out-of-body
experience, and "miracle" cure. Core: Capricious or accidental loss versus psychic
experiences (also capricious), or body versus spirit (body is vulnerable, spirit protects, magically undoes).

Irene. Loss of opportunities no longer possible, reflected especially in negative relationship with daughter—never finding niche, wrong turnings—versus transcendence through service to others. Core: Lost opportunities versus service.

Annette. Loss through accommodation to various restrictions for the sake of shelter
and security, which various communication activities make bearable and transcend.
The restriction of communication would make other losses unbearable. Core: Security in restriction versus communication.

Britt. Loss of hearing restricts otherwise exciting, challenging, and structured life as
army nurse; exposure to different ways of living, to alternate lives, which also
means various separations from loved ones, which she describes as characterized
by same stages as bereavement. Core: Separation versus alternate lives.

Inez. Betrayal by others, especially men in triangular relationships but also by friends,
career supervisor, rapists, different cultural values, transcended by service in the
form of healing others. Core: Betrayal versus healing.

Sissy. Loss through loss of status and through sister's alcoholism as alternate life,
versus status, "fun." Status concerns of mother made her marry a man she didn't

TABLE 1 Fifty-three loss and transcendence life themes (*Continued*)

love, who subsequently died, freeing her to marry a man she did love. Sister as her opposite, requiring help, job, responsibility, and yet children have turned out well. Motivation by status and resultant losses and transcendences; lives through sister. Core: Both loss and transcendence through status and alternate life.

Denise. Physical and mental abuse by others with consequently low self-esteem, "I'm weird"; transcended by the strength of others and proof that she can survive. Core: Abuse versus survival.

Kendall. The unconventional leads to many losses, problems with parents, aunt's death, her own rare disease, schools, illegitimate child, thwarted career ambition, lack of substantial relationship, loss of truth through the falseness of others; transcended by ironic sense of humor and unconventional activism, behavior and beliefs. Core: Loss and transcendence through unconventionality.

Sibyl. Conflict with mother, with daughter, with herself over who she is. Others define her self by assigning importance through work; transcended by being acknowledged by others as productive. Core: Identity loss versus identity as productive and important.

Charyn. Family conflict results in necessity for alignments that can be both treacherous and rewarding. "Being in the middle is neat." Such alignments spread to other relationships. Both loss and transcendence through alignment in conflicts. Transcendence through service to the disabled who are without family (and alignments). Core: Conflicts versus service, both mediated by alignments.

Frances. Sexual problems and perversion (incestual molestation, transvestism, sexual disinterest, etc.) resulting in chronic fear; transcended by general transcendence activities—music, religion, prayer, and especially ESP. Core: Sexual perversion versus psychic and spiritual experiences.

Sue. Communication with God, parents, self, teachers, husband, child, as source of both loss and transcendence. Loss of important relationships through lack of communication; transcendence by dedication to God, communication with others, various communication activities (teaching, sign language, etc.), and proximity to those loved. Dedication to the idealized or unattainable (husband, son, God, parents, friends) mediated by communication or its lack. Core: Communication as mediator for idealized relationships, both lost and preserved.

Winnie. Loss through sinful and wild childhood, upsetting parents, versus redemption through religion, which is also a part of marriage. Core: Sin versus redemption.

Babs. Emotional withdrawal, schizoid personality, a husband sick with jealousy, and a pervasive paranoia throughout much of the protocol; transcended by work achievement and by splitting the self into two, showing devotion to husband with social conservativeness to allay guilt and jealousy, on the one hand, and aggressive, goal-seeking, sociable, role-related, successful behavior at work on the other, which is enjoyable. Core: Paranoid and schizoid self versus successful work self—both as split self.

Yves. Overly structured childhood led to lessening self-confidence and strength, which led to pervasive fear; this is transcended by strength from environment, support in work and by second husband, male mentors. She allows status to create her. Core: Lack of self-confidence versus strength from others.

Harriet. Loss through distance from people, sense of not belonging, loneliness; this is transcended through mothering service to others—children, students, patients,

TABLE 1 Fifty-three loss and transcendence life themes (*Continued*)

suicidal individuals, even animals, although the set-apartness returns, is finally accepted. Core: Distance from others versus closeness through mothering service.

Opal. Loss through everyday struggle with insoluble problems such as alcoholism, domination of mother-in-law, the tragedies of others—in this sense, others control this life; this is transcended by the gradual removal of the problems, improvement in children, death of major relationship, rewarding job. Core: Problems of others versus release.

Greer. Passivity, 20 years of waiting for husband one way or another, marking time, isolation, his love affair, her passivity in the face of all his changes, her life circumstances defined by husband and by daughters, doormat, could not stand alone; versus physical activity and particularly therapy, which led to work and more self-confidence. Moving as metaphor. Core: Passivity (marking time) versus move toward independence.

Faith. Obstacles to artistic development (parents' unactualized potential, lack of education, family responsibilities, critical rejection, accidents, tragic love affair); transcended with the assistance of a succession of mentors (librarians, husband, art teachers); foremost among these is her husband. There is an uncanny timing to her connection with these mentors. Core: Obstacles versus destined mentors with felicitous timing.

Nora. Negative relationships characterized by lack of love with father, mother, son, daughter, the hoarding of injuries, insults from same, with bitter, sarcastic, hypercritical resentment; transcended by getting away, travel, being on the road, seeing how others "survive." Core: Bitter relationships versus getting away.

Vicki. Vicariousness characterized her parents' attitudes toward her, pushing her toward expected roles; she found it easier to follow rules and make no decisions until a nervous breakdown released her from their demands. There followed three marriages to manipulative men to avoid manipulative parents; a fourth marriage resulted in children, through whom she lives in return. Core: Self as object of manipulation and vicariousness, transcended by vicarious life.

Tess. Lack of competence and self-confidence (because self unemerged) manifested in major losses in work and relationships; transcended by son as someone who loves and accepts her unquestioningly, also by drugs, alcohol, and fantasy including fairy tales. Only her face and body are accepted, never her whole self. Her body goes from one man to another and is abused. Core: Incompetent unemerged self versus general transcendence—drugs, alcohol, unquestioning acceptance, and fantasy. (Unquestioning acceptance *is* fantasy.)

Judith. Tension between unpredictability and stability, with both losses and transcendence on this dimension. Loss: Unpredictability in mother, fiancé, impregnability, uterine tumor; transcended by traveling, ritual, work, adoption circumstances, humor. Core: Major unpredictabilities versus minor ones.

Willa. Loss through long history of alcoholism of father, aunt, brother, husband; transcended by fun in daily activities, comfort, volunteer work, which can be threatened by loss of money. Core: Alcoholism in others versus "fun" in the moment.

Oona. Negative relationships with husband, children, and others, characterized by jealousy, rivalry, alcoholism, and unfaithfulness, leading to interference with career; transcended by hope and by fantasy. Core: Negative relationships versus fantasy.

Queenie. Loss through sensitivity to criticism of behavior by husband, by mother, by

TABLE 1 Fifty-three loss and transcendence life themes (*Continued*)

psychologist, by daughter; this is transcended by other aspects of the relationship with husband and children, by cooking, and by political activity connected with cooking. She feeds others. Core: Biting criticism overcome by feeding others.

Elaine. Loss through death of mother, abuses by stepmother, alcoholic husband who nearly wrecked her career, the marriages of her brother, father, and self to unsuitable people, the loss of job to boss's friend; this is overcome by a logical methodical approach to her work as manager and director of various business, community, and religious activities, by personal achievement and triumph in business and theater; she experiences considerable time pressure to get all her activities accomplished (loss of time is experienced as approaching death in the L/T paradigm)—she wards off death by filling time to the brim. Core: Unsuitable and destructive relationships versus achievements multiplied by saving time (and vice versa).

Jaclyn. Loss in relationships with men through sexual irresolution and dysfunction; this has kept her from education and work and any achievement, as well as from being a "woman." Transcended by a vegetative existence in abject poverty, watching TV, playing cards, since she feels incapable of everyday functioning, of moving from the domination of a destructive man, and of getting her own house and job. Core: Sexual dysfunction versus vegetative existence (loss transcended by loss).

Janet. Sudden loss of relationships, separation from parents, divorce, abrupt death of two children, betrayal of sister with husband, shock, near loss of self expressed in fugue states and suicide attempt; this has been transcended by a great sexual relationship with a long-term lover and business success. Core: Sudden relationship loss versus stability.

Yvonne. Loss of education not obtained, of art not pursued, and particularly loss of the world as it was; this is transcended by emphasis on traditional values in marriage, children, grandchildren, work, and by hypercritical attitude toward those who diverge. Core: Loss of world as it was versus traditional values.

Vera. Has allowed others to determine and dominate her major decisions and how she has led her life (mother, first husband, father-in-law, second husband, brutal psychiatrist, daughter), leaving lasting regret over wasted time, work not done, education not obtained; sacrifice; also severe guilt over her part in these relationships, selfishness, unkindness. A subtheme of motivation for monetary reasons is noted. Transcended by support of friends, children, grandchildren, nursing, faith, rationalization, grieving through. Core: Domination and guilt versus external support.

Ursula. Loss through hardship, rootlessness, rape, poverty, lack of education and self-development owing to the handicap of dyslexia, abuse of self, failing health; this is transcended by current pursuit of education, support of females (mother, teachers, children), church, job, late-blooming talent, and humor. Core: Underdeveloped and abused self versus supported and developing self.

Germaine. An idyllic past, a sheltered childhood, protection by siblings, the importance of religion, an ideal marriage—all have been shattered by deaths, of father, husband, sister, baby, false pregnancy, but particularly the death of the ideal marriage about 10 years ago, for which she still mourns. Core: The ideal as shelter versus its death by exposure.

Alice. Loss through accidents and congenital handicap, particularly of a son with Down's syndrome, who inflicts further losses to image of self as rescuer, to her

TABLE 1 Fifty-three loss and transcendence life themes (*Continued*)

sense of justice, her relationship with husband, her life style, and to health. This is transcended by high intellectual activity, humor and sarcasm, her relationship with her daughter, and artistic activities as a return to the artist she might have been. Core: Unjust handicap versus intellect and talent, or gift, both inborn.

Pilot Cases

Gisella. Loss of ideal self and world through loss of energy, childhood ideal that was, politics, war, health, self-confidence, father's mental health. Transcended by Victoria, B.C. and antique book collection (world as it was), selling (objects for survival), political activity for an ideal world, sports, acceptance of single life's independence and freedom. Core: Loss of ideal self and world versus buying and selling of both past and present (time).

Ilona. Losses through lack of education, marriage, chance to be a nurse, alcoholism, welfare, divorce with five children, versus survival through kindness of others, factory jobs, and especially children becoming what she wanted through her efforts. Core: Survival struggle versus vicarious self-creation.

Aurora. Loss of idealized self, home, children, parents, husband, and family, as well as time for these, especially loss of males; transcended by work, symbols of relationships, romanticism, relationships, organization to yield more time, and especially by son who is ideal. Core: Idealized relationships versus real ones.

Tori. Loss through time limits, disillusion with academia, sexism, tenure process, lack of childhood intellectual and artistic environment, alcoholism, things as they should be. Transcended in writing, meditation, the humanistic way of being, activism, teaching, music, debate, and relationships with daughter and husband, in which she stresses psychic components. Core: Identity split by time limits versus spiritual growth.

Em. Losses through the deaths of relationships—parents, siblings, first husband, children, self as artist. These are transcended by art on the topics of death and birth, also a lover-mentor, gardening, support for women, identification with American Indians—all signifying rebirth. Core: Death of relationships versus rebirth through art.

NUMBER AND UNIQUENESS OF THEMES

The first thing that strikes us in reviewing the L/T life themes is their diversity. Although there are superficial similarities among some themes, such as the impact of alcoholism or physical abuse or the different ways in which self is experienced, certainly no two themes seem alike.

As indicated above, the themes are reported in two ways; there are the expanded or extended, full-life L/T themes and the short, summary, core themes. These may be seen as two levels. First is the thematic level itself, expressed in the abstract issue, often a conflict, that is, the common denominator of loss, versus the common denominator of transcendence. The second level of the theme is the support level of the first, the major events and experiences from which the core theme emerges; in other words, it is how the core theme is expressed in the individual's life.

The *expanded* L/T life themes are the patterns of loss and patterns of transcendence and how they are interrelated. They are based on the major events and experiences in the protocol; no major event or experience is omitted in determining the theme simply because it does not seem to fit a pattern. In other words, it is not fair to be selective to prove a point. Sometimes the very variety of forms of transcendence represents a pattern, expressed by the interviewee as "having fun," for example. Where several themes appear, they are always seen as interrelated; none is totally independent of the others, because they reside in the same individual, in related incidents, behaviors, outlooks.

The most interesting observation about the *expanded* themes is that, even when several involve superficially common events, they seem to have their idiosyncratic application in individual lives. For example, "disrupted relationships" are common to most or perhaps all lives to a greater or lesser degree. But when one takes into account *which* relationships are disrupted (family, childhood, work, male or female, etc.), *how* they are disrupted (moves, rape, betrayal, erosive fighting, death, other people), *why* they are disrupted (personalities, war, jealousy, accident, physical or mental illness), the *response* to the disruption (depression, challenge, fantasy, passivity, escape, changed behavior, faith, art, living through others), and the *metaphorical meanings* of disruption, one discovers great variability in the L/T life themes.

The *core* themes express the life themes in the briefest possible manner, either summarizing the major theme or selecting one theme that seems preeminent among several related ones (which have been connected into an overall theme). The core themes are ways of "evening out" or "smoothing out" differences among people, in the way one smoothes a curve, and the result is that several individuals were rated as the same on one pole or another. For example, three individuals are rated as transcending mainly through service to others—a highly socially desirable mode in females and one in which they are virtually trained by society. Their extended life themes, however, show that the three are very different, because the context of service varies from one to another; service that transcends distance from others differs from service that transcends lost opportunities or family conflicts. The character of the service and the motivations, feelings, satisfactions, decisions, and regrets differentiate these three even further when one reads the protocols.

In trying to express a core theme, one is dependent on words and chooses one word over another, resulting in the appearance of *more* diversity than is perhaps warranted. For example, consider the core themes "restriction versus freedom" and "dependence versus liberation." Could not the word "freedom" be substituted in the second theme for "liberation"? Quite possibly, but the word "liberation" is a better choice than the word "freedom" in this case, because the women's liberation movement is a salient aspect of this woman's life, and also it is the word *she* uses. It has the connotation of enslavement, which is not applicable to the life of the first individual, who is restricted by home, religion, rules, and even institutions but never actually enslaved. Often it seems wise to use the words of the interviewee in order to be as accurate as possible.

The core themes are useful for categorizing and investigating themes *across* individuals. However, just as the label "schizophrenic" cannot summarize an individual but is useful for treatment, so the label of a core L/T theme must not be taken as a reduction of the individual to a single element.

Finally, when several aspects of themes are salient, it is possible for different raters to see all the aspects but to choose different words to describe them in a core manner. Let us look at Sue's L/T theme, for example. One can see her theme as involving communication, the loss of relationship, the recurring pattern of love and loss of her husband, the pervasiveness of religion in her life. The final statement could be "lost relationships versus religion, both mediated by communication," or it could be "dedication to the unattainable (husband, son, God) mediated by communication or its lack," or even "communication versus noncommunication." One rater preferred the word "communing" because it conveys the religious nature of her communication, in contrast to Melanie's, for example.

ETIOLOGY: ORIGINS OF THEMES

This brings us to the question of how L/T life themes develop, whether their sources, like those of waterfalls, are cataclysms, underground springs, or melting snows.

L/T life themes seem to have three sources. One is some external event or situation, often traumatic, often precipitating conflict, and often occurring in childhood or adolescence, such as the loss of a parent. A second source is the internal perception or cognitive organization of the individual, by which she *sees* the events as forming a pattern. Still a third source seems to be the internalization of both parents; when these parents are very different from each other, and additionally in conflict, a split self and resultant L/T life theme may emerge. However, a traumatic life event results in certain internal perceptions, and these, in turn, may be based on nontraumatic external events, so these sources do not necessarily preclude each other.

The roots of these themes may or may not be traumatic childhood experiences (see Weenolsen, 1986c). For example, one root commonly found is that of parents with opposite values who are in conflict (Lorellen's case). In other words, a *susceptibility* or predisposition to a certain loss or transcendence pattern can often be traced to childhood. Inez's transcendence pattern is seen at the age of 3, but the loss pattern seems to begin later. Of course, there is always the possibility that a more detailed history might reveal earlier etiology.

For the psychodynamic psychologist, the root trauma is often sexual in nature. But to me it seems that the basic conflict is between life and death, actually or metaphorically, and I believe this is even basic to, or underlies, sexual conflict, as will be shown. While past unresolved relationships may continue to be acted out in present relationships, they also have their effects on the individual's development. As has been pointed out, losses represent not only past losses and the ultimate death of self but also their relationship to each other and to the various levels of loss, primary, secondary, holistic, self-conceptual, and metaphorical. Transcendences represent life, immortality, and rebirth at various levels.

For those whose L/T themes seem to originate in specific external life events, quite a variety of these events are mentioned as foundational: the sudden death of a parent at an early age, the gift of an art book, the assassination of a public figure, the unexpected divorce of parents, and so forth. Often, there is a cluster of events, such as repeated beatings, mental and sexual abuse, alcoholic violence, inordinate restriction, and fighting, on the one hand, and occasions of family community, being saved from death, and positive medical experiences, on the other. There are more loss events in childhood and adolescence than transcendence events as apparent sources of themes, or as first events in a long line of similar ones. However, even when the events seem isolated and as close to "causal" as one can get, utmost care must be taken in recognizing that there is still a context in which these events have occurred. The death of a parent took place in a family so warm and happy as to make the event doubly tragic, or the family is uniquely capable of carrying on. Or that death took place in a family so stressed by divisiveness as to make the surviving child feel guilty, or victorious, or relieved. *The clues to these contexts, often long past memory, are probably within the contexts of the similar events that succeeded them.* The context of an event, as well as the personality of the interviewee, may also explain why similar events, such as deaths of parents, can have such dramatically different impacts on different interviewees.

It is possible that a traumatic childhood event, which often leaves a wake of other difficult events (secondary, holistic, self-conceptual, and metaphorical losses) prepares the child to see life in terms of this event, prematurely in terms of death, for example, which may translate into unpredictable comings and goings of individuals, intimacy as threat, attachment as more secure it if is materialistic rather than emotional. It is possible that among later events, those more salient to such an individual are those that remind her of the death; that is, she responds to such events differently from the way she would have responded had the parent not died, with more vigilance, or more regret, or more effort—all seeding theme.

In such a way an L/T life theme having a predominantly external source may begin its formation. It must be emphasized that such a formation is not beyond the individual's control; she is creating her life and self by responding selectively and idiosyncratically to that event, even though the event was beyond her control, something that happened to her, as it did not happen to the majority of children her age. In this example we are generally looking at off-time losses, which seem to wreak havoc (though not always) as do off-time deaths. But even to the extent that a death is controllable by the individual who dies—for example, that she or he was engaged in coronary-prone behavior—to this extent the child may feel betrayed by the needs for achievement that may lead to death (see Chapter 10). None of this need be on a conscious level. The child's worth has been invalidated. Children's anger at being "deserted" by the dead parent, unreasonable as it seems, is perhaps not altogether without reason on an intuitive level. Also, the child's creation of self is out of this raw fabric of self and environment interaction.

Another phenomenon appears in the case histories of those whose themes seem to be of external origin, and that is a pattern of *repeated external events* apparently beyond the individual's control. Lorellen, for example, endured repeated instances of sexual violence (three rapes, three abortions, etc.). Alice sustained repeated instances of accidents and handicaps of relatives (not genetically based). The marriage of Willa to an alcoholic (he wasn't to begin with) seems like very bad luck after a history of alcoholism in father, aunt, uncles, and brother. Frances's history of involvements with sexual perversion sounds like a bizarre series of accidents as it is related in the protocol. Clinicians often observe that individuals tend to marry their fathers or remarry their first spouses, their second being so like the first, especially dominating or restrictive ones (easy to find in a culture that has promoted male dominance), and this has certainly been true of a number of our interviewees. They escaped from restrictive homes into restrictive marriages. Why this apparent accidental attraction to circumstances that repeat previous losses? Anna Freud (1946) used the term "repetition compulsion" to describe the situation, an aspect of transference within the psychoanalytic setting.

The L/T answer may be that previous losses were not satisfactorily transcended, that the interviewees keep setting the same problems for themselves so that they can overcome them, that creating similar losses in a life gives one the opportunity to transcend them and, in so doing, transcend the original loss for which they are metaphors. If Lorellen could deal with a second rape in a satisfactory manner, she would be dealing with the first one as well and with the whole problem of rape (and its meaning to her). This type of transcendence is often greater than the transcendence of a single direct loss; it leads to the *affect* of transcendence, thus making the risk-taking worthwhile. A phenomenon similar to the psychoanalytic concept of transference may be occurring, except that the transference is not necessarily to the individual or the analyst in a therapeutic setting but to the event in an entire context of self and life meaning, so that it can be worked through or result in integration. Some psychodynamacists tend to explain by defining; a woman marries an abusive husband for the second time because she is a masochist. In the L/T paradigm, the individual has experienced a loss that is a death to part of the self in the sense that part of self has been destroyed; the terror is always that all of self may die; the individual risks additional metaphorical or actual death for the possibility of life, self, and meaning creation and enhancement. It should be observed here that the repeated losses are metaphors of the original loss, not simply displacements, as in the Freudian paradigm, because transcendence results in a re-creation of the entire self structure, rather than one event or aspect.

But something else is going on with Lorellen and others like her, who suffer such patterns of apparently "unlucky" losses. They are saying, in effect, that such losses should not have happened and therefore will not. A woman should be able to go to isolated places without being raped. For another example, Paula's repeated loss of men to other women is based on unrealistic expectations that intimate relationships *should* be completely interdependent, mutually fulfilling of all needs. These individuals see their relationship to the world somewhat unrealistically, and *they are repeatedly trying to rearrange the world, or reshape it,* so that rape and "the other woman" will disappear, rather than accommodating themselves to the "reality." Their creative efforts are focused on tasks less susceptible of success rather than on themselves. They are experiencing loss of the world as it should be—a world without loss, without any form of death, the "fundamental illusion." But perhaps they engage in trying to actual-ize or real-ize the fundamental illusion because they see self as less likely to be successfully re-created. The answer to why they do this may lie in the period in which they learned how they differ from societal ideals, the later childhood and early teen years. They respond by trying to create the ideal world. Then they themselves will be ideal. (See Chapter 8, on individual development.)

Of course, there is another explanation for patterns of repeated traumatic events, one given by a number of interviewees. This explanation is usually some version of Karma—that they are destined by some cosmic plan or entity to overcome losses in relationships sustained in a previous existence or losses they have caused to others, that through this they will grow, learn, become enlightened. Although I would not dismiss the religious answer by any means, I see in this the creation of self, life, and meaning through the transcendence of loss, including loss metaphorical of previous losses unsuccessfully transcended—simply once removed to the cosmic level!

Let us turn now to individuals whose L/T life themes seem to have originated internally. There are a number of observations to be made. First, and most obvious, just because an individual gives a diffuse account of childhood does not mean that it happened that way. Key events may have been forgotten. There may indeed have been an external event, or a cluster of them, operating perhaps idiosyncratically to create a pattern.

Second, even though an L/T life theme cannot be traced to a single event, there is often a value, or standard, or attitude within the external environment that seems related to the theme. For example, Sibyl met her husband-to-be in the course of her work, traveling through a wide area, performing a service for people. She states that she was "important," and therefore he asked who she was, and others knew who she was and introduced her because of that importance. But her assessment of the situation is clearly an idiosyncratic one, as her work was of a middle level of prestige (similar to being a visiting nurse) rather than a high level. However, she alludes to her father as having been "prominent" (also a questionable assessment), to herself as having been "watched" in college because important things were expected of her and as having received prestigious awards. An attitude toward prominence as desirable seems to have been in the home. This attitude was, in a sense, external to her before she identified with it, took it to herself, and began the lifelong pattern of interpreting people and events in terms of their "importance." In the L/T paradigm, people who are important may be too important to die, a theoretical interpretation borne out by data on longevity which show that those of higher socioeconomic status live longer, probably because of improved health care, more knowledge of healthful life styles, higher intellect, better work satisfaction, and more money for a healthier life (Palmore, 1970, 1974; Birren & Sloane, 1980).

The third root of an L/T life theme is the internalization of two different and conflicting parents. To the child, the parents are omnipotent and can overcome death's many metaphors. Death is not final and irreversible until the child is about 9 or 10 (Lonetto, 1980; Wass & Corr, 1984a, 1984b), an age at which the omnipotence of the parents is just beginning to be dubious. This doubt reaches its height during the teenage years when the full realization of death and its many metaphors, the limitations of life, is apprehended with the cognitive period of formal operations (Piaget, 1952). (See Chapter 8.)

The child who would save his life has two models for survival. If these are very different from each other but supplement and support each other, if the parents appreciate and value these differences, the child can internalize aspects of both and remain whole. If, however, the two parents are in conflict, modes of survival are in conflict; the child must choose, must repress one mode for another. Lorellen chose her father's way of being in the world and found that it led to the many deaths of her life and her father's as well. Now she is repressing this part of herself and choosing her father's opposite, her mother's stability and security. Perhaps she and her baby will survive this way. There are a number of examples of internalization of parental conflict to a greater or lesser degree. For better or worse, the child *is* both of her parents; they survive, they transcend loss, and she emulates and becomes them.

AWARENESS OF THEME

How aware are individuals of their L/T life themes? We asked each interviewee the following question:

"When you think about your life, do you see some sort of theme(s)

to it? If so, what do you feel it is?" (Suggest "pattern" if they're stuck.)

Of the 48 interviewees, 15 responded that they did not see a theme to their lives and 33 responded that they did. Of those who did see a theme, 31 saw only one and 2 saw two themes.

The interviewees were then asked:

"If you were another person looking at your life, would you see any theme(s) to it?"

Twelve reported that others would not see a theme, 31 replied that others would see one theme, 1 did not know, and the data on 4 were missing. Of those who replied that others would see a theme, all 31 felt others would see only one theme. However, it should be noted that these questions came at the end of the interview, when time was growing short, and it is possible that with more time the respondents would have seen more themes.

Finally, for those who had reported seeing a theme or themes in their lives, we coded these themes as being either different from the theme the rater saw, the same as the theme the rater saw, or containing elements of both sameness and difference, that is, mixed. Usually the last category meant that the individual saw one pole, say the loss pole, but did not see the transcendence pole of her theme. With this code, 29 saw a theme different from that of the rater, usually stated in terms of a value that had not been mentioned much, if at all, in the protocol, such as "doing good"; 16 responded with a theme that was only partly what the rater saw; 3 saw themselves as the rater saw them. When putting themselves in the place of others seeing their lives, they came closer to seeing their life themes as the rater saw them. Part of the problem here is undoubtedly that the interviewees have not been trained to look at their lives within this paradigm. The *interrater* reliabilities on this were very high; it does appear that the themes were not artifacts of the rater (see Appendix B).

The conclusion from these data is that, by and large, interviewees are not aware or are only partially aware of their L/T life themes. This indicates that they are not consciously dictating the thematic course of their lives or not acting out their lives according to a conscious pattern. This is especially interesting in view of the finding that most interviewees report an active life review process. (See Chapter 7, "Life Meaning.")

One other check on L/T life theme awareness was performed. According to the theoretical formulation, a life theme may take the form of a recurring conflict (as found by Weenolsen, 1978, and as is shown in the preceding section on origins); therefore interviewees were asked:

"Do you think there has been a central conflict or group of conflicts in your life, which you have found hard to resolve?"

Thirty-six of the interviewees replied in the affirmative and 12 in the negative. Here the agreement between the interviewee and the rater was much higher. Fourteen were different from the rater, mainly in that they saw no conflict where the rater did; 15 saw the same conflict as the rater; and the conflict seen by 19 interviewees agreed partially with that of the rater. For example, Lexie saw her conflict as "being versus doing," one aspect of the conflict that the rater saw as split self, a conflict of identities. This was also highly relevant to the theme of her life. As is apparent from the above statistics, no life was entirely conflict-free, as seen by the rater, although not all conflicts were thematic of the life history.

EVENT SALIENCE

Even though both externally and internally originated L/T life themes seem to be fairly well demarcated, a personal reconstruction of the life is going on in both instances, and there is no way to be sure to what extent subsequent events make previous events more salient. For example, Alice, whose recent life has been extremely difficult because of the birth a few years ago of a retarded child, begins her interview with the observation that a sibling was handicapped. Later, it becomes clear that this handicap was a minor one. One wonders whether its salience was present before the birth of her child—quite possibly not. In our efforts to make sense of present life, seek coherence, find causes or explanations, we may resurrect the heretofore inconsequential.

CONSISTENCY OF LIFE THEME

Would individuals who give a certain theme at 40 have given the same one at 20? Obviously, the question is not finally answerable without a longitudinal study of some type, but we can make a few educated guesses. We can, for example, hypothesize that L/T life themes during life periods that are more adjacent should be more similar than themes of life periods farther apart, just as personality is more likely to be consistent in adjacent life periods (Kagan & Moss, 1962; Brim & Kagan, 1980). That is, we might expect a theme of a 30-year-old to be quite similar to the one she expressed when she was 25; when she is older some change is likely, if only in the supporting life events. Perhaps some losses will drop away, and new ones or more effective modes of transcendence will arise—or the reverse. When we look at the case history of Germaine, we can readily believe that her theme might have been different before the death of her ideal husband 10 years ago—perhaps 10 years ago he was not ideal? It is hard to believe that a great change in L/T theme will occur soon in Lorellen's life. However, she is making an active attempt to change the balance of loss and stability; if she succeeds, then eventually as the salience of loss events recedes and that of transcendence events increases, there may be a modification of her theme. Further, my findings of family life themes that extend over generations (Weenolsen, 1978) lead me to expect considerable consistency over the life span, especially when the themes seem to have arisen from the values and orientations of the parents, as in Sibyl's case.

RECURRING THEMES ACROSS PROTOCOLS

Although each L/T theme is unique to the individual by virtue of supporting events, two categories of themes recur across the protocols. The first category includes L/T life themes that are similar, such as the similarity observed above between "restriction versus freedom" and "dependence versus liberation." The second category includes other single themes that occur across the protocols but are not in themselves L/T life themes. We will examine these two categories of recurring themes in turn, to determine what light, if any, they cast on the course of human development.

There are three recurring L/T life themes. The first and most frequent theme concerns crucial issues in *self-creation,* expressed most patently in such themes as self-submergence versus self-emergence; self-mergence versus self-emergence; identity loss versus identity as productivity and importance; paranoid and schizoid self versus successful work—both as split self; incompetent and unemerged self versus unquestioning acceptance and fantasy; underdeveloped and abused self versus supported and developing self; identity split by time limits versus spiritual growth. In each of the above protocols the individual experiences herself as incomplete, or split in some fashion. Probably the most serious "loss" that an individual can sustain is loss of self, without which there is no integrated self to love and work; the ultimate expression of loss of self is, of course, death.

However, self-creation is less obviously an issue in many of the other protocols. For example, the theme of injury versus healing is injury to self, which Lorellen says may be irreparable, versus healing of self and others. For Marjorie, one must become oneself in order to have a self to lose or let go within a greater cosmic consciousness; her self was fragmented for a while by events beyond her control. Melanie experiences self as part of a community that she actively creates, rather than simply losing herself in groups as a defensive maneuver; the more of group and community she creates, the more of self she creates as well. Elaine actively creates community as well, but it is an expression of herself, an achievement. The struggle for liberation as an expression of self versus the temptation to lose oneself in the security of dependence is the issue for Heather and to a lesser extent for a number of other interviewees. For Theo, the splintering and temporary cohesion describe the life and self as well.

Several interviewees transcend losses to a greater or lesser extent by living through alternate lives that are either worse and make them feel fortunate or more exciting and take them out of themselves; they transcend the limits of one life, one self, by partaking in many, as do the service- and community-oriented. Denise defines her self as "weird" and, for her, survival means keeping the self together; she depends on others to define her as something better than she thinks she is. Yves similarly gains her support from others in order to overcome crises in self-confidence—lack of confidence in the integrity of self, capable of *doing*. However, strength from others can become a tyranny; the payment for the strength of others often seems to be allowing them to define who one is. This is true of Crista, whose husband repeatedly told her she did not know what she wanted in response to her many years of need for city living; of Opal, whose life was defined by the problems of others and who achieved gradual emergence only as circumstances released her from those others; of Greer, waiting for her husband one way or another for 20 years; and of Queenie, who adds to other selves by feeding, in order to overcome their subtracting criticism. Jaclyn has drawn strength from a man to the point of his dominion over her, because her sexual dysfunction has discounted her womanhood, and as a result she leads a vegetative existence. For Yvonne, loss of the world as it was is repeatedly taken as a personal loss. The main theme for Ursula clearly revolves around the educated self, who will be a different self, an artist and a writer.

Finally, we can see a number of protocols as involving an integrated self as opposed to a split self. A number of these interviewees speak in terms of emergence. Marjorie has attained enough identity to be able to merge with a larger consciousness; she emphasizes the necessity for individuation first, or one is schizophrenic. Melanie is clearly herself, and to be herself is to be connected with others. Heather is insisting on her identity, possibly at the expense of her marriage. The integrated self may become integrated enough to be part of the divine plan; we sense this as a refuge when the self has not emerged, as is perhaps true of Winnie, Gwen, and Frances, where transcendence of overwhelming loss has been too difficult, or there has been little loss to transcend. A higher integration that results in one form of life meaning, commitment beyond self, where individuation has occurred, seems to be in process with Marjorie, Della, Sue, Harriet, Faith, and Judith.

As noted in the theoretical formulation underlying this research, the creation of self, one that is more meaningful rather than less so, is a crucial aspect of human development. These protocols constitute a record of self-creation, which may be categorized as unemerged, living alternate lives, split, individuating or struggling to integrate, or integrated. These categories may be seen further as different levels of the L/T process, as *mourning* the unemerged self, as *searching* for some means of individuation or *replacing* by unifying, and as *integrating* or having integrated the parts of self into a functioning whole, losses transcended or in transcendence, life made sense of, the potential self finally emerged, finally born, through the creative process involving decisions, commitments, and so forth. (See a fuller discussion of this material in Chapter 6, "The Self.")

A second way to view these themes is in Koestler's paradigm of the irreconcilability of the individual as a whole individual with the individual as part of another whole (societal), who can still maintain his or her individuality, as Frank Barron and I have observed (Weenolsen & Barron, 1979). Issues of freedom and restriction, emergence and submergence, dependence and self-reliance, shelter and exposure, control and its lack, security, transcendence through something outside the self such as service, divinity, psychic phenomena—all can be seen as issues of the individual as a whole and the individual as part of a greater whole. For many, it is union with something beyond self, which cannot die, that endows life with meaning; for others, being part of a family, for example, is crippling.

The third recurring L/T life theme is rather a dimension of the themes than a theme in itself, or perhaps a theme of the themes. Taking control of one's life, wresting freedom or liberation for oneself from others, actively shaping one's life rather than passively accepting it, doing rather than mourning, serving others rather than remaining apart, communicating rather than remaining silent, overcoming obstacles, dealing with a problem rather than getting away from it, achieving rather than allowing the devastation of loss to overwhelm, overcoming a lack (of education etc.) rather than living with it—all seem to belong on a unified dimension that one can conceptualize as active versus passive, independent versus dependent, or control versus lack of control. Repeatedly in these protocols women seem to shrink in identity when they are less active. There seems to be less and less of self when a woman is swallowed up by circumstances and important others. This finding may be seen as similar to the findings of Baruch, Barnett, and Rivers (1983) on the importance of mastery. On the other hand, when a woman becomes more active and assertive, although many losses may result, she reports enhancement of life and self, vitality, energy, meaning. Because passivity in women is our societal ideal, and living through others rather than living in oneself is the prescription for femininity (Gilligan, 1979, 1982; Rubin, 1979), one can see that the creation of self and its concomitant meaningfulness can be a special problem for women. However, our findings dovetail with those of mental health practitioners who rate the more active (and masculine) dimensions as healthier. Seligman's (1975) paradigm of learned helplessness seems apposite to the issue of activity versus passivity here; one who is taking an active part in shaping her life and self into more meaningful directions is less likely to learn that she can do nothing or that she is helpless in the face of controlling others and circumstances. Many of my interviewees seemed to have learned that they were helpless, like Jaclyn, who at the age of 50, after years of being controlled, simply *believes* she is incapable of moving or working, and so she is. Having lost her "womanhood" because of sexual dysfunction, she has become the expression of femininity prescribed in our society in its most extreme form, leading a vegetative existence of almost total passivity. (See Chapter 10, on psychopathology, for Jaclyn's life history.)

Turning to the themes that recur *across* protocols but are not necessarily the major L/T life themes, we find many that are theoretically relevant and a number that are especially frequent.

One theme that emerges across protocols is the notion that the interviewee sets out to create the home she did not have as a child. Tori says, "Garth and I create in our family what we did not have." There may have been a certain element, such as "warmth" or "stability," lacking in the childhood. This is clearly an attempt to replace a past loss so that self and meaning may be integrated. One senses that if the interviewee can create this home for her child, she herself will at last have the childhood she never had. There is, in other words, an ongoing metaphorical re-creation.

Related to this is the notion of creating the family she never had in another way, by finding or creating substitute families. The theater was "home" for several, a boarding house for one, political and social movements for others, actual substitute families for still others. One wonders if it is the real or the ideal family that is missing from these lives; certainly, some of the interviewees expressed expectations of what a family *should* be like that were more appropriate for television—perhaps where they got them.

Still another theme is that of mothering the parent, often in the parent's last days or months on earth. This is a transcendent experience for our interviewees. Not only may the strained relationships be re-created in more loving form, but also there is a new concept of self as competent (Tess) or becoming somehow better (Em). Perhaps pain, suffering, and dying do some good after all, in that they elicit love and "better selves."

A somewhat related group of themes concerned major decisions, particularly those related to marriage. A number of women speculate on whether an alternative marriage would have been right for them; some dwell on missed chances at length. "I would have led a different life" (Aurora) and it would have been a better one, unencumbered with realities as is the dream. Others regretted not having divorced sooner. Several (like Lexie) saw that they had expected their husbands to substitute for the world they left behind when they were pregnant and new mothers, and this simply did not happen. Still others felt a kind of community of womanhood with mothers and daughters and tried to pass this from generation to generation.

A different theme is that of special dreams of a house. The interviewees report recurring dreams of a house that have idiosyncratic meaning for them, which many described in extensive detail. There seems to be a relationship between the house and the L/T life theme, life and self circumstances, and loss-transcendence poles in the individual. "The house is my life," says Em.

Still another theme, a conflict between living in the city and in the country, seems to be a conflict between different life styles or ways of being in the world. It is also related to feeling more or less alive. This may be partly a reflection of the sociocultural value that emerged in the 1960s and 1970s, which sees fulfillment in going back to the land, unity with nature, and deadness in the technological advances implicit in city living, in contrast to seeing variety in city places, persons, and activities, and potential for alternate lives, and sameness, drabness, emptiness in country life. When asked their favorite places, 18 chose the country or nature, 14 chose a foreign locale (not emphasizing city or country), 5 chose a town or city, and 5 chose to be wherever they are.

Still another theme that occurs across protocols is, not surprisingly, a conflict between family and career. Although it was not itself the major life theme of any one protocol, it contributed to the life themes of a number, such as Lexie. Because this is an issue of particular importance to women in this society (Gilligan, 1977, 1982; Rubin, 1979) it may be seen as a historically specific phenomenon, although not, I think, a cohort-specific phenomenon. Women of all ages were wrestling with the issue to a greater or lesser extent. In mid-life they sometimes had to struggle with the demands of their husbands as well as with the labor market in order to gain entry and reasonable treatment. The younger women tended to see themselves as having to give up one for the other, at least temporarily, and experiencing considerable loss no matter what their choice. Answers to questions about satisfaction with children and satisfaction with work, while demonstrating more belief that children bring satisfaction than that work yields satisfaction, bring the dilemma into relief. Whether or not they had children of their own, 22 women felt they would definitely have children, 3 felt they would definitely not, and 17 had mixed feelings about having children. With regard to work experiences, whether or not they were currently working, 16 were rated as gaining satisfaction in work, 6 as not feeling satisfaction, and 26 as having mixed experiences. Social desirability may have inflated the mother satisfaction numbers, but it is at least clear that enough satisfaction is perceived in both areas to make a conflict painful when there must be a choice.

When women were asked if it was better to be a man than a woman, 11 thought it was better to be a man, 19 felt it was better to be a woman, 7 thought both were equally desirable, and 9 felt neither was better. The major reason given for the advantage of being a man, in this and related questions, was that men had the advantage in the workplace and did not have to have a conflict between work and family. The women also report that adolescence was the worst life period, and middle age (thirties, forties, and fifties), the best.

One very interesting theme, especially among more transcendent individuals, was that parents who had been cruel or had not done well in some way inspired their daughters to do better. This resulted in a number of surprising answers to the question, "Do you think your (mother, father) influenced you for the better, for the worse, or somewhat in between?" After detailing childhood mistreatment that might be expected to promote neurosis rather than healthy growth, a number of interviewees responded "for the better," because it taught them to be more independent or kinder, to overcome obstacles at any cost, or some other strength, or they would never have been so motivated to succeed. In other words, a positive value was found in cruelty, failure, indifference, and various forms of abuse.

There were other, more expected themes. There were children who pleased their mothers as extensions of themselves, or who disappointed by rejecting values or not actualizing the potential the parents saw in them. The grief of conflicts with children was reported by many mothers, including Crista, Marjorie, Heather, Judith, Elaine, Vera, Alice, and Em. Motherhood was not all it was cracked up to be, but many still felt they would not have missed it. As was reported in Chapter 1, physical abuse and alcoholism were devastating to more than 40 percent.

CONCLUSIONS: L/T LIFE THEMES IN THE THERAPEUTIC SETTING

It can be helpful for therapists to employ the notion of L/T life themes in clinical practice for a number of reasons. First, the L/T life theme emphasizes the life-and-death nature of the struggle the client is undergoing. Second, the therapist can understand the ways in which the client's life is "coded" for life and for death. Third, the therapist can understand the metaphorical nature of loss, by which it represents other losses (especially with the addition of the metaphorical system). She or he can seek the original loss and develop ways of working that through, as is frequently done in psychoanalysis for different reasons. Psychodrama and other modes of acting out are especially helpful, with attention paid to the subsequent losses of the same type that are, in essence, repetitions of the primary loss. Fourth, attention can be paid to the modes of transcendence and their value within the L/T process. These are the strengths of the client. The client cannot be a vacuum, with losses removed and nothing substituted. Substitution of transcendence modes *before* working through of losses can be of value; for example, a return to previous loved general transcendence behaviors, such as taking nature walks, moviegoing, playing tennis, letter writing, and going to the opera, can be encouraged and supported before the client feels ready for them. Fifth, it must be remembered that the client will always have *some* L/T life theme. The goal of the therapist is to make the loss poles less severe and more within the control of the individual and to make the transcendence more balanced among the three types and more functional. Sixth, the therapist must be careful to think of the client's welfare in terms of *her* values rather than his own. The L/T system focuses on how the client perceives life events and relationships and much less on what really happened.

5

Metaphorical Systems

"It was like we were looking out our own windows. Everybody has a window, that you look out and see the world. Because I saw something a certain way, I assumed he saw it the same way. . . ."

A certain premise of the L/T paradigm is that there is no such thing as pure experience. There is indeed an external world, but it is not directly accessible to any of us. We filter objective reality through our own spectacles, and the prescription for these spectacles varies from individual to individual. That which is experienced as external reality actually differs from person to person, be it a common, ordinary table, a human face, or a Bergman movie.

The reality of experience can neither be apprehended nor communicated. We perceive and communicate by metaphor. Nothing is ever merely what it is; it is also what it stands for or represents in our system. Misunderstandings arise when my metaphor is perceived by you within your own metaphorical system.

In this chapter I briefly discuss the prevalence of metaphor in our lives, as brilliantly set forth in Lakoff and Johnson's work *Metaphors we live by* (1980). Examples of metaphors as they extend into entire systems are followed by a brief discussion of what the metaphorical system represents—the metaphorical life-and-death struggle. A metaphorical analysis of behavior is performed on the histories of Crista, Annette, and Kara; in the latter history a metaphorical system is briefly diagrammed. Finally, a number of conclusions are drawn about the relationship of metaphorical systems to life and self development.

FROM METAPHORS TO METAPHORICAL SYSTEMS

Lakoff and Johnson (1980) demonstrate that we live by metaphors of which we are unaware. According to them, "the essence of metaphor is understanding and experiencing one kind of thing in terms of another" (p. 5). But rather than defining metaphor as a linguistic device or a rational equation, Lakoff and Johnson believe the metaphors we live by have an experiential basis. They give a number of examples of their thesis. In everyday life we speak as if *argument* were *war;* we talk of attacking weak points, being on target, using strategy, claims that are indefensible, and shooting down arguments. We view *time* as *money* in that we speak of wasting or saving or spending or investing or borrowing or losing time. In similar fashion Lakoff and Johnson demonstrate how metaphor pervades our lives without our being aware of it, how we speak in metaphors and live by them, and how we construe, understand, and create meaning in our everyday experience by employing these metaphors.

Of course, we are situated within our culture, and such metaphors as those above are shared among us. However, according to the L/T perspective, there is even more that is metaphorical about our lives. Each of us has a unique metaphorical system, experientially based, of which the L/T theme is the shorthand. Our metaphorical system is our network of losses that represent death to us and transcendences that represent life, immortality, rebirth, or resurrection.

The spectacles through which we see our world are calibrated according to our individual metaphorical systems, or the ways in which we have structured our experience thus far. Because of this, an object (1) represents itself but also (2) represents our own relationship to it, (3) its relationship to other objects and (4) other selves, and finally (5) its place in a world of which we are continuously attempting to create some meaning or make some sense. Thus, no object can be experienced in exactly the same way by two individuals. One way this can be demonstrated is simply by having several people "associate" to a common object. My students associate to the word "sunflower," for instance. They begin by such associations as "yellow" and "seed" but then quickly move to idiosyncratic associations such as "Aztec" and "swing set," reflecting their own metaphorical systems based on experience. The contents of these systems, though not all fully present and active in our minds, are still part of us and influence our interpretations of our experience.

If symbols represent objects and objects also represent symbols, how much more can this be said of more complex objects, relationships, and experiences? This becomes an extremely important principle when we refer to loss. The implication is that loss is not a pure experience but represents other, often similar or similarly perceived, losses as well. One of my interviewees, Paula, had been rejected by men in a number of serious relationships. She could not speak of one relationship without referring to the others. She even told one lover that she would not tolerate his working with another woman because a previous lover of hers had fallen in love with a woman under similar circumstances. She viewed herself as one who had lost love, and in doing so she seemed to perpetrate further loss of love; that is, she showed more unreasonable possessiveness, questioning, demands, jealousy of women, and other characteristics that would destroy the basic trust necessary to a relationship.

It appears that we each carry within us an entire metaphorical structure or system whereby no experience is pure; rather it is experienced in the context of others that have gone before. The L/T life theme seems to be a kind of shorthand for that structure. And it is in the context of that metaphorical system that the world is viewed.

I may tell you that I love trees, and you may rejoin that you love the ocean. Now, to tell you why I love trees and what they mean to me would be an extremely complex task (other than my having been a dryad in a previous existence, an explanation for which some of my friends have opted). Until this moment, I've never really tried to put this into words.

Some years ago I was participating in a group guided-fantasy experience. We were supposed to enter our bodies, explore, and see what we could find. I entered through my back, for some inexplicable reason, a stage with curtains drawn to let me in; poked my "head" up through my neck and into my head, and was astounded at what was there—a huge gray archetypal forest, enormous oaks and redwoods in the mists of time, ancient, with cobwebby lichen dripping from their branches, incredibly deep and dark, the sunlight filtering through, glimpses of an aquamarine sky above the gray—a forest that had existed long before me and that would go on long after I was dead—and yet all of this was inside me! I was eternal, because the forest was!

When I was a child I dreamed I was in danger and flew to a tree, which opened, and inside the trunk was a woman with a candle who beckoned me to safety. Later, as a teenager, I sculpted her as the Madonna.

I could rub my skin raw against the bark to enter a tree and to be part of it. I express love by embracing, but even when my arms encircle the trunk of a tree it is not enough, because it is not the whole I am embracing, or that embraces me, and we exist on different planes, so the tree does not feel my love, nor I its love. I alone feel my own love. The tree is the home of Pan, dryads, other gods and goddesses of the woods, Ceres or Cybele fruit of the earth; it is nourished and nourishing, changing and eternal, hideout of my childhood despair, wind-tossed, haunted, life-giving, a forest veiling the mysterious, where I and only I belong, mysteries which will be revealed just beyond, mysteries I almost know the answer to, then never revealing but concealing more until the journey is the revelation. The tree is velvet leaf and all the greens grayed into forest, lacy against the sky, pine needles sharp to touch and bending to my fingertip, whispering, lemony and pine smells, swaying and nursery log, grubs under bark dank, bird homes, great bowls like cancers, baby seedlings, slashed and logged, lightning- and-fire-riven. If I were to go and live among the trees, I know I would die, and they would be witnesses uncaring—I know this with my logical mind, and yet that is what I secretly long to do. Each place I live must have a special tree. Where I live now in Seattle, there is an extraordinary pine with one cone, and beside it an aspen shimmering. In Chicago a superb oak sent its branches across my balcony, eucalyptus trees with owls in them in Santa Cruz, a tulip tree in Venice and in Palos Verdes, a *Bauhinia purpurea* (orchid tree) that my husband cut down when we were separated—instinctively I think he knew it was our marriage, that I would never stay—all my trees, endlessly life-giving and refreshing to my spirit as is religion to others.

I sense this is only the beginning—one aspect of my metaphorical system.

And you thought a tree was a trunk with a bunch of leaves!

Is that what the ocean—or whatever thing you love—means to you? (Pick a *thing* for a moment; with a *person* it is too easy to say you love him or her for courage, kindness, a sense of humor, and on and on, never getting below the surface.)

And yet, if we stop with these statements, if I say to you I love trees and the forest and you say you love water and the ocean, what has happened? I've begun to share my metaphorical system with you, and you with me, but neither of us has received the system of the other. We may both conclude that we have something in common: we love nature, or we love. It is also possible that we love what is life-affirming and hate or fear what is life-denying and that different things represent these to us. A friend of mine confides the "cabin fever" he and his family experience living in the woods. Where there is safety and security for me (and I realize a Freudian would have a field day with my uterine forest symbolism), there is danger for him.

Notice that in this simple attempt to begin to share my metaphorical system with you, I wrote that I love trees, and I went on to try to communicate what trees were—I deliberately sidestepped the more difficult task of defining love!

From the L/T perspective, a metaphorical system is our personal encoding of what represents loss and death to us and what represents transcendence and rebirth (Weenolsen, 1987a). Each loss symbolizes other losses, each transcendence other transcendences, each person other persons, each event other events. All symbolize who we are and who we would become. And all are linked in a unique network, in which everything is related to something else. This metaphorical system constitutes the pair of Adlerian spectacles through which we see the world. Our relationships with others are metaphors of other relationships, and we deal with others in our present lives as we have dealt with others in the past, even though we often struggle against doing so; we tend to trust or mistrust, depend or strain away, be kind or cruel, be jealous or forgiving. The metaphorical system comprises metaphors of life and death as we have created them over our lives. The most salient of these metaphors form the shorthand for the metaphorical system, the L/T life theme, which we discussed in the preceding chapter.

At the moment I am writing this, a woman in brown cords and a hooded navy jacket, with the weathered face of a street person, a huge tote bag slung over her shoulder, is walking up the street. She has left the sidewalk and moves along the outside of the line of parked cars. She comes to a white compact station wagon and circles it several times, not an easy task because it is parked very close to a maroon car, so that she has to squeeze between the front of the white and the back of the maroon. She does this three, four, five times—I've lost count. Then she moves on. How does she perceive the sidewalk? Not as the place for pedestrians, as most of us do! And the street? Not as a place to get hit by a car! What about the white car—what does it mean to her that it is part of a ritual? What place does it have in her metaphorical system, so different from our own? I wonder—is she looking for a car to steal? Is she drunk? Crazy? That is the system through which I perceive, and, because I am a psychologist, and she doesn't stagger, and she didn't try the doors of the white car to gain entry, I lean toward schizophrenia as an explanation. I see her metaphorical system as sufficiently different from that of most of the rest of us that I label it, and I am concerned for the welfare of such an individual.

Logically, I know there may be a perfectly sane explanation for the actions that struck me as so peculiar.

METAPHORICAL SYSTEMS IN COMMUNICATION

These metaphorical systems are the reasons why we may "know" someone for years and suddenly discover one day that we do not "know" him, why husbands and wives do not "communicate" even though they talk, why the phrase "where I'm coming from" has become so popular—it alludes to the metaphorical system. Each metaphorical system is, of course, unique and extremely complex, and, relatively speaking, we only gain small insights into them in the life histories. Because it would be so difficult and impractical to learn the metaphorical system of everyone with whom we come into contact, we have developed conventions of communication, and we assume we understand each other. Even superficial communications often conceal others.

I believe Freud was right about transference as far as he went. But I believe there is much more transference going on, not just from analysand to analyst or father figure but also from person to person, thing to thing, thing to person, situation to situation. The whole becomes a system in which transferences are linked to each other. One might even think of it as a delusional system, such as that which besets the paranoid, except that it is more benign. One might also think of it as an *ill*usional system, since nothing is as it is but is only as it appears to be, only what we make of it.

LIFE HISTORIES

Let us turn to the stories of Crista, Annette, and Kara to see what they can reveal about metaphorical systems, what they consist of, their pervasiveness, how they manifest, develop, and influence our lives. On each we will be performing what amounts to a metaphorical analysis of behavior.

Crista

"I lost part of myself in the struggle for where I lived."

Now in her early forties, Crista lives in a beautifully appointed home of redwood and stained glass.

Crista grew up taking responsibility for the conflict between her mother, who was usually depressed, and her father, an angry perfectionist. She herself was a "good girl." Her earliest memories are of being helpful, climbing on chairs to dust and wipe the dishes. She feels now that she got into the habit of helping others and being responsible for them at that early age, without stopping to think about what she herself might want, because of her mother's manipulative depression and perhaps also because her father loved perfection. "My very favorite thing was to go downtown to San Francisco [on the] street-car. . . . I always loved to go downtown. Some kind of atmosphere. I realized that the downtown area was somehow more sophisticated. I became aware very early of where I was, where I liked to be. I loved the big stores and restaurants. It was an event for me to do that, and something I continued to do clear into adulthood."

During her adolescence, Crista's father became alcoholic, her mother's depression worsened, and Crista took on more and more of the household responsibility. The conflict between her parents erupted into physical violence; one night her father threatened them with a knife and they fled the house. However, Crista's mother did not believe in divorce, and eventually they returned.

Crista managed to keep her turbulent home life separate from her school life, where she was fairly popular and successful. At that time, more than anything else, "I wanted our family to be happy and peaceful."

Continuing her identity as helper, Crista enrolled in nursing school, but she hated the hospital environment. She told her mother that she wanted to quit, "absolutely the first time I had ever looked at what I wanted to do," and her mother, in bed with her depression, pulled the covers over her head and said, "Oh, my god, I just don't know what you're going to do if you don't become a nurse." Because Crista had no idea of what she *did* want to do, she finished her training and specialized in obstetrics, where she was successful.

Crista was attracted to her husband because he seemed to be an "exact contrast" to her father, although in the end this did not prove to be the case. Their marriage took place partly because "I had nowhere to go." By this time, however, even though Crista didn't know anything about her desires and motives, she had discovered one thing about herself: she loved the city and hated the country. Unfortunately, her husband's work required that they live in the suburbs, which began a conflict that has continued to this day. Even when she told him how she felt about the city, he didn't believe she really knew what she wanted, and he discounted her desires. In their various suburban and country homes she felt alone and friendless, even though she had children, and she cried a lot. Her husband was very patient with her, and she did manage to make a few friends and get to the city occasionally.

"I feel that what is uniquely me thrives in the city," she says. She does not know why, although there are childhood memories of visiting the country and feeling uncomfortable there.

Crista's life changed dramatically in her thirties. After having given birth to her three daughters, she returned to nursing, where she got "a lot of strokes." She also went into therapy, where "I learned how to deal with my mother, that I was not responsible if she was going to drink herself into oblivion, or kill herself, or whatever. There was only so much I could do." This represented an emancipation for her, from "all those years of taking care of" her mother, of feeling sole responsibility for everyone to the exclusion of herself. "Boy, if I was ever in a real pattern. . . ." Therapy showed her it was okay to want. It helped her deal with her husband, who, while appearing quiet and soft-spoken, was "actually a very strong, controlling person," like her father and, in a different way, her mother. She also faced the fact that even when she knew what she wanted, especially to live in the city, she tended to back off from assertion.

Crista tried to switch from nursing to another field in the area of artistic environmental design; her few accomplishments in this area, including design of their beautiful home, gave her great joy. But the field is a depressed one, and much as she loved the work, she has been unable to find employment. So she is taking brief training to go into still another field, because she loves the atmosphere of her potential workplace.

Crista sees herself as still living where others want her to live rather than where she wants to live. There has always been some ostensible reason—a long commute for her husband, the welfare of her daughters, a financial investment—to remain in suburbs or country rather than make a final move to the city. It has always been "a few more years, a few more years," and then they would move. However, she is now thinking in terms of alternatives, a job in the city, a part-time life there, although she protests that she would not be splitting up her family, the horror of family strife and split having been planted in her childhood.

Asked how she sees her life theme, Crista responds, "One thing that bothers me is that so far I haven't gotten to where I am really comfortable, and it seems the decisions I make don't lead me to [a comfortable place], but yet, looking at all the given choices, with that one theme of never in all these years being settled, or really at peace with where I am—that bothers me—a negative theme. A positive theme: I do see myself as a nurturing person, mother, and I see this in my relationship with other people."

Running through Crista's history is concern for environment, particularly visual, expressed mainly in her conflict between country (or suburbs) and city living, but also in her dislike of the various nursing environments, her choice of an alternative career designing environments, and her choice of a third career because of environmental atmosphere. The conflict seems rooted in the childhood development of being helpful and responsible, being a "good girl," perhaps because her father loved and insisted on perfection in many aspects of their family life, perhaps to "save" her mother's equilibrium and eventually her life. This helpfulness was at the expense of assertion of her own desires and, indeed, of her even being aware of them. The penalty for imperfection and nonhelping, which threatened child and adolescent for years, was family violence and breakup, as well as the death of parents. All this came to pass, in spite of her best efforts. Helping others, responsibility for others, was always at the expense of her own identity emergence. However, there is a kind of death on either side of the conflict.

This life theme comes out in her recurring dream: "I have a dream that I go into a house, and it has many rooms, and it's a maze, and the rooms are never laid out right, and I keep finding more rooms, but they're never right. The windows are always too high, I can't see out [laughs]. I didn't have it for awhile after we moved here, but I had one recently, very similar. I was finding—oh, look—there are more and more rooms, and I think, how can I make this into something that is united. It never is cohesive. There's lots of space, but not in the right order. . . . There is an air of expectation. I'm finally going to find the right room."

Imperfection in environment is paid for with noncohesiveness, not being united. The right environment *is* cohesive. Is environment an expression of the self and is the self therefore noncohesive?

She handled her conflict by crying a lot, being depressed (the way her mother handled conflict), but also through therapy, which helped her to become more assertive. Now she is looking forward to a practical change; certainly her work and therapy have provided her with many satisfactions, and her outlook is good.

"I have this fantasy of having this gorgeous flat in San Francisco filled with art, and I have a neat job, and my husband and I are on a continual high just from living, and the kids are happy."

The mystery of her love for the city has remained. She says, "The place I still especially love is [the city]. I love the natural beauty—the bay, the sky, and the man-made beauty that is integrated with the buildings. I love the buildings. I love the bridge. I don't love all the buildings. I love the hills. It's a combination of the natural. . . . [Buildings] mean life. I see life going on there. When I look out and see no houses and no people—I don't see life like I see when I see a building. I hate little teeny-tiny hot, country, dusty crossroads towns [laughs]. I feel such desolation. I sense despair. To me, a person can live in an old run-down flat and still be kind of alive, but to live in some old ramshackle place in the country, somehow part of me would not be alive."

In this we see very clearly the metaphorical relationships of death to the country and to the loss of city for Crista whereas city represents life. The city-country dichotomy is a life-death one for her. She also expresses a sense of loss in that the part of her life she lived outside the city can never be recovered:

"I have lost part of what was uniquely me. I lost part of myself in the struggle for where I lived." (Do you think you could get it back?) "No, it's gone. I said to my husband recently, I was quite upset and I said: 'I didn't get to roll my baby buggy along the sidewalk. It's gone. I can't get it back.' We had been through all that conflict, and that doesn't mean I can't develop or utilize what's left [of my life], but I feel I did lose something. I gave it up. I let it go. . . . That brought some feelings [tears]. That's okay, though. I know they're there. Without in the beginning even realizing . . . I didn't define it until I was already so far into it. . . . People either understand or they don't."

In the loss and transcendence process, Crista still seems to be in the searching stage, searching for a career and a living situation that is right for her. Her orientation was rated as being to loss, but she feels that she is moving toward a solution. She sees her own conflict as one of control, and certainly this is a way of looking at her life theme on a simpler level. She was in conflict for control with her parents, with her husband, and with her children.

It is appropriate to note the importance of the visual to Crista. She states that the worst loss, which would make life meaningless to her, would be the loss of eyesight. Her highest function on the Myers-Briggs Personality Index (Myers, 1962, 1977) was in perception, which was very high at 45 and denotes flexibility and adaptability to novelty. Such a high score might even suggest a *need* for novelty and variety, more likely in the plethora of city stimuli than in what she perceives as the sameness of country.

Crista was one of the few interviewees for whom life has no meaning. "We are born, we live, we die. It's the same thing over and over." She has not really overcome the loss of life in the city and senses that she has lost the self that might have been created in this environment.

Crista's L/T life theme, then, is concern with environment, particularly, visual, expressed in a lifelong conflict between country and city living, which are metaphorically related to death and life. What keeps her in the country is the necessity to be helpful, which is rooted in childhood, when she was reared to help, and to submerge her own interests for those of others; if she did not, the threat was family violence, breakup, and death. Responsibility for others brings its own rewards but is at the expense of her own identity emergence, of which the environment is an expression. The core theme is country versus city as an expression of self-submergence through helping versus emergence.

In this sense, we see Crista's struggle as one over emerging identity. She fused with others to save her environment, family, and relatives and could not emerge as one who wanted, as one who had desires and motives in her own right. Her emergence as an individual is comparatively late, and it is still a struggle. Still, the focus of her marriage and her career on the city-country conflict suggests another dimension to the entire issue of loss and transcendence. Is it possible that the unemerged, those whose identity is not yet out of the shell, so to speak, focus on loss as a way of forming an identity? Is having lost better than remaining empty?

Theoretical analysis

Metaphorically, to nurture others is to give them life. Crista has given life to others, and this in turn might have been life-giving to her but it was not, perhaps because it was a requirement, under duress, too early in her development, rather than a voluntary commitment. However, had she not nurtured, those lives might have been taken from her, threatening her own survival. The loss of primary caretakers from whom sustenance has been derived must always seem threatening to the child, a loss of nourishment and a loss of self. Crista's mother might have died of depression (metaphorically), her father might have killed them all, or left. Crista was a "good" little girl, trying to preserve the flimsy structure of her family and her life by doing dishes, dusting, and other family tasks. As Crista gave life to others, she was assured that her life would continue as it was, and that she would continue, but not that she would become. Repressing, rigidly holding herself together as she did her family—these were safe but nonfruitioning strategies. Assertion of self, of desires or wants, might be met with violence. She became a family holding itself together, "not rocking the boat."

She also became a nurse, virtually by default; she didn't know who she was or who she wanted to be. She had no desires of her own, having ministered to those of others. Always a helper, even though it felt wrong, she continued in the only role she knew, finding some satisfaction as well as discomfort in it later on.

Crista knew one thing about herself by the end of adolescence; the "city" was life to her and "country," including suburbia, was death. This seems to have begun early in childhood, when city was escape from an unhappy home. But she also sensed that our environments play a large part in creating who we are. She mourns the self she might have been, the alternate life, wheeling the baby pram down city streets. "I have lost a part of myself. . . . It's gone. I can't get it back." The implication is that there is less of life—the city— in her self than there might have been, that she is not as alive or vital as she would have been had the city become a part of her. She has been giving up a more vital self through childhood and marriage in order not to lose her family, nurturing so as not to lose nurture, sustaining to be sustained. Her struggle might be seen as accepting one form of death to protect herself against another, exchanging spiritual or inner life for physical life. Her husband has been her father, a kindlier one to be sure, but still controlling and delineating whom she may become. Their family has been her natal family, and occasionally she has been her mother, responding with depression. Had the natal family been more stable, one wonders if the loss of unity in her marital family might have been not quite as threatening—she would not have been losing her husband and primary caregiver.

I believe Crista sees many aspects of her life, from minute details to the larger events and decisions, in terms of this city versus country dichotomy. There is evidence of the pervasiveness of this theme in her responses to many questions. She loves buildings, and without vision to see them life would be meaningless. She had training in architectural design and loved every minute of it, although she sees little hope of entering the field professionally. She lives with her family in the house she herself designed (in a rural suburb), but still yearns for the city. She has chosen to pursue a different job in a large, award-winning architectural complex, nicknamed City in the Forest. She describes the children in terms of being happy in the suburbs, needing school continuity, not being ready to move to the city. We learn little about her husband beyond their conflict. Her relationship, surroundings, occupation, and thoughts represent the city versus country dichotomy, which in turn represents life versus death. The metaphorical system is far-reaching and complex because so much of her life hinges on it. Although a city versus country conflict was present in a number of protocols to varying degrees, in no protocol was it as pervasive as in Crista's.

Perhaps most telling, the emotions engendered by the conflict are still raw, never allayed. Tears spring to her eyes over the many manifestations of the conflict, some of which happened 20 years ago. The loss seems to be felt as keenly as the loss of a beloved human being, which it is—of herself.

In trying to explain her feelings, Crista employs the words "comfort," "comfortable," and "uncomfortable" a great deal. She is never "comfortable" in her country surroundings. They are not where she belongs, and there is a sense of being alien, a stranger. In the country there is a lack of comfort or of being comforted, perhaps nurtured. Although not specifically mentioned, it seems to be the dimension of space and her place in it that troubles her. She loves to re-create space according to her own design. As Piaget (1952) and Bowlby (1969) both pointed out, the dimension of space is an important issue for the toddler. The toddler must discover where she or he belongs in space, must learn the meanings of over, under, back, and front, both linguistically and kinesthetically. It might not be too great a leap to assume that if something goes wrong with that learning, if it is interfered with in some fashion, if the child is either enclosed in a confined space for long periods or excluded from certain spaces, this could lead to a problem of defining the self in terms of that dimension of the world in which we live.

Finally, Crista tells us that the decisions and choices she has been making all these years never seem to have led her out of this dilemma, to a way of being in the city. In this she seems to be taking some responsibility for the lack of resolution. To explain this by instancing the metaphorical links between nurturing and life and death, city and country, illuminates much; but she married or created a man who would keep her from full life and self-development, perhaps controlling him in the same way her mother controlled her father, by laying down her life. The city represents life and, in the final analysis, she has stayed away from it.

Annette

"I think that the way to get along with a person is knowing what to say and what not to say."

Annette, a petite blond woman in her mid-sixties, feels that she had a normal, quiet childhood. Her family moved around quite a bit because her father's business required it, but she still had her siblings to play with. Their upbringing was a conventional one; their father's business necessitated a certain degree of propriety in their behavior. However, apparently there were hidden problems between the parents that were never aired in front of the children; when their father went away for a while in her early childhood, she and her siblings were mystified; he returned because her mother was having difficulties raising the children by herself. Their divorce when she was 18 also came as a surprise. Her mother had kept years of unhappiness to herself, but the children found an account of these years in a diary after her death; they burned it because they felt it was private and later regretted this loss of history.

Annette feels that she and her siblings were immature compared to children today. "We never did anything on our own. We never did anything without [our mother's] consent. I notice that my grandchildren are so forward, and they speak out so much, where we wouldn't think of it." She feels that the way children are raised today is an improvement "because I didn't really mature until high school. I dated very little, and we never thought of doing some of the things that the children do now. I notice that with my daughter, when she got to be eighteen, she was more or less immature, but she wanted to be on her own and move into her own apartment. We never would have thought of it. I think it really helps them in marriage, too, because then they are on their own and know more about what life is about. We were too sheltered as far as I was concerned."

Annette's teen years were happy ones. She and her siblings "had a lot of activities and house parties, and who could eat the most waffles. Everyone knew everyone because it was . . . a small town. We didn't have any of these drug abusers or drinking that we have now. They all drank milk . . . you hardly ever even drank coffee."

In high school Annette had a boyfriend with whom she went to dances and shows, but there was nothing romantic between them. "I was always uneasy with boys because they wanted something that—I wasn't romantically inclined . . . [until about] twenty-two."

It was on her graduation from high school that Annette's parents were divorced, a traumatic time for her. "The only way we knew that they were going to get the divorce was my mother said to us: 'How would you like to spend your summer vacation in Reno?' We said: 'Great, and how come?' She said: 'Your father and I are getting a divorce.' Why, we were just shocked, because we had no idea. My father had been away a lot because of his traveling." In the course of his travels, he met a woman whom he subsequently married and regretted marrying. "He said he lost his children. . . . We never had any closeness after that, and he always felt badly about that." His new wife was jealous of his children and didn't invite them over much. "That was one of the sad things in our life, that we weren't close to him."

Her parents sent Annette to college for an education in teaching because she loved to read so much, but she disliked the courses, switched to business, and got a job. She had been very shy from her childhood on, but she became more independent as she worked. In her twenties she met and married her husband. He was quiet also, "prim and proper, but one thing I liked about him was that he had a job and . . . he was steady. I liked that because it was a secure thing . . . and I thought if I was going to get married, I would want someone that could support me. . . . He was very careful about things, neat, and he didn't smoke or drink, and that was something I liked. He was very comfortable to be with" but liked the outdoors much more than she did.

Marriage required an enormous adjustment on Annette's part. "I cried my whole first year of marriage, because . . . I had been independent and had my own money. . . . He didn't believe in joint savings accounts or commercial accounts; he was the head of the family. He ran everything. You did what he said. You went to bed as he said. And that was so different from what I had before. I think one of the things was . . . that we were raised in an easygoing family. . . . Getting married and finding your life is entirely different from what you ever thought, it was a great change for me," and then came several children. "I think if I'd have had a lot of nerve, and had been foregoing [sic], I never would have stayed married, because I would get out and walk, and try to get rid of the resentments, the feelings, because I knew I had to stay married. I couldn't support myself." After about 7 years of marriage "I learned to cope with a lot of this, and know what to say and what not to say, and to get around things."

One of the things that helped Annette through this period was a good friend who took care of her children one afternoon a week so that she could go to the movies. "If my husband knew that, he would have just felt terrible to think that I would do that, I would have pleasure while he had to work. He resented me having to stay home and not do anything, supposedly."

Annette had a number of secrets, such as her afternoons off, which she keeps from her husband to this day, because she feels it would hurt him to know. "I think he would be hurt, because he thinks we never have any secrets. But I think that the way to get along with a person is knowing what to say and what not to say. And I didn't know how to cope. . . . I have to remember my husband has his own feelings, and I have mine. We've been married forty years. You see, if I don't make it now, I never will [laughs]. I've heard about people getting a divorce, you know, after the children are grown," as her own parents did. "We have a very good marriage now, because he has learned to understand me, and he has found I am an individual. That's why I have my little room here. I can come in and play my piano, sew and knit, listen to the radio. He doesn't like to listen to the radio, he doesn't like to hear any noise, and he doesn't like to read much. . . . I want time to myself, and he would like to be with me every single minute, so there are a lot of compromises. . . . He likes the outdoors. He would hike up a mountain every day, if he could."

He was "very jealous of our children." He didn't tell her this in so many words, but she feels his actions did. He'd "put them to bed, get rid of them, do something with them, because he wanted to do things with me, and whenever they were around they had to be very quiet. They were never allowed—they had to stay in their rooms. And the television was never allowed in the living room; it was always in their bedroom. And we had one radio then, and we listened to certain programs on the radio. But we did get television. They could each choose one program each day, and we watched television no more than two hours a day. . . . He says that watching TV or reading before six o'clock is like taking a drink in the morning, that's wasting time." When she was raising the children "I felt that what he said would be the law," but "I got my work done by, say, one o'clock, and I read until about four, or did other things. . . . When I first started to read, my mother would bring me books and I would hide them. . . . Then when I went back to work," in her forties, that took that reading time away. "I was either at work under the supervision of someone, or I was at home under his supervision." So they finally worked out a compromise.

In her forties Annette took a job in a bookstore to help them out financially, because her husband was worried about money. It meant a great change for her, but she loved books, particularly romantic novels; the job proved a blessing in disguise. She gained a great deal of confidence through meeting the public.

Meanwhile, her daughter married a man who was strict like her father, and her son, somewhat estranged by his father's demands, went into the armed forces where he did well. He, too, has since married. Both of the children are very strict with their own children. "I think it's really good, in fact, I wish that nowadays parents were more strict with their children, took more of an interest in what they do. . . . They lose track of respect." Meanwhile, her husband "felt like he had me again. He didn't have all that competition, me trying to keep the kids in order."

Annette and her husband retired in their sixties. Her husband wants to move out of state to live on a farm in the wilderness, but she refuses to leave her friends in the area. He doesn't like the area. "He hates it. He doesn't like living here. . . . He feels there are too many people." She tries to ignore his feelings. "If I felt that it really would make a difference to him, I would move." She doesn't want to move out of the area because "it would be so entirely away from anything that I'm familiar with. I like the familiar." Another source of disagreement between them is their church friends. She goes to church; he doesn't. "He thinks he knows everything there is to know. . . . He will read the Bible, he can quote the Bible, but he's not having someone else tell him how to believe, because he already knows how to believe. . . . He leads a very Christian life, in fact, his morals are almost too high for these times." He's very critical of promiscuity and pornography.

Annette believes that "your life has been laid out for you" and points to what she views as certain "synchronicities" (see Jung, 1971) in her own life, which became important turning points for her.

Her mother died when Annette was in her thirties. "She stayed with us, and she died in our house. I took care of her, and that was a sad time. . . . They just told her to go home to die, really, although we never did discuss it. I wish we had now. I think now if anyone in my family were going to die that we would talk about it, because it's more open now."

When she thinks of what dying is like, Annette thinks of "how fast your mind can speak, without you making the words, like a thought. . . . I would like to believe you would be surrounded by people you were familiar with, and you would make contact just by mind."

She had one dream that came true. She dreamed there was something wrong with a grandchild, and this proved to be the case, although it was not a terribly serious problem.

She believes that her marital difficulties "helped me grow and build character. Because if you don't become something [make something] of your life, but you are just bland, you haven't accomplished anything. Why are we here?"

Annette has another secret from her husband. There's a little "earpiece down by the radio that my husband doesn't know about. He knows I have it there, and I just tell him I have it there in case I can't sleep in the night. . . . When he wakes me up at two in the morning, and talks from two to four, I can't just sit there and lie and listen to him, so I put my earpiece in my ear, and I listen to the talk shows, because he never expects me to answer. He's talking about the world problems, what they should do in this country, how things are these days. How we should plan, how we are to program this. I've heard it so many times. So that's another thing. You have to learn to do these things when you're married, so you can stand your life. So it works out, very nicely, and we get along just beautifully. And then I can listen with both ears, can't you? [laughter]."

She believes she has resolved her marital conflict by answering back to her husband in her mind only. "If I answer back to him in my mind . . . I say in my mind very fast answers. But we stay out of conflict that way. I do put my foot down if it is really something that is going to concern me. . . . Then he'll just stomp out, but afterwards he will come around." She says that her husband is very demonstrative and loving.

Annette says that the worst thing that could happen to her would be losing her sight. "Losing sight would be almost tragic. Although there are many sightless people that get along in this world. I'd have to learn braille right away because what would I do without reading? . . . It's very relaxing to me. Maybe you might fantasize. . . . You kind of live through another person . . . like Steinbeck's works. I don't know if you ever read *Pastures of heaven* or *Travels with Charley*. . . . He's so descriptive. It just kind of puts you in that place. I like to read biographies and find out how other people lived. . . . I read novels, historical novels. . . . I don't like too much history. I've been reading a lot of Harlequin novels. They're romantic . . . boy meets girl, they fight, they get married, but it also tells about the different countries, and the different things that they do. . . . I always say that they're for people over sixty and girls about thirteen."

Annette believes that life has meaning, "that we are here for some purpose, and that if we aren't careful, and don't notice this that's going around us, and just exist, that we aren't doing what we're meant for."

The source of her need for security may have been the Depression, which she remembers as a difficult time, although she felt sheltered. Her personality type shows her highest function as judging. Whether the need for scheduling and planning, evidenced by her high judging function, was a result of her strict upbringing and marital relationship, or the reason for it, is a matter of speculation.

Annette's life may be seen as a set of interrelated themes. First, there are the losses resulting from restriction both in her childhood and in her marriage, losses that, while interfering with her maturation process, kept her sheltered and secure, two high needs arising perhaps from her Depression experience (see Elder, 1974). Second, there is the theme of communication. She and her siblings were not told of the impending divorce of her parents, and this was a shock. She and her mother did not speak of her mother's unhappiness in her marriage; the children burned her means of communication, her diary, which they regretted. Nor did they speak of the mother's impending death, denying it instead, also a matter of regret. She also notes her shyness from childhood to her mid-twenties, manifested by incidents of inability to communicate. Her husband forbids or restricts forms of communication, radio, television, books, as wasting time, and she has to hide them.

However, communication, or its lack, not only has been involved in loss to Annette but also has been the mode of transcendence. Reading is a method of leading an alternate life; she enjoys romantic fantasies and travels. One of the high points of her life was her job in the bookstore, where she read and communicated with others regarding communication. Lack of communication with her husband—her secret afternoons, her earpiece, the hiding of books, her "mind speak" instead of voice speak—probably provided a safety valve that saved her marriage and her security, kept her sheltered.

Thus this theme of communication may be seen as actualizing the theme of security, and its restriction is a form of loss. Sometimes the restriction of communication is accepted and gotten around in order not to lose security. In this other sense, one might see Annette's theme as one of accommodation to restriction for the sake of shelter and security, which communication makes bearable and transcends, a theme congruent with her personality profile. Core theme: Security in restriction versus communication.

Life meaning as part of an unknown divine plan, where a life is laid out, and synchronicity that keeps it on track (all secure and orderly) are exemplified by an incident in which she transcended loss by a communication activity, a turning point in her life.

Annette's protocol is rated high loss, high transcendence, in the replacing stage, replacing restrictive loss with survival mechanisms, even though she protests that she has had a "good life." Her major methods of transcendence are situational (the earpiece, etc.) and general (fantasy, reading). She was not always generally transcendent.

Theoretical analysis

Some of the pain in Annette's protocol can be seen as emanating from a situation that required her to return metaphorically to the womb. She had emerged enough to be independent, overcome her shyness, earn a living, and become autonomous and in control of her life. Even her childhood upbringing, while conservative and with a concern for propriety, had been fairly "easygoing." However, when faced with the possibility of marrying, some of her major concerns seemed to be for shelter and security. Once married, she found herself hemmed about with restrictions, with the responsibility for money and her welfare, and even the details of how she lived her life, devolving on her husband rather than herself. It was as if she had to unlearn growth, to go back to crawling after she had learned to walk. She cried the whole first year of marriage at the pain of this new confinement.

However, she did find ways to grow *around* her husband and her life circumstances when she could not continue to grow *straight*. Basically, she used a lesson taught her by her natal family: not everything must be revealed. A certain amount of discretion about what is said and what is not said can be protective, can make life bearable for both her husband and her herself, and the needs of both can then be met.

Thus, in a sense, Annette leads two lives, the life required of her by her husband and her own secret alternative life consisting of forbidden movies, reading, television, radio, as well as church fellowship. If her husband knew, he might judge her actions harshly as deceit; she feels he would be hurt. Annette's marriage has been based on seeming to be what she is not— compliant with her husband's demands and values. Annette seems to have maintained this false self system (see Laing, 1976) by rationalization and other ego defense mechanisms; indeed, the false self now seems integrated with the true, and no longer false. Of course, we have no idea how much her husband really does not know. By the way, it should be pointed out that being false to others is not necessarily false to oneself, not necessarily a false *self* system. Annette's background including selective communication may not be a false self system, although we gather from her rationalizations that it is.

Like the retired couple in Tillie Olsen's *Tell me a riddle* (1961), Annette and her husband have a severe conflict over where to spend their remaining days. Her husband, always a lover of mountains and finally retired, would complete his life-self on a farm in wilder country; Annette would complete what is uniquely her self by remaining with the familiar church, friends, and surroundings, which must make her feel sheltered and secure. "Everything makes me feel alive here." This is a dilemma for which resolutions must be difficult, either Annette's or her husband's solution rendering the other incomplete, although compromises are imaginable.

We can see Annette's metaphorical system as a web or network of finely interconnected lines representing what may be communicated and what may not be within the two lives she leads. Care in what she tells her husband probably became second nature to her: not alluding to anything she read, saw on television, heard on the radio, not mentioning anything said by friends and relatives who dropped by to lend a forbidden book or revealed confidences when babysitting her children so she could go to a movie; acceding to "his law" while planning a different course of action; pretending to hear his orations on world problems with one ear while listening to talk shows with the other;

perhaps even fantasizing about her latest Harlequin romance or other places, other lives forming her own secret life while she does some task within her husband's. In a sense, within this secret or other life of hers, Annette lives the lives of other people still, through biographies, for example. "You kind of live through another person." She "answers back" to her husband in her mind while being externally compliant. This secret inner life "so you can stand your life" seems to have helped her to survive as a reasonably well-integrated person, to continue her birth as a person in the face of life-constricting circumstances. Friends, church, and the concepts of shelter and security are also major aspects of her metaphorical system, or how she sees the world and makes decisions regarding it. Finally, she envisions death as the ability of two minds to communicate with each other without the necessity for speech; she hopes it is this way. Her major mode of transcendence, communication, also transcends death. This suggests that transcendence through communication is metaphorically related to life and that constrictions, with their resultant losses, are metaphorically related to death. In a twist or paradox typical of a number of the protocols, however, the life constrictions are in turn motivated by the desire for shelter or security, accepted in payment for these, shelter perhaps from the storm.

The importance of communication has arisen in several of the L/T life themes, but a comparison of communication in Annette's metaphorical system with that in Sue's illustrates the essential uniqueness of each system. For Annette, both communication and noncommunication facilitate security and shelter, as well as the transcendence of the restrictions of shelter. Through communication, an alternate self is created which experiences a rich variety of other lives, both historical and romantic, in other times and places, all of which would be directly unattainable by Annette in her present circumstances. Were normal enriching experiences open to her, this alternate self might not be needed. For Sue, you will recall, communication or its lack mediates her dedication to the idealized or unattainable relationships—with her husband, God, parents, friends, the children she teaches, the son from whom she intermittently separates. Noncommunication is never a virtue for Sue; it is responsible for separating her from loved ones (although it maintains her idealization of them).

Security is also a frequent theme of the life histories. I see the need for security as basically a fear of its lack and what this might imply, lack of food, clothing, shelter, safety, and the other necessities to maintain existence.

In the third history, Kara's, I diagram a metaphorical system.

Kara

"A lot of people join [the armed forces] when they are eighteen, and they are trading one set of parents for another, because they control your life, tell you where to go, what to do."

Kara is divorced, childless, and in her early thirties. She relates her life story with wit and gusto, occasionally punctuated by obscene gestures.

Kara was raised in a small midwestern town in accordance with strict religious principles. All through her childhood she rebelled against parental restrictions, which were often enforced with severe beatings. "My parents were very authoritarian, and my life was very controlled." She felt "cramped . . . I was always a mouthy, aggressive kid. Still am. . . . My parents would discipline you physically, and I think that tends to make you more independent. . . . They'd belt me, whack me. Held certain beliefs. . . . Don't knock a kid in the head, the lord gave a kid a rear for a reason. . . . I was ready to leave home only 48 hours after I graduated from high school. . . . All of their lives and energy went into supporting the kids, making a family. Even though I didn't agree with their discipline, I think they behaved in honorable ways, not neglecting us, we were always taken care of."

However, in high school she felt a need for birth control, which she didn't get. To the contrary, "about in ninth grade, there was this guy in the street, and we got caught making out one night, and my mother drug me to the priest for salvation, and that ended boyfriends." High school was otherwise notable for teachers who turned her on to science.

On Kara's eighteenth birthday she packed her bags and left home. "It was great, I was gonna be in charge of my own life, nobody telling me what time to come in, and looking forward to me making all my decisions. . . . My mother was upset, crying the entire time." The university was miles away "which I was grateful for, I wanted that distance, 'I'll send you postcards.' "

"About forty-eight hours after I left home, let's make it seventy-two, all hell broke loose," in the form of socializing, meeting people, going to bars, hanging out, and becoming an atheist. She also experimented with drugs and was busted for stealing a small item:

"It was only twenty days, and in a way I was grateful for that, because there was a little old lady ahead of me that had taken sheets from a department store, and the judge had given her twenty days. 'Oh, if this little lady got twenty days, I'm gonna get months.' But it was a standard kick, he was giving everybody twenty days. . . . Well, twenty days is nothing, a year would scare me. . . . The jail was new and clean, and there was . . . an interesting group of people. . . . There were a number of Indians in there that had been caught stealing foods in supermarkets. And then about four or five days later my father found out. . . . So he came down in tears: 'Oh, I can't tell your mother you're in jail. Let me pay the fine and get you out of here.' . . . So there were all these people in jail, and we didn't want to go. Other people were looking at us as if we were crazy. I didn't want to be indebted to my father."

Her father did get her out and took her home, where she fought with her parents the entire time, so she went back to college. A few days later her parents had her picked up and shipped to a psychiatric hospital because she was into drugs.

" 'We don't want to do this, but we don't know how else to save you,' you know, my mother was the type: 'Marijuana one day, heroin tomorrow!' . . . It was kind of a nice hospital. . . . We used to go out and party. . . . There was another guy from my hometown. . . . We had some real crazies, and we also had young kids whose parents didn't want to have them because they drank beer and stuff. So they throw them in the hospital. This guy, when I first went in, he was leaving, so we were helping. He was a very hip type, into smoking and listening to Jimi Hendrix records. He had all his friends in security positions with keys and stuff. So they smuggled all his possessions out, and the day after I came in was his escape day, but we were getting along real well, so he decided he didn't want to go. Now it was time to reverse everything. He smuggled all his stuff back in, except they got caught, and they busted us all in solitary, these small cells. They take away the mattresses during the day, and they come in with a partial mattress at night. If you try to lay down during the day they kick the bars. It was part of the discipline. . . . There was an elderly ward above us, people who didn't have money for a rest home. . . . You would see old people working in the cafeteria. They'd fall out of a wheelchair, and they said: 'Oh, leave them, they're just putting on an act.' It was really disgusting."

After Kara and her boyfriend got out of the hospital, they lived together for a while and then broke up because "I am really hard-headed, I can be really bitchy and bossy, domineering. I did pick up some of my parents' habits." He embarked on training for a career, in which Kara encouraged him; he achieved his goal and then found himself unable to get a job until he had an operation he could not afford. He committed suicide. "He was laying there on the floor, and I sat there and cussed him out because . . . if he had ever done it, we were supposed to go together. And he went alone, and I was pissed that he had gone alone."

After this, Kara and some friends of hers went for pregnancy tests, and they all found out that they were pregnant at the same time. "So we were all pregnant, and the only way to get an abortion there at that time was if you were in the middle of committing suicide they would consider an abortion, in other words, if you had the knife in your chest. There was no birth control information or anything like that. . . . I mean, my total sex education was from my parents saying: 'Don't let boys touch your chest because that gets them too excited.' . . . I thought I'd never get pregnant, you know, I am not the type. I'd just skip that one."

She went to another town, had the baby, and it was adopted out. "I know that I could cope with living off a very mediocre income, welfare, living in a one-room place; I couldn't see putting a kid through that." She plans to locate her child when she or he turns 18.

Kara was involved with a lot of drugs and also with Marxists and SDS (Students for a Democratic Society) organizations all through her twenties. She was also an atheist. "Actually, I was a confirmed atheist. In the middle of [an] earthquake I had this strange realization that I was going to die—the bed's going this way [making swaying and jerking motions]. I'm up on the mountain and thought I was going to be at the bottom in a few minutes. This is the time to find out if you believe in god or not, and I said no, not even that will stop the earthquake. In the middle of the earthquake, I became an atheist."

Kara returned to college while doing odd jobs and won debate trophies all around her state—"me and my big mouth"—the same mouth that got her into so much difficulty in her personal relationships. Now in her twenties, she met a man who wanted to marry her, but she wanted her independence. "The main thing in leaving my parents was that I wanted to establish my own independence. . . . I knew that if I got tied down with a marriage and a kid, I'd have to give up that freedom." Independence for Kara means control over her own life in the context of the lifelong constriction of her parents and her church, as well as various institutions.

There followed a period of relationships and hunting for a career that would go somewhere. "If I don't get to move up and become an executive somewhere along the line, forget it. I don't want to be in a little cubicle pushing papers for a minimum wage." It was then that she decided to join the armed forces, having made extremely high scores in the tests, and she further decided to go to radar school. "I figured it would be an excellent technical education in terms of electronics . . . and also I'd be having my education benefits when I got back out." It was at this point in the interview that she observed the similarity between parents and the service: her daily life was minutely controlled.

At the urging of her boyfriend she married him, and he followed her around the country on her various assignments. Conflicts between them arose and increased until "I found myself several times being thrown across the room. . . . He was big. . . . He was afraid of being rejected. He was jovial all the time, and consequently suppressed any time he felt [upset]—then every now and then he'd blow up and it would be like World War III. . . . People just loved him. They thought that he was wonderful, that he could never hurt a fly, and it was true 360 days a year. Five days a year he was just completely whacko." At one point, "he had me on the floor, saying: 'All right, I'm going to teach you stuff, lay down on the floor!' To run out the door was impossible. . . . I had to be back to base the next morning to work. . . . He was standing on the table, I didn't know it at the time. He said: 'Now, where am I? Keep your eyes closed and tell me where I am.' I said: 'Oh, you're over by the couch.' 'You're wrong, I'm on top of the table, and I'm going to jump on top of your head and smash your skull in.' . . . He has a lithium imbalance. . . . When he was Dr. Jekyll, he was just beautiful. . . . It was a complete flip. . . . Once I must have said something . . . the next thing I knew I was flying across the room, and I bounced off a wall and slid to the floor. . . . It's really stupid . . . but he's still the only man I really love. And it was so close, it was like when I left for the service right after boot camp, I went back first and we were standing in the airport, and I'm sobbing, and he's crying . . . we were so close." Thus, violent physical control is the form this relationship took when it was not going well. Control became a brutal game.

When Kara got out of the service she went west to study science again and was offered high-powered jobs in industry, which she turned down because she wanted to spend enough time in college. One day when she was on the phone trying to arrange bail for a roommate who had just been busted, her husband appeared at the front door with a witness, saying, "Sign these divorce papers." One of their major conflicts had been that he wanted a kid, and she didn't want to be tied down. "All these men want kids. I thought it was supposed to be women who wanted kids. . . . I'm running into all these men that want kids. . . . Then about six months later I got a notice in the mail that I'd been divorced. I thought: 'Jesus, don't we get to go to court? Don't I get to say anything?' . . . I guess I hadn't realized how much I really was emotionally heartbroken. I couldn't come home and study. I enjoyed the lectures, everything was clear, I understood it, but . . . I was too depressed. . . . I spent another year basically alone," although her friends were great to her.

She got her present job as manager of one of a chain of stores and has another male roommate; "unfortunately . . . I get into these really impulsive relationships. It was like my husband. I met him when I was waitressing in a restaurant and the lunch shift was pretty much over, and I was ahead, so I was sitting down talking to him, and the nice restaurant owner didn't appreciate that, and I said: 'Well, all my work is done,' and she said: 'Well, get up anyway.' She was the type that liked to see everyone looking busy. I have this tendency to just—if you're right, you're right, and if you're not—get screwed! And I came up the end of the day, and I had her make my severance check, and I managed to track him down about two weeks later, and the next day he moved in." Kara takes control of both work and love situations, by both rejection and initiative.

Kara's worst experience was the divorce. Her best was 2 years in the armed forces: "The complexity of the work, working on the flight line, every day. . . . They are the boneyard of the services, plus we had all kinds of aircraft. We were part of a reconnaissance wing. We had the U-2's in there, we had all the T-35's, beautiful planes, that NASA would fly in. Just the working environment. I love aircraft. We'd sometimes ride the helicopters out to the ranges, the parachute would come out. . . . We'd be hanging out the back end watching the land and the city." She plans to go back into this kind of work, but these jobs are in the city and she wants to live in the country. Her ex-husband has remarried and has the child he wants.

"If I became sufficiently established to be able to afford a nanny, I could very easily [have children]. I've told my ex-husband, I talk to him from time to time, I say: 'Well, I'm getting my act together, grab the kid and enough diapers to get you up here.' . . . and I say: 'We'll do it when I get things settled again, when I get sufficiently stable, maybe I'll have kids.' . . . I'm really not into changing diapers for several years. . . . The only reason I would really think about [having kids] would be because, like with my husband, I really loved him and sooner or later if things were really right, I wouldn't mind us having a kid, I wouldn't mind his kid."

When asked about the disadvantages of having kids, Kara responds, "There's the danger of them becoming teenagers. Nowadays, they tend to run the family. In my day, the parents ran it right up 'til the day you left home. But I've seen an awful lot of families, and I don't know if it's California or what, but by the time they start turning 12 or 13, kids start calling a lot of the shots. . . . I would expect certain behavior like . . . you don't bring kids over for wild parties to get drunk and destroy the place, you're not going to take the family car out hot-rodding." The issue around having children is clearly one of control, again.

Currently, Kara worries about growing older. "You're getting that face that doesn't look 22 any more, and you're still running around in Levis. . . . I've had a number of people tell me that I should start dressing in a more appropriate way [for my age] . . . but I really don't give a flying fuck what they think. . . . I dress appropriately for what I'm doing." As for her home, she wants to have her own little house in the country.

With regard to support systems, Kara feels a sense of responsibility for providing for her parents as they grow older. She misses the camaraderie she had in the armed forces and feels very much alone. She almost always refers to her ex-husband without the "ex" and is still grieving for him. She sees herself as a winner because "I believe in my own philosophy, outlook and morality, the ways I treat people . . . even on my job . . . when they tend to give me bullshit, I tend to tell them to get lost. . . . There again it ties into children. . . . A lot of people in a lot of jobs take an awful lot of bullshit out of fear for survival—how am I going to take care of my family and my kids?" Kids not only run the home but also control whether or not you can quit your job. She feels like a loser "probably in my personal, close relationships with men. . . . And by and large I get emotionally involved with people, and then I probably end up trying to fit them into my pattern of life, and then sometimes they tell me to fuck off, but by then my heart, you know, I've invested a lot of emotion in [the relationship]."

One could think of the "flight" or the "parachute" as a metaphor for Kara's life. She parachutes out of any situation that restricts her; she simply bails out and enjoys the view. Her need for freedom translates into a need to overcome restrictions imposed by religion, monogamous relationships, work, children, and hence control of reproductive processes. Her insistence on freedom generates a great deal of strife and loss. That she joined the armed services is not a contradiction either intuitively or practically, because she considered it only temporary, and a test, pretty much of a nine-to-five job after boot camp. The army gave her a support network and restriction she paradoxically rejected and needed. Restriction is metaphorical of home, religion, intimacy.

Kara was rated high loss, low transcendence and currently loss oriented, predominantly yearning, but moving to the searching stage, yearning for her husband, searching for the right career and life style. This is a good illustration of how one may be in somewhat different, adjacent stages in the two major areas of one's life, love and work. Kara was one of the few people who believed life had no meaning; but meaninglessness for her meant "being" in prison—locked away" from life and relationships, the loss pole she is having difficulty in overcoming. She is not yet ready to proceed with the re-creation of self as an older person.

In summary, Kara's L/T life theme is loss of freedom through the restrictions imposed by religion, family, monogamous relationships, work, and the possibility of children, versus independence, freedom from control. She "parachutes" out of any situation that restricts her, enjoys the view, and takes control. Core theme: Restriction versus freedom.

Theoretical analysis

It would be instructive to lay out or verbally diagram a metaphorical system such as Kara's in order to explore the relationships between key issues and the major life events or people that symbolize them.

We could see the major issue of Kara's life as the issue of control. Who controls her self-life, Kara or someone else? Control by others is perceived as restriction; control by herself is perceived as independence or freedom. Kara sees her family, boyfriend, children, religion, the armed forces, and her jobs all in terms of where control lies.

We would start the diagram of Kara's metaphorical system with "control" as the central issue. The diagram will look somewhat like a sociogram. We can use the equivalence sign (=) to indicate symbolism. A two-way arrow from the left of the word "control" leads to the word "restriction" and another from the right leads to "freedom." Now, what symbolizes restriction for Kara, and what symbolizes freedom? And how do certain concepts symbolize each other?

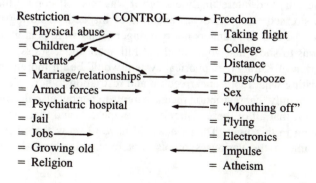

For Kara, restriction is symbolized by, and symbolizes, her parents, physical abuse, jail, the psychiatric hospital, religion, growing old, and having children. There are also aspects of restriction in her marriage and other intimate relationships that are partly associated with physical abuse; while beating her, her husband wouldn't let her up, wouldn't let her leave or even open her eyes; indeed, he took complete control of her, and at least twice during these beatings she thought she was going to die. The armed forces are associated with control by others, but it is a control that she chooses and is associated with some of her most transcendent experiences: flight and the electronics work she enjoys, and at which she excels. Since she associates her parents with the armed forces (probably not as restrictive regarding drugs, drinking, and other personal habits), being in the service and having a good experience with it may have been a way of working through parent-child relationships into something more satisfying. Her occupations as well give her opportunities to wrest control, if only by quitting when her freedom is curtailed. Jobs, then, symbolize restriction and freedom, like the armed forces and relationships.

On the other side, the first symbol of freedom seems to have been "mouthing off," although it had painful consequences. She took control verbally many times at home, on jobs, in debates. Other modes of freedom were taking flight, getting distance from restriction, college, indulging in the forbidden, including sex, drugs, and booze, as well as becoming an atheist. Flying planes seems to have been one of her most transcendent experiences, combined as it was with her work in electronics. It will be noted that most of these freedoms seem to have been breaking bonds, going beyond limits, freedom *from* rather than freedom *toward*. A common factor in many of these freedom activities was impulsive behavior and freedom to act on impulse—have a drink, quit a job, invite a man to move in—rather than thinking things through. Impulsive behavior in her childhood was probably squashed rather than moderately allowed, although I believe impulsivity may be a genetically based personality characteristic. (See Chapter 10, on personality and psychopathology.) In any event, while impulsivity is associated with freedom for Kara, many of the consequences are definitely restrictions, particularly in her romantic and work relationships. Impulsivity may be seen as lack of self-control, or control over the self by the self, and interestingly enough it was this self-control that the armed forces stressed. Kara gives an example of inspections during which wrinkles under the bed and hangers not two fingers apart were penalized; she felt the aim was to show that you would not fall apart under stress.

The diagram of Kara's metaphorical system would be far more complex than simply listing what represents freedom and restriction to her. We would have to show not only that restriction means parents to her but also that parents mean restriction, that all of these symbols are reciprocal, and that each takes on new meaning in this light. Then we would have to show the other inter-relationships among the various symbols. For example, physical abuse is associated with parents, religion ("the lord gave a kid a rear for a reason"), the psychiatric hospital, probably jail, intimate relationships, and undoubtedly children—abused becoming abuser. Then we would have to show the association between the important issues listed and other issues that do not fit neatly into the category of either restriction or freedom. For example, "meaninglessness" to Kara is "prison—being locked away." So one of the things we would equate to jail would be meaninglessness, but this also equates meaninglessness with restriction, the loss pole of Kara's L/T theme. Then we would want to make note of the crossovers; for example, drugs on the freedom side also are associated with both the psychiatric hospital and jail (of her friends), but as jail is equated to meaninglessness (among other things), we have within Kara's metaphorical system the equation of drugs with freedom and meaninglessness, which must manifest as one of the many paradoxes or conflicts troubling her. Drugs are also associated with relationships, good and bad; we begin to have a deeper understanding of who Kara is. Our diagram would be completed by adding in as many of the details of Kara's life as we know and defining their place in the network. It will be noted that our analysis could proceed along all the levels of L/T suggested in Chapters 2 and 3— primary, secondary, holistic, self-conceptual—all within the metaphorical. The fuller the life history, the more detailed the diagramming and understanding of the metaphorical system would be.

Thus we now have an insight into Kara, how she experiences her world in everyday life, where she is "coming from." If she were in your office applying for a job, you would know far more essentially about her than a battery of personality tests could tell you. You might want to either put her in charge of something or have her working alone. You could understand how she feels and thinks and could even make limited predictions about her.

If you were a counselor, you would work with her strengths and her paradoxes; she controlled her life once by accepting control (in the armed forces). Perhaps this fusion would work for an intimate relationship. Seeing how her impulsivity also controls her might be of benefit to her. She has much to work with to make her life more fulfilling once the metaphorical system is understood.

Kara, like all of us, lives and acts out of a unique metaphorical system, which is complex but not beyond our understanding. What conclusions might we draw for the relationships between two human beings? Could we sketch the metaphorical systems of families, groups, and nations?

CONCLUSIONS: CHARACTERISTICS OF METAPHORICAL SYSTEMS

The life histories in this chapter demonstrate examples of metaphorical systems, what they are, how they operate, and how a metaphorical analysis of

behavior can be performed. It would be possible to perform a more microscopic, "Piagetian" kind of analysis with more data.

A number of conclusions across the protocols can be drawn. First, the
metaphorical system is pervasive. The individual sees herself, the important
others and events in her life, and the other—workplace, community, and
country, world or society at large—from the vantage point of her metaphorical
system, or way of symbolizing what people and things mean. I believe that
even the supposedly insignificant is seen and interpreted through this metaphorical system, because small and insignificant happenings are related to
larger ones.

Second, not only are people and events interpreted through the metaphorical system but also the choices, decisions, and commitments of an
individual are made from within this system. The individual often attempts
to select what she perceives as promoting her transcendence or her metaphors
of it. In this way, she creates her life out of her metaphorical system, and it
would be difficult to do otherwise, because this is what she sees. To the extent
that her life creates her, she creates herself as well. Obviously, sometimes
she makes wrong decisions; what she thought would promote transcendence
results in loss, and this also creates her.

Third, metaphorical systems are probably resistant to change, as they
lead to a life and self that perpetuate them, but change is certainly possible.
We could think of therapy and counseling as attempts to adjust the metaphorical
system. We suspect that repression (possibly healthy) of aspects of herself
helps Della to maintain and grow in a metaphorical system, one pole of which
is related to her religion. Cults, the unexpected, time-irrelevant losses, brainwashing, disasters, life-threatening disease, changes in lifestyle such as aerobic
exercise, and many of the general transcendence mechanisms (drugs, movies,
music, etc.) may all promote at least temporary change in the system. Perhaps
this is why travel, vacation, and other leisure activities are so beneficial. One's
"perspective" is changed a bit, and it feels better to escape the narrow confines
of one's belief systems and thought processes.

Fourth, it almost goes without saying that no two metaphorical systems
are the same, simply because no two persons or their lives are the same.
When we reduce a metaphorical system to a few words, an L/T life theme,
sometimes we get the same words—"healing," for example, in Lorellen's
and Inez's systems. And yet, how very different are their metaphorical systems
and even their metaphors of healing. Healing means something different to
each of them and probably to each of us as well. (We need only begin to
associate to it beyond the first few obvious concepts to demonstrate this, as
with the sunflower.)

Fifth, the implications of the different metaphorical systems for communication between individuals are disconcerting. Communication is difficult,
an illusion to some extent. Undoubtedly this is why conventions of language
are invoked. When we begin a conversation with comments on the weather,

or what are deemed "superficial" topics, it is to establish the bond of a shared metaphor, from which it is hoped more sharing of things *not* held in common will radiate.

Sixth, metaphorical communication is both a tool and a source of mythology—family, religious, and national. The family myth of who we are, what we have done, and why establishes a shared metaphorical system, without which members go their own way. Parents experience outside forces in their children's lives, such as peers and the teen culture, which woo their children away from the family myth or metaphorical system, replacing it with a strange one. Then the parent says, "I have lost my son." (See Chapter 9, on relationships.) A traitor breaks from the country's mythology and must be punished for it lest others begin to divine the truth behind the mythological. Two lovers, separated for a year, return to find they have changed, their frail mythology built through letters and phone calls no match for metaphorical systems that may not have had much in common anyway. The cry "You've changed!" may simply be a way of saying, "I know your metaphorical system better now, and it's incongruent with the myth. You misled me." Clothing, home furnishings, perfume, jewelry, makeup, automobiles, all material possessions are attempts to express a metaphorical system—either our own or one that we think is consonant with the metaphorical system to which we want to appeal. When Goffman (1959) so perceptively describes the behavior of waiters and waitresses, he is really showing that they behave in congruence with aspects of the metaphorical systems, or shared mythologies (of restaurants and food), of those they serve.

The woman who walks in the street and circles white cars has returned many times since I began this chapter. She is always wearing the same clothes, and occasionally she munches a roll. I have seen her in a downtown park, aloneness like a cape invisibly shrouding her shoulders, she covering notebook pages with impossibly minuscule handwriting. Who is she? How is it for her, being in the world so differently from myself? What do we mean to her, you and I, the street, the parked cars, the sidewalk?

In the metaphorical system, each loss symbolizes other losses and ultimately death, each transcendence other transcendences and ultimately life, each person other persons, each event other events, each word other words. Even so minor an item as a dress or a different food symbolizes who we are and who we would become. All are linked in a unique network, in which everything is representative of something else.

Nothing is irrelevant!

6

The Self

If I were to say to you, "Tell me about yourself," you would probably respond with your name, age, sex, occupation, important people in your life, hobbies, a few dreams for the future, perhaps. You would be defining yourself by your external attributes or the life you lead, that which can be observed by others. Of course, you also *feel* like a 37-year-old male marriage and family counselor and marathon runner, with a wonderful wife who is an anthropologist and two sons, but is that *who* you really are? Even if you pile detail on detail of your body and life, are you really satisfied that *that* is who you are? How about adding a detailed autobiography and interviews with your parents, wife, friends, sons, co-workers, and bosses—does that define you well enough? You might want to add that you are very sensitive, concerned about nuclear war, shy when talking in front of a group of people, intelligent, love nature, have a good sense of humor, and enjoy eating out, all kinds of music, and going to the theater—does that describe you? It does thousands of others! Just check the personal ads in the *New York Review of Books*!

Perhaps if you could tape a cassette describing all the feelings you have ever had, the inner experiences that were going on at the same time the outer experiences occurred, that would give us a better idea of who you are. How did you feel, moment to moment, as you learned to ride your bike, got lost in the woods when you were nine, talked with your boss for the first time, went through the wedding ceremony, played peekaboo with your son, heard a friend had been killed in an auto accident? *Now* have you given us a better sense of who you are?

All of these, and a million other incidents, are perhaps disjointed; they are also incidents that have happened to many of you who read these words. What is it about them that makes them uniquely you and no one else? What is the thread that runs through all of these experiences and feelings? Is it simply the *combination* that gives you that sense of separateness, uniqueness, of continuing, the sense of self, the sense that "I am, I was, I shall be," that "I" being a fixed identity or thing like a sunflower, not immutable (but neither is a sunflower) yet continuing from birth to death?

When you were 3 your dad gave you a ball for your birthday, and the two of you played with it for hours—you'd forgotten that, hadn't you? When you were 7 the teacher called on you, and you didn't know the answer. When you were 11 the kids said you could join their club. When you were 15 you were elected class representative, but still you felt like an outsider. When you were 19 you fell madly in love, and your girl left you for someone else. You wanted to die then, but 3 years later you met a woman far more wonderful than any other, and you were married.

Are you the same person today who played ball with your dad, couldn't answer the teacher's question, joined the club, was elected class representative, was rejected in love, married your wife, and on and on? You felt like a whole self at 3, 7, 11, 15, 19, and 22. Of course, at 11 you were not the person who married at 22, you could not foresee the future; but at 22 you were the person who joined the club at 11. Why is it that we have a complete sense of self at every age, and yet today that sense of self includes so much more than it did 5 or 10 years ago?

Perhaps the sense of self is just that, like the kinesthetic sense or the sense of sight, rather than an object. And yet the body is an object, and it is part of the self; we would not be content to fully equate the body with the self. In my families classes I assign a project: "Who am I, and how did I get to be that way?" Most students leave their bodies out of their descriptions entirely.

In this chapter I begin with a brief review of those main strands of contemporary research that are most relevant to the L/T concept. Then I outline an L/T conceptualization of the self, followed by illustrative material from the cases of Lexie, Babs, and Sibyl. I conclude with tentative suggestions from these histories, as well as others, for the possibility of "types" of selves, which may be stages in self-development.

STUDIES OF THE SELF

At what age do humans begin to have a sense of self? Brooks-Gunn has studied the recognition of self as object in the mirror, on the hypothesis that if a baby recognizes himself, he must have a sense that he exists, that there is a self to recognize (Lewis & Brooks-Gunn, 1979). This self-recognition develops during the first 2 years of life. Such experimental evidence dovetails with Mahler's (1968) view that the first 2 years of life represent a period of symbiosis and gradual separation and individuation. Kaplan (1978) sees this as a second or psychological birth. It is my view, however, that this psychological birth is a lifelong process and that the stages Mahler describes are only the first.

Significant progress in the notion of self as structure has been made by Kohut (1977, 1984). The child's structure consists of exhibitionistic and grandiose needs, idealizing needs, and alter ego or twinship needs. The structure is acquired by a process termed "transmuting internalization," episodes of empathic attunement between self and other (parents, therapist, friends). As an existentialist, I believe these concepts can be translated into needs to be significant (see Adler, in Ansbacher & Ansbacher, 1959), so that one is not overwhelmed or smothered to death, as well as needs to idealize heroes (Becker, 1973), who transcend death, and needs to survive through another. Kohut advocates the strengthening of self-structure in the clinical setting, a most important view in contemporary psychotherapy. An intriguing comparison of the self-psychology of Kohut and Rogers (Kahn, 1985) shows similarities in their views of the role of other in self-structuralization, unconditional positive regard, empathy, and a belief that humans "have a tendency toward growth, health and fulfillment."

Kegan (1982, 1983) and others have applied the Piagetian notions of assimilation and accommodation to object relations theory, describing how the infant, through the first circular reactions, learns boundaries or, in my view, what she can control (self) and what she cannot control (other), and this becomes more and more complexly defined throughout life. Psychopathology develops when that which is defined as part of the self is redefined by the other, or is under the other's control, that is, when the boundaries are not maintained (see Chapter 10). Self as process has also been emphasized by James (1890) and more recently by Blasi (1983).

Kreilkamp (1976) points up the contradictions between conceptions of a natural self oriented toward finding the true self, toward self-actualization and fulfillment (the theories of Rogers and Maslow), and a social self, oriented toward the welfare of others and socially constructed by them as well. The contrast here may be between the inner self and the social facade.

M. B. Smith (1978) prefers the notion of selfhood to the notion of self; selfhood does not reify the self as something "thing-like, substantive or concrete." He points out that statements about selfhood are self-reflective, that we speak of being self-aware, self-conscious, of self-concept, self-cognition, and these, indeed, are the major areas of empirical investigation. As Kelly (1955) would remind us, we are not born selves—we *construe* ourselves, and Smith (1985) shows that construed selfhood is both historical and cultural. He also shows how selfhood can be constituted metaphorically, along lines similar to those suggested by Lakoff and Johnson (1980).

Holland (1985), in his investigation of identity, proposed the term "identity theme" for the "continuing core of personality," a pattern or personal style that he abstracts from great and small life events, just as we abstract the L/T life theme, which must be a self theme as well. Holland asked whether this identity theme could be changed, examining lives like G. B. Shaw's, and found that it could not.

The relationship of the self to society has been a major area of investigation. Koestler (1971) thought of the self as both a whole and a subpart of a whole society, or a social holon. Because the self is both autonomous and dependent, it is in a conflict that cannot be resolved. In a similar vein, Kreilkamp (1976) warns of the social "corroding" of the self. On the other hand, Slater (1976) warns that the tradition of individualism leads to a distortion of the individual, and Bellah, Madsen, Sullivan, Swidler, and Tipton (1985) set forth the thesis that individualism can destroy commitment to one another and consequently community. While Broughton (1983) sees the relationship of self to society, and also history, as crucial to self-definition, these opposing views of the self-society relationship are yet to be resolved. Different cultures, be they shame, guilt, or other, create different selves, and these in turn affirm the culture (White & Kirkpatrick, 1985; Marsella, De Vos, & Hsu, 1985). As the meanings of objects and relationships differ, so must selves. (See Chapter 11, on culture.) Other major aspects of the self that have been studied are self-concept (Wylie, 1979), self-reflection, self-perception (Bem, 1972), and self-evaluation (Wegner & Vallacher, 1980). Concepts of the social self, as enunciated by James (1870), Mead (1934), Gergen and Davis (1985), Goffman (1959), and Sarbin (1986), are discussed in the next section.

One of the most fascinating perspectives on the self is suggested by Markus and Nurius (1986) in their concept of "possible selves." It is their view that individuals are motivated not only in accordance with who they are but also by who they would like to become (the ideal self), as well as the selves they could become and the selves they fear they might become. In addition, "possible selves furnish the criteria against which outcomes are evaluated" (p. 956). A person will respond to a broken lunch date in the context of whatever possible positive or negative selves she may hold. "In fact, one of the dramatic differences between self-perception and the perception of others can be found in the simple fact that when we perceive ourselves, we see not only our present capacities and states, but also our potential" (p. 964). To this concept of possible selves as motivators I would add the lost self, or the past I's and me's, as described below.

AN L/T CONCEPTUALIZATION OF THE SELF

Self as Structure

The self can best be conceived as comprising the I and the me's (James, 1870), in accordance with Mead's (1934) symbolic interactionist position, which will be modified for our purposes. The me's are the various roles in society that are undertaken by the individual, such as husband, father, engineer, Episcopalian, Democrat. We perform these roles in the situations that elicit them (Sarbin, 1968); often we are treated as if our entire identity were a single role; and our behavior changes according to which role we feel we are being called on to perform (Goffman, 1959). The I is the experiencing and executive part of the self; it is in this part of the self that we interpret our me's, our lives, and our concept of self (or how the self knows itself). The I reflects, construes, and integrates in a fashion that will be most *meaningful* to the self, as will be seen.

Within the self, there are two different kinds of me's: (1) those that are still actively engaged in transactions between the individual and society are the transcendent me's and are currently involved in transcending loss, and (2) those that are inactive, that only define previous activity in the external world, are the lost me's. The engineer was once a waiter, a student, a choir singer, the class historian, a fisherman, a rejected lover. He no longer participates in these activities; he has lost them to the past, but they are not lost to memory. In defining who he was, they help him define who he has become and who he yet may be; he is, in this sense, always partly who he was, and he examines his life, experiences it, responds to it, selects from it, and attempts to control it within the context of what he was as well as what he is and hopes to be. These lost me's enrich his life and still participate in its construction. He can empathize with the fellow office worker who has just been deserted by his wife, partly out of the pain of his own rejection, and he can share how he transcended, building intimacy with a friend from his own past loss and transcendence. Thus, although the transcendent me's define his present role interactions with society, the lost me's are part of his self, both in concept and in self-construction.

In the same way, there are two different kinds of I, the transcendent I and the lost I. The transcendent I is that part of self which integrates the activities of the various transcendent me's and structures the concept of self as well as life meaning. Its tools are the various mechanisms of defense, coping, adaptation, and mastery. From its repertoire, the transcendent I selects its mechanisms. First, it selects on the basis of those mechanisms that were employed by the self previously, were experienced as successful in handling actual or threatened loss, and have therefore become part of the "style" or "personality disposition" of the individual. Second, the transcendent I selects on the basis of the situation in which the me is involved, different loss situations calling for different transcendence mechanisms. To the extent that the transcendent I can successfully select or match the mechanism to the situation, that mechanism will be appropriate and loss will be minimized. Third, the transcendent I selects the mechanism that will construct the "best" meaning from the experience in which the me is involved and will aid in the restructuring of self-concept in a positive direction, toward growth and away from annihilation. In sum, the transcendent I is responsible for the integration of the total self.

Conflict may occur when the best mechanism for the situation is not readily available in the repertoire, or when it is not consonant with the "best" meaning for the individual. For example, the best defense for a soldier, outnumbered and outmaneuvered by the enemy, may indeed be flight, but this may be incongruent with the concept of self as heroic, devoted, and patriotic and inconsistent with ideals that give life meaning, such as honor and the triumph of good. The soldier might elect to remain, paradoxically choosing annihilation of self in order that an ideal concept of his self may prevail in the memory of others—a concept in memory of which his self will have no awareness. His entire loss and transcendence structure will have led to this decision.

On the other hand, the appropriate mechanism for a situation may have been employed with such painful consequences in past situations that the individual, while recognizing its appropriateness, avoids it. An abscessed tooth might best be pulled; if the choice is not to have it done, the risk is the spread of infection. Inappropriate selection of transcendence mechanisms is a function of pathology, as will be seen.

The second sector of the I is the lost I, which contains all the transcendence mechanisms, meanings, and self concepts that previously defined the individual. It is the rich storehouse from which the transcendent I may draw. If present, possibly more mature defense mechanisms or strategies are inappropriate to a sudden overwhelming catastrophe experienced by the transcendent me, the transcendent I may reach into the storehouse of the lost I and draw forth a lost mechanism or meaning, a less mature one perhaps, such as fantasy or projection or a past religious faith. An example will illustrate the relationships among the four aspects of the self.

A woman has been employed for 20 years as an administrative assistant to the president of a large insurance corporation and has been devoted to her work. Unexpectedly, through a reorganization of the company, her boss is out, and the new president has brought his own long-time assistant with him. She is given the choice of resigning or taking another position of much lower interest, status, and salary within the firm. Her common defense mechanisms within the transcendent I are humor and altruism, neither of which seems adequate to her present problem. Her lost me's include a long climb through the ranks, job hunts in which she was repeatedly rejected, being fired several times for incompetence and insubordination, and an attractive youthful appearance that got her jobs in the past but is no longer applicable. She sees her present crisis in the context of these lost me's as well as the context of impact on other transcendent me's (she will no longer be able to donate substantial sums to her political party) and the context of the lost I, which includes her past self-concept as alienated and inadequate. Her present transcendent self-concept has been one of competent and fulfilling functioning, but suddenly it is moving into the lost area. In the context of the lost self, her past is happening to her all over again.

Objectively, of course, there are many possible ways for her to handle this situation, such as seeking a new job outside the company, retraining in a different field, accepting inferior employment, taking a trip around the world (she has saved a lot). But her handling of the situation and her perception and integration of the newly lost me and I, as well as transcendent I, will be influenced by the previously lost me's and I as well as the transcendent I. The transcendent I might reach into the lost I and find all sorts of possible strategies, such as throwing a rock through the new president's window, as she threw one through the school principal's when she was eight, or returning to the religion of her teens, which taught that misfortunes are blessings in disguise, that you could have faith that disaster had meaning, and that this meaning would become apparent. The process of transcending her loss will involve complex interactions among all parts of the self; she will transcend in some fashion, that is, she will cope somehow for better or worse; and this coping either will be in such a way as to add meaning to her life, to triumph, overcome, and grow in self-concept, or will be incomplete or inadequate, resulting in pathology of some sort, loss piled on loss, physical illness perhaps, depression that does not lift, and diminution of self-concept.

The individual may thus be seen as structure and process. The structure is the self, comprising the lost self and the transcendent self; the lost self includes the lost I and the lost me's, and the transcendent self includes the transcendent I and the transcendent me's. The process is one of perpetual loss and transcendence occurring as the dynamic functioning among the various aspects of the total self in response to its interactions with other selves and with society. This dynamic interaction may be seen as analogous to the dynamic equilibrium between assimilation and accommodation described by Piaget (1952) with reference to cognitive structure and process.

The following diagram illustrates the basic structure-process relationship (Fig. 1).

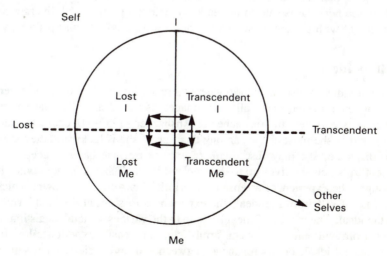

FIGURE 1

This diagram cannot show the shifting proportions of the various sectors of self to the whole, or the shifting shape and dimensions of the total self. Although the various implications should become clear later, a few examples may hint at the range of possibilities. As we grow older, for instance, it is possible that the lost sector grows larger than the transcendent sector in proportion to the total self. Also, the personality of an individual with a very large lost me section might be quite different from the personality of someone whose bulk was in the transcendent I sector. The implications for development and personality, as well as the extent to which the various types of imbalance may be reflected in pathological behavior, are discussed in succeeding chapters.

Self as Concept

How the self views itself is self-concept (see Wylie, 1979). The self looks into itself as into a mirror and sees an image that may be at variance with the image others see (this is in contrast to Cooley's 1902 notion of the self looking to society as its mirror). The anorexic sees herself as obese, and all the reassuring concepts that others have of her as thin cannot persuade her otherwise. Fatness is relative, of limited objective reality. Objective reality is, in the final analysis, only a consensus, one with which the anorexic disagrees, because she sees. So the self perceives itself on a myriad of dimensions, as bright-humored but with a tendency toward irascibility in the face of small frustrations, talented at pottery, terrified of pain, warm toward members of the preferred sex but with a pronounced tendency toward fickleness, nails brittle, boss of dubious integrity, and on over every detail of body, external behaviors, intentions, emotions, relationships, and experiences. To the extent that the individual sees herself and her relations to the world as others see her, she is said to be reality oriented; a pronounced divergence in agreement with the consensus moves her toward deviance and pathology.

Self as Ideal

The individual is also in a world where there are ideals of who she is; parents, school, church, and peers all have images of the ideal individual she may become (see Adler, in Ansbacher & Ansbacher, 1959). Because the ideals vary, either she must choose among them or, if she is lucky and they are not too disparate, she may fuse them. In either case, she has a concept of the extent to which she lives up to this societal ideal. If she does not come close enough, she experiences a sense of inferiority, as Adler has shown, which is the loss of self from the ideal; she experiences loss because of not living up to the ideal. The inner self-ideal lives up to the various societal ideals imposed on it from without. The nonconformist can more easily experience loss from the societal ideal, or discrepancies between self and societal ideal self, and not experience a loss to the self-ideal, or possibly even experience a gain. It is his ideal to revolt against the norms.

Laing's (1976) brilliant vision of the self includes the realization that when the self conforms too closely to the ideal from which it is really distant—that is, when the me's are too alien to the I's—the me's become what he terms the "false self." Thus, the self experiences itself as split rather than unitary. The I may disown the me's and split off even further, resulting in psychopathology, such as schizophrenia, multiple personality, other dissociation, or fugue, depending on the circumstances. I will examine this process in Chapter 10, on the reconceptualization of psychopathology.

Self as Myth

The self, particularly the integrating I, is engaged in continuous mythmaking about self and life. Life events are puzzle pieces that must be rearranged, often painstakingly, before a coherent picture emerges. Sometimes the pieces must be trimmed in spots, or painted different colors, or dispensed with entirely. The process of recounting experiences over and over with minute changes as the rationale of behavior and meaning is constructed is the process of mythology (and also of bereavement!). The story of a divorce, as told by the ex-wife and the ex-husband independently, may be unrecognizable as the same story from one to the other, and yet both may be telling the "truth." The story must conform with the myth of self as being forgiving, for example, or cooperative, or doing everything in one's power to preserve the marriage (but the other just wouldn't . . . listen . . . understand . . . consider). As mentioned above, the myth (with its metaphorical system and theme) is the pair of spectacles through which we see ourselves and, like all other myths, is a mixture of truth and fiction. A friend is someone who believes your myth and even helps in its construction by prompting questions.

Relationship of Life to Self: Identity

We consider the individual's self and life as two aspects of a unity, the inner aspect and the outer. Reifying the self as if it were a structure, thinking of it as comprising the self as subject (the feeling and integrating I) and the self object (the role-related me's in Mead's terms, 1934), helps us to talk about it. It also helps to think of the external aspects of self (self as object to others, behaviors, life) and the internal aspects (feelings, experiences, values) as the life-self entity, or identity. It is important to point this out because many psychologists seem to concentrate on the external lives, events, and behaviors, whereas I consider that the internal experiences are as important and are accessible by methods such as the life review. Supposedly, accounts of external behaviors are more accurate because they can be counted and statistically analyzed; actually, with the exception of the simplest facts, objective facts are as open to various interpretations as are subjective facts. So, the term "identity" designates the external and internal aspects of the individual, self, and life.

The meaningfulness of the outer aspect, one's life, is related to the meaningfulness of the inner, the self. We strive to make the life experience meaningful, because only then do we ourselves take on meaning. Somehow we intuit that a meaningless life could not give birth to a meaningful self. Nor would a meaningful self lead a meaningless life. We strive to create a life that is an expression of the self we conceptualize as meaningful. When our lives are not expressions of our selves, as we conceive them, there is a sense of dysphoria (such as boredom, frustration, depression, anger, anxiety). This is because we intuit at some level that we create our selves and that both our life experiences and how we interpret them are crucial to this creation. Further, this must be the authentic self, rather than the false self described above.

The creation of a life and a self that are meaningful requires many decisions, choices, rejections, and commitments. These result in conflicts, crises, regrets, and affirmations, because the paths to meaning are not always clear. The self emerges as one who has made these life choices, has been rent by that conflict, has resolved on this commitment. We attempt to make the choices or decisions that will enhance the meaning of our life and therefore enhance our self, that will, in short, create or generate the self. We regret the life decision that has resulted in meaninglessness or in a less meaningful re-creation of life and self.

When we experience a great life loss, we experience a great loss of self as well. If a loved one dies, it is common to say, "I have lost part of myself." This is true. We mourn both losses, although we think we mourn only one. We are bereaved of love, of a related life role, of the part of the self that loved and was loved, of the meaning of self and life with which that love endowed us, and finally of part of the paradigm through which we construed that meaning. We may say, "Life has no meaning." This requires a vast restructuring of life, self, meaning, and the rules for construction of these. The spectacles through which we see our selves and our lives may darken for a time.

Transcendent I has the concept of self, but it is within self and part of self, not outside looking in. So it is subject to the same distortions as those of an individual within the universe trying to comprehend the universe.

Self and Other

Other is simply all that is not self. It may be a specific other individual, all of environment surrounding the body, a group of others, the societal other, or the "generalized" other to whom Mead (1934) refers when he speaks of "taking the role" of the generalized other to define one's own role expectations.

The most convenient boundary between self and other is where the body leaves off.

On another level, the concept of other is a tricky one because it can only be held within an individual. It is therefore subject to distortion, projection, misunderstanding, idiosyncratic associations, and disagreement about its nature and values between one self and another self. In that sense, it has always a subjective element, although it is treated as if it were objective. Further, the self is a specific other for other selves and is also part of the generalized other. As such, it is not as distinct from other as subjectively perceived.

The Abused Self

What are the consequences to the self when it is abused? We have a record in both the literature (Bass & Thornton, 1983; Finkelhor, 1984, 1986) and my life histories. The child who is attacked by an omnipotent, omniscient other, who is told he is not who he feels himself to be, is at a loss on several counts. If he is not who he feels himself to be (1) his true self may stop growing; (2) he is either someone else whom he does not know, a stranger to himself, or no one at all; and (3) his feelings, his perceptions of self and other, must be wrong; reality is distorted, is not as he thought it was; and he can enter the twilight zone of unreality. His parents or teachers tell him he is not who he is in order to bind him to their *own* notions of his identity, because their own notions are part of who *they* are, and they would have him extend their selves and therefore their lives, immortalize them. In a wonderful film, *The Maze*, the well-meaning father of the great schizophrenic artist William Kurelek maintains to the end that his son should have been a physician. The son has painted unforgettable scenes of his madness.

The physically neglected learns that she is not worth the nurture of food, drink, comfort, warmth, and medical care—that she is, indeed, unworthy of life, like Tess, who was not worth the milk she drank.

When the self is abused severely, it may fragment into the multiple personalities of a Billy Milligan (Keyes, 1981) or a Sibyl (Schreiber, 1974). The abused become abusers, a cycle difficult to break (Finkelhor, 1986). Others who are sexually abused, perhaps from infancy by those they trusted, have anger, hatred, and distrust at their deepest levels. As we cannot have other thrust upon us without *becoming* other to some degree, the sexually abused, who cannot turn what has been done to him outward, turns it in, becoming depressed, nontrusting of intimacy. Many who read these words have battled back from physical, mental, and/or sexual abuse and know how difficult their battles have been.

Self as Creation

I have said that individuals are always in the process of creating lives and selves that are more or less meaningful. But many people feel that they already exist as complete entities and that life is a series of events that happen to them, over which they have only a modicum of control. Why do they believe this?

It is comforting to believe that the self is a given, that life exists outside ourselves, perhaps even that it was foreordained, that it is part of our Karma. When we believe this, we need not be responsible for our lives and we can escape blame when things go wrong. Helplessness and lack of control and responsibility protect us. The idea that we create our lives and our selves is threatening to us, and we would rather not believe it.

It is true that, as Heidegger (1962; see also Kierkegaard, 1946) observed, we are "thrown" into our life circumstances; we probably did not choose the affluent country of our birth over a nation where many children starve. Unless we do believe in Karma—and Karma consoles—being born to parents who abuse us mentally, physically, and sexually was another instance of our "thrownness." Nor are we responsible for the congenital or genetic weaknesses of eyes, lungs, heart, temperament, or mind that sooner or later afflict so many of us. In addition, throughout our lives other circumstances arise over which we may feel we have less control—our nation plunged into war, economic depression, or wholesale slaughter of our race.

How, then, can it be claimed that life, self, and their meaning are processes of creation rather than objective facts having independent existence, like the Devil's Tower in Nebraska?

First, let us reexamine the relationship between life and self. I have said that your life is the outward expression of who you are, at least to some degree; when there is incongruence between life and self, you are alienated, as factory workers may be from their work (see Marx, in Ollman, 1971). Your life does not exist independently of your self. But that is only part of the story. Your self is the inward expression of your life. You become what you do, whom you are with, where you are. Mothers become their children, their homes; after a while this is all they know. This is part of the anguish of choosing a career. You are choosing who you are to become. If you decide to be a computer analyst, you know you will be a very different person than if you become a nurse. You will work with machines instead of people. Printouts instead of people's problems will haunt your dreams at night. Computer analysts socialize differently, have different values, beliefs, standards, attitudes, perhaps even voting habits and religions.

You have chosen to lead your life one way rather than another, and in that sense you are creating one life rather than another. But that life will also create your self, will fill your thoughts and feelings with some things rather than other things. You are choosing your inner landscape. You will retain your sense of self, of being the same person, of wholeness or integrity, but that self will develop differently. Of course, that same self chose computing rather than nursing, probably because the work was more congruent with who the self was. The seeds of who you can become are within you at birth, nourished or blighted, trained or growing wild in childhood.

Thus, as you create your life, you create your self. Further, you will define your self not only by what you do, and where and with whom you do it, but also by your past, which is the story of your life and who you are. You are the one who has made this choice, those decisions, that commitment and who has, in consequence, lived through these events.

As for meaning, we create lives and selves that are meaningful in two ways. First, we create meaning by choosing one life event, friend, career, or leisure activity over all the others available to us. There are myriad options, almost all of which are open to you, the reader, at this moment. You can stop reading this book and head for the beach, be it a mile or a thousand miles away, by foot or by thumbing a ride. This might be more meaningful to you. You can quit your job and join the Peace Corps, become a shopping-bag lady or gentleman, pig out on candy, get drunk, dance down the street, go mad, swipe a can of detergent, make an obscene phone call to your mother, go to the library and read up on labor relations—your choices of where to be, who to be with, what to do, and where to do it are infinite. We simply tend to dismiss most of our choices without thought. An obscene call to our mothers would be a meaningless activity for us—most of us.

You will decide on a certain activity because experience has proved or you imagine, that it is a meaningful one for you. For example, going to the beach is not a haphazard decision. Although you may not ponder it too heavily and may not be in touch with what the beach means to you, let us consider what beach means to some. It means warmth, sun, sand between toes, breeze, pounding surf, salt smells and tastes, cold waves on the body, tide pools, a tan that will be attractive to the preferred sex, meetings with friends old and new, hot dogs and ice cream, the promise of sex, and maybe love. In sum, what is meaningful about the beach for many is a variety of sensual and possibly emotional gratifications.

However, to Lorellen it meant rape, and a consequent move toward meaninglessness.

Second, we create meaning by interpreting our life events in accordance with our paradigms, or spectacles, or metaphorical systems. This is done through the life review, as indicated in Chapter 7, "Life Meaning." We have a sense of our lives and selves as they should be, or the ideal against which we measure them. We feel the degrees of discrepancy between actual and ideal, and we try to interpret our lives and selves as closer to the ideal. Two men who lost their jobs have different pairs of spectacles or metaphorical systems through which to view the loss. If we are all on the same train, we will each experience the journey in our own idiosyncratic fashions, and the trip will have a different meaning for each of us. In addition to the ideal possible selves, Markus and Nurius (1986) have pointed out that we may try to avoid the negative possible self, the criminal, the addict, or the bag lady.

Action within our lives and interpretation within our selves, then, are the two ways in which we create a meaningful life-self entity, or identity.

Even though the self grows, in the sense that it continues to experience and then becomes one who has experienced, do most of us have a feeling of lack before the self has become what it will be? Perhaps the feelings of dissatisfaction or even dysphoria are feelings of not being completed self. Perhaps we have no way of knowing. When I was 30 I had my first pair of contact lenses; they were a revelation. I saw much that I had never seen before (although, oddly enough, I had dreamed of what I saw). Perhaps, for many of us, self feels perfect, unified, whole, complete, simply because we do not know anything else.

There are, of course, many who do not feel like themselves, or unified, or complete. We will study some case histories of such people, because they shed light on the thesis of this paradigm, that even though self may feel unified, complete, and continuing to be the same as it was, it is not. It is continuing to be who it can be and who it has been before, but it is also being created and re-created from moment to moment, not simply in the womb, but throughout childhood, adolescence, youth and young adulthood, middle age, old age, and the process of dying, after which it vanishes mysteriously. The self is a developing entity, rather than a whole and complete entity. It is always in the process of birth.

The self is continually created out of its body, senses, abilities, beliefs, experiences, and those who tell it who it is. A human seed can only become human, and many of its characteristics are genetically blueprinted before birth (see Rogers, 1961; Thomas & Chess, 1977), but the interaction with experience of self, as far as it has developed at any given point, re-creates the self anew, and to the extent that we choose our experiences, we choose how we will be re-created.

The self, then, is ever in process, rather than a static structure, ever developing, rather than simply being, ever becoming more alive or more dead. We can think of the self as always growing, rather than as magically a whole at birth, 16, 21, 30, 50, 67, or 83. The self is moving toward giving more life to itself, or further birth or emergence on the life-death continuum, or it is moving toward death. As we have seen, some loss-oriented individuals, in trying to cut their losses or defend against loss, move toward self-destruction, splitting; they become rigid and impermeable, are shrinking rather than expanding. If it is the nature of human beings to be born as buds, gradually open until they are in full bloom, and then begin to brown at the edges, the brown creeping toward the heart of the flower, until the dead petals fall, fertilizing the earth beneath—if this is the nature of humans, some buds seems to brown at the tip and then open, and others seem to die without ever opening fully or at all. The causes often are too much water or not enough for an extended period of time, or root shock, or a cold snap, or not enough sun, or a virus—something in the nature of the plant or the environment.

The case histories give us insight into the nature of the self and how it develops. The I is the part of the self that must integrate who I am at present with what's happening to me, moving my outer life to my inner self. I must continuously integrate into unity, in assimilation-accommodation, Piagetian fashion, or I will experience my self and life as split. Some who do not feel like themselves are confusing self with other. The specific process and development of the birth and growth of the lost and transcendent self I describe in Chapter 8, on individual development.

LIFE HISTORIES

We turn now to the emergence of a number of selves—Lexie, Babs, and Sibyl.

Lexie

"I have lost myself."

Lexie is a woman in her twenties who lives with her common-law husband and several small children.

Her home in the midwest was a happy one, her parents counterbalancing each other in that one was an intellectual and distant, while the other was vivacious. She was "unpopular" at school because she was a "smart mouth," although she was the leader of a neighborhood gang. She remembers that fantasy played an important part in her childhood, both through games and in the form of putting on plays, which she wrote and directed. She describes two teachers, one a good influence, because "she trusted me," and the other a bad one. In high school she became one of a group of outcasts or nonconformists, so she felt more popular. "All my adolescent anger came out against the school. . . . I was unique. It kinda drove them crazy because I was good. I followed the rules and was very outspoken against them. They could never quite pin me down as the one causing all this trouble all the time. . . . So that was fine. I enjoyed that . . . I think I felt more a victim of my peers in childhood, but in adolescence I wasn't any more. I was a leader of my peers . . . the times shifted to where I fit into them real well."

Lexie also discovered "that I could attract men, and I always was in shock when someone was attracted to me, because I was used to the long history of being the scourge. . . . I did graduate a virgin" (one of two, and everyone knew who they were).

When Lexie graduated from high school, she came to California and met her present common-law husband at a commune. Their relationship was an on-again, off-again situation for awhile.

"I got pregnant and had an abortion. . . . It was before it was legal, actually. . . . I never had to lie so much in my life." She had to talk to "two psychiatrists, and convince them I was going to go crazy. I went to the welfare office then to pay for it. I lied about where I lived. I lied about everything up and down. The abortion—I remember waking up to total euphoria. Every time I have a kid, I've been totally euphoric."

Her parents were divorced when she was in her teens. "I think both of them fell into . . . very traditional role patterns. . . . My mother got sick of it and didn't see any (other) way out. . . . My father also [realized] he was not going to go out there and kill all the dragons." Conformity betrays, and the metaphor of success is in terms of fantasy. Lexie provided a great deal of emotional support for her father during this time, and yet he remarried without inviting her to the wedding, which upset her.

She participated in a leadership capacity with a number of community agencies, as well as in community theater; this gave her a sense of family and a chance to "play executive."

A drastic change in Lexie's life came about when she and her boyfriend became committed to each other, moved in together, and had several children. When the children came she stopped working, and this has been a source of conflict for her over the past 5 or 6 years. Her contacts with other people became nonexistent, and her need for her husband became stronger, "because I got a lot of things from the outside world before" she had children and had to stay home. She sees him as providing a balance for her, just as her parents did for each other; "he's strong in places I'm not"; she tends to get more upset about things. Now "all of a sudden I wasn't getting to 'up' my ego."

"I think one of the reasons I did fall in love with him was I was playing with all of these men and all of these games which I enjoyed tremendously. But then he sorta walked in and said: 'Would you like to sleep with me tonight?' I was just floored by his ignoring all that flirting and playing. . . . He was going right to it. It wasn't like someone from the street saying: 'Hey, baby, do you want to fuck?' There was a relationship there. There was this straightforward . . . and it wasn't all of this game-playing. I remained faithful when it got down to brass tacks. I had a lot of flirtation. I really enjoyed the flirtation. Now, all of a sudden, I didn't have that any more, plus my whole body's run over from a truck" (her pregnancy). "All of a sudden I'm looking to [my husband] to provide something he's never provided for me. I'm really angry with him that he isn't, and it took me a while to sort all that through."

In this quotation we see first that the game playing, pretense, and fantasy has extended itself from childhood through the theater into adulthood. Honesty, straightforwardness, and reality are in conflict with lying, pretense, and fantasy in Lexie's system. She lied to obtain an abortion, she liked her husband's straightforwardness, she enjoyed the game playing of flirtation, and she fell for a man who did not play games. Second, we see a theme that runs through many women's histories: expecting men to provide all that their pregnancy forces them to leave behind. However, having a child *did* put Lexie in touch with the softer, more intuitive side of herself. She says having a child was a decision, rather than merely a matter of luck (as it was for some other interviewees), "fool that I was!"

The theme of split between fantasy and reality is repeated: "I feel like my options are basically to either put my children in child care or to remain isolated from an exciting adult world. Neither of those options are good for me. So I spend a lot of time spinning fantasies of what would be better—as a more community-oriented situation . . . where women and small children are not totally cut off from other kinds of real adult work. I do make the choice not to put my children in full-time day care and go off and do something. . . . I'm still surprised how much on an emotional level I don't want to leave them. I was expecting myself to plunge them off on to babysitters or whatever, and go off and continue doing whatever. . . . I also have a bias of being raised by someone that thinks you're wonderful . . . that is good for them. So it's an emotional thing and also a 'should'."

Lexie is expressing very well the severe conflict that many women undergo between giving their children the advantages of being raised by their mother and giving up "the exciting adult world." Her way of handling it is through fantasy. If she had a choice between coming back as a man or as a woman, she would come back as a man "because men don't have to make the same choices between children and career."

Lexie was asked why she and her husband never legally married. She replied: "[The reason] sorta changed as the times went on. At first, it was 'the state is corrupt, religion is corrupt, so I'm not going to have either of them mucking about in my relationship.' Then we sorta grew out of that phase; there's a period when we'd talk about it, but not quite get around to it. The last time we really talked about it was when I was pregnant. That's when we changed from my name to his name. There's a couple of reasons why we—why I didn't want to at that time. One was that I didn't like the idea of getting married because I was pregnant. . . . I somehow felt that getting married at that point negated what had gone before. It was like that wasn't real, now we're going to do it for real. I didn't want to buy into that. There's also just a tickle in not being married. We'd be talking to someone and they'd become a friend or something, and it will just come up that we're not actually married. They're always so surprised. It's like, oh, we've been together [many] years, and oh, we're not married. It's always just a laugh. I think we both enjoy those remnants of our revolutionary past."

The theme of nonconforming is repeated here, with the additional element of a split between what is "real" and what isn't "real."

Besides fantasy, Lexie has also handled the conflict through a somewhat successful creative endeavor involving children on a part-time basis, although this has by no means solved the conflict.

When asked for her best experience, Lexie thinks of it as a toss-up between two polarized experiences, herself as executive running community activities and directing plays, and also herself with her children, which involves "flashes of incredible joy, in some ways a lot deeper than the executive self." These two identities "are not synthesized yet. Maybe they will be later on. But I see those as two different people that haven't quite figured out how to meet."

Lexie keeps a journal, which is what she would save if the house burned down. When asked what this journal means to her, she asserts that it is "evidence that I am." The reality of her existence must be confirmed! Later, in the sentence completion section, she said, "I have lost—myself. . . . I was afraid when I was pregnant the second time that I was going to lose whatever remnants of myself that were still there. . . . My first child I lost myself, and my second child gave me back myself, my self-competence [sic]. . . . I totally got shot to hell with my first child, incompetent, you know."

The search for a whole, unsplit identity seems to be continuing. In this search, the whole hippie movement influenced her positively, because it "really reinforced who I was, my sense of being able to do whatever I wanted to, of not feeling like I needed to fit into a particular mode. . . . I still believe in it, even though the culture no longer reinforces it." In reminiscing further about the hippie movement, she says, "We are creating a new world, but it's taking a whole lot longer than one ever thought it would." This world was going to be "love and peace and tolerance . . . all that flower-child hippie stuff . . . the non-materialistic approach, and I really buy that" (using the materialistic metaphor). "And I see a lot of peers now who see it as that was then, and that wasn't real . . . and now are after the dollar. That disappoints me." Once again, the lines between reality and fantasy are blurred, and the result is disappointment.

In speaking of the place she loves the most, Lexie sees it as "a very strange town; to me it feels like there are two forces, sort of a dark force and an enlightened force. You see a lot of people . . . caught in a destructive, heavy dope, heavy booze situation, and at the same time . . . that air of enlightenment or spiritual awareness."

When asked about the appearance she thinks she presents to others, she says she's seen as "kinda scuzzy and unkempt" and would like to appear "sexy, casual," although she's not sure the latter is "real."

With regard to the feminist movement, Lexie felt she was "playing both sides of the fence" because she was an executive, but then when she had her children she was "furious at the feminist movement. I felt real unprepared for what I came up against. . . . All the things that my feminist self-image relied on was being in the working world, and a certain way of thinking which gets sort of shot to shit after you have a baby. All of that was gone. Somehow I was bad, I was a housewife. . . . I felt really furious and undone by them [the feminists]. Then my feminine self was shot to shit, and what was left? I was no longer sexy, desirable, playing that game 'cause you can't play that game when you're a mother. And I was no longer an executive career woman playing that game. What identity was there for me to latch on to that was a positive identity?" An identity is something one latches on to, a game one plays, not a growth from seed.

Although Lexie does not see a theme in her life, she says others observe her as always having run-ins, battling against something, aggressive, split.

And a central conflict for her is "being versus doing. . . . I always feel I should be doing more." This is set against "being able to go to the park and just enjoy it . . . look at the trees and it's also cosmic. . . . And I sit there thinking I should do something. . . . I have period fantasies, the Gothic mansion with all the servants keeping house. Of course, I'm the mistress of the castle, not a mere peon queen . . . a large group of people working, and you're more or less in control and power. You're administrating all the house and all these people, benevolent and kind and lazy."

On her personality test, Lexie's particularly high score of 49 in intuition well reflects her concern with potentiality rather than actuality, which in her case is expressed mainly by fantasy, since much other expression is blocked. One is reminded of the findings of Henry and Simms (1970) that actors and actresses are role diffused (see Erickson, 1950) and have not achieved a sense of identity—their roles give them temporary ones. Certainly, Lexie's sense of unreal self is confirming here, as is her conflict between roles. Lexie rated her "career versus child" conflict as one of her most stressful life events.

Overall, the theme that recurs in Lexie's life history is one of splitting, mainly of identity. The split of her parents, of herself between career and motherhood, from her body in an out-of-body experience, from society in the form of various deviant activities and fighting, between being and doing, between forms of womanhood, feminine versus feminist—this splitting results in a recurrent loss of identity, to which she refers in various parts of the interview. Her journals give her "evidence that I am," as if no other evidence existed, and for that reason they are the most precious things she owns. She lost herself partly when she had her first child, although this was returned to her by her second child. Her entire history is told in terms of splits, the dark force versus the enlightened force in her favorite town, the good teacher and the bad one, the complementary relationships of her parents, between herself and her husband. Even her involvement in career is in the theater, where she can pretend to family, and as a community worker, where she "plays at being executive," and the relationships with men have been flirtations, playing a game—never quite real, with the exception of her "husband." Much of her transcendence of this lost identity and the splits associated with it have been in the form of fantasy; in addition she has found an identity in nonconformism, also a game.

For Lexie the meaning of life is "feelings of joy and love"—the very words she uses to describe the advantages of motherhood. When asked, "True or false: Most people lead lives of quiet desperation," she corrects the statement: "Most *mothers*—true." In the L/T paradigm, she seems to be in the searching stage.

Lexie's overall theme is splitting of self (or identity) expressed in split parents, split between career and motherhood, from her body, with society, between being and doing, between forms of womanhood, between light and dark forces, between reality and pretense; this splitting results in recurrent loss of identity. It is transcended by fantasy and by transient satisfactions from both sides of splits. The core theme is self versus self, or split self.

Theoretical analysis

From Lexie's story we learn much about the nature of loss, metaphorical systems and their roots, and the self.

First, Lexie is "two different people that haven't quite figured out how to meet." She must have "evidence that I am" and states that "I have lost myself." Laing (1976) would say that she lacks "primary ontological security." We must ask, with Lexie, who she is and if she ever was. She seems to have spent much of her life playing games, pretending, fantasizing, enacting roles, "playing" executive, striving to be either a mother or a career woman as a way of "latching on" to an identity, appearing "scuzzy and unkempt" when she would like to appear otherwise, but unsure about which, if either, is really herself. In other words, Lexie conveys a sense of lost identity, and yet we have no evidence that her identity was ever hers to lose. She appears to be unborn, or unemerged.

In all of the life reviews we are shown how great losses are forms of death to parts of the selves that undergo them, but enough of the self usually survives to carry on, to re-create. For Lexie, something of her seems to have died too soon; she endures the greatest loss while still living—the loss of self.

Lexie's entire metaphorical system is made of splits—where she is, who teaches her, raises her, marries her, her life (she is even a Libra, whose symbol is the scales). It is through these spectacles that she sees the world. These splits are metaphors of her split identity, and many are judged as being real or fantasy. It seems to be the fantasy that she enjoys more, but the problem with fantasy (for Lexie) is that it is unreal.

When we look to the roots of the metaphorical system, we find a number of possibilities in her childhood. First, she was a smart, aggressive kid who alienated others. This seems to have been a facet of her personality, not her parents. Second, her father was distant, her mother warm. When they split, she helped her father, who then rejected her. Third, she was a bright, imaginative child, given to fantasy (plays), which was rewarded with companionship; she speaks of the feelings of family in the theater. Certainly, we can understand the seeds of Lexie's identity problem in this childhood, but it is not convincing. She also refers to her incompetence as well as to tensions around the concept of trust. These suggest a long period of unresolved psychosocial crises in the Eriksonian paradigm (Erikson, 1950).

More convincing, perhaps, is the contribution to her development made by the historical period of the 1960s, to which the above factors of her childhood made her particularly vulnerable. The 1960s was a period of dreams in American history (probably many of them rooted in fantasy), of acting out fantasies and giving them life. There was much breaking with tradition, a culmination of which was the career-versus-child conflict of many women. Possibly the distance of her father, certainly her penchant for fantasy may have made her vulnerable to this high-impact historical environment.

Lexie is faced with alternate selves that will give rise to alternate futures. She can be a mother or a career woman who pretends—acts, plays the executive. Being a mother deprives her of fantasy and rewards her with joy— she transcends the deprivations by pretending. The false self system is too much a part of Lexie's identity for her to let it go, and this is the paradox with which she must deal. The solution to the split is to choose one or to alternate; time, the measure of life, becomes crucial—endings are implicit in time running out.

Lexie's solutions have been with her for a long time. She tries to view splits as "balance"; her mother and father balanced each other, as do she and her husband. Being unborn, one cannot die. Being unmarried, one cannot be divorced. Commitment is withheld—to child, to mate, to career. Being without a career, one is condemned to neither following nor failure. Looking scuzzy, one need not reveal or attract, and one can pretend that it is appearance only, and appearance implies something real beneath it. Being nonconforming protects from the commitments to tradition and from being rejected by tradition. One cannot lose what one does not have.

I believe Lexie does indeed have a self, an identity, although she is as yet unaware of it. She is the one about whom all of the above could be written. Her true self comprises what is false as well, as it does with all of us to a greater or lesser degree. First, always, there are dreams. Unreality has a reality all its own, and falsity rings true.

Our next case history demonstrates two major modes of self-creation, the alter ego or alternate self and the split self. Babs is a modishly suited lady in her mid-forties, quick of wit. She is one of the few interviewees who chose to come to my office rather than be interviewed at home.

Babs

"I remember being terrified of all kinds of situations. . . . I developed a guard against very close relationships . . . not letting anybody get close enough to hurt me."

Babs's mother was a "taciturn, stern woman" who was loving nevertheless. A schoolteacher from the midwest, she was a strict disciplinarian, a religious conservative, active, aggressive, stubborn, "demanded . . . strict adherence to her mores and life style, critical of others." Her influence was both good and bad. She gave Babs a sense of wanting to be a high achiever, to strive for excellence, but she was rigid and made Babs rebellious. Her father was gentle, kind, and considerate, a strict disciplinarian like her mother but not as aggressive. His is a "good mind, but it isn't an educated mind." His influence on her was for the better because of his gentleness, his concern for others, and his sensitivity. Babs's aunt also provided a refreshing influence because she had a sense of fun and "enjoyed the lighter side."

A traumatic incident occurred when Babs was about three or four. Her uncle, who had played with her a great deal, was drafted. When he left, it was "like having a father leave." Six months later they received notice of his death. Babs recalls "crying myself to sleep and waking up with nightmares."

Babs's brother was "a very happy child, just the opposite" of Babs. "He developed problems later. See, my problems got straightened out later [laughs]." He married, had children, "and then decided that he wasn't getting enough sex at home, so had to go out and screw around, got divorced, a very bitter divorce that separated him from his children, and he has just become a drifter and a ne'er-do-well. He totally lost all focus in life. He calls me birthdays, Christmas. I'm disappointed in him, especially because of the way he treats my parents—very badly," because of their constantly pushing religion on him, for which he blames them. "He's a borderline alcoholic now."

Babs did not have a happy childhood. The discipline included a good deal of spanking, using hands, the back of a brush, and "a good white board." She was spanked about every other day when she was 8, 9, and 10 years old, and her last spanking took place when she was 16, but she was never injured enough to see a physician. School was difficult for her, which upset her mother. "I was very, very withdrawn when I went to school as a kindergartner, and I never got over that until probably some time during my high school years. I had a lot of emotional problems as a child. I was out of school a lot . . . and I was on nerve medicine which they called it at that time. I felt no one liked me, and I was the strange kid at school, and everybody picked on me. I don't know if they did or not," she laughs. Her fondest memory is of seeing her dad drive by in the school bus and wave to her. "I was an impossible child for my mother [laughs]. [She] couldn't understand any of this, and would force me into school and social situations, and she would generally take the school administrator's or teacher's side against me on every issue [laughs]. . . . I got to the point that I had no social interface with any other children. . . . I was totally a loner . . . I wouldn't play at recesses . . . I would sit by myself in the cafeteria. I was terrified [to go to school] . . . I don't know why. I was terrified until I reached about the seventh grade." Then she became rebellious and a troublemaker, called teachers names, got into fights, and her mother was called to school for new reasons. "I was a child that definitely needed a lot of professional help" and didn't get it. "I remember being terrified of all kinds of situations." Further, she thought she was a fat child, but now when she looks at pictures of herself, she realizes she was not.

In her teens Babs went through a "self-inflicted isolation," although in high school she did develop several friendships, which she believes probably were not as emotional as those of other children. "I developed a guard against very close relationships because I had felt so persecuted throughout grammar school. I was frightened of people, of being hurt, and I built a defense against that by simply not letting anybody get close enough to hurt me. I had no boyfriends through high school. I was very strictly regulated by my parents. My life revolved around the church. I didn't participate in any high school extracurricular activities." She did not learn to flirt like the other children and figured she must be boring.

After high school Babs and her friends were packed off to a church college. "My parents were glad to see me go," and it was a relief for her as well. "I majored in education, and I got about as far as practice teaching and decided I really did hate that. I didn't like the children any better at 20 years old than I liked them when I was 10 [laughs]. . . . I also decided at the age of nine that I was never going to have children, a commitment that I have stuck with throughout life. And I think I decided that because I was so miserable as a child. . . . I was never going to bring another kid into this world to be so miserable." She should have gone into business, that was where her interests lay, but at the time she thought all a woman could do in business was to be a secretary, and she hated that.

After quitting college, she spent 2 years as a dental assistant. A friend asked her to go out on a blind date, and "it turned out to be my husband, strangely enough." He was outgoing, gregarious, fun-loving, talented, handsome, a dozen years older, "a superb conversationalist," and had great plans for the future. However, he was a nonpracticing member of another religious faith, and her parents "all but disinherited me. They were on our doorstep almost every weekend, and sometimes during the week, getting me out of work, harassing me. They wanted me to get out of the marriage. . . . It was very difficult for him, and he tried to handle that the best he could. I came apart. After having gone through the kind of childhood that I went through, I couldn't handle my parents at that time, and . . . I was an emotional wreck. We finally packed up and moved back east, and I didn't tell my parents where I was for almost two years." She didn't work because her husband wanted to support her, but it was very boring.

However, eventually she had to go to work, because her husband "fell into a pattern of leaving jobs, not staying employed." So she had to increase her salary and achieve more and more as time went on. He had health problems, became withdrawn, had "illusions of starting his own business. He tried that several times. It didn't work . . . mostly because he didn't pursue it. He would put everything together and then not do anything. And because we had to keep a roof over our heads and keep eating, I continued to try to attain greater goals." Fortunately, she had excellent mentors and was able to work herself up the ladder. She feels her husband influenced her for the better in a negative way, because "I had to become a really strong person to be able to deal with the problems that he presented for me. Strangely enough, I loved my husband—it was the first emotional tie I had had in my life. . . . Very good relationship sexually, and sometimes I wonder if that wasn't what kept us together, very honestly. The sexual aspect of our marriage was absolutely fantastic."

A strong role model for Babs during these difficult years was her sister-in-law, whose husband (Babs's husband's brother) "ran around with everything in skirts and became an alcoholic," while she was saddled with half a dozen kids. "Yet through it all, she is one of the toughest, strongest ladies that I have ever known. She was determined to straighten out his ass [laughs]. . . . She was a street-fighting kid, and she would go and pull him out of bars. I've known her to go pull him out of a brothel in bed with somebody, grabbed that little sucker by the—[laughs]. Made such a scene that he was so embarrassed that he—you know." She did this for a dozen years, and finally he began staying home more, got a job, became interested in the children. "She was determined to turn him around, and she did it with love, with might, with every possible tool available. I model myself after her." Later in the interview, Babs talks about how she is two selves, and the person on the outside in business is modeled after this woman. "I can handle the rest of the world that way, but I still can't handle my husband that way [laughs]."

During her early thirties, Babs made a suicide attempt. "He had second mortgaged our house and had gotten behind in all the payments. The government put a lien against our home and put a sign on the door [laughs]: 'Seized for back taxes.' And I hadn't known that." In addition, her husband had been so jealous that he didn't want her to have any friends. He became more reclusive as she became more outgoing, the result of having to be more aggressive in order to achieve on the job. "So we were becoming opposites. . . . He was jealous of everyone in my life. Even though there were never any other men in my life, he imagined there were." There was a "constant problem of not knowing what to say for fear he would take it the wrong way. There was never any physical abuse, but the mental stress of having to deal with a constant jealous mentality—he was jealous of his brothers when they came—he thought his brothers were eyeing me. He thought his cousins were eyeing me. He thought strange people in restaurants [laughs] were making eyes at me. I mean, the man got a little sick [laughs]." Babs had been contemplating suicide a lot, took an overdose of sleeping pills, and slept for a day and a half. When she woke up "I decided it was time that I grew up a little, and either I had to leave this man, or I had to decide to stay with him and deal with it . . . and killing myself was not the answer. Unfortunately, I decided to stay with him, and partly because he was very, very dependent on me, partly because I believed that he was going to do better, and probably mostly because of sex."

Babs's solution was a novel one. "I split myself in two. I became one person at home with my husband, and another person with the outside world where my husband wasn't with me or involved. . . . When I was with my husband, I was a devoted wife who spent all of her time waiting on him and supporting him, trying to allay his fears that he was going to lose me to some other man . . . being careful not to give him any wrong impressions." Whenever they were with other people, she acted conservative, withdrawn, and focused entirely on him. In the outside world of work, however, "for goal-setting, achieving, I became an aggressive person who would achieve these goals at almost no matter what the cost. And I became outgoing. I worked up a role of a fun person, a person who could handle a lot, could work under pressure without breaking, and run things." Her jobs got better, she got a lot of respect from her peers and friends. But, in looking back, she wishes she had left her husband.

Meanwhile, they moved around the country, made amends with her mother and father, and her husband never found work. Now in his fifties, he seems to have settled into his health problems, which include migraine, back, thyroid, arthritis, ulcers, heart attack, and angina. Babs attributes this to his having been spoiled by a wealthy family and being very talented, with a high IQ. He doesn't work partly because he has "always believed he should have something better. Whatever job was offered to him, he felt that it should have been a better job. It should have paid more money. They asked him to do menial things. This is his idea. I mean, once in a while somebody may ask you to do something menial [laughs]. I have to clean the toilet bowls at home, right?"

Now in her forties, Babs says, "I'm still contemplating divorce. I'm going to be contemplating it for the rest of my life [laughs]." As her husband's health got worse, her jobs got better, and "I began to feel responsible for him, and I had to deal with a lot of guilt concerning the fact that I didn't put my foot down in earlier years." She stays faithful because he's so jealous and keeps tabs on her, asks her where she's been, and with whom. In recent years, she's resolved to leave him "because I think that's probably the only way that he's going to be able to get hold of his life, and I also believe that his health will improve." What worked for her—being forced into the outside world to become independent—might work for her husband, she believes. Further, there's no more sex in their marriage, because he takes so much medicine for his pain that he is impotent. Asked if she has a time frame for leaving her husband, Babs responds with a laugh, "Yes, I have a time frame every month. . . . I've resolved those things before. I'm not sure that I will, because I have a great deal of guilt concerning it. I'm always afraid that, sure as hell I leave the bastard, and he'll drop dead three months later."

Babs remains successful in sales and has gone out of her way to make friends and have a social life in spite of her husband's objections. When asked if she wishes anything had been different about her twenties, she responds, "I wish I had left my husband," and she has the same response for her thirties and forties. When asked if she has any regrets, she says she regrets having married, that marriage was a wrong decision, but that not having children was a right one. If Babs could write her own epitaph it would read, "This lady should have never married but she did one thing right, she didn't have kids." However, her most difficult experience was leaving a job after many years with the company, which was headed for bankruptcy. "As much as the company meant to me, and as much as I had invested in it, I wasn't interested in watching it to the last dying breath."

When she looks back on her life 5 years from now, Babs hopes that either she'll be divorced or her husband will be dead. When she looks back on her life at the end of it, she hopes to be able to say that she gave others the strength to achieve. If she could have anything she wanted, it would be . a rich husband who traveled all the time, so she could work, party, and have affairs. If she could come back in another life as anyone she pleased, she would return as the madam of a brothel of very high-priced call ladies—she'd have it made. Her sentence completions describe both time and life as like a "prison," her highest peak experience as being her "work environment," the world as a place where "things can be enjoyed," and she says she has lost "years of happiness." She was very frightened when Kennedy and others were assassinated; these events caused her to search harder for security and independence. Thus, security and independence seem to be metaphorically equivalent to protection from death in her system. She fantasizes about parties, having people to dinner, going on trips with people—all without pressure. In fact, she makes up whole stories about this.

Babs sees her life theme as being a supporter of others—her parents, her church, her husband, the people who work for her, and those she works for—all these substitute for being a nurturing mother. She's unhappy about this, hasn't done enough for herself, such as writing essays, but her husband demands too much of her time outside work. Someone else looking at her life would see "a woman who never learns her lesson." She says she's also had a lot of guilt all her life, "as early as I can remember. This was part of what contributed to me being so frightened as a child. I felt guilty—I don't know [why]. I guess guilty for—fear that I was going to do something that would displease my parents."

Babs's L/T life theme would define her losses as including emotional withdrawal, schizoid personality, lack of trust, persecution in childhood, and a husband sick with jealousy and pervasive paranoia throughout much of her protocol. These are transcended by work achievement and by splitting the self into two, showing devotion to her husband with social conservativeness to allay guilt and jealousy, and showing aggressive, goal-seeking, sociable, role-related, successful behavior at work, which is enjoyable. The core theme is paranoid and schizoid self versus successful work self—both as split self.

This protocol is rated as being high loss, low transcendence, the loss seeming to overwhelm the transcendence, although there is a considerable amount of the latter; I believe that another individual with Babs's experiences might have become flagrantly psychotic, and Babs has defended against this at great cost. The protocol as a whole would be rated as in the searching stage, but she is also moving toward replacing; she has friends and activities outside her home. Her personality profile shows a tilt toward introversion, fairly high intuition, and high thinking and perceiving factors. This kind of person is quiet, reserved, has theoretical interests, and is logical, unusually more interested in ideas than parties or small talk (Myers, 1962, 1977). I think this describes Babs as she has been, but she is moving toward extroversion, being alert and outspoken.

Theoretical analysis

Babs teaches us a great deal about the creation of self, as well as of alternate selves, in order to survive.

The reasons why Babs remains in her marriage, even though it is the part of her life she regrets most and she resolves over and over to leave it, are undoubtedly complex. We must begin with the reasons she gives us. First, she says she remained in the marriage because the sex was so fantastic, although there has been none for 4 years. Babs felt that she could never find sex that good with anyone else, but she also says she has been faithful to her husband and would like to have affairs. Perhaps she had one or two unfortunate affairs before marriage, or perhaps her self-image is so poor she feels she will not attract another man (a problem for the middle-aged woman). In any case, as her husband is now impotent, we must look to other reasons—her feelings of guilt for not having insisted he shape up earlier in the marriage and her anticipatory guilt over his demise if she left him now.

Guilt has been with Babs ever since she can remember. It is now a personality characteristic rather than simply a response to a specific life situation, as it is with many of us. There are two powerful roots of her guilt, both extending into her early childhood. The first is the unusual amount of corporal punishment she endured. It is true that parents punished physically more in those days than they do now, but a beating every other day seems extravagant for any era. Being severely punished must send many messages to the child about his or her lack of worth, lovability, and so forth, but one of the major messages is also that the child is guilty of being bad—and *the child is as guilty as the magnitude of the pain endured*. Babs has been severely punished, therefore guilty, ever since she can remember—perhaps the meaning of original sin for her.

We have seen in other cases of physically abused children that not only does guilt develop, but also guilt is a metaphor for having caused loss, hence death, to another. The guilty person has done this and will continue. What is worse, the guilty child who is severely punished wants to cause the death of the punishing other, so that in the child's mind that is part of why she or he is being punished. It is not surprising that Babs anticipates her husband would die if she left him; she has already told us she wishes him dead in 5 years. She is metaphorically guilty of killing him. Thus remaining with him is proper punishment!

Another root of Babs's guilt is the extremely strict, conservative, fundamentalist church in which she grew up, a church that condemns much of what is ordinary social behavior in our society. Kicking over the traces after such a strict upbringing occurs several times in the histories (see Kara's history in Chapter 5), and this is what Babs's brother did—women, gambling, alcohol, divorce, and self-destruction, blaming (and punishing) his parents all the while. Babs's response was more moderate, but both fulfilled the implicit prophecies of their parents and either did things to be guilty of or simply remained punished. And both have punished their parents in return.

Religion has had an insidiously damaging effect on Babs's life, in the context of parental influences. According to her account, it is religion misused. This religion promises salvation in return for following the strict codes; therefore, breaking the codes is death. If one can be punished, however, one might still be redeemed. The punishment may be in the form of extended suffering.

Religious experience is a form of general transcendence and can be one of the highest forms, winning the battle over death, but for Babs the general transcendence was perverted, religion-ism like alcoholism, and her salvation has lain in turning against it, in metaphorically choosing death. She now lives in hell, or perhaps purgatory, where church and parents might say she belongs (for marrying outside her faith as well as the rest).

The other major feature of Babs's protocol is the amount of splitting that has occurred, which I think has been mainly defensive (and which must also be defended against). Babs is right in her assessment of herself as having needed professional guidance. She was remarkably fearful and isolated, not daring to get near anyone for fear of being hurt. Those closest to her, her mother and father, had certainly hurt her. She may also have feared hurting, striking back. She did not trust (the first psychosocial development task, according to Erikson, 1950), and the foundations of a paranoid, possibly schizophrenic, disorder seem to have been present. Instead of continuing in fear and isolation, however, she turned to anger and rebellion; she finally did hit back, anger displaced from mother to teachers and peers, but her mother was also affected in the process. She had to suffer trips to school to hear about her naughty daughter, probably a bitter pill for a teacher, and sweet revenge for the child.

It is said that we meet life's challenges with either flight or fight. We can think of Babs's fear the first 13 years of her life as flight; then she turned and fought instead, probably in her case a far healthier response. In trying to seize some control over her environment (and she views the first 18 years of her life as the worst, because of lack of control), she undoubtedly met with the kind of limited success that started her on the road to relatively healthy adaptation rather than permanent psychosis. She was still not allowed to develop the ordinary social skills in high school (flirting, dating, etc.) so necessary to forming good relationships, but she had friends for the first time. Thus she moved from a schizoid childhood, split off from others and the world, to some kind of unity, enough to assert her preferences and leave college when it was inappropriate for her, fall in love, marry, have a good sexual adjustment, and go to work. She married the aspect of her self that she wanted to create—fun-loving, outgoing, with zestful future plans, gregarious. She was creating herself further.

Another split took place after her suicide attempt, when she became two people, clearly as a defense against the death of her self. One person was devoted to her husband, waiting on him, supporting him, very careful of all she said and did in front of others, conservative, and withdrawn—much as she had been before. The other person she specifically refers to as a "role" being played, intimating it was not her real self—achieving, a fun person who could handle a lot of work and run things. The first self maintained her marriage and was, in effect, punished. The second self, for which I believe there had been inherent potential, was rewarded with friends, fun, respect, good jobs. The second self is, I think, taking over and perhaps will eventually help her break from her husband and the necessity of being her first self. Her second self is also likely to attract other men. Some might see the second self as a false self system, but I see it as the healthy part of herself that was repressed for so long and is finally allowed to emerge.

The final major example of splitting seems to have occurred in her husband, whose self seems to have moved from a positive unity to one suffering both physical and emotional losses. Paranoid herself, Babs married someone who must have had the seeds of paranoia already within him, betrayed by his body and fearing betrayal by her, fearing loss of body and love, death in two forms. He appears jealous and hypochondriacal; she dismisses his illnesses as something he could get beyond if he had to, not quite real. Yet, he has a real foundation for his fears; he seems to have real illnesses, real pain, and is certainly really in danger of losing her despite all her assurances. There is a split here between her reassurance and her wish for their separation and his death, which is probably the reality-based cause of his mistrust. She began life with a certain degree of paranoia, and now she has married one susceptible to it and unwittingly feeds it.

For Babs, her split between two selves has saved her life, and it works. It should be noted that splitting as a reaction to severe physical abuse in children seems to be common. In fact, in cases of multiple personality (another form of splitting, fragmentation), approximately 95% have been physically or sexually abused as children. The splitting, in these cases is also defensive; for example in The minds of Billy Milligan (Keyes, 1981), one personality is the "keeper of the pain" and has the responsibility for "taking the spot" whenever pain is being inflicted.

Another form of self-creation also in evidence in Babs's case is the alter ego or alternative self. In this case, the role as aggressive, achieving extrovert was the personality of her sister-in-law, with whom she identified because they had such similar problems and had married two brothers. Babs sees this woman's life as her own; the lines between self and other are blurred—she becomes the other, is successful at it. She is now a role model to others!

Our last illustration is the story of Sibyl, for whom a traumatic event interfered in the creation of identity.

Sibyl

"The chief problem that I . . . always had . . . was [not] having a sense of self."

In her early sixties, Sibyl is petite and silver-haired. She was raised in a farming community in the east, "an ideal place to grow up," she feels. "You always have so many other people . . . and other situations . . . to try yourself out on. . . . You are always an individual, and you can always contribute to the community. I can remember at age two standing on the stage and making my first recitation. . . . You have so many other adults feeding back to you, giving you feedback . . . which I consider a real plus, and one of the reasons I feel that I survived."

Of her parents, Sibyl says they were good but nonnurturing. "My mother is the kind of person who never really thought of anybody but herself. So in consequence, my father spent all his time thinking of my mother." Her mother never approved of her and doesn't to this day—she is in her mid-eighties. "My mother handled things by becoming ill. [She] ruled by weakness rather than by [strength]. . . . My father was a Mr. Milquetoast," kind but ineffectual. "They never fought. In my family, nobody ever confronted anything . . . never any bickering or fighting. One always maintains an exterior calm, no matter what's going on underneath the surface . . . take into consideration what the neighbors might think." Sibyl's grandparents were nonjudgmental and lived on the farm as well. A highlight was to go south each summer to visit other relatives.

Sibyl had the whole great outdoors to play in and also loved reading. In school "my first grade schoolteacher and I were friends for years. It became apparent very early that I was an accomplished reader. I can remember being taken to the other rooms to demonstrate my reading ability which, when I think about it, was a horrible thing to put on a kid. I don't think I ever learned to read, I just read." Her brightness didn't win her any popularity contests in school, until she emerged as a leader in junior high.

A major incident in Sibyl's life happened in first grade. Her sister was born, the twin of a dead baby. Sibyl remembers the little white box in which the infant was placed, but there was no service. Death was commonplace in that community, very open, and children were included in any rites. It was around this time that Sibyl, who had always been a rebellious individualist, became conforming. Because there were so many years between her and her sister, they didn't play much together, but there were no real problems until Sibyl was a teen. "I was practically grown up, and she was still a brat."

Adolescence, and particularly high school, were a lot of fun, but "The chief problem that I had, and always had, which manifested itself, was having quite a problem of having a sense of self, and that manifested itself in my adolescence. This is something which was difficult. On one hand, I could see that I always achieved, and I always progressed. On the other hand, it was unbelievable." (Was it almost like the person who was achieving wasn't really you?) "That's right. It's taken me many years to lose that [laugh]. I think I have much more of a sense of self [now]." (When did you achieve that sense?) "Oh, probably only in the last ten years." (Some people say you don't change much as an adult.) "Oh, my gosh! If you don't change, you're dead!" Sibyl likes to try out a lot of different things and not stay with one thing indefinitely, and she has many interests.

It had been assumed that Sibyl would go to a university where "I knew some of the dignitaries there," because of family connections. But she wanted to attend a liberal arts college in the city. This was considered impractical, so she compromised on still a third university and majored in home economics, which would give her a job. "I was elected secretary of the freshman class at the beginning, joined a sorority, became president and vice-president of the sorority, belonged to a couple of honorary societies, did everything there was to do," including attending the ballet, the symphony, and plays. In college she honed her "people skills." "My senior year I received the highest honor that is given anyone. . . . It's laughable now when I think of the title. I was honorary Captain. . . . It was for the one who had contributed the most to the college during the time they were there. . . . It was very gratifying . . . because it indicated that all the work I had done because I enjoyed doing it— that someone felt it was worthwhile."

Sibyl had a boyfriend in college. When asked if he was important in her life, she replied, "I tried to make it an important thing." They had the same background and values, but he made a derogatory remark about someone from another nation, and this had such an impact on her that she would not marry him. "I had never heard of discrimination at that point. . . . People were people." They did continue a "tentative arrangement," however, not breaking off completely.

Sibyl was hired as a home advisor for the third largest county in the state. She taught rural women's groups home economics skills and organized 4-H clubs. Even after she married, she continued this work, the first female allowed to do so. When you married, you were supposed to resign. She was also paid the largest salary.

The man who was to marry Sibyl spotted her at lunch in a cafeteria. He "kept asking people: 'Who is she?' Well, everybody knew who I was 'cause I was a fairly important person in that county with that job." He learned her identity but no one knew her well enough to introduce him. Some days later he saw her talking with the owner of another restaurant, whom she obviously knew. He knew her, too, and "forced an introduction. . . . About three months later, he asked me for a date, and we went out, and five days later we got engaged. And then I had to go back and tell the other young man." She didn't like her husband at first because "he was so sarcastic. I hope he hears. He knows this. He was tall, handsome, a graduate of Columbia, and just a very nice young man."

They had two children, and Sibyl quit work to raise them, which proved somewhat frustrating. "There were a number of years there when I wasn't doing much of anything, other than stuff in the community," before she returned to part-time work. Her children are different from each other. One was an easy child and the other individualistic and "able to speak her own piece, whether it was the way she yelled at you, or looked at you, or spit her food out at you, and early learned how to manipulate her brother. I used to say: 'Don't let her get away with that, sock her if necessary.' He never would. . . . I've often wondered, is it heredity? Is it the way I acted that brought out this kind of response?" She feels her son's characteristics are like those of her father, whom he hardly knew, and her daughter's are like her mother-in-law's.

Of this period of her life, her twenties, Sibyl says, "I regressed. Having a family was not enough positive feedback for me. I lost the confidence that I had gained when I was in college and when I worked." In her early thirties, Sibyl was having anxiety attacks and sought therapy, which proved beneficial. "I began to realize there was such a thing as thinking about what I wanted. I had never had any idea of that before. For 30 years almost everything I had done had been for my mother." (What were you doing for your mother?) "Just existing, really. I realized that I had married my husband, that was my decision, and upset the family because he had a middle name of [Umberto]— that's foreign [laughs]. . . . All my life I'd been trying to solve her problems, take care of her, and there really had never been much room for me. . . . She is such a dependent person that somebody else has to almost exist for her. You keep hoping you have her jacked up to the point where she'll take off on her own, but never ever had it happened. . . . As one of my therapists said: 'Your mother is a crazy-maker'." (Double bind?) "Oh, my god, one after another. I think the one way I can express most clearly is her telling me it's okay for you to be smart, but don't ever let anybody know it." Sibyl's marital family attended therapy with her. They also embarked on a systematic search for a church and found one with "people out there who thought like I did."

Sibyl feels she was an inadequate, immature parent, and this was compounded by the problem of raising children in the 1960s in a relatively affluent neighborhood. Her daughter said to her once, "Do you know that I went all the way through high school and college, and I never heard one person mention the word 'job'?" She deliberately flunked a course in college because "I'm interested in the psychology of learning. I don't have the faintest idea what it's like to flunk anything." Because of this she did not graduate on time, and Sibyl and her husband said they wouldn't pay for more than 4 years; she'd have to return on her own, which she did, successfully.

Sibyl and her husband sought therapy as their children were leaving home, for "some unsolved problems. . . . A whole new world was opening up without kids around. Once you lose that cement, you gotta find something else." Part of the problem was "my inability to state flatly what it was I wanted." She and her daughter get on better now, but things were "rough, let me tell you." Her daughter would say, " 'Well, it certainly all depends on your role models [laughter]'. . . . It's obvious that you can tell what her role models were [laughter]." When she finished college, she floundered, and Sibyl and her husband refused to support her. "I think parents are not tough enough with their kids." They felt their children would be better off without parents on the scene. Their son had been in the Peace Corps, and they'd always wanted to emulate him, so they applied, were accepted, sold the house, and went to Africa. Their primary motivation was to force their daughter to live on her own. She was living in the woods, but she found a place to live with someone when her parents seemed serious about leaving. "If you call her bluff [laughs]. . . . If I hadn't had all the therapy, if I hadn't done all the changing and growing that I did, I would have never had the strength to do that kind of thing. . . . Mary would have been a lost soul, I think. I think she was going to put off growing up forever. . . . She never would have produced anything, never would have become a productive member of society, as I see so many of her contemporaries [laughs], and I think there was a time there when the struggle to give up was almost greater than the struggle to move forward. With kids you've got to let them know that they're not going to wreck you. If they're gonna wreck anybody, they're gonna wreck themselves only. . . . And somehow or other I've been able to separate myself enough that I was gonna save myself."

Now in their sixties, Sibyl and her husband had a marvelous time in Africa. On her return, Sibyl decided that from now on her time was going to be paid for. She got a creative, satisfying community job, and when that changed she went into real estate. "People buying and selling in real estate—I can't think of anybody who needs more help."

Sibyl had had breast lumps for many years, so she was relatively prepared when one of them turned out to be cancer. Her husband was due to go into the hospital for elective surgery, but when her malignancy was discovered, she went instead and had a mastectomy. She had read everything she could about breast disease in the library and had experience with people who had died of it. She spent "a lot of time with a friend who was ill a year [a man]. That was a growth experience, believe me . . . to be able to share some-body's—it was somebody who knew he was dying, and he wasn't terribly ill up until the last three months. It's a good experience to have. And I was amazed at myself that I let myself in for it, but it turned out to be a positive experience." She used her own surgery as a growth experience as well and had support from her family. Some years before she had returned from South America with a special good luck charm, which she had lost several years before surgery. On her way to the surgery, the day she was entering the hospital, she reached down the back of the front seat to pull out a stuck seat belt, and found the charm. She felt this was a good omen and cried and cried.

Sibyl's main fantasy has been "about being an expert in something. I've always admired experts. I am an expert in something, but not the kind that is generally recognized or paid." At one time she was a member of a city planning commission. "It's an experience to sit in back of the table and have to make decisions, rather than sitting out front having all these ideas for those people back of the table [laughs]. . . . You have to think of the greater good. When you're out front, you're thinking of what's right for you."

Sibyl has some telepathic abilities. She can think of relatives and friends and have them think of her at the same time. "I save a lot of long-distance expenses [laughs] by thinking about them enough, and then they get the message and they call me, and it's on their nickel rather than on mine." She sees her pattern in life as "I've tried to be open to new experiences" and feels others cherish her friendship. Her main conflict has been hard to resolve, "my lack of sense of self, and the conflict with my mother." Her highest peak experience has been a religious one with her church: "You grow, you feel yourself expanding."

Sibyl's main conflict seems to have been one of separation, first from her mother and then from her daughter. Being part of them, she could not be her self or have a sense of self. Perhaps this was why being important was significant to her, reciting on the stage, reading to the various classes, being elected and having honors, being known to dignitaries, being regarded as having an important job—these told her not only *who* she was but also *that* she was. When she stayed at home to tend children, there wasn't enough feedback telling her who she was and she became anxious, sought therapy. Therapy seemed to separate her enough from her mother to later separate from her daughter. The dependence of both was not good for her own development. The L/T life theme, then, is conflict with mother, with daughter, and with herself over who she is. Others define her self by assigning importance through work. Loss of self is transcended by being acknowledged by others as productive and important. Core theme: Identity loss versus identity as productive and important.

Sibyl's protocol is a good example of a loss-oriented history moving toward transcendence. Because the major loss is the most serious one, loss of self, it would be scored as loss-oriented but moving toward transcendence orientation in the last 10 years, that is, her late fifties and early sixties. Thus, great strides in growth can be achieved later in life. "The whole purpose of life is to grow. And if you have children, the purpose is to hopefully . . . get to the point where they're your friends [laughs] and not your adversaries."

Theoretical analysis

Sibyl says that her main problem has been lack of a sense of self. We wonder what that means exactly, and she cannot explain it any better than essentially to repeat it. Later she says that under therapy she realized that everything she'd done had been for her mother, not even for her husband and children. Her mother was dependent on her, apparently lived through her. Sibyl would try to get her mother "jacked up to the point where she'll take off on her own" and give Sibyl independence, but it never happened, and her mother had to lean on Sibyl for support. This leaning took the form of defining how she should live her life and of never being satisfied, no matter how hard Sibyl tried to please. Her daughter also depended on her, although her personality was quite different. Sibyl had to go to drastic lengths to get her to stand on her own feet, quite possibly sensitized by her experience with her mother, transferring the struggle with the mother to the struggle with the daughter and transcending the loss of mother through the daughter. When people leaned on Sibyl, they demanded of her that she be whom they needed, rather than herself. Her self was smothered, could not emerge or develop. She did not know who she was, the person her mother needed her to be and later the person her daughter needed her to be.

I think that this lack of self was complicated by, and partly rooted in, what seems to have been a family value, a concern for feelings of "importance" within the community. Sibyl may have been particularly vulnerable to this concern because her father, a nobody at home, was a somebody in the community. There he counted for something, validated his worth, and perhaps Sibyl seized on this to raise her father in her own eyes. Of course, her mother, too, was concerned about what neighbors might think. The maintenance of the "false front" or "false family self," repressing problems or the "true family self," seems to have reached a comparatively high state of the art here. There is a point at which the false front to others is maintained to such a degree that, even in private, some semblance of it must be maintained as well, lest the seam rip, the hypocrisy be too blatantly exposed, to the family and to those outside. The price, of course, is that the false family self gains a life of its own, and the true individual selves that comprise it are devitalized, undernourished.

Another possible root of this lack of self was the death of the twin sister when Sibyl was about five or six. Until this time, Sibyl seems to have been developing normally, with a good dose of rebellion thrown in. Developmental psychologists say that children tend to become more conforming at this time anyway. But it is only temporary. Sibyl's conformity persisted. We know from thanatologists that when children experience the death of a sibling, they fear it will happen to them. To Sibyl's 5-year-old mind, the twin may even have been punished; to be good might be to survive. Existentialists like Maddi

(1976) warn against conformity for conformity's sake as an inauthentic way of being in the world. Sibyl's false self may have taken root or gathered impetus at this time. It may be that Sibyl was good so that her mother would not grieve, Sibyl taking the place of the dead child, stillborn. Or she may have become conforming with the mother, omnipotent other, capable of killing her own babe in the womb, in order to stave off her mother's lethal judgment against her offspring, to protect herself from death at her mother's hands.

Sibyl defined herself through feedback from the community, and when this feedback disappeared while she was at home raising children, she began to disintegrate. In a sense, she worked out her problem with her mother on her daughter; when she separated her daughter from her, metaphorically she separated from her mother—with the individuation normally carried out in childhood. And she may even have brought such a situation about by behaving toward her daughter as her mother had toward her.

Sibyl's long list of achievements, like the honorary college award, told her that "someone felt it was worthwhile." Our immediate reaction is, but didn't *she* think it was worthwhile, and wouldn't that be enough? Evidently not. Sibyl must receive assurance from outside herself, the assurance she never received from her mother. A need not satisfied at a critical time may precipitate an insatiable hunger. Her mother, the caregiver, the life giver, never told her she was worthy of life. Her community with "adults feeding back to you . . . one of the reasons I feel I survived," indicates the life-giving, nurturing aspect of this approval that "feeds" her. "Importance" or being set above others in some fashion, being unique, was partly Sibyl's way of seeming more individuated, more of a self than she was. With the accretion of many parts of a false self, consensually validated by a society that kept saying, in effect, "Yes, you really exist, and that existence is worthwhile," she could maintain an illusion of a self. The recognition of achievements were the trappings that concealed emptiness, or the "hollow" person, to use Sarbin's metaphor (1979). "Importance" made her alive. The root word in "importance" is "import," or meaning, and it seems appropriate in Sibyl's case to equate importance with meaning, a justification for living, throughout most of her life. What threatened her importance (staying home with her children, when she regressed) threatened her survival, and she began to decompensate.

Sibyl believes that if she had not compelled individuation, her daughter would have "put off growing up forever," a key to her own metaphorical system. But perhaps so would Sibyl. She feels that "the purpose of life is to grow," and in the last 10 years, her late fifties and early sixties, Sibyl seems to have been carrying out that purpose.

CONCLUSIONS: TYPES AND STAGES OF THE SELF

In the above case histories I have shown how the self is created through the transcendence of loss; this self may be more or less meaningful, it may be false or true, split or whole, merged, submerged, unemerged (unborn), or emerged, defined and created by others or by the self, struggling to be born or unborn.

Other histories are also exemplary of the self-creation process. As Inez heals others, she creates a self who heals and who is healed of her many betrayals; she gives life rather than being killed. Lorellen has experienced and introjected the split of other, her parents being polar opposites; her self is split in consequence, reflecting these opposites; the self has experienced much bodily damage, which can injure the spiritual aspect as well as her child's vital essence; something greater than herself, above and beyond, must help her, something that is pure life must overcome the death in her. Gwen, threatened with extinction from so many capricious sources, invents or becomes attuned to the psychic realm, where self cannot be destroyed. We do not know if this represents a split—she *does* distance herself from other by switching from "I" to "you."

We have found that two parents may be two sides of the self. If a parent dies, that side of the self dies as well or becomes frozen in time, idealized or forever condemned. Being immobile and lifeless, this is a death of self that must be overcome (see Elaine in Chapter 12). If two parents are extremely different and at war with each other, the conflict may be represented within the self of the child as a split; Lorellen and Lexie spring to mind as illustrations. When one is a child, one's parents are omniscient and omnipotent; the child is immortal by identification until she or he is an adolescent, when the parents, in effect, become destined to die; being like them is no guarantee of security, and adolescents must seek their own. When parents are split, which part will lead to security and which to destruction? Lorellen chose her father's path for a while; the result was devastating for him and for herself. The source of her split is comprehensible; now, possibly too late, she looks for security in her mother's way, in conventionality and stability.

It is clear from the histories that parents damage their children by *invalidating who they are*. Parents have dreams and expectations of their child; as the child deviates, the parents either resist or show delight. Invalidation can take many forms. For example, parents can try to make children into carbon copies of themselves or into ideals they have of how their children should be. Patty's father showed her how to eat, dress, and attend cultural events in order to join the level of the society at which he thought she belonged. She had to fight and rebel to become herself. For some children, the punishment of rebellion is so severe, threatening to the fragile existence of their selves, that they become inauthentic selves and experience self-destruction in madness (see Laing, 1976). Paula's parents tried to compel her and her brother to be who they were not; in compelling overachievement, they gave their children little opportunity to make mistakes and become competent on their own. Parents like Crista's force children to conform to an ideal, on pain of the parents' destruction; these children have difficulty finding out who they need to become; often they live years of being who they are not. Theo's mother was disapproving. She *created* a child of whom she would disapprove!

Many other accounts of invalidation show how damaging attacks on the true self can be. That Robin was required by her employer to take a lie detector test created the possibility that she was a liar and a thief, against which she had to fight, both externally and internally. That Gwen had to have a pelvic examination in her early teens created her as a possibly incestuous daughter, which she was not. These are traumatic experiences for the interviewees, because they may be being re-created by the other in ways they are not; their self-concepts are affected as well. And there is always a temptation to be as other perceives them, especially to obey or believe omniscient, omnipotent parents. By the same token, parents and others can create a positive identity by encouraging the child to become who she really is.

As we are treated, so we are created. The work of Rosenthal and Jacobson (1968) has made this frighteningly clear with their self-fulfilling prophecy experiments. This is why it is so difficult to fight against sexism and racism. It is hard to deny what others say you are; indeed, then you become one who denies the stereotype! In similar fashion, the abused self is created (see Chapter 10, on psychopathology).

We have also seen that when a daughter has been hurt by her parent, she seeks to heal the wound in herself by mothering her child, making a nest of her home like the one she never had. The re-creation of the family in the image of an ideal, or in the image of family past, is the effort of the parent, although sometimes the child does not cooperate. To comfort another is to feel comforted; to heal is to be healed. In this very real sense, what one does to another, one does to herself.

Members of the family, occasionally friends, and particularly siblings, become the alternate selves through which the self experiences the lives it might have lived, the self it might have become or might yet be. This is related to the notion of "possible selves" mentioned above (Markus & Nurius, 1986) and also Kohut's theory of twinship needs (1977). One woman (Sissy), from the security of her low-risk life and home, spent much of the interview discussing her sister, who was alcoholic, married several times, whose children had problems, but oddly enough seemed to be straightening out, and they loved their mother in spite of all. I kept trying to bring the interview back to what I *thought* was the topic; it finally dawned on me that this *was* the topic, that this woman had lived her sister's life as well as her own, vicariously, nonrisking, apparently puzzled to find in it something her own life lacked. Parents unwittingly cause a blurring between self and sibling by making unfavorable comparisons; if there is something wrong with who I am becoming, perhaps I should be more like my brother, but is that really me? I waver between becoming who I am and becoming who he is; I may compromise by trying to be a little of both, or I may reject who I am supposed to be entirely, even those aspects that are really me.

Babs "became" her sister-in-law as her assertive, social, successful self. We do not know how false this is, but it seems to be successful. We assume that Paula and her brother were both incompetent at survival tasks because they shared the overwhelmingly competent home; but there may have been considerable identification between them. A negative interaction between one parent and a child will be experienced by the sibling as applying to himself as well, even if he is the "good" one—witness the look of puzzlement on the "good" sibling's face when he wins approval at the expense of his brother. The message is double. "You are good and your brother is bad." "But I am my brother, so I am bad." Or "I must reject my brother, because I am so much like him, I may become bad." The importance of this identification of siblings with each other has been overlooked until very recently (see Bank & Kahn, 1982) in the concern for identification with parents; sibling influences must be recognized to understand the creation of self.

Thus, different family members are aspects of the self. When a self has identified with another self, cruelty, betrayal, or abuse by that other self is experienced as inflicted by one's own self as well. If I have defined myself in terms of another who abuses me, I abuse myself, and my self is an abuser. This explains many paradoxes, such as why an abusing parent was almost always abused as a child and usually vowed never to inflict such harm on his own children. Being abused by another, from whom he was not yet distinct, made him an abuser as well. His rage at the abused child is that the child continues to elicit the part of himself that he would rather not acknowledge. It is also the rage he felt as the abused—he hits back at his parent; the child's screams are his own but also those of his parent. Once again, self and other are not distinct. These boundary issues may become pathological.

Further, he has not worked through his own abuse as a child; when he hits his daughter, he is making the impossible demand that she somehow overcome his abuse of her, because then, metaphorically, she will be over-coming his own childhood abuse, fighting his own abusive parent, re-creating the abused self inside him into a fighter and avenger. Of course, she cannot do this, and her helplessness is his own, enraging him still further.

We *need* to live the lives of others as well as our own. We become less limited; we are renewed as parts of ourselves are created in the interchange of social relations. We are given more choices as we hear of other's choices. We help in the decision process of others, as well as our own. We are "reincarnated" into the lives of others before our own lives are ended. Costume parties are fun because we can become someone else for awhile.

Thus, the stuff or material from which the self is created is the self (including genetic components), the family, friends, the larger environment, and life events. The process of self-creation is the transcendence of loss, or the L/T process, which includes yearning, searching, replacing, and integrating the story or myth of who the self is, one example of this being the life history. It has been clearly shown in the histories so far that self-creation is a neverending process throughout the life span rather than ending at an arbitrary age. It is mainly within the searching and replacing stages that the choices, decisions, and commitments that will define the self are made—choices of occupation, mate, friends, clothes, hobbies. The self thus has considerable freedom as to who it will be, limited mainly by who it is now, the life crises or circumstances of the moment, and its own concept.

The self will experience itself and life as more meaningful the more alive or vital it is, and less meaningful the closer it moves to death and its metaphors on the life-death continuum. Newly created parts of the self may seem false (the imposter phenomenon). This is because we assume there is a solid self, which we experience as unchanging, and therefore any change may seem false. You can think back to an activity which is now an integral part of your life but which, when you first began, seemed doubtful. Perhaps you didn't like jogging when you first began; now you have several T-shirts, jogging pants and shoes, a rhythm, jogging friends, and you define yourself as partly a jogger. At first, when friends asked, you deprecated your efforts, saying you could only run a mile (or a block!). To do otherwise would have been to claim a false self. There is an idea that there is a one and only true self, created perhaps by God, meant to be, a self we have to find or get to know. This seems to be an illusion.

My self-concept is my idea of who I am. If I believe I am honest, I am more likely to return the extra $5 the grocery clerk unwittingly handed me in change. She will tell me I am honest. Thus both I, in my decision to return the money, and the clerk, in her praise and respect, will confirm my definition of myself. The reward of consistent behavior is self-definition, or being told that one has a self that really exists. Inconsistent parents tell children that the real existence of the other is in doubt and thus put their own existence as a unitary, consistent self in doubt as well. This is the source of the child's insecurity with inconsistency. Neither she nor her parents are real selves!

As we do, we become. Then we do as we have become.

It is a thesis of the L/T paradigm that the self is always in the process of becoming, creation, emergence, even birth, rather than being a fixed entity by a given age. However, analysis of the life reviews demonstrates that individuals differ in their sense of self; some, being relatively "unborn," are most loss oriented; others live alternate lives through other selves; others seem "split" or fragmented in Laing's sense (1976); and finally some have a more "kinesthetic" sense of wholeness, are integrated.

Thus, I tentatively offer four "types" of self and their modes of being in the world. First are the *unemerged*, like Tess, who are relatively unborn. Second are those who are *submerged* in the beings of another and whose modes are alternate lives, living the lives of another, like Robin and Sissy. Third are the *dismerged*, whose mode of being is to try to break away from the submerged; because they are only partly successful, they are split in two or fragmented into many, part of which is the real self, and part of which is false. Babs, Lorellen, and Lexie are good examples of this. Finally, there are the *emerged*, whose mode of being is integrated and whole, like Faith and Judith.

The types of selves are adaptive in their ways. The unemerged or unborn self is protected, unknowing in the womb, because that which is unborn cannot die. Even very young children develop a knowledge or awareness, from social cues, that they are dying (Bluebond-Langner, 1978) but, of course, the unborn do not. Those who live the lives of others are not restricted to their own and can remain distracted from their own deaths, secure in that they do not do what others do that leads to *their* deaths. The split (or fragmented or multiple) selves are more like the integrated, having different I's and me's not knit together, called upon for different protective tasks, much as were Billy Milligan's personalities (Keyes, 1981). The integrated have many me's and two major I's that are unity, a type of ego strength (Barron, 1979). These four types of selves can range from mild to severe pathology, according to cultural definitions, although the integrated selves have less pathology.

The above stages are structural and are not related to age. They are probably irreversible except in cases of organic pathology, such as organic brain disorder. They may form a hierarchy, because progressively less loss and more transcendence is involved. Most "lost" is the unemerged or "unborn" self, inauthentic, not knowing who she is, being what others tell her to be, not feeling a "sense of self." A bit farther along is the self who leads other people's lives and finds vicarious defeat and triumph, as well as puzzles that she cannot acknowledge in her own life. The split self can be a defense against an unborn self, the child forced to conform, to be a model child, until schizophrenia gives him other voices (see Laing, 1976). As we will see in Chapter 10 on psychopathology, much pathology is defensive, and the defense is against the greater annihilation of the structure of the self.

Since some of those who are split report themselves as having lived alternate lives in the past (as Babs did), and some of those who are integrated report having been split, there is a possibility that these are actual *stages* of self-creation; however, extensive research specifically addressing this possibility would have to be performed to confirm a stage theory of self.

The above theoretical material and empirical findings on the self have major implications for clinical intervention. As will be seen in Chapter 12, "Time and Death," it is a central proposition of the L/T approach that life is ever changing, that all change includes loss, that loss is a form of death, and therefore that all counseling is, in effect, bereavement or grief counseling. The individual is in mourning for loved ones or lost expectations, to be sure, but also for the part of the self that has died, that must move into the lost sector, because the roles, plans, hopes, dreams, and illusions have died as well. These losses must be assimilated and accommodated into the self structure. The clinician whose approach is L/T in nature, who recognizes life and self structures and processes and the L/T process and stages inherent in them, will treat and understand the whole person with a depth of analysis heretofore unavailable to him. The clinician will help his client in self-reflection and self-evaluation, to revise self-perception in a healthy manner, to redefine who she is and is becoming.

7

Life Meaning

In this chapter I discuss some of the philosophical issues underlying the question of life meaning. Then I briefly review the literature, the methods of this part of the study, and the findings. The histories of Patty, Alice, and Nora illustrate issues of meaning and meaninglessness; data implicating the "life review" as a process of meaning creation are presented. Finally, I draw conclusions within the context of existential philosophy and psychology.

INTRODUCTION: OF MEANING AND MYTH

Whenever we ask "What is the meaning of my life?" we perform an act of faith. Implicit in the question is the affirmation that there is, indeed, some meaning and that our task is only to discover it. Life is a mine, and its meaning is the ore laid down eons ago when the earth was new.

We slide over that far more devastating question "*Is* there a meaning to my life?" By answering the first question, we are better able to repress the second. By unilaterally defining the meaning of our existence, we may eliminate the necessity not only of determining whether that meaning really exists but also of facing the fact that the determination is impossible. We are like passengers at an airport who know when our flight is due to leave and its proposed trajectory, cruising altitude, destination, and estimated arrival time; for peace of mind, we must not ask whether it will fly and land at all! We repress alternative possibilities—crash on takeoff, rough winds, iced wings, innumerable engine malfunctions, a bomb in the luggage compartment, desperate hijackers. As Becker (1973) so eloquently argued, we *must* repress in order to continue living, or we could become immobilized, like the catatonic schizophrenic, by fear of the dangers that beset every phase of our existence. If queried, we rationalize by citing statistics showing that planes are safer than autos or the cigarettes the questioner is smoking; better still, we focus on the goal of our flight—the successful conclusion of a business transaction, a growth-enhancing vacation richly deserved, or reunion with a long-absent loved one. If our goals are worthy, then so is the means to them; our goals protect us from annihilation. They are like validation stamps on the risks we take. By giving meaning to the flight, they help us repress the question of whether or not it will take place. People who do not successfully repress cannot fly.

Yet, repression is never completely successful. We are not totally oblivious in every fiber of our being. Somewhere in our tensed muscles, our dreams, our acts of penitence, we know.

The question of meaning, then, is the question of ultimate purpose, of whether there is a goal toward which all the events of our lives, great and small, are inexorably driven. We ask if we, in our eventual though limited wisdom, or someone or something of higher wisdom, will see these seemingly disconnected happenings in some coherent pattern, if they are merely random scraps of cloth gathered together in random piles, or tapestries whose theme we are too close to discern but whose every figure, thread, and stitch is essential to a unique, inevitable, and meaningful design. As we live our lives, loss piles on loss, friends weave in and out, we move or are moved from one space to another, we love and leave or are left, we drop one occupation and take up another.

We need to know that our lives are a landscape, rather than a senseless spattering of paint on canvas. Such knowledge gives us the strength to continue.

When we ask if life has meaning, we are asking if our selves have meaning, if we are worth something or worthless. Life meaning is self meaning. "Is life worth living?" and "Am I worth living?" are two sides of the same question. The fact of death is a sign of worthlessness that we must overcome. We are probably asking, in addition, why there is pain and loss and whether the pleasures of life can outweigh the pain. If we answer in the negative, what is there to keep us alive—except perhaps the fear of death and dying? In feelings of worth lie our survival.

If life has no meaning, then it does not matter what we do with it. The choices over which we agonize are absurd. They are like throws of dice; they may catapult us into one series of events or another, and one series may be a happier one than another, or more disastrous. The immediate payoffs are to be dealt with in the moment only, but with no sense or logic to expectations, intentions, or ultimate consequences, which are always loss; the house always has the edge.

If God is dead, so are we.

Freud (1923, reprinted 1955) and others have noted that it is impossible to conceive of our own death in terms of our own nonexistence. We are conscious beings who cannot imagine nonconsciousness. Even when we sleep, we dream. If nonconsciousness is black, we still remember it as being so. It is just as difficult to conceive of life as meaningless, as a series of random events that have no pattern, that ultimately do not matter, because they matter very much to us and because we are always able to make some sense of the past. We are pattern-making creatures. And yet, there is the haunting possibility that we may see pattern and meaning where there are really none. This is the supreme terror—not death, not life with its myriad losses—but that the meaning we see is illusory, that we have "made it all up" and, like other acts of our creation, it can disintegrate. The illusion of meaning is the ultimate defense mechanism. It keeps us sane. The overuse or abuse of this illusion occurs in delusions of reference, paranoia, exaggerated defense.

Thus, imagining meaninglessness is perhaps as impossible as imagining one's own death. But if we cannot define meaninglessness, except to say that it is the absence of meaning, we can experience it. The meaningless experience may be either a trauma so overwhelming that we cannot deal with it or an event so minuscule as to go unnoticed, or so alien as to be noninterpretable within our personal paradigm. Meaninglessness is often our first reaction to personal tragedy. Why should a brilliant artist lose his sight at the height of his career? Why should a child so full of joy, potential, and love die of leukemia? Meaninglessness here is the lack of reason or justification. There is no cause for the effect. It makes no sense. Such meaninglessness may be so devastating as to require a major reintegration of life and self.

But there is another form of meaninglessness, and that is the way in which our lives relate to our selves, a kind of discrepancy between life and self. We may say, for example, that our work is meaningless because, as Marx pointed out (see Ollman, 1971), it may utilize only a small fraction of who we are, a hand making a few prescribed motions on the assembly line; we—that is, our selves—become alienated from our work, our work is strange and foreign to who we are; but then we also become alienated from the part of us that does the work, thus experiencing the modern fragmentation. When Laing (1976) speaks of the false self, he is alluding to a similar kind of split in our identity. The self, which we must present to the world in order to survive, is too different from who we are, who we think we are, or who we want to be. The fragmentation is like losing an arm or a leg, but it is a psychic loss. And yet such fragmentation may be defensive. The individual with a false self is too much at odds with who he really is and may split to defend himself, like a man whose arm, caught in machinery, must be amputated to save his life. Disowning parts of the self may salvage meaning from an otherwise meaningless existence. An example of the split self is Lexie, who describes herself as "two different people that haven't quite figured out how to meet."

It is far safer to see this meaning of our lives not as something we have created, but as a priori. We want to feel that our lives could not have been otherwise. This is the great attraction of astrology, divining of omens, and other forms of foretelling the future—not simply knowledge of what will happen, but the solace that it is predetermined, and this must be for a reason. We are comforted and protected by the belief that pain, loss, and disease are part of some grand plan, present at our birth. We would take umbrage at Julius Caesar's words, "The fault, dear Brutus, is not in our stars, but in ourselves" (Shakespeare, *Julius Caesar*, act 1, scene 2, lines 133–134), preferring to see our destinies in the fixed and eternal starscape, very much to blame! We want to think of ourselves as *discovering* a meaning that already exists, rather than *creating* it from the raw material of our lives. We have less confidence in our selves, our abilities to create, than we have in a God whom we may, indeed, have created.

If the meaning of our lives is determined at our birth, so too are the events. We are relieved of the responsibility of our choices, but we are also deprived of the freedom to make them. Our choices are, in a sense, already made for us, and if this is so we are incapable of morality. Our "goodness" and our "badness" are as original as sin in the Garden of Eden. This contradicts our phenomenological experience of having choice. And if we have choice, then the design of our lives is no longer fixed and immutable but is in the process of construction; we ourselves are the creators. (It may be, however, that our choices do not matter, that we grow as we are destined, from within, in spite of what occurs without.)

Even if some events in our lives were predestined, for instance, our meeting with a certain individual, it is possible that we do create the meaning of our lives; perhaps we were predestined to create it! Underlying our every choice is a value that, when we recognize it, tells us who and what we want to become. This value represents a judgment about the relative importance of various losses and the ways of transcending them. It is easiest to see this in our major choices, but if we examine even our most minor decisions, we can trace them back to a revelation of our major values. An analogy is Freud's (1901, reprinted 1960) tracing of minor slips of tongue and action to major conflicts.

For example, we may ask ourselves why we chose a certain occupation and respond that it paid well, it was interesting, we liked the people we would work with, it offered security, it was in the small town, or the exotic city, or the outdoors, we enjoy working with our hands, it was the only work available and we had a family to feed, and so on. If we then ask ourselves about the particular advantages of our work that we have mentioned—what it is about working with the land that is important—we get at underlying values. Examination of a group of choices in this manner clarifies our whole value structure, and we could even construct a hierarchy. These values will always say something about which losses are toughest to bear, which ways of transcending are better than others, and how we see ourselves and wish to see ourselves in relation to these. Thus, our value system is implicit in our metaphorical system; in fact, we could restate a metaphorical system in terms of values!

When we are in conflict, it is between underlying values and the differing life meanings that their enactment will yield. Which experience will yield more of what is transcendence to us, and which of loss? Sometimes, when we can recognize these, our choice is made easier.

We have given a meaning to our past. As today becomes yesterday, it takes its place in our logic of our life's design. Tomorrow will not be senseless, because there are always connections with today and yesterday, in our jobs, the people we know, and our own selves. If these connections are suddenly abrogated, if we wake up alone in the hospital remembering nothing, we will be "thrown" into the senselessness and panic that characterize the existential crisis (see Kierkegaard, 1946; Heidegger, 1962).

In my abnormal psychology classes I ask my students to perform an exercise popular in Gestalt psychotherapy. One student tells me, in front of the class, about some task he must perform. Then I have him reword the statement to the effect that he *chooses* to perform this task. "I *have* to go to work on Monday" becomes "I *want* to go to work on Monday." We discuss in some detail what will happen if he *doesn't* go to work on Monday. It is borne home to the students that all their actions are matters of choice, not necessity. By actions that promote their survival, they choose life over death, but they do not have to! Although this notion can be carried to extremes (in Chapter 10 I discuss thinking of the Holocaust in terms of choice), the viewpoint that we have much more responsibility for the course of our lives than we admit is helpful in seeing how our actions are based on values and how we operate within these values to create a life that is more or less meaningful.

While the creation of meaning is based on the values that underlie our transcendence of loss, that which we believe meaningful is implicitly stated in the story we tell ourselves of what we are about. We are each engaged in creating the myth of who we are, what we do, how we do it, and, most important perhaps, why we do it. The concept of self is formed out of this myth. The most important inheritor of the myth is therefore the self, because the myth specifies not only the shape, content, and quality of self but also how others will receive it. The self is engaged in constantly checking with others to be sure that the myth is correctly received and repeated. The frequent fact that it is not correctly repeated results in the "conflicting stories" we hear about divorce, presidents, and nations. A family myth may take precedence over an individual myth, for example, resulting in the scapegoating of an individual, laying responsibility for all that is wrong on one person, somewhat as Jesus took on Himself the sins of all humans. This may represent complete invalidation of the personal myth of the scapegoat, against which she may hopelessly argue and struggle. Or she may change her myth to conform with the family's, taking on herself the sins of the family and working through some kind of redemption. On the one hand, she is ousted by the family; on the other, she may preserve her membership by acceding. Meanwhile, the myths of the others are safeguarded, their salvation ensured, their unity affirmed.

The creation of meaning progresses with the creation of one's own myth over the life span. It is *about* the transcendence of loss. Referring ahead to our account of individual life span development, we can readily see that this begins with the progressive individuation of self from other, the definition of self as having bodily dimensions, as being able to accomplish various tasks. We can take as our prototype the infant girl who must gradually attain control over her environment, which ensures survival. She is learning who she is by the reactions she inspires in everything that is not herself, for example, the immobility of the dining room table against which she falls; she is the one who wants a cup of milk, pushes a doll from one place to another, buries her head in her mother's lap, and sucks her thumb. Already she is beginning the story of who she is according to the responses of her environment and what others tell her, how they react to her, as well as her own perceptions. These may be quite distorted, according to important others, like parents. The shadow over the chair is a ghost, and no matter how much the light shows it to be a coat, there is still something ghostly about it—it could change form, just as ice cream changes form. The surprising potential of some objects lends an unknown potential to others, limited only by imagination. She is learning what reality is, according to her culture. If she does not, she will be "insane."

At this point, the whole matter of "meaning" becomes crucial to competent living. Words have meanings; these meanings change with inflections of the voice or movements of the hand. Meanings are then linguistic, metaphorical, distorted, or far greater than they first appear. Too much inconsistency of meaning in the environment results in confusion, meanings inappropriately or inadequately learned, the extreme result of which may even be schizophrenia (Bateson, 1972). In Laing's paradigm (1976), if one cannot function adequately in the world because one cannot understand its meanings, one is threatened with annihilation. The only safety would lie in a closed feedback loop, that is, one's own, idiosyncratic meanings! In the individual whom we term psychologically impaired, communicated meanings are perceived in distorted form, and the creation of life meaning may then be immature, idiosyncratic, or fantastic (see *Pathways to madness*, Henry, 1971). We see evidence of this not only in schizophrenia but also in the cognitive aspects of depression, where the meaning of an event is interpreted with excessive pessimism (Adler, in Ansbacher & Ansbacher, 1959; Beck, Rush, Shaw, & Emery, 1980; Lazarus, 1966).

Our myth is our statement, to ourselves and to others, that our lives have meaning, and what that is. It is a way of adjusting reality to fit the illusion we have of ourselves as actualizing possibilities. Our friends accept our myth and perceive us less as who we are than as who we would like to be. Our enemies wound by trying to kill the myth. To be put on the defensive is to have to defend the myth against distortion by others. It is not only the father that Freud's sons murdered (1923, reprinted 1955) but also the myth he sought to perpetuate of himself in and through his sons. When we become disillusioned in a relationship with a friend, we are ceasing to see her as congruent with her own myth; we may very well be making up an alternative myth about her, one less threatening to the myth of our own self. Our friends may assist us. This is where the virtue of "talking out" a loss lies; it is a process of re-creation.

One of the major ways in which we create our myth of self is in the design of our appearance. As we shall see in Chapter 8, on individual development, teenagers try on new looks every day, "outlandish" clothing combinations that are more like costumes, sophisticated hairstyles, makeup that emphasizes eyes over mouth or vice versa, a sexy walk or business stride, artistic jewelry, simple handwriting or curlicues, a variety of knicknacks on the shelf. These make different and often contradictory or even clashing statements about who they are. Part of this is a matter of fashion, and the degree to which they are fashionable is also self-defining; but part is a way of discovering which *me* fits best, feels more comfortable, exciting, promising, or whatever is important, according to their values. Feedback from others regarding their different styles will help them decide. But they are choosing among images, the classical traditionalist, the rugged individualist or outdoor type, the exotic or artistic, the punk rebel; their clothes are chosen partly for convenience but mostly to convey the myth. The important result is that, by making such a statement of who she is, the individual is treated as such, which helps her in becoming who she wants to be.

In the final analysis we cannot answer with any certainty the question "What is the meaning of my life?" We create our own myth of meaning, but we never know if this mythic meaning is an illusion. If we seek consensual validation among our peers, we find it variable and unpredictable. They will validate what does not threaten them. In a sense, we are salespersons of our own myth; if we can convince others, they treat us as if the myth were true, and we become more persuaded of its validity ourselves. We are confirmed in the myth of our identity, that it matters, and why, achieving continuity or immortality of a sort.

We live our lives with the expectation of meaning. We persuade ourselves that what has been meaningful in the past will be so again. This is another manifestation of the fundamental illusion.

We live our lives as though they do have meaning, never knowing whether we live a lie or, indeed, whether we will ever know. This is the bedrock of faith. Most of us choose to live this meaningfulness, although some choose to regard the whole enterprise of existence as absurd (Sartre, 1964, 1969). Bishops James Pike (personal communication, 1951, 1968) believed that when one had a great deal of evidence pointing to a causal relationship, such as

that for the connection between smoking and cancer, it became *logical* to
make the small "leap of faith" to arrive at the suggested conclusion. In these
cases, irrational faith becomes the rational human activity. But disagreement
may exist over the extent of the evidence, for the cancer-smoking connection
or the life-meaning connection. Becker (1973) saw the human tragedy as
inherent in the singular knowledge that one will die. That that death and all
the other deaths which have been one's life may not have meaning compounds
the tragedy. Just as the soldier dies for something, one needs to feel one lives
for something, that suffering has value. If one does not live for something,
death also is meaningless.

Both individuals and institutions have defined the meaning of life in terms
of mystical transcendence of some type. Some religions promise an end to
death, life everlasting, Heaven, reincarnation, Nirvana, Satori—all some form
of being beyond this life, beyond small deaths or the great one, that is,
immortality in some form. There are rules to follow in order to attain escape
from meaninglessness, and following these rules confers meaning on life.
Such rules may include selfless love of others, kindness, ritual, prayer, meditation, self-flagellation, fasting, forsaking material comforts. Life's meaning
becomes escape from ultimate loss by embracing daily losses. It becomes
denial of much of the condition of living (see Becker, 1973).

BACKGROUND AND PROPOSALS

Traditionally, questions of life meaning and related issues of death meaning
have been the province of existentially oriented philosophers and religious
thinkers (Sartre, 1964; Tillich, 1952; Buber, 1961; Heidegger, 1962; Kierkegaard, 1946; Koestenbaum, 1976). Writers of fiction have also explored
questions of meaning, notably Tolstoy in *The death of Ivan Illych* (1960) and
Camus (1946, 1948). However, a number of existentially oriented clinical
psychologists and other social scientists have also defined life meaning as a
central problem of human existence (Frankl, 1963; Maddi, 1976; Binswanger,
1958; Boss, 1957; May, 1977; Becker, 1973; Laing, 1976; Moustakas, 1958;
Fromm, 1967; Gendlin, 1962). In the works of these writers, other centrally
related issues are stressed, such as courage, thrownness, dread, neurosis,
creativity, psychosis, death anxiety, aloneness, decision, freedom, responsibility, conflict, and commitment. However, no empirical study has addressed
issues of life meaning in a life span developmental context (see Weenolsen,
1982, 1985, 1987c).

In his splendid and comprehensive work synthesizing the fields of existential philosophy and psychology, Yalom (1981) summarizes the various
meanings of the phrase "life meaning." He sees them as falling into two
categories, which he terms "cosmic meaning" and "personal secular meaning,"
sometimes called "terrestrial meaning" by philosophers. According to Yalom,
cosmic meaning rests within Western religious traditions; the individual was

put on earth by a divine, all-knowing, and intentional entity; his or her life is part of the divine plan, and living in accordance with this plan will result in ultimate reward, the joyful transcendence of death. A sense of cosmic meaning "lifts the individual out" of him or herself and is, according to Frankl (1963),.far superior to secular meaning. Personal secular meaning is the purpose in an individual life, which Yalom believes is embodied in altruism (one of the defense mechanisms according to Vaillant, 1977), dedication to a cause, and creativity, which help the self go beyond the self, as well as hedonism and self-actualization, which are based within the self. Yalom believes that cosmic meaning is distinguished by a sense of coherence in the life plan, whereas personal secular meaning is distinguished by a sense of individual purpose.

Yalom (1981) agrees with Frankl that personal meaning that does not lead to self-transcendence, that is, hedonism and self-actualization, may actually make meaningful relationships impossible, because the individual is immersed in the self and cannot reach out. He speculates that "there is a gradual evolution of meanings throughout an individual's life cycle" from the teen preoccupation with self to Erikson's (1950) stage of generativity or concern with matters beyond the self. Yalom cites Vaillant's (1977) study and other evidence that altruism and self-transcendent behavior increase with age but concludes that many women have had altruism forced on them in younger years and evolve to a dangerous preoccupation with self in middle age (pp. 440–441)!

Although my empirical findings are congruent with Yalom's superb scholarly integration of philosophy and psychology, I believe that there are several problems with his life cycle discussion. First, I think it is dangerous to make value judgments on which type of life meaning is more desirable, higher, or better. Individuals who find or create cosmic meaning may be snuggling into the arms of a god who takes over much of the responsibility for their existence; or they may not have thought out their position but simply accepted it— dangerous when trauma and tragedy challenge beliefs, as they must; or they may be otherwise repressing, displacing, or employing Calvinist-like concepts to appear to be one of the elect. In other words, no system of meaning can be judged superior, even one that can nest individual purpose within cosmic plan, as my taxonomy suggests.

Second, Yalom makes the distinction between individual meaning as purposive and cosmic meaning as giving coherence. My findings suggest that the individual life meaning may include a sense of purpose *and* life coherence, the sense of purpose lending coherence to a life. The cosmic meaning often includes a sense of divine purpose, as we shall see. Yalom's important distinction between purpose and coherence is better served, I think, by applying both concepts to both types of meaning, cosmic and individual, and analyzing the life meanings in terms of both.

Third, Yalom's dismissal of women, as, in effect, regressing in their search for meaning as they grow older, is arguable. Their altruism has not necessarily been imposed; many women find personal and cosmic meaning in their nurturant roles; to say that in middle years many women become "concerned primarily with themselves rather than with others" is to forget their continuing roles as mothers, wives, children of aging parents, grandmothers, volunteers, and valuable contributors to the business community. There is evidence to suggest that white middle-class men in their forties may allow the more nurturant side of their selves to emerge (Levinson, 1978; Vaillant, 1977), and women may allow the more assertive side of their selves to emerge (Rubin, 1979; Livson, 1977); that in middle age the contrasex elements of men and women may be permitted expression (Jung, 1971); and that men may move toward more passive mastery of the environment, and women may move toward more active mastery (Guttman, 1968). However, a more accurate account of the experience of both men and women may be to say that altruism takes many forms, which include supporting a family or nurturing it. Nor must we overlook the fact that many people find self-fulfillment in altruism. Altruism is not necessarily the opposite of concern with self! Nor must we forget that many are more capable of concern for others when they start with a sure sense of identity as a base (Erikson, 1950; Vaillant, 1977; Laing, 1976). In *If you want to write* (1938, reprinted 1987), Brenda Ueland's main thesis is that it's important to do what we love; it is out of selves who are loving that we relate to others.

Finally, whereas Yalom's perception that the meaning of meaning may evolve over the life cycle is a laudable insight, and one that I have urged, I question his application of Erikson's theory. Adolescents and young and middle-aged adults are not only concerned with self necessarily. Concerns with community, the world, hunger, nuclear energy, racism, and pollution are extremely important to teenagers newly raised to the cognitive stage of formal operations. The increased interiority that Jung (1971) and Neugarten (1968) observe over the life span, the socially promulgated role of mentor, the social desirability of certain forms of "altruism" as roles, particularly in middle-class males, all make the entire issue of the evolution of personal meaning from self to self-transcendence complex.

Having taken exception to 2 pages out of 524, I would like to say that I think this book makes one of the major contributions to the fields of existentialism and human development.

In previous studies of life meaning, investigators have sought to define the topic for the interviewees, either explicitly or implicitly, or the interviewees have initially defined life meaning (cf. Crumbaugh & Maholick, 1974; Braun & Domino, 1978; Klinger, 1977). Although this is proper research procedure, it has the unfortunate result of creating the phenomenon whose existence it seeks to validate. In this study, the term was not defined and the *meaning* of life meaning was left to the interviewees. Self meaning was implicit in all questions of life meaning, according to this paradigm.

In this study, 11 issues concerning life (and self) meaning were investigated: (1) How pervasive is the belief that life has meaning? That it is meaningless? (2) What do people *mean* by the "meaning of life"? (3) What makes life meaningless? (4) Can we begin to develop a taxonomy of life meanings, one that is related to other major dimensions of the individual's life? (5) What is the relationship between belief in life meaning (and in one meaning specifically) and one's stage in the L/T process as well as (6) one's orientation to either loss or transcendence? (7) Is the life meaning reflected in the loss and transcendence life theme and, if so, how? (8) Is life meaning found (as Frankl, 1963, believed) or created? (9) If it is created, how? What is the *method* of meaning creation? (10) How conscious are individuals of the creation of meaning as a developmental task? (11) Can we trace the development of the *meaning* of meaning?

FINDINGS: LIFE AND SELF MEANING

Does Life Have Meaning?

The question that interviewees answered was, "Do you believe life has meaning?" As indicated above, great care was taken *not* to define terms. The results were as follows: 38 of 48 women responded that life did indeed have meaning, 8 said it did not, and 2 did not know. There were no significant differences by age or marital-employment status, an indication that the perception of life meaning is not necessarily an attribute of being single or married, employed or unemployed, old or young.

Definition and Classification of Meaning—A Taxonomy

The interviewees were asked, "When we talk about the meaning of life, how would you define it?" The definitions of meaning in the interviewees' answers could be categorized into four groups.

In the first group, it is clear that what the interviewees interpreted as "meaning" is a kind of cosmic purpose; the *purpose* of one's life is designed by, and residing in, a supreme being, and it is preordained. Della's views are typical of this position. She says, "I think God places us in each life to accomplish, to be fruitful, and for me that's our relationship with other people, that sharing Christ with them, sharing love with them. The only Bible that they might read, or the only Christ they might see might be in me."

In the second group there is still cosmic purpose, deriving from beyond the self, but it does not emanate from a divine being or plan; rather it is part of a process of ultimate personal, social, and spiritual growth. Lorellen exhibits this meaning when she says, "The meaning of life is evolution—personal, social, and spiritual". She sees this as part of a cosmic evolution, the development of humanity, and not simply in individual terms.

The third definition of meaning is still one of purpose, but it is a specific one that resides in the individual, such as an achievement of some kind or a goal, that is, in terms of what gives or would give meaning to that particular individual's life. Examples are "Education," "Doing something worthwhile for others in a service or philosophical way," and "I think we have to be productive, make a contribution of some kind." In each of these cases, the interviewee had been engaged in specific activities that reflected these meaning definitions. For example, at age 55 Ursula discovered that she was dyslexic, which explained her aborted education. She returned to school as she had always longed to do, took special training, and even won a short story contest. (See Chapter 8, on individual development, for her full history.)

Finally, the fourth group speaks of a personal purpose that is more general and not pursued via specific activities, such as "loving," "being happy," "sharing with friends," and "feelings of joy and love." To love, to share, to be joyful are values. They may be hedonistic or spiritual. They usually were not mentioned in the rest of the interview. The concentration is on being in the moment, rather than in the past or future. Purpose is immediate.

Thus, we have a fourfold taxonomy of "meaning of life" definitions, two originating beyond the self and two originating within the self. These can be labeled cosmic-specific, cosmic-general, individual-specific, and individual-general. The concept of purpose becomes one of values or "oughts" as the life meaning moves from cosmic-specific to individual-general. This suggests a taxonomy that might prove useful in further investigations.

Definition of Meaninglessness

"Is there anything without which life would be meaningless?" was a way of asking the question of meaning in reverse. Loss of love, not unexpectedly, headed the list; losses of love objects, of child, church, God, husband, friends, "others to share with" were stressed. Loss-oriented individuals tended to answer that life would be meaningless without something they had already lost or were currently in danger of losing, thereby inadvertently suggesting that their lives were meaningless. For example, a life without "love" would be meaningless for a number of interviewees whose protocols revealed great difficulty in retaining love or considerable loss of love. On the other hand, the transcendent individual might respond either with a loss she had never sustained or with a clear implication of attempting to overcome it. Example: "Loss of a child, loss of body capabilities, body health, or ability to get around. That would be a real *test* for me."

Another example: A woman who describes herself as a visual person tells us, "It would be very difficult for me to live without my eyes. I could be in a wheelchair easier, because for me the whole thing is seeing, and if I couldn't see, I just don't know where I'd put my focus. I know I would live, but it would change everything that I know is me. I could give up my legs." From one who transcends through communication, especially reading: "Losing my sight would be almost tragic. Although there are many sightless people that get along in this world I'd have to learn braille right away, because what would I do without reading? I love to read." From one who faces the possibility of needing to take control of her senile mother: "I think at the point when I had lost all of my faculties, then life is meaningless. I never want to be in a position where someone has to take total physical care of me." From a woman for whom restriction of independence was thematic: "If I were locked away in some prison and couldn't see the outside. If I couldn't or didn't have access to people over a long period of time. Maybe I could go to Alaska for lots of money and do some technical work, and be isolated, but it wouldn't be something I could do all my life. I'd have to be able to get back to people and have relationships." From another, separated from her child, partly for the child's welfare, and who transcends through religion: "God. I've even questioned whether or not I could do without my son, and he would be the next one I would answer." (How did you happen to question that?) "Just in proposing how much of a commitment I was making to God, if God should make that decision that I would be without my son, even if his physical being, or through death, that I would be separated from him. It seemed like that was a questioning in seeing if I really had given everything up for Christ. You can talk about that 'til you're blue, if faced with that, I'm not sure how I'd react. But because I believe that He wants our ultimate good, He would only do that if He thought that was best." Other things without which life would be meaningless are the ocean; the sun; emotions; moments of joy; love, friendship, and affection; and happiness. Finally: "You have to have a response from life. I think that's why some people are so unhappy, is that they don't see any results from their being there. If you can once get a person to feel that their being alive makes a difference, even if it's a very small thing"— from a woman who volunteers actively in suicide prevention.

Relationship to Loss and Transcendence

Loss-oriented individuals tell their histories mostly in terms of the losses they have sustained. Transcendence-oriented individuals recount their lives in terms of overcoming and growth. There was a tendency among the loss oriented, or those who were struggling with a particular loss that was thematic of the protocol, to answer that life had meaning in terms of a positive outcome to their struggle. For example, the answer that love was the meaning of life was given by a number of respondents in whom repeated loss of love was thematic of their lives. Implicitly, they were therefore suggesting that life might not have meaning, because it seemed filled with loss of love. The loss oriented answered in terms of what they did not have, whereas the transcendence oriented replied in terms of losses overcome. Those who answered in terms of their losses were in the grieving or searching stage of the L/T process.

Those who saw their lives in terms of overcoming and re-creation were in the replacing or reintegrating stage. These responses were often reflected in the L/T life theme.

Life Meaning Found or Created?

Frankl (1963) believed that individuals must search for and find the meaning of their lives, which for him originated in divine design (the cosmic-specific class of the above taxonomy); to say that individuals can invent meaning was, to him, absurd. Frankl's position seems incongruous with the existential view that, even though individuals are "thrown" into their particular life circumstances (Heidegger, 1962), they must take responsibility for how they respond, for their own decisions, conflicts, and commitments—indeed, they create their own meaningful lives and selves in this sense.

In this study, those who believe that meaning originated in divine design, and who simply trusted in this, did not see themselves as creating life meaning. But those who saw life meaning in terms of spiritual growth, specific life purposes, or general abstract goals, such as happiness, were much more likely to see themselves as active in life meaning creation.

Life Review as Process of Meaning Creation

One method of life and self meaning creation seems to be the process of life review. There is some disagreement in the clinical and popular literature as to whether this is an end-of-life phenomenon or an ongoing, lifelong process. Butler and Lewis (1983) see the life review as a universal phenomenon during the final years. It results in depression or acceptance. This process of reminiscence does not necessarily happen in therapy but can be conducted with friends or alone. It may include creative products or working out problems with relationships, and Butler and Lewis see it as a healing process. There is also a popular view. The 65-year-old man retires and writes his autobiography, entitling it something like "Summing up"; the dying woman conducts a life review with a therapist to come to terms with her life. However, both Sarbin (1986) and Gergen and Davis (1985) have indicated the belief that, viewed as a personal narrative, there is support for the notion of continuity over the life span.

I have found that individuals report they are conducting a virtually continuous review throughout their lives and that this is what forms the conscious process of meaning creation. The interviewees were asked whether they ever conducted a life review similar to the life history they had just completed, at what age they had started thinking about such questions, what importance they attributed to the life review, and its uses. Seventy-one percent reported that they think about such questions often or occasionally, 29 percent reported that they think about them rarely or never, only one claiming that she never thought about such questions. It is, of course, possible that those who review their lives rarely or never do so in a different manner, by fragmented accounts to friends or reflection on different issues. On the other hand, those who agree to participate in this kind of study might be more inclined to introspective evaluation than those who do not volunteer.

Neither age nor loss-transcendence status seemed to be associated with frequency of life review. Women of all ages, marital-employment groups, and loss-transcendence orientations felt a life review was important—98 percent of our sample—thus its importance is not restricted to older people or those who are loss oriented, as is perhaps popularly believed. The reasons for reviewing their lives fell into three categories: planning for a better future, dealing with present problems, and wrestling with philosophical issues such as the ultimate meaning of life and self or the evaluation of how they are doing in reference to good-bad criteria.

Most interviewees report having engaged in the process of life review from before the age of 30. Most also reported that their life reviews had increased or stayed the same as they grew older, rather than decreasing. However, four interviewees expressed a caveat. They observed that too much review of one's life could be not only depressing but also possibly somewhat paralyzing. The feeling was that one must get on with the business of life: "You can dwell on things too much." "You can't change the past." "You shouldn't go through life not weighing things, but don't dwell on things." "I firmly feel that you oughta kind of forget yesterday. Tomorrow is important . . . you don't rest on past laurels. . . . I hate to dredge up downers. . . . You tend to lose your self-confidence."

It is apparent from the data that the life review as it is conducted across the life span serves several purposes. First, it is a form of rationalizing, reordering, or reconstructing reality along thematic lines. It is a method of mythologizing. The man who gives his friends a blow-by-blow account of how he was fired from his job is not objective; the boss's words are rearranged, the customer's complaint is subtly blown up to seem even more unreasonable; the loyal co-worker's praise of his past record becomes more high-flown. Indeed, members of his family who must hear the tale told a number of times might notice the subtle changes the story undergoes at each retelling, were it not for the part they themselves are taking in the construction of the myth. If the boss were to hear the new story a few months later, he might not recognize himself, the employee, the incident, or even the company!

The second purpose of the life review is to form a platform from which to launch future conduct. Evaluation of where we have been in relation to where we want to be, where we are, how we got there, and lessons that have been learned—all are considered by many to assist and guide decisions regarding the future. Third, and related to the other two, is the purpose of evaluation or judgment of the congruence between our behaviors and our standards, and the possible readjustment of either our perception of our behavior, or our actual behavior, to agree more closely with our values.

Two additional points must be made regarding the life review. First, it is probably not always a conscious or deliberate process. For example, the mere telling of a section of our life to a friend is a life review of sorts and accomplishes some of the same goals. It is part of the process of evaluation and myth construction. Second, the quality of the life review may be different at different ages; indeed, it may be quite different at the end of life, when one is facing death. There may be more of an urgency to complete the story in final draft!

Development of Meaning

We can turn to the literature of life span development to see how the notion of meaning develops. (For a discussion of many facets of this question, see Lee & Noam, 1983.)

Meaning requires interpretation, and we interpret our life events according to our individual paradigms or theories. From birth to death, each of us is engaged in the continuous process of seeking to make sense of our life experience. As infants we begin to construct our own pretheories about the world out of the information that comes to us through our senses (Piaget, 1952). We find that a certain smell, a certain touch to the lips, the feeling of liquid trickling down our throats are all associated with comfort, warmth, drowsiness, and content. This is our world and the meaning of it. As we grow older, we read the meaning of an angry or smiling face, we learn that "hi!" is approach or nearing, that "all gone" is disappearance, and all the other symbolism of language. Things have functions; they are to be used for certain purposes and not for others. Later, ideas, such as fairies and goblins, can exist without sensory referents.

Thus, gradually, life experiences and their interpretation exhibit rules; they become instrumental, semantic, symbolic, conceptual, and metaphorical, as well as sensory—the product of an increasingly complex organism interacting dialectically with the world. A person or object represents not only itself but also our relationship to it, its relationship to other objects as well as other selves, and finally its place in a world of which we are continuously attempting to create some meaning or make some sense. The meaning of experience is created on different levels at different stages of development. Fire warms the 2-year-old, but it may also cook the food or burn the hand. The teenager understands very well what is meant by "lighting my fire," whose burn may be infinitely more painful than that of the fire on the hearth. To the adult, fire may also consume or purge, may burn white-hot in the noon of life, or may be more peacefully banked in the evening.

Eventually, we move to a point where the "meaningful" takes on larger connotations. We ask if life has meaning, or makes sense, because we become capable of envisioning an entire lifetime in the context of its limitations, that is, its metaphorical deaths. We deplore the meaningless tragedy. We cannot "understand" or "comprehend" the deaths of 6 million in the Holocaust. To die may seem absurd. "Life has no meaning." This requires a vast restructuring of 'life, self, meaning, and the rules for construction of that meaning. We develop a system of beliefs, values, and attitudes, our philosophy, by which we evaluate our lives as worthy of continuing or not. ("Unworthiness" leads to psychopathology.)

LIFE HISTORIES

The following histories of Patty, Alice, and Nora further illustrate the premise that life meaning and meaninglessness are related to losses and their transcendence. Loss, for example, of love, is associated with meaninglessness and transcendence with meaningfulness. This is further confirmation that life-self meaning is created through the transcendence of loss.

Patty

"It made us realize, after experiencing so much death . . . I think to appreciate more of the here and now. . . . To have a child is really a miracle."

Pregnant and in her early thirties, Patty talks to me in her kitchen, between many phone inquiries about the sensorimotor development classes she runs for normal preschool children.

Patty's father came from a wealthy family; his father was famous for his inventions. However, Patty's father felt that wealth destroys, because he had seen so much alcoholism and infidelity. He was a truck driver and then became a successful salesman, but he banked his money rather than spending it ostentatiously. Patty had a very good relationship with him. He encouraged her to read and taught her not to lie, especially to "your parents, your doctor and your attorney," or they couldn't help you when you had a problem. His family had all died when he was young. "It was extremely important that I learn to be independent, because there was nobody in the family that my parents wanted me to live with in the event of their mutual death. . . . [It] would have meant . . . a foster situation. . . . So they wanted me to be able to care for me. . . . When it came to making a decision about can I go some place, or can I have a quarter, or can I go to the show with my friend, can I ride my bike alone—it was kinda put back on me. Do you think that's a good decision? So at an early age I had to take responsibility for my actions. The consequences of those actions . . . good or bad—they were always there to help me out in case I blew it. But it was: 'Let her blow a lot, and let her figure it out'."

Patty's mother was mechanically inclined, an artist who had not been able to afford art school but had continued her art and also made Patty's clothes, "the source of greatest joy to me." Her father was kind and sentimental, but her mother was not. "He and I would watch a movie, and sit there and cry, and Mother'd say: 'Come on, you guys, it's just a movie'." Her mother and father never said a cross word to each other, but Patty now realizes "they must have kept up a great front. I never ever saw them contradict each other . . . talk back . . . swear. . . . I never remember hearing raised voices."

Patty lived in the same middle-class house and neighborhood most of her life. She had eye and teeth problems as a child, and because she was not well coordinated, she was a poor athlete. Her mother and teachers tended to be protective of her. She sees the same kind of overprotection in her parents' attitude toward her young child, whom she describes as a "high risk-taker"; her pediatrician predicts casts and stitches. "Perhaps I overcompensated," for her own protected childhood by allowing her daughter "a lot of freedom." When her daughter climbs, her parents tell her to stop or she'll fall, and Patty sees this as inculcating the same lack of self-confidence she experienced as a child, feeling that she is seeing in her parents' treatment of her daughter how she herself was raised.

Another special relationship for Patty in her childhood was with her grandmother, who cooked special dishes for her, picked flowers with her, and was a great companion.

A major problem for Patty was her lack of self-confidence, particularly in athletic and academic situations. "I was put in with the smart kids, but I wasn't the one walking around with the 130 IQ. So I was in the top group, but the bottom of the top group. . . . I could never perform to where the top kids were performing." Patty feels her mother gave her a sense of appreciation for art, as well as "sticktuitiveness," but made her feel inferior without meaning to, because she couldn't do crafts as well as her mother. "I see some of the things that I did not commit myself to do because of fear that I was going to become injured. I felt I really missed some enriching opportunities."

When Patty reached junior high, she became aware of racism. She was no longer allowed to play with her best friend because her friend looked Mexican. However, Patty became successful academically and popular in school. "I finally figured out the school game. Basically, you make the teacher feel really good about themselves, and you're always really nice to them, and very polite, and have your homework done on time, blah, blah, blah, and you're going to succeed. That's where it was at. I no longer decided I had to be brilliant. I just had to play the game." Patty got "talked into" running for student body president in high school. She was the only girl running for a high office. It was between herself and a boy, "a jock, but he was really stupid." She had a lot of friends who told her she'd won the election in their homerooms, plus the vice-principal of the school, who told her she'd won overall and called her parents with the good news. The next day it was announced that the boy had won. Years later she found out her father had visited the principal to ask what had happened. He just "could not accept the fact of a girl being a student body president," so had given the victory to the boy. Patty was devastated by this experience and never went out for elections again.

By the time she got to high school, it was clear that Patty's father had plans for her future. He would bring home notebooks from a renowned university and say, "There's no reason why you can't become a biologist . . . [or] a chemist. You'd love chemistry." His only hope was that "you never try to be a goddam school teacher. . . . I've never known one that ever had enough sense to pour piss out of a boot." Patty responded that he didn't have to worry, she was going to "get married and live happily ever after." However, she wasn't as confident as she sounded. "I was feeling ugly. I had a definite case of the uglies. I was skinny, my hair was [not] blonde. I was nearsighted. I had to wear glasses and just didn't feel attractive. And I was no longer feeling real smart because my grades were beginning to slip." She got up the nerve to ask a boy to go to a dance, and they dated regularly after that. "That's what I needed—a boyfriend. I needed some self-confidence." She managed to put on some weight, and she was feeling "womanly" because she had her first sexual contacts with this boy. "He really felt he was in love with me, and I was not really convinced I was in love with him, but I was in love with the idea of having a boyfriend, and . . . with the idea of Friday night getting to get dressed up to go out . . . to the college activities . . . to a movie . . . with a boy. . . . Until he started getting really possessive during the summer, and I realized . . . it was getting down to, was I going to lose my virginity to this man?" They broke up. She persuaded her mother to let her bleach her hair and cut it. "Contacts and bleached hair, I mean, I was a different person!"

She met another young man to whom she was strongly attracted—"animal magnetism." Fearing he might be Mexican because he was so dark, she brought him home for approval. Her parents approved, and they fell in love. However, neighbors started putting pressure on her parents to break them up because, even though he was not Mexican, he looked it. "How could I degrade my parents dating this Mexican?" So they broke up, got together, broke up again. She went to college, and he enlisted. She dated up a storm and had "many sexual encounters." Her father gave her all the money she needed for college. He was still "breeding me to be the rich man's wife. We would take two weeks off and go to San Francisco to see a play, go to the Hilton. Then my dad would spend money. That's when the money would come out. 'I'm going to teach you how to eat, and how you drink, and how you dance in public, and this is how you go to the theater. . . . And this is how you go to the museum.' And he took me to Columbia and showed me where he went to school. 'You know, this is available, Patty, you just have to pull it together to get here.' So they made a real effort to show me that I didn't have to be a housewife in a small town. That they had the money, the means, the expertise to offer me more than that."

In college, Patty had another boyfriend who fell in love with her and wanted to marry her. He bought her an engagement ring, "and I just felt terrible about it." She said, "Oh, my god, I can't really marry you. Did you think I was going to marry you?" At college she also met blacks and Jews, and by her junior year she realized she wasn't married and had better start thinking about her future. She decided to teach elementary school, and subsequently her grades, which had been low, shot up.

It had been 3 years since Patty had seen her old Mexican-looking boyfriend. He came back from Vietnam and "I told my parents, you know, I'm twenty years old, I'm going to see him, period. You can withdraw my fees, you can kick me out of the house. . . . I've waited three years, I have dated twenty men, professors, teachers, athletes, students. . . . I want to see him." So they dated and decided to live together. In retrospect, Patty feels that the fight with her parents to stay with her boyfriend made her a strong person and was therefore good for her. He got an entry-level job, but "basically he came back from Vietnam a very different person, a very violent person. He drank a lot. He'd go from being very passionate, being very cold, being very withdrawn. I couldn't take it. It was like, you need some help, isn't there someone in the VA that helps you guys that wake up at night screaming [laughs]? He wasn't really willing to admit that he had a problem." They broke up. "I just said, God, how could I ever marry this person? He's crazy!" Patty continued dating in college and got pregnant. "At this point you did not practice birth control" in this particular state. "You could not get birth control without your parents' signature. Even though you were twenty-one years old, it didn't matter. You were not married."

Patty was about to graduate from college and start a new job. She had to tell her parents about her pregnancy, but, to her surprise, they took it very well, with no recriminations. "They bought me a trip to England for a graduation present, and my mom and I were going to London for an abortion. . . . We had a wonderful time." She was feeling guilty and assured them that she was pregnant by a boy she hardly knew, which was the truth, rather than by the boyfriend to whom they objected. "We were walking into the abortion clinic. My mother leans over and says: 'Well, don't feel too bad. Actually, you're pretty lucky. I had to go through this when I was fifteen, when I was alone!' It was like, I thought I knew everything about my mother in the whole world. . . . She knew when I was in college I was active sexually. We would laugh about it. You know, this guy was a jerk, he was great, or whatever. I just looked at her and I don't believe it. It was like we really touched base, really connected." The rest of the trip was a positive experience.

Some time after this experience Patty married her old boyfriend, but the relationship was a tragic one. She watched him hurt a dog he loved, alienate himself from his parents, and destroy everything that meant something to him. She realized she could not help him and was herself "losing contact with reality." She supported him for 2 years and did all she could for him, to no avail. The final incident? "He threw a glass at me, and I thought, that's just past my face. . . . He was waking up at night shaking and screaming. It was really sad to have seen this person just destroyed. Anyway, so I realized, you know, this guy could kill me. As much as I love him, I'll always love him, he's going to kill me." So she left, went to stay with a friend, and filed for divorce. Some time later he called her and begged her to take him back, said he was seeing a therapist. But she figured she'd been in love with him for 10 years and had to do something else. "I just have to pretend like he's dead," although he isn't—he's married to someone else.

"I met my present husband in a human relations workshop. By then a lot of this hurt had healed. I wanted a relationship, I wanted a child. I wanted a family." She realized her husband was the type of person she wanted to marry, someone who was "pretty even" and who could work things out verbally. The decision was more of an intellectual than an emotional one for them both, but it's worked out well. They have one child and are expecting another.

After her first child, Patty got pregnant again. The "child was born with many anomalies, and did not live more than a couple of hours. It was just extremely devastating to both of us. It was the compounded guilt of not wanting the child in the first place." The baby had not been active while she was carrying it, she had bled, and there had been confusion as to when it was due. But "you face in this life what you're dealt. . . . I just thought, something is wrong . . . I had this mess that was a boy." Not long after this, within a few months of each other, three of her husband's closest relatives died. "My husband's afraid to have another child. He couldn't take another loss." They found themselves putting all their hopes and dreams into their daughter, and "it isn't healthy for her. . . . I felt like we needed rejuvenation in this family," so she secretly got drunk one day, came home, and said: "Let's make love." She left out her diaphragm, and announced a few weeks later that she was pregnant. "I think deep down he is happy, and if he ever confronted me with, did you do that intentionally, I would certainly 'fess up. . . . It's the only time I've ever been deceitful with him." In some ways, their year of deaths has enriched their lives. "It made us look at life. I mean, this year we couldn't afford it, but damn we got on the plane and went to Disneyland on Christmas. I mean, why wait until your kid's old enough to remember it? I may not be here six years from now, he may not. Let's do it now . . . charge it and go. So what if it takes us four months to pay for it. Once in a while let's do it. And I think that's been a healthy turnabout for us. It's made us realize after experiencing so much death so quickly, it's got us to an attorney and had a will made, and that kind of thing. . . . I think to appreciate more of the here and now. And also to appreciate our daughter. To have a child is really a miracle [laughs]. It does work. So, anyhow, the last years have been heavy."

Patty started her own business running an athletic program for preschoolers. "I'm right out in front. If I blow it, it's so obviously me. I have all of my retirement money in it. So if my business doesn't make it, my old age, the security of it, is questionable." So far she is successful.

Patty talks of what she's learned, having a child. "All those years of being a teacher, it was so easy to tell parents: 'If you would just do this. . . [laughs]. Now I look back, I think, oh my god, how did I ever be so naive. You don't know until you have your own. It's humbling."

Patty regrets never having developed a hobby, because she misses a sense of creating. She also regrets having hurt people, like the student who wanted to marry her, and also "I have used people for my own self-interest. That I regret. I don't like to use people."

When asked what she thinks death will be like, she responds, "That's the last door we open [laughs]. I think I probably feared it a lot more until I'd seen so much of it." She watched her grandmother and her mother-in-law die, she herself having just given birth, and although these were opposite experiences, there was a resemblance. A baby lacks control and is gaining it, control of its arms and legs; someone who is dying has control and is losing it. "Truly, she was stepping beyond." Patty's other grandmother is being kept "zapped up on 30–40 milligrams of Thorazine three times a day. She's 90 years old. She's just sitting there like a zombie now. And I think, why doesn't somebody O.D. her? I wish they would let her die. She's physically fine, but she's going to start starving herself, because she's so out of it she can't eat."

As for the meaning of life, Patty sees it as "how we act in a given circumstance—our total response to our environment, to all of the stimuli around"—individual-general. Life becomes meaningless when we lose control of our environment, Patty feels. "For myself, I feel like each of the major tragic points in my life—they're still there, and they're always going to hurt, and that's what being alive is. You go to your grave with your hurts and your joys." She feels as though the whole civil rights movement influenced her life. "Like my parents were selling me a bill of goods about the whole status thing, and it was always, you accept people for who they are. I managed to get out past from where they are."

Patty's L/T life theme emerges from her losses through multiple family deaths over a relatively short period of time, as well as the loss to insanity of the man she loved—she must pretend he is dead. There are also losses through pretenses, surfaces and appearances of things, which are connected with these deaths. Her transcendence is through both the birth of children and her work with children; indeed, she states that her highest peak experience has been "giving birth." In the L/T paradigm, pretense is inauthentic and therefore a form of not being one's self, or death. The core theme, then, is death versus birth.

Patty's protocol is rated as transcendence-oriented, in the replacing stage. But the stages of grieving and searching are still clearly visible.

Theoretical analysis

In some lives, the perpetual conflict between life and death is less metaphorical and more overt. Because there has been so much death in Patty's life, it cannot be far from her thoughts, and extraordinary measures must be taken to keep death at bay a little longer and more effectively.

The history of off-time loss due to death began with Patty's father; he lost most of his family when he was very young. This may be why he and his wife took rather unusual precautions to provide for Patty if their deaths, too, should be untimely—discussing the subject, molding her character to be responsible early on, looking toward who might raise her. Patty seems to have grown up in a family where death was regarded as possibly an off-time or time-irrelevant event, rather than on time—the common method of defending against death. In this context, even small decisions, such as going to a movie with a friend or riding her bike alone, were training in responsibility for herself, because the deaths of her parents could leave her with these decisions at any time. These decisions could also, of course, lead to her own death, since death was capricious. As we have seen, the child only gradually achieves an identity separate from the parents. If death could come to them at any time, it could come to Patty.

Another feature of Patty's upbringing was the tension between pretense, or lying about who one is, and telling the truth. Patty's father had been reared in a well-to-do home, where he saw what he considered to be the evils of wealth—alcoholism, infidelity, and disillusionment. When he himself became well-to-do, he first eschewed the trappings of money, banking it instead. This may have been a way of keeping the evils of money at bay, by denying his wealth. If you don't show it, you don't have it (a kind of reversal of the Calvinistic approach in which to display goodness worthy of being among the elect is to give the illusion to self and others that one *is*!). This defense is rooted in the magical child and is a form of both denial and reaction formation.

Patty's father seems to have reacted against pretentiousness by pretending not to have the capacity for it. However, later in Patty's life, things seem to have changed. There was the racism, the concern for appearances when she was dating someone who simply looked unacceptable (Mexican) but was in actuality of Mediterranean extraction. There was the unveiling to her of her possible new position in life, that her parents could purchase for her a status superior to that for which her childhood in a small town seemed to have destined her. It was as if the childhood was all pretense, and now the high-prestige university, money, and professional career were all the realities to which she was entitled. But which was authentic and which was sham? Identity was endangered here. (See Henry, 1971.)

In the L/T paradigm, pretense of any kind is inauthentic behavior; it is being not who you are, but how you want to appear to others. It is being who others want you to be. It endows others with the power to create your self, instead of your retaining that power. Others will create in their own image, because this is what they know, rather than growing you from the *seed* of you, developing you from who you really are and can be. Or others create you in the image of one who will defend their own being; if you are generous, to whom will you give? To me, of course, and therefore I will endeavor to make you generous! In this way the self as object, the me's or roles, all define who the self is, and the part becomes the whole. Self as subject can be lost. Pretense as inauthenticity is then a form of death of self, one with which we all contend to a greater or lesser degree. For Patty, the pretense was a major facet of her L/T life theme, one that she feels she has gotten beyond; she apparently does not see as pretense the deception over her present pregnancy.

Patty's father does caution her that there are people with whom it is unwise to pretend—family, doctors, and lawyers. If they do not know the real self, how can they help that self when it is in trouble? If you have deceived the very important people in your life, they know a false self whom they will cultivate, protect, and nourish instead of the true self. The great danger of pretense, of course, is that, assisted by others, you become who you are not, instead of who you are. Pretense as defense was originally used by Patty's father to defend against other forms of death—alcoholism and infidelity— although one suspects that his parents used it as well. But this defense, cautions her father, must be used selectively, or it can turn on you.

Can death find the real you among all your disguises? If death kills off the person you pretend to be, are you safe? If life is a costume ball, will death be fooled into accepting the mask, so that the real you can escape? If you constantly deny yourself, saying, "It's not me, it's someone else," you may escape death by being no one—by not being. One way of avoiding death is to kill yourself. All the children we never had cannot die.

Patty and her husband had a series of deaths in their family. What had happened to Patty's father, what he had feared would happen to her in childhood, actually happened to her and her husband—the deaths of important relatives, primarily her husband's, over a short period. The most devastating was the birth of a "mess of a son" with many anomalies, who died shortly after.

This was especially devastating, because Patty has given birth to transcend death; she gives birth to children by training their sensorimotor development— completing them, as it were—as well as by having her own children. She teaches in defiance of her father's contempt for the profession (she has taught elementary school as well). She has been forced to kill one child, although it brought her closer to her mother, and now there is another child who never would have been completed had she not taken such good care of herself. In this she is guilty. So, like her father, she uses the defense of pretense and pretends to her husband that she accidentally left out the diaphragm. She does this in the context of all the recent deaths. Their family needs "rejuvenation." She does it for their daughter, on whom they have come to depend too much for life. Patty is overcoming death by using the only weapon she knows that is stronger, and that is birth.

For Patty, watching her relatives die was clearly a reversal of the birth process, another side of the coin, antithetical and yet the same. The newborn comes into the world without physical control and gains it; the old person goes out of the world losing it. She seems to sense a coming and going from the same place. She reports, as many do, feeling better about death after being in its presence. It is less fearsome.

In the first pages of this book we asked how, in a life filled with death, one could create meaning. For Patty, birth, with its metaphors, is the way.

Alice

"I had some adventurous view of myself as a female white knight on the horse [laughs], running to people's rescue and righting wrongs. . . . What I'm angry about is . . . that this happened to my kid . . . and I feel he got cheated."

Alice, in her mid-forties, bright and witty, lives in a beautifully appointed city apartment overlooking the ocean. A gourmet cook, she is preparing some of her specialties, offering me tastes. Two little boys, aged 3 and 4, play in the adjoining family room. The 3-year-old, David, is good-looking, very quiet, sober, a model child throughout the 5-hour interview. The 4-year-old, Jeffy, has Down's syndrome, and is an affectionate, exuberant boy who is insistently into everything, including my tape recorder. He's a handful, and Alice grows impatient with him.

Adopted at birth, Alice begins the interview by observing that, as a child, she was a tomboy, accident prone, and was hit by a car. (It is common for people to announce at least one pole of their L/T life theme in the first sentence or two of the interview, without, of course, being aware of it.) She welcomed the birth of her slightly handicapped brother, but felt jealous because her parents spoiled him, and she felt pushed aside. However, she articulated her feelings to her parents and felt this situation was resolved.

Generally Alice was a happy, inquisitive child, talented in arts and crafts. "I did have a temper, however [laughs] . . . I have always been infuriated by anything I saw as injustice, and as you know there's quite a bit of it around, so I often lost my temper." When a handicapped girl was deliberately tripped at school, Alice almost "tore the head off" the malefactor. "I had some adventurous view of myself as a female white knight on the horse [laughs], running to people's rescue and righting wrongs, and all of that. I was so patriotic and caught up in God, country, flag—anything, any cause could bring me to tears of sentiment [laughs]."

Alice was closer to her mother than her father, who seemed rather distant, gruff, and conservative. They lived in a "controlled, moderate, rather quiet household," and she mistakenly thought they were poor. She regrets that she was too sheltered as a child, because she didn't learn until later in her twenties "what the world was really like." Her mother kept "trying to make me into the lady that she thought I would be. She had a little difficult job on her hands, there. I admire her tenacity. She certainly was inventive about trying new approaches. But she was, however, very narrow in her view about what a person should be . . . and so she hung some pretty good guilt trips on me. . . . And I thought she was absolutely right. I always had the feeling of needing to fight to be me." Although she appeared indulged and loved, she felt manipulated by her mother. "She wanted me to be . . . a carbon copy of herself."

Alice's adolescence was a fairly happy one. She pursued her interest in crafts, particularly sculpture, and wanted to be an artist. However, her mother raised her to be an "old-fashioned, stereotyped . . . homemaker" and did not think education for a woman was important. Her father did, but what he thought didn't count. "He was, especially for his age, one of those unusual people who looked at the person and not the sex, and felt that a mind especially should be developed to its full potential, and it didn't matter whether it was a girl or a boy. In that particular respect he had more interest in my mind than he had in my brother's."

Alice also had a grandfather who taught her a lot before she attended school, and they used to sneak ice cream before meals. He was "very indulgent," and he died when Alice was in her teens, after which both her parents became more important to her.

Alice graduated from high school and, after a battle with her parents, went to art school. While there, in her late teens, "I came to realize how important my father was . . . how important it was to please him. At art school they have something they call 'mid-semester blues'," which Alice experienced. "Prior to that time, I'd been relatively carefree. I wasn't accustomed to being disturbed or upset about things. It turned out that I was concerned about my father, and what he thought of me, and how well I was doing. . . . It was a revelation to me to realize that I cared so much." Around this time her father died. "I felt cheated of the time that we could have spent together, with me having a different perspective, rather than arguing with him and fighting with him. I was more ready to commune with him." She wished she had had more opportunity to learn from him.

A few months after her father died, Alice suddenly changed her plans to study sculpture in Europe and married a man of whom both her parents had disapproved. "I perceived him incorrectly, and thought he was someone that he wasn't." He lied a lot, was "canny enough to find out what was important to me and then profess to feel the same way about it," and Alice was naive. His motive was to get married, and apparently he wanted to do a "little social climbing," although she says "there wasn't that much to climb." When asked why she married him, Alice responds, "That's what I kept asking myself later." She thought she was in love with him and thinks that probably the death of her father had something to do with it. However, this marriage changed her life completely in that she gave up art school and all her plans and ambitions.

They moved east about a year after her marriage, and Alice gave birth to her daughter. "So becoming a wife and . . . later a mother kept me away from [art]." However, she divorced her husband and got a job rather than return to art school. This was a major turning point for her. She decided not to pursue art because "I didn't think it would be good for my daughter." Most of the artists were hippies or beatniks, as they were called then, and unconventional. That life was fine for those who wanted it, but "I didn't think it was fair of me to stick her with it . . . so I thought the best thing to do was to try to provide an environment for her that was as close to the one my parents had provided for me as possible, and that's essentially what I spent the next fifteen years doing." She and her daughter were "highly companionable" and had such a good relationship that she laughs, "It's too bad she had to grow up." However, "had I been childless, there is no question in my mind that I would have gone back" to pursue an art career and finish college. She tried to do it in addition to working and raising her daughter, but it was too difficult, although she made the highest grades during that brief experience.

Alice did, however, work in art-related jobs, although she found both career opportunities and decent salaries were "denied to me because I was a woman." Also, she hadn't finished college. However, she did newspaper layouts and advertising art for a department store and then went to work in county government. She'd never learned typing because she'd been afraid she'd end up as a typist. "Civil Service gave me a fair shake."

Alice tells in detail of a traumatic event in her life, when she lost her daughter in the San Diego Zoo. She was looking at curios, turned to display one to her daughter, and found her gone. She searched behind the counter, outside on the patio, and started to panic, running down paths, seeking her in the ladies' room, asking people. "I started thinking all the worst things . . . even went down and looked in the creek, half expecting to find her floating face down. . . . I was starting to become irrational, thinking if I couldn't find her I'd never go home again." Shortly before the zoo closed, her daughter came walking toward her, having visited the elephants. "It affected my attitude toward her . . . because I valued her much more after that. . . . Initially I had felt sort of burdened with the responsibility of raising her by myself, and that life had not been good to me."

Alice remarried very briefly, thinking she'd had her fling, and the "sensible" thing to do was to settle down, for her daughter's sake. After they'd been "sensibly" married for 3 months, she did the "sensible" thing and unmarried him—got a divorce so he couldn't claim her daughter later.

Alice's divorces and "my mother's rigid ideas about life, people, ladies" made her feel "a failure . . . and I withdrew. I was like an animal going into a cave to lick its wounds. . . . I spent most of my twenties observing. I'd always been a participant." However, she doesn't regret this period because she learned a lot about the world and herself and became more realistic. One thing that helped her a great deal was joining a social group. "It drew me out. I started becoming active again." It still means a lot to her.

"When I hit thirty, all of a sudden I decided it was time to liberalize Alice. I had been locked into this Victorian view of myself and women, and that was contributing to my feeling like a failure." She'd had a health scare, and her physician had recommended sexual experience for it. She knew she would have to conceal such activity from her mother, which she didn't like, and her "respect meant a great deal to me, and I knew that if she were aware of this, she would not respect me." After a few years, she realized that she respected herself, and that was what mattered. So she had become more active sexually.

Work was important to Alice when she was in her thirties, and she had to be careful not to neglect her daughter because of it. She became ambitious, took over supervisory duties, and became successful "by sheer brow power." She became more disciplined and analytical, less dependent on intuition. She felt very responsible toward the people under her. "I don't like to see them get a dirty deal or get stepped on." She also had a "perfectionist streak" and did quite a bit of "crusading. We have other terms for it in the county. It's called shit-disturbing. A little complimentary term!" She gradually worked her way to the top, still without the college degree, a position "which was verboten, and especially for women."

Alice married her third husband, Perry, when she was in her late thirties. Of her husband, she laughs, "I have to contend with him every day." When asked if his influence on her has been for better or worse, she responds, "I'm still trying to answer that question. It depends on the day. Things were fine . . . in the early part of our marriage. . . . I don't know if 'setback' is the right word, but there's sure been a strain and a change since Jeffy was born. . . . They say it works a hardship on the family. Well, it's working one on this family." The quality of life improved with this marriage and her children, but her day-to-day activities and stress load worsened.

The birth of Jeffy 4 years ago was a traumatic experience for Alice. She had nearly died on several occasions from hemorrhaging, which gave her a sense of drifting. When Jeffy was born she had placenta previa, and "my blood pressure dropped down to 14 over 10. I even passed the point, I didn't even feel cold. It was comfortable, tempting; I knew that if I wanted to let go, I could die. However, I didn't know there was anything wrong with Jeffy, and I had no reason to want to die." Immediately after his birth, however, she experienced intense grief and did want to die. Since then she has not.

Before having David, Alice ascertained that he would be normal by having amniocentesis. "I said I'd had Tweedledum, and I wasn't going to have Tweedledumdum." Amniocentesis is stressful, because one is well into the pregnancy, it is weeks before the results are known, and an abortion is planned if the news is bad. In this case the news was good, particularly because David was a boy and her husband wanted one so badly.

Jeffy has affected their lives in a lot of ways. They moved to the city, where he could get proper training and help, giving up a happier place in the country. Alice thinks of Jeffy as one of the important people in her life "in a tragic way. David is important because he's like the great white hope for us [laughs]." David was a noisy, demanding, difficult baby, but now is so quiet he needs to be loosened up. Jeffy looks like Perry, except for his blue eyes, which are like Alice's and are "almost a saving grace for him with me. . . . Yes, we're going to give him up, I'm hoping not before he's 18." Alice is trying to give him a normal life. She believes kids get kicked around in institutions. Both families had agreed to "place him" while Alice was still in the hospital after giving birth to him, but Alice was distressed at the prospect, and fortunately their pediatrician felt it might be a mistake. He assured them that Jeffy would not be "a basket case" and that more could be done for him than they imagined. Perry was the one who wanted to "place him" earlier, but he decided to let Alice have him for a few years because she needed him, "and then we would be done with this nonsense and place him [laughs]. And much as he tried not to, he's become attached to him." At first, they lived in an environment that was supportive of a Down's syndrome child, but for a while they were in a more difficult environment that was not only not supportive but also very hostile. Consequently, Jeffy got on Perry's nerves, and Alice got annoyed with this. "I hate to say that I'm personally bitter about his condition, angry about it. And they talk about phases that you go through. I don't think I'll ever get over it. He has a lot of spunk, and I feel he got cheated." Alice's voice breaks, and she tends to something in the oven.

Alice doesn't see any disadvantages to motherhood—only benefits. You do feel the pain of your children, but raising her daughter was a relatively painless experience, and Jeffy's "just a fluke." Motherhood gives one emotional fulfillment, "rounds you out as a person . . . takes you out of yourself, and not much else would. . . . It's a growing experience." Alice stopped work to devote herself to her children. "David was such an uptight little kid. He's a little perfectionist himself in some ways, and I felt he needed me to cheer him up and make him quit being so serious and such a little sobersides, relax and enjoy life more." But later she speaks of loss: "I lost my baby, in a way, I lost Jeffy, and all of the hopes and expectations that we had for him. I also discovered along the way that David is not a substitute for Jeffy. David is David. I spend the vast majority of my time just going along with Jeffy in a rather normal way . . . the day-to-day routines, and only occasionally allow myself to be maudlin. . . . I don't think it's healthy to dwell on unhappiness."

Health is a concern to Alice. "Some of my activities are restricted at the moment, because I've damaged my spine." She hopes it is only tension and stress that make her cervical vertebrae so painful, and she uses traction every night. She has unusual muscle fatigue. The doctors don't know what is wrong, but all of this has made her more emotional. It "causes my muscles to burn and ache without provocation, and it affects my dexterity, and I think it's affecting my eyes, too. I think that's why my eyes get so fatigued. . . . It's all very distressing." She quietly went "half berserk with worry" over a breast lump, which has turned out to be benign. "Actually, I'm in marvelous condition other than the fact that I'm dying of something rare," she laughs. She does take medication for a minor condition. She and Perry occasionally attend a group for parents of handicapped children, aided by volunteer counselors.

Currently, Alice has returned to sculpting, is taking lessons, and has sold a few pieces to friends. She feels she is more emotional than she used to be, although there is less exuberance and anger in her now. "I am more moved, I think. When it hurts, it doesn't seem like it's for the good [laughs]," apparently in contrast to the past, when hurt could make her more understanding. She has tried to be better informed so that she could vote intelligently. "I think it's important to remember to be practical in trying to achieve goals, and to question . . . whether the goals are worthy. . . . I have a lot of trouble justifying tearing everything down in order to make everything better. . . . I see the need for more caution. . . . There are a lot of things happening now with society here that distress me, and are making me contemplate leaving. Crime, and the type of blind pursuit for change, that I see destroying things rather than building, and tearing down old traditions—obviously I'm tradition-minded. I don't like erasing our past. I like the idea that we have something as mankind and humans and families, something that's lasting . . . that has some meaning, although I realize that in terms of the cosmos we are fleeting. . . . I disapprove of erasing the differences between people. I think we should cherish them." She doesn't approve of the struggle over "who's going to run the show today" and doesn't participate in it any more than is "necessary for me to get by and protect me and mine."

Alice enjoys cooking and sculpting because of the sensual gratification in doing things with her hands. She does mind the messes, particularly stepping in the food that Jeffy is always spilling. Her most important possessions are silver and china mementos that "are a combination of sentimental value and real value," handed down through the family.

Some of her most precious jewelry, her "link with heredity," has been stolen. She's "family-minded" and she values the time spent with relatives that some of her china embodies. She takes pleasure in success, which she defines as "achieving your goals, soufflé, quieting the kids down," and the success of others pleases her immensely. She hopes that in the next few years they will have set up an estate for David—not for Jeffy, because someone might be able to "manipulate it." She also hopes she'll be doing more art. Being a woman she feels has been a disadvantage, because "it's inhibited me from doing things that I have wanted to do most of my life," staying out after dark to play with the kids, access to the car. "I always had people worrying about what I was doing because I was a girl. It's boring to be constantly worrying everybody. Then, of course, in terms of adult life and career opportunities, there's no denying that there's still an awful lot of inequality out there. . . . Women don't get a fair shake." But "it's better to be a woman," have children, be more perceptive, have higher verbal skills, feel more of life. As for her age, in terms of career her present age is a disadvantage, but in terms of life appreciation it's an advantage. The thirties are the best age, because "your body's still holding together reasonably well . . . you can exercise some control over your life."

Alice feels she has gone downhill in the last few years. "At one point, for a long time, I was steadily mellowing. I saw that as a very good change. I feel that in the last few years I have not responded as well to stress as I might, and that I have undone some of that mellowing process. I would like to get back to it. As a matter of fact, I intend to." Asked to define "mellowing," she responds, "Being able to take life in my stride a little better, and not have it throw me, and being more tolerant of myself and others." While she doesn't feel like a failure, she feels "like I've wasted a lot of time. . . . There have been missed opportunities."

One of her secrets is "radical viewpoints on certain topics," which would "upset other people, things that I see as practical and expedient, but that are kind of shocking. . . . One topical area would have to do with selective breeding."

Her dream of a house is "an old Victorian . . . and there was a sense of foreboding about it. It was almost empty." Once she dreamed the answer to a problem they were having at work. She fantasizes a lot, particularly on what might be the scenario of something that she is going to do, like this interview!

Alice sees as a pattern her traditional life, growing up, marrying, having kids, with the "usual American variation with the divorces." Her central conflict has been "trouble resolving my role and my mother's—our interaction—much more difficulty than my daughter and I seem to be having, because I gave her more leeway," and "my mother really doesn't want me to do that." She doesn't believe life has meaning. "God has never given me a personal message in order to convince me. . . . I wouldn't rule it out." And she's not sure there's a point to existence. However, she believes we put subjective meaning into it. She lives because she enjoys life, particularly experience, senses, intellect, beauty.

Alice describes at length an incident that took place recently and gave a lot of meaning to their lives, although it was a tragedy. Some close friends had a year-old baby who died of a congenital defect. The child's development had been gradually slowing, and one day he just gave out a cry and froze rigid. Perry tried to rescue him with cardiopulmonary resuscitation, to no avail. Alice and Perry discovered that "we worked well together as a team in a crisis. . . . I started to admire him more and more again after this experience. . . . [It] has had a positive effect on us. I would never tell them that, because it sounds terrible." They did all they could to help the family through the tragic ordeal.

Alice's story shows a pattern of loss through accident and particularly congenital handicap, as exampled by her son with Down's syndrome, who inflicts further losses to her image of self as rescuer, to her sense of justice, and to her relationship with her husband, her life style, and her health. This is transcended by intellectual activity, humor, her relationship with her daughter, and artistic activities, as a return to what she might have been. The core theme is unjust handicap versus intellect and talent, or gift. In a sense, neither the handicap nor the gift is fair, and both are inborn or congenital, or circumstances into which she is "thrown."

Her protocol is rated as loss oriented, in the grieving stage; she is still grieving for her son and also for who she might have been.

Theoretical analysis

The relation between meaning and metaphorical system is well illustrated in Alice's story.

We see her grieving for the tragedy of her son (whose ebullience forms a sharp contrast to her view of him). Her grief is profound and prolonged, and we must ask if there is anything about Alice or her life that deepens the grief, that makes it especially difficult for her to handle, as she herself has observed. In her recent life there is much sorrow, anger, disillusionment, ill health, and a feeling that the growth or "mellowing" of recent years has been reversed.

One concept through which Alice interpreted her life and world, an important aspect of her metaphorical system from early on, was the concept of justice. The first instance she mentions is that of the birth of her brother when she was eight. Slightly handicapped, he got too much attention, and she felt pushed aside; that is, he and his handicap were sources of being cheated, or unfairness, to Alice. She had to have it out with her parents, and the imbalance was righted to her satisfaction. Indeed, later, her father was even more impressed with her mind than with her brother's, in spite of her being female. It is possible that Alice's treatment of Jeffy, and particularly her annoyance with him, is another way of righting the imbalance between herself and her brother. This may be the way she wishes her parents had treated her brother. Because they did not, she does. Jeffy is her brother. It wouldn't be fair to show him any favoritism; on the contrary, she is careful that this is reserved for David (herself).

In school Alice righted wrongs like a "female knight on a white horse"; the instance she selects to tell us about was when a handicapped girl was tripped. Her sense of right and justice encompassed God, the country, the American flag, and other causes, which could bring tears to her eyes. Her mother "manipulated" her, trying to get Alice to live as she thought right, inculcating strict notions of right and wrong. When her father died, Alice felt "cheated." She married a man who perverted the truth. When her daughter was born, she didn't feel it would be "fair" to "stick" her with beatnik artists and hippies. At work she also did quite a bit of "crusading," or "shit-disturbing," and even though there was unfair discrimination against women, she managed to reach a top position. When she had Jeffy, she felt he also was cheated. Finally, she feels she has grown more realistic about the world and country, and this translates into disillusionment. She deplores the tearing down of tradition (what was always "right"), the crime, the loss of meaning in the erasure of the past as well as the differences between people. Tradition gives life meaning, whether it be in a personal possession handed down by beloved relatives or the ways in which the country functions. Perhaps it is more accurate to say that tradition provides the stuff of which the individual can make his or her own meaning. Alice no longer participates; it is as if the God, country, and flag that brought tears to her eyes as a child have betrayed her. She is cheated personally and cosmically, "although I realize in terms of the cosmos we are very fleeting." Injustice is winning over the knight on the white horse, and she now only battles when it is necessary. Even her body is betraying her (for a discussion of illness as betrayal, see the section on physical pathology in Chapter 10).

Thus, fairness and justice—that is, the losses of life evenly meted out and for good reason, as well as traditional ways of doing things changed only for good reason—have been the pair of spectacles through which Alice has seen, interpreted, and created her life and world and made sense of it. The birth of Jeffy was a multiple blow for Alice: he is "Tweedledum" in a home of highly gifted, intelligent people who prize this intelligence; he represents loss of hope and possibility, the "ideal child" to his parents, as well as the tough life for which he is destined; no estate will be set up lest he be "manipulated" out of it; and besides all this, Alice must be asking herself at some level how her father would feel about her son, he who valued intelligence so highly, how disappointed he would be, this father who still lives in Alice and will never die—is he rejecting her son and her? Finally, Jeffy's birth represents a cataclysmic injustice. It is as if the possible existence of Platonic justice, immanent in the nature of things, has been destroyed. When Jeffy was born, not only did Alice have to contend with the potential and actual tragedies that did, and will, ensue, as well as family conflicts, but also her own way of creating meaning was challenged and, it seems, the spectacles were shattered. Her metaphorical system is fragmented. This is why I think the birth of Jeffy has been even harder on Alice than on some other mothers of handicapped children, and the grieving stage has been prolonged.

Alice, like us all to some extent, has fallen victim to the fundamental illusion. There is no death, no change; in this case, there is no change in the way things happen. Justice and tradition triumph. Alice shows that there is another corollary to the fundamental illusion. When there is change, it is predictable, and thus nonchanging or changeless. Babies are born—healthy. Tradition changes—traditionally. Both personal and cosmic meaning were destroyed in the birth of Jeffy.

But there is something else. Try as we might, we cannot ignore whisperings. What about David—the great white hope? What about the David who was such a normal, noisy, demanding, and difficult baby, now so quiet, serious, and perfectionistic, the model child? What is going on in that beautiful, curly little head? Can we banish from our minds the resemblance of David to those model children in thousands of case histories—those who later developed such severe pathology? (See Laing, 1976.) Can we ignore the reasons why David might do exactly that? Remember our concept of alternate lives. As Jeffy is treated, so is David. Remember that David is guilty of falling short of "white hope"; so are we all. David bears the weight of his parents' doubly dashed hopes, dreams, and meaning on compliant little shoulders. Perhaps it is not only Jeffy over whom Alice grieves.

Nora

> "I wanted to set a torch to her bedroom. I wanted to burn it! . . . They only seem to remember the bad things. . . . I don't understand what you get out of it [motherhood]. Maybe you get out of it the satisfaction at that moment yourself, when you see your kids in a ball game. Maybe that's what you're supposed to get out of it."

Nora is almost 60, obese, with steel gray hair, a sallow complexion, and black eyes. She walks with difficulty and smells of urine, probably because of her kidney disease. Her husband passes in and out of the den where we are talking; he looks as though he tries not to get upset, possibly because of his high blood pressure. Every 15 or 20 minutes Nora tells him to check the mailbox for their Social Security check. Her speech is pressured, angry, explosive, and bitterly sarcastic during much of the history.

Nora's mother and father were divorced when she was very young. She was awarded to her father, but the papers were sealed, and she does not know why. Her father remarried, and Nora enjoyed her stepmother, who was young and lively. She lost track of her real mother until one day she simply stepped out from behind a beautiful parked car at school and introduced herself and her new husband. Nora ran home terrified to her stepmother. After that, she was kidnapped alternately by her mother and father over a period of years. While with her mother, she hung around the small gift shop her mother owned, and for which she worked very hard. Her father also was a hard worker and mentally, and occasionally physically, abused her stepmother, as he had her mother. Nora lived most of the time with her father but paid occasional visits to her mother, with whom she did not get along, she thinks because of the things her father said about her. "See, I don't remember much about the (divorce and custody), there were stories. People tell me today I had a lousy childhood when they hear about all this, and I tell them I didn't, because I had a father that I knew loved me above all things. Later on, since I've had more communication with my mother (of course he's dead so I can't ask him), I've had reasons to wonder if he really did, but at that time I had a house, I had warmth, food, and always had security. . . . They say 'you didn't have a mother's love.' I say, 'yes, I did, I had a stepmother's love'."

Nora remembers with embarrassment that she could not always attend school but would have to go with her dad in his delivery truck when he was sick. He picked up his dairy load at four in the morning, and if he had a hacking cough or cold she'd run the milk for him. "It used to be mortifying. All the kids would be going to school, and you'd be jumping on and off the truck. . . . He had an iron hand, an iron fist, I guess you'd call it. . . . He was great at giving out orders."

Nora has happier memories. She used to visit her mother's place of business in Chinatown. "Oh, how I wanted to be an FBI agent, and get everybody for narcotics. Chinatown was spooky in those days, all these Chinese people. I consider it now very daring that as a kid I was allowed to go up and down those streets. . . . I always had a girlfriend with me." She collected Chinese bric-a-brac and also fantasized about being a nun, because she loved them at the Catholic school she attended. "They were beautiful people, so kind to us."

Unfortunately, Nora's father transferred her from Catholic school to public school in junior high, which proved to be a difficult transition for her. It was hard going to school with boys. "And the disruption in the classroom was something I couldn't believe. We weren't used to disruption, nuns just had those little clickers and that's all, they'd click those little things and you'd come right to attention. . . . I wasn't used to teachers who lost their temper. I had one teacher who . . . would pick up her shoe and throw it across the room. I was used to the serenity of the nuns."

Nora's one regret about her childhood was that she didn't enjoy her father more. She wishes they had traveled together, but "his life was nothing but work. He died at 58 years old. I can't see where he had any enjoyment out of life. . . . I wish I had spent more time asking him to do things." However, she also recalled that he never gave her money, he always took it. As a kid she worked cutting apricots for drying sheds, and her father was there at the end of the season to take her check. He took her stepmother's paycheck from the cannery, too. "I didn't think too much about it then, but today I think about how humiliating it is, that if I missed my ride to school, I had to go to the corner grocery store to charge the money off as a can of tomato sauce in order to take the bus to school. None of us had a dime in our pocket."

By the time Nora was 18, she was dating Arnie, the man who was to be her husband. Her father did not like him. "He didn't think Arnie was a good enough worker. . . . He took Arnie on his truck with him a couple of times . . . and my father had magnetism, it just overflowed out of him. He could speak 6 languages, and he'd treat all his customers like they were queens, everybody loved him. . . . All the ladies confided in him, he was like a father confessor. . . . Arnie was a quiet, shy little kid. However, my dad did see one thing in Arnie that I didn't see. He told me [we] were not suited for each other because I like people, and he figured that Arnie didn't. Which there was some truth in. Our first couple of years of marriage were very stormy." At one point, Nora's father gave her an ultimatum. Either she break off with her boyfriend, graduate from high school, and then go out to work and bring home some money, or he would throw her out. With the help of a social worker, she moved out into the Y, got a job, and lived happily on her own.

She and Arnie married, but there were problems, particularly his jealousy. "One of the reasons why I did like Arnie was because I thought his jealousy was beautiful. But afterwards it turned out to be a *pain*. . . . At first, when somebody's jealous, you think how wonderful it is, he wants me. But after a while, when you've had one roaring battle after another, it's terrible." After their marriage it was even worse. "Many, many nights I cried for my dad— isn't it funny?"

At the time when Arnie and Nora had a year-old baby, Arnie and her father both "deserted" her, Arnie for the service and her father to return to sheepherding in the midwest. "He and my stepmother got a divorce. Of course, my stepmother made the big mistake of thinking that the minute her step-daughter was out of the house, everything was going to be wonderful. She didn't realize that his need for her was over. She had fulfilled a function." Each of them tried to get Nora to testify for him or her in court, but she refused and played golf on the day of the divorce. "If anything I'd testify for my stepmother over my daddy, anyway, because I felt that she got a bad deal."

When Arnie and Nora's father left, Nora took her baby to live with her mother-in-law. "She's one of the most beautiful persons that ever graced this earth." Nora stayed with her during the time Arnie was in the service, while he was writing nasty, jealous letters asking her who she was going with. As soon as he got home he started accusing her again. She got a job, figuring that she might have to leave him and support her daughter. One night they had a battle, as the result of which he changed completely. The jealousy "stopped cold." But even though he no longer exhibited jealousy, he still had a terrific temper. "I guess I was afraid of Arnie. . . . The fights were terrible. . . . I used to get so *sick* at our table. . . . Arnie would make the kids eat evèrything on their plate [Nora pounds the table with each word]. They gotta eat it. I used to see Jeannie get sick to her stomach to eat fish. I don't know why he did it. . . . See, my dad wouldn't do that to me. We had an old-fashioned soup, the chicken would be cleaned, and then the whole chicken would be dropped in the pot, and the whole onion. Well, those onions would part, and they would just slurp around in the soup—chee, when I looked at my dish and I would see those onions, I would get sick, nauseated, and my dad would just reach over and take his spoon, take all the onions and put them in his dish—never had to eat none of it. . . . Why do you force your kids to eat something they don't like?"

Nora's regret during this period was that her husband did not return to school and become a teacher. "All we thought about was hurry up and get our little house and our chintzy furniture, and get started on a family." He spent his entire life driving a truck, which she views as a waste of time. As for her thirties, Nora replies, "They went by too fast. They were Little League, Middle League, Bluebirds, Fly-up's, Boy Scouts, you name it, it was too fast. You wonder where they went. Typing all afternoon at a school for free, setting up the library for the Catholic school that Harve went to, holiday parties, birthday parties, spaghetti feeds. . . . I remember a lady friend that worked with me . . . said: 'You never, never had five minutes to even get out of the car. You'd drive up, honk the horn for Jeannie, and you didn't even have five minutes to come in and get a cup of coffee, you'd just swoop on down the driveway. You never had no time for anybody.' "

When the children reached their teens, Nora and Arnie started having difficulties. Jeannie had been a very beautiful and obedient child, but her father's rules and regulations alienated her. She had to be in by midnight, and during the week she was to come home and get supper. "I think Jeannie resented mostly the fact that her father didn't trust her. She wasn't allowed to run at night. . . . Now when it came to his son, our son . . . he was allowed to stay out until 2:00 in the morning" because he was a boy. (Nora relates much of this with hostility.) When Jeannie turned 18, "all of a sudden with the help of a neighbor she ran off and got married. . . . I remember the night I found out she had run off. I wanted to set a torch to her bedroom, I wanted to burn it [with hatred]. I couldn't believe that she would do it to me. It was just such a stinking shock. I always maintain that kids have to get their courage from somebody else, and it's usually an adult. . . . And in this instance, it was a neighbor lady across the street, my friend, the one I'd gone to school

with [biting sarcasm], who was giving her the backup she needed [explosive]."
Jeannie is paying for this mistake in that she has a "lousy relationship with
her husband."

Years later, Nora took a course in child psychology, which she wishes
had preceded her having children. "Because I was a firm believer in strict
obedience, too. When I tell you to do something, do it, don't give me any
argument. I used to tell my kids, I never gave my dad *any* argument. I never
asked my dad why, or how come I have to do it. He'd tell me I was to do
it, I did it. If he said pluck a chicken at 11 o'clock that night, I plucked a
chicken at 11 that night. I didn't argue with him, or say, gee, I have to be
up for school at 6. The chicken was there, and the order was there, there it
was. I used to tell my kids, god, can't you do . . . anything without an
argument? Just do it. Just *do* it!" In a child psychology course, Nora thinks
she would have learned how to manipulate. She sees women who work in
the office as "great manipulators." She believes people would rather be manipulated than given a direct order. Perhaps her daughter would not have left
home if Nora had learned to manipulate, although the precipitating factor was
her father giving her a spanking after she was 18, which she brought on
herself with her stubbornness. Nora and Arnie also sought counseling to try
to break up the relationship between her daughter and her husband-to-be. "We
went to a Catholic priest who . . . gave us the worst advice we ever had:
'Let 'em see each other as much as they want to'." Now they wish they'd
sent their daughter off to Europe.

Nora's regret about these years is that they went too fast. She remembers
that Saturday nights were their special nights for treats and watching TV. "I
spent a lot of time brushing Jeannie's hair, she had beautiful blonde hair. I
didn't take time to play games with them, Monopoly and things like that that
a lot of people play with their kids. But we did have a closeness—I *think*."
Unfortunately, the children seem only to remember the negative things. Her
son remembers her spanking his sister. "When you ask your kids about what
they remember about their home life, seems like they only remember the bad
things, not the good things. Come home from work and head right out for
Little League, and sit there cold, watching your kid play ball, god, is this
ever going to end? All that attendance at Little League, selling hot dogs,
Middle League, and Fly-up and flying off in a plane, you'd think he'd remember that: 'Oh, no, I remember the spanking you gave Jeannie one time
because she couldn't learn her arithmetic. What a terrible spanking that was!'
That's what he remembers about home life. That's unfair. What happened to
all the good things you shared with them, picnics, days at the beach, fancy
things you did with each other, going to look at the trees at Christmas. What
happened to all those things? Where are they? They only seem to remember
the bad things. I don't understand it." (You feel a sense of loss?) "Oh, sure.
I see other women . . . who didn't put as much into being a mother as I did,
and got better results in the end. I have a girlfriend, her daughter remembers

her all the time with flowers. . . . Hey, I don't get flowers. I got flowers on Valentine's Day because my son had forgotten my birthday. He thought 'I'd better come up with something' so he sent me flowers on Valentine's Day. Gee, I put so much more into it than she did, how come her daughter thinks so much of her and . . . you're just out in left field some place. . . . I really worry about that. Maybe a course that would help parents realize, no matter how much they do for their kids, maybe what they do isn't important to the kids. I don't know what the answer is. I went through Little League, Middle League, Pony, high school baseball, college baseball, and where am I? Harve hung up his glove, I hung up mine, practically, and I don't understand what you get out of it. Maybe you get out of it the satisfaction at that moment yourself, when you see your kids in a ball game, maybe that's what you're supposed to get out of it. Maybe you're not supposed to hope that some day they'll remember all the things you did for them, how many hours you gave up for them." (Did you enjoy it?) "Oh yeah, I loved it, 'cause I played a little ball on the side before I left home, girls' softball. We traveled, that was one thing my dad let me do. We traveled with the team."

"I told my grandson, I was just kidding him, I said: 'I don't know if it's worth having kids.' He said: 'What do you mean, grandma?' I says: 'You put in so much and you get out so little. . . . You think about it.' He's twenty. 'Think how much your mother is putting into you, and are you ever going to do for her as many things as she's done for you? Not that you're supposed to do anything. Ask yourself: 'Am I going to be around when my mother needs me, when my mother has a lonely moment?' He said: 'Well, my mother's independent.' 'Not that independent,' I says. 'No woman's that independent that they can surrender their children to another woman or to another life, and get nothing in the end, sit back and say, well, gee, he's having a wonderful life. I'm happy for him. They'll still feel that loneliness and wonder why they're not included'."

When Nora thinks of other things she could have been doing, she says she could have been sitting down once in a while instead of always running, driving. She could have been taking courses, bowling, had a few pieces of jewelry instead of letting her daughter have everything.

The forties were good years for Nora, working, socializing with friends from the office, her children gone. However, she was still concerned about her daughter. "Her first husband she went around with a hoop through his nose. She didn't want that after a few years. The second time she married a man that put a hoop through *her* nose, then she figured out she didn't want a hoop through her nose." He came back from Vietnam with a terrible temper, "tearing doors off the walls, smashing the stove to smithereens, if you could believe it." For a while Nora could hardly stand her daughter after the marriage, "with her hair down her back like Mama Cass. She was a *mess*," raising a lot of animals, as a result of which their yard was "a tragedy."

She sums up her forties: "I got more complacent. I became more liberal really in my thinking, especially toward black people. I never had much to do with black people. Then I started working with them . . . and got to see them as human beings like me and you. Also, like I used to tell my husband: 'You know, they bleed the same way we do, and they cry the same way we do'." She became more liberal toward Mexicans, too. "After my two trips to Mexico, I said: 'You Mexicans don't have nothing to be ashamed of. Why do you act so funny and argumentative, like you got a chip on your shoulder. . . ? All you have to have on your shoulder is pride." She does wish she had traveled more, especially that she and Arnie had traveled with the children. After wondering if it was worth doing as much as she did for them, she finds herself wishing she'd done more.

Of her fifties, Nora says, "They're fun years," even though her husband had a heart attack. At this point she recounts an incident that really distressed her. "At that time I was upset with my son. I think this is something that ought to go down, because I've always wondered about Harve. The day that Arnie had his coronary . . . I called Harve and said: 'Your father's having problems, you'd better get over to the hospital.' I don't know why you call your kids, I really don't know, why do you call anybody?" When they got to the hospital, they found there was going to be a long wait before the doctors would know anything definite, and Harve decided to continue on his camping trip with his friends. Nora was shocked: "My God, Harve, do you realize I would give anything in the world if I could have helped my dad out the day he died? Do you realize that my dad laid down in the desert and died, and nobody even helped him, that nobody even knew what his last words were— that nobody even offered him a drink of water? And you stand there and tell me that this man, who has spent his whole life working for you and doing for you and being a dad, father to you, you don't want to stay? I said, I don't even want to talk to you. . . . Then I marched out of the hospital and got in my car." Once home, she found that Harve's friends had decided not to leave after all. "Of course, I felt so bad when my dad died, oh my god." Nora tells the whole long story of how she heard about her father's death with great emotion. "So I always felt bad about it that I—we had reconciled during the years—he had come and stayed with me. And you know the thing that I really felt bad was the morning that he was going to leave to go down to look for property, he came in the kitchen, and I can still feel the emotion, every bit of my heart wanted me to put my arms around my dad, tell him not to go, to wait. . . . But I still was smarting from leaving home, still that was in the back of my mind, to think that I was forced into it, and stuff like that has always made me smart. . . . And then I told Harve, I said: 'Do you know what I would give to be able to put my arms around my dad and tell him how much I love him? And you have a chance, a simple thing to stay by your father, and you want to go off camping, and it'll be there a thousand years, and maybe your dad will be dead.' Well, I'll tell you I never understood that, and to this day I don't understand it. I don't know how anybody could ever explain it to me."

One of the bitter things Nora remembers about her father's death was her mother saying, "Well, thank God that son of a bitch is dead." Nora felt like hitting her, especially since her dad had always told her to respect her mother. "God, Arnie tells me that I'm like my mother sometimes, and I think that's an insult. I think the woman's balmy. I hope she hasn't influenced me at all. Woman's crazy. I think she's nuts. This business that because you give birth to a child, that the child owes you something for the rest of your life. . . . I remember one Mother's Day when I was particularly stirred by the priest's sermon [she's very sarcastic here], I called her up and thanked her for being born, god, she thought that was the best compliment I could have ever given her. . . . I finally realized that she had carried me 9 months, and she had struggled to have me [dramatic] and went through the agony. Well, I think she's crazy, and like I told her, any slut can have a kid." Nora still continues a bitter feud with her mother. Her mother felt Nora owed her the inheritance from her father. Nora saves her "nasty" letters in case they ever go to court. They don't speak to each other any more, they just write or communicate via a third person, and her mother's letters address her by her last name. "Two years ago you hurt me a lot, Mrs. V. I never got over it, and I never will. So I go to my grave with my pain and a broken heart." Nora says, "I got that one last month." Her mother has also returned to Nora all the gifts she's ever given her in one huge package and is threatening to sue her over some other possessions. Grimly, Nora observes that it's a good thing her father taught her to *laugh* at life.

Of her fifties, Nora says she wishes she had worked less and traveled more. She feels she has handled her problems "very poorly" and seeks solace in doing things "where you can lose yourself and not think about things."

Nora has a number of regrets. One is marrying at such an early age, before "you've explored life, been every place, seen things, especially a person who likes to travel like me. Now to travel is a fight. Maybe with another man it wouldn't be." Arnie likes his regular schedule and doesn't want to break it with travel. She also regrets working as hard as she did and retiring early. "I miss the whole routine, bored stiff staying home." Her most important possession is a diamond ring, which she wanted so badly that she bought it for herself. Another was a mink stole, in which she had planned to be buried, but it was stolen. She spends most of her time "looking at four walls," reading, listening to music, watching TV, and gardening. "I used to look for antiques, but I decided, what do we need all this stuff for, just have to give it to somebody like my daughter. She doesn't go in for those kind of things, so who do you give that kind of stuff to after you leave the world?"

The prospect of eventually having to go on dialysis worries her. Either she would have to put a machine in her house, and there's no place for it, or she'd have to go to the hospital three times a week. She also has problems with blood pressure and obesity, and her son says she needs a counselor "desperately [laughs]. . . . He thinks I have too many hostilities," but she indicates *he's* her main hostility. What makes her happy is "just getting on the road again, like Willie Nelson says." What makes her sad is her relationship to her children. The women's movement seems important to her because she feels women don't earn as much as men. "Wages, for instance, god, I was talking to my cousin's kid the other day. He makes $1500 sticking a nozzle of a gas thing in an airplane, while a secretary going up the ranks may make $1200 if she's lucky. Well, boy, if that isn't getting robbed, there's something wrong there. I think it's terrible."

Nora finds the question about how much control she feels she has over her life a difficult one to answer "because a lot of the things I would do I can't do because I've got Arnie. I would do a lot of things differently. For instance, I'd be long gone from here, I'd be traveling. I wouldn't hesitate about taking a trip to Paris. I wouldn't want to go first class, I'd go third class. I could bum it over there. But I can't do it with him. I have to think, well he won't go, so I can't go. He doesn't want to go. Yet, if conditions were reversed, and he said go, I would go. See, that's the difference. . . . I'll go sit in a lousy boat in Oregon and freeze to death, just to catch a fish that I won't catch, but he won't turn around and do something I want to do that means a lot to me . . . and it constantly holds me back. If I could go with somebody, like my lady friend, he wouldn't care if I went, but to go by myself right now, I don't feel like I can go, so I figure that he controls that." (Why do you feel you can't go by yourself?) "Well, I don't feel I have it all together enough to go by myself. I don't speak the language. I think I could get in trouble. . . . If I was starting all over today I'd be an airline hostess, so I could travel [laughs]. Seeing new people, seeing the different places, walking around and looking at other people and seeing how they survive—survival, boy, when you go into Mexico, you wonder how they survive, but they do. They seem to be happy."

When asked if her children realize she might not survive 5 years, Nora responds: "Yes, they know it. I don't think it touches their life that much. I think Harve feels that—my son has a beautiful attitude toward life. He doesn't want anybody's problems. . . . I also feel that, in the last couple of years, he's taken two old *shoes* which are his mother and father, and tossed them in the cupboard. We go away, and he comes over here, comes in and stays here for two days. We come home and he goes home. We never see him. . . . Now we're going away tomorrow, and he's coming Saturday. He'll come over, and he'll leave a mess, and I'll have to come home and clean it. He talks love, but I don't believe he means it, and I hate it, I hate it coming from him. I'd just as soon he not spout love, because if he loved, he'd have time. He has time for everything else . . . everything in this world, but he doesn't have no time to do that little golf game with his father any more, he has no time. And I don't believe that he loves anybody but himself. My daughter thinks it's wonderful that her brother has found the answer to life"— not becoming involved in other people's problems.

For her epitaph, Nora chooses the following: "Here was a woman who loved, and who would have loved to have been loved." She has already made her own funeral arrangements, because she felt it was something she could do for her family. As for the future, 5 years from now, she feels that she won't be here, because of her kidneys. When asked if she'd thought of making the trip to Europe in light of this, she says, "Oh yes, but I'm still waiting for Arnie to make up his mind. I feel that he should go with me." She doesn't feel she's made any contribution to the world, although on probe she recollects, "I brought two children into the world. I guess that's the most important thing I've done. I haven't gotten in any trouble, never been in jail. Haven't caused the government any problems, or people."

Our interview was interrupted by a phone call from a neighbor who wanted to know how she was, evidently so that she could convey this information to Nora's mother, because Nora and her mother are not on speaking terms. "This is what we do, we play games."

Her most memorable and recurrent dream is of "fish in clear water." She's had the dream for a number of years. "I think it means good fortune." She did have a nightmare recently in which she heard weird music and felt as though she was coming back from death. "Isn't that a terrible feeling?" She woke up to find that the music was on television, accompanying the story of an old medicine man who was combating evil influences by shaking Indian dolls. On her sentence completions Nora says, "I have lost—faith in people" and "My highest peak experience has been—the children's graduations." She perceives no life theme. To questions about conflict and life meaning, she sees the conflict with her daughter as the major one. The meaning of life is to "grow within yourself," and it *should* be "love and kindness." It is love and family unity that make life worthwhile.

According to Nora's account of her life, the major aspects have been negative relationships with her mother, husband, son, and daughter and an ambivalent relationship with her father, half idealized and half broken— exacerbated by his death. "I think people have lousy relationships with people." There has been transcendence by positive relationships with her stepmother and mother-in-law, which relationships are given little space in the history, however, and transcendence by the idealization of her father and by travel. Her theme, therefore, is negative relationships characterized by lack of love and the hoarding of injuries and insults, with bitter, sarcastic, hypercritical resentment; transcended by getting away, travel, being on the road, seeing how others "survive." This is escape or undoing, passive rather than active overcoming. Core theme: Bitter relationships versus getting away. The history is rated as loss oriented, grieving stage. Anger is one form of grief.

Theoretical analysis

For Nora, the meaning of life is growing within oneself and should be love and kindness. Love and family unity make life worthwhile. The focus of most of her history is hatred, unkindness, and family *disunity*. Thus, there is an implicit statement in her history that her life has no meaning, that it is not worthwhile. This was true in a number of the case histories. What was most meaningful or worthwhile was precisely what was lacking.

The evidence for relative meaninglessness is abundant. Nora inveighs against her mother from the earliest years until the present (at far greater length than we can report). This is a 56-year-old feud. They don't break off, they don't make up, they just continue hurting each other. Nora sees her greatest conflict, however, as not with her mother but with her daughter. She reports at greatest length on the conflict between herself and her son. Her account of her husband's heart attack is completely in terms of how their son did not respond and her regrets over her father—a loss not worked through.

Once again we see that a previous loss, not worked through, potentiates a present one. The relationship between Nora and her father ruptured when he gave her the ultimatum. While they got back together again after several years, the bitterness she still felt prevented her from telling him she loved him on what was to be their last day together. He went to his death unforgiven; as usual, the unforgiveness is far more traumatic for the unforgiving than for the unforgiven. His death still looms large in her mind, the night she learned of it, the circumstances. She, the unforgiving, is ultimately the unforgiven, because she cannot forgive herself. Death forecloses all possibilities of reconciliation. Nora has learned this the hard way. She doesn't want Harve to learn it the same way she did. However, as she talks to him about it, it sounds accusatory, and, of course, it is herself she is accusing.

Alienated by her father (as Nora was by hers), Nora's daughter leaves her much as Nora left her father; Jeannie was aided by Nora's friend, just as Nora was aided by the social worker at the Y. Nora's anger is her father's. Nora identifies not only with her father but also with her daughter, but now her daughter exhibits aspects of Nora that she cannot forgive—that are unforgiven.

Nora is dying. She represses this fact quite well, but her awareness of it does emerge when she speaks of not being here in 5 years, of having made burial arrangements, of not living to see Europe. She blames this on Arnie, but when pressed and probed, she lacks the confidence to go, perhaps because of her illness. Nora is dying as her father did, unforgiving and unforgiven. She cannot seem to turn this around, but it makes the solution to her difficult relationships that much more urgent. And yet, if Harve will go on a camping trip while his dad is in intensive care, how will he react when his mother is terminal—perhaps not too long from now? I think it is this that bothers Nora; her father's death and her husband's serious illness foreshadow her own fate. Will her son or daughter be there to give her a drink of water, as she was not for her father? Water is especially important to the kidney patient!

Nora does not seem capable of transforming negative relationships into the loving ones that give life meaning. The next best thing is to get away from them, to escape, and this is through travel. The love and lack of travel—her mode of transcendence—come up over and over in the history. She regrets not having traveled more with her father and her children. She's trying to persuade her husband to go. She wants to "lose" herself and not think about things (like losing herself, perhaps). If she had her life to live over, she would not have married until her late twenties, and she would have been an airline hostess so she could travel and see how others "survive," because that is what she sees when she travels—survival.

Nora's epitaph would be, "Here was a woman who loved, and who would have loved to have been loved." She loved her children, but it was not returned. There is a sense of waste, disappointment, and meaninglessness. What was all her busy motherhood for, with never a minute to stop for a chat, if her children do not love her, avoid her, and seem to despise her? These losses weigh heavily as the ultimate loss is upon her, with less and less chance to recoup and no indication that her children want to. Her mother's letters speak of pain and broken heart, but that is what Nora feels. As is often the case, there is a family pattern that is difficult to break. Nora, her mother, her father, her husband all seem to drive their children from them. Nora's children will have difficulty breaking the pattern.

Psychodynamically oriented psychologists would see in Nora's story an unresolved Oedipus complex. Cognitive psychologists would see the destructive pattern of negative thinking, a habit difficult to break without therapy. Both of these positions help us in understanding Nora, I think. There is the final realization, though, that death can be a gift, throwing into relief conflicts and tasks so that they can be resolved, if possible. Further, Nora teaches us that not to forgive is to die unforgiven, that cruelty kills, both the life and the self, and that the meaningless life is the one in which losses are inadequately transcended. In this case, bitterness seems to have its satisfactions, like revenge, but its effect is salt water on the thirsty tongue.

CONCLUSIONS

I began this chapter by asking a number of questions about the concept of life meaning. I wanted to know what people *mean* by the concept, how pervasive the belief in life meaning might be, the process of meaning creation, the degree to which individuals are aware of their own life meaning and the process of its creation, the relationship between life meaning and L/T orientation, and the possibility of a taxonomy.

I have found that individuals interpret life meaning in different ways, from which a taxonomy emerges: cosmic-specific, cosmic-general, individual-specific, and individual-general. Most of my interviewees believed that life had meaning. The meaning ascribed was related to their L/T orientation, in that those who found life meaningful were those who had attained whatever it was that made life meaningful (to some degree) and were transcendence oriented. Others, like Nora, might claim love or family unity as meaningful and, not having attained it, were loss-oriented, with the meaning of life in doubt. In some ways, Patty might be seen as having endured the most loss objectively—

so many deaths for her young years—and yet she is transcendence oriented, focused on overcoming by replacement and re-creation. Meaning creation seems to be an active process of life review over the life span, both individually and with friends. Although individuals may not be aware that they are creating meaning, they are, of course, aware that they review their lives.

A mystery remains. Why do people like Alice and, to a greater extent, Nora become "stuck" in loss, while others like Patty seem able to move forward? I do not believe that the whole complex of reasons can be teased out from these three histories or all the histories combined. But there are certainly suggestions. Nora seems to have been trained in habits of bitterness by both her father and her mother; she was used as a weapon by each against the other. Metaphorically, this meant that she was taught she was a killer, and she carries this on metaphorically to this day. She kills with bitter words. It is a habit, an identity she cannot escape. We sense a perverse pleasure, like an addiction. Old wounds never heal. A long period of travel might be refreshing to her; without a husband to upbraid, she might be turned outward to others, addiction broken. On the road she would be "on the wagon." Nora reminds us that we carry our losses within us, precious parts of ourselves. Alice teaches the importance of reexamining values when they are threatened; intelligence has always been highly prized by Alice and her family. The worst that could befall them would be a retarded child. She expects to breed high intellectual capacity, to clone herself and leave herself to the world with an estate. Must she, and can she, replace with something else the priority intellect has always held in her life? Her neck is stiff and inflexible, and she is "sick unto death," in existential crisis. Intellect is who she is, and it will die with no replacement. Perhaps Jeffy has something to teach her—of great benefit when she finally learns about David. Patty grieves and works through each loss as it occurs. She will not have to work through each loss again as others befall her.

Life and self meaning are idiosyncratic. In the days that followed the explosion of the space shuttle Challenger, I asked my students what meaning, if any, this had for them. These were some of the meanings they saw: (1) Some said it meant we should no longer be in space; (2) for another, there was an association with her mother's death; (3) another student saw an equation of malfunctioning machinery with the emotionless, inhuman, impersonal reports of the media; (4) another said it meant we should not take anything for granted; (5) another pointed to the construction of "heroism"—before the tragedy we had not known the names of the astronauts. These and various other attributions actually made the experience more meaningful.

Throughout this chapter we have talked of life meaning. We create life meaning by transcending loss—overcoming death and its many metaphors. But life and self are the external and internal aspects of the same entity. A meaningful life bestows meaning on the self. And without life meaning, the self is meaningless.

8

Loss and Transcendence in Individual Development

In the first seven chapters of this book I have presented both quantitative and qualitative data on human development within the framework of such concepts as loss, transcendence, meaning, L/T life themes, metaphorical systems, the lost and transcendent self, and the fundamental illusion. I have also performed a metaphorical analysis and interpretation of life histories, in order to demonstrate the practical application of these concepts. However, there is a whole body of traditional clinical and empirical literature in the field of life span development. In this chapter I propose to reconceptualize some of this traditional literature to show that it is congruent with an L/T interpretation. The L/T approach is not necessarily inconsistent with psychodynamic, behaviorist, and cognitive viewpoints because it is a fundamental metaphor underlying them. The L/T framework can be of help in a number of schools of thought, and these in turn can inform the L/T framework. Certainly this is an ambitious undertaking for a mere chapter in a book. The treatment in this chapter is meant to be merely suggestive and far from exhaustive.

I will now proceed to review some of the major literature in the field of human development, from birth to death, showing how the traditional literature fleshes out the L/T approach and how the L/T approach reinterprets traditional literature. I will begin by employing the convention of the generic "he," following a male from birth onward, to minimize confusion of female pronouns for both child and mother; however, I will note where gender differences occur and will later alternate gender designations. The chapter concludes with the story of Ursula, whose history and its metaphorical analysis illustrates the truly life span nature of human development.

BIRTH

A living being has begun in a womb of darkness, moisture, and unvarying warmth; he is thrust into a place of light, cold, dryness, unaccustomed noise, and pressures on various parts of the body. From birth onward, these elements vary as they have not prenatally. Air fills his lungs. He cries. Rank (1973) considered birth not only a trauma but, being the first, a prototype for those to come. Some doubt this because birth is not usually, if ever, a conscious recollection and has not been told in words, as have losses later in life by victims of flood or accident; also, perhaps they doubt because birth is the lot of every man and woman (although births vary in difficulty). But memory need not be conscious, and it need not depend on the verbalization that the baby lacks. The newborn infant has responded to the experience with his reflexes, and these sensations and responses may remain within the individual at some level, within nerves and tissues, perhaps (as Reich, 1951, would have it), within the unconscious as defined by Freud and Rank. In our paradigm, it is the first experience of loss—from uterine (homeostatic) equilibrium, relative changelessness, a kind of death to which Freud (1920, reprinted 1955) once believed we had an instinct to return.

Birth is also the first time we "leave home."

INFANCY AND EARLY CHILDHOOD

Heidegger (1962) wrote that a human being is "thrown" into his life circumstances. This is easily demonstrated. The country of his birth may be rich or impoverished. His primary caretaker may be loving or abusive. Much of the infant's future will be influenced by whether it is a girl or a boy. Finally, the infant is born with certain genetically determined predispositions and characteristics such as those described by Thomas and Chess (1977). These include tendencies to activity or passivity, a happy mood or a sad one, regularity or irregularity in sleeping, eating, and excreting habits, greater or lesser distractability, adaptability, threshold of responsiveness (how loud must the noise *be* to startle him?), attention span, persistence, and intensity of reactions. No matter what the circumstances into which the individual is thrown, it is his response to these (the root meaning of response-ability) that will shape the course of his development.

Piaget (1952) believed that the child's cognitive structure began, just like that of a skyscraper, with a foundation; instead of cement there were physical capacities, reflexes, senses, and motor abilities. Personality, emotional, social, and other structures or systems begin with the same foundation, much of it inherent in the genes, or part of the blueprint Rogers (1961) envisioned. So, too, I believe, an individual's loss and transcendence structure begins, a major aspect of the physical, mental, personality, social, and spiritual systems. This foundation, with which the child is born, becomes the base on which the entire edifice of the human person will be erected, although ever-changing with each new experience.

The newborn's initial reflexes include the Moro or startle, crying, clinging, sucking, following, and grasping, many of which he may exercise at birth. All of these are attachment behaviors (Bowlby, 1969) that bond him to his mother (or primary caretaker) and his mother to him, without which he could not survive. But also, within our paradigm, these reflexes protect the infant from loss to sight, to grasp, to touch, or to warmth. Whenever the infant experiences a loss of warmth or breast, for example, he responds with reflexive behavior that will transcend that loss. Transcendence of loss in the infant is the innate push toward survival, without which the neonate would experience the ultimate loss of his own life.

During this period of life, there is no differentiation of self from other, of subject from object (to extrapolate from Jung, 1971). The infant *is* his hand, his mother's face, the ceiling, the mobile, the breast or bottle. But soon the face moves from sight or cannot be grasped, the breast is not available for sucking, with resultant loss of comfort, the body is removed from contact comfort and laid in its bassinet. With all these losses, differentiation of self from other begins. These are the first losses the individual incurs in his life, losses over which his reflexes give him only a modicum of control, varying from infant to infant and more dramatically from caretaker to caretaker. There are as yet no other methods for transcendence of loss in his repertoire. One might hypothesize that those for whom control of their lives later becomes an issue may be metaphorically reenacting neonatal struggles.

When the infant's reflexes work for him by transcending loss, when his crying brings his caretaker to him, for instance, his L/T structure is developing. If he is reasonably successful, he will learn to *trust* that the loss will be overcome in the future, and by his own efforts (to extrapolate from Erikson, 1950). To the extent that he is unsuccessful, that he is left to cry, for instance, or that the body to which he clings is torn from him, mistrust of self-other will occur. Because self-other is undifferentiated at this time, mistrust and loss of *other* must be phenomenologically experienced as mistrust or loss of *self*. To the extent that the results of his reflexive efforts are inconsistent or capricious, he is learning that fate or luck controls outcomes.

In the neonate's behavior, we can trace the stages of transcendence as they first occur. Food, bright objects, and warmth are his earliest goals and are innate. However, it is in the nature of human life that he be separated from them periodically, which sets the course for later goal-seeking behavior (Buhler & Massarik, 1968). One would not have goals if one had everything one needed and desired. The infant attempts to transcend loss through his reflexive capacities, but when the breast or the bright object or the mother's face reappears, it is always within the context of their loss, which has preceded the reappearance, and thus neither the goal nor the transcending infant is quite the same as what was lost. This is analogous to the Piagetian process of assimilation and accommodation, through which the *cognitive* structure is ever-changing (Piaget, 1952, 1976).

The infant's crying is his first "mourning" behavior (grieving), and searching is his second. When he gets what he wants (which is never quite the same as what he wanted), he is being "trained" in the model that the resolution of mourning is replacement and he integrates this into his L/T structure, so a minusculely new structure will greet the next loss—harder crying, or flailing arms, or body twisting in search, perhaps. This is growth.

Just as the infant builds his cognitive structure initially by developing various schemas, such as the grasping schema, through primary, secondary, and tertiary circular reactions and other sensorimotor stages (Piaget, 1952), he is also building his L/T structure by differentiating self from other. He is learning that he controls the hand and that it is part of him, as the rattle is not. The hand has feeling and sensation; the rattle does not, although it has other properties—it makes a sound when shaken that the hand alone does not make. This differentiation of self from other can be seen as originating in attempts to transcend loss of object from view (the mother's face, perhaps) or from grasp, as well as in transcendence of loss of social interaction through smiling, clinging, and later through the other proximity behaviors observed in the locomoting child (Bowlby, 1969). Assimilation and accommodation are the processes by which the individual builds his cognitive structure (Piaget, 1952). Assimilation describes the process by which the infant "breaks down" a bit of experience into particles that his cognitive structure can take in, as digestive chemicals break down a piece of food for incorporation (Flavell, 1963). The structure then undergoes the changes necessary to fit in or accommodate the new experience. In the same fashion, the L/T structure is operating to differentiate self from other, beginning at birth; later, the differentiation of I from me becomes increasingly important.

The concept of object permanence in its stage-by-stage development (Piaget, 1952) is crucial to an understanding of how the individual structures L/T. At first, the object is lost to view and ceases to exist for the baby. Later, there is evidence of his searching in his looking to where it was last seen. Gradually he learns that something lost exists in a specific other place, and its discovery will yield to search. Eventually (by about 18 months), he learns that it may exist in one of several places. Throughout these experiences, he is susceptible to distraction, or the replacement of the lost object with something else, since the values of the objects that are lost or are replacements have not yet been differentiated. Thus, the stage development of object permanence in the baby is the prototype of the stage development of the L/T structure; it demonstrates the development of the four stages of the L/T process—grieving, searching, replacing, and integrating.

This is also the first paradigm of faith and belief in the existence of what one cannot see, or religion, one of the general transcendence mechanisms (see Chapter 11). The more lost things are found, the more the baby builds a structure of expectation—or faith—that things can be found. If he tends to find them himself, he builds the faith that *he* can find; if helped by an omnipotent, omniscient other (the parent), he learns dependence on others. Thus, the foundations of these personality dispositions are being laid (including genetic predispositions). In our society, our goal is an individual who is reasonably affiliative and reasonably independent; this suggests that an optimal balance should be provided for the baby in these early experiences.

Differentiation of self from other, and also of other from other, and fear of loss of specific other are manifested at about the age of 7 months by the "stranger anxiety" syndrome, a function of proximity; the infant cannot bear to be handed to a stranger, even with his mother standing a few feet away. The separation anxiety of the 12-month-old is a similar attempt at transcending anticipatory loss; he can be handed to a stranger, but his mother cannot go out the door, or he screams after her and struggles to get down and join her. Eventually, she can be away from him for increasingly longer periods; she is a "permanent object"—she can continue to exist beyond his sight and hearing. His learning that she will return (the promise of the great religious leaders, Christ, Buddha, Quetzalcoatl) is a function of his concept of time. There is a future in which the permanent object will reappear.

At about the age of 8 months, the disappearance of the mother can be made into the game of peekaboo (an antecedent of child and adult fascination with magic). The sight of mother or of another is lost and then found, which gives pleasure in that it repeatedly overcomes anxiety that the other, and hence the self, may be lost forever. The repeated reappearance of what has been momentarily lost is reassuring to the baby, who is discovering loss from his self in the progressive differentiation of self from other; that is, he continually finds that what he thought was part of his self is part of other and beyond his control. That which we fear, we seek out and overcome, until overcoming is a habit to replace fear—a very early prototype of the reaction formation defense mechanism as well as adult ludic activities involving danger, such as rock climbing and race car driving. Loss to self (death) is repeatedly overcome.

The 8-month-old who drops things over the side of his chair to have them retrieved by his mother is also experimenting with loss in space (as well as sound, sight, and time). His mother will transcend these losses by retrieval. He extends control over his environment through her.

At two, the game of peekaboo is elaborated into the game of hide-and-seek; the child who can remain lost the longest is the victor. There is comfort in knowing he is not *really* lost. On finally being found in a department store, one little girl told her frantic mother, "I wasn't lost. *I* knew where I was."

At three, the games of pin-the-tail and blindman's buff elaborate further on transcendence of loss to sight. Games such as these form good bases for defense mechanisms. The placement of the child's self in relation to others has consequences of success or failure. He learns to argue or rationalize. He learns the consequences of investing (cathecting) his emotions in various individuals and activities.

As the baby begins to move through space, he experiences his own loss of familiar minienvironments and seeks to overcome that loss by frequent return to the proximity of his mother (Bowlby, 1969). He extends familiarity to a few more square feet of room, to other rooms, to the world just outside the door. He also learns of other losses in space and form: he builds a block tower and knocks it down; he cannot complete a puzzle; his favorite TV program ends; his older brother takes his train.

Possessions become extremely important to him; because at first he does not completely distinguish between self and other, his possessions are himself, and he mourns their loss by crying, searching, complaining to his mother, who will replace. With the attainment of object permanence and the onset of symbolic representation in imitation, memory, and language, losses of possessions now become more salient, because he can remember them. A favorite doll is broken, and the crying that had remedied previous losses with replacements in some form cannot remedy this one; the memory of its form remains—of what it looked like, what he did with it. The child is beginning to learn that some objects are indeed *not* permanent, are lost forever, and the part of him that played with a toy in a certain way is also lost. These two stages of relationship to possessions—first, possessions as part of self, and second, possessions as distinct from self, but whose experience still remains part of the lost self in memory—are laying the foundation for a lifelong relationship of self to possessions and a greater or lesser definition of identity as being confirmed by them. They are also the prototype of attachment to form, against which the Eastern religious mystics warn.

The child is also experiencing a loss of predictability in his world, with the introduction of other playmates; they do not act as he, his parents, and his siblings do; they do not play fair, pay him great attention, let him win because he's younger, or hang on his every word; they live in different houses, come from different places, eat different foods, have parents who are angrier or nicer. The circumstances into which they have been *thrown* are different from his own. All unpredictability involves the danger of loss, and these dangers are transcended by certain rules. One never gets into a car with a stranger, even if she offers candy.

Increased socialization involves a system of rewards and punishments that are losses but that gradually become predictable, as with toilet training. What was once acceptable no longer is. Mastery of his environment is an innate drive in the child (White, 1975), a necessary condition of adaptation, but leads to still further differentiation of self from other, and other threatens, whereas self does not. (Not yet.) The 2-year-old tries to do many things that are beyond his present skills, to dress and feed himself, to fix the broken pedal on the trike. Many instances of distress at this age can be traced to frustrated attempts at mastery that will minimize loss. Transcendence is secured by making things more predictable, by balancing the predictable with the novel, as the world widens from home, to yard, to other houses on the street and nursery school.

The concept of time in the 2-year-old is still rudimentary, as Piaget (1970) points out; time is the language associated with some activity, such as lunch time, nap time, or story time. It gradually becomes differentiated into morning, afternoon, and night, then yesterday, today, and tomorrow, and finally past, present, and future. It becomes the measure of our losses and our transcendences that are related to our activities (see Chapter 12). Yesterday's activities and relationships are lost, today's are happening, tomorrow we will transcend today's losses with replacement; we will go to the playground or have hot dogs for lunch. The child is being trained to look to tomorrow for transcendences, the earliest prototype of hope; he is also being trained to delay gratification and not live in the here and now as the humanists and existentialists suggest. He is not being trained to fully accept loss today in the same way that he accepted the disappearance of an object when he was a month old. Hence, the exhortation to parents to be consistent and to keep promises may be inadvisable in that the child must eventually unlearn these in the real world. Life is not necessarily fair, just, or consistent, nor does it always keep its promises.

He learns to put things away in their proper places, so they will not be lost in some fashion, either broken or out of his possession. He resists this, because he is not yet cognitively capable of conceiving of a loss that has not yet occurred, and the boredom involved in straightening up represents a loss of stimulation. He learns to return things to their proper form, such as making his bed, or he will lose sleep because of discomfort, and there is an aesthetic value in proper form that his parents are mysteriously unwilling to lose (they have formed an attachment to proper form, which he has not, in his newly attained skill of recognizing sameness in changed form—an unmade bed is a bed).

Mother and father are important to the child in their nurturant and power-giving role (Bandura & Walters, 1963), which is simply their ability to transcend the child's losses in many different ways, thereby modeling the various transcendence mechanisms so that he may eventually use them himself. They transcend the child's broken doll with replacement, promise, or hope (tomorrow), bandage his knee and assure that the blood and skin are not significant losses; they turn out to be right. Identification takes place because it implies the ability to transcend his losses. This underlies the sexual (or life-giving, life-maintaining) aspects that the psychoanalyst sees as promoting identification. To the extent that the parents cannot always transcend his loss, the child must extend his own abilities through mastery and competence. And yet, to the child's egocentric view (Piaget, 1952), his parents experience no losses of their own and are in this sense perfect. They exist only to transcend his loss. A crying parent is a puzzle to the child and a frightening one.

The child has been structuring L/T through differentiation of self from other, but also through differentiation of I and me's (Mead, 1934). Until the age of three, I and me are confused linguistically and probably also experientially. "Me do it myself," the 2-year-old insists. By 3 he is just beginning to sense that he is an object to others, just as they are to him, and that his objectness does not include his whole self but only that part he turns to the world, the face, the me. "I" is not object.

To illustrate further, the little girl is Linda's friend, Mommy's and Daddy's daughter, Jeffrey's sister, kitty's or dolly's mother, and her behavior differs in these various roles. She is finding that, although something of her is always changing, something of her is also the same and can stand back and look at herself and make some of her actions similar in different situations. She will play doctor with Jeffrey and read a book with her daddy, but some of her thoughts will be the same in both cases. There are inner and outer aspects of her identity, I, me's, self, and life. While even in solitude she may be taking the roles in imagination, part of her purely experiences. I is different from me.

Until now, under normal circumstances, the child's structuring of loss and transcendence through differentiation of self from other, and of I from me, has been progressing in a relatively sheltered environment, home and neighborhood. With entrance into preschool, the unfamiliar environment is substituted with the loss of many routines and their replacement with new ones. Each small bit of learning requires a progressive redefinition of his self. For example, he must learn to share; that is, he must learn the circumstances under which he must agree to the loss of an object as well as to the loss of the teacher's attention or comfort. At nursery school his possessions are only his for the moment, but at home he has them when he goes to bed at night and when he wakes in the morning, and these possessions are extensions of himself, as they are not at school. The experience of loss is, in a sense, extended as it is transcended. Others now have power to cause loss (teachers, playmates) as well as to transcend it.

With the development of memory, his objects become invested with experience that is not lost if it can be recaptured. He must learn what is real and what is imaginary, a form of training, because everything is initially real to him, including what is magical (Piaget, 1974). In our culture, what occurs solely in the mind—the dream, the imaginary playmate, the fantasy—is not only not as "real" as events that can be apprehended by the senses and validated by more than one person but also of less value. The preschool child makes no difference between his "mind's eye" and his physiological eye. But the dreams and fantasies of the child are trained out of him as being of less worth. "It's *only* your imagination, *only* a dream," and the child must lose a most exciting part of himself through this training. Hallucinations and visions are madness and are to be feared. This is not true of other cultures. The Plains Indians engaged in vision quests to confirm their identities, and their visions were respected by all; hallucinogens such as peyote are used by southwestern and Mexican tribes to give them specific information (Chiang & Maslow, 1977; de Ropp, 1960; Weil, 1972).

The ambivalence of the culture toward the child's perception of dreams and fantasies, the imagined rather than the sensationally perceived, would appear extraordinary, but it becomes more understandable within the L/T paradigm. On the one hand, the parents "put down" dreams and fantasies, even becoming alarmed if they seem to exceed the parents' conception of what is normal. The shadow in the closet is definitely an overcoat, not a ghost. As is true of childhood games like peekaboo, it is fun to experience fear (of loss) so that one can be reassured. On the other hand, fantasy in the form of fairy tales, Santa Claus, the Easter bunny, and the stork is condoned or encouraged up to a certain age. These are the fantasies that transmit the values of the culture, the major one of which is the transcendence of ultimate loss in the form of evil (evil kills). The prince and princess live happily ever after, attaining immortality, transcending ogres, spells, giants, and witches, usually through heroism, steadfastness, and other virtues that are sterotypically male and female. Death and its metaphors can be overcome through adherence to societal values. This is society's way of promoting the denial of death, until perhaps the child is judged tough enough to face it. Then he must "put away childish things"; he would be ashamed to continue "believing" past the age of 6. The veil is being drawn from his eyes; there is no good-hearted saint distributing gifts to children of the world; on the contrary, there is want and starvation. The inculcation of favorite fairy tales by the parents is also their opportunity to relive their own "fundamental illusions," when they believed, before they knew, vicarious denial. If I spit out that bite of the apple from the Tree of Knowledge, will the apple be whole again?

Now illusion must be circumscribed, restricted perhaps to church or Sunday mornings; the rest, they think, is survival. The illusion that is allowed to enrich the life of the young is taken from them as they grow older, but others unwittingly replace it, and form the general transcendence mechanisms, as we shall see.

Music is not as necessary to survival as water, but without it we die younger.

The 6-year-old who finds candy or a coin under his pillow in replacement for a tooth is learning that lost parts of the self can be replaced with something that gives pleasure to other parts of the self. The giving of the coin is a sweetening of the lesson of impermanence. Just as he learned that solid objects have permanence, he is learning that parts of his self do not. The coin distracts him, and especially his parents, from ultimate implications (will my eye fall out, too?). Actually, the coin is in payment for pain and fear, to quiet expression of it, to instruct in repression. This is how loss is to be transcended. It also teaches that parts of the body can be bought (a tooth is worth a quarter), that a price can be put upon him, as it eventually will be in our society. (We could teach him otherwise, what we preach, that no one, whole or part, is expendable, that we cannot pay him for tooth, or leg, or entire self, that he "cannot be bought," a moral stance. But this is one of the many inconsistencies between values uttered and practiced, and we may do him a favor by teaching him the inconsistency with which he must live.)

MIDDLE CHILDHOOD

The long process of socialization entails training in what is considered by society as ideal, as well as the structuring of the self in ways that either approximate or differ from that ideal. For example, Western society, through teachers primarily, informs the child that the ideal individual is always on time to school, never absent, speaks under specific conditions (does not speak to friends during class), does his homework in a prescribed manner with his name in the upper right-hand corner, follows certain standards of dress, is in certain places at certain times and needs permission to be in other places at those times, and does not swear, kick, cry, or otherwise exhibit inappropriate emotional behavior.

To the extent that the child is discovering that he falls short of this ideal, he is experiencing loss to himself from the self-ideal; he not only does not conform to all the ideal expectations of society but also finds he cannot, for such conformity involves too great a delay of gratification, or not enough reward, or there is simply too much to remember, or sitting still for such long periods cramps muscle and spirit. Being scolded for moving is worth the price. He is learning of the discrepancy between how he should be and how he is, and this difference is experienced as a loss from the ideal he has of himself. It also involves loss of approval, love, and security. He transcends his loss with various types of replacement, some socially sanctioned and some labeled deviant. He can try to act out other ideals—the nonconformist, the antihero, the autonomous, the class clown—or he can simply allow himself to be not quite perfect, perceiving that none around him is, evolving a kinder self-ideal, which is the measure of the extent to which he must conform to the societal ideal—a measure he himself has decided on and a check on a too stringent superego.

As the child progresses through this school socialization, as his L/T structure is gaining in complexity, he may discover that he gives many right answers in math, that he is sometimes late, that he has a tendency to cry, that he loses at baseball but wins at chess, that he is frequently nominated but never elected, and so forth. Through the wide variation of loss and transcendence, he is learning to define the I and me's of his self. The period of 6 to 12, in which the psychosocial crisis of industry versus inferiority is salient (Erikson, 1950), is nothing less than the accelerated buildup of a wider repertoire of methods of transcendence specific to the wider types of situations he encounters.

School is the model for the world; he is learning how to handle his peers, deal with authority, do the least to get by—a variety of small component skills that lay the foundation for the skills to be required of him as an adult. Interpersonal relations, community, country, and universe—all of these have prescriptions for thought and behavior that define his self, insofar as he obeys, ignores, understands, or defies them. He learns that disobedience entails loss through punishment—loss of comfort, pleasure, companionship or love from others, according to the specific penalty. Whereas before socialization, all other, including the ideal, was part of his self, as he becomes differentiated from the other, and from the ideal, he loses both the ideal other from the other and the ideal self, until eventually he is a solitary individual. The striving for mastery and competence includes not only the necessity for adaptation but also the wish and need to know the extent of his loss in order to satisfactorily transcend it. Each day, each moment in school, each microscopic behavior demands his attention, and to the extent that he is inattentive, he remains uninformed and incompetent and experiences loss from societal ideal. To the extent that he develops requisite skills, he transcends loss from societal ideal, and his self approaches it. The paradox that loss through conformity may be far greater than loss through nonconformity is not a conscious issue until his teens or later.

In addition, the child from 6 to 12 is learning a form of Janusian thinking; societal ideals differ from societal practices, but not too much, or the society's survival would be threatened. There is, for instance, the ideal of honesty; and learning when it should be adhered to, the circumstances under which one is likely to be caught, and the sliding scale of punishments for various levels of dishonesty is a complex task. Cheating on exams, although dishonest, is not as likely to be discovered or severely punished as stealing money from someone's house. To steal achievement—that is, to cause relative loss of achievement to someone—is not as serious as to steal the rewards of achievement. Losses are hierarchized. The child is also learning exploitation and manipulative skills, all without appearing to do so, because they are against societal ideals, although our society as it is presently set up could not function without them. The learning, of course, entails loss (of face, perhaps?) and transcendence (through gaming someone else?), and the personality trait of relative honesty or relative dishonesty is developing. If the individual tends to lose in reciprocal relationships, not be as clever at exploitation or manipulation perhaps, not be elected class leader, he can always become "more" honest than others and gain points of a sort that way. Many of the ideal societal values are taken on by "losers" as consolation prizes.

Still, like losers everywhere, he helps to shape the race, which would be quite different if only the winners ran. The 4-minute mile would be unbroken still. The race may be to the swift, but some credit is to the slow. Haydn was an also-ran.

In the Piagetian paradigm of the concrete child, the child's differentiation of himself progresses from recognition of his body in the mirror to the assessment that others give him as he grows, entailing profound loss to the extent to which the child's physical appearance deviates from the ideal. The preteen and the teen spend long hours in front of the mirror assessing appearance, trying various stratagems to bring the self closer to society's ideal (combing hair into different styles, wearing different combinations of clothing, females experimenting with makeup, etc.). The feeling that one is unattractive, especially overweight, is prevalent during these years, as reported by my interviewees. The preteen or teen checks out each change in his appearance with peers, seeking consensual validation of his closer approximation to the ideal (see Stryker, 1984). (This form of interaction concerning physical appearance among preteeners and teenagers is analogous to the mutual grooming observed in ape societies.) With the lessening of Piagetian or cognitive egocentrism (he may not see himself from another's viewpoint) and the attainment of formal operations (or the ability to think abstractly), also with the impetus to physical attractiveness grounded in pubertal development, this attempt at conformity to the ideal physical appearance reaches its zenith in the teen years.

ADOLESCENCE

Adolescence, perhaps even more than childhood, is historically and culturally defined. Differential timing of physical maturation in teenage boys and girls has been found to be a source of anguish and to be associated with behavioral differences in development. Among teenage boys in particular, slower physical maturation is associated with poorer athletic skill, lower leadership, compensatory "clowning," less interpersonal social skill, and delayed heterosexual maturity, whereas advanced maturation signals development of the reverse (Jones & Bayley, 1971). Among females the situation is somewhat reversed, with females who reach puberty sooner experiencing more self-consciousness, although the effects of differential maturation rates are not as substantial. At any rate, slower physical maturation in a boy may define losses to the ideal self-concept as, for instance, athletic star, class leader, sexually successful. Pubertal changes in themselves signify a loss to the old self and the emergence of a new one. Either way, there are losses that must be transcended in some manner.

The teen years entail profound encounters with loss and the necessity for transcendence. Often, having attained the cognitive stage of formal operations (Piaget, 1952), the teenager is able to contemplate loss in the abstract. The sense of past, present, and future over greater distances of time is emerging, and there is a real sense of what has been lost already and threats of future loss, which must be dealt with.

According to Erikson (1950), adolescence is the period of the "psychosocial moratorium." The adolescent is allowed to delay mate and work choices, explore options. This involves a definition of self that is nothing less than defining "who I'm not," a loss of the possibility of certain roles, as he "tries them on" like costumes in his struggle between identity and role diffusion. During the latency period of industry, he was concerned with specific component tasks and skills; now he is concerned with the clusters of tasks and skills that define social and occupational roles, or me's. He learns he is not a rock singer because he lacks the talent; he is not a budding president because he lacks money and persuasive skills and can't even get elected class secretary; he is not a doctor or nurse because he faints at the sight of blood—and organic chemistry books!

In the late teens and early twenties, this differentiation involves learning about not only what he is not, what he lacks to make a role possible, but also what the role itself lacks. The illusion of glamour fades as the teenager learns the years of hardship that are virtually prescribed for the novice actress; the tedium of meetings or other chores that are a realistic part of the business or academic career; the qualities of character, such as manipulativeness or political-mindedness, that are at odds with newly developing values but may be involved in the previously idealized roles of lawyer or salesman.

He is going to select a me that will be incorporated into, and change, his whole self L/T structure, and he is going to make the selection to a greater or lesser extent blind; no amount of information can convey to him what it really means to lead the life of a restaurant manager day by day. This is scary. Meanings, previous me's, parts of self-concept will all be moving into the lost sector, to make room for a new me that must gradually take up major space and affect the transcendent I. And that me may not prove compatible with the rest of self. This represents an extended loss of innocence. In choosing a me, he will conform to the pressures of society to select and the pressures of the specific institution into which he has selected himself. Heretofore, *nonconformity* has entailed painful losses—the loss of friends, approval, and good grades and always losses to self-concept. He is unprepared for the losses *conformity* entails, often experienced as major surgery. Society has glossed the surgery with ritual and promise as other societies gloss circumcision, clitoridectomy, and tattooing.

At the same time, there is a growing awareness of the losses in the community and the world—losses through hunger, poverty, violence, prejudice against race, age, sex, religion, occupation—which can now be abstractly comprehended because of decentering; there are a capacity for empathy and a desire to transcend these losses in some fashion as the mature defense mechanism of altruism takes root (Vaillant, 1977). This desire, of course, is experienced differently, partly depending on membership in a minority or majority.

The adolescent is also discovering that the omnipotence and omniscience of his parents are more and more severely restricted. His parents make mistakes, they don't know everything, they are defeated, they develop angina, arthritis, malignancy, sometimes they are unjust, they must struggle to cope; as the teenager discovers this, he is discovering his own future limitations as well, for, to the degree that he has identified with his parents' omniscience and omnipotence and their possibility for himself, he must also identify with their limitations. Part of the anger toward parents at this time is undoubtedly displacement of anger for their limiting of him in this sense. (And part of their anger toward him is at this growing reflection of their limitations!) This naturally leads to a rebellion by the teenager against limitations; curfews become metaphors of much larger restrictions that he is just discovering. In panic over his new understanding, the teenager attempts to seize control over his future with the much observed struggle for autonomy, which is really an attempt not to lose what he is just recognizing as already seeded for loss.

Teenage attempts at socially unsanctioned transcendence are also displacements of sudden helplessness in the face of ultimate limitations. Alcohol, drug use, and sexual promiscuity are pleasurable, but they are also all ways of "beating time" and the loss that it implied, if only for a few hours. It has been seen that, in a sense, parental concerns for material things, future security, hard work, thrift, and all the other virtues they have sought to instill in him have gotten them nothing more than the limitations and losses they now suffer, and to follow in the parental footsteps is suddenly absurd. He sees this absurdity and throws it back to them, and they resent his vision because it makes light of their lives, their sacrifices, and the repression and hope that have been necessary to give him life.

At the same time, these limitations and losses are real and can be averted not only by beating time, the measure of loss, but also by attacking the losses and limitations themselves; with new zeal and idealism, the teenager or youth becomes involved in making the world a better place, working with troubled children, picketing the great corporation that tricks mothers in undeveloped countries into using prepared milk formula, demonstrating against nuclear power plants and apartheid, raising organic vegetables. The struggle for autonomy becomes not only familial but societal, as society is recognized as the larger parent who will limit life and growth, its quantity and quality. There is nothing that cannot be accomplished if we all pull together, and parents are too preoccupied with their own vague, selfish affairs to "*do* something." That those selfish affairs include putting food on the table so the teenager can have a full stomach on which to continue his activism is hardly perceived. Both teenager and parents can accuse each other of being out of touch with

reality at this stage; the teenager may view his "inactive" parents with contempt, and the parents, hurt by this opinion, which is such a far cry from the
high esteem in which they were held just a few years ago, still view him as
a kid who "doesn't know the score." The conflict of, or gap between, generations is at its height; each perceives different losses and sees different
modes of transcendence as more effective. Both parents and children lose
each other a little at this time, parents often looking to the lessons of the past
and teenagers to the possibilities of the future, where parents had already
looked and found the clash of illusion with reality.

One of the surprises in my case histories was the number of interviewees
who reported feeling like an "outsider" during their teen years, alienated,
isolated, not one of the group. Even those who had been, by objective signs,
"popular" (i.e., cheerleader, class vice-president, active in several clubs)
reported this sense of being on the outside looking in. Space is one of the
first dimensions on which we learn to exist, and the inside-outside dichotomy
is a notion with which many children experiment in play (as are over-under,
front-behind, etc.). This understanding of space—one cannot be inside and
outside at the same time—continues on a metaphorical level, but a value
judgment is now placed on it. Inside is "good," and outside is "bad." Further,
a common theme across protocols was the importance of a special place or
space, the country or the city, for example. One lives in the right space, dies
in the wrong one. The destruction of space, a home, is acutely painful; several
interviewees reported that their houses had burned to the ground and past
lives thus destroyed. A common dream was of space, distorted, empty, or
filled, meaningful within the context of the L/T life themes (of these, more
in Chapter 9, on relationships and families).

Graduations from junior high school, high school, and college serve as
rites of passage, as deadlines of the psychosocial moratorium. These rites are
supposed to be greeted with celebration and joy, diploma, parties, perhaps a
watch to signify the new importance of time. They are valuable, as are other
"passage" rituals, in that they function as mandates to behave as if the transcendent aspects of the passage obviated the various loss aspects, as if death
did not exist. Of course, the losses are profound: losses of friends, structure,
environment, behavior, peer support, relationships, possibilities, a chunk of
future, relative financial freedom, limited responsibility, loss of safety if they
face the draft and possibly war, loss of predictable forms of anxiety, which
are supplanted by unpredictable forms (final exams replaced by job evaluations
or exploding shells), even loss of boredom, which is the negative aspect of
predictability. These losses obviously vary with the investment of self that
has gone into the educational experience. If they were faced and admitted
full expression, entry into adult life might be considerably delayed. Such
rituals are promissory notes from society, the larger parent, assuring the
participant that other good things will replace the losses incurred, as the tooth
was replaced by the coin. These rituals are also rewards for following society's

mandates to learn and believe in its promises; society in the form of school, parents, community makes the individual the center of attention for a day.

Loss of virginity symbolizes different things to parents and children, this symbolism varying with religious and social upbringing (as well as with historical cohort). In Western literature, to parents and, in a very different sense, to children, loss of virginity represents a loss of innocence. The innocence lost is of sexuality, the parents often having repressed their knowledge of the child's other sexual activity, including masturbation. The innocence lost is also of evil, the blackest form of which is death; the child, like Eve, partakes of the forbidden fruit from the Tree of Knowledge. Now he knows. To the parent, the child now knows sexual orgasm for the first time. Sexual orgasm is a metaphor of death, "le petit mort"; the frigid or impotent individual who is preorgasmic is very often afraid of loss of control, afraid to die. Both orgasm and death are experienced as blackness; the little death is more fearful because it is pleasurable and so could tempt to further dalliance with the larger one. Indeed, some adolescents add strangling and suffocation to the instant of orgasm, reporting that this intensifies pleasure! Until now, the child has been innocent of the magnitude of loss that must be incurred over the life cycle, culminating in death. Thus, to the parent, at some level her child's loss of virginity is his first experience with the death of self. The full tragedy of having brought into the world a life and love destined to death probably descends on the parents at this point, which is often at just the age of 35 or 40, when their own death is becoming more salient and realizable. For them, the waning of sexual power and attractiveness or even the return to chaste "virginity" will signal further progress toward the great death, *dont et dans la ronde*. To the child, loss of virginity coincides with the cognitive period during which he can comprehend the abstract, including death. Lorellen and others report that sex was a form of rebellion against limits. It is often enough a mixed, traumatic, or disappointing experience, one of the little deaths with which life is filled, frequently unattended by the pleasure that had been expected, and with which it is later associated, because of technical ignorance, guilt, fear, or performance anxiety. Thus, knowledge of evil or the loss of innocence, loss of virginity, and death are all equated in our culture, an equation not always conscious. However, a more psychoanalytic interpretation would consider sex to be the life force and aggression the death force, sex bestowing a momentary immortality.

The teenager's loss of innocence about sex, death, and evil in the world seems paradoxically related to a characteristic aspect of adolescence, that of increased risk taking, or a plunge into new loss possibilities. He races his car or motorcycle, thumbs rides with the unknown, experiments with mind-altering drugs and music, fights, with weapons possibly, frequents amusement parks and arcades and "smash" dances, and may try out delinquent behaviors. The explanation for this behavior is probably fourfold.

First, there is a natural delight in novel stimulation, the thrill of a roller coaster ride, which is probably coordinate with sexual development and a counter to the increased pressures of school boredom. These pressures include a brutal "training out" or brainwashing of altered states that enrich life; only one consciousness is permitted at school and at homework, the alpha dealing with the logical and the concrete. Many risk-taking experiences alter consciousness, perhaps for only a period of seconds. Boredom is deadening, and novel stimulation is revitalizing.

Second, sexuality is less repressed than it used to be, but death and aggression are still the great taboo. The teenager violates this taboo with "smash" dancing, chains, red skulls on leather jackets, in defiance of a death he is just beginning to comprehend.

Third, as the teenager is not yet allowed to prove his competence in adult roles, he tries to prove himself in substitute activities, whatever is open to him. In other societies, teenagers are already full participants in the life and work of their group (Munroe, Munroe, & Whiting, 1981; Whiting & Child, 1973; Munroe & Munroe, 1975; Whiting & Whiting, 1975; Vogt, 1970; Triandis, 1980; Chagnon, 1977); the hunting, gathering, fishing, building, and nurturing all entail purposeful activity that constitutes a real and necessary contribution and risk enough. In our society, teenagers spend years in activities that seem only remotely related to the world for which they are supposedly preparing. The culture is handed down through years of hours spent sitting, listening, taking in, repeating, rather than stories told by the old ones around the campfire after the day's work. Arbitrary laws, orginally meant to protect the teenager from exploitation, now keep him out of the job market, where he might be too much of a threat. Technology keeps whatever job he gets at entry level. The rhythm imposed thus on growing is not necessarily "natural." It may be more natural for the notoriously difficult early teenager to sling hash at the local fast-food outlet, earn money for clothes, feel competent, be physically active, stay out of trouble, get bored with the limited vistas of such work, and *then* develop a motivation for higher education, returning to school. Probably nothing short of a revolution will make education itself an experience of ecstasy (Leonard, 1968).

Fourth, with the increased capacity for abstract thought and time perspective, the magnitude of loss in life is beginning to be comprehended, and, through risk taking, the teenager symbolically proves his transcendence of death and all its metaphors. Each risk pays off in thrills and extended life, showing that loss is not real, confirming the fundamental illusion. Then a friend foolishly dives into a foot of water. . . .

Another paradox of the preteen and teenage years is the desire to be just like everyone else, at the same time that one is undergoing rapid individuation. Partly, this can be seen as an unconscious transference of the identification process from parents to peers, in order to be accepted by them, with all the associated rewards of support, friendship, approval, sex—a teenage mode of transcending loss. Partly, it is the discovering of the universal within the unique; the universal is associated with other selves, warmth, companionship, and the unique is associated with aloneness, against which there is a cultural mandate and which is painful (Becker, 1973). There is protection in numbers. Slater (1976) is eloquent on the conflict between the cultural mandate of independence and the resultant emotional isolation and destruction of limited environmental resources. In our culture, solitariness is equated with loneliness, against which there is a social mandate as powerful as that for independence. We do not train our children in the rewards of solitude, although it is possible that some of our lives will be spent alone. That great accomplishments in the arts, as well as many spiritual experiences, are usually achieved in solitude is anathema to teenagers and another instance of lack of proper training. The film *Walkabout* shows a teenager of another culture, Australian aborigine, trained quite differently. I think Slater misses the fact that teenagers have been trained to herd, and wastefulness of material and human resources occurs in the company of others.

For the rest of her life, the individual will oscillate between recognition of the common bond she has with all humans—the surprising universality of her own intensely individual fears, anxieties, rages, joys, and hopes—and the progressive individuation that makes her more and more different from other selves as she grows older (Jung, 1971; Koestler, 1971; Becker, 1973). She will pass the piano practice room and hear an unknown other playing the same Chopin nocturne that she plays, at once empathizing with the discipline, struggle, and euphoria that the other experiences and recognizing that she herself plays it—and feels it—as no other. When she is 20, she is similar enough to others to form a bond of intimacy, marriage for instance, with any number of others; when she is 40, she may be too different; kindness and caring may be broadened to include many others; she will know the universe of hunger, delight, fear, revenge, laughter, and love so well, but now there will be depths that are hers alone.

YOUNG ADULTHOOD

With the end of teen years, the individual chooses either to "postpone adulthood" by further education and preparation or to begin the life of an adult. This choice partly depends on his place in the social structure and in the historical period; if he is of lower socioeconomic status or in a depressed economy, he may have to get a job to support himself and others (Elder, 1974). Or he may manage to support himself through college. There is evidence that the early twenties are evolving as a new period of socially sanctioned extended moratorium (Kimmel, 1974; Levinson, 1978) with an associated extension of the identity versus role-diffusion psychosocial crisis, just as adolescence and childhood evolved from a time when a child was regarded simply as a small adult (Aries, 1962). Without optimal resolution of this crisis, there can be no successful resolution of the intimacy versus isolation crisis, requiring merging of one identity with another (Erikson, 1950), and indeed the rise in alternative life styles may reflect this.

The tasks of the twenties are generally marriage, parenthood, and starting a career; however, these tasks increasingly seem to be postponed. The sexual revolution, allowing sexual fulfillment outside marriage with the advent of the pill; the increasing education or training needed to enter many occupations; the women's liberation movement and correlative postponement of parenthood for careers; the problems of mismatch between population growth and energy or other natural resources which lead to a lessening social mandate to procreate; the enormous growth of technology resulting in career retraining for many— these are all credited with the change in timing of major life events. The notion of age clocks—that individuals in a society can define age-appropriate behavior and plan their lives accordingly—is changing (Neugarten, 1987). In recent years it is recognized that this timing is no longer as rigid as it once was. Individuals postpone children, return to school, and switch careers in mid-life.

At whatever point the individual selects an occupation and begins either vocational/professional training or actual work in the field, he experiences the losses of all other alternatives. He must gradually, through socialization into his new role, experience the losses of the parts of self that would have been appropriate for other occupations but are not appropriate for his chosen one. The budding musician must leave that part of himself behind when he enters medical school; he may use the defense mechanisms of intellectualization or anticipation to tell himself that, once he is established, he can play with the local orchestra part-time. But Barron (1972) has found that first-year art students often do not yet identify themselves as artists; rather they identify themselves in terms of alternative occupations that they have finally selected against or to which they might return. This split identity can be as psychically painful as the loss of a physical limb, and indeed the phenomenon of phantom limb may prevail in the analogy of phantom role, that which is lost but still feels present and is indeed still present in the lost self.

Faith, an artist in my sample, was accorded the identity of "artist" very early in life, by parents who gave her an art book, teachers who praised and hung her work, and librarians who let her into expensive print collections. But many individuals are not as fortunate.

On the job there is the progressive disillusion that firsthand experience entails: a loss of ideals, a distortion of the me of self to goals, with a concomitant distortion of the I. If the distortions required of the self in a particular job become too severe, the individual may seek another occupation. However, disillusion is the losing of illusions and the progressive salience of reality; it does not necessarily result in the *affect* of disillusionment; on the contrary it can be most satisfying.

Socialization into a job entails the acceptance of beliefs, attitudes, and values that may be alien. An invisible contract exists between the large corporation and the employee, often implicit rather than patent. It reads something like this:

> *The product of the company is important because it makes our work, and therefore ourselves, important. The founders, whose pictures gaze down benignly from the reception area walls, are to be revered. We do this [list of activities and attitudes] and we do not do that. We are a unit now, and you are a part of this unit. You are to be loyal, competent, and believe in what we are doing. In return, we supply you with the wherewithal to live and with a meaning for your existence.*

The individual who selects an occupation is also selecting an identity. At a party, it is common to ask, "What do you do?" The reply is: "I *am* a computer programmer" or a nurse or an electrical engineer. Thus, even linguistically, what we do defines who we are. Our occupation becomes our identity. The process is as follows. Each occupation has a stereotype or an image of itself in the minds of others. As soon as we announce our occupation, we will be treated according to that image or stereotype. We will be expected to respond to that treatment in stereotyped ways. We will behave as we are expected to behave. We will perceive ourselves as behaving in these ways, that is, as objects. For the sake of cognitive consistency, we try not to see ourselves as behaving differently from the way we feel; besides, we receive validation from others for our consistent behavior, and to some extent we exist in accordance with this validation from others. Then we begin to *feel* as we behave. Then we see ourselves as both feeling and behaving like our occupation. And thus, through a feedback process, we become how we feel and behave—we *become* our occupation.

When a person chooses an occupation, she or he is selecting far more. Clothing will be largely determined by that occupation. The clothing of a waitress is different from that of a lawyer and so is the salary. So is the status or prestige, the extent to which others respect what we have to say and validate our existences as worthwhile. When we select an occupation we also choose our friends. The Strong Vocational Interest Blank demonstrates that people of similar occupations have similar interests, so we are choosing our interests and also our topics of conversation, even though we are unaware of this initially. We are also opting for certain ways of socializing over others—skiing requires more money than tennis. Our life style also will be largely determined by our occupation, both what we can afford and the nature of it. Upper-middle-class people are more aware of healthy life styles, the importance of exercise, particularly if one's occupation is sedentary, the occasions on which counseling may be appropriate, the desirability of fruits and vegetables, poultry and fish, unsaturated fats and fiber, the dangers of smoking.

Finally, the person selecting an occupation is also selecting environments; she or he chooses to work in a hospital or a business office or a factory and will probably live in a neighborhood of families of similar socioeconomic status. The children will very likely attend schools in that neighborhood. Teachers ask to teach in better districts with fewer discipline problems, and the best teachers tend to have their requests accepted because they have more occupational options. So, in a very real sense, the person choosing an occupation is choosing much of the future for self, spouse, and children.

In the Marxist paradigm, work may alienate the worker from himself. On the assembly line, along the firetrails, in the kitchen, behind the x-ray machine, if the individual cannot integrate some meaning of his work into the L/T structure, he loses his time and his life to no avail. We cannot assume that there is more intrinsic worth in one specific occupation than another. Rather, there is a balance of losses and transcendences within an occupation for a specific individual as he builds his own "life structure" (Levinson, 1978), self structure, and L/T structure. The matters to be balanced have grown more complex in past decades (Turkel, 1975; Berger, 1969). For some years salary was no longer the highest consideration of many workers. While salary has grown more important again in recent years, other factors are significant as well; security, intrinsic satisfaction with the tasks, feelings of worthwhileness, happiness with co-workers and bosses, and fringe benefits are all of great concern (Davis & Cherns, 1975; Yankelovich, 1981; Applegath, 1982). Levinson (1978) and Rubin (1979) have illustrated the importance of considering what *meaning* an individual's work has to that individual, and these illustrations are often reminiscent of Frankl's (1963) thesis that meaning is the object of human search in every area of life. Levinson's subjects appraised and reappraised their work in terms of its meaning for them, its intrinsic worth, its impact for good or ill on their life styles, the satisfaction and enjoyment inherent in it.

An individual trades her time, which is her life, her distance from death, for the wherewithal to live her life; she loses alternative ways to spend her time, the coin of her existence. In what existentialists term the dialectic between the individual's present and her death, between being-in-itself and being-for-itself (Sartre, 1969), there is a dialectic between work and death as well, as can be seen in the reports of an overwhelming number of my interviewees that they reevaluate work (and other major aspects of their lives), be they 25 or 65, throughout their lifetimes, rather than simply at the end of life. The work must transcend the loss it incurs of time, of other choices, of health, novelty, joy, and this transcendence includes not only the skills, mastery, and competence required for it but also the contribution it must make to building the self and L/T structures.

Work and love are the two major issues of the twenties and, in different forms, of our entire lives. The median age of first marriage is 22.5 for women and 24.4 for men (U.S. Bureau of the Census, 1986). Although the com-

mitment to one intimate relationship in the twenties is one culmination of
learning how to be intimate, to relate to another on a less and less superficial
level, such learning has been going on since childhood. This intimate relating
moves from the knowledge of two me's to the empathy and intuition of two
I's. However, just as the child has actually loved his ideals of who his parents
were, rather than the parents themselves, and has discovered this in adolescence, he runs great risk of marrying an illusion in his twenties. Once again,
the wedding day is the day on which all other possibilities are lost. There is
a projection of all ideal qualities on the selected mate, in the attempt to
transcend this loss; in a sense, nothing is lost if the mate is all, and others
cannot compare, and we can maintain cognitive consonance. To the extent
that this illusion is successfully maintained (bolstered by society in the joyous
solemnity of the ritual, in approval and mythmaking), the couple will feel
unconflicted on their wedding day. They will see each other as all, the fulfillment of a societal myth that is necessary to the culture's stability and
survival.

The ambivalence, the so-called crying for joy, is a mourning for the loss
of illusion once again. Mothers and fathers cry not only for the loss of role,
relationship, and beloved children but also in displacement of their own clearer
grasp of the realities involved. Relatives congratulate the couple on their
acceptance of the societal mandate with gay laughter and sly winks to one
another, supposedly pregnant with sexual innuendo but in reality of grimmer
meaning. (Is that a note of sadism in Uncle Charlie's hearty toast?) They
know something the young couple does not—the reality beyond the illusion—
but they're not telling. The young couple are validating their elders' choices,
and why should they escape death, or the limitations of life in which the older
ones unwittingly ensnared themselves when they succumbed to the same
societal pressures? The bride particularly becomes the embodiment of the
loveliest of illusions for a day. She may even have selected an "illusion veil"
for her bridal headdress! When the veil is lifted for the consummatory kiss,
the couple is supposed to see and welcome each other as they truly are—and
the illusion is complete! 'Til death us do part. . . .

The much-vaunted adjustment that subsequent marital life entails (Papalia
& Olds, 1986) may be readily understood from the L/T perspective. Marriage
represents rebirth, leaving home, expulsion from the womb. The transcendent
married me in the L/T self structure of each individual is learning the various
duties of its role from society and from each other and is growing and taking
up more space within the L/T structure than some of the other me's, particularly
the single me and the engaged me, which must be moved into the lost me
sector along with all its activities, single friends, freedoms, and especially
expectations. These losses are, of course, registered in the transcendent I,
which must integrate both the meaning and the self-concept, still caught
between the myth of what we thought our married selves would be like and
the reality of how we are. To the extent that the myth and the reality are too

discrepant, or transcendence mechanisms are limited, or meaning and self-concept are difficult to integrate, the adjustment may be defined as a difficult one. To the extent that integration is easier, the transcendent married me may be strengthened in each L/T structure, and the couple may experience growth, a deepening of love, a stronger transcendent I, best described by Maslow's (1968) "peak experiences" and "beta needs," and indeed the love may become a general transcendence mechanism, pervading the entire self, giving meaning to the lost as well as to the transcendent sectors. If all my past has been leading up to this, it has all been worth it. Some of the self has been given up for the total marital entity that the two me's now are, the *we,* and this may be experienced either as progressive loss of self or as self being part of a greater entity. Analysis of the case histories yields the conclusion that the transcendent married me undergoes quite a bit of variation in the amount of space it takes up over the life cycle, marriage being experienced as more freeing in some periods and more constricting in others.

The married couple sets up house, or the outward and visible expression of their transcendent mergence. The part that friends, art, religion, TV, alcohol, and other general transcendence mechanisms will be assigned in their lives may be seen in their choice of possessions—wide space and multiple seating capacity, a bar perhaps, a certain kind of art selected before a modest TV, religious symbols. The home is set up for transcendence, a haven and refuge from the stress of the outside world, a womb in which to regain one's homeostatic equilibrium, impregnable to loss. It may also be experienced as a kind of death, "housewife's syndrome," the fear of leaving home or agoraphobia, which is reaction formation, panic over not being able to leave the womb simultaneous with a prospective expulsion, or a defense against *needing* to leave. (The syndrome may serve the purpose of birth eventually. See Chapter 10, on personality and psychopathology.)

The evidence of others as well as my own (Moos, 1976; Dohrenwend & Dohrenwend, 1974; Papalia & Olds, 1986) indicates that new parenthood represents a severe crisis to the majority of people studied. When looked at in the context of the L/T paradigm, the reasons are quite clear. New parenthood involves a plethora of losses—privacy, freedom to break routine, previous habits, time together, money, some sexual intimacy (on the average, 3 months of disrupted marital relations)—previous activities for which diapers, feeding, formula preparation, cleaning up, rocking and singing, and so forth must be substituted. Identity changes with changed bahaviors. The new parents are suddenly in an extremely confining structure, bounded by the baby's needs seven 24-hour days a week, and these all obtain if the baby is relatively healthy and problem-free! These losses stretch into a seemingly unending future for the couple, variably transcended by love for the baby and each other, as well as specific coping and defense mechanisms—babysitters, vacations, task sharing, hobbies (sublimation), planning (anticipation), humor, and repression. Much of the transcendence of the parents must be shifted to the future as it never has been before; not only must security be planned but also the future is seen in terms of the baby's growth, and the baby becomes an extension of their own selves, their own growth and transcendence.

In addition, the baby provides a different form of transcendence for the parents; as it grows to childhood and beyond, it is a daily reminder of their own lost childhoods, a help in understanding their own pasts and in integrating further meaning. Against the smoothness of the baby's skin, the hand of the 25-year-old is suddenly wrinkled as it had not been before, and there is a realization of one's own progress through time. Baby will see years that parents will not, a new century perhaps.

The parents of the new baby will often find themselves "in mourning for the perfect child expected" (Kanner, 1976). She may have been born deaf, or with clubfoot or a strawberry mark, or she may just look different. Sooner or later, as she becomes what she is seeded to become, this mourning process may deepen; she is not as bright, talented, pretty, angelic, popular, or happy as her parents have bent every effort to make her; and yet she is delightfully so much more than they had envisioned and touching in her full humanity. She doesn't see as we see, and she insists on going her own way, dancing oblivious toward daily disaster that, somehow, does not occur.

Part of our sense of tragedy in the fate of Anne Frank and the children of the concentration camps is that they were never allowed to grow into their idealized adult selves. But, by the nature of their humanity, they could never have fulfilled our illusions of what they might have been.

Parents found a family on a dream. Their family will be ideal, loving, together, mutually supportive, a warm place where each member can become the best she can be with the loving help of every other member, a place of cozy fires, loving meals, refuge from pain and injustice in the outside world, glowing holiday celebrations, in short, a place that is different from the family in which each parent grew up; they will not let their children down as their own parents have. They will be more generous, provide more clothes and education, never spank but simply reason, always listen, be there whenever needed—all things to each other and to their children. Many of my interviewees, like Marjorie, expressed their desire to provide for their children the home they felt they never had. In fact, this was a theme across the protocols. In becoming the parent they wanted their parents to be, they will transcend their own sense of loss from the ideal; their ideal parenting will provide love and security for the children whom they identify with themselves. They will ideally parent the child within themselves, thus regaining what they have lost. It is illusion once again. They do not count on their sons and daughters becoming individuals who do not want what their parents offer because they have different values.

These new parents will be rejected to a greater or lesser extent because both generations are partially products of different ages. They will discover, as they must, that "their" children were never really theirs, that they were only on loan, given into their care for a little while. They will wonder at the mystery of when they really lost "their" children—was it on the child's wedding day, or was it farther back in the high school years, quarrel by frustrating quarrel, or was it on that first misty day of kindergarten, when a tiny hand was relinquished to the world, or earlier still? The mystery of where their children have gone is like the mystery of death, because their children were never really theirs and were never really the children the parents thought they were, but mysterious little beings still evolving their selves and lives, separate L/T structures, in which their parents have moved into the lost sector.

The parents experience the death of the child who never was and the death of themselves in the child's eyes.

The parents will have to struggle not to reject in turn, but to accept and transcend this loss from the ideal, to accept their children as they are and are becoming, to found their loving relationships on an everyday reality as they do with friends and acquaintances, rather than an impossible ideal. Otherwise, their family runs the risk of becoming pathogenic, in modes brilliantly evoked by Jules Henry's book *Pathways to madness* (1971) and also by Bermann in *Scapegoat* (1973), in which loss is piled on loss, and transcendence is maladaptive.

Henry lived for several weeks with a number of families, each of which had at least one psychotic child. He found that the relationship of the parents to dimensions such as time and space was bizarre; food was an occasion for schizophrenogenic interactions; transcendence mechanisms were inappropriate, often placing children in actual jeopardy; a mother rescues her toddler from the road only at the last moment; a father leads his young son into physical danger; meals promised for delivery in a few moments are hours in the making and then taste awful. In the Bermann study, the psychiatrist similarly went into a home to determine why a young boy was reported to be an impossible behavior problem at school and a perfectly adequate child at home. He found this to be true indeed, but the maladaptive transcendence of many problems was common here as well; transcendence for one family member caused loss to another that could not be resolved and remained hidden beneath what Henry would term "sham." L/T process and structure within family life is complicated by the fact that each individual has an L/T structure, as does each dyad within the family, each triad, and finally the family as a whole (see Chapter 9). Both of these studies demonstrated losses stockpiled, transcendence incomplete, or worse, pathologically dependent on the loss of others.

Another major new area of L/T at the young adult stage of development is the management of finances. Depending on income, how one manages finances is indicative of how one transcends loss in general, one's choices and basic values. Some have only enough for bare subsistence; L/T is finely balanced hard work for bread, and nothing is left over for general transcendence (which may partially account for the higher incidence of schizophrenia in people of lower socioeconomic status). All spending also involves the loss of possibilities in the choices being made, and decisions on how to expend one's resources may very nicely reflect the L/T structure of the individual. An emphasis on saving for the future is an attempt to store up the years one saves for; the spendthrift knows future has an end point and despairs of it, losing self in a welter of things that may exist longer than she does; the miser fears her future lack of competence to earn enough for subsistence and saves against starvation, illness, rejection, aloneness. For many, extra money is spent on general transcendence—TV, travel, alcohol, music, drugs, art—and excessive expenditure in this realm may denote a paucity of specific mechanisms, an unhappiness with daily life, or an attempt to extract meaning to the last drop.

Responsibility cuts across the parental, occupational, and financial sectors of young lives. Responsibilities usually involve postponement or loss of hedonic gratification, which postponement society has mandated in the form of laws, prescription, and ritual for the sake of its own ultimate survival. Some responsibilities are civil—voting on issues about which it is one's duty to become informed, cooperating with authorities on various levels, filling out forms, paying taxes, behaving in prescribed manners in specific situations (such as not leaving the scene of a car accident). A major loss deriving from the necessary assumption of responsibility may be boredom, or the loss of an optimum level of stimulation from what is novel. Also, responsibility may take too much time, the measure of one's distance from death, which might be put to more satisfying use. It has been estimated that the average American currently works more than 4 months a year to pay her taxes, which often go to projects of which she may disapprove, such as the buildup of the military, the space program, foreign aid, tobacco subsidies, "irrelevant" research.

MIDDLE ADULTHOOD

A crisis occurs when loss threatens to engulf existing transcendence mechanisms, be they specific, dispositional, or general. At no stage in life is this truer than the mid-life period. It is the point at which all losses, present, past, and future, suddenly catch up with the individual, threatening to overwhelm. It is also the point at which many dispositional transcendence mechanisms are becoming progressively maladaptive and less dependable; the winning smile will no longer clinch the sale because the corners of the mouth are turning down. It is the point at which the major questions become "Is this all there is?" and "What's the point of it all?" Life has reneged on the promises we thought it made: the love is not eternal; the children deviate from the dreams we had of them; even the badges of success at work are unsatisfying; we have done all we were supposed to do, but there is no reward; something is missing; foam has no substance, and neither have clouds. The questions of middle age are the hardest, questions of ultimate values. There is a growing sense of "last chances." I may never love again, rise higher on the career ladder, see the wedding-cake castle of Monaco and dance down its narrow, crown-chandeliered streets. All I've done, and how I've lived—is it all meaningless? This was Ivan Illych's question (Tolstoy, 1960).

Middle age, or middle adulthood, extends from roughly 35 or 40 to 55 or 65, depending on the socioeconomic status of the definer, with working classes perceiving it as a younger age bracket than middle classes (Neugarten, 1968). The period of midlife transition occurs from 38 or 40 to about 43 or 45. For some of my interviewees, the period was a gentle transition; for others it was crisis. Farrell and Rosenberg (1981) report that not all men go through a mid-life crisis.

Traditionally, the major losses associated with middle adulthood are the waning of sexual attractiveness and loss of sexual experience that it may herald; correlationally, the ebbing of procreative and sexual functioning, evidenced by menopause and decreased potency; the possible "empty nest" syndrome in parents who may mourn the loss of children leaving home to establish their own households, and the consequent loss of role functions associated with parenthood; the frequent recognition that professionally one has reached a plateau, has gone as far as one is likely to go in terms of promotions and salary increases, is not going to attain the heights once dreamed of; the onset of more frequent and disabling physical restrictions (this is the period in which many chronic diseases often first appear); frequently, the death of one's parents, with the concomitant realization that one is now part of the older generation, next to go; the more acute perception that time is limited and there may not be enough of it left to do all one had planned, and, as Levinson has so eloquently pointed out, the consequent necessity to revise the dream; the decline in feelings of worth and self-esteem associated with losses in the above areas. The decline is proportionate to the investment of self one has made in these areas as well as to what the culture of the individual is telling her about her worth and the worth of the area. Finally, there is the salience of increased prospective or anticipatory loss in all of the above areas. The doctor who could cure everything when we were young, no longer can. There may never be another day without pain or discomfort of some kind.

We will consider each of the above losses and modes of transcending them briefly before moving on to a more general consideration of L/T in this period.

As the individual grows older, he looks less and less like himself. The reflection in the mirror is becoming a shock. We carry pictures in our minds of how we appeared when we were younger, and adjustment of these pictures to reality seems to proceed by "catch-up" jolts rather than gradually, like the real changes. Repression aids us in our blindness to fine lines until they are wrinkles. We approach mirror and camera with our "best face" on, smile, tighten muscles, but every so often we are caught by surprise. As we age, gravity pulls the mouth down in an uncharacteristic expression of bitterness or opinionation. We look so different from the way we feel, and increasingly we are treated the way we look rather than the way we think we really are. Evidence has accumulated that we tend to *act* the way we are treated when we are children (Rosenthal & Jacobson, 1968), and there is no reason to think we respond differently as adults. So when nature molds lines of "worry," "anger," or "depression" in our faces (they are rarely interpreted as "wisdom" or "fulfillment" except in our observations of the physiognomy of other races and/or cultures), we are seen that way and we respond that way. The rest of the body changes similarly; flab accumulates, hair thins and grays, skin pales. We do not look the way we feel, but increasingly we feel badly about the way we look. The me seems less and less representative of the I.

One of the major reasons for our concern with changed appearance is worry over diminishing sexual attractiveness. The topic of "sex" is such a value-laden one in our society that it may be impossible to strip it to essential meaning. In a sense, sex is the great leveler; no matter how poor, uneducated, underemployed, scurrilous, or even scrofulous an individual may be, if he has the basic sexual equipment (he need only imply capacity to use it), he may take his pride in that; his existence is justified. That we do not focus on similar natural functions such as the capacity to defecate, bleed, tremble, or perspire as sources of esteem or worth may clue us to the blinding nature of sexual values. It would be quite possible to build the justification for laudable defecation in place of sex on billboards, television, in college courses (agriculture), innuendo, pleasure cruises, and so forth—although the reader may doubt it. (I offer it as a short story theme, if I don't write it first.) Breathing as a cult has its adherents. At any rate, we are a genital rather than an anal society, for which Freud would give thanks, and the uses of sexuality are to bring people together, overcome hostilities, procreate the race, have fun, and provide a democratic base on which nearly all people may be equal, at least to begin with. As they age, they are less equal, and so less human and less entitled to the benefits of humanity such as income, compassion, and political power.

With regard to sexual functioning, there is a set of propositions which states: (1) more is better, three orgasms a night is superior to three a week; (2) older is less attractive, unless it's a man with money (see De Beauvoir, 1972); (3) older has fewer and less intense orgasms and a likelihood of impotence or declining lubrication; (4) older is sexually inferior; (5) older is therefore inferior, period. These propositions—the result of a materialistic and mechanistic society—begin haunting individuals in our culture around the age of 20, when, to maintain worth, each of us must become partnered if we aren't, keep that partner from all the more sexually attractive partners around, get another partner when our sexual inferiority finally catches up with us and we lose this one, lie about our age, and fight all aging signs diligently. When we hit 40, we expect rejections to increase exponentially, and so we perceive that they do. We cooperatively fulfill prophecies by more numerous episodes of impotence, painful intercourse, vaginismus. We are an obsessive society. We smother all thoughts of death and spirit by obsessing on sex, counting it, quantifying it. Sex is screen, distraction. What is it that we are hiding from?

The menopausal woman and the impotent man are objects of derision. In a mechanistic society, anything that breaks down in normal functioning, interrupting the stimulus-response flow that protects us from thought, may be kicked or laughed at with impunity, cars or humans. But whatever we do to others, ultimately we are doing to ourselves, and at some level the laughers know this. By their laughter at parents today, they inflict pain on themselves tomorrow. Their laughter will echo down the hallways of their minds.·

Research in the area of sexual functioning, particularly that of Masters and Johnson (1966, 1970, 1981), has gone a long way toward dispelling myths, but unfortunately not stereotypes. Sexual functioning in males does indeed very gradually decline on a purely physiological basis as they age. With regular activity, however, it continues indefinitely, with intensity of orgasm in both males and females only minimally lessened and apparently dependent on muscle tone, which can be maintained. The key lies in that prescription of "regular activity" (Masters & Johnson, 1981; Hunt, 1974). Elderly widows don't have partners, being devalued as elderly males are not (De Beauvoir, 1972) and also greatly outnumbering elderly males. Sexual interest, as opposed to physiological functioning, reaches its zenith in males at the age of approximately 18 and then gradually declines. In females, sexual interest culminates in the late thirties and remains at that level for an indefinite period. Just as a woman is at her height of interest, she is undergoing what Sontag describes as the "humiliating process of sexual disqualification" (1972). Whether the differences between males and females are physiological or cultural in basis is yet to be resolved.

In our society, lying is the most common mode of transcending changed appearance and decreased sexual attractiveness and functioning. The goal is to appear Calvinistically one of the "elect"—the young or younger. It begins with lies about age, hair color, eventually face lift and other lifts, bolstered by swallowing vitamins, hormone injections, jogging, swimming, tennis, and yoga. The transcendence is less than complete and satisfactory, however. The self does not become younger, and what is incorporated into the self is a split between I and me, reality and appearance. The part of me that must lie to retain sexual activity a little longer must be reflected in a self-concept of one whose worth is partially a lie. On the other side, the price of integrity is high, sexual deprivation occurring sooner. The woman who does not color her gray appears odd; she must be uninterested in sex, not quite human, undemocratic. The double standard of which De Beauvoir (1972) writes with such eloquent anger allows a man's hair to be distinguished when it is gray if he has status to match.

Related to sexual deprivation is touch deprivation. Although there appears to be no research confirming this, it would be logical to hypothesize that babies are touched most of all and that as we age we are touched less (except by the impersonal nurse or doctor, which is more like invasion). As more than one-third of marriages end in *dissolution* and the other two-thirds are often filled with *disillusion,* this decline in touching and being touched seems inevitable.

Folklore has it that when the children take flight, one or both parents may suffer from empty nest syndrome, which may include feelings of depression, boredom, anxiety, uselessness, and a host of psychosomatic ills. The mother in particular may suffer from role loss, at a time when she is going through menopause and feelings of decline in attractiveness that may be emphasized by the blooming of her teenage daughter. But the results of research in the area show that, for most, life satisfaction in married couples goes up in this period (see Rubin, 1979); Neugarten, 1968, 1987). There is the lessening of stress connected with children. Couples have more time for each other and for the leisure activities of which they have dreamed, particularly travel. Women have been "saving" up projects that they will do when they have free time, courses they will take, lost me's that they may now resurrect. Although a father may regret that he did not spend as much time with his children as he now wishes he had, and the opportunities for such nurturance are now slimmer, overall this is a relatively happy period.

However, there may be a serious problem here. The 20-year-old who gave up acting, biking, and career aspirations to devote her life to her family, who squirreled away those lost me's, is now trying to bring them back into a different self. She has sciatica and riding is painful; her ingenue acting efforts that gained raves of "talented" and "promising" in the little theaters of her youth must now be switched to character parts, where more is expected of the older and experienced. In other words, it is when she returns to acting that she becomes a "failure," if only for a time. From the perspective of the 20-year-old, she could always catch up; the 40-year-old knows better.

The empty nest may be filled with grandchildren (see Cherlin & Furstenberg, 1986). Grandparenthood is a new role for the individual during this period, and although grandparental behaviors are popularly defined (gifts, babysitting, visits, having the family to holiday feasts, giving advice only when asked), they seem on the whole to be satisfying. Grandparents are fond of observing that they now have all the joys of the children with none of the hassles. As soon as baby wets, they can hand her back to Daddy.

The new challenges presented by the empty nest, particularly to women, are related to challenges of professional change. Lillian Rubin, in *Women of a certain age* (1979), writes movingly of the risks, guilts, and joys midlife women experience when returning to school or embarking on a new career. As observed above, some women "go back" or try to. All during her period of marriage and motherhood, the amateur "historian" has been reading history books, dreaming of the day when she can return to school, obtain a doctorate, perhaps become an assistant professor, and then rise to heights unlimited. But she has changed and the world as she once knew it has also changed, a world where graduate students had university representatives practically lined up outside their doors to hire them. The time is lost. She will transcend this loss of time and opportunity in the same way that many men do when they find that, in mid-career, their opportunities are closing down.

The midstream career change is becoming more common with the opening of new job fields, in computer-related industries, for example, and the closing of others because of population reapportionment, fewer children attending school (this is changing), more older adults, and the longer life span. Here again, however, the me of the old job must move into the lost sector, and the new me must be socialized into the new job with consequent restructuring and redefinition of the self. The process is similar to that undergone when the first job was chosen in the twenties. But it may be more painful. The individual must change his definition of self from "I am a high school counselor" to "I am a computer programmer," and one can see the dramatic loss that this poses—the lost friends and colleagues, activities, meanings. If I can be changed so devastatingly, then surely I am not me, but who am I? For too long the individual has had one most important me and, as the humanistic psychologist points out, this can be deleterious to growth. Maslow (1971) describes the self- actualized individual as defining himself in terms of his work because he loves it so much that it is one with his metamotivations, such as beauty, truth, and justice. However, Bugental (Chiang & Maslow, 1977) seems more on target in pointing out the dangers of defining self in terms of restricted me. If I am my arm, my breasts, my job as train conductor, I had better not lose them, or I am annihilated. After all, the me of myself is an object; it is how I am treated by others. I had better not treat myself as an object, or identify too closely with the others who do.

The mid-career change for women may not be a question of self-fulfillment. Inflation makes the two-income family more of a necessity, less of a luxury, and divorce has increased the number of single-parent households headed by females who must work to survive (Papalia & Olds, 1986). Woman's image is a reflection of what society expects of her and is rapidly changing from full-time motherhood to mother-worker (Baruch et al., 1983).

Individuals in their forties are often growing out of the patriarchal image they had of "their" company when they were in their twenties, particularly if they have been with it for a while. Little instances of their lessening value show that their company doesn't love them as much as Daddy does, unconditionally, in spite of age and heart disease and an occasional screw-up with the client. They will predecease their company as they will not predecease their father; the company will see to it. The perspective of the 40-year-old is changing like a fog lifting from a field. The idealized relationship between company and employee is ending, as between computer and programmer. We recall that it began with the 20-year-old's necessity to choose one occupation and foreclose all other possibilities and the necessity to see his choice as the best. Now we see that the relationship has been merely reciprocal all along. Neither the computer nor the company was human, and the phrase "the company feels that . . ." was a lie. The company has no feelings.

In his poem "Prospice," Robert Browning wrote of a time when "the snows begin, and the blasts denote I am nearing the place" (1922, p. 222), the metaphor of physical decline approaching death. In middle adulthood, breezes very often precede the wintry blasts, but they are multitudinous (Papalia & Olds, 1986). The forties are the common age at which bifocals are needed; gum disease, having had an earlier start in the thirties, now threatens future dentures; increased insomnia, episodes of vertigo, muscular aches, ailments of almost any organ, lumps benign and otherwise, hemorrhoids, decreased vital capacity, breathlessness, longer periods of convalescence from colds and flu, longer wound-healing—the list is endless. Some of the symptoms are more foreboding than others, but all are suggestive of catastrophe. The index of hypochondriasis goes up in MMPI records (Barron, 1979), and the individual may die a different death with each symptom. The fact is that, barring accidents, sooner or later one of these symptoms, or the disease it heralds, will prove fatal.

Losses are becoming less often chosen, more often imposed. That they are now of internal origin is more sinister in implication; the body, part of the self that one could always count on, direct, and control, is becoming increasingly unreliable. Betrayal springs from within. Because the I does not feel at one with the body, there is a tendency toward splitting, I from me, and increased objectification of the body. I feel fine, if only my hand would stop shaking. The body becomes part of the world, the threat, the enemy, the other who will condemn. Denial is the frequent transcendence mode to handle depression. In many ways, it is the reverse of depression. When depressed, often one has faced facts, although one may be integrating them in an unnecessarily gloomy cognitive light (Beck, Rush, Shaw, & Emery, 1980). One transcends by plunging into healthy practices and visualizing the positive consequences. Sometimes these happen, weight is lost, muscle and skin toned, blood pressure down. Denial comes in handy for ignoring the fact that these improvements are only temporary.

The severe illness and/or death of parents, which may be accompanied by heavy personal and financial responsibility just as one is trying to launch the youngsters, is often a watershed, a kind of life span continental divide. No matter how many miles or degrees of understanding away, the parents were a bulwark against adversity, sources of support, counseling, and financial help perhaps, and, on an unconscious level, a womb to return to if the world got to be too much. Until our parents die, it is they who will care for us on our own deathbeds, as they did when we were sick children. Now, it will be our spouse, perhaps, or a child who does not yet fully understand suffering, or strangers. Our parents were our last shield against mortality. We could not die as long as they lived. Over and beyond the grief we feel over the loss of them personally, the me who has been child, however revised, must move into the lost. When we lose our parents, our childhood becomes irrecoverable.

And more. We lose the childhoods we could have had, the parents we always wanted but could never quite mold—more approving of our careers or life styles, more affectionate, less prone to anger or indifference. The possibility of the family that might have been is also gone, no matter how unrealistic this possibility had become when we were grown with children of our own. Pretenses about it, however, tend to be externalized. We praise the dead aloud, at the same time admitting to our consciousness the failure in relationship that can now never be rectified. We see the same failures reflected in our relationships with our own children. After long trying to be like our parents, at last, in our forties, we are too much like them. The dying of our parents is thus a time of guilt, regret, and further loss of illusion, as they are no longer present to maintain fictions, which we in kindness and guilt maintained to their faces. For the first time, we may be faced with moral questions concerning euthanasia, suicide, and institutionalization, all fertile ground for guilt no matter how we decide. The guilt is like sin, original and inescapable. (See Chapter 12, on death.)

Others we know, too, are beginning to die (they so rarely did before)— Sally's mother at only 42 of cancer, the famous actor at only 48 of heart attack. We are losing acquaintances, friends, family, idols as we did not before, and the me who related to these also moves into the lost sector of the self. Still, the obituary columns we have begun to read show many who survive to 80, dubious comfort.

The time perspective is foreshortened. When we are children, eternity is from Thanksgiving to Christmas; as we grow older, life passes like the journey on a road so frequently traversed that we are at our destination before we know it. Now is the time priorities must be reset, goals hierarchized and/or eliminated. The society that sets store by accomplishments measured in terms of career, title, money, prizes has in effect set a price on our heads. We must either agree with those values, and with our price, or determine that there are things more important. One of the most common modes of transcendence is a move from future orientation to present orientation. We who have missed so much in the present times which are now passed, are smelling flowers. "Où sont les neiges d'antan?" the poet asks (Villon, 1960), and we respond by walking in the snows today. New values, new meanings may be constructed in which we can accept ourselves and the worth of our lives as we could not before. The fact is, we have failed to a greater or lesser extent as parents, jobholders, citizens, lovers, friends, and all the other me's of our selves. The actual never reached the aspired. We must come to terms with this or succumb to stagnation, preoccupation with bodily decline, despair (Erikson, 1950).

Each of the above losses and its transcendence redefines the concept of self that has been constructed over the years; the loss of roles (Sarbin, 1968), insofar as they have defined the self, is equivalent to the loss of me's, and the I may have less to integrate. The individual will transcend these according to the L/T structure she or he has built up over the years, as well as the specific transcendence modes dictated by each loss situation. As we have seen, common specific strategies include trying to appear younger than we are, which leads others to treat us as younger and ourselves to feel younger—an illusion of course (you're only as young as you feel); finding new activities (replacement); and what Vaillant (1977) terms the "mature defense mechanisms" of altruism, suppression, humor, anticipation, and sublimation, although of course, neurotic and immature (and even psychotic) defenses may also be employed.

The mid-life transition is resolved in a number of ways. There is either a recommitment to the marriage, or separation and divorce. Divorce is often an act of faith; the divorcing person believes that a better relationship is possible. Similarly, with one's career, there is either a recommitment or a new career. In both marriage and career, however, there is change as a result of recommitment. Those who decide to remain married do so after counseling, soul-searching, experimenting with other relationships, marathon marriage retreats. They renegotiate the marriage contract, typically leaving more room for the development of separate identities. Thus, mid-life transition is not necessarily an occasion of upheaval. One of my interviewees commented that she had not had a "mid-life crisis, because I didn't know I was supposed to have one." (She was one of two who reported this.)

There are other resolutions as well. The 40- and 50-year-olds become mentors to the young. They grow in their concern for, and contribution to, their community and world. Their being-in-the-world will have made a difference. Their grown children become delightful companions rather than burdensome responsibilities, because parents can now free their children to make "mistakes," having learned that so many mistakes are occasions for growth. Mid-lifers have a renewed sense of freedom and choice—if they are willing to take the consequences, they no longer feel "compelled" to do *anything*. They are discovering the rewards of solitude, in reflection and in the renewal of long-buried creativity. There is no longer a need to please others or to conform in the superficial ways that used to seem necessary.

A new compassion for the human predicament arises. The 40-year-old man who has been bent on achievement and the actualization of his animus may newly discover and permit the anima in himself, the nurturant needs and feelings that have been necessarily repressed (Jung, 1971); the woman may become more assertive, and now that her nurturant needs have been satisfied and her homemaker role is ending, she may move toward fuller actualization of her other abilities. The man may become more caring, the woman more materially productive. In these bloomings of the contrasex aspects of the self (Jung, 1971), the self may become more whole.

One of the major modes of transcendence that arises during this period is a progressive sense of interiority (Jung, 1971; Neugarten, 1968); the individual's thoughts, values, feelings, intuitions, and spiritual stirrings become increasingly important, so that the phsyical loss is of less significance. It is as if the landscape of the mind, or inner space, expands with the contraction of the external landscape; or it may be seen as a form of overcoming physical obstacles by spiritual strength.

Possessions or material things seem to take on new meaning at this time (Csikszentmihalyi & Rochberg-Halton, 1981; Weenolsen, 1978). They are a way of preserving what is lost, of keeping relationships alive that death or distance have disrupted. The crystal bowl that now holds a place of honor on the family dining room table, overflowing with fresh fruit, once held fruit trifles, plum pudding, and other festive desserts at the home of the beloved aunt on holiday occasions, when the entire family met, and the now aged were in their primes, and the now mature were wide-eyed children, and the family squabbles seem forgotten in the haze of remembered embraces and excited chatter. The bowl is a loyalty, which the present children will preserve, with stories of times they never knew, told to the children they do not know as yet, as they pass to adulthood.

It can be seen that mid-life transition bears only a superficial resemblance to adolescence within the L/T paradigm. The identity crisis is there once again, but it is in the context of other identities, emerging values, lost me's and I. The finitude of time and life, the approach of new losses, the necessity of conversion from physical to other resources—all are appreciated in a way that was impossible during the teenage years.

SENESCENCE

Personality considerations aside for the moment, if we were to diagram the lost self and the transcendent self in the child and again in the adult, we would find a much larger proportion of transcendent self in the child. In fact, the infant has only a cluster of molecular behaviors in the lost sector. In the middle years, there is likely to be more of a balance. With the older person, the situation is reversed somewhat, a far larger and expanding proportion of self being in the lost sector, as transcendent self, coping mechanisms, and role-related me's, gradually contract. The transformation of self that has been included in transcendence is moving in a new direction. I am all that I have been, but I am not now what I once was.

The age at which senescence is perceived to begin is most commonly the age of retirement, which represents one of the major losses of the period. The loss is a complex one, with component losses of financial reward, role activities that define how one spends the major portion of one's time, relationships with co-workers that often extend beyond working hours if only in gossip, the structuring of one's time, and, most important, the concept of self as enacting the role that the work entails. Like high school graduation, it may be memorialized by the farewell dinner, speeches, and a gold watch, a peculiar symbol in view of the fact that time will probably be less structured than it was and its measurement less required; it may be a reaction formation or denial that time is limited, a replacement of time lost, a wish to the retiree of long time before death, or a memorial of time gone, like a grave marker. At any rate, in our inimitable cultural fashion the celebration conceals and denies the plethora of losses involved. The retiree is enjoined to be happy; the metaphor of retirement from work as retirement from life, or yet another step toward death, is blurred, but accounts for tears; the prospective retirees, on whom the last years of work may indeed hang heavy, are to metamorphose sorrow to joy as a way of dealing with anticipatory mourning. Their turns will come. Meanwhile, those retiring are sallying forth into the sunset.

And they frequently do. If they are healthy and financially secure, they may purchase a motor home and travel the country, join the American Association of Retired Persons for supportive networking and various benefits, subscribe to *Modern maturity*, watch reruns of "Over Easy" on television to see how others have solved similar problems, and enjoy the title of senior citizen (the new euphemism—there are no junior citizens) with its occasional fringe benefits of merchant, movie, and national park discounts. They have earned their leisure, if they managed to put a little aside or have a company pension to pay the taxes on the home they thought they owned. Otherwise, years of trying to survive on fixed Social Security and Medicare (sometimes during runaway inflation) may be grim. They may have to subsist on dog food, depend on nutrition programs such as Meals on Wheels if they are shut-ins, and even die of hypothermia during cold spells when there is no money left for heat—or of drugs inadvisably combined because of inadequate research into the idiosyncratic effects of drugs on the elderly. They may have saved all their lives for retirement, acquiring a decent nest egg, only to "spend down" all of it on a costly disease like Alzheimer's before they are eligible for government help. Many senior citizens find their nest eggs gone in a year. Losses that would stagger a younger person must often be met by the frail or ill. The poor elderly are less attractive than the wealthy elderly; if they become incontinent, ill, disoriented, they may have a darker problem with which to grapple; abuse of the elderly by their children is only just coming out of the closet (Pedrick-Cornell & Gelles, 1982). One can only guess at the effects on self and self-concept. However, solutions to some of these problems are also proliferating. SAGE is now giving the elderly a sense of potential; the Grey Panthers, the American Association of Retired Persons, and similar organizations, headed by such activists as Gay Luce and Maggie Kuhn, began the kind of political fight that seems necessary to gain any minority in this country fair play, compassion, and legislative help.

Further losses of the period include increased physical restrictions (Birren & Sloane, 1980) in sensory areas as acuity of taste, sight, hearing, kinesthetic feedback; loss of teeth, muscular flexibility, skin tone; and losses associated with common diseases of the circulatory system, cancer, rheumatoid arthritis, and so forth. It is often necessary to spend more time attending to health. Jogging in place becomes a symbol of the Red Queen's caution to Alice that one often has to run very hard just to keep up.

Other losses include loss of attractive self-image, loss of friends, companions, and spouse through death; loss of grandchildren as they, too, move off to establish households; loss of home, as restricted financial circumstances or loss of spouse or children frequently make a move to smaller quarters mandatory during the fifties and sixties; loss of "the world as it was"—future shock quite frequently catches up with the individual in this period. The whooping crane is becoming extinct. Loss of self-esteem is perhaps one of the greatest losses endured during senescence; she feels she has learned so much, but no one will listen; indeed, no one even touches her any more. Antique furniture gains in value as it grows older, but not human beings.

Here we must distinguish between the losses associated with normal aging and those caused by disease. For example, one stereotype of old age is the onset of senility, and yet only 10 to 20 percent ever experience severe cognitive decline, most over the age of 80. It is a temptation to attribute chronic back condition to age if the person is old but to accident or the carelessness of youth if the sufferer is young. (There is the story of the elderly gentleman who visited his physician with a complaint of pain in his right knee. His doctor told him, "You have to expect problems like this at your age," to which the gentleman replied, "But doctor, my left knee is the same age as my right one.") The distinction between normal aging and disease process is an important one because we are more likely to be able to cure disease than to reverse the effects of age, although an ability to slow down the aging process may not be too far off.

There has been a long-standing controversy in the field of gerontology over whether a principal mode of transcendence for healthy functioning at this age is disengagement from society (Neugarten, 1968)—from work, friends, and interests—or activity (Birren & Sloane, 1980) in new areas that replace the old, such as leisure occupations, travel, new work roles, and involvement with community service. The resolution of this controversy has been the recognition that disengagement may constitute healthy functioning for some types of personality, which have had their roots in such responses in the individual's past, whereas for others, activity is the best solution. Both disengagement and activity entail replacement of some sort, either through defense mechanisms such as withdrawal or through specific substitute activity. The myth or story we tell oneselves of our life will be quite different if we have withdrawn than if we are still integrating new me's into our structure. And we cannot know to what extent we choose replacement (or activity) for intrinsic worth of the activity or because we are uneasy with the story we would have to tell if we stopped.

As the transcendence mechanism of interiority increases, there is an increased emphasis on memory of past events and their integration into a life review (Butler, 1968; Butler & Lewis, 1983). As my research has shown, individuals report ongoing review and evaluation throughout their lives, but the quality of life review in old age is different. Its main purpose is to make sense of what is done, rather than to plan the future. The individual may not be able to remember what he had for breakfast this morning, but he can remember an event from his childhood with glowing clarity. It is true that this may be a sign of organic brain disorder, especially when accompanied by disorientation as to time, person, and place, as well as other indicators (R. Kahn, personal communication, 1977). However, the lost sector of the individual may be far richer than the transcendent sector in terms of experience, and reliving its events may provide an emotional satisfaction that cannot be elicited from busy children, dead friends and relatives, work colleagues one no longer sees, and restricted activity. Further, the periodic reevaluation of his life in which the individual has been engaged over the cycle takes on new urgency as its end approaches. The story that he has been telling of how he lived his life, smoothing out ruffled relationships, adding significance where there was little, explaining a dubious action in more acceptable terms, constructing and reconstructing meaning over and over again to give self substance—all is drawing to a close and must be put into final form, like the last draft of a manuscript. The time will come when no changes can be made. The sense of personal urgency in this activity is not readily explainable, unless we believe we will be held accountable in a new existence or are concerned with the memory of ourselves that will remain in our children and in the world. But this final life review, this construction of meaning and integration into a finished self, must be performed. The self must not die unfinished for some reason. This is one illustration of death as final transcendence.

If reminiscence becomes too obsessive, the self may become more isolated from the present. Lost images may fill his mind, but he is incapable of communicating their beauty, humor, horror, glory, significance, the pungency of their taste or smell. He has experienced them and integrated them in his unique fashion, and try as he may, he cannot convey that experience to his listeners. In a replay of the generation gap, his listeners may be more concerned with the urgent business of daily living. If he wants companionship, he learns to keep these riches to himself or exchange them only with one of his own age, whose story may be a bit dull, but who is amenable to a reciprocal arrangement.

DYING

Finally, there is dying. All the other leavetakings of one's life have been prototypes of the final one, and how one has transcended the others may be of help now. As we have seen, there have been many small and great deaths, of hope, career, illusion, pets, children, parents, friends, possessions, physical wholeness, possibilities. These are all projects of love, and that death should overcome love seems unacceptable. In the Erikson (1950) paradigm, individuals may face the prospect of their own death with integrity or with despair; if they have integrated their lives into meaningfulness, they may accept death as the end, or as the stopping point in a long journey that continues in spirit.

For many, death itself is not as fearsome as the process of it, the actual dying with its pain, loneliness, feelings of abandonment, loss of control and independence in making decisions about one's treatment as others take over, the ritual denial and pretense in which one is forced to engage with staff and relatives surrounding one's condition. The individual is transformed from all he is and ever was into a dying person; that is his role, in which he is trained through his interactions with others, and he is suddenly seen as a dying person only. As such, he must participate in rituals of sham, as Henry (1971) would have called them, and of which Glaser and Strauss have so eloquently written (1965, 1968; Strauss & Glaser, 1985). The "good patient" must pretend he is getting better, never speak of his doubts and fears, not complain or try to take a hand in his own treatment, but obey and cooperate completely, and speak only of neutral subjects like the weather or the hospital food, and preferably of the immediate future only, as allusions to longer time might embarrass others—relatives, friends, and staff alike. He must pretend to accept all assurances, ignoring whispered conferences in the hall, thereby shielding the living from what they, too, must eventually endure.

Fortunately, alternative approaches to dying have developed (Stoddard, 1978; Davidson, 1978; Rossman, 1977; Wilcox & Sutton, 1985). The hospital is still the best place to be cured, but it may not be the best place to die. Extreme life-prolonging measures may not be what the patient chooses. The hospice movement, under the direction of Dr. Cecily Saunders, has taken hold in England and is now spreading in the United States. At this writing there are over 1100 hospices in the United States (Kane, Wales, Bernstein, Leibowitz, & Kaplan, 1984). The hospice provides home care and support for those who wish to die at home, visits to hospital patients by trained volunteers, and freestanding institutions that seek to minimize the negative aspects of dying. Pain relief is a top priority (S. Lack, personal communication, 1979). The individual can maintain the independence he craves as long as possible. The hospital, geared to treatment and cure, can prolong his life, but when the quality of life becomes unacceptable, he can opt out. The ultimate goal of the new movement is to assist the individual to "live his dying" (S. Lack, personal communication, 1979; Kubler-Ross, 1971).

Dying is also the experience of becoming less like oneself; one feels that self is splitting from the body. As observed above, we each carry with us a picture of self as we were when younger than we are now, as children when we are teenagers, as 20-year-olds when we are middle-aged, as in our prime when we are old. Perhaps we have never looked like our real selves, or how we feel we should look; perhaps the mirror has always given back startling reflections, and we appear blander, more sorrowful, more superficial, or more attractive than we know we are. But in dying, the discrepancy is accelerated. It is an odd experience to feel the various parts of the body break down, that body which has been identified as the self for so long; one begins to feel detached, as if an old friend were leaving on a journey over which one has no control; it seems strange that the various parts of the body that worked pretty well for so long, no longer do. There is a sense of going on, or of going away, of splitting off rather than ending. The treatments have thinned luxuriant chestnut hair (never mind that it had grayed); disease has mutilated and wasted us almost beyond recognition. As we entered life not recognizing our hands as part of who we are, we leave it in the same way—these hands so wrinkled, bony, and veined are simply not ourselves. Perhaps in infancy and in dying we are closer to the truth of our identity, that our bodies are not who we are.

Roman Catholics administer extreme unction at the last moment, but this is one of the only positive rites of passage we have for the dying, and what event better merits one? Surely, dying, as much as birth, graduations, weddings, birthdays, and anniversaries, is worthy of some ritual assistance to help the individual with his last integration of self-concept, to tell himself the story of how it was and is, to provide meaning. (See Chapter 12, on death.)

We think we have no control over the length of our lives, that we helplessly await a "bullet with our name on it," but within the L/T paradigm this cannot be. Predictors of longevity (Palmore, 1970, 1974) are not only actuarial (race, sex, ethnicity, and genetic endowment—our "thrownness"—over which we have no control) but also physical functioning (cardiovascular disease, smoking, exercise), intelligence, and work satisfaction, all of which are susceptible of some manipulation on our part. High socioeconomic status also increases longevity (Butler & Lewis, 1983; Birren & Sloane, 1980) because, with increased wealth and status, we are better able to maintain our health. When the proportion of loss to transcendence in our L/T structure becomes unbearably great, frank suicide may become our choice (rather than the more dishonest forms, such as smoking). When that proportion is relatively equal, we may not be motivated enough to extend our lives by adopting healthier life styles and habits.

Now that the mandatory age for retirement has been extended from 65 to 70, it will be interesting to see if our concept of senescence also recedes 5 years; one would predict that it will. One would also predict that, since longevity is associated with work satisfaction, we will see some extension of the average life span. The psychological correlates of disease would support this prediction (although the stress of being on the job longer might lead to more stress-related diseases). (See Chapter 10 for a fuller discussion.)

OTHER ASPECTS OF THE LIFE SPAN

The losses outlined above are those which are commonly on time during the life span, and their transcendence, including the revision of self, is typical of the life period. But some of these losses can occur off time. A baby may be born to a child of 12 out of wedlock; divorce, separation, or death of spouse may occur at any time from adolescence to old age; biological predisposition may lead to the onset of disease off time. The off-time sustainment of losses that are normally on time will often be more traumatic and require modes of transcendence different from those normally employed. The preteen who bears an infant may lose it to adoption, lose education to go out to work and support it, lose other chances at marriage, revise her friends to include those who are more understanding, change her relationship to her parents, and certainly alter her concept of self in her efforts to transcend. These are heavy requirements for a self barely formed.

Time-irrelevant events such as natural disasters—earthquake, flood, fire, tornado, or other "acts of God"—can occur at any time during the life cycle, with their attendant train of losses both direct and indirect. Accident may maim, kill, and/or traumatize the individual or one close to her. Crime may victimize. Friends are lost and replaced throughout the life cycle, although the various on-time losses outlined above will accelerate this. Most devastating may be the accident of historical period; the stock market may crash, war may be declared, treason, witch-hunt, or dishonesty may haunt high places. The Great Depression affected parents and children at various points in their life cycle quite differently (Elder, 1974).

Moves from house, neighborhood, state, or country can occur at any time during the life span. Their attendant losses are those of structure, relationships, familiarities, sights, sounds, and activities; the long lazy bike ride under arching trees to the department store is replaced by a bus trip. Moves teach a child the "expendability" of human relationships; that people are replaceable or interchangeable and yet unique, like some parts of her body—her tooth under the pillow; that commitment too deep is unwise. These children lose the vista and rhythm of growing up in a community, of continuity in other individuals and in themselves. Lastly, moves require the individual in a new neighborhood to enact a new role, to behave like the societal ideal for a while, once she has found out and learned the community version, to conceal herself until enough of the new me has been incorporated.

Moves are a function of the dimension of proximity in space that proved so important in babyhood. As the individual grows older, she must range farther and farther from the original source; if she is fortunate, she becomes her own source, or as the humanists say "centered," or she finds a version of the source that she can carry with her, such as her God. Still, distances become longer, from a different room, to school, community, country, world, and universe, in mind if not in body, and the attachment bond that first united her with her mother is the prototype of the bond to country, for example, whose honor she may have to go to war to defend. All subsequent bonds are metaphors of the original and preserve it to the extent they preserve themselves. The ambivalence in our society over dependence-independence is also a function of proximity in space.

Choice points occur all through the life cycle, ranging from decisions on what to wear (so as not to lose that chance at an important job or beau), what to eat (so the body's wholeness and attractiveness may be retained or enhanced), what medication to take in order to successfully overcome present discomfort, to the major decisions on whom to marry, what work to do. Any one of these can have repercussions far beyond the apparently limited scope of the decision made. It is the awareness of these possibilities, how all decisions foreclose other possibilities, and how the most innocent decisions, such as to market at noon, can lead to death, that has its manifestation in pathological indecisiveness (see Chapter 10).

Transcendence mechanisms specific to the situation have been stressed in the above account, but dispositional and general transcendence modes will also be employed. They are discussed in detail in subsequent chapters. But the stages of transcendence, the grieving or yearning and searching of the mourning period and the replacement and integration of the resolution period, are present in some form with every loss listed above. They can serve as a guide to counseling and assistance in instances of pathology.

Ritual seems to serve the function of informing the individual how she should feel, particularly in the face of loss. It reshapes emotions that otherwise might be dangerous to the integrity of the society and thus is a safety valve and a societal survival mechanism.

In reviewing loss and transcendence through the life span, the question of biology versus culture must arise. To what extent, for example, are losses in the work or sexual area a result of decreased physical functioning, and to what extent are they a result of cultural conditioning? Longitudinal and sequential research investigations, as well as cross-cultural research, may point to answers for this question. However, there is a large, as yet quantitatively undetermined, proportion of variance accounted for by cultural variables. Some of the suffering and/or decline of each period of the life span can be averted because it is not physiological, not a function of age, but rather a function of culture.

In every age period we seem to descend into the stereotypes and myths associated with that period. Some of these are pure fiction, and some are loosely based on fact. But the culture dictates age-appropriate behavior by defining it, less now than previously. It explains behavior in terms of age, which is not explanation but merely descriptive and circular. The effect is insidious. To extend Sarbin (1968), we know the role expectations of each life period and we are, in effect, trained to behave as we do. The penalties for nonconformity are degrees of ostracism or shunning, ranging from vague social isolation to institutionalization (Szasz, 1964). Awareness of the enormous cultural demands to behave in a certain fashion, to lose as we lose, to transcend as we transcend, to deny, conceal, lie, pretend, employ reaction formation, fantasize, withdraw as a whole segment of society, aggress passively—awareness of these demands and possible alternatives may lead us to perceive without prejudice the inherent losses and transcendences of every age and not to impose further on them.

If this culture were evaluated in terms of preponderance of defense mechanisms, we might find an unhealthy proportion of immature, neurotic, and psychotic mechanisms predominating, as defined by Vaillant (1977). And we might find that we can change them, that many of the above losses need not be typical of the age period, and that there are healthier modes of transcendence, such as a view of life as moving onward from physical to spiritual.

LIFE HISTORY

No single life history can illustrate all of the theoretical issues and insights described above; indeed, much of the metaphorical analysis of the life histories is on a different level from the traditional and will not illuminate, for example, Piagetian development, although Piagetian concepts such as those of assimilation and accommodation are applicable to the process of loss and transcendence, as we have seen. The theoretical interpretation given above illuminates the life span nature of development, and the life history of Ursula illustrates it.

Ursula

"It doesn't matter if there's a hundred million people better than I am. The point is that I found joy in doing it, and it was something that I had wanted to do my entire life."

In an old, run-down house nested within a wooded community, birds flit through the rooms, their cages everywhere. Outside, in the rocky yard, about 15 solitary cats sit, sleep, or roam, all strays previously dumped in the park next door. Ursula feeds them on her meager income.

Ursula is a small woman who looks older than her stated age of 54, with long white hair straggling around her face. She is toothless, with sparkling dark eyes and a bubbly, intelligent personality. We are looking over her backyard, "The cats are wild, won't let you touch 'em. See my peach tree? Isn't it absolutely splendid? One peach [laughs]. I watch it. When it gets ripe I'm going to eat it."

Ursula's childhood was spent wandering from place to place with her four siblings and her parents, migrant workers trying to homestead. Her mother had to be very resourceful to feed and shelter the family as they wandered from place to place. Each child was born in a different state. Ursula recalls one bit of land where "there were all kinds of scorpions and snakes." They lived in a tent and hauled water. Once when they were camped under oak trees, it started to rain. The next day their mother had them get "all the cardboard boxes we could, especially refrigerator boxes or anything that had a little bit of wood on them, to build a little structure. She covered it with cardboard, and then she painted it with oil paint. That made it water repellant. . . . We at least had a place to stretch out. . . . At Christmas time she made Christmas wreaths out of the oak leaves, because they were like the holly leaves, put a big red bow on them. . . . She was somewhat of an artist. . . . We went out and sold them. That put food in our stomachs. . . . She knew every edible plant," because often they had absolutely nothing to eat. "She raised a garden, we'd sell produce." The only child to be born in a house died of pneumonia. Ursula's mother also started them in the Latter-day Saints religion, after trying out a number of others. "And she even tried the Spiritualists, and she said: 'Don't ever tangle with them, whatever you do. 'Cause they'll drive you crazy, they rattle the windows, they knock on the walls'."

Ursula describes her father as believing "the grass was greener on the other side of the hill," as he moved the family in search of a dream: a job and a home. He had asthma, "so he was always wheezing and saying: 'I can't work, I can't do anything'." Her mother also had heart trouble. She believed in Ursula's father, being "gullible," but finally "began to lose faith and divorced him" after 22 years.

The family's travels had the effect of making Ursula shy and withdrawn in school. This, together with undiagnosed learning disabilities, contributed to many difficulties. Dyslexia was not diagnosed until Ursula was in her fifties and then only by chance. "I had trouble in school from the beginning. . . . And if anybody even said hello to me, I just broke out and cried. . . . And one little girl said: 'Go say hello to her, and she'll cry.'. . . And so she did, and I busted out crying. . . . And the teachers didn't even dare speak to me." Her educational difficulties also troubled her. "They gave me a math book, none of the rest of the children in the school had it. So then I felt degraded." One time Ursula and her siblings missed the bus. So Ursula had to carry the younger ones across the creek, because there was no bridge, and she arrived at school sopping wet. Another day her brother had 11 cents to buy lunch; he'd earned it, but the school officials kept them all after school, demanding to know where he'd gotten the money, because they knew Ursula and her family were poor. "I wouldn't tell them, because I thought it was none of their business. . . . Well then it began to get dark, so they wanted to take me home." Ursula refused to ride with them, so they followed her in a car to be sure she got home safely, and she gave them the slip by running across an orchard. She characterizes herself as extremely rebellious as a result of her hard life, her educational difficulties, and her shyness.

During her adolescence, Ursula worked a great deal. "I was a good worker in agriculture, picking fruits, vegetables. . . . It made me feel good that I was good at something, because certainly I wasn't at school." She feels that one thing has remained with her all her life, and that is that no matter what happened, she has always been able to obtain and keep a job. "That definitely builds your self-esteem." She quit school in the eighth grade, at the age of 15.

Ursula's first marriage was to a "nice young man," who had to go overseas and whom her mother persuaded her to divorce. Ursula believes this was a tragedy, that her life would have gone smoothly if she'd stayed with him. "We would have done the same thing as the average American. We talked about buying a place, having a family." She had a child who died during delivery.

Ursula comments on the discrepancy between the individual myth and the family myth. "I find myself absolutely amazed when I get with my sisters. . . . I will say: 'You know, if it wasn't that I knew we was talking about the same thing, I would think it was something totally different!' 'Cause the same incident, every one of us have a totally different outlook on it."

Ursula had three children when she was in her twenties, one the result of rape. "It was my personality more than anything, 'cause if I'd have been faster, I'd have knocked him in the head or something. But I was withdrawn." Another child is the son of her second husband. This child's grandmother had been teaching him to talk, and when she died, he stopped talking. But he did sing in the car: "I see a service station. I see a house. I see a little dog. The sun is shining." And then the boy would add, "And my grandma died." Then he would sing some more, always ending it with, "And my grandma died." Ursula separated from this child's father while she was pregnant with yet another child. She had been walking 4 miles to and from a job, but one night she got so sick that she went to the hospital. He never even checked to find out why she hadn't come home. Later he divorced her on the grounds that she was unstable, because she hadn't come home! Therefore he did not need to pay her child support.

Ursula tells of an incident, a "miracle" that happened to her when she was taking the children through the Arizona desert in an old panel truck and had a flat tire. She couldn't get the jack to work. "Well, the sweat was pouring off me, and . . . we could just die of heat." She heard muttering in the truck, and yelled, " 'What are you muttering about?' And this little quivering voice comes back and says: 'Can't a body pray in peace?' . . . And I thought: 'Well, now, that's stupid. Here I've been working and working and working, and I never once thought of prayer'." Then she saw billows of dust that turned out to be a sports car, whose driver helped her.

Ursula's third husband worked in construction as an electrician, was an alcoholic, but bright. His father had raised all the children on booze except the oldest one, because he'd decided the oldest would become a doctor or a lawyer. Ursula married him because she wanted a father for her children, but he beat and abused both herself and them. Once he almost strangled a child. "He put the belt around Betsy's neck, and I thought he was just going to hold it there while he talked to her, and he jerked her out of her chair, and I had visions of her head rolling one way and her body another." At one point

Ursula got so annoyed with his constantly telling the children, "Your mother and I are going to die," that she told Betsy her dad was going to die but her mother wasn't. Betsy repeated this to her dad one night, and that put an end to it. The final incident: "I was about seven months along with Angie . . . and he came home drunk and rammed his fingers down my throat, and put his hands around my neck to choke me. Then he threw me across the room, and I laid on the hassock . . . and ran out the door. I said to myself: 'One day he's going to kill you'." She told him to leave.

In her forties Ursula married a fourth time, again to provide a father for the children. He also was an alcoholic, although he was able to hold a job. However, he was under the domination of a well-to-do mother. He seems to have wanted a mother in his wife as well. "I didn't want to be a mother. I wanted to be a wife, and I wouldn't compete with her." He left Ursula about 5 years ago and went back east to be near his mother. Ursula sends him a Christmas card, and he phones.

In her late forties, Ursula had major surgery. After a hysterectomy, she found that part of her bowel protruded, and they wanted to do surgery again, but she didn't have any more medical insurance and they were not sure the surgery would be permanently successful. "I don't have a heck of a lot of faith in doctors anyway. . . . I just literally hate hospitals." So she continues to live with this rectocele, which "can be fatal if it ruptures, but what the heck? Can you imagine going and having surgery every year? That's not me." She blames physicians for not having warned her to stay less physically active after the hysterectomy; she was mopping the floor soon afterward when she first felt the pain.

Today, Ursula works in janitorial maintenance, where she feels she is learning a lot, although "I wish they had a course in it." Recently she had to repair Exit lights and didn't know how to do so. One of her children was having trouble in school but was helped so much by a private tutor that Ursula decided to consult her, and that was how she discovered that she was dyslexic. Her local junior college has special programs for the learning disabled, and she hopes to become a high school graduate. Educational grants are her major source of income in winter. Her income is approximately $5000 per year with these grants, but when she doesn't have the rent, the Latter-day Saints bishop makes out a check. Church members also bring her food if she needs it.

Ursula has always wanted to be a writer. "I always thought it was stupid because I couldn't read and write, and here I wanted to be a writer." Ursula brings out a short story for which she received a $100 award at college. "I also wanted to illustrate." Her art instructor had them do a self-portrait, and 2 weeks later another. Ursula shows them to me, and the improvement is truly remarkable. "It doesn't matter if there's a hundred million people better than I am. The point is that I found joy in doing it, and it was something that I had wanted to do my entire life. . . . After all these years I found that it was possible. . . . I had an experience about five years ago in Sunday

school. I was holding a little boy on my lap and drawing a picture for him.
. . . He told me to draw a car, so I drew a Volkswagen. . . . And he had
big blue eyes, and he looked up at me and said: 'The car's broken' [laughs]."
Ursula tells each incident in detail like a storyteller. "If you use the right word
in the right spot, it can be so dynamic. And the reason for the picture is 'cause
all people can't hear what you're saying in that word." She wants to do
children's stories primarily. "I need a lot of education. I know I've got a lot
to go. But I'm having fun while I'm going." When Ursula thinks back to all
the years when she was trying not to make a complete fool of herself in her
reading and writing, she thinks her newly blooming literacy is a miracle. This
is largely due to the encouragement she has had from English teachers. She
feels that some day she will get a book published.

When we list Ursula's major losses and transcendences, a pattern emerges.
According to Ursula, her major losses are the excessive traveling she had to
endure as a child, with consequent shyness and withdrawal at school and
disrupted education; this is laid at the feet of a father she remembers as a
powerless dreamer—things would be better elsewhere, and he was often too
sick to assist in their survival; there was hardship in her childhood, they often
went hungry; there was the loss of a husband through her own decision,
influenced by her mother, and there were subsequent husbands who were
abusive or alcoholic or both; there is her health, failing for some time; finally,
there has been a lifelong dyslexia that has kept her from the reading, writing,
and illustrating she has longed to do—indeed, she feels the entire course of
her life has been influenced by this lack.

But many modes of transcendence have been open to Ursula, including
the extraordinary resourcefulness of her mother; the support of female children
and a junior college teacher, who believes in her; her job, church, talents,
and their recent development; and, not least, her sense of humor. Both literally
and figuratively, hers is a rocky garden; she removes the rocks one at a time,
and only a small patch is cleared. Eventually things may take root. Indeed,
the garden is not even her own.

The expanded L/T life theme is thus loss through hardship, rootlessness,
poverty, and lack of education and self-development, owing to the handicap
of dyslexia, abuse of self, failing health, transcended by the current pursuit
of education, support of females (mother, teachers, children), church, job
and late-blooming talent, and humor. The core theme is underdeveloped and
abused self, versus the supported and developing self.

She is rated as transcendence oriented in the replacing stage, high loss,
high transcendence.

Theoretical analysis

Some theories of life span development hold that our development is
virtually finished by the end of adolescence, and the rest is repair; or that our
cognitive or moral development is completed by our twenties; or that we are

going through the adult psychosocial crises of generativity versus stagnation, followed by integrity versus despair (at Ursula's age); or that in our forties and fifties we have reached the summits of our careers, from which lofty heights we now mentor the young. Although Ursula has demonstrated generativity in her rearing of children, she is turning to another form at a (relatively) later age. None of the theoretical viewpoints seems descriptive and/or interpretive of the major thrust of Ursula's life, although many of the stages defined in the foregoing section of this chapter are undoubtedly applicable. Ursula learned by a process of assimilation and accommodation, but *what* she learned was difficult and disrupted.

Ursula's story is that of a human being who has many talents, but, like seeds, they fell on hard, barren, and rocky ground, not taking root. The focus of her childhood was physical survival. Education—the flowering of who she was and all she could be—was denied her because of disability, shyness, and rootlessness. Ursula is, at the very least, a natural storyteller; others were reading, learning, and practicing their craft while she was illiterate, incapable of its very rudiments.

Ursula's concept of who she was, slow and incapable, was exacerbated by marriage to men who *beat* who she was and who her children were. Physical death in different forms threatened, as it had all during childhood. Perhaps Ursula deserved these beatings because she was slow (in her own view).

The seeds did not die. Transcendence for Ursula was creating shelter and food, and her mother showed her how to do it well. In turn, she feeds the homeless. Ursula was also a hard worker who merited pay, a loved and loving mother, a ward of the church. Finally, in a tiny crevice of her life, a seed has rooted and sprung to flower. Ursula is doing what she loves at the age of 54, and also what she can do. She is not stupid, only disabled, something that can be overcome. She is talented; there is a tangible reward for her stories. She is becoming much more of who she can be with a rush, and at an age when others are mentoring.

How is it that the seed did not die, as it has for so many others? We look to Ursula herself for answers. She tells the story of a life of hardship matter-of-factly and with no self-pity. Indeed, she tells it as a succession of stories (which space permitted me only to suggest), transcending in the very act of telling, building that aspect of herself denied so long. She demonstrates the "mature" defense mechanisms of anticipation (education), humor, and sublimation (storytelling and illustration). She feels deeply the loss of past education, but rather than grieving, she is replacing and integrating. She finds help through others. She had the splendid model of a mother who raised her children against incredible odds, resourcefully, cheerfully, and well—a daily battle against starvation and exposure.

Finally, Ursula is doing what she loves, transcending the loss of education with the consequent re-creation of the undeveloped self. Thus she creates an identity that is worthwhile and meaningful.

The manifestations of developmental loss and transcendence as shown in individual lives are demonstrated above. But loss and transcendence within each individual carries with it serious implications for that individual's relationships—dyadic, familial, generational, and group. It is to these that we now turn.

9

Loss and Transcendence in Relationships

If the individual's structure of self is always undergoing transformation, with some of the transcendent self moving into the lost (me's and I); if the lost self is always the framework or context within which the transcendent self operates; if the shape, content, process, and concept of self and its meaningfulness are always changing, with different aspects expanding and contracting, growing or diminishing—what then can be said of the relationship of the entire self to another self undergoing the same process? In other words, if we are always changing, how do we relate to others who are changing as well?

In this chapter I will discuss some fundamental issues in the relationships of dyads, families, groups, and generations, respectively, all from the L/T perspective. I will illustrate these from the lives of the interviewees.

DYADS

Love, in its myriad permutations, is one of the greatest forms of transcendence available to us (see Aron & Aron, 1986). We try to bring more love into our lives, or to avert a threatened loss of love. This love may have many faces and may be of different degrees of intensity. It may be love of a woman for her mate, a father for his child, a friend for her friend; love of nature, art, work, God; love of that which can bring us love—money or fame, perhaps; love of approval, prestige, or other pallid imitations of intimacy; superficial love of the many, if the love of the few is denied us. The yearning and searching for love, the replacement of a lost love object, the integration into self—these constitute stages in the transcendence of lost love.

One of the most important experiences in life is the love between one individual and a member of the preferred sex, most often between a man and a woman. We are raised on the powerful cultural myth that there is one and only one right person for each of us. Plato expressed this, in his *Symposium* (in Jowett, 1956), as the creation of a whole individual who was riven in two and then shot to earth, each half forever to seek the other. Our social myths and fairy tales teach that there is one other individual for us who is perfect, who will fulfill all needs and desires, physical, emotional, mental, and spiritual. We will marry and remain together forever, two units blending into one union of eternal bliss. It is possible, it exists, we have only to find it. Perhaps we pass each other on the street and do not recognize—we must be ever alert! We long for this ideal relationship, and we begin our quest, vigilant to possibilities. The longing is so deep we actually manage to create the illusion of its fulfillment for a while.

The process seems to work in the following manner. Each of us carries a picture of this individual and this relationship in our minds. Her sexual preferences will be kinky or conservative; she will have a sense of humor (implicit is that it will be like our own); she will be kind, warm, tolerant, religious, strong, sociable, sexy, affectionate, intelligent, loyal, attractive, open-minded, possibly employed, financially secure, not too dependent, not too independent, and so forth. These are the qualities most often mentioned in my human development courses, when I ask university students what they want most in a mate. Walster and Walster (1978) report similar attributes.

Then we meet an individual with whom we are compatible. It occurs to us that she may be *the one*. We may start ticking off the characteristics for which we have been searching. Intelligent? Yes. Kind? She did put a quarter in the street musician's box. Sexy? Most assuredly. Sense of humor? Actually, she doesn't smile or laugh much, but she loves Doonesbury. Unaware, we are filling in the gaps, endowing her with whatever is lacking to bring us both to the ideal. Further, she is doing the same thing. The longing for the ultimately intimate relationship has enabled us to create the illusion of completeness. We are two conspirators, weaving the intricate web of illusions that will permit us to realize our dreams. We do not see each other as we really are (if we *are*, really), but as we want the other to be. And we cooperate by changing ourselves in little ways as we sense any strain in the fabric; we dress a little more conservatively, or more casually, tone down the laughter, or guffaw, make ourselves into the image we are learning the other wants. Some me's are relegated to the lost. Others, which will facilitate the relationship, become more salient. The I cooperates by redefining the self. We mold, distort, and change. My interviewee, Nadine, didn't really like football, but "You do a lot of things when you like the person you're with."

If we are successful in our deception of self and other, we may even marry.

Just as each individual has his or her own L/T structure, so too does each relationship. It has been created using the societal ideal as a template. The mythical or archetypal marriage has certain characteristics, which the two lovers act out according to their unique personalities, their social class, and so forth. These are interpretations, of course, and subject to distortion. Their relationship becomes a version of the ideal, and then they say that they have *found* what they have in fact *created*. "I have found my own true love."

Analogous to the individual L/T structure, the structure of the relationship between two people comprises the *transcendent we*, the *transcendent us*, the *lost we*, and the *lost us*. Taking a marriage as our example of such a relationship, we find that the transcendent role-related us contains all the presently active ways of interacting with society: the transcendent us raises children, goes to church, plays bridge on Friday nights and tennis on Sunday mornings, fixes up the house. When there are many such activities, the relationship may be stronger than when there are few. The lost us's are the activities in which the couple have engaged but no longer do, such as courtship, or making do on a lower income, and as with the individual structure, they remain in memory. The transcendent we contains the coping behaviors and mechanisms that are presently employed by the couple as a unit and structure the concept of the relationship, its meaning, myth, and emotional tone. The lost we includes mechanisms not currently employed and the concepts of relationships that were previously defined but are no longer applicable. For example, in the past, disagreements may have been settled by making love; now they may be settled by bickering or fighting, productively or nonproductively. The transcendent we integrates the activities of the various us's and also the story the couple tells each other and the world around them about who they are as a unit and how they function. They are a happily married couple, for instance, who put their relationship ahead of their individual interests, who vacation together, who divide the decision-making processes along traditional sex-stereotyped lines, who are pillars of society. If the relationship changes drastically—if, for instance, too many of the activities of the transcendent us move into the lost us, and there is not much left between the couple except quick breakfasts—the story the we devises may undergo revision; we allow the other to go his own way, we believe in freedom of the individual.

The impact of such changes on the two individual selves is registered first in the me's and then in the I, and the self is redefined as having a different kind of marriage. These stories have the status of myth, in that they are created to propagate societal values as well as individual values and meaning. Changes may be viewed as discrepancies. The relationship is the expression of the archetypal marriage myth and how the specific marriage fulfills that archetype. A change in the expression threatens the archetype, and so the prescription is for less change. Even when the expression changes, the revision of the myth may lag behind.

It thus becomes apparent that the marital relationship, and indeed any dyadic relationship, has an L/T structure of its own. This structure may best be seen as the relative intersection of two L/T structures at their transcendence points (Fig. 2). It will be seen that the intersection occurs between the transcendent me's first; if the relationship progresses, parts of the transcendent I's may be included in this mergence. Complete mergence would appear as the superimposition of one circle exactly on another and is obviously impossible. We can never wholly know another, or we would be that other. Lost selves are too individually defining; no life, so no lost self, can ever be exactly like another. Yet it is precisely this mergence, this other half or mirror image, for which so many long and seek, and precisely the illusion that it is possible (a manifestation of the fundamental illusion) that dooms most relationships before they start.

If we are lucky, the illusion works for a while. Ultimately, it fails. It fails partly because the ideal relationship is a construct, an illusion, a place to arrive and remain forever, like Heaven. Once we get there, we will be there, and there is nowhere else to go. But no relationships are static, because individuals are not. They only appear so. Each individual in the relationship is undergoing constant revision of his or her L/T structure, of which we spoke earlier; the pond freezes over in winter, it floods its banks in spring, it dries up in a summer of drought, and the marshes choke its waters, a myriad of new creatures breed in the stagnation, the color changes from blues and greens to browns and golds with the shallower depth, and beavers build their dams. To say we love the pond is a fallacy unless we love it in all its permutations; then it is the many ponds we love, yesterday's and tomorrow's. Like the pond, we ourselves may have frozen over, or are breeding new species of thoughts, feelings, and visions and new ways of being in the world.

It is possible to maintain the illusion of no change for a while, but true changelessness is impossible. A relationship either expands or contracts, deepens or shallows. When a relationship appears static, it is actually contracting. The appearance of being static is the attempt of both to avoid the shrinking that is already in progress, to hold the fabric to its original size. The symptoms of a marriage or other relationship in this difficulty need no esoteric understanding to spot. Emotional interaction, either positive or negative, is at a minimum; anger would rend the fabric. If the couple is fighting, the relationship may at least be moving in one direction or another, brought on by the changes in each L/T structure. Another symptom is boredom, which is an impasse in the structure of either the relationship or the individual; flow is sluggish, stagnant; the individual, in attempting to hold on to the relationship, tries not to change herself.

In the traditional marriage it has been woman's place to change as little

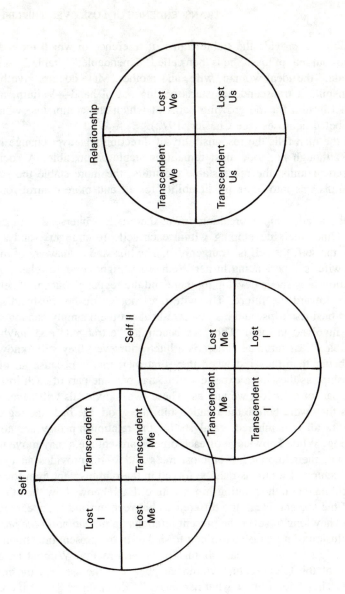

FIGURE 2

as possible, to provide the stable frame of reference in which the man can grow without fear of loss. She is then called "dependable," "stable," "serene," "helpmate," the ideal woman, wife, and mother. Male doctors give her antigrowth pills if transcendence starts getting out of hand—Valium, meprobamate, Librium for the growing pains of which she complains, which are often labeled neuroses (see Chesler, 1972).

To the man falls the responsibility of directing whatever change is necessary, although he, too, must remain as stable as possible. A society is composed of units; the more stable the units, the more stable the society, which translates into more predictability for all and more control for those on top.

If the relationship is breaking down, there is less intersection of the two selves. Other me's developing within each self are strangers, and as they redefine the self, the self is stranger also. The husband is unaware of the new me the wife is experiencing in her Wednesday night ceramics class, and all the relationships she is developing there and the revising concept of self with its move toward the future. The wife does not go on her husband's more frequent business trips, and his few words about them simply cannot convey the me involved in them. They are becoming "estranged" and maybe "incompatible," less intimate. There is a hitch, however; they still "know each other" better than they did when they first met; this is because all of their relationship, as they have experienced it, has become part of each lost I and me and part of *their* lost we and us. These two individuals will never be the same as they were before the relationship; the good, the bad, the regret, the elation are all remembered, catalysts for the relationship they are now experiencing. While knowledge of each other's present me's may move toward the casual, their knowledge of most me's and I still provides an intimacy from which cruel weapons may be forged in their ambivalent fight to at once sever and maintain the relationship structure. Each knows how the other falls short of the societal ideal, the differences between me and I, appearance and reality. They long to sever the present relationship but *maintain the past one*, or the illusion of it that is so difficult to shake. In the present they blame each other for loss of what is past, both illusion and reality. Without an understanding of the L/T structure within and between themselves, the mystery remains. They "don't know what happened." "He changed," as if it could be an accusation, something he could have prevented. "She's not the girl I married"—her fault, of course. As Aurora says, "You marry because one fits the other, and when one changes, the other one gets lost and can't figure out what it's all about." They are married to static images of each other and had expected them to remain as portraits on a museum wall. Their marriage is a victim of the fundamental illusion.

They are not be faulted for this. The institution of marriage, established to provide stability in society, regulation of sexual activity, homes for children, fulfillment of civic responsibilities—to minimize the losses that would ensue in anarchies—has led them to expect changelessness. Much of the me involved in husband and in wife is prescribed, a long list of behaviors to be expected, from taking out the garbage, bringing home the paycheck, to scouring the kitchen floor. In spite of these me's, and even if they remain relatively changeless within the L/T structure—questionable with all the possible events of unemployment, children, illness, disaster, and so forth—even if the husband-me and the wife-me do not change much, all other me's, as well as interaction within the individual and relationship L/T structures, are changing. Considering the protracted length and speeded pace of life, as well as the changes brought about by technology, that one marriage could endure for a lifetime seems more a miracle than a reasonable expectation. The tragedy is that such endurance may require so much distortion of self toward the goal of sustaining marriage as to be of questionable benefit to the individuals involved.

In our culture, relationships are judged successful or failed by their length and how they end. A marriage may have been successful for 14 years, but if it ends in divorce in the fifteenth year (possibly because it was so successful that the individuals grew enough to grow out of it), it is labeled a failed marriage.

Much pain in relationships arises because there is always one person in the dyad who knows more about the relationship than does the other. For example, in an incipient relationship between a man and a woman, there is always one who sees greater possibilities for the relationship. These perceived possibilities are influenced by the need to "find" the ideal mate. Thus, the greater expectation is predicated on illusion, rather than knowledge. A woman may see her new friend as ideal for her, simply because she does not know him well; for her, the possibilities of the relationship are still limitless; he, on the other hand, knows the extent to which he distorts himself when he is with her, or that her blithe assumption of the norm of fidelity is a thing of the past for him, or that her lack of commitment to his political values must limit them, or that there is someone else, or has been someone else, with whom he feels better matched physically and intellectually. How conscious this knowledge is will vary from individual to individual; but the relationship is still a pretty good one, and he may want to explore it a little further before ending it. When he finally does end it, she is mystified, hurt, betrayed. Even as she has begun to see constraints—he must spend so much time in his political activities, and museums hold more interest for her—she clings to the illusion. What is going on within the structure of the relationship is that they are not telling themselves the same story about it. She has been betrayed by the person she thought he was, but not by the person he is. He has given little hints, or perhaps openly commented on their differences, and she has argued or ignored rather than accepted, out of her need for the ultimate. Janet comes close to understanding this process as she observes, "There's probably not more than one person in love when a marriage takes place."

Some relationships grow and deepen; the structures are changing in similar directions at relatively similar paces. There is a maxim that a good marriage requires hard work. This work includes open communication, which assures the exchange of information about structural changes within each individual self and the exploration of alternatives to move them in a similar direction. Shared activities and experiences, while not resulting in identical structural components, keep structures similar enough. Loss is shared, as is yearning; replacement is sought together through similar transcendence modes; both integrate together in the relationship structure (for example, the loss of a child) and create the meaning of their relationship.

A central issue in human relationships is the conflict between mergence and individuation, that is, being all of who one is and can become versus submerging one's feelings, thoughts, interests, and needs beneath those of a significant "other" in order to be one entity. As Yalom (1981) has shown, the penalty for individuation is isolation; the more one becomes who one is, the less one is like everyone else, and the less chance there is for commonality and bonding. On the other hand, the penalty for mergence is often the loss of one's self. Koestler (1971) saw this as the conflict between the whole (society) and the subpart of the whole (the individual). Many young people express the "urge to merge," the longing to find a mate with whom to unite as one. However, both mergence and individuation can result in the death of the self; metaphorically, mergence leads to death by smothering or asphyxiation, and individuation leads to death by exposure to the elements. It is for this reason that individuals often vacillate between mergence and individuation, now leaning toward one pole, now toward the other. Both are forms of transcendence, going beyond what we are, and both can result in death. The advantages of losing one's self in another include escape from responsibility and therefore from guilt, and less painful awareness of the self. But ultimately the self is lost. The advantages of individuation include the transcendence of the old, incomplete, undifferentiated self and the creation of new humanity, growth, revitalization, and life; the disadvantages are aloneness, responsibility, and guilt. On the other hand, individuation *within* a relationship can lead to emergence; Faith's husband encouraged her to be all she could be in the field of art, and she temporarily sacrificed her art so that her husband could take a new job.

Findings that attraction in relationships is based on perceived similarity between individuals (Byrne, 1969) tempt one to revert to a Freudian narcissistic explanation; the beloved other is as much like the self as possible, so that one is in love with another me of the self—that Platonic other half—or in love with oneself in permissible fashion. Horney (1950) perceptively viewed love as a "neurotic solution" when carried to extremes. One can bury oneself in the "womb" of the other and never die. Erikson (1950) saw that the fusion of two people in the intimate relationship was successful only if each had achieved his or her own identity first. Finally, a feminist view of the "perfect relationship" myth would see it as the bill of goods sold to American women, particularly in the thirties, forties, and fifties, to submerge identity so that the husband's identity might prevail—male identity perceived as more valuable to society than female, particularly by males! (See Chesler, 1972; Friedan, 1963.)

The possible course of a marital relationship within the L/T framework has been expounded on as an example of a dyad because it is so important. At the same time, many other relationships may be ongoing for each member of the dyad, one or more of which may become threatening to the dyad itself, resulting in sexual jealousy.

Sexual jealousy has a number of components; one is possessiveness (Clanton & Smith, 1977; Hupka, 1977, 1982, personal communication; Aronson, 1984). But if we indeed regard an other as our possession, if we regard ourselves as possessing that other's body, mind, soul, and emotions, I's and me's, lost and transcendent selves, what we possess today simply does not exist tomorrow, or next month, or 3 years from now. We must therefore constantly take possession of, or repossess, one who is different. Mentally, we hold their image, and our image of ourselves, as they both were when they were "right" for each other. But in the L/T view, commitment entails expectations of changes that are unpredictable, faith in the ability to work through these changes together, acceptance of what is necessary, but unknown, for the growth of the other.

Sexual jealousy is also experienced as painful to the extent that it is experienced as rejection of our selves. What is it about our self that has become unlovable? What is it about the other man or woman that is "better"? Is it his techniques of love-making, perhaps, or that pert way she has of tossing her hair, his empathy, her wit? We may try to emulate the me of that threatening other, or excoriate our own shortcomings as we conceive them. We miss the point entirely that selves, their L/T structures, merge at their natural intersections, which will best promote the expansion or growth needed at that time of life, and that as these structures change, so do these intersections. The urge of the L/T structure is to grow and integrate, rather than to shrink and dedifferentiate, in the Jungian paradigm, and as the structures change, the others with whom these can grow best may change as well. Thus, within the L/T paradigm, what is going on when two people move apart is not a rejection of the self, but a mismatch that is increasing either in reality or in perception (and perception *is* reality). To try to hold the relationship still, like a snapshot, is absurd, even though societal values attempt inculcation with the belief that we should do just that. Rather, within this paradigm, it makes more sense emotionally and rationally to want very much whatever will promote the growth of those we love, even if this means letting go, sooner or later, to a greater or lesser degree.

When we experience sexual jealousy, we feel as though we are being killed. It is true that an aspect of our identity and existence is in danger of being destroyed; the part that related to the other individual, with all the possibilities, plans, hopes, expectations of longings finally fulfilled, dreams, ways of living, feelings of unity in groups, protection of mergence—all this is threatened. A vital part of our life and self may be destroyed, and we are vigilant against that destruction.

Sexual jealousy is one of a number of negative aspects of love; indeed love, the supreme goal and blessing, may be a profoundly negative experience associated with catastrophic loss, as shown in the case histories. The pain of the all-consuming one-to-one relationship has been labeled "romantic" love, and much of the richness of life itself is excluded in this type of involvement. Solomon and Corbit (1974) describe this kind of love as fitting their opponent processes model of addiction; individuals within this kind of relationship feel they cannot live without each other; they have withdrawal symptoms if they are apart, fill their waking moments with thoughts of the beloved, and orient most or all of their lives toward being with each other, just as the addict orients most of his or her efforts toward procurement and experience of drugs.

A continuum of intensity and involvement of self characterizes the range of our relationships from the most intimate to the nodding acquaintance. These are defined by degree of mergence of L/T structures. Many friendships occupy as much self territory as love relationships. Another dimension may be more formally recognized in friendships than it is in love relationships, and that is reciprocality. Friends assist each other in transcending loss, and they do it "evenly." A "network" of friends representing various capacities for transcending loss makes us more secure within the society. Thus, friends preserve our existence—our life and our self—literally and metaphorically, just as enemies threaten it.

CASE HISTORY ILLUSTRATIONS

In the above paragraphs, major relationships have been interpreted according to central premises of the L/T paradigm. Let us turn now to an examination of the marriages and major love affairs of our interviewees for illustrations of these principles. In effect, we have been discussing the many births and deaths of relationships, as well as of individual selves within these relationships. Mergence and individuation can both lead to death of the self by suffocation (asphyxiation, smothering) or by isolation (exposure). Individuation within a relationship can lead to emergence. Sexual infidelity kills, as does betrayal of trust.

Among my interviewees, the major dyadic relationships span the range of mergence from unemergence through submergence, dismergence to emergence. However, other studies can be read as demonstrating similar issues under different rubrics such as dependency, autonomy, and control (Rubin, 1979; Scarf, 1987; Baruch, Barnet, & Rivers, 1983). I begin with examples of submergence.

When I arrived at Heather's home, she demanded to see my ID through the window. Satisfied with this, she opened her door, and I was greeted by two huge dogs; she assured me they would kill me if I attempted to harm her. I was willing to leave at this point, but she explained that her husband insisted on these precautions. This turned out to be part of her L/T life theme (as with so many of the first words and/or incidents of the interviews). Heather's husband is a law enforcement officer and agrees with her on the need to be careful of the violence in the world, as evidenced by assassinations and the murder of a prominent family in their neighborhood.

Heather says she married early: "I wanted to be in love . . . so I started out being the way my mom was with my dad, and then later on in life I found out that wasn't really me, so I'm being more myself." This gradual individuation of Heather is a continuous source of tension between herself and her husband. He has opposed her working as a secretary in a retail store, as well as this interview; she didn't ask his "permission" as she would have in the past, because she knew he wouldn't give it. When he gets angry, he does not speak to her for days. Heather's conflict is between individuation and submergence, which also means security and survival, as her husband will protect her from the world of violence. In discussing her mother's emerging independence, Heather says it's easier for her mother because she's not afraid of losing her husband, whereas for Heather this is a real risk.

I have quoted Heather at some length because we can see her as submerged, but struggling toward individuation, which may necessitate dismergence and emergence. This threatens her husband; he will not be the same person as he was, because he will no longer be married to the woman he originally wed.

Other examples of submergence and dismergence abound. Robin was the unemerged product of a structured home and a Catholic education. Her boyfriend moved in with her, was fired from his job, became lazy, and let Robin support him for 2 years. She allowed him to do this because she was afraid she couldn't stand alone. However, she met another man, and this gave her the courage finally to kick her boyfriend out. When the new romance cooled, she felt so insecure she would call up her friends every night, trying to spend each night with someone. Now, at 25, she is more secure in her independence; she can enjoy being with herself or with others. She is finally out of the womb.

Winnie's struggle to be born and individuate took the form of rebellion against a very straight, traditional, conservative family. (This happens to many teens; see Family section of this chapter.) She merged with her husband within a fundamentalist, born-again Christian religion; this is submergence rather than emergence, because she and her husband leave all decisions, guilt, and responsibility to God.

Greer believes her ex-husband "was looking for a very submissive, quiet person." From age 21 to 41, she feels her life revolved around "waiting for him one way or another." He impregnated her without her consent and had a number of extramarital affairs. At his own request, he was transferred to another area of the country, without his family, so that he could be with a lover. He and Greer stayed married, partly for financial reasons and partly "because the thought of being on my own was just paralyzing." Greer began to see a psychiatrist, asking, " 'What's wrong with me?'—the traditional woman's question—it had to be my fault." She began developing her career and had a brief affair with the husband of her husband's lover. Her husband started drinking, but Greer still couldn't separate from him. He could still get her to drop everything and move to another part of the country with him. When he was going to be transferred for a few months, she actually begged him not to go and leave her alone again.

"All this period of time I almost collapsed. I just did crazy things, begging him that I would turn over all my paychecks to him for anything he wanted. I just can't take it, I might commit suicide—just reverting back to the total scares, just going to pieces. He'd drink very heavily, and we'd have terrible arguments, and in the meantime he'd be off dating, and he told me he was, but then I couldn't understand that."

Finally, she was divorced at 40, and a women's support group helped her validate who she was and who she was becoming. She feels very good about her profession and her financial progress, but bad about her children and her relationship to men. Of her disappointment in her daughter, who decided not to go to college and who has also rejected Greer's values, Greer says, "God, think of the things I could have done with my life. So it's been a time of feeling like what I did as a mother is down the tubes." Of men, she says, "I think I'm less confident about my relationship to men at this point. I think I've regressed. . . . I don't feel as confident about my ability to have a strong male-female relationship. I've been dating somebody for six years, and the last couple of years it's gotten worse. I'm fearful now of going out and starting. . . . I know I don't look old, but I'm accepting that I'm older. Nobody's going to be interested in me. I'm shying away from [making] contacts. I want to meet people, but I . . . don't take the initiative." Her present lover became impotent in the last few years, but she hesitates to try to find someone else. "It's like I'm waiting for something outside, and I'm not able to do it myself."

As we have seen, Crista was submerged, fulfilling the needs of her birth family while she was growing up. If she did not help, her mother might die. "I never wanted anything." [A great part of an individual's developing identity is being aware of one's own needs and wants, trying to fulfill them. To the extent that we do this, we know who we are.] This pattern extended into Crista's marriage, one of the many reported by my interviewees in which the husband made all the important decisions, such as where they should live. He told her that she didn't really know what she wanted.

At 32, Denise's fourth husband is finally giving her the "strength" to survive. She feels "weirdness" runs in the family. "Oh, Jimmy," she takes responsibility for a minor goof, "I've messed up somewhere." Her interview is littered with judgments of herself, like "not stupid, but somewhere along that line," and "not qualified." Abused as a child and relatively unborn, she summarizes her four marriages: "I'm still looking for people to take care of me."

A number of women reported that they were married to "controlling" husbands. Obviously, this is a way of submerging one's life, self-development, needs, and desires to those of another human being. One gains security, stability, safety, and snug protection, like a baby wrapped in swaddling clothes. One does not exhibit the Moro or "startle" reflex. One feels as though one cannot fall, is being tightly held, even in the crib. However, one cannot crawl in swaddling blankets, let alone walk or run.

Annette, Crista, Yves, and Marjorie were all married to controlling or restrictive husbands. Della reports that her husband "made all the decisions," as does Vicki. Yves says, "If I went to the grocery store, and I was gone a little longer than he thought I should have been, he wanted an explanation. 'Where have you been? What took so long? Why did you spend so much money? Why didn't you get this?' My self confidence—what I had when I married him—just went down, down, down. . . . It was a devastating fifteen years." She stayed with him because she was "afraid of trying to make it on my own. How am I going to support three little children?" For Annette, at 65, restriction was indeed security and shelter from the storm. She learned to tell her husband what he wanted to hear; she got a friend to baby-sit once a week so she could go to a movie—her husband strongly disapproved of movies as wasted time. She also sneaked books and hid them. Secretly she listens to the radio with a special earpiece while her husband expatiates on the state of the world in the middle of the night. "You have to learn to do these things when you're married, so you can stand your life. So it works out very nicely, and we get along just beautifully. And then, I can listen with both ears, can't you? [laughs]." Communication is part of Annette's L/T life theme.

One frequent manifestation of submergence has been the mental, physical, and sexual abuse that many of my interviewees have undergone in their marriages. Either they loved their husbands so much that they endured life-threatening behavior, or they feared being alone, like Robin and Greer. Em had to protect her children from her husband's alcoholic violence. Elaine tells us, "One time he threw me against a door, which had louvered windows, and it was glass, and it cut my back all up, and I fell on the floor, and I slid down and hit my shoulders and wrenched my neck. It was a terrazzo floor. . . . He would hit me or wrench my arm. I learned to get out [laughs]. He was jealous of what I did. A few times he would insist that he was going to go somewhere, and I would hide the car keys, so he couldn't have the car. He was just roaring drunk. And, of course, he would take after me, and grab me, and try to make me tell where the car keys were. Or, he'd try to get an argument started, and I'd try to avoid it. And [that] made him angrier, he would start swinging at me, 'cause I wouldn't answer his questions properly, I wouldn't argue . . . I'd just go somewhere and park the car. Just sit." (What did you think about?) "How long it would be 'til I could go back home. I don't like to remember it [tears]."

Kara describes the ex-husband she still loves as "Dr. Jekyll and Mr. Hyde." At one point he "had me on the floor [saying], 'I'm going to jump on top your head and smash your skull in.' He had a lithium imbalance." Kara says that when he was Dr. Jekyll he was a beautiful person, everybody loved him, he was smart, a good student. But when he "flipped out . . . I was sitting in a chair, and the next thing I knew, I was flying across the room . . . and I bounced off a wall and slid to the floor." Once, he nearly threw her down into a courtyard, but a guard saved her. This is the only man Kara has ever really loved. "We were so close."

Ursula tells of the time she was 7 months pregnant and "very heavy. He came home and rammed his fingers down my throat, and put his hands around my neck to choke me. And then he threw me across the room, and I laid on the hassock and also lit closer to the door, and I ran out. He scared me to death. I said to myself: 'One day he's going to kill you.' So that was the end of that. I told him to get out, and he went. It was really rough, because when he was sober, he was really terrific."

Patty also left her first husband, a healthy decision, because he returned from Vietnam a different man, who'd wake up screaming at night and was "a very violent person. He drank a lot. He'd go from being very passionate, being very cold, being very withdrawn. I couldn't take it." Tess was in an abusive relationship, and often physically threatened within a heavy drug culture.

Jaclyn's entire life history is one of mental abuse and subservience around sexual issues. At 20, she met and married Jeb, but could not have orgasms; for this he berated her constantly as being less than a complete woman. Counselors made her feel at fault. In her thirties, they became friends with another couple, Len and Celie, who turned them on to nudist camps, group sex, and wife swapping, pressuring Jaclyn to participate. Len, a self-styled guru, decided to "cure" Jaclyn, and there were heavy sessions in which he attempted to therapeutize the three of them, tell Celie not to feel jealous, and so forth. After years of this, Jeb divorced Jaclyn, and Len and Celie took her in. She now lives in a shack on their property. Len lives with Celie but visits Jaclyn every day. Jaclyn and Celie are also friends. Jaclyn has no money, not much work history, few job skills, and Len keeps threatening to kick her out. She spends her days watching TV, playing solitaire, doing aerobics, as well as some gardening and accounting work for Len. Thus, she has spent 30 years of her adult life a victim of sexual dysfunction and under the domination of men, her father, a psychiatrist, Jeb, and Len. Len is now a good deal older and mostly impotent, for which he blames Jaclyn. Jaclyn is trying to figure out a way to move, get a job, and make a life for herself, but she's been doing this for years. (See Chapter 10 for full case.)

Admittedly, Jaclyn's story is an extreme one. Most of the women abused by men got out.

Still another mode of submergence for many of the women was that of enduring other problems around sexuality. Some reported a sexual jealousy on the part of their mates that was often unrealistic; this served to keep them in line, restrict their activities and behavior and ultimately their growth. They had difficulty in fully becoming who they were, under the threat of violent jealousy. Others endured sexual jealousy in themselves, as their husbands became unfaithful to them, while they themselves often remained loyal. When one mate betrays another, the resultant distrust extends to all other areas of the relationship. If you betray me sexually, how can I trust you with my other thoughts, needs, feelings? Worse, an aspect of who I thought I was, in a loving, exclusive, trusting relationship—a large section of myself—is destroyed. Over 25 percent of the women interviewed expressed anguish about this issue.

Janet had a sister whose own life was a myriad of problems with men, marriages, children, and alcohol. While Janet was in the hospital giving birth, her sister came down to "help out" and seduced Janet's husband. "She was really helping me out!" Janet laughs. Later, after the death of one 6-year-old daughter from leukemia and the suicide of a teenage son, Janet began an affair with a man; it is a happy, long-lasting experience that she feels has saved her sanity and her life.

Vera's husband, an alcoholic, ran away with his secretary, divorcing Vera when she was 60. She went to bed and nearly died of depression and starvation, but her children roused her, and others helped her to return to the nursing field. Oona and her husband have had a marriage that is on and off, sexually in a rut. They've attended a marriage encounter, but her husband won't return. "They're all a bunch of phonies." He caught gonorrhea from a casual contact and had to tell Oona. Oona has wanted to return to nursing, even though she has four children, aged 2 to 15, but she thinks her husband wants to "keep me pregnant, busy with kids, out of trouble, at home, and then he could do as he pleased. I feel somewhat resentful." He has a new business and doesn't get home until late; Oona can't be sure if this is due to work or sex. So they are in a standoff but appear to be moving toward divorce, toward dismergence. Oona finds her return to school fulfilling. Like a number of the interviewees, Oona discovered how she really felt when her husband had to go away for a few days. She was surprised to find how much she enjoyed being on her own and not having to think about him. Like Heather, Oona is emerging.

When Queenie, now 50, suspected her husband of infidelity, she hired a private detective to find him out. She took the children away for a weekend, knowing he would have his lover over. "I didn't really count on finding black,

black hair on my pillow, but I did." She had been forced to quit a part-time job she liked, because it took her away from him some evenings. Eventually, she divorced him. "I should have divorced earlier . . . [but] I didn't know where the money would come from." Queenie expresses the fears of a large number of women in abusive marriages. After they split, her husband began living with a woman who claimed to be a psychologist and told him Queenie was raising the kids all wrong, so he would call her up and berate her, but her daughter lit into him one day and the calls ended. Queenie is now happily remarried.

Babs was raised in a strict fundamentalist home and grew up terrified of all kinds of situations, withdrawn and alone. Her parents disinherited her when she married Don, who seemed to have grandiose notions about the kind of work he could do, but always failed. Their sex was "fantastic," and this was "the first emotional tie I had had in my life," but their financial situation became so desperate that she went out to work. She became sociable, as he became reclusive and jealous, believing that men in restaurants and even her brothers and cousins were "eyeing me." Throughout the protocol, Babs says she wishes she had divorced him, hopes one day she will, and knows she won't, because he's sick and she'd feel guilty if he died. She believes guilt was ingrained in her from childhood.

As we saw in the chapter on loss, Inez has a history of being betrayed by men, usually in triangular relationships. Nora thought her young husband's jealousy was "beautiful" until it got to be "a pain" with "one roaring battle after another." Then they had one big blowup, during which she told him to stop being jealous or she'd leave him. "He reversed his nature," and they never had another problem with it. As a child and adolescent, Ronnie was the object of a number of sexual overtures from relatives and husbands of best friends. Then she and her husband moved next door to a beautiful woman, whose husband was frequently away, and who always jogged around the neighborhood in hot pants. The common item of gossip was, "Whose husband is she after?" "Miss Hot Pants" often asked Ronnie's husband over to fix the plumbing. Ronnie finally found out they'd been having an affair for a year. It meant nothing to him, he claimed, and he severed it. Interestingly, he'd become very jealous of her when she went back to work during this period. Because of her husband's affair, she had an "almost affair" with a client, but he was a bounder and she didn't let it go further. Ronnie and her husband are now renegotiating their relationship.

In the first part of this chapter I wrote of the illusory component in relationships, the longing to believe what one wants to in order to create the relationship in one's image of it. There is so much evidence of this throughout the case histories already presented that I will give only a few further illustrations. We will note, however, that often the illusion is that the husbands are *different* from previous husbands or fathers, when actually they turn out to be the same on some vital attribute, like control. As Scarf (1987) has shown, we often repeat relationships of the past, which I have shown may become thematic.

Janet says of her husband that he "had a dark side I hadn't seen before." Over and over, this kind of comment recurs in the histories. Crista thought the man she married was the opposite of her controlling father, but he turned out to be very controlling indeed. Babs's husband "changed, or he probably didn't change, he probably was the same person. But he fell into a pattern of leaving jobs, not staying employed. It became more and more necessary for me to work all the time, to increase my salary, do better in my job, achieve . . . and he became more and more withdrawn over the years." Willa's husband *developed* an alcohol problem (but alcohol ran in her family). Germaine's husband, dead 10 years, had only one flaw: he liked strong, smelly cheeses. Indeed, the dead husbands, like Germaine's and Gwen's, seem too ideal to have existed. Even Vera's dead husband, an alcoholic unfaithful with his secretary, apparently divorced her because he'd committed some crime, might be caught, and didn't want her to have to make monetary restitution!

I have expounded on the stories of submerged and individuating women at some length. But what of those in relationships characterized by the emergence of two total individuals in union, and the continuing emergence of each, as well as the relationship?

The truly emergent relationship is characterized by a recognition of respect and support for each individual, rather than the subservence of one's needs, feelings, desires, beliefs, and values so that the other may flourish. A number of the marriages typify these; briefly, we will review Faith, Melanie, Tori, Nadine, Judith, and Em.

Faith's first love was a man who wanted to install a buzzer in his workspace in the garage so she would be at "his beck and call." That ended *that* engagement! Her mother had held back her father's great artistic abilities; this determined Faith to "make sure that my husband reached his full potential." From her youngest years, Faith had wanted to be an artist, and her husband supported her in this. But when he had an opportunity for a major career advance in another city, "which seemed like the end of the world to me," she thought, "how could you prevent a man from doing something as wonderful as that?" She talked him into going, deciding to put her own art career in neutral, and in gratitude he sent her to study art for 6 weeks in Paris. As luck would have it, she linked up with a mentor and her art progressed in quantum leaps. Her husband made arrangements to give her the solitude she needed to work. Later, she helped him develop a heretofore hidden talent in wood carving. He arranged a retrospective of her work. The entire history is one of a husband and wife who supported each other in actualizing their potential in their careers and who both became successful. Somehow they were able to avoid repetition of her parents' relationship, which, as Scarf (1987) shows, might have endangered their marriage.

Judith's husband's work has taken them all over the country. However,

Judith enjoys the unpredictability of moving and has a job that makes it easy for her to relocate. In fact, their one major problem seems to have arisen with her husband's retirement. He'd been hanging around the house too much and wanting her to stay with him. But she continues with her career, and "I told him I married him for better or worse, but not for lunch." He got another job. When asked her opinion of women's lib, she responds, "I don't think we should lower ourselves to equality. I think we're above it."

Melanie's marriage is nested within a communal arrangement with another couple. She had been married previously, but they had grown away from each other and were finding it an incredible strain to try to remain what they were not. Her present husband helped her end that relationship. She compares both her husband and her lover to friends and brothers. There is no jealousy among the four, and they talk about their feelings freely. It seems like an ideal situation, which developed very gradually. The other woman involved is a homemaker and misses having a career, but other than that, the four are happy.

Nadine describes her married years as "the happiest years of my life." A dancer, who has both taught and exhibited, Nadine was particularly happy when her husband learned ballroom dancing as well. As both of them loved the water, it seemed only natural that they should bring their dancing talents to cruises, and this has been one of their most enjoyable activities together. Thus, similar loves and (transcendence) activities have drawn them together.

Yvonne, now 60, shows that partners do not need to be "equal" in every way to have an emergent relationship. She and her husband both own and work in a janitorial cleaning service, but he is the head of the family, just as her father was. "My dad believed it was the duty of the man to support the wife." A "good mother would put both him and his children first, and was there all the time. . . . And, of course, infidelity was out." Yvonne takes pride in having raised children who are good and respect their parents, not like other children these days, whose mothers "don't want to be bothered" because "they just want to have a good time." In Yvonne's house, her man is the boss, and she's happy that way. "Any big decision my husband makes," although they do talk it over. "I never interfered" with her husband's discipline of the children. "When my husband spoke, I did not speak." This *sounds* like a submergent relationship, and indeed Yvonne misses not having had an education or having been an artist; but her marital relationship fulfills her ideal, is based on mutual respect, is as she feels it should be, and she is not diminished by it. Rather, she is enhanced. Her identity is not suppressed; it is fulfilled.

At 30, and a highly successful professional woman, Tori has already experienced a series of "deep, long, intense" and nurturing relationships. She is still friends with all but one of her former lovers. She and Garth had been friends for years, but started spending more time together. Tori tells us how that relationship developed: "It was instantaneous. That connection was so deep our minds worked together like hand and glove. Our senses of humor, everything about our characters, was absolutely eerie. . . . I had always been attracted to him, but I never thought that he would be attracted back to me. Because I was 27 and he was 38, and he seemed to me like a full-grown man. Whereas I was still really coming to terms with being an adult, particularly the prolonged adolescence of graduate school. . . .

"And I had had dreams about Garth the year before, erotic dreams, but I never thought of pursuing them, because he seemed just unattainable to me, and I thought he saw me as a little sister. He'd always been just as drawn to me as I was to him. . . . We would sit and talk for five hours, and that's real magic when your minds work together that way." He was going away for a week, and Tori kissed him goodbye and then sighed to a friend, "I'm in love." "And I had a week alone, and Garth and I had been throwing out a lot of signals that day like, what if we both meditate together on Wednesday night while we're apart?" They were also planning other things they could do together when Garth got back. "So we were throwing out little signals, which I was sensing, plus I've never been wrong when I've been attracted to somebody that they've been attracted to me. And I always think, and I thought this time, this is going to be the time that I'm not. But I never have been wrong. If it's been a real strong thing, then it's always been there on the other side, too."

"So I just debated and deliberated [about] this new man in my life, representing everything that was possible. And we meditated. We found out later that we had meditated at exactly the same time. We'd received the same images. I had images all week of what he was doing, like I would experience what he was doing. It was a very psychic week in terms of the connection. . . . And so Garth came back a day early and said: 'Well, I thought a lot about you.' And I said: 'Well, I did, too.' And it removed all the intellectual doubts of it. And we slept together that night, and it was just like, well, of course, we're always going to be together now, and we're gonna get married." Garth told Tori that he was willing to move from the house he had built and lived in for 8 years. Although he had never intended to have any more children, "within two days he's saying: 'Well, I guess the question is just how many kids we're going to have.'

"So it was just like walking into a universe where there was no time and no space. Garth and I both experienced this is what life—our whole lives— have been about, coming together. Our whole lives have been to bring us to this point, and from this point on, this is life as it should be. And he had given up that he would ever remarry, or ever find a partner. He had just built himself [a house] . . . which became our place. Everything had come together at the exact right time for our lives to join. And it was a sense that we had been looking for—we had always wanted life to be the way it should be, and always been disappointed in that. And here was a relationship where everything was as it should be. There were no disappointments. It was like we were one person. And sure there are things that you work out in those beginning months, but it was all in the context of absolute perfection.

"The other thing that was really eerie about it was that Garth and I had started on our path of spiritual development" in the early 1970s, at the same time, when he had left his wife and children, and "started to read Eastern psychology and do a lot of meditation and body work. And that was when I started to take TM, live away from home, get involved in the antiwar movement, start reading Alan Watts. So even though we were eleven years apart [in age], spiritually and psychically we were in the same space. . . . So it was just as if we had converged and then come together, and it was very clear that a child had to come out of that." Two children have been born so far; the first is a female, bearing Tori's last name, which she had retained, and the second is a male, with Garth's last name. Their relationship continues strong to this day. (See Chapter 12 for a full account of Tori's history.)

Thus, dyadic relationships have lost and transcendent aspects. They promote mergence or individuation and may be characterized as unemerged, submerged, dismerged, or emerged, as we have classified the selves within these relationships. The picture becomes more complex in families.

FAMILY

Within the family there are the L/T structures of the individual members, the various dyadic structures of relationships between each two members, triadic structures, and lastly, the L/T structure of the entire family; this, of course, includes the lost and transcendent aspects. (For accounts of these structures, see Satir, 1972, 1967; Bowen, 1978; Scarf, 1987; Horne & Ohlsen, 1982; Hoffman, 1981.)

One manifestation of this family structure is the myth of the family, or the story each family tells itself and others about how they are constructed, how they fit the societal ideal, how they function, and their meaning.

A child is born. She will be healthy, loving, beautiful, happy, successful. She is a dream at her birth, born ideal, and every manifestation to the contrary is a loss that must be transcended in some way. Should she represent too great a loss, departing too far from expectations, she may be rejected. In the same fashion, a family is born. It will be warm, caring, a refuge that is all things to all members, who will consist of two parents and two-plus children. That it may "give birth" to other families—single-parent head of household, divorced, widowed, childless, same-sex, communal, polygamous—cannot be recognized initially, because these differ from the ideal.

The family member me of the mother is different from that of the son, and yet these me's, as well as the me's of the other family members, build the family L/T structure. Each member must work out individual L/T structure within the family structure.

The family that "works" is the one in which one individual's transcendence is perceived as the transcendence of all, and one member's loss is a loss to all. Further, the functional family is one in which the family myth is congruent with the individual member myths. This is the transcending family. In the dysfunctional family, the individual myth is destroyed by the family myth, or there is a constant tension between the two. If I believe that I am strong but my family bruits about stories of my weakness, I am in a triple bind. Either I must contradict these accounts and interpretations of my actions— and ultimately be ejected, because I am disturbing the bonds forged through this mythology—or I must accede, remain part of my family, and not be who I am. Or I must become weak. This is the dilemma of the scapegoat.

When the family transcends inadequately, it either dies, changing form radically, or becomes pathogenic, its individual members ill-equipped for transcendence individually (see Henry, 1971). Then one member's transcendence is at the expense of another's and is thus another member's loss. The family mythology re-creates one who is blamed (see Satir, 1972). A member is sacrificed, and during this period false unity pervades the remnant. Of course, after the sacrificed member is gone (dead, institutionalized, or run away), another from their number must be chosen and the process begins anew. Otherwise, this family will have to face the "real" issues, family secrets of abuse or inferiority or betrayal or impending death (see Bermann, 1973), and the family will disintegrate.

Families, like individuals, incur losses that are on time, off time, and time irrelevant. All the stages of mourning and resolution—the grieving (yearning), searching, replacement, and integration—occur in family transcendence of loss; families will develop coping, adaptation, and defense mechanisms that are, in a sense, dispositional to them, as well as situational and general. They will withdraw to their rooms, or fight, or call a "family council," or seek outside assistance, or scapegoat a member, or agree to hierarchical autocracy, with father as head, mother second, eldest child third, and so on. The integration will be the story the family members tell each other of how they perceived a loss, who was responsible, what really happened, how they transcended the event, and what it means to them as a family. This will constitute revision of the family concept (who we are) and family myth (how we got to be that way). The role of each individual in the story will be interpreted until the story becomes a myth, or stylized truth handed down to generations and friends, but mainly a creation of meaning. All changes in the L/T structure of the family affect the individual, dyadic, and triadic structures within it; they are channeled through the family member me's. They revise the individual concept of self to include a me that belongs to the revised family structure.

Conflicts arise in families because one or more members threaten radical alteration to the structure, and therefore the myth, family metaphorical system, and theme. This may be through an abrogation of role-related activities, such as when a mother who has always stayed home "suddenly" goes out to work or school, breaking her implicit contract to remain as she was, shattering the fundamental illusion. The child who leaves home at 15 is altering the L/T structure by imposing an off-time loss; her action must be dealt with legally and practically and must be explained to other members of the family in justificatory fashion, as well as to the community. As Haan (1977) points out, families must "constantly redefine themselves." If the redefinition is off-time, it is a more traumatic loss, more like a death. The attempt of the family is to remain congruent with the ideal of a certain developmental pace, that is, to be on time; relative changelessness or staticity provides an illusion of stability in which losses are minimized and progress toward metaphorical death—of family and members—is less perceptible.

Families develop typical general transcendence mechanisms that go under the rubric of "togetherness," a cultural ideal. They play Monopoly together, or rent a movie cassette to watch on Sunday nights, or take a camping vacation once a year. These activities may produce considerable struggle, if not down-right misery, such as boredom in the adults who must play at the child's level, compromises on a PG-rated movie, horrible incidents at the corner eatery where the children must sit and squirm too long and parents must try to hold down the noise and damage; me's that are quite different from each other must do the same thing so that whole revisions of self do not go unknown, resulting in breakup. During the child's teenage years, midlife parent and teen may suddenly not "know" each other, because both may be undergoing identity transformations at a more rapid pace. This "togetherness" principle has much in common with "romantic love"; it is "romantic family"; each is a Procrustean bed on which to fit the transformations of individual growth. Each can be painful. Particularly in the area of values, wide changes in individuals are likely to be the genesis of much anxiety, hostility, and sorrow.

That each member of a family has his or her individual role (Satir, 1972; Horne & Ohlsen, 1982) that contributes to the totality is nicely illustrated in Bermann's *Scapegoat* (1973). In this family, it is the function of the young boy to be a scapegoat for the family problem (in this case, the mortal illness of the father); it is the function of his older brother to be the weapon of the family, carrying out the scapegoating activities. The web of family relationships might disintegrate were any member to step from his or her role. This is, of course, a pathological instance. The scapegoat distracts the family, not only from the problem of the father's impending death, and how they relate to it, but also from the way the family functions. He, in his turn, sacrifices himself to keep the family together—to keep death from spreading. He dies to the family's continued life, however tenuous. Family is survival through mergence, rather than death through isolation and exposure.

Jules Henry, in his brilliant account of pathogenic families, *Pathways to Madness* (1971), illuminates the myriad ways in which parental distortions of reality are trained into the children. It is through their parents that the children perceive and construct their worlds. Such distortions include time, which can be measured objectively but is experienced subjectively; for example, family members show their inconsiderateness of each other through abuse of time, making others wait hours for a meal, promising something on time and not delivering, abusing the words that are connected with time, such as "tomorrow" and "later." Space also is distorted, particularly as a dimension of safety or danger, the mother restricting or freeing the space of her child in an inappropriate fashion, leaving the 2-year-old in the middle of the road, but not allowing the 13-year-old to leave the house because something might happen to him. The meaning of food is also commonly distorted in these families, and food is used as a weapon; unpleasant food is served, alternative food demanded, food refused or urged; indeed, food, often seen as a symbol of affection in Freudian literature, is the frequent battleground in these families, where affection and hostility are confounded. Food is nurture and life-giving; to reject it or make it unpleasant is to reject life and invalidate those who provide it. Sham and the double bind are related distortions, in which there is always a double reality of what is expressed and what is felt, resulting in self-deception as well as deception of others. (I illustrate this in my classes by telling a student to come to me as I push her away, and then I tell her to go away as I draw her toward me. "Come here, go away.") Still another distortion occurs in the manifestation of love, confused with hostility, manipulativeness, and aggressiveness. We have seen how our interviewees identified jealousy with love. In the same way, objects, people, availability to each other, and motion are perceived in distorted fashion, as are a host of bodily functions. The losses implicit in these distorted perceptions within the parents are perpetuated in the lives of their children, rather than transcended in their own lives. Or they are inappropriately transcended, resulting in further losses of the type they are meant to transcend.

To the extent that the child is being trained in a distorted view of reality, that is, does not perceive time, space, motion, food, and feelings as his culture does, he is being trained to lose. Great artists can distort to artistic purpose (cf. Eugene Ionesco, *A stroll in the air*, as well as the surrealistic painters, and the novels of Gabriel Garcia Marquez); by the unique association of one event with another, they can often set forth a greater truth. But they are aware of the distortion, and that awareness is their power; the distortion is not accidental; they dramatize the reality as they perceive it and would have us know it. The members of Henry's families are unaware and have not consciously designed their distortions to a higher goal.

Such family problems very often can be resolved only by family breakup or family therapy (see Haley, 1978; Minuchin, 1974; Satir, 1967, 1972; Horne & Ohlsen, 1982; Hoffman, 1981).

In our interviews with women, we can trace loss and transcendence through a number of aspects of family existence. These aspects are the interviewees' emergence from their birth families, visions of the ideal family, participation in metaphorical families, experiences with their parents, experience of home, disappointments and joys they feel with their children, experiences of giving birth, and dreams of houses. We will discuss these in turn.

Emergence and Individuation

Some interviewees, like Paula and Kendall, show us the difficulties of emerging from overwhelmingly competent parents. They must fight their parents to become who they are. Kendall succeeds by moving a continent away, having a baby, and having lesbian and heterosexual affairs, some of which she reveals to family friends, shaming her parents. Paula is now separate but is continually reminded that she cannot be as successful as her parents, who would dictate not only relationships but also the very food she eats. Crista as helper never found what *she* wanted, became the nurse her *mother* wanted instead, and was unable to assert her love for city life. Tess is not worth the milk her mother gives her; she has rebelled unsuccessfully and is still unborn. At 25 Winnie recollects her wild adolescence, trying to separate from her parents, but now she merges with God within her husband and children. Both of them are "born again"; they use the Bible as a guide and so perceive that they have no control over their lives and therefore no responsibility or guilt; their lives are given over to God—they leave everything in his (competent) hands.

Other interviewees perceive their parents as having merged into one. Kendall describes her parents' interactions that drove her sister and herself "up the wall." "It's like they have these little routines, their little chats down, like: 'Anything interesting in the paper, dear? Do you want a cup of tea, dear? Oh, I don't know, dear, are you making a cup of tea? Okay, if you're making one.' They're just like a little double act." Kendall and her sister, as well as Paula, Kara, Winnie, Tess, Heather, Oona, and others, must rebel in order to individuate. Greer perceives her parents as merged into one. Faith's struggle to individuate was influenced by her mother's oneness with the role of mother and her lack of development of her musical gifts. Faith says, "I wouldn't do that to my own kids; I would let them feel I was a separate person on my own, besides being a mother."

Ideal Family

A sense of loss of the ideal family was expressed by a number of the interviewees and transcended in different ways. For example, Marjorie set out to create for her children the home, the nest, she had never had as a child. Her father had committed suicide when she was six; her stepfather had molested both Marjorie and her younger sister for many years. She discovered, however, that her children did not want the ideal family she had set out to provide for them. They had other ideals. Finally, more painful than letting her children go was the necessity of letting her ideal family dream go.

A number of interviewees, like Kara, talked about what they had never done as a family. Winnie set about creating the religious home she had missed as a child.

Metaphorical Families

Related to the concept of the ideal family is what I have termed the "metaphorical family." Typically, the interviewee's home had been seriously disrupted in some way. She found or created another group, to whom she referred as her "family." For example, Lexie likens the theater to a family, and it seems to be this aspect of theatrical experience that she misses the most. For Kara, the product of an overstrict home, both the armed forces and the hospital seemed to function as supportive, and relatively nonpunitive, families. Melanie and her husband joined another family in a communal arrangement that has metaphorical family overtones; Melanie came from a very traditional, family-oriented background and both loves and needs this support. Paula seems to have sought for family substitutes as a refuge from her overwhelmingly competent mother and father. She found a political group—"it was like a real family"—and an art cooperative: "For years, the co-op was my family, and that's one of the problems I'm going through, leaving home." In all of these, the ideal family is implied, and the mourning over its loss seems as deep as mourning over the loss of a real family might be. For Theo, the theater "provides me with an extended family"; she also owns a house that she compares to the theater, where she takes in a number of boarders; "it's a place where my son can come."

Related to the notion of metaphorical family is the single relationship that is compared to family experience. Marjorie describes her best friend: "We have been mothers for each other, as well as sisters and friends." To Della, living in a dorm "was like having sisters I hadn't had before." With misty gratitude, Gwen recalls that when she was beaten and kicked out of her home as a child and teenager—a frequent event—she could knock on any door in the neighborhood, and none would be closed to her.

These women and others are expressing a need for family intimacy; if they do not find it in their natal families, or if they are separated from those families, they attempt to create it in other societal groups or relationships. Later in this chapter we will see that simple groups are usually predicated on a single task; groups that become metaphorical families may provide support and working-through opportunities throughout a whole spectrum of roles, relationships, and life experiences. Unfortunately, such metaphorical families do not seek family therapy!

However, not all metaphorical families provide positive experiences for their members. I am reminded of one academic department at a university;

each member seemed to have one of the roles (computer, blamer, distractor, peacemaker, scapegoat, etc.) described by Satir (1972) and others! This particular metaphorical family was described to me by an erstwhile member as incestuous and dysfunctional, both in communication and in action. Each year, groups of students held a revolution without, presumably, understanding how the dysfunction of this particular system influenced them to rebel. The entire experience was rated by my informant as "a season in hell."

Experience of Home

A number of the interviewees reported that loss of a home during childhood had been a traumatic experience for them. For others, home and often the surrounding country seemed idealized as a place of refuge or sunny enjoyment. Lorellen expresses the feelings of a number when she recalls "this beautiful home in the country with trees—a great place to play and grow—just turned to ashes. It was like, wow, things can change pretty drastically." Later they moved again when her parents divorced. "I used to have bad dreams about not being able to go home." Yves also endured the trauma of a house that burned to the ground when she was small. Still in her crib, she was wheeled out the door on Christmas Eve, an event she remembers. Fire and burnt-out buildings still disturb her. For Sue, moving into a big house when she was six was a traumatic and overwhelming experience. Ursula recalls her migratory childhood and the cardboard boxes that her mother painted to make them water repellent so that they could live in them when they worked in the fields in the southwest. Winnie's parents finally sold the house in which she was raised, and she tells us this hurt for a long while. Sissy is proud of the beautiful new house that she and her husband built; she feels it will be "a monument long after we're gone."

Grown Children

Interviewees expressed both joy and disappointment in their grown children. Often this was linked with the extent to which the children perpetuated some aspects of the parents' selves. If Nadine's son dances, as she does, the dancing will continue even after she stops. She wants to pass on to him that which gives her so much pleasure, and she finds it hard to believe that it does not pleasure her son as well. Indeed, she would "pass on" her dancing like a trait or a legacy, if she could. But hers is the loss of the ideal child, echoed by so many other women. "He just grew his own way, and it wasn't the way we wanted. His father would have loved an athlete. I would have loved someone that was a better student." In a fire she would save her son's baby pictures, perhaps because they are what remain of the ideal child—before he "grew his own way."

Ronnie wishes her child had been able to adjust to college, and to become the great pianist promised throughout childhood.

Nora is one of the most eloquent parents on her disappointment in her children. She grieves over a childhood they claim they never had and over what they have become. In her bitingly sarcastic voice, she tells us: "Saturday night was our little pizza night. We all watched TV together. I spent a lot of time brushing Nancy's hair. She had beautiful black hair. Unfortunately, one of the things Nick remembers about home was me spanking his sister. . . . Come home from work and head right out for Little League, and sit there cold, watching your kid play ball, God is this ever going to end? . . . Selling hot dogs, Middle League, and Fly-up and flying off a plane, you'd think he'd remember that. 'Oh no, I remember the spanking you gave Nancy one time 'cause she couldn't learn her times tables. What a terrible spanking that was.' . . . That's unfair, what happened to all the good things you shared with them, picnics, days at beach, fancy things you did with each other, going to New York at Christmas time to look at the trees, on the train, and what happened to all those things? Where are they? . . . I have a girlfriend, her daughter remembers her all the time with flowers. . . . I got flowers on Valentine's Day because my son had forgotten my birthday. . . . I don't understand what you get out of it. Maybe you get out of it the satisfaction at that moment yourself, when you see your kids in a ball game, maybe that's what you're supposed to get out of it. Maybe you're not supposed to hope that some day they'll remember all the things you did for them, how many hours you gave them."

Nora goes on to recall that she did enjoy these activities. But now her son seems to avoid her, and when her husband had a heart attack, she couldn't even get her son to the hospital. That her daughter ran away from home and married someone of whom she disapproves also embitters Nora.

Greer also expresses regrets. Her daughter decided not to attend college and exhibits values alien to those of her parents. "It's just like all that time I spent, did she ever hear a word I said? . . . God, what did I spend so much time of my life on, why did I spend all those years? God, think of the things I could have done with my life. [I'm] feeling like all that I did as a mother is down the tubes. The men she's choosing are rejects, no education, party, play, drink. . . . The way she keeps house, the way they live—pigs, as far as I'm concerned, never saving any money, not having any plans toward the future." As for her son, he's had many minor brushes with the law and is possibly gay. He seems to have money without having a job.

Sibyl and her husband were so concerned that their adult children remained too dependent on them for too long that they actually joined the Peace Corps! When they returned, their children were independent and doing beautifully. Judith, like others, expressed concern about the life style of her child, that she was living with someone, for example, but felt that she and her husband must accept their grown children or run the risk of losing them. This acceptance seemed to work out very well. Judith is also disappointed that her daughter quit college and that both her children are goalless.

Other parents were happy with the way their children turned out. Harriet glows with pride in her several children and their families; they are happy and productive, although there were behaviors that she and her husband had to force themselves to accept. Vicki feels that the experiences with her two preteen children have been "the best that I can think of in my life." She praises the positive attitude of her son. "You can do something for a child, and you just get thanks, but Rex will walk in and say: 'Dad, you put the trellis in the backyard, gee it looks great!' . . . I never had to spank him. When he was little, he started to put something in the light plug, and I just lifted my hand and said: 'Don't do that,' and he pulled his hand back and got big tears in his eyes, because he was doing something he shouldn't."

Women whose children did not "turn out" well tended to blame themselves. They were in mourning for the ideal child, and they felt that somehow it was their fault. "What did I do wrong?" a number of them asked. They had lost aspects of both potential and actual lives and selves.

Dreams of a House

Dreams of a house were more common than any other topic and seemed to embody aspects of selves or families, particularly conflicts. Crista, an interior designer whose lifelong struggle had been to live in the vital city rather than the dead country, dreams: "I go into a house, and it has many rooms, and it's a maze, and they're never laid out right, and I keep finding more rooms, but they're never right. The windows are always too high, I can't see out [laughs]. I didn't have it for a while after we moved in here, but I had one recently, very similar. It was finding—oh look, there are more rooms and more rooms, and I think, how can I make this into something that is united. It never is cohesive. There's lots of space, but not in the right order." (Is there anyone else there besides yourself?) "No." (How do you feel?) "There's a great air of expectation—oh, I'm finally going to—this is going to be perfect—find just the right room, or the right set of—I'm looking with great expectation, and I don't find it." (Has your room changed much?) "No." (When did you first have it?) "I don't know. Since before my early thirties— I'd had quite violent dreams, nightmares. So the dreams changed. I'd wake up screaming and shouting. Since my teens. [There was] a lot of stress in my life." (What does this dream mean to you?) "Well, it means that I am not yet personally in a position in my life where I feel really comfortable and at one with my surroundings. I either make a conflict or find a conflict."

In answer to the question about recurrent dreams, Vicki responds, "It didn't mean a lot to me. It meant a lot to the psychiatrist [laughs]. It was a power struggle dream. Of course, I didn't realize that. It was a dream about a house in the Berkeley Hills that I used to drive by all the time, and for some reason I was moving into it. And after I moved in, I realized that there was a huge swimming pool in the backyard that was all filled with algae and floating lily pads. It was all overgrown. And I was moving into it with my ex-husband, the kids' father. This person that used to live in the house raised anacondas, and he had a second story built like 3 feet higher than the first story with an opening between that was all heated. It was a very explicit dream—where these things lived—and apparently he died in some horrible accident. And so they had been left without any care for some time. I don't remember now in the dream who told me all this, but anyhow, one of the anacondas appeared in the garden, and we had to throw—well, and the cat that I had at the time walked by and didn't see it, and it was about to eat the cat. And I had to throw a tablecloth on its head to hide it from the cat so it wouldn't see the cat and get the cat away from it, and then I called the snake removal company, and they came with a truck with 'snake removal' on the side [laughs]. And I explained this problem to them, and told them I didn't really want the snakes killed, they weren't really bothering us, and they hadn't done anything wrong, but if they could somehow secure them to the area they were supposed to be in, it would be nice." The psychiatrist interpreted this as a power struggle, similar to struggles ongoing in her life at the time.

For Jaclyn, living below poverty level, whose main struggle throughout her life has been with feeling inadequate as a sexual being and who is living in a one-room shack on her lover's land, there is a structure in which she is continually discovering more rooms: "And then, from there there'll be another room. I think this has something to do with the type of claustrophobia I feel here. It goes way back. Even when I was a kid I didn't have a room of my own until I was 12." (How do you feel in this dream?) "Oh, thrilled at all these rooms. It's wonderful. Even though I can't believe what I was dreaming, because the room could go off from here, and be much huger than it is on the outside."

Vera was deserted by her husband for another woman. He was an alcoholic who finally died of his disease. She is just beginning to get over the devastation of these experiences. "For many years, all the time I was married to my second husband, I dreamed that he was gone, and I was looking for him. I was going through big houses and little houses and rooms, trying to find him. 'Cause he used to disappear so easily." (What were the houses like?) "Just houses with many rooms and nooks and crannies [laughs]."

Ursula, whose life story I told in the chapter on individual development, recounts the following dream: "I've had [it] many times. It's kind of odd. It doesn't make any sense to me. A house that I go into, and when I get there I think, Oh, I've been here before. It's a funny little house, the rooms are kind of random. They aren't decorated with any particular style, they're just kind of—maybe like people—all different. I haven't had it now for more than a year, but I usually dream it 2 or 3 times a year. Have had it as long as I can remember. I feel puzzled, because there's never any people there, and yet the house looks lived in. So I don't know where the people are. I like the house because always there's warm sun coming in through the window, so it's pleasant." (Is there an outside area?) "It's got a very small yard, and it's very close to the road. Strange." (Are the rooms furnished?) "Yeah, somebody lives there, but there's nobody there. That's the puzzling part. It's all furnished, and the dishes are in the sink, and it's just like somebody's there, and yet there's no one. Every time I'm there, I say: 'Oh, I've been here before. Here I am again.' Maybe it's a collection of places I've been, I don't know."

Alice tells of a dream she had in late childhood: "It was an old Victorian house, and it was almost empty. It didn't have much in it, and I didn't run into people in it either. It wasn't as though I actually encountered anything. I didn't like that place particularly. I was not at all happy when I realized I was dreaming about it again."

Harriet recounts her recurrent dream, which she has had for the last 5 or 10 years: "It's of a big house, and it's not always the same house. It's usually my house, no specific house; they're different houses, but they're always large, and they're usually mine. I remember one, for instance, where the house was huge, but it was so big that there were people living up on the third and fourth floors of it that I didn't even know they were there. And yet I'm quite sure that it was my house. . . . Sometimes I'm planning things, or wandering around trying to find something in the house. The most recent house I was in was a large house in the field. The large house symbol comes back frequently . . . and it's usually an old house. We've lived in large houses always." (What are the people like?) "As I said, it varies from time to time, and I don't think the people make much difference." (What would the house be saying to you?) "I think it's mostly my fantasies of having people in my house." Harriet goes on to reveal her fantasy of having an old person, a middle-aged couple, a child or two, and maybe a baby living in her house, "in other words, having an intergenerational household." She describes where each could live in her own, current, large house, and feels she would enjoy this.

Yves's house is "haunted, but I never see a ghost. In my mind, I've seen this house in my childhood. I always want to write a story about it. I go inside. The rooms are empty, dusty. Sometimes there's sunlight coming through a dusty window—kinda a movie set type place. I never encounter anybody, it's just I enjoy going there." (Why?) "Intrigue." Yves recalls her grandparents' house when she was a child and the ghost story her grandfather told about someone walking through the house, a one-legged man with a wooden leg. (If the house could speak to you, what do you think it would say?) "I guess you tend to feel there's a ghost in a house. The house draws the personality of whoever lived there, and if they could talk to you the person or the house, they could tell you a lot of things. It would be interesting, the stories they could tell. Maybe they'd impart some kind of wisdom that I could use."

Gisella notes that "the only dream that made a mark on me is that I'm wandering through a Victorian house, and I can see the panelling . . . the wallpaper is very clear—and it looks very Victorian, or very English. And that's made me feel that maybe I'm reincarnated from a Victorian time. I feel I had lived in that house." (How do you feel about it?) "Mysterious. Dreamed it just once, when I was in my middle twenties."

Family Themes

In the course of research done with three-generation families for a study by Mihlyi Csikszentmihalyi (Weenolsen, 1978; see Csikszentmihalyi & Rochberg-Halton, 1981), I discovered that individuals within families had life themes as I have indicated, but also that families themselves had themes and that the individual and family themes were closely related. For instance, in one family I found the life theme of each individual centered on alienation, but the family theme included alienation as well, and each member (unwittingly) cooperated in the alienation of each other from other family members, from friends, and especially from the community. In another three-generation family, there were individual and family themes partially centering on the issue of security. Hess and Handel (1959) have also found family and generation themes running through various L/T structures. How can we explain this?

Perhaps in no other area of human functioning is the role of the lost self more evident than in the area of family themes. I noted in Chapter 4, on L/T life themes, that individuals appear to set for themselves certain past loss experiences to be re-created and transcended in the present. What is past is lost in the sense that it cannot be appreciably altered; perhaps a relative will finally explain the mystery of an aunt's suicide, so that we view it with more compassion and less horror, and in turn we experience more guilt over our former reactions and assumptions; or perhaps we can finally come to the conviction that the child who died of leukemia has gone to God, or the son who died in Vietnam has contributed to our disillusion with war and thus to a better world; but our capacity to alter the past is generally limited to rationalization or to unexpected information and so, in large measure, is "lost." Thus, our only hope to recapture what we have lost, and redirect it, may be to re-create past situations in the present to work them through. However, a parent who re-creates her abusive natal family in the present marital one is also exposing her child to abuse, which may become thematic for the child as well. Thus, in actuality, she may perpetuate aspects of her own L/T life theme—its lost aspects—and the theme becomes a family one.

Scarf (1987), whose most recent book, *Intimate partners*, has just come to my attention as I am finishing this book, has data from which she draws similar conclusions. She believes that couples may be attracted to each other because they see in the budding relationship the possibility of "re-creating and struggling to master old family concerns and difficulties. . . . It's as if family dilemmas that had never found their satisfactory resolutions needed to be resurrected . . . so that individuals could work on those problems once again." She sees this as "unconscious collusion" (p. 41) and traces the patterns through families in "genograms." This also seems to echo my broad interpretation of the Freudian concept of transference (see Chapter 12), as well as Anna Freud's (1946) notion of "repetition compulsion." To the extent that the children are affected, the thematic aspect becomes repeated and thus part of a *family* theme. Scarf (1987) especially has noted triangular "family patterns" and terms these "blueprints for being"—denoting the prescriptive qualities of family themes.

I emphasize my own view that not all relations between a man and a woman are predetermined by their parents' relationships. The relationship of Faith to her husband is one example of the ability to transcend previous family patterns, rather than being predestined to repeat them. We need to explore this fascinating and highly useful topic with much more research.

GENERATIONS

The presence of several generations in a family defines the integration aspect of that family more than any other. It includes the incorporation of the historical moment into the family, the sense of continuity and transcendence over time— that is, more than a single life—and over losses experienced only indirectly. Within the L/T generational structure are the lost L/T structures of individuals now gone; their final integrations and meanings are immortalized in myth. The individual can sense his or her own prospective continuity in intergenerational relationships.

Each person is at work on her own myth. The relationships of the units of family within generations may be of a predominantly loss-imposing nature, with much malicious gossip and fighting, the presence (or absence) of black sheep, who were usually too different in values or life styles, and long conversations of hostile and justificatory content—all attempts to rescue personal myths, as one would one's shadow if that is all that is left, but the vilifications of others seem unavoidable. Or the relationships may be of a predominantly transcending nature, strong in traditional ritual. It is almost a maxim that family members who do not see much of each other get along best; they do not need to know each other very well; they simply resurrect old family me's for the Christmas dinner or funeral, the common denominators being compliments, a hearty cheerfulness, kind gossip, loud condemnation of something safe like the weather or the national politics. These are attachment bond-building and can be indulged in by almost anyone for a few hours without the more individuated and unique me's showing through to define just how separate the members have become.

As I have indicated above, L/T life themes can also be seen within the various generations of a single family. The integration stage of the L/T process in particular becomes a story handed down as a family tradition, ritual, or possession. "We are descended from those who came over on the Mayflower, and we have always exhibited the independence, adventurousness, courage, and spirit of our forefathers." Possessions, in particular, are a tangible way of holding generations together and a form of preserving a relationship or an individual who has gone beyond. The Wedgwood vase on the living room table holds not only today's fresh-cut flowers but also the flowers picked by great-grandmother when she was a girl, to allay her mother's anger when she had done something wrong. Flowers in the Wedgwood vase are forgiveness in this family. To the visitor, they are simply flowers.

Much more work needs to be done on the possible perpetuation of L/T life themes, or some aspects of them, within multigenerational families, and the above can be considered only as suggestive.

GROUPS

Kreilkamp (1976), in his book *The Corrosion of Self*, has said, "We need each other to cooperate and get necessary things accomplished. Babies need people taking care of them if they are to grow up, if they are to develop. Finally, as Goffman makes clear, grown-up people need one another to maintain a sense of purpose, to maintain definitions of reality, to maintain a sense of identity; we get support from one another just as inevitably as we get what Laing calls invalidation from one another. Both processes—support and invalidation—are interwoven and cannot be separated from one another" (p. 218).

Obviously, major sources of this interpersonal support and invalidation are the groups to which we belong. The family is the preeminent group for most of us, and its tasks are the most complex in creating our identity through the transcendence of loss.

However, most of us belong to many other groups as well, which also support or invalidate us. They differ from the family group in that they are usually task-oriented and therefore focused on a narrower range of behavior and expectations.

For example, the local precinct political group may concentrate on getting a state senator elected; the behaviors required of this group—meetings, door-to-door campaigning, mailing parties, coffees for the candidate, telephone canvassing—are all focused on a single goal. The senatorial candidate represents certain positions on issues such as water pollution, care for the homeless, improved transportation, and licensing of services; these obviously represent losses that must be transcended in some manner. Thus, the precinct worker is engaged in the transcendence of community loss, which he also feels may become his own. In similar fashion, the church group, the city board of education, and the university faculty senate are engaged in overcoming problems and re-creating themselves, their group, and those they represent and influence in a mode they believe will be better. Each of us probably belongs to a number of such groups. Yalom (1985) lists just a few therapeutic groups, for example, "obesity, adjustment after divorce, chronic pain, sexual dysfunction, rape victims, epilepsy, myocardial infarction, hemodialysis" (p. 11), to which we could add Alcoholics Anonymous, Mothers Against Drunk Driving, Parents Without Partners, the American Association for Retired Persons, the American Civil Liberties Union, and all the committees to which we belong at work. As such, the task-oriented group has a transcendence-oriented purpose.

The group has an L/T structure of its own, just as individuals and families do, and the L/T structures of the individuals intersect with it at one me only, the group membership me. Each group me is defined by its place in the group according to the group's needs; that is, there is the leader or alpha me, second-in-command beta me, and, last, omega me, possibly scapegoat. Thus, the entire L/T structure of the individual will define the quality of his membership in the group, and the group will validate his structure to a greater or lesser degree according to his participation in the group task.

Although the purpose of the group is generally focused on some task, actually belonging to the group may be far more important to the individual than the task to be accomplished. The task is usually one of larger dimensions and meaning than the individual's own life and one that the individual could not accomplish on his own. Therefore, as the group is successful, the individual transcends his own limitations and attains immortality of a sort, in that the changes the group has wrought may outlive him. Further, as the group supports him in this one aspect of existence, he may *feel* as though his entire life and self have been validated.

Yalom (1985) perceives the "common group tensions" that arise in therapeutic groups. However, these tensions are present in other groups as well. For example, he points out the struggle for dominance that is characteristic of every newly forming group, until each person has his or her place and the group has achieved a certain cohesiveness (see Sherif, Harvey, Whiter, and Sherif, 1961). When a new person enters the group, the struggle begins anew, as has been observed by both social and comparative psychologists. Yalom also comments on the conflict between a desire on the part of group members to support each other and feelings of sibling rivalry. Most important for our purposes is the conflict "between the desire to immerse oneself in the comforting waters of the group, and the fear of losing one's precious individuality" (p. 161), the conflict between mergence and individuation, two different forms of death that characterize all human relationships, and on which dimension each human being vacillates between one pole and another.

Becker (1973) has observed the need for a hero as an object of transference to preserve us from death metaphorically. The group leader may function in this fashion. Or the task may be one of "heroic" proportions in transcending loss. When the group is successful, each member shares in the heroism, obtaining a kind of immortality if the transcendence continues for a long time, as did the signers of the Declaration of Independence. When the group is not "working," and there is more loss than transcendence for the members involved, its form may be changed, peacefully or by "revolution" (re-evolution); the old form dies, and the new one is born. *Group* meaning becomes part of each individual's *life* meaning.

The members of the group tell each other the "story" of what they are about (group concept), how well they are succeeding, the importance of the part each member plays. The story is a myth, of course, subject to a construed consensus of the individuals involved. It is the task of each member to believe the myth and perpetuate it by word and deed. The Ku Klux Klan is based on the myth of specific threats that one race poses for another; that these threats are nonexistent, that they might be seen by outsiders as constituting a reaction-formation type of defense, displacing the threat of death on a specific race (if the race is checked, so is death and all its forms, and the members of the Ku Klux Klan will live forever)—all this is beside the point.

Other problems of group participation arise not only when the group is not working but also when a group member's investment of his L/T structure is out of proportion to the task requirement of the group. In that sense, he may feel he "possesses" more of the group than he does, or be jealous of someone else who seems to "possess" more, say, the leadership. Or he may see other forms of transcendence as more workable. Or he may not earn enough of his reward. (For a fuller discussion of the group as society, see Chapter 11, on culture and society.)

Thus, there are risks in group membership. The risk to the member is that her identity may be invalidated or destroyed. But there is also a possibility that her identity may be enhanced. The other group members are alternate selves, whose lives she may join along the dimension of the task. Adler's vision of the child's struggle for significance within the family (Ansbacher & Ansbacher, 1959) has its primordial repetition in each group of which the individual is a member; if she was killed by her family, she may be given life by the group; but also, she will fear another murder.

CONCLUSIONS

It is clear from the foregoing discussion of dyads, families, generations, and groups that the loss to be transcended in each is a metaphor of the ultimate loss and that its transcendence is a form of immortality. Humans huddle together in the presence of death; they peer into each other's faces to avoid the face of death. In each case, the individual "survives" physical death within either the lost sectors of those who survive her, or the children, possessions, and stories handed down from generation to generation, or group accomplishments. Were an individual, by some miracle, created on a desert, were she to spend her life there, she would be like the proverbial tree falling in the Amazon. Would she make a noise?

This is the threat of isolation, that forms of immortality are denied to the individual, and she is left alone in undistracted contemplation of her death. However, the positive face of isolation is solitude, fertile soil for general transcendence, when the artist paints, composes, or writes in blissful imitation of her Creator, who, by some accounts at least, was quite alone.

Toward an L/T Reconceptualization of Personality, Emotions, and Psychopathology

One function of emotions, motivations, and personality, both normal and pathological, is literal and metaphorical survival. A related function is the infliction of death on others. We are safe from those whom we destroy. The clinician may ask the source of the client's handwashing compulsion; he may be assured that the underlying aim is personal salvation, and that the energy with which such actions are undertaken is the same energy with which we save our lives. On the battlefield, the strength with which we fight is similar to the strength with which clients often cling to dysfunctional behavior; the problem is that, on the battlefield, the threat of death is readily apparent; in the counselor's office, often it is not.

We cannot survive without inflicting death, either directly on the plants and animals we eat, wear, smoke, and shelter under or metaphorically on those over whom we triumph. Ultimately, we are destroying a planet, that is, changing its energy from a consumable form to a nonconsumable form. At the same time we cannot live, inflicting death, without being part of the dying process. "In the midst of life. . . ." (*Book of common prayer*, 1789, p. 332).

What makes a specific behavior pathological is that the client is avoiding one form of death by inflicting on himself another. Pathology is transcendence of loss by another loss that does not lead to future transcendence, indeed, that leads to greater loss. The integrity of the self is threatened with denial or extinction, so, ironically, the man suffering from psychopathology has chosen an alternative mode of destroying himself. We saw this clearly in the case of Babs's husband, whose paranoia was gradually losing him the relationship with Babs about which he is paranoid. The disordered individual is like a criminal who must choose between hanging and lethal injection. By selecting depression, she avoids agoraphobia.

In this chapter I offer some suggestions toward an L/T reconceptualization of personality, emotions, and psychopathology. Obviously, this is only a beginning. I offer interpretations that, while incorporating much of the traditional, demonstrate the value of probing to the underlying substratum of the life-and-death struggle in which we are all engaged. Four life histories show some specific applications to paranoia (a return to Babs), depression (Vera), psychosexual disorders (Frances), and personality disorder, sexual dysfunction and sadomasochism (Jaclyn). I conclude with suggested applications for clinicians in the therapeutic setting, as well as for everyday life.

PERSONALITY

Personality traits, needs, styles, types, and patterns can be viewed as modes of transcending loss. The salient personality traits in any individual are those that have helped him survive; they have been reinforced by that survival. They represent the triumph of life over death. As behaviorists show us, if the schedule of such reinforcement is variable (a condition of life), extinction is difficult or unlikely. Tess, whom we met in Chapter 2, "Loss," still uses her little girl ways because they helped her win out over her sisters for her father's affection.

In the past decade there has been increasing recognition of the biological basis of many personality traits (Thomas & Chess, 1977; Barron, 1979; Parke & Asher, 1983), although many are mere biological predispositions that need environmental conditions to be actualized. These biological predispositions could be seen as enhancing survival in sociobiological fashion (see Wilson, 1975).

For example, research has shown that infants are born with certain temperament characteristics (Thomas & Chess, 1977), and those that are gender-appropriate tend to be reinforced by the society and therefore to remain stable over time (Kagan & Moss, 1962). Neonates vary on nine different temperament dimensions (Thomas & Chess, 1977): "quality of mood" (happy or sad), "adaptability" to a situation, "intensity" of reactions to a situation, "threshold of responsiveness" to new stimuli, "approach or withdrawal" to new stimuli, "activity level" (active or passive), "rhythmicity" (regularity of bodily functions), "distractibility," and "persistence" and "attention span." Each of these characteristics promotes survival in different ways, to a greater or lesser extent. For example, the happy baby may be cuddled more. The crying baby may provoke more anxious attention. The baby who cries harder for food may get food sooner. Further, there is evidence that such characteristics as introversion versus extroversion (Jung, 1971; Barron, 1979), schizophrenia (Arieti, 1974), depression, manic depression, and addictive behaviors are inherited (Arieti, 1978) and therefore biologically based.

Throughout life many individuals attempt to cultivate a personality that will make survival easier. For example, a friendly disposition makes one more attractive on the job and in the home, but overfriendliness may drive people away. Friendliness is nonthreatening; the message it conveys is that available resources will not be seized, that their possession will be worked out. When friendliness becomes abasement or masochism, the temptation to kill may be aroused with concomitant guilt, and the overfriendly individual is blamed. Or, as with other species, abasement may signal the dominance of the other within the hierarchy, thus sparing the abased one's life (Wilson, 1975). Or, overfriendliness may make too obvious the manipulativeness in the "average" friendliness, laying bare hypocrisy. Both the arousal of guilt and the revelation of one's own ulterior motives are threatening.

Aggressiveness is an obvious example of a personality trait or need (Murray, 1938) that promotes survival through loss to another; the aggressive woman protects herself against even a hint of threat, grasping the business opportunity more firmly and more quickly than the man beside her. Threat of failure is threat of annihilation, so she may exhibit a high need for achievement, or motive to avoid failure (McClelland, 1961). The job may be lost, and with it the wherewithal to buy food, shelter, and clothing. She may be exceptionally vigilant, interpreting actions of others as threat where none exists, the ultimate form of which is paranoia. She may refer to her world as "dog-eat-dog," a place where one must guard against being "stabbed in the back," or a "rat race." For her, death is by violence, which she seeks to inflict on others before they do it to her. "He who lives by the sword shall die by the sword." Thus, we see in this analysis that loss and transcendence underlie not only a personality trait but also motivation, emotion, psychopathology if carried to extremes, and an implicit world and death view.

The affiliative individual (Murray, 1938) seeks protection through group participation; he identifies the group gains with his own. The political party will win, and so will he; the group's life is longer than his, so he wins immortality. In exaggerated instances he may so submerge himself in the group, as Koestler observes (1949), that he fails to completely individuate— death by never having been completely born, stillbirth or asphyxiation. Because there is less of life in him, he is bored and boring. He may exhibit a high need for succorance from friends and relatives, reburying himself in the womb, if full identity and intimate love are not forthcoming. When friends and relatives respond, his miseries multiply. They commiserate with him, a counterfeit love that will sustain him if he cannot have the real thing. A related need is for approval, to replace warmth. Thus both accomplishments and personal disasters have similar uses, to draw others to himself. In payment for affiliation or approval, he permits others to define who he is, to define his me's; he experiences annihilation when the definition proves faulty, so he must constantly seek reassurance from others that he exists (see Laing, 1976). This was one reason why each loss of a job was so damaging to Tess.

Similarly, we may analyze other personality traits, needs, and motives (Murray, 1938). When we are nurturant, we care for others through great and little losses, which both represent our own and help to distract us from them. We also parent ourselves when we parent others, as we have seen in Marjorie's case. We protect ourselves from loss by abasement or deference to others, so they will not inflict losses on us from the stance of superior power; by ordering our lives to the smallest detail, so that we may survive on islands of design in the universal chaos; by ever changing (can death hit a moving target?), not committing ourselves profoundly to one occupation, relationship, or plan, so that the inevitable event of its loss cannot cut too deeply; by creating something that will outlive us; by honing our critical faculty to tear down what others have created, denying them afterlife; by cooperating with others so that we may receive our fair share; by giving to others so that they may say we live in reasonable hope of heaven.

Personality traits with inner-outer dimensions are particularly helpful to us in seeing the L/T substratum, for example, introversion-extroversion (Jung, 1971; Myers, 1962, 1977) or internal-external locus of control (Rokeach, 1968). The introvert finds safety within himself, holds himself inside so that he cannot be attacked from without, builds his world inside himself like a fortification, is more close-mouthed, intersects his me's with others as little as possible because such intersections are risky, lives within himself, perhaps vividly and richly; the danger, of course, is that he will be attacked from within and have only himself to fall back on in gradual disintegration, the most severe form of which is schizophrenia. The withdrawal of the schizoid or of the schizophrenic is maladaptive, transcendence pathological. Those who are isolated are exposed to the elements and to wandering tribes without protection. The extrovert, on the other hand, looks to others to transcend for him; when they fail him, what resources has he left? He also may not have developed enough of the ego strength needed to combat schizophrenia (Barron, 1979).

Similarly, the internal individual attributes loss and its control to his own efforts, whereas the external individual looks for this control in others, blaming others for loss. Crosscutting this distinction are findings that we generally tend to attribute our success to our own efforts and our failures to unfortunate external events (Jones & Nisbett, 1972); when judging others, however, we attribute their success to sources without and blame their abilities, characters, and so forth for their failures—an amusing commentary on human nature! In any event, it is both control of loss and attribution of loss and its transcendence with which we are concerned. We may, for instance, have a tendency to dominate or lead in our interactions with others, the better to control outcomes and assure ourselves greater protection against metaphors of death than we think others can afford us. Some of us want to fly the plane!

Many of these personality traits, motives, and needs have been reified as general transcendence mechanisms in our culture. The need for change becomes the general transcendence mechanism of travel, often prescribed; if the need is satisfied in this fashion, it may not be fulfilled by changing jobs, husbands, houses, and other less socially desirable forms of instability. Creativity becomes art, performed or appreciated; aggressiveness becomes athletic games or competition. Succorance, nurturance, and abasement needs (Murray, 1938) are fulfilled in religion and charity. We are, of course, inclined to employ a general transcendence mechanism that is congruent with our personality traits, salient or complementary; the person higher on the need for change may travel more. Travel may even become his occupation. (See Chapter 11 for a more detailed discussion.)

The several meanings of the term "personality" are often considered to be mutually exclusive. They are actually emphases on the different sectors of the self and are thus closely related. Traditional behaviorists would rather speak of behaviors, the activities of the me's, that is, stimulus and response histories, behavioral activities that can be counted and that are tangible to any or all of the five senses of the counter, so that even a statement such as "I feel fine" is interpreted only as the behavior of stating that one feels fine and has no other "inner" referent (Skinner, 1938, 1971; Sarbin, 1968). A behaviorist cannot conclude that the speaker feels or does not feel fine, or indeed that she feels at all. Sarbin (1979) would say he is enacting the *role* of feeling fine.

This viewpoint is not unrelated to the popular notion of personality, which is also external. You say of this one that she has a good personality and of that one that he does not. We have a general idea of what you mean. We assume she is probably bright-eyed, cheerful, smiles and laughs often and appropriately, is warm, helpful, and so on down the favorable adjectives of The Adjective Check List (Gough, 1952), with a good dose of female stereotype thrown in. We know he is probably too quiet or too loud, sullen, negative, overly aggressive, perhaps aloof. In our society, we value the above traits as positive or negative. Anthropologists know there are, and have been, societies where traits that we value as positive are negative, and vice versa (Benedict, 1934). As we have seen, one of the major tasks of the teen years is to try on, not just different roles, but also different personality traits. Can she become the "girl next door" without doing too much violence to who she really is, which she is only just discovering, supposing she really *is* someone? Both the behaviorist and the popular views of personality are operative in the transcendent me sector of the self.

A third meaning of the term "personality" is that of an inner structure, with an assumption that external behavior is a manifestation of this. In the Freudian paradigm we speak of the id, the ego, and the superego, their relative strengths or weaknesses, how they relate to one another, defend against each other, and conflict, and how the individual with such a structure comports himself in the social situation, his relationship to reality (Freud, 1923, reprinted

1955). One of the major issues in personality psychology (deriving from this paradigm) has been whether the individual behaves consistently across situations, because he has certain stable traits, or to what extent the situation dictates his behavior (Rorer & Widiger, 1983). To extrapolate from Bem's (1972) example, is the individual shy in front of a large lecture class, at a party, and in a one-on-one meeting with a student in his office, or is he shy at the party and warmly at ease in his office? It is believed that if the latter is true, a situational determination of shyness, rather than a trait of shyness, is being demonstrated. However, I believe that to be shy consistently in one set of situations and to be consistently un-self-conscious is another set could be interpreted as a stable personality disposition!

From the loss and transcendence perspective, there is an inner personality—the lost and transcendent I, and the lost me—and an outer personality or group of transcendent me's that may vary according to the situation of each particular me. The relationship among these facets of personality may be candid or obscure. The personality is the structure with which an individual transcends both threatened and actual loss, both inwardly and externally. Haan (1977) observed, "It seems reasonable to assume that all coping, defensive and fragmentary actions are within the armamentarium of all people, and can be brought into play according to the person's interactional needs with different situations, here various stress situations. However, the different processes are clearly not equipotential, since people have histories, and therefore preferences as to what has worked for them in the past" (p. 171). These preferences form the basis of personality traits, the reactions or responses, defense mechanisms, that people most often use in different situations over time. They move from the transcendent I to the transcendent me—we think before we act (and then we think some more!). The individual transcends in the stages and processes I have outlined, and each defense mechanism may be considered a form of mourning or resolution.

Thus, defense mechanisms may be viewed as similar to personality traits, ways of handling loss or its threat. We may withdraw from loss, sometimes wisely but sometimes maladaptively; we may lose more by withdrawal from the loss situation than by remaining within it. Habitual withdrawal is considered pathological unless there is a gain; the hermit is wise, instead of crazy; if the mystic hears voices in a culture that accepts them, rather than having them viewed as a symptom, she may be sainted.

We may deny that we have sustained loss; denial may be a successful way of handling loss on a short-term basis but maladaptive in the long term. Haan (1977) cites the example of the woman who denies the lump in her breast; if she does so for too long, her denial may kill her. On the other hand, Wolff, Friedman, Hofer, and Mason (1964) compared parents of fatally ill leukemic children who denied the seriousness of their children's illness, with parents who recognized it. Parents who successfully denied had a lower excretion of 17-hydroxycorticosteroids in their urinary output, implying that their denial may actually have protected them from physiological stress (we cannot be sure of the direction; however, it may be that people who have such low output are deniers). In view of the evidence linking stress (reaction to a loss situation) with disease, it seems that denial might protect the individual from disease. It might even be wise for counselors to encourage denial in some circumstances, a view that would horrify many contemporary clinicians. Goleman (1987) cites recent contradictory evidence: self-deception may be helpful, or it may lead to disease, if carried on for a long time. The time element may be the crucial factor in the helpfulness or harm.

We also rationalize or intellectualize our losses, calling them "blessings in disguise," seeing profounder losses in their stead had we been successful in escaping them, and attributing more culturally acceptable reasons to the losses we cause others. We suppress or deliberately postpone handling our losses until we are readier to deal with them (Scarlett O'Hara will "think of it tomorrow"). We react against the anticipation of loss by behaving contrarily, the strength of our reaction formation being proportional to the strength of our oppositional desires. We project our losses onto others; if we have been rejected by a lover, we may shrink from the disgusting spectacle of secret loves everywhere. We displace our loss of face on the job by hitting out at husband, instead of boss. We fashion our loss into a joke and gain the warmth of others laughing with us (probably a mature form of isolation or dissociation). If we can laugh at something scary, it is not dangerous. We transcend the loss to others through altruism; we ourselves can never lose when we prevent loss to others, or we are meeting the challenges to others that we do not have, gaining pleasure in the competence we demonstrate. Vaillant's fine work on defense mechanisms (1977) shows that we probably develop them from the psychotic and immature ones of childhood through the neurotic to the mature (we hope)—sublimation, suppression, anticipation, humor, and altruism. In all of these we transcend death in some form.

EMOTIONS

Emotions are the feelings we have about our various losses and transcendencies. Joy, love, delight, gaiety, and hope are examples of transcendent emotions, whereas hatred, anxiety, guilt, anger, and regret are emotions associated with loss. When we reverse them, feeling joy over loss, finding transcendence in hatred, or when we display flattened affect, it is indicative of either pathology or the possibility that loss on the primary level yields transcendence on other levels. When a situation evokes both loss and transcendence, we say we have "mixed emotions," and then we analyze the ways in which the situation represents both loss and transcendence to us. We have mixed feelings about moving to the large city. On the one hand, there are all the cultural events in which we take delight, the wide variety of people to meet, shopping opportunities, resources for our interests; on the other hand, we'll miss the trees, the small town, our friends, the relative sense of safety. If we have a choice in the move, we may be indecisive, draw up a balance sheet of pros and cons, trying to quantify safety and stimulation. This country-city dichotomy was a conflict for Crista and a number of other interviewees.

Guilt is the experience we have consequent on causing loss to another, which may be a crime or a sin, depending on whether it falls under the secular or the religious arm of society. There is more sin than crime (a crime is a sin, but a sin is not necessarily a crime); even the contemplation of causing loss to another prompts excoriations from conscience, except in the psychopath. Because we cannot exist without causing loss to others (humans, animals, and plants), we have formulated the doctrine of original sin, to which we are born. Confession, repentance, and forgiveness may mitigate guilt feelings in the Christian religion. To live ascetically is to cause the least loss possible to others, although more to ourselves. Lethe, the river of forgetfulness, erases loss from memory; we try to dip into it and drink, music or alcohol. Or Alzheimer's?

Jealousy is the emotion we feel when threatened with the loss of a loved person, or a sales territory, to another (see Clanton & Smith, 1977; Huplea, 1977, 1982, personal communication); envy is what we feel when someone has something we wish were ours—object, success, prestige, or possession (see Schoeck, 1966). Nostalgia is the loss of the familiar, or what might have been had life continued as it was; regret, the loss of possibility; hope, the transcendence of present difficulties in the future; despair, the loss of hope. Loving transcends the distance between selves (the loss of perfect mergence), bestowing on us alternate lives to lead besides our own. Love is truly a gift of life.

We feel hatred toward those who cause us loss; because those we love are most capable of causing us loss, knowing what is dearest to us and taking it from us, we can hate most deeply those we love. In war, it is necessary to hate a faceless enemy in order to kill him, so we stereotype him with hateful characteristics. We say he is ruthless, brutal, cunning, cruel, inhuman—all the traits we need in ourselves in order to kill him. We say he would destroy all that is good in our lives, all we value, personalizing hatred, because we might not otherwise kill on behalf of the faceless ones on our side. We especially hate feeling negative emotions, because we sense that we incorporate them into our selves, where they may fester and poison our entire L/T structure. One of the greatest sources of familial frustration is to be compelled to negative emotions, forced to feel ingratitude and murderous impulse by and toward those we love. Families can manipulate this to an exquisite form of torture and never be aware that they are doing so. Bateson's (1972) double bind, in which an individual is induced to feel two conflicting emotions at once, is an illustration of this. Come here, go away.

Loneliness is loss of relatedness, of former or ideal companionship, warmth, sexual satisfaction, good conversation, of being with another and within another and feeling that other with and within us—all of which we have been promised since fairy tales. The obverse of loneliness may be companionship; our dictionary and our values would certainly have it so. Being alone is often equated with loneliness. But its obverse might also be solitude, the ability to be with and within ourselves, which may also be fulfilling. In our culture, we train children in social skills, and when they find themselves alone at different points in their lives, they cannot make of themselves companions. They tend to lose themselves. Self alone is of no worth— a tragedy.

Anxiety is often an aspect of depression, as are anger and guilt. The interrelationship of these four negative emotions is unclear and puzzling, unless we use the concept of identity as a substrate. These four emotions are all reactions to threats to our survival. We lash out in anger at him who would kill us; or we are anxious lest we be killed; or we are guilty of killing those who threatened us; or we are depressed because we are dying. To this interrelationship we might add that envy and jealousy are the emotions we feel toward those (such as a lover) who may kill off some aspects of who we are or might become (our possibilities).

PERSONALITY, STRESSFUL LIFE EVENTS, AND DISEASE

Historically, there have been numerous attempts to associate specific diseases with specific personality characteristics, emotions, or problems in early childhood (Plaut & Friedman, 1981). Freudian psychoanalysts in particular defined a number of major illnesses as psychosomatic, such as bronchial asthma, rheumatoid arthritis, ulcerative colitis, essential hypertension, neurodermatitis, thyrotoxicosis, and duodenal or peptic ulcer. In the psychoanalytic framework, asthma was the result of an infant in conflict with the mother over its crying, resulting in inhibition of the expiratory acts of crying or communication, more popularly conceived as "smotherlove"; arthritis represented difficulty in handling hostile impulses; ulcerative colitis resulted from loss of hope in task accomplishment; neurodermatitis was the result of a complex interrelationship among exhibitionism, guilt, and masochism; thyrotoxicosis was the consequence of great death fear; and an ulcer resulted from the frustration of oral dependency in childhood, with ensuing longing for love manifested by the secretion of too much gastric acid (Alexander, 1950). Research attempting to demonstrate these specific associations between psyche and soma has had mixed results, and this "theory of specificity" generally goes unproved. These psychosomatic diseases are typical of the view that a physical illness symbolizes a psychic problem. Susan Sontag (1979) brilliantly inveighs against this notion, particularly as it might apply to cancer or tuberculosis. However, connections between soma and psyche make intuitive sense—the person is a unity.

In recent years there have been exciting new research developments concerning links among personality factors, stressful life events, disease, and healing. The old Cartesian mind-body split may be overcome. I will give brief examples from the literature on infectious diseases, heart disease, and cancer and then discuss the implications for L/T moral philosophy and therapy.

The relatively new discipline of psychoneuroimmunology yields evidence that psychosocial factors may influence the central nervous system, the endocrine and hormonal systems, and neurotransmitters (Maclean & Reichlin, 1981), in ways that suppress immunity and lead to disease or enhance immunity and help resist disease (Ader & Cohen, 1981). For example, in a number of different experiments, Ader and Cohen (1981) were able to *behaviorally condition* the suppression of the immune response in mice and rats.

With regard to infectious diseases, Kasl, Evans, and Niederman (1979) studied infectious mononucleosis in West Point cadets and found that those under greater stress were more likely to develop the disease. Plaut and Friedman (1981) speculate that psychosocial factors influence the host of a pathogen in such a way that the individual is more susceptible to infectious diseases, because the immunologic status is changed. There seems to be evidence of immune system suppression due to psychosocial factors in streptococcal disease, dental caries, diabetes, and respiratory infections as well as mononucleosis.

Among the autoimmune diseases, cited by Solomon (1981), in which psychosocial factors may play a part are rheumatoid arthritis, thyroiditis, acquired hemolytic anemia, systemic lupus erythematosus, and myasthenia gravis. Other diseases so influenced that may be autoimmune are multiple sclerosis, Graves' disease, ulcerative colitis, pernicious anemia, idiopathic thrombocytopenic purpura, and diabetes. Solomon states that the central nervous system and the neuroendocrine system seem to have a role in regulating immunity, although this has not been proved. There may be a genetic predisposition to such diseases, mediated by reaction to stress and also by psychological defenses. The research shows that rheumatoid arthritis patients tend toward "more masochism, self-sacrifice, denial of hostility, compliance-subservience, depression, and sensitivity to anger, and are described as always having been nervous, tense, worried, highly strung, moody individuals" (Solomon, 1981, p. 179). The progression of their disease seems to depend on their psychological defense mechanisms.

Just as loss is a common dimension of many psychosomatic reactions and infectious diseases, it is also the common dimension of diseases not traditionally regarded as psychosomatic. A personality aspect has been recognized as possible in heart disease and in cancer, two leading causes of death assumed heretofore to be purely physical in cause and nature. Patients with these two diseases seem to have contrasting personalities; whereas the cancer patient may tend toward feelings of helplessness and hopelessness, giving up in the face of loss, the heart patient, like Sisyphus, persists in an impossible task doomed to failure, continuing to roll the boulder uphill against incredible odds (Jenkins, 1971). These are two very different ways of handling loss.

With regard to cancer, there is some evidence that stressful life events and personality factors may tend to suppress the immune system but that the issue may not be stress as much as how the stress is handled. Bernard Fox (1981) sums up the situation: "We are being drawn closer and closer, in view of recent studies, to the firm position that PF [psychosocial factors] in the human may indeed affect cancer incidence. But we are not yet securely in that position" (p. 10). He defines PF as (1) personality characteristics and (2) stresses and sees the immune system as the mediating factor between PF and disease. Goodkin, Antoni, and Blaney (1986) have found that personality factors may influence the progression of precancerous cervical lesions. Women who had a generally negative view of life and a greater number of stressful life events had greater precancerous change. Psychological health in childhood predicts later physical health, according to a longitudinal prospective study by Carolyn Thomas. She cited "high self-esteem, a warm relationship with parents, an optimistic outlook, an outgoing temperament, the ability to cope with stress" as possibly protective against major disease (Anderson, 1982, p. 56). Bartrop, Luckhurst, Lazarus, Kiloh, and Penny (1977) reported the suppression of immune systems in surviving spouses 2 months after bereavement, with a strengthening at about 4 months. These studies are among a number of similar ones showing the importance of attitude in the development of physical changes and/or illness. However, there is still controversy concerning such factors as the stage of cancer and the measures used.

The coronary-prone type of person, described as engaging in type A behavior by Friedman and co-workers (1974, 1984), is competitive, achievement-oriented, time-pressured, aggressive, hasty and impatient, restless, hyperalert, and explosive in speech. In contrast, type B behavior is more relaxed. In addition, the type A person tends to neglect aspects of his life other than work, is on the go, drinks, eats, and speaks more rapidly, works overtime, and often does two or more things at once (i.e., reads, eats, and talks on the phone). Recently, R. Williams and his colleagues at Duke University have implicated hostility or "cynical contempt" as possibly the most damaging type A characteristic (Wood, 1986). Other recent studies do not replicate the finding that the type A individual is more coronary prone, although Friedman and Rosenman argue that the personality measures were questionable (Fischman, 1987). Jenkins (1976) has cited evidence for increased risk of coronary disease as a result of such stressful life changes as divorce or bereavement. In any event, within the L/T paradigm, it is *time,* the measure of life, that heart patients are battling in innumerable ways so as not to lose it! (See Chapter 12, "Time and Death".) In addition, hostility, or the urge to metaphorically kill another, may kill oneself.

There are numerous other studies of psychosocial factors and illness. For example, Vaillant (1979) found that occupational progress and dissatisfaction as well as other psychosocial factors could predict physical illness over 40 years; this was while controlling for such known longevity factors as obesity, genetics, and smoking. I have reviewed some of the persuasive evidence on stressful life events accumulated by Holmes, Rahe, and Masuda in Chapter 1, on methodology.

Evidence for personality and psychosocial factors in healing and health (as well as disease) is also accumulating (Ornstein & Sobel, 1987). Some alternative therapists claim that individuals with AIDS, which involves suppression of the immune system, can be helped by various mental practices (Serinus, 1986). If our outlook on the world can be changed, we may indeed have more control over our health. The work of Seligman (1975) on learned helplessness suggests a possible link among control over stress, depression, and the immune system. Loss of power may increase the incidence of illness, according to McClelland and Jemmott (1980). It is possible that power may also be conceptualized as control, opposed to helplessness. The importance of how stress is handled (Maier & Laudenslager, 1985) lends added significance to the existential notion of "response-ability." It may actually save one's life to feel responsible (in control, empowered).

There is some evidence for the healing possibilities of caring for others, imagery, relaxation, and having a social network as a buffer to stress (Maier & Laudenslager, 1985; Ornstein & Sobel, 1987). Friedman and Ulmer (1984) have been demonstrating that the type A personality can be changed. Ornstein and Sobel (1987) observe that many societies and religions emphasize the importance of caring for and serving others (as against being hostile); this might promote not only the health of the community but also that of the individual.

The picture is complex, because physical and mental pathologies are determined by a number of other factors, including constitutional or genetic predisposition, history of L/T, and the type of loss situation, as well as personality traits, stressful life events, and development. Within the L/T perspective, physical and mental pathology are not only inseparable but also inevitable aspects of each other; they are seen as resulting from or as forms of inappropriate, incomplete, maladaptive, and/or ineffectual transcendence.

All loss threatens or is experienced by the entire self, and any pathology, physical or mental, is a manifestation of this. A stressful life event may be cognitively appraised as threatening to one individual and not to others (Beck, Rush, Shaw, & Emery, 1985; Lazarus, 1966) because that individual may be particularly vigilant, have a history of loss surrounding similar events, be aware that he lacks certain capacities to cope, and so forth. Consider possible reactions to a note from the boss suggesting a meeting in her office at 10 a.m. One individual may experience simple curiosity; another, optimism about promotion; another, fear of being fired, which may increase adrenaline or gastric secretion, which may in turn intensify the emotion of fear. The individual who habitually perceives events as more threatening (or negative) or who is loss oriented would be more likely to exhibit more pathology, physical, mental, or both. The possibilities of loss become infinite and engulfing, because the self is not integrated enough, strong enough, or whole enough to cope. However, even disintegration has its uses, if it can lead to manipulation or exploitation of others.

The literature cited above may be read as indicative that loss may be associated with the onset of illness. Many findings suggest that everyone experiences loss; it is the way loss, or threat of loss, is handled that may evoke disease.

There are major implications for moral philosophy and for therapy.

Psychosocial loss—a stressful life event mediated by the individual's personality and consequent response—may lead to physical disease and death for the individual. Thus it can be argued that one who inflicts stress on an individual, in the workplace or in the family, is engaged in a killing act. If the immune system is lowered when the boss consistently denigrates his subordinate, or the parent terrifies her child, the boss or the parent may be committing an act of murder for which he or she holds no less responsibility than the knifer. If those who mediate loss—the friend, relative, teacher, minister, nurse, or social worker—do not make every effort to help the lost individual respond, gain control, take power, and be optimistic, they also may be mediating a murder. At some level I believe many of us know this, and it is our inability to thus preserve life in the face of inadequate resources and inhuman caseloads that leads us to burnout. The flame in us dies as we take on the deaths of others.

Elsewhere I have noted that we are in a continuous metaphorical struggle between life and death; we straddle a continuum on which we move back and forth, sometimes closer to death, sometimes closer to life. This applies to each of us as an individual. Now, it appears that the metaphorical struggle is not simply one in which we are engaged for ourselves. As friends, relatives, bosses, and professionals, we also play a crucial role in the metaphorical struggles of those we know and work with. At any moment we may be killing, preserving, or enhancing life. The implications are that cruelty takes lives and kindness saves them. If life is of value and murder is a sin, then so is cruelty.

A basic weapon in the therapist's armamentarium is the presentation of options that the client does not see. But the counselor is doing more than this without, perhaps, realizing it. She or he is rallying the forces of hope, before the immune system of the client is too long depressed. The old-fashioned virtues of love and faith may conquer death, for a while. She or he saves the lives of many more than those who are frankly suicidal. As do we all!

PSYCHOPATHOLOGY

Pathology may be psychological, or it may be physical. It may be a biologically based psychological problem or a psychologically based physical problem. There is increasing recognition of the interplay between both; indeed, no problem seems entirely physical or psychological. A disorder such as depression results in physical manifestations such as eating and sleeping problems. A physical disorder such as kidney disease often results in depression. With many disorders, there is a ''chicken-egg'' issue. The old Cartesian division between mind and body seems increasingly inaccurate.

Pathology represents either the inability of the individual to transcend a loss, or a loss as yet untranscended, or a transcendence that is more loss-inflicting than the loss it transcends. The loss may be one of bodily defense against an invading microorganism, or the loss of a job. As we saw in Chapter 2, each primary loss brings a host of others in its wake, indeed is reflected on five levels. Inadequate transcendence of loss may occur at any stage of the L/T process, and the individual may become fixated in that stage, resulting in pathology. The process of pathology can be traced through all four stages in the mourning and resolution phases, in hopeless grieving, searching, replacement, or integration.

For example, after the death of his wife, a man may become so preoccupied with his loss that he cannot move on to the next stage of searching; he remains in his apartment, work has suddenly lost its savor, he watches TV, drinks, and, to friends who try to help him by suggesting he attend the church social, he responds, "I'll never find another like her." The general transcendence mechanisms (in this case drinking and TV) are only temporary anodynes of grief, whose effects wear off too soon. He cannot move to the next stage. He may be diagnosed as experiencing reactive depression or "uncomplicated bereavement" (see Diagnostic and Statistical Manual III-R); if too severe, with a history of similar episodes, the depression may be seen as endogenous depression; fixation at the grieving stage may become his behavioral style and may have some constitutional element or predisposition. Further, he may lose interest in eating and exercise and may be unable to sleep, all predisposing him to physical illness. Feelings of hopelessness or helplessness may eventually prevail; the individual may even lose desire for anything—"I can't seem to find anything I want any more"—so that searching, the next stage, becomes fruitless. Suicide may result. Vera, when her husband left her for another woman, went to bed, stopped eating, and might have died had it not been for friends and relatives urging her toward her nursing degree. A number of other interviewees reported mothers who, in grief, just "went to bed over the whole thing" for years.

In the next stage of searching for a replacement, the affect of depression may be replaced by feelings of assertiveness, energy, and even anger. A good example is the teenager who is "searching" for something. She must "put away childish things," but she is unsure of what is childish. Her losses have been, and are, many: loss of security, financial dependence, being allowed to be irresponsible; loss of her parents as omnipotent and omniscient; loss of timelessness. She is seeking answers but she does not know the questions, so her "search" is couched in vague terms; or she may say she is searching for herself, who she is, what she is to become. Implicit in this is that she *is* someone, if she can only find out who. She has discovered that her parents cannot tell her who she is, only who they want her to be; they have their own ideal, and she falls short of it and is guilty of causing loss to them. But the imposition of an ideal on her self has been unfair; she resents it. She asks her friends who she is, and they seem to know better. She may decide to "seek her fortune" in the world; she is a self who will spring to life as soon as she is in the right circumstances like magic-colored rocks that become plants when covered with water. She will "discover" this self; she does not see herself as constructing her self. She searches in subcultures, schools, jobs, cults, and general transcendence activities such as drugs and alcohol. She encounters limitations in all of these and searches elsewhere. If she becomes too discrepant from her parents' ideal she may "act out" and angrily become the opposite of the ideal, a juvenile delinquent, engaging in petty theft, arson, drugs, prostitution, perhaps. It is probable that many criminals or people guilty of antisocial behavior are fixated in this searching stage; they know they are not the ideal, so perhaps they are its obverse. The criminal may also be seen as replacing what is lost to her with someone else's property, identity, or life. Depressives who move from grieving to searching have new energy with which to commit suicide. Replacement may be death.

The initial stage of resolution, or the replacement of what has been lost, is not like finding a lost heirloom ring in an unused drawer; it is a process. The individual creates another "me" in a relationship or a new career, for instance. Some other me's move from the transcendent sector into the lost sector, the punk rocker must cut his "slavelock"; self-concept must be adjusted, which in turn modifies the new me, which modifies the self-concept in an equilibrating process (see Piaget, 1952). But there can be snags here as well.

All illustration of fixation at the replacement stage is the high school English teacher who has lost her job in the job squeeze resulting from declining birth rates. There are openings in computer programming, so she begins training in this field. But the me who was a teacher is having difficulty moving into the lost sector. She harbors the secret hope that the education job market will improve (as, indeed, it is beginning to) and that she can return to this more satisfying life. She still feels like a high school teacher, probably behaves and dresses like one; her friends, the organizations to which she belongs, how she relates to others (she tends to be a bit didactic, perhaps) are all part of the me that must be let go. The high school teacher me moves only slowly toward its destination. She is undergoing what is commonly called an identity crisis, with attendant anxiety, conflict, and bouts of depression, different from the teenager's initial search for identity, since the teacher must discard one identity for another. At some point she is neither a high school teacher nor a computer programmer. How her family sees her is also undergoing revision. Old ideals must be given up, as well as old concepts of significance. It is probable that this identity crisis will be resolved eventually, that the high school teacher me will move into the lost sector and the computer programmer me will grow and consolidate itself in the transcendent sector. If not, she becomes fixated in the replacement stage; physical and emotional pathology may deepen and anxiety become chronic. The specific time-related diseases, heart and ulcers, may have their highest incidence in these individuals; the pressure to achieve is great *because identity must be consolidated*. Yet, there is often an equal and opposite attraction toward nonconsolidation, so that other identities need not be given up. Anxiety would be the predominant affect of those fixated at the replacement stage.

Integration also may not be completed, and fixation here is seen as characteristic of the neuroses, particularly of existential conflict over the meaning of life and the apparent futility and absurdity of doing anything (see Sartre's *Nausea*, 1964); this must be distinguished from the hopelessness and inaction that characterize the grieving stage. In the integration stage, the individual continues to function competently in role-related activities but is struggling to find meaning, to integrate a concept of self as purposeful, transcending in the sense of being part of something high and beyond self. Some must tell their stories over and over compulsively in the attempt to make sense of their lives. The individual knows who he is (identity, self-concept) but is still working on the myth of how he got to be that way.

Healthy individuals have both specific situational and general transcendence mechanisms in their repertoires, as well as dispositional ones. Some individuals may be classified as employing predominantly dispositional mechanisms; they meet every crisis with their small repertoire, with sweet persuasiveness or angry explosions, no matter what the situation. Others are competent predominantly in situational transcendence, and still others in general transcendence, with a final group who employ combinations of two or all three. A general transcendence mechanism may become the dominant mode of coping for an individual because she or he lacks competence in situational or dispositional transcendence, and this incompetence may be an etiological factor. For example, many people use alcohol and drugs, appreciate music and the arts, watch TV, or attend movies; all are characterized by timelessness, a rest from time-pressured activity, a sense of flow, peak experiences, or even transcendent joy, perhaps (Csikszentmihalyi, 1975). Death is deferred. But such an individual may become an addict, employing the defense mechanisms of denial and repression to excess. He is less functioning in his role-related activities; indeed, his role becomes "addict" (see Sarbin, 1968, 1979).

Serious mental pathology may be seen in terms of the permeability of the various sectors of the self. The boundaries may be calcified and relatively impermeable or may be weakened and too permeable. For example, a common feature of some types of schizophrenia is the inability to mark off time; the lost me's drift into the transcendent me sector, and the defense mechanisms of childhood such as fantasy and projection, normally relegated to the lost, show up in the transcendent I. This is analogous to Freud's eruption of the id impulses through the repression barrier into the ego (1923, reprinted 1961). Catatonia, on the other hand, is a form of petrifaction (Laing, 1976) or calcification. When any kind of movement in any direction is threatening, the best defense is immobility. Dissociative states (amnesia, sleepwalking, fugue, multiple personality) split off the lost me's and I from the transcendent. Contrarily, in regression, the lost me's overwhelm the transcendent. In all cases, the individual has not been able to build and strengthen her L/T structure in the "normal" way.

SPECIFIC PATHOLOGIES

When we reinterpret a few representative examples of specific pathologies, we see the application of the L/T framework. For example, chronic depression is the recognition that death in its myriad forms ultimately cannot be overcome. The individual displaces the recognition onto specific life events, saying "I have lost my lover" or "I have lost my job" or "my cat" or "my grandmother's pencil box." She gives specific attributions for depression, often wandering from one life event to another. It is not only the life events that have gone untranscended but also the ultimate loss they represent, and for which she is in perpetual mourning. It is less threatening to be depressed over a lost lover than one's ultimate annihilation. Depressed people are often in flight, whereas the more surgent, like Faith, respond to the same threat by fight. On the life-death continuum, the depressed are moving toward death.

Something else is going on with the depressed person. She acquiesces to loss. "If I don't try, I can't lose." Thus she is in flight from life as well as death, because she will not try to live. Depression over loss protects her from further loss. But a flight from life is a form of suicide. While each small *act* of self-killing is intentional, the ultimate intention to kill is often pre-conscious or unconscious.

Maggie Scarf's research on depression in women (1980) shows that women have a higher incidence of depression than men for both biological and cultural reasons. They may have a biological predisposition to depression, but the culture compels them to identify themselves in terms of others (husbands, children). When these significant or "dominant others" (Arieti, 1978) leave, the woman's identity is partially destroyed and, to reframe in L/T terms, she continues to kill off the other parts of herself with depression rather than live only as a part-self.

The depressed person acquires power over those surrounding her, family, work colleagues, and friends. She controls others with the threat of self-annihilation, nibbling at her food, giving away her possessions. This reminds others of the death they are free to choose for themselves as well. They resent her for reminding them of material repressed with such great difficulty and for arousing in them their own despair and death inclinations. If they can save her life, metaphorically they save their own. If they can convince her life is worth living, they convince themselves, at least for a time. If she dies, they have not tried as hard as they could, they have not cared enough, their buried resentment against her has killed her. They deserve to die.

As Freud (1917, reprinted 1957) saw, depression is a form of hostility, and it can kill. The depressed person cannot control the events over which she believes she is depressed, but metaphorically she controls dying by controlling her own and that of others. She is wrenching control over the uncontrollable, controlling symbolically that which she cannot control in actuality, destroying in others what is dying in her. She will not easily give up this phantom control.

Eating disorders such as anorexia, bulimia, and bulimarexia involve similar issues, killing with sustenance, extending power over family, life, and death. They arise just as the teen becomes cognitively capable of conceiving of her own death.

The hypochondriac has illnesses that are not really there, magnifies minor symptoms, cannot be reassured that the medical evidence shows the ailment is minor or nonexistent. Of course, the hypochondriac is right. Even if the fatal illness does not exist today, one day it will. The test results will come back positive, surgery will be needed, or medication, or radiation, or "nothing more can be done." The hypochondriac is practicing. Maybe with enough practice he will be able to meet that final day with more equanimity than he would without practice—practice makes perfect. He cannot practice accidents (as the "accident-prone" person does), but he can practice disease with all its trappings of stethoscopes, ether smells, tests, and white uniforms. He sets his sights on death, not life. When he dies, there will be no more fear. Each time he is told he will live longer, he overcomes death yet awhile. When he goes to the physician, he is not *really* saying, "This pain worries me. It may be serious." He is saying, "Help me, Doctor. I'm going to die some day. Give me a pill—or a philosophy. How do *you* face it. Talk to me about death, and maybe you can talk me out of it." The physician does not hear this; she only knows that a nuisance is taking valuable time and resources, and yet she must avoid risk of a malpractice suit by attending silly symptoms!

When the day finally arrives, and the hypochondriac is diagnosed as seriously ill, he is often relieved and even lighthearted, at least for a while. He jokes bravely in the face of death. He is like the prisoner whose sentence is finally converted from "indefinite" to 7 years. The hypochondriac won't have all the other diseases he suspected all these years—he won't live long enough to get them! This is an occasion of celebration. He is dying of heart disease—no more cancer worries for him!

The hypochondriac, like the depressed, is disliked, mocked, and avoided because he digs up what the rest of us bury. The rise in hypochondriasis with age (Barron, 1979) is reasonable. When one is young, a twinge in the chest may be a pulled muscle. One might even view the increased vigilance of the hypochondriac as adaptive. He may get to the doctor soon enough to treat the early stages of a disease.

The paranoid is vigilant against all the enemies that may assail him from different directions, as we saw with Babs's husband. The more of other that he lets into himself, the more aspects of himself may die without his even being aware. Laing's (1976) paradigm is of great assistance here, the notion of the other that may overwhelm and engulf the self so that it ceases to exist or dies or, worst of all, becomes other. The hypochondriac and the paranoid are alike in that both fear destruction from myriad directions. The paranoid is jealous of other lives. No one can live a life without stealing from his. Life is a well that can run dry. But "even paranoids have enemies" (B. Eben, personal communication, 1983). The paranoid is, indeed, in danger of being destroyed.

Cases of multiple personality as recounted in *The lives of Billy Milligan* (Keyes, 1981) and *Sibyl* (Schreiber, 1974) are probably more common than has been thought heretofore, and over 90 percent of them can be traced to severe abuse in childhood. Typically, the individual "splits" into different personalities, each capable of handling different aspects of survival. For example, in the case of Billy Milligan, David took the pain, Tommy was called to the "spot" when escape was needed from ropes or cuffs or strait-jackets. Ragen was there for strength. Some of the other personalities were more self-creating than loss-overcoming, like those who were artists. The "undesirables" had their uses as well. We are all like multiple personalities in that there are different facets of ourselves to overcome different problems and re-create.

Shyness is not considered a serious disorder, and yet it causes great pain (Zimbardo, 1984). The shy person's subconscious rationale is, "If I am invisible, I cannot be hurt. You cannot strike me if you cannot see me." In my classrooms, some very bright students are quiet all quarter (although they may have more of worth to contribute than some who "babble on"). Their ideas are dear to them; their ideas are who they are, and they cannot be destroyed by logic or mockery if they are held inside instead of being displayed. These students do not die by exposure of their ignorance. Others, on the other hand, need affirmation that their thoughts and they themselves exist and are worthwhile. They expose themselves. The risks and the rewards are great. They are perhaps less in danger of feeling destroyed than the shy ones if "something happens" and their ideas are unworthy (of course, the good professor will never let this happen), but they will gain in self-esteem if the ideas are good. They are, of course, also motivated by the excitement of ideas. Thus, once again, there is the conflict between mergence versus individuation, exposure and isolation, dying of either, as Yalom (1981) has shown.

The phobic is aware that all choices can lead to death. Daily life is a game of Russian roulette. If he can keep death manageable, he can go on with his life. The trick is to figure out where death is most likely to be hiding in wait and avoid the area, to circumscribe death, confine it to snakes, or bridges, or airplanes. He manages to do this for a while. He stays away from elevators, and he is safe; there is a rewarding feeling of relief, which, as behaviorists point out, reinforces the phobia! Unfortunately, often enough, the fears begin to spread and also to increase into panic attacks. Other objects, situations, and people are dangerous. He can't avoid everything, and yet he can't afford to show his fear of the wind at work, when the huge rattling windows could shatter at any moment or the swaying building could tip over, or they'd think he was crazy. The panic rises. He tries not to show it, but they are looking at him strangely, asking if he is all right.

Phobias appear to be fears of open places, flying, spiders, and so forth, but are actually the ultimate terror. They arise when the individual's growth (life) is blocked. Phobias are the ultimate terror scaled down to a more manageable fear that can be avoided. Death can be the ultimate transcendence (see Chapter 12), and when other forms of transcendence are not being experienced, death's metaphors—phobias and other psychopathologies—develop. Behaviorists have had success in treating phobias, a success Freudians eschew because they feel treatment of symptoms does not get at the underlying problem. Within the L/T framework, both are right. Eventually the patient must deal with what he really fears, his death. The behaviorist (unknowingly) thrusts transcendence on the individual, who, transcending fear, is transcending it also as a metaphor—she is being conditioned to cope with death.

Agoraphobia has been called "housewives' syndrome." In many it arises because the woman needs to "grow out," but she is shrinking in. If she "grows out" she may "outgrow" her marriage and family. She must choose between two forms of death. As an agoraphobic she is experiencing mergence at the expense of individuation (see Yalom, 1981), or death by suffocation. Her fear is of "open spaces" beyond the home, or death by exposure. She remains within cozy confines, the swaddling clothes of her infancy, rather than venture out. Should she become depressed and choose the "suicide" of the world outside, she might be rewarded with new experiences and stimulation, and perhaps eventually her agoraphobia would be overcome.

It is often observed that the mentally disordered person distorts reality to a greater or lesser degree, depending on the severity of the pathology; that is, he does not agree with his society's interpretation of reality. He may even be suffering from delusions—of grandeur or persecution, for example. However, these delusions are only exaggerated illusions, whose content is a life-and-death matter, concerned at the very least with the survival of his identity.

LIFE HISTORIES

The above represent a few suggestions for the ways in which the L/T existential viewpoint can illuminate some facets of personality, emotion, motivation, and psychopathology, always remembering the role of biological and environmental determinants. We turn now to the case histories of Vera, Frances, and Jaclyn to help us understand the role of loss transcendence further.

Vera's story is an admixture of abasement, sacrifice, guilt, nonliving, suicidal depression, and the support of others.

Vera

"I developed . . . a Christian sort of crucifixion about myself."

Vera, in her mid-sixties, thin and attractive, was raised in a tiny midwestern town by a kind but withdrawn father and a hypochondriacal mother who was angry, gloomy, and impatient and frightened the children with threats of her own imminent death. Her brother, some years older, was jealous, violent, and hit her often over the years. "They said he tried to smother me when I was a baby."

While Vera was still a child, her father became ill and disabled; her mother, who had always had a maid, had to go out and become a maid herself to support the family. She was bitter about this.

Poor finances continued to plague the family throughout Vera's adolescence. As a result, her mother made her take "stupid" courses in domestic sciences and business so that she could start bringing in more than her mother made cleaning houses. Actually, Vera wanted to be a journalist. Another loss for her at this point was that "I was reared with definite prejudices against the Indians. . . . I missed the whole culture of Indian life."

On her graduation, Vera married, because everyone else was doing it and it seemed like a solution to her problems. She feels she yielded up control of her life at this point, although she did have a daughter, who remains close to her to this day. They lived near her husband's parents; his mother was a fine, deep, understanding woman, but his father "was crude, extremely domineering. She tolerated him, and he tried to dominate me, of course, and my child. . . . I was discontented. I think I was a poor wife, and I was determined to get out of there. . . . I think the early years of my marriage were actually bearable because on Saturday night I would go downtown and watch people."

At Vera's instigation they moved to California, where they endured extreme poverty and sacrificed to buy a piece of land and build a small house. She and her husband separated because of Vera's unhappiness. Because of this, her husband underwent military reclassification, was drafted and sent overseas, and was killed.

"It was terrible, because we didn't know that he was dead or alive." Her daughter had written him letters, and a letter came stamped "Missing in Action."

"She knew her father was gone then, and she tried to protect me. When I came home at the end of the shift, I couldn't find her, and she was across the street. She was about ten at the time. The girl she was with said: 'You have to tell your mother.' And she said it was nothing. She didn't know that I already knew it. I had received a telegram. I was trying to protect her, and she was trying to protect me. So we got together on it, and she cried, and she said: 'I'll never cry again!' . . . And she didn't."

Vera carries the guilt of his death with her to this day, not only for his sake but also because his death hurt her daughter. She feels it was selfish of her not to act in her daughter's best interests by remaining with him.

She met someone else, whom she married after a brief courtship and with whom she was very much in love. Unfortunately, he was an alcoholic. Her daughter sensed his instability and didn't like him. "The first five years of our marriage were pretty terrible. I realized immediately I had married an alcoholic. He drank even in the mornings. So, for five years it was pretty terrible, and it was a terrible thing to put on my daughter. . . . It blighted her whole life. He was not cruel to her physically, but we led such an unstable life she felt unstable herself."

Two surgeries in quick succession awakened in Vera an interest in medicine, and while she regrets that she did not return to college at this time, she did take nurse training and then got a good job. Her husband, who was fired from jobs for drinking, wanted her to stay home, because he felt he would drink less with more support from her. She finally acceded to his demands, although he seems to have agreed to her real estate license and job because they needed the money. Eventually she gave this up as well. "He strangely enough tapered off on the drinking, was able to get control of it. . . . He decided he would practice the principles of AA, but he didn't have enough in common—he felt too much pride to associate with people who were in it. He would never go. . . . He wanted me in the home when he came home as a sort of supportive thing. And those are the years I have the most regret about. That I didn't go back to school then and there, because I still would have had time at least to become a registered nurse. He didn't want me to do anything except stay in the house and be there when he was there. It gave him some superior feeling that at last he could support me, and he was in the driver's seat. This lasted quite a number of years. He was dry for about twelve years, and we had a marvelous time. . . . I could relax and I would be safe." During Vera's forties, "I devoted myself to him, and the house, a little bit of entertaining. To keep from going bananas I took up sewing with a vengeance, sewing and tailoring, very dull I think now [laughs] looking back on it. . . . He didn't like nursing. His family looked on nursing as a sort of servant thing, sort of a nonprofession. So I gave it up, and I just subjected to—and quite honestly I seemed to be quite happy just for the fact that he was happy."

Meanwhile, her daughter went to college, embarked on a successful career, and gave Vera grandchildren, all a source of happiness to her. Vera's own religious faith increased, also making her life more positive.

Vera was happy passing the time quietly as she did, passively, and yet she regrets not having been more active, done more, particularly with her education and nursing. "I wish I had used the time instead of wasting it, definitely. And I wasted years even in my early fifties that could have been used to good advantage. I think that I traveled with such a guilty conscience after my first husband was killed, that I was determined, no matter what the cost, to make the second one a success. I developed some kind of mania about it, a Christian sort of crucifixion of myself. That I was going to do it, no matter how much I was punished, that I was going to do the right thing in this marriage, and not be discontented."

However, eventually the marriage broke up. "I think what you learn from living with an alcoholic is that you're always sitting on a time bomb, and that they are never cured. And that, as he told me later, there was never a day that he didn't want lots of drinks, and that . . . because I was instrumental in him quitting, he held it against me. . . . Instability ran in the family, and he had aunts and family that had been in institutions, all from drinking. His own father died, a brilliant man . . . died drinking."

"So, after ten years of this marvelous sobriety he, apparently in the business, got into something that was on the shady side, trying to make money faster. And he had begun an affair with an unattractive woman who worked for him. . . . He kept everything very secretive in his business. He wanted me to feel dependent on him. . . . But at the same time he also needed her, because she apparently did most of the hard work. . . . I entertained her, and was kind to her, and it was a classic situation where the wife finds out last." Of those 10 years of sobriety, successful work, and good marriage "he later said that these were the happiest years of his life. But all of a sudden, everything crashed." Vera was in her mid-fifties when he "came home and informed me that he wanted to leave, and he wanted a divorce, and he wanted it quickly. And I asked him if there was someone else, and he said: 'Yes.' I had no idea who it was. . . . So he walked out on us, by 'us' I mean myself and my family. And I was in a state of total shock. I was a vegetable, and I had close to a breakdown. Looking back on it, I think I did have a breakdown. I spent most of my time in bed, and only got up when somebody made me get up. In fact, I wanted to sign myself into an institution and just about did. The thing that kept me from it was the fact that I was the only person my kids had, because they were both only children. They depended on me so much as stability in their life—my daughter and her husband and their . . . children."

Vera later "pieced together" the real story, that her husband was in a hurry for the divorce in order to gallantly protect her by seeing to it that she retained the money, in case he was prosecuted. He even said that he hoped to be able to come home some day. To what extent Vera mythologized his concern for her we cannot tell. She told him to come back, that they would find a way together. She sees him as having sacrificed for her. "It was just like a Greek tragedy in which everybody was designed to just really die."

Vera sought help from a psychiatrist, who excused her husband's behavior on the grounds of the tedium of his work—a rationalization Vera regards as "brutal." Vera became anorexic, suffered continual vomiting, was weak and suicidal. However, a minister, a friend, and her children all helped her through the ordeal. Her friend was the one who suggested she go back to nursing. She describes the return to college as initially bewildering:

"I decided in some thread in my mind that I would go back to school and pick up on pharmacology, 'cause I knew I was way behind in anything that had happened in all those years." She went to enroll at the local college "and I was so shattered . . . all these young children were there in miniskirts. And I thought, what could I do? I don't even know how to make out an application. Strangely enough, the director of nursing was still there after all those years. She said: 'Don't worry about it. Bring the forms over here to the office, and we will help you'." Vera began her studies anew. "I could barely drive to the college, and I would come home and go straight to bed. And I never got up except to go to the bathroom and try to eat a little something. . . . It was as if a weakness had descended on me that I couldn't move. You see, all these years that I had given up, and all these years that I had banked on a successful marriage, because I felt I had sacrificed myself for nothing."

Separated from her husband, Vera did well in nursing class and got a job. "They later said that I came in like a wraith, and they didn't see how I could ever function because I was so thin. . . . And I purposely asked for the 3–11 shift, so that I wouldn't be home [tears] for dinner during the dinner hour, because . . . when a man doesn't drink, why food is very important, and then when they do drink, it becomes unimportant." His office was in sight of her home. "And I could see when the lights went out. And he said: 'When the lights go out, I want you to put the supper on the table.' So I could still see his office."

He had gone back to drinking, his business went under, and Vera got the divorce herself so as not to be burdened with his debts. "He went down, down into degradation. It was incredible how he just became so coarse and terrible. And he never married her at all, even after the divorce. She later said to me: 'I wouldn't have him now that I know he's an alcoholic.' After she had helped destroy him, you see." (How?) "She'd had the affair with him, and after he began to drink, she didn't realize what a volcanic situation it was. And she said: 'Come to my house and drink, you're not an alcoholic.' So she encouraged him to drink with her, and she didn't realize that this was like throwing gasoline on a fire. When she found it out, then she rejected him. He said to me later she turned out to be very shallow. . . . But I do know that what little financial accumulation that we had, he gave it to me. He said: 'I want it for my freedom. You can have it if you give me my freedom.' Which was a terrible thing to hear. I suffered total rejection, total."

He subsequently died, and Vera feels guilty about that as well. "I realize that I failed him in many ways because, when a person is a drinker, the way to handle them is to never condemn them. And I did a lot of condemnation, a great deal. . . . I wish I had been kinder to him." In his last months, he wanted Vera to return and take care of him, but Vera knew her children would never forgive her if she did this, so she did not.

Vera bought a small home, continues her work as a nurse, and is in close contact with her children. "My life is pretty dull. . . . I think I was selfish in creating a situation where my daughter lost her father in a war, and that preyed on my mind and still does. And then marrying somebody in a sense without too much thought again. And I don't know whether anybody ever really plans their life, but I think my daughter's often criticized me and told me that the reason my life didn't turn out well was because I didn't plan it well. [Laughs] My marriage lasted longer than some do now, even the first one." The daughter who has saved her life seems quite critical of it.

Vera has been happy these last years. However, she has recently suffered the onset of irreversible eye disease which is robbing her of her vision and consequently the ability to read, which is terribly important to her. When asked if she has any secrets, Vera responds, "Probably about how bad a person I was. I think I'm the type that punishes myself a lot. I would like to be perfect, more near perfection, less impatient. I'm better at that now that I'm at this age." This seems thematic of her history and strongly suggests that, as her guilt seems no secret to us, it goes far deeper than her review would indicate.

As her life theme, Vera sees a "pattern to it, that I have often thought with my heart rather than my mind, and that was a mistake." Others would see "a pretty good set of rules, honesty and that sort of thing. . . . They probably don't see how really weak and mushy I am inside." Her central conflict was that she was always "chronically discontented."

Toward the end of the interview, Vera returns to her feelings of guilt about her daughter. She feels she should have been "thinking more of her health, cooking better meals, and knowing more about nutrition, and not hurting her by remarrying the wrong kind of person. It took its toll on her. . . . You keep asking for forgiveness and you're supposed to be able to accept it. That's the whole basis of Christianity."

Vera rated the alcoholism of her husband and the problems with her eyesight at 96 and 95, respectively, approximately as stressful as the death of a spouse (98), divorce (99), and marital separation (97). These are the most stressful events in Vera's life by far, and one must note that they extended over a great part of her life and of the interview.

On the Myers-Briggs Personality Index, Vera is type INFP (introverted, intuitive, feeling, perceptive), with high intuitive and feeling scores. This type "cares about learning, ideals, language and independent projects" (Myers, 1962, 1977), reflected in her unactualized interest in journalism, perhaps. Vera's was one of the most loss-oriented protocols. She is rated at high loss, low transcendence, in the grieving stage of the L/T process, although there are signs of movement into the searching and replacement stages in the more recent past. However, the entire protocol is rated, not just the present, and it is one of grieving and guilt.

Thematically, Vera has allowed others to determine and dominate her major decisions and how she's led her life (mother, first husband, father-in-law, second husband, brutal psychiatrist, daughter), leaving lasting regret over wasted time, work not done, education not obtained and sacrifice, as well as severe guilt over her part in these relationships, selfishness, and unkindness. A subtheme of motivation for monetary reasons is noted. The support of friends, children, grandchildren, nursing, faith, rationalization, and grieving through have assisted Vera toward transcendence. The core theme is one of domination, sacrifice, and guilt versus external support.

One also wonders if guilt is a form of transcendence somehow—because guilt absolves by inflicting suitable punishment on the guilt-ridden.

Theoretical analysis

"I developed . . . a Christian sort of crucifixion about myself," Vera tells us. There are several elements to the Christian crucifixion. Christ sacrificed himself to redeem human guilt. There is abasement in his story, as well as submission. There is the love of a God who gave his only begotten son.

Sacrifice and guilt are interwoven into a single theme in Vera's story. Her brother's physical torment of her was an outstanding feature of the first years of her life. Their mother threatened them with her own death, about which it is reasonable to assume they must have felt some guilt. Both of these may have been the major feeder roots of Vera's sacrifice and guilt orientation.

In addition, the message of the mother was always that love dies, and because it is the love of the primary caretaker, without whom the infant dies, it had to be experienced as a threat of their own demise. Vera uses the same word to characterize both her mother and herself; "discontented." This suggests that the natural identification of Vera with her "dying" mother actually took place, at least to some degree.

Vera sees much of her life in terms of submission and abasement to the domination of others. First she submitted to her mother's threats and her brother's physical abuse; later her mother's insistence that she forgo college and dreams of journalism; later still her first father-in-law's domination of her and her child. Vera refers to the "sacrifice" she and her husband made to get a little piece of land and build some shelter. Her alcoholic second husband insisted she give up her career to "support" him at home and yet viewed nursing as a form of servitude (he forbade one form of abasement, substituting another). The guilt over her first husband's death led to her determination to stay in her second marriage "no matter how much I was punished," and she stayed partly *because* she was punished (when one is punished for a bad deed, the deed is erased, it will not occur again; her second husband would not die). Vera responded to the abandonment of her second husband with depression and the gradual ebbing away of life functions. Even the devoted daughter seems to dominate, threatens her with never seeing her again if she cares for her dying ex-husband and characterizes her life as one that "didn't turn out well." When asked about small losses, Vera says, "it always bugs me when people are rude," a form of domination, devaluing, small losses metaphorical of larger ones.

The major loss we see in this protocol is a variation on the theme of self-destruction. One can destroy oneself in many ways—by not living life to the fullest, by sacrificing one's self for others needlessly, by not eating, by being addicted to alcohol or addicted to someone who is. Vera illustrates the metaphorical equivalence of the difficulties of her second husband and their breakup with death when she said, "It was just like a Greek tragedy in which everybody was designed to just really die."

We usually think of life and death as an either-or situation; that is, one is either alive or dead. Vera's life history shows the life-and-death continuum, on which each of us is usually moving in one direction or the other, becoming more alive or more dead. The humanistic psychologist's concept of self-actualization (Maslow, 1968) is relevant here, a form of becoming more one's self, more fully alive rather than less. Vera seems to have had difficulty with this, possibly because of such an inauspicious childhood, inhospitable to growth. Roots growing in the barren top inch of sand are easily uplifted by the vagaries of any wandering breeze.

Clinically, there is much of the depressive in Vera's story. Freud (1917, reprinted 1951) saw depression as hostility turned inward, and we get small hints of anger throughout her protocol (she fought with her mother, condemned her second husband's alcoholism, rudeness bugs her), but considering what she has suffered, there seems to be very little. Anger may have been too dangerous; her one attempt at self-assertion ended in the death of another—anger can kill. Thus, if we carry Freud's explanation a little deeper, beyond anger to the concept that anger kills, actually and metaphorically, all of self or part of self on the life-death continuum, we have a more complete interpretation of Vera's life.

Arieti (1978) sees that depression is a result of loss, either the loss of the "dominant other" or the loss of the "dominant goal"; again, the explanation goes almost far enough. In Vera's case, the dominant other has been her mother, brother, father-in-law, and her husbands, and the dominant goal has been her career, but the dominant others have forbidden the dominant goal. Clearly, loss of dominant goals and dominant others characterize Vera's life, as well as *threatened* loss over extended periods of time (her mother and her husband). As we saw in Chapter 2, threat is also loss. The losses are forms of death; parts of the self can never be recovered. A different, perhaps more vital self would have emerged had Vera gone to college, become a journalist instead of marrying her first husband, losing him, having her child, and marrying for her; or had she even been able to fight her brother off. In marrying an alcoholic, she may have married a punisher (the prototype of whom was her brother). A behaviorist might see Vera as having been conditioned to guilt, a conditioned response to the pairing together of her mother's dying and her brother's abuse over the years—the abuse became punishment for her part in her mother's dying. The pairing together of the two stimuli could have caused anger that turned inward.

We cannot look at the losses in Vera's life and see them as unrelated, even if they are related only to death, as I have shown. Vera herself demonstrates many interrelationships. She would not have remained with the second marriage if the first had not come to such a devastating end, if her daughter had not had consequent problems for which Vera was to blame.

Vera was guilty. Ultimately, what one is guilty of is precipitating a murder, the death of another either partially on the life-death continuum or completely. She killed her first husband, gave less life to her daughter than she should have, was probably partly responsible for her mother's condition, killed her second husband by condemning his alcoholism and driving him to the arms of another and to renewed alcoholism. (All this is Vera's experience and judgment of herself, of course, not ours.) For this she beats herself, as her brother did. Her guilt preceded her sins; if she was punished, then she must be guilty, and no sacrifice is too great a price to pay; besides, sacrifice wards off punishment.

Vera (like us all) has killed throughout her life. Perhaps this is the meaning of being born to original sin—that we cannot survive without inflicting death in its myriad forms on all that surrounds us.

Frances gives a bizarre history of sexual perversion that began in childhood and was repeated in several adult relationships. Her history poses tantalizing questions about the advantages of repeated losses.

Frances

"I felt used."

Now in her forties, Frances has short red curly hair, and her eyes do not seem to focus properly. Later I learn she is congenitally blind in one eye. As we sit in her homey kitchen, which seems to have meals in various stages of preparation and decomposition, people and animals are wandering in and out, looking us over, injecting comments, meows, and barks.

Frances got along better with her father than her mother, because he didn't try to run her life, as her mother did. A farmer by trade, he was "a softee," although he was mean when drunk, and she was afraid of him. Her mother worked in a hospital kitchen, was conscientious, kept house well, and tried to make Frances's decisions for her. The relationship between her parents was okay; her mother "kowtowed" to her father to keep the peace. A good friend played cowboys and Indians and hiked and swam with her until she moved away, which was "devastating" to Frances. She had a half-sister who was mentally retarded and was not on the scene much. "I wish I had had a sister or a brother that had been a normal child. . . . I didn't like being alone. . . . I was envious of kids that had brothers and sisters. . . . [My sister] was home part of the time before Mom got her into a hospital." Her mother and father couldn't handle her, and her grandparents kept her for a while but "wouldn't acknowledge something was wrong," even though they couldn't handle her either. "She was not well controlled. . . . She couldn't brush her teeth, comb her hair. She could eat, but her manners were bad. . . . She would have tantrums." Frances's mother got a lot of ridicule from relatives because they thought she was cruel to put her sister away, although she came home sometimes. "She wasn't quite mentally all there, and it wasn't like a normal relationship between sisters." Frances expresses much regret over the sister she didn't have.

School was generally a good experience for Frances. However, in sixth grade she started her period, and the occasion was a traumatic one. "It happened at school one day, and one of the kids told me I had a red spot on my dress. My mother is prudish and she didn't really talk to me. My dad was the one that talked to me, but he didn't go into that. I was terribly embarrassed." The principal sent her home, her mother gave her a pad, and "I had to clean everything up, and it scared me to death." The next day at school she could hardly look at the boys.

In seventh grade another traumatic incident occurred: "My dad was still drinking, and at that time quite heavy. And since I was afraid of him, and didn't know any better, he came home and wanted me to do things with him. You know what I'm talking about. And mainly what he wanted me to do was masturbate him. And because I was scared of him, and because I hadn't been around or been told too much, I didn't—I knew it wasn't right, but yet I didn't know how to get out of it. . . . I was afraid of him. So I go ahead and do it, and as time went on through seventh grade, he would buy me a dress or give me ten dollars or something. Of course, at that time it was nice because we didn't have a lot of money. Mom didn't have money to go out and buy school clothes and stuff." Frances maintains that there was a definite connection between the gifts and her sexual activities for her father. She didn't realize the experience was affecting her badly until later.

Frances was raised strictly. She wasn't allowed to go to dances or out with boys. "My parents, even though Dad did what he did, they were also very strict religiously . . . So I had to sneak." She tried to learn dancing at noon classes at school, but often there were cousins present who might tell her parents, so that fizzled.

The relationship between Frances and her father continued until she was 15. Although it never progressed farther than mutual masturbation, "he threatened to have intercourse . . . when I turned sixteen. . . . I hated it . . . I don't know if I felt guilty, but I felt like I wanted to get out of it and didn't know how." She was afraid he would hurt her when she didn't comply.

They moved to a farming "hick town," which she hated. There were many lower-class people and people of other races. Her family forbade her association with them. Relatively friendless, she did find one good girlfriend, of whom her mother disapproved because the friend's "mother was divorced, and my mother had a thing about divorced mothers, and she thought Peg was wild. Peg was boy-crazy, but she wasn't—she was a little bit—but not as bad as Mom had her made out. For years my folks [called] Peg's mom the town whore and all that, which was not true." One bond between Frances and Peg was that Peg was also a victim of sexual abuse by her stepfather and her uncle. She understood why Frances dreaded going home after school.

Frances found that her relationship with her father was beginning to affect how she felt about boys. "I was a little bit afraid of boys. I hung back. . . . Now my mother never knew about this . . . I would tell Mom I was going over to Peg's house for a night, which I did, but we'd go out and we'd walk up and down the streets and flirt with the boys and sometimes we did get in the cars with them [laughs]. Luckily nothing ever happened. . . . I was afraid of sex . . . I began to get the concept that that's all the boys wanted." Peg and Frances had a fight one night because Frances refused to go with a boy about whom "I heard that if he didn't get what he wanted, that he could get kinda rough, and could make it rough for you. . . . The bad part about that town was there was nothing to do except go to the movies."

Frances finally broke off sexual contact with her father when she was 15. They were in the process of moving from town to a farm. "So during the move Mom wanted me to go out with Dad and move. So I went in the pickup, and on the way out, of course he wanted—he wanted—you know what. And I refused. I don't know—for some reason I had gotten to that point where I couldn't do it any more. Because I was older. I was beginning to feel a sense of guilt. I knew it wasn't right. I didn't want to continue . . . I felt used. I knew he had a problem because I knew he drank, and I figured either he wasn't getting it from my mom, or there was some psychological mental thing wrong there somewhere, but still I didn't really hate him then. . . . He went on that I'd promised him. . . . I countered back that he had promised me something and he hadn't fulfilled it. Of course, he said: 'Oh, I'll make up for it' . . . and I just said: 'No, I'm not gonna do it anymore.' And I did threaten to tell Mother. . . . He said something like she wouldn't believe me. We got out to the farm. By this time he was angry. But I was also upset. I was crying. I jumped out of the pickup and ran through the fence and into the house, and at that time the beds were already in the bedrooms, and I ran into my bedroom which was the front one, and I slammed the door and threw myself across the bed. I was scared to death because I was afraid he was going to come in there and rape me. . . . No phone, and it was half a mile from town. No real close neighbors . . . and they couldn't have heard anything. But you know he didn't come in, and boy I prayed—I prayed hard [laughter]. I heard the pickup start, and he left." Frances also remembers: "Sometimes after we moved out to the farm, and I'd be sitting at the breakfast table—I'd have my bathrobe on—he'd come in and he'd reach in and try to play around and stuff. And Mom would be standing right there. She saw it and she'd ignore it. Whether she was afraid of him or decided not to make an issue of it, I'll never understand." Gradually his drinking eased off to a lost weekend every few months, and the sexual harrassment seems to have eased, also.

Although Frances didn't have any special ambitions during her adolescence, she did play the piano and the violin for the school orchestra at dinners, choirs, and glee clubs, which she loved. Her interest in music stemmed from positive childhood experiences—people who owned a piano on which she played, an aunt who played, and wonderful piano teachers. It was while playing music that she felt confidence in herself, as she became more and more afraid of boys. "I wish Mom had given me more self-confidence and self-worth, that I could do things. They did not let me drive. Daddy was going to teach me . . . because of Mother's reaction it never really got off the ground. Because I'm blind in one eye," congenitally, "she didn't want me to drive . . . and she tried to shelter me and run my life a lot. . . . She tried to choose my friends. . . . I just didn't let her. . . . If I wanted to buy a dress, and she didn't like it, I bought it anyway." When Frances wanted to date a Mexican boy, "they told me that if I dated him, they would disown me, and I would never get that piano," pointing to the living room. "And Daddy said if he came in the yard, he'd shoot him."

Frances and Paul, a boy she met in seventh grade, had been writing to each other off and on for 5 years, because they lived in different towns. "You might say we fell in love through letters." He visited for about a month, and things became pretty serious, but "again my mother did not like him. She thought he was too sissified. She thought he was lazy." They separated for a while, and Frances went to college to major in music education but got discouraged when she flunked chemistry, and there were no more interesting music courses to take, so she left. She dated Paul off and on, because by now he was in the armed forces. She felt he was generous, kind, treated her well, and that they had many interests in common.

After leaving college, Frances obtained jobs through friends and particularly loved being in an office, answering the phone, being on her own for the first time in her life (college dorms had been strictly supervised). Eventually Frances and Paul married and had children, who were very different from each other temperamentally. Married life was not good for Frances, however. "I started getting more inside myself. I wasn't around people then because I was home with the kids. Paul was not a sociable person. We didn't have many friends. . . . I withdrew. It was bad." Paul was gone overseas a lot, and she raised the children alone. She got involved in church, playing the organ for the choir.

"When Paul came back from overseas, he began wearing my underpanties. At first I thought it was strange, but then I thought, well, it's a phase that he will grow out of. On top of doing that he would masturbate, sometimes not directly in front of me, but we'd be in bed, and you know, I'd know what he was doing. . . . I began to feel rejection, of course . . . that he preferred doing that. It went from panties to pantyhose to bras . . . I didn't understand." Paul joined up again, and they moved to a place where Frances was again isolated with her two boys. "I got pretty stuck out there, and that's when I really began to crawl inside myself, become very withdrawn." She had a lot of back pain, which the doctors attributed to depression. As for Paul, "his problem kept getting progressively worse. He got to the nightgowns, and I had a lot of anxiety because I used to think, what if a fire broke out, and we were upstairs and he was dressed this way? . . . Another thing he did that was quite peculiar. . . . He'd come home . . . and the first thing he'd do is head for the bathroom. He would take enemas . . . almost every night . . . he'd be in there for a half hour to an hour. And one night in his sleep he said: 'I wish I was a woman.' And when I confronted with him, of course he denied [it]. . . . And I do get premonitions, and one night I did have a premonition that we would not make it. But because I was so insecure, and being out there with [the kids] with no job training, no nothing, and the way my health was, I didn't know what else to do. . . . Paul began to retreat from people to some degree. . . . If company came over sometimes he would literally go into the bedroom and go to bed. . . . Those four years were miserable . . . I did remember praying and asking the Lord to help me understand what was wrong with him."

Paul and Frances moved again, and Frances moved in with her mother for a time, but she couldn't cope with the "interference" with childrearing. She and Paul found a small house, but his brother and his family moved in with them for several months, which was difficult. The brother was lazy. She had a premonition that their living quarters were only temporary, but didn't know why. Then one night she, Paul's brother, and his wife saw a program about transvestites on TV (Paul had gone to bed). There was a man on the program who said he felt "like a woman trapped in a man's body," and Frances felt like a "light bulb went off"; she finally understood. Their sex life had become almost nonexistent, because he was only interested when he was dressed in women's things, having progressed to lipstick and wigs. "It was the shocks I went through." She confronted him about the TV program, and "within three hours that marriage was gone. . . .It was horrible, and he was crying and I was crying." That night she told Paul's brother and his wife, who didn't believe it until she spotted a pair of pantyhose on Paul under his trousers.

They separated, and Frances moved back to a town that felt like home to her. She had to tell the children the truth; they were teenagers and wouldn't accept anything else. They cried for three nights but have finally worked out a decent relationship with their father, who occasionally visits. Paul vacillated between begging her to come back and saying it would never work, until Frances couldn't stand it any longer and filed for divorce. She got a part-time job as a salesperson. A new friend helped her overcome her shyness, and they went to singles dances, where Frances gradually felt more at ease.

Frances got into a rehabilitation training program because of her eye and did scheduling and phone work with the Salvation Army for a few months; she'd been petrified of doing this but "that was another of the best things that ever happened to me." She moved in with a woman her own age and began dating the woman's son, a musician, whom she subsequently married. He is 15 years younger and is "self-centered. He wanted to handle everything, be in control . . . I would say immature." She married out of insecurity and was tired of being alone. What "attracted me was his strong personality. He made me feel like a little girl sometimes, and sexually, see, he didn't try anything. In fact, he didn't even show much interest in it. Well, see, because of what I'd been through, I felt: Oh great, I don't have to worry." She moved in with him and his mother, who is domineering. However, eventually she divorced him because he had no interest in sex.

She met the man she dates currently at a dance. He's a sweet guy who could probably never handle the children or support the family. "I thought: Gee, won't I ever find somebody who's normal that way?" It turns out that her current lover is normal and they have a great relationship, although "sometimes I found with him, it's weird, sometimes I feel almost detached." He lives with her, her children, and her second ex-husband's domineering mother-in-law, who is in crisis and needs a place to stay. "But there are still times when I wish he wasn't here. I wish it was just me. I need some space." They've arranged for him to be away a couple of nights a week. Also, working as a bank teller, she's found the pressure too great, lately her nerves are shot, and she's considering a job offer at a church, where she could be an organist.

Frances prays a lot and also gets premonitions or hunches. "I prayed for the right man, and I think I've had some premonitions about that. One night I dreamt that I was at a . . . dance. The dream was vague and yet the emotion was stronger than anything I've ever felt. In the dream I saw the man I would marry . . . somebody that I knew I would end up with for the rest of my life." Another time she was praying and "got this feeling of another geographical place. . . . It was almost an unreal feeling. I was here but yet I felt like I was somewhere else." A friend of hers had a vision and "saw me on a ranch somewhere. She described the man I would end up with." She has had strong premonitions that she would get a certain job or that a specific home or relationship would be temporary. Once she was warned by a hunch not to go out with a certain man, but she ignored it and "ended up with a fight on my hands."

For Frances, sexual problems and perversion (incestual molestation, transvestism, sexual disinterest, etc.) result in chronic fear. These are transcended by general transcendence activities—music, religion, prayer, and especially ESP. Her core theme is sexual perversion versus psychic and spiritual experience. There is little of situational transcendence in her protocol, because the root experience occurred when she was too young to exercise any control over a sexual attack that went on for years, perpetrated by the father, condoned by the mother.

Frances's protocol is generally loss oriented, placing her in the searching stage—for a good job and for a good mate. She seems to be working things through, and she eventually does what needs to be done, refuses her father, leaves her husbands, does not allow a domineering mother or mother-in-law to cow her. There seems to be a basic assertiveness in her personality which helps her.

Theoretical analysis

According to her own account, Frances's first experience with sexuality in any form was the embarrassing and frightening red bloodstain on her dress at school and going home to clean it up, completely ignorant of what was happening and very frightened. Her father had apparently discussed sex with her, probably in the highly restrictive vein in which they raised her, but she had no knowledge of menstruation. She must have thought there was "something wrong" with her, just as there was "something wrong" with her father and later her husbands.

Her second experience a year later was her father's molestation of her, which lasted approximately 3 years, until she refused. She hated it but submitted because she was afraid—a fear stemming from early childhood, although apparently he'd only "slapped" her a few times, usually when drunk. Her escape from his sexual abuse culminated in a terror of being raped—a threat he'd made many times. In addition, she'd always seen her mother afraid of him; even when he put his hand down Frances's bathrobe at breakfast, her mother pretended not to see. What had her mother feared—sex or beating? They had to be linked in her mind. This sexual perversion, abnormality, "something wrong" sexually was among Frances's earliest and most traumatic teenage experiences.

One can imagine how confusing Frances's childhood must have been for her. Her mother overprotected her because there was something wrong with her; she was blind in one eye, congenitally, born to it like the original sin of her fundamentalist religion, already punished and consequently guilty. Yet her mother did nothing to protect Frances from a serious and specific threat—her father. Her mother and father were both so religiously strict with her about boys that she couldn't even participate in normal high school activities, and yet her father was sexually molesting her on a regular basis. (Perhaps he was jealous?) Right and wrong were both very important and very mixed up.

It often happens that if a child has a problem with one parent, she or he becomes closer to the other. In Frances's case, this could not work. Her mother not only did not save her but also tried to dominate her to such an extent that Frances might never have emerged as herself if she had submitted. Fortunately, she resisted.

However, the damage was done. Frances was scared of boys as well as other life situations, such as working. She married a man who was kind, treated her well, and became a transvestite, feeling like a woman trapped in the body of a man. Her mother spotted him as being "sissified" but Frances did not. He was not interested in sex with her, so in marrying him she protected herself from sexual abuse ("I felt used") by a male figure, even though she needed and wanted a healthy relationship. I believe it was fear, rooted in her father's treatment of her, that led Frances (without realizing it) to marry someone sexually nonthreatening. The pattern was repeated when her second husband was simply not interested and never had been. She is involved currently in a normal sexual relationship but feels "detached" at times, as though it is unreal. Her pushing him away from her may be for reasons other than their good sexual relationship, of course. But I suspect "detachment" was her defense during her father's molestation of her. It is a common one used by prostitutes and others in repugnant sexual experiences, as well as those whose lives are threatened. Thus, men who are not interested in her sexually protect Frances from the maleness of her father, and sexually normal men threaten her, because they *are* her father. She transcends partly through this protection. The nonheterosexually oriented men also converted her father to asexuality metaphorically; that is, they turned her father off her, something she must have yearned for those long years. This is how and why the L/T life theme of Frances seems to have been created.

Frances's father threatened violence, which is metaphorically a form of death, unless Frances performed sexually, a form of life—thus associating life with death, making them one. Her mother threatened to keep her from emerging, also a form of death. Frances is frightened all the time. Metaphorically it is death she fears—nonemergence of self in a job, death in sexuality.

She overcomes both through the resources of her own personality and through creating what she has lacked. She has created a sister in girlfriends many times. These sisters are older, take charge as her older, mentally retarded sister could not. Frances also overcomes with that which is *beyond* life and death: religion, prayer, ESP hunches, premonitions, precognition, and music, especially in church, which is a double transcendence. Her parents once threatened to take this away from her in the form of her piano, but she has it still.

Although it is probable that Frances would benefit from an extended course of psychotherapy, considering her losses she transcends well and is gradually making progress.

We have seen in Frances's story how a traumatic incident, actually a series of incidents, seems to have set up a lifelong pattern of similar losses and, further, the logic of how this came to be.

Jaclyn's story is a more difficult one. At 50 she appears to be a woman who has not really negotiated the midlife issues but is always on the verge of doing so. This happens when both sides of a conflict appear equal in strength and power and when any resolution yields more to be feared than the conflict itself. Jaclyn leads a vegetative existence, giving us insight into issues of meaning and meaninglessness as they are related to pathology.

Jaclyn

"The only thing I ever felt very confident about was my intelligence, and then you find out this doesn't mean a thing. Being smart, as such, you just offend people mostly. . . . I wasn't woman enough because I didn't have [a climax]."

Jaclyn is a beautiful woman who appears younger than her stated age of 50. She reminds me of an auburn-haired Geraldine Chaplin; there is a kind of brooding mystery about her. Jaclyn lives in a shed with a spooked cat (the only animal in all my interviews who would not let me near her). The shed is on land owned by Leonard, who is married to Celie but spends 2 weeks per month with Jaclyn as well. Her income is well below the poverty level, and she does odd jobs for Len in order to subsist.

Jaclyn's childhood in the midwest was one of following her itinerant-worker father from town to town. She had no brothers or sisters, but she adored school and cried whenever she had to miss it. Because her father had to move around so much to find work, Jaclyn often had to switch schools. "I didn't even get to finish that first year. I got notes from my teachers, and they would give me my grades in an envelope . . . to take on to the next school. . . . I went to 9 different schools one year," and she was always terrified of these changes. "My mother and I were very close, because we were alone a lot together. . . . We'd go into these little apartments or tourist cabins, and she'd just scrub it from one end to the other. . . . My dad would come home with his tool bag, and she'd start packing . . . and we'd take off the next day. I'd usually go to school in the morning and get a note from the teacher, and off we'd go. And I remember waiting at union halls for my dad. I can remember sitting out in the car and reading every sign that I could see [laughs], to pass the time. Or sitting inside of them, and the smelly old spitoons. He had a particular odor I will never forget [laughter]. . . . I got excellent grades, which I was very proud of. I related well to the teachers. I thought they were something like gods. I loved reading." However, as the new girl, Jaclyn would often find herself between warring factions of students. She learned to handle this by becoming a loner. She was teased a lot when she first entered each school; the teachers would help her, she'd adjust, and then it was time to move on. Cats were substitutes for friends.

Jaclyn's relationship with her mother was a good one, partly because they were alone together so much but also because her mother trusted her— almost too much; it made Jaclyn feel too responsible. Jaclyn also liked her father until a few years before the divorce, when she lost respect for him. "I guess I wanted him to love me. I was a teenager. I think that was something I sought right up until shortly before he died. I couldn't trust him. He would lie . . . it turned me off completely. . . . He cared too much what people thought. He would sell you out. If there were other kids at the house when I was little, he'd fuss over them and put me down. . . . He had been on his own since seven . . . and I guess he was going through life seeking a mother. So he was very phony. I don't think he had any real values that were his." However, he did work hard to support them. Thus both Jaclyn and her father were seeking the love of a parent.

Jaclyn relates one of her more traumatic childhood memories: "I started my periods, which was very upsetting because I was so much younger. Most schools I'd gone to had no provisions whatsoever. . . . I felt like an oddball, and I flowed very heavily, and I had to get up and leave the room. . . . I used to carry paper bags to cover my bust, because I didn't want them to be seen. I was so different."

In spite of the frequent moves, Jaclyn was way ahead in school, but her mother wouldn't let her be accelerated for fear she'd be behind in the next school district. However, Jaclyn was finally skipped and took college courses in high school. When asked her peak experience in life, Jaclyn responded, "Passing tests." She usually got A's and was encouraged to go to a top university, but she didn't know about scholarships and was also tired of school. She wanted to be a veterinarian.

The high school courtship between Jaclyn and Jeb, her husband-to-be, was a rocky one. They dated regularly, and then he stood her up one night, for which she "grieved terribly." She got herself together and began dating again; then Jeb came back into the picture just long enough to break up Jaclyn and her new boyfriend, before he began dating her best friend, which "was like a slap in the face. He told me he planned to marry me," but their relationship was on and off a lot before this finally happened. "If I had ever been in love, I think I'd fallen out of love by the time he had turned this strong attention to me. . . . I finally decided that I should get married. And also I finally slept with him. And I didn't think after you'd slept with somebody you could get married to someone else." Jeb gave Jaclyn the choice between marriage and college but was proud of her intellectual abilities.

Jaclyn got pregnant right away. Having been told the probability of her getting pregnant was remote because of a "tipped uterus," she hadn't been using birth control. The baby was an accident, and she felt trapped. Meanwhile, her husband had dreaded the service. "That's one of the things I remember being upset about. He cried. He thought he was going to have to go into the service. He completely came apart. And I was pregnant and I had to baby *him*, nurse *him*. He was just a little boy, and that . . . was a big disillusionment." He stayed out first because he married her and then because she was pregnant.

Jeb forbade her working, but she took responsibility for their finances and managed well on what little they had. She enjoyed "working at being a good mother," but not motherhood itself, not her baby. She believed in keeping him clean, letting him sleep, but not much actual loving. Their social life was mainly with her husband's family, and his siblings were extremely jealous if anyone got anything, so there was no closeness. Her mother always gave Jeb expensive gifts "because he'd never had anything," so the siblings thought Jaclyn was rich and spoiled.

As for the relationship between Jeb and Jaclyn, "we had some bad times. We fought over sex a great deal. Apparently we were both too ignorant, because I kept looking for the magical climax, and he used that as—I wasn't woman enough because I didn't have one. Oh, I had masturbated, but I didn't think that was sex. . . . I thought the two were two separate worlds entirely. We got into wars that were just horrible over sex. . . . I sought help from doctors, and from friends and other people. We really never got any good advice. And I wish we would have, because we would have saved an awful lot of upset [laughter]. And that became one of his tools against me. I used it as a tool against him for a long time, as a denial. . . . Some people . . . were telling me how selfish I was . . . denying him. That at least I could be happy making him happy. I worked on that, and it helped—a lot. But he always would promise everything when I became a 'full woman'."

Jaclyn sought help from a counselor, who told her she didn't have to talk about sex, but "hell, this was over 50% of my problem. So he finally asked to have Jeb come in. And Jeb . . . told him I had not had sex with him for three months, which was not really the truth. It had only been a month. And he told me, well, your problem is in your sexual attitude, and dismissed me. . . . And he completely agreed and took sides with my husband. So that is really bad when you try professional help and they're just as hung up as you are." Jaclyn had even gone to counselors *before* they got married to see if they were compatible, but they said they weren't set up for that, "we're only set up for after you're married and have problems."

Married, and with two babies, Jaclyn returned to night school at the neighboring community college, but it was too difficult. Her father returned to stay with them and "made it hell to study. He would interrupt me like a two-year-old. . . . I cried and cried when I quit. Maybe it wasn't the outside of me, [maybe] it was myself. . . . We keep ourselves inside those confines whether men put the walls up or not. We help them maintain it." However, her husband had been proud of her. They were called "intellectuals" among their friends and acquaintances, and her husband felt this raised their status. As for Jeb, he was a salesman but had always wanted to drive trucks. He finally switched occupations and loved it. Their financial circumstances were the best ever, but it was at this time that they got a divorce. The circumstances leading to the divorce stemmed from their friendship with another, older couple, Leonard and his wife Celie.

It turned out that Len and Celie were nudists and wanted Jeb and Jaclyn to try it. They said many of the nudists were psychics, which Jaclyn had been reading a lot about. So Jaclyn decided to give it a try. "So we went up, and have you ever been so still and so tied up that you actually hurt? Just ached? I spent a day like that [laughs], but Oh, my children and my husband just loved it." Jaclyn couldn't bring herself to go back, but her father died, and they had to be in the area of a certain nudist camp that Jeb, Len, and Celie had been pressuring Jaclyn to try. They were all very much into idealism, spiritualism, and beauty, and Jaclyn felt this was great for the family, although she couldn't get comfortable about it.

"But it turns out the camps were going through a sexual revolution, and they were into swinging, which is swapping mates. It was very new. . . . And, of course, because I thought there was something wrong with me, and my husband was very interested in this idea, we got involved in the swapping. And all it really did was make it all worse for me, because it would end up that I was a cold duck, because I still didn't climax, and it was a real negative put-down all the way around. My husband was turning the gals on, and he enjoyed that. But I don't think any couple who is getting along well, and has a good sex life, would bother with swapping. I think you've got sick couples that go into it. . . . Sex was on a purely payment basis. It was worse than any kind of prostitution. You are given to the other man so that my husband has the right to go to bed with his wife. If you have two couples, they're not usually both going to be interested in the opposite partner. So the others go along with it to alleviate guilt. . . . And they talk about [how] this should having meaning, and there should be love besides the physical attraction, and it really boiled down—they would just hop in and hop out, and I'd had enough of that." When Jeb took off with Celie, he returned raving about how spontaneous it had been and how easy, and Jaclyn felt betrayed. Jaclyn and Len had remained behind, talking.

At this point Jaclyn made a suicide attempt. She turned on the car in the garage, but Jeb found her and plied her with coffee and vodka. She called

Len, whom she thought of as a god and a guru, and he spent a lot of time talking with her about her hang-ups, while Jeb and Celie made love. This didn't bother Len, he claimed, because they had an agreement, but actually he was "very undone with her. . . . And my husband had a definite cruel streak"; he would find a person's weakness and dig at it. Before long he "started putting these little needles" into Celie. "She got down on her hands and knees, begging him" not to leave her for Jaclyn, but he ignored her.

Meanwhile, Len was conducting both private and group psychotherapy with all of them. He thought of himself as a therapist, although he didn't have a degree, and they had some painful times. "The only thing I ever felt very confident about was my intelligence, and then you find out this doesn't mean a thing. Being smart, as such, you just offend people mostly. Len pointed these things out to me a lot." They both felt she was "using it as a display, as this is who I am," that this was offensive. "I'd done a lot of reading, and I was trying to have it win things for me, because I felt I wasn't capable of much of anything. I'd bought the myth that a woman doesn't know anything," mainly from her husband, who wanted to maintain his superiority and would carefully not show her how to do mechanical things around the house, even messing things up for her after she filed for separation and he had to move out. He said: "I'm not going to pay for anything if you're not living with me, and you're not going to get a penny."

(At this point in our interview, Celie dropped by for a visit; plain, fat, scraggly hair. After a few words, she left, and the interview continued.)

Len decided to teach Jaclyn to climax and then return her to Jeb so that they could work out a better relationship. The teaching worked temporarily, but the relationships worsened all around. The children were upset because their dad was sleeping with Celie but denying it, lying to them. Also, he would call them up and tell them he was going to kill himself. After he'd found his own place to live, the children started acting strangely about visiting their dad. It turned out he had raped the daughter when she was 10 and was continuing his sexual abuse of her. She returned one day in trauma, saying, "Well, I guess I fixed him. I wouldn't sleep with him." Up until the rape, "it had been a little bit at a time. He had masturbated in front of her, and of course my daughter had gone through her Lolita-like stage, and I knew before this that there had been a lot of sexual play. I thought it was innocent," but some psychics helped her tell Jeb that he was "stimulating" the daughter too much when he played with her. "And so this had gone underground. I found out afterwards. So the sexual play had gone on and on, and I guess she was old enough to tease."

Their separation turned into a divorce, which Jaclyn filed for, and Jeb was "violent about it. I guess it was possession. And the kids were both gonna stay with me, and he didn't feel he should have to pay anything." Then Jaclyn and her teenage son got into a fight over his freedom and she sent him to his dad for discipline; Jeb let him have the run of the house for sexual experimentation, which he liked, and he decided to stay.

This suited Len; in fact, he'd promoted it because he didn't like another male in the picture. "He doesn't appear to me now to be anything like I thought he was. If he was ever like I thought he was I don't know, 'cause I had him right next to God. I thought he knew everything. He said: 'You have to follow me totally and completely, and trust me, or you don't love me.' And so I trusted him, and I did what he said." When Jaclyn filed for divorce she thought Jeb and Celie were going to stay together, but they broke up, so Len felt he had to stay with Celie, especially since she had been sick a long time. "I don't think Len ever had intended to marry me, though I thought he did. . . . Now how could I be so dumb? But I was. [Laughter] Len put the pressure on Celie and Jaclyn to live on the same property with him, and they are now good friends.

Meanwhile Jaclyn was taking government job training in clerical work; unfortunately, she had to turn down job offers because she, her mother, and her daughter were in a serious car accident. Jaclyn was pinned under the car when a man in a suit walked up. "He looked at me under the car, and he turned and walked away." Len claimed that all this happened because Jaclyn had not followed his advice when she took in a girlfriend who had just gotten out of a mental hospital. "And this was the powers that be, punishing me. . . . I had gone against what Len had to say."

Currently, Jaclyn lives in the shed on Len's land, and Len spends half his time with Celie in their house a few yards away and half his time with Jaclyn. Jaclyn describes herself as being in a communal marriage. She wishes she had the confidence and ability to get a job and move out, but she does not. Len alternates between forbidding her to leave and ordering her out; he has, on occasion, turned off the electricity when he was displeased with her, and he's taken away her key, so he can walk in on her anytime. He continues to believe "sex is the only thing that's important in life," but he tends to be impotent, and is also dirty and undesirable, and he blames this on Jaclyn (he is now in his seventies). Their relationship has gone on for about 15 years. Jaclyn has completely lost contact with her son, whom she believes to have married, had children, divorced, and remarried, so she is not in contact with these grandchildren, either. But she has a close relationship with her daughter and her children. She wishes she had broken off with Len many years ago, when she had more confidence to restart her life. She spends her days doing odd jobs on the property including keeping books, watching television, doing some yoga, playing card games like solitaire, and caring for her plants and her spooked cat. She doesn't know if she could "work, and get a home, and make the kind of payments they're expecting." She thinks perhaps she could practice her typing or get that job as a "girl Friday" that she's read about. She reminisces about how Len used to be, his teachings about Christ and the golden rule, and all the psychic experiences they had together. For instance, once they went into a restaurant and sent strong feelings of love to a solemn waitress and got her "turned around so she was working and doing more, and smiling." But she says that "finding Len was not who I thought he was, was devastating." If she could write her own epitaph it would read, "She could have done a lot more"; [laughs].

Jaclyn fantasizes about "an expanding home" with many rooms. She tried a women's group, but they could only offer her shelter; she couldn't bring her plants and animals and "those are my responsibility. I can't walk off and leave them." She could leave them with Celie, but Len wouldn't let her, "he wants to fight me." Her favorite song is "Somewhere My Love," because it makes "the promise that life does renew and end at the beginning." She had one clairvoyant experience in which she saw her husband endangered by a fire, which was true.

Jaclyn sees as her life theme a pattern. "I was dead set not to be with any man like my father. And I think I've been with two who are very much like my father." Her husband lied a lot, and Len withheld things. Her dad would buy his new wife things Jaclyn needed and give any money she asked for to Jeb. Her main conflict now is in trying to resolve the problems between herself and Len so that there "can be a relationship left," but "the only resolving is to end it. I think I have hoped somewhere that it wouldn't all have been pointless."

Jaclyn's L/T life theme includes loss in relationships with males through sexual irresolution and dysfunction; this has kept her from education, work, and achievement, as well as from being a "woman." These losses are now transcended by a vegetative existence in abject poverty, watching TV, and playing cards, because she feels incapable of everyday functioning, of moving from the domination of a destructive man and getting her own home and job. The core theme, then, is sexual dysfunction versus vegetative existence.

The Myers-Briggs Personality Index rates Jaclyn as highly introverted, highly intuitive, thinking, and perceiving, with a good balance between perceiving and judging. These individuals are "quiet, reserved, brilliant in exams . . . logical, interested mainly in ideas . . . need to choose careers where some strong interest can be used and useful" (Myers, 1962, 1977).

The entire protocol is rated as loss oriented, in the grieving (yearning) stage. She seems to live in the past and exist in the present.

Theoretical analysis

No exploration of meaning would be complete without a study of its obverse, the experience of meaninglessness.

"The only thing I ever felt confident about was my intelligence," Jaclyn tells us, and apparently with good reason. Despite a childhood extremely unfavorable to educational attainment, Jaclyn succeeded, was accelerated, had all A's, took college courses early, and could have entered a prestigious university. Even today, 30 years later, her peak experience is defined as "passing tests." It is as if 30 years had not happened. She might have become another person, all that she could be, but was blocked by poverty, the difficulties of combining education with rearing children, her father, who would not let her study, and general disapproval and devaluation. Jeb was proud of her intellect but does not seem to have helped her; indeed, in his ambivalence he opposed her becoming superior to him by knowing too much. Her "guru" helped her devalue intelligence; it is offensive, she used it as display, to define who she was, and ultimately this possibly strongest part of her was denied. (In another environment it might have been affirmed and encouraged.) What was left?

Being a "woman." But this had always been problematic. The male who taught her about male-female relationships at the outset of her life lied and devalued her in front of others, and, no matter how justified, he was responsible for the obstacles to her achievement and friendships, that is, the family's frequent moves. The onset of menstruation and sexual development was early and made her feel like an "oddball." She was in an apparently masochistic relationship with her husband-to-be by early high school. He stood her up, broke up her relationship with another, and dated her best friend—"a slap in the face"—before informing her (not asking) of his intentions to marry her. They slept together before their marriage and were apparently concerned enough about sexual compatibility to seek counseling then. She married Jeb because she had slept with him and therefore felt she had no choice. For a while she had to mother him because he was so frightened of the army, but this power reversal was unique and brief. Their marriage settled into a "war" over sex. Somehow femininity was defined as being able to have an orgasm during intercourse (not masturbation). Jaclyn could not. But she did get trapped by a male child, whom she mothered well but did not enjoy. She denied sex to Jeb as a weapon, and he said she was not a "full woman." Her reward when she became one would be things they would have and do. A family counselor took her husband's side, as did her friends and family. Her mother was giving Jeb expensive gifts she could ill afford, and Jaclyn at one point described him as having wooed her mother as much as her—as a woman or as the mother of his bride to be? Were the gifts a dowry? A bribe? By example and by advice, the only message she received was to submit.

Jeb and Jaclyn became friends with Celie and Len. That sexuality was something to be concretely rewarded was evident when Jaclyn was traded to the mates of women with whom Jeb wanted to sleep. This confirmed her less than "full womanhood" when Jeb began swinging and his relationship with Celie became serious. Jaclyn attempted suicide, although Jeb was in the house when she did this, and she is not sure she wanted to die; she believes now that she thought she would be found. In the L/T paradigm, when a person attempts suicide, it is because too much of himself or herself has already died, or been aborted, or has never been born. The part of Jaclyn that was growing mind had been aborted, and the womanhood as Jeb defined it had not been born. Interestingly, motherhood did not count in the definition. Then who was Jaclyn and who was she becoming? She was mind denied, and she was becoming woman-never-having-been. Whether or not the suicide attempt was "serious," on the life-death continuum Jaclyn was moving too close to death.

Len seems to have completed the destruction of Jaclyn as becoming. They developed a therapist-client relationship, but unfortunately Len had neither the training nor what one might call the "natural talent" for therapy. He made egregious elementary errors, and he did the worst possible thing. He disconfirmed the major strength in Jaclyn—her confidence in her intellect. (I don't say that no therapist would do this *ever*, but it had better be done by someone who knows what she's about!)

Jeb deepened the devaluation of Jaclyn by his sex play with their daughter, culminating in his rape of her when she was nine. This was quadruply destructive of Jaclyn: it was injury to the daughter she loved; it was placing that daughter in Jaclyn's stead and thereby effacing Jaclyn as an individual; it challenged her capacity for the most basic function of a mother, that of protection; and finally it was driving a wedge between Jaclyn and the only other person to whom she was close. Fortunately, their bond survived this. In this particular family the sexual molestation and rape of the daughter could have been diabolical, had to have been intended as such.

Jaclyn was ultimately deprived of her son, his healthy development as well as his presence, completing the cycle of destructive associations with all the males in her life—father, Jeb, Len, son, and even the man who left her pinned under her overturned vehicle. What is left *of* her? What is left *to* her? Still startlingly beautiful at 50, she lives a mainly vegetative existence, wishing she could do something else, find a place to herself, work just enough hours a week to eke out a living. But all the possibilities have problems. Meanwhile, an aging Len shuts off her electric power but forbids her to leave, keeps the key but orders her to go, demands sexual favors from her and blames her when he cannot follow up his demands, takes her to a psychic fair and is insulted when she get more time with a reader, tells her she should be sexually active and comes to her unclean, "smacking" his false teeth at her, and spoiling for a fight.

This is also a story of idealization, power, and sadomasochistic relating. Jaclyn idealized her teachers. They were "gods" to her, and she succeeded in pleasing them. They were her allies and friends. Then she idealized Len; he was her guru, who trained her in psychic abilities but demanded complete obedience in return. When she disregarded his advice, the "powers that be" punished her with a car accident. (Or he turned off her power—electric!) This belief in psychic powers beyond human explains part of why she has remained with him. He is also older than she, now in his seventies, the father she always wanted—she remarks on their resemblance. A father is all-powerful, can protect a little girl from death.

To what extent Len and Jeb were sadists and to what extent Jaclyn created them out of her own masochistic needs we cannot judge, but undoubtedly both are somewhat true. A masochistic need is a need to die, to be destroyed, and this has been largely fulfilled in Jaclyn. However, her situation is changing, and she may need to move toward living after all these years of dying—a prospect as frightening to Jaclyn as is the prospect of dying to most of us. Living is dying to someone like Jaclyn, who must ultimately become a stranger to her self of 50 years if she moves in that direction, destroying much of who she is now.

We idealize another individual because she or he overcomes death, either actually or metaphorically. Len overcame death by power, which extended beyond the human, Jaclyn believed. The example of the waitress is actually an instance of kindness breeding kindness; there is not necessarily anything supernatural about it, and Jaclyn is much too intelligent not to know that with her mind. She *needed* to believe in something beyond, an eternal life that transcends death. This gave her life meaning. The many moves of childhood showed her how uncertain her life was. She paid the price in submission to Len, as well as Jeb, withholding only one thing from them, that which they most demanded, her confirmation of their masculine sexuality—which is life—through orgasm. In this withholding, undoubtedly not deliberate, Jaclyn maintained a tiny corner of power and of life. The sadomasochistic bond is like this. Ultimately, the masochist has power over the sadist, confirming or denying his power, and the sadist submits to the masochist by dominating him. The balance of life and death is kept more even than we imagine. Further, often the masochist is creating guilt in the sadist, a powerful weapon.

The relationship between Len and Jaclyn is changing because his physical and psychic power is waning. She has been beaten down, and how much more can he degrade her? He is not able to do what she requires of him, and this frightens her. He could do the ultimate and send her away into life, but then he would no longer have confirmation of his power around him. He could lose control of Celie as well, because part of his control of her is through the presence of Jaclyn. The balance of power could shift.

Jaclyn says she hopes that the whole association between herself and Len, with its corollary relationships with her husband, son, daughter, and Celie, will not all turn out to have been "pointless." If something is salvaged, then it will not, but if she leaves it entirely, it will (according to her way of seeing it). Something that is pointless is, of course, meaningless. If the relationship ends, her story of the last 15 to 20 years of her life will lack both coherence and purpose. It will probably have to be revised radically.

Jaclyn has experienced many losses in her life—the loss of her self as intelligent and her self as woman, of her husband to Celie and also her daughter, of Len as god and guru and therefore of all he taught and she believed, of her son, and of a home of her own, which she now craves more than anything—all including losses of possibility, illusion, hope, alternative lives, but especially loss of self as she might have been. I have said that all losses are transcended in some fashion, because we do go on. Jaclyn transcended the losses of her daughter and their bond by rebuilding it into something good. This is what is meant by transcendence conventionally, an overcoming and re-creation, a moving from something negative to something positive and greater than one's self. But most of Jaclyn's losses seem to be transcended by other losses. This also is possible. Jaclyn transcended the losses of her husband by her association with Len and Celie, the counselor, her son, and even her daughter. Overcoming a loss with another loss may cushion the impact of the first loss; more important, when one seeks out and/or accepts loss, along with its redefinition of who one is, one is protected from subsequent loss. If Jaclyn never attained "womanhood," she could not lose it. If she gave up power, it could not be wrested from her. Thus, overcoming loss with another loss is also a method of transcending loss; it re-creates the self in the image of one who has lost, loses, and will lose—what society cruelly calls "a loser." It is like having a definite jail sentence instead of an indeterminate one, with its painful concomitant hope. Losing can protect one from loss. If I have a lot of chips and lose a few in a game, I do not feel it. If I have only a few chips, I feel the loss of each one. But if I have no chips, I cannot lose, and I am free not to continue (unless I borrow or fantasize).

Jaclyn says life would be meaningless without a belief in the absolute. But she no longer believes in Len, her metaphor of the absolute, god and guru, so their whole relationship and much of her life may be pointless. She remains trying to convert it to something meaningful once again, to recapture the possibilities it had, although the enterprise seems hopeless. She engages in general transcendence (cards, TV, yoga, etc.) because dispositional and situational transcendence fail her; in her this also seems to be an act of self-destruction, merely "killing time"—the measure of her life.

There seems to be a "fundamental illusion" here, that the situation will always be as it is now. Of course, it is already changing, and she is going to look at other places to live tomorrow, with Len's agreement (she doesn't know how temporary) and some money from her mother. She is almost bound to move toward living, a very painful process of self re-creation. If she seeks out death, she will not need someone to protect her from it.

CONCLUSION: THE USES OF PATHOLOGY

We can see from the above that pathology is useful for the survival of the self. Although we refer to defense mechanisms as binding anxiety and protecting us from pathology, the pathologies themselves are defense mechanisms. They defend us from death.

Pathologies (like emotions, motivations, and personality traits) defend us in several ways. First, both physical and mental disorders permit us to escape from problems that are insoluble and/or intolerable. These are the escapes that are condoned by society. Anything from the common cold, to neurosis, to cancer, to psychosis is like the bugle call to retreat from the world. We climb into our beds, or hole up in our rooms (or in our minds), so that we do not have to cope. Perhaps our problems will magically disappear while we are gone. There may be the added bonus of sympathy from friends and relatives, hospital visits, cards and flowers or, at the very least, an enjoyable new acquaintanceship with the daily soap operas we always miss because we are at work. By removing us from the "rat race" of daily living, pathology saves us from losing more. We who have lost the race can no longer lose it!

Pathology, therefore, can be reinforcing if it is not too painful. By the time we discover it really is not worth the price we pay, it may be too late; we may be too ill mentally, physically, or both to recover. The depressive may be so rewarded by his environment that it is especially difficult to climb out of the well of his depression. One of the great dangers of which therapists warn relatives is too much sympathy or concern. The therapist herself must be careful.

Pathology is rewarded because the assumption is made that the individual is a victim with no control over his well-being. Whereas the existentialist alerts the individual to his reponsibility for all that befalls him, the humanist objects that, if we are responsible for our disorders, then we are also held to blame. Responsibility and blame are two sides of the same coin. Cancer victims may be blamed for cancer, especially if they are smokers. Susan Sontag has pointed this out eloquently in *Illness as metaphor* (1979). The answer to this dilemma is, I believe, somewhere in between. The individual is probably more responsible than we think, tempted to loss and even death by virtue of the transcendence possible, but he may be walking along the street and a piano may fall on his head. Of course, he chose to walk along that street at that instant, but. . . .

I was at a convention in Chicago some years ago where a renowned humanist stated that we are responsible for all that befalls us. My companion, who happened to be a very large, muscular Jewish professor, questioned this: "Are the Jews responsible for the Holocaust?" "Yes," came the undaunted but daunting reply. My friend strode to the front of the 500-person gathering, towered over the red-faced humanist, and said, "Good! Then you're responsible for what I'm about to do to you." There was nearly a riot, but I thought he had made his point quite well.

The fact is that pathology rewards us, *whether or not* we are responsible for it, in whole or in part.

Pathology has another use. Like trivia, it is a way of focusing on a small death so as to forget the larger one (to reframe Becker's 1973 analysis of Rank; also see Menaker, 1982). It distracts us from greater dangers. We saw this in the case of a phobia that distracts us from the greater fear, a form of displacement.

As we have seen in the case histories, pathologies defend us from being destroyed by other pathologies, germs, the control of others, exposure, isolation, and so forth. They often give us the opportunity to *choose* our losses instead of having them thrust on us. In this way, pathology may defend against an even greater destruction of our life and self. What would we do without our pathologies?

Finally, pathology may ensure our survival in still another way. The more we let other into our self, the more self, as it exists at any point in time, is threatened with change, in other words, with annihilation of previous form; the more a me is merged with or redefined by the me of another, the more repercussions there will be for other parts of the self—transcendent, lost, concept, myth, and meaning. Therefore, some individuals will minimize contact with others to achieve stability, the negative face of which is stagnation, lest, as Laing (1976) points out, they be overwhelmed and cease to exist. This may take the form of introversion, withdrawal, schizoid tendencies, or schizophrenia. The more of other that is shut out, the less of self that needs to be revised, the more sense of continuity the individual may achieve. In one of fragile ego strength (Barron, 1979), where sense of continuity is shaky, schizoid pathology may be a defense. A different individual—the change-seeker, the wanderer—seeks to take in as much of other as possible. Other is life, other does not die, and incorporating it leads to immortality of a sort, unless one dies by asphyxiation! This individual may be extroverted, emotionally labile, one who skates across the surface of things, an excitement-seeker, impulsive, or even sociopathic. In psychopathology, the loss is increasingly difficult to replace and integrate. The death of true self is the one loss that cannot be replaced, for which no substitute can be found.

The mental health professional, faced with the patient in the therapeutic setting, must ask of herself and of her client the following question: "*Who* dies, and *how*?" Ultimately she will find herself fighting one form of death with another.

Cultural and Societal Manifestations of Loss and Transcendence

Once upon a time there was a group of woman friends who gathered together weekly, year in and year out, to knit and gossip about their husbands and young children and exchange cookie recipes. They were all normal except two. One managed to function reasonably well in daily activities but was comparatively mute at the meetings, silently wondering how they could talk of cookies when they would all die. The other, a long-time member of the group, in and out of mental institutions, was mad, an embarrassment, her quietude occasionally broken by a comment that had nothing to do with cookies, or knit one, purl two, or husbands' infidelities, or children's precocious sayings. This was an obvious manifestation of her insanity, but the women immediately responded to her, even though she had betrayed all they valued by turning her back on it in madness. They responded because they were kind, curious, and most of all because they wanted no relapse before dessert, which was usually a rich torte. One night the mute one popped the question, "How can you sit here and talk about cookies, when we will all die?" The mad one reproved her gently, "But that's just the point."

In this true fable we see the importance of trivial activities as distractors from death (see Becker, 1973). Knitting, chattering, eating something rich, and exchanging cookie recipes are all endowed with special importance. This chapter is divided into two sections. In the first I examine the cultural metaphors of loss and transcendence, and in the second the societal manifestations. Although the notions of society and culture overlap, in my definition of culture I emphasize the beliefs, arts, and behaviors characteristic of a group of people. As Brislin (1983) notes, definitions of culture may include man-made objects and responses to them, behaviors, symbols, and shared knowledge and concepts, all of which would be applicable here. In my notion of society I emphasize the organization, relationships, and institutions of that group, and in the approaches below restrict my theoretical views to Western culture, although there are many applications to other cultures. The stories of Tori and Harriet assist us in understanding many aspects.

CULTURAL METAPHORS OF LOSS AND TRANSCENDENCE

When we communicate in metaphor, we make an "implicit comparison or analogy" between the explicit term we are employing and the thought or object of our comparison (Morris, 1975); an extended metaphor becomes an allegory or a parable. In any culture, there are many metaphors of loss through death— the time-boundedness and the constriction of possibilities that death implies— and metaphors of transcendence, such as art, religion, music, literature, travel, movies, television, mysticism, meditation, paranormal experience, drugs, alcohol, nature, and athletics. To the degree that each of these is culturally specific, for example, that certain types of music are specific to a culture, they may be termed cultural metaphors of L/T. Participation in any of these metaphorical activities is a general transcendence mechanism, and different individuals choose different mechanisms according to their individual L/T structures. We call most of these mechanisms "leisure" activities, by which we imply that they are not as necessary as "work" activities; they do not carry the onus of responsibility or survival. Actually, for the integration of meaning into the self structure, they are essential.

Becker's (1973) interpretation of Kierkegaard includes a delineation of the tragic human existential dilemma; a man cannot face the reality of his limitations including his death, and yet he, alone of all living creatures, is aware of them. The general transcendence mechanisms are ways of dealing with this dilemma metaphorically, through escape from, conquest of, or even mergence with death (analogous to the paradigm of identification with the aggressor). Thus, in cultural metaphors, we experience the grieving, searching, replacement, and integration stages of transcendence of loss, but we do so metaphorically. The transcendence of loss that we experience in general transcendence becomes a rehearsal for the ultimate transcendence of the ultimate loss.

Some general transcendence mechanisms are acceptable in our culture to the degree that they assist others in transcendence. For example, transcendence through drugs and alcohol is not as highly valued as transcendence through the arts. When an individual drinks or gets stoned, she is not assisting anyone's transcendence but her own. When she paints the ocean, she is helping many. Further, joining with many in the appreciation of a work of art or in religious services is more highly valued by the society, because it perpetuates the myths of transcending, assisting in their reification, and because it promotes the unity of individuals and their conformity to the values of the society represented by the artwork, the being together that society must facilitate to survive. (To confirm this, one need only recollect the condemnation of Tchaikovsky's music in Russia as being too bourgeois and capitalistic, of Wagner's as being anticommunist and romantic.) Even the solitary drinker is condemned more than the convivial drinker, although she may actually imbibe less; she is considered at greater risk of alcoholism, of addiction to a general transcendence mechanism that not only may be disastrous for her family but also is non-productive and may eventually deprive individuals in the society of their lives, whether by accident or by the necessity of supporting her.

Thus, the extent to which general transcendence mechanisms are culturally approved becomes, once again, a matter of how much time is transcended, how much life is illusorily extended, the aggregate time of a group being of more value than the solitary time of an individual. Often, however, the general transcendence may become one's lifework: she is a professional athlete or musician, which is acceptable, and we do not think of her as addicted to golf or music because she provides for others, must do it even when she does not feel like it, experiences the work-related hassles, and is productive; the "professional" drug addict or pusher is even respected by certain elements of a subculture for providing for others, often because he is a rich man in a poor neighborhood; other cultures such as the Zinacantecos of Mexico (Vogt, 1970) limit drug and alcohol experiences to religious rituals.

When general transcendence mechanisms are overused, it is often because specific transcendence mechanisms are weak or maladaptive, a form of pathology relative to the society.

An examination of some general transcendence mechanisms as cultural metaphors of loss and transcendence should provide some clarification.

Loss in an *athletic* contest or *game*, such as tennis or chess, is a loss to the me of the self, which is then registered in the I, compelling a reintegration of the concept of self. What is lost to the self is the concept of I as competent, able to win, as living up to the ideal self. As such, it is a preview or metaphor of the gradual loss of competence as one ages and the total loss of competence that death will inflict; the emotional intensity with which such a loss is received may be in direct proportion to the individual's fear of death.

Still, the game is played, and partly for the reason that its loss can be transcended in a way that death cannot. "It's only a game," is the phrase that minimizes the loss of self, objectifies it. "I'll win next time" is the same as saying "I'll live next time" metaphorically. Of course, this cannot be true, unless one believes in afterlife. (It will be a different person who wins next time, one who has lost before.) But to lose is not permanent in tennis. Even losers walk away. To say it is only a game is an attempt at the metaphor of life as a game. The chessboard can be closed, the "men" secreted in their individual nests, and then one can turn to something else, secure in the knowledge that he, like the chessmen, can be resurrected. The playing pieces of many games are "men" (never women), capable of inflicting loss and arousing emotions, substitutes for the daily wars with more serious wins and losses.

Competition is an overt way of inflicting loss on oneself as a form of rehearsal and as an assurance of immortality. Just as death only happens to someone else, we can demonstrate this by inflicting the metaphor of ultimate loss, that is, defeat, on another person. The injunction to "be a good sport" is analogous to the injunction to "be a good patient," to smile, deny loss, brave it out (Strauss & Glaser, 1985). It is bad form to remind others of their mortality on the tennis court or in the hospital room.

Some individuals are motivated to make a practice of such contests as a way of accumulating immortality. The regular participation in sports, games, or dangerous activities such as mountain climbing or car racing represents the regular conquest of death to the individual, as if by multiplying conquests of form to achieve a habit pattern one can eventually achieve the final conquest. Csikszentmihalyi (1975a, 1975b) sees these activities as resulting in the "flow experience," which is for the sake of itself. A characteristic of such experience is that time is transcended, just as it is transcended in death, and by returning to time one also symbolically returns to life. Further, one has enjoyed the timelessness in which the time-bounded self has been transcended with a perfect integration of the I and the me. The promise of fulfillment in the ultimate timelessness is implicit.

All art is a way of preserving life from loss and is loved for that preservation (just as parents are loved for the same reason). Stokes (1965) says "Art is based on the need to correct all man-made things," including institutions, "hence the aesthetic core in rituals" (p. 8). We respond to feelings of "conflict, grief, loss and sadness as the spring of art" (Stokes, 1961, p. 9), and we respond because they correspond to our own feelings. Stokes (1965) writes that we both absorb art and are absorbed by it, that is, we identify empathically and transcend the stress of our lives by merging with the timeless incident depicted. Read (1967) believes art overcomes the divorce between individuals and also between humans and nature. Since this divorce takes different forms in different epochs, masterpieces of the past may be "dismissed as no longer relevant" (p. 30). (We don't look at The Assumption of the Virgin today in the same way that fourteenth-century men and women did.)

An individual perceives a work of art in the context of his own L/T structure. He may look at a still life consisting of a bowl of fruit and a jug of wine, while similar fruit and wine await him on his dinner table at home. Yet similar is not same. Long after his own are consumed in time, their prototypes will be preserved on the museum wall, with no loss of freshness, color, or moisture. Art is a way of making time stand still, of denying decay. Further, this painting is the prototype of other fruit and jugs of wine long gone, long forgotten, consumed in the contexts of lost environments and relationships. In a sense, the wine is the same as that he shared with his first love on a windy hill, daring truancy from school, transcending loss with love, losing self in other, moving farther from childhood, parents, home. It is also the wine shared with long-lost friends in college; it is the wine of an altered state when new verities were perceived. In short, it is very much part of his L/T structure. Lastly, it is the wine that the artist shared, which is lost to the observer in that he may never know its precise taste, sensation, effect, and emotion. He can only approximate it. The artist reaches across the centuries to him with an experience that both can share through his painting.

Malraux (1949) also observed the function of art as transcendence. "After having served for the creation of a supernal world, plastic art was chiefly, over many centuries, the means of creating an imagined or transfigured world" (p. 14). For many centuries, the function of art was to "deepen and adorn [humanity's] communion with the universe," (p. 16), transcending the dilemma to which Becker (1973) alludes. For example, Rembrandt "showers his [paintings] with light so as to raise them above the norm of humanity" (p. 61). Religion, that other important general transcendence mechanism, was one of the major subjects of art for centuries; many paintings portrayed the Assumption of the Virgin, the Last Supper, the Crucifixion, the Cleansing of the Temple, and the Pieta, as well as topics from "pagan" religions, myths such as the birth of Venus, and the many love affairs of the gods. As the historical subject replaced the religious, there was a greater move toward the representational, that is, conformity with the senses (Malraux, 1949); transcendence moved from the heavens beyond to immortality on earth, and in a sense Heaven and Hell were lost, perhaps as life on earth became more tolerable—perhaps also with the revolutions in humanity's relation to the rest of creation brought forth by Copernicus and Darwin (Barron, 1979).

Portraits transcend death by preserving a body, a personality, and in a sense the being of the artist who painted them. Landscapes go beyond preservation to the same transcendence many of us experience in nature settings, on the beach, in the mountains (see Bierstadt's and Churchill's apocalyptic visions!). Paintings also give us perspective on loss by distancing us from it. Photographs may do the same.

Because L/T structures differ, one work of art has meaning for one select group of people, whose L/T structures resonate to that of the artist. The artist achieves universality and hence popularity to the degree that her L/T structure, out of which she has created her work, is similar to that of her beholders. Fashions in art come and go, as history molds the L/T structures of cohorts of individuals. Pop art, dadaism, surrealism, romanticism, and impressionism all have had their followers; they reflected and transcended the losses of their particular historical times. They also reflected the current saviors from death; when pop art was in vogue, technology would save mankind. It is no accident that the great works of landscape arose from the industrial revolution, when the wilderness experience was being lost. Stokes (1965) observes that the impressionists were in reaction to "the new aesthetic poverty of the streets" (p. 46). He further notes that contemporary art "aims at symbolizing states of mind through the means of external forms" (Stokes, 1961, p. 40). When a culture is "attuned to actual or potential traumatic experience, famine, earthquake, or cultural chaos, art increases its abstraction" (p. 43), because distortion is a defense mechanism in which the ego is confused with objects or in how it relates to reality. Thus, artworks reflect not only the losses of the time but also their transcendence. But transcendence brings its own losses, as has technology, and these also must be transcended, so the fashions change.

Literature actually instructs us in how to deal with loss. Stories, plays, and novels contain plots with human beings who have dispositions toward specific transcendence mechanisms. The characters are in conflict between loss and loss; lover is pitted against lover (D. H. Lawrence's *Women in love*), parent against child (Shakespeare's *King Lear*), allegiance to country or political party against personal survival (Koestler's *Darkness at noon*), brother against brother and one way of life versus another (Mitchell's *Gone with the wind*), aspects of the self against other aspects of the self (Marguerite Young's *Miss Macintosh, my darling*, and Garcia Marquez's *One hundred years of solitude*), society versus the individual (Ralph Ellison's *The invisible man* and Shirley Jackson's "The lottery"), man against woman (Alice Walker's *The color purple*). Plot can be seen as loss and transcendence in its myriad permutations. If it is good literature, it is said to contain an element of the universal, which means it addresses universal forms of loss and how individuals transcend them. These stories constitute rehearsal of loss and its transcendence, and they are a form of transcendence for us in themselves, in that time is suspended as we read or watch. *Romeo and Juliet* is a story of love that transcends death by embracing it. It is representative of the peculiar fact that the depth of love cannot be gauged, experienced, or expressed without reference to its eventual loss. Transcendence is relative to loss. There can be no transcendence without loss. Heaven is dull. (It might be a nice place to visit. . . .)

Science fiction (e.g., Frank Herbert's Dune series) promises a future beyond death, made believable by continued loss; if we cannot actually be alive in the twenty-first century or on other planets in other galaxies, we can experience them in imagination. And perhaps tomorrow another civilization, far advanced beyond our own, will make death obsolete. Biography instructs us in the losses of great men and women and in their transcendence through great works and service to humankind, in spite of the insuperable odds that we ourselves experience. The lesson and the hope are that we, too, may aspire. Numerous works of nonfiction instruct us in the specific and general transcendence mechanisms of our culture; they tell us "how to." The quest for knowledge in academic texts of philosophy, physics, anthropology, psychology, and so forth is the search for explanation of different aspects of life in the hope of understanding, meaning, and prediction. They train in specific transcendence needs; Inez, the physician, must know anatomy, chemistry, and pharmacology in order to heal.

Historical works tell us of the successful or unsuccessful transcendence of losses to men and nations—of the searching of the conquistadors for El Dorado, the man of gold, actually a king who yearly anointed his body with resin, covered himself in gold dust, and plunged into Lake Guatavita in Bogata (Chapman, 1967); the search for the Seven Cities of Cibola, and for the Fountain of Youth; of the replacement forced on the conversos of Inquisitorial Spain, who had to choose between loss of religion and death by torture and the stake, as the nation itself tried to avoid the "contamination" of Jewish, Mohammedan and Protestant religions, and thus to avoid loss to the Catholic religion (Lea, 1906; Plaidy, 1967). Historical accounts attempt the final phase of integration in the light of how it all turned out; they mythologize; they tell us a story of the meaning of all these events, and they do not all agree; the integration of the American Revolution in British historical texts is quite different from American ones.

Poems often express the yearning (Tennyson's "In memoriam"), searching (Poe's "The raven" and "Annabel Lee"), replacement (Frost's "The road not taken" and Christina Rossetti's "Look in my eyes"), and integration phases (Browning's "Porphyria's lover") of specific transcendence, as well as general transcendence (Emily Dickinson's "I taste a liquor never brewed," Omar Khayyám's "Rubáiyát," De la Mare's "The listener"). They are the emotional expressions of our L/T experiences and they say what we cannot, saying it with a beauty that uplifts or deepens our feelings. Our favorite poems will reflect our own L/T structure, which of the stages predominates, what means life to us and what means death; we choose these poems accordingly. (Do grieving and searching predominate in Poe?)

Music may be "absolute" or contain lyrics, with the stories, emotions, and themes of our L/T structure. (I am reminded by my colleague and professor of music, Dr. Louis Christensen, that music is never "wordless"—it always says something.) The "absolute" music of orchestral pieces, concertos and symphonies, gives us feelings of completion and closure by virtue of the repetition of theme and rhythm (Meyer, 1956), a completion that "goes unresolved in daily life." By this repetition, expectation is evoked; there is a feeling of suspense, which is then satisfied. For example, uniformity of rhythm and melody is established and then embellished with deviation of some kind, with chromaticism, perhaps, which in alternating major and minor modes emotionally means grieving to us and is associated with intense feelings of "sadness, suffering and anguish," also expressed by slower tempo. Meyer sees loud dissonance as a means to arouse our emotions, and consonance to

soften or calm them. Examples of these might be heard in a contrast between
Shostakovich and Debussy. Music that is all dissonance or consonance is
boring, just as a life would be. L/T parallels might link the chromatic music
with the grieving phase of mourning and the consonant with the integrative
phase; it is the emotions of these L/T stages that we feel when we listen. In
listening to music, when we "keep time," we transcend it, the time or rhythm
often being a reflection of ongoingness in our biological rhythm, the pounding
heart, the heated sexual pulsation.

Silberman (1963) asserted that the musician cannot possibly be communicating the same emotion to the listener as the listener receives. This
seems substantiated by recent findings that many listeners do not even *hear*
music as it is actually played, sometimes perceiving a tone in a pair of notes
as higher when it is actually lower, and also as ascending or descending,
depending on the playback speed (Deutsch, 1987). We might observe that
the L/T structures of the composer, the performer, and the listener are different,
and they will deal with music from these differing structures. However, there
are degrees of exception. Martial and religious music do contain and communicate the universally experienced emotions associated with militarism and
religiosity in Western culture (indeed, they may dictate them), and, while
these experiences are felt as unique, they also include some commonality and
are more likely to be played in group settings than in the solitude of the living
room. These two categories of music impart the feelings of marching or praying
with others in a unity that makes one of many.

"When you listen [to music] you hear what you are" is an old aphorism
(Seashore, 1947, p. 201); different people respond to music in the context
"of [our] past total experience," p. 208, that is, our apperception. Seashore
believed that we evoke musical images from all our past association, just as
we would greet an old friend with all our memory images of her. I would
add that not only the lost I and lost me but also the transcendent I and
transcendent me, including our future hopes and fears, are the context in
which we experience the meaning of absolute music. But even absolute music
often has a title with content. Beethoven's "Farewell to the piano" expresses
the farewells we all must make, more beautifully than we can ourselves and
yet, in its very survival of the man himself and in the continuity of the melody
with its inevitable rising, makes farewell a continuing experience rather than
a final one, moving us to another plane, loving that which we must leave,
loving even the process of leaving.

Much of absolute music gives us this sense of continuity, especially the
long legato passages of Schumann, Chopin, and Mozart, or Sinding's "Rustle
of spring." Continuity is an aspect of transcendence; we go on as the music
does in never-ending time, we become part of the music, and it continues
when we do not. Farnsworth (1969) showed that the eminence hierarchies of
classical composers were stable among different groups of individuals in

different countries over the period from 1938 to 1964. Composers included Bach, Beethoven, Wagner, Mozart, Brahms, Haydn, Palestrina, Handel, Schubert, Debussy, and Chopin; the universality of these composers over time and country (in Western cultures) is, we suspect, due to the transcendence of the universal time in music, even though time may be perceived very differently in different cultures and different historical epochs.

Traphagan and Traphagan (1986) correlate emotion and meaning in music to recent developments in physics. They believe that the listener intuitively recognizes the similarity between the structure and patterning of music to those of physical reality. The matter and energy of the universe has an implicit order to it, which is reflected in music, our reception and perception of it. This affects us viscerally and is emotionally meaningful to us because we are part of that physical reality, structure, patterning, and order. In L/T terms we might see this as the ongoingness of transcendence.

In music with lyrics and stories, we find popular songs and operas replete with L/T themes, particularly loss of love. They are popular because they sing to the underlying motivations that are universal in the L/T structures of us all. Themes of loss in popular music include parting from a loved one in some manner; long journeys ("By the Time I Get to Phoenix" and "Wandering"); nostalgia, or the longing for lost time ("Those Were the Days"); loss of mind ("She's Not There"); loss of home ("Going Home"; home is often not only the home of childhood, parents, and friends but also the home of Heaven after death); from the self-ideal (Janice Ian who learned at seventeen, that "love was made for beauty queens. . . ."); loss of understanding between generations (Cat Stevens' "Father and son"); loss of illusion (Judy Collins' "Clouds"; only their illusions, like life and love, are recalled); loss of kindness and compassion (Boy George singing "Do you really want to hurt me?").

Then there are the traditions of counterrevolutionary music ("Where have all the flowers gone?") and the great Black spirituals, transcending the losses of the present life by looking to Heaven ("Sometimes I feel like a motherless chile'"), emphasizing replacement of some sort. Other pieces of music, both classical and popular, assist transcendence through reference to other general transcendence mechanisms, such as altered states of consciousness in the drug experience and disco dancing ("Lucy in the sky with diamonds" and "Saturday night fever"). The L/T structure of a relationship may also be commemorated by a song ("The anniversary waltz"). A number of interviewees commented that one piece of music was especially meaningful to them; it was playing during that first candlelight dinner with a lover long ago, or it was his favorite, or it conveys their feelings, how things were for them. It becomes "our song." Many of the above songs are in the grieving/yearning phase of L/T and express our own yearning.

Themes from opera include sexual jealousy and loss of love (*Carmen*); loss of love, beauty, and ultimately life (*La Traviata*—The Lost One); the quest for something lost, the Holy Grail, its loss symbolizing loss of innocence and holiness (*Lohengrin*); loss of soul (*Faust*); loss of identity (*The barber of Seville*); loss of Heaven (*Don Juan*).

To extend this brief sample list of songs and operas demonstrating the L/T theme that pervades our music is unnecessary. The reader may simply refer to her own favorites.

In an interview on the "Today Show," pianist Ivan Pogorolich (1986) described the significance of musicianship. "We make dead things alive," he said. He went on to explain that the composers were dead, but he brought them back in a way that mere machines could not. This was how he believed he was of service.

Travel is the general transcendence mechanism by which we explore and experience the alternative possibilities for life that we ourselves have not chosen. When we chose the city life over the small town or country life, skyscrapers over wilderness, hamburgers and malts over sukiyaki, dresses over saris, cosmetics over veils, the Mojave desert over the African veldt, Montana blizzards over Gobi mirages, Kansas tornadoes over Scandinavian northern lights—when we chose one life style, culture, language, society, government, geography, climate over the many others available to us, we eliminated whole worlds of thought, feeling, human interaction, sights, customs, and sounds from our experience. We may not believe these are choices but just as, from the existential perspective, we choose life over death, or living over dying, so at every moment of our existence we are choosing the boundaries of that life, even if the choice is between one room and another room in the same house.

When we travel to the corner café, or to Aux Deux Maggots in Paris, we become who we might have been for a little while; of course, we are not really who we might have been, because we are always *who* we are, no matter *where* we are. No matter where I go, I'm always here.

In India, my Canadian friends were horrified, guilt-ridden, and sickened by the skeletal beggars of Benares with their begging bowls, because my friends cannot conceive of the highest goal of life as being privileged to die in that holy city, as do the Hindus. Experiencing a little of other lives so vastly different from our own enriches us, transcending the loss of all the possibilities we have not chosen. We experience the inconveniences of life that others take for granted, returning to our own inconveniences, which are preferable to us because we are accustomed to them; we thus transcend the loss of other possibilities by confirming what we have chosen. There are instances, of course, when this does not happen. Anthropologist Janet Siskind (1975) found it difficult to return to her own culture after staying long enough with the Sharanahua in Peru to feel like them, an experience common to those of her profession.

Time is transcended through leisure travel in that accomplishment is not necessary; one never grows older during a trip, especially if time is the measure of things to be gotten done. Strangers in strange lands are undifferentiated and as a class have always been there, always done things in their traditional way. When we watch the changing of the guard at Buckingham Palace or listen to the Beefeaters tell their grisly stories at the Tower of London, we see uniforms and marches similar to those of centuries ago; we do not distinguish the humans within the uniforms, and so they have for us a certain immortality. This England, its castles and traditions, are those of Queen Victoria, Shakespeare, the Stuarts, Tudors, and Elizabethans, and we pleasantly delude ourselves that we have gone back in history.

When I went with my family to Gettysburg, I dreaded not being able to find the history there for the commerciality; indeed, I despaired of it. But, as fate would have it, the motels were full, and we stayed in a haunted house on the battlefield, through which the spirits of the past glided as we slept. And early the next morning I saw the mists over the fields, and the men fighting in the mists, and I knew the hills they had come from, and the ravines where they would go, who would win, lose, and die; oddly enough my four young children "saw" them too—folie à cinq (but my husband, being sane, did not!).

Alcohol and drug experiences are much like those of travel, in that we experience other forms of being in the world, other or altered states of consciousness. And, like travel, these experiences are dependent on who we are, often the aspects of ourselves that we have repressed or not chosen to be. The woman under the influence of alcohol may be free to be hostile, weepy, sexy, or convivial, more so than she allows herself in real life because this aspect of herself might threaten loss of some kind. The drug experience (Weil, 1972; de Ropp, 1960) is notoriously a function of who is undergoing it; by expansion of awareness and sensory experience, she discovers more of who she is and might be. The loss from return to normal consciousness may be so great that she chooses to spend less and less of her time in the normal state. As with other general transcendence mechanisms, the individual is often not transcending a specific problem or situation but the problem of being alive; it is probable that the addict to any general transcendence mechanism has a paucity of specific mechanisms and wants to "get away from it all." (If the addiction is biologically based, the lessening of situational and dispositional mechanisms may follow rather than precede the addiction.) She must meet with disapproval within any productive society, because she is likely to produce less than her share, compelling others to produce for her, or at least give her a dollar for "bus fare." Also, as with other general transcendence mechanisms, time stands still, or slows to the point where an eternity of experience can be encompassed in a moment.

The movement to widen horizons through the holistic, the mystical, and paranormal experiences, as well as through psychedelic drugs, might well be a result of the loss of fantasy, imagination, and dream, which are so early trained out of the child as being valueless, an attempt at recapturing the magical experience because it is of help in expanding consciousness and giving an extra dimension of meaning to our lives. All cultures prescribe the experiences that are to be valued and those that are to be devalued, and these prescriptions lend cohesion and identity to the culture. One wonders what values in our culture would be threatened were children not trained to eschew the magical—probably the values of achievement, competition, materialism, and others which the hippie drug culture rejected. It takes no great imagination to surmise what would happen if our entire culture returned to a full appreciation of the magical—dream, fantasy, the paranormal and/or the drug experience. First, there would probably be a serious breakdown in the production of goods and services, a great social loss, and then, after chaos, the birth of a different society—with other losses to transcend!

Transcendence in religion lies in the promise that all losses will be erased in some other dimension, beyond life and time. We will be reunited with our loved ones. There will be a purging and falling away of sin, leaving us as perfect wholes. There will be mergence with the supreme, all-being, all-creating, all-joyous. Those who have caused us pain and loss in this life, and have gotten away with it, will obtain their "just reward," preferably hideous, in the next. Because vengeance as an emotion is sinful or self-defeating, we can let go of it in this life, accepting loss, if we know some abstract law of justice will make all things equal in the next.

Religious practices promise some form of transcendence in the life of the spirit. This may be through salvation, as in the myth of bodily resurrection, through remaining in the present, as in meditation, through the wheel of life, death, and rebirth, as with Karma, when suffering and eternal loss are the price to be paid for never ending. The stories of the Bible, beginning with Genesis and ending with the Apocalypse, are all stories of loss and its transcendence. Religion also assists in transcendence through acceptance. In the Christian religion, turning the other cheek purifies us of vengeance. In the Jewish religion, we leave it to Him who claimed it was His. In the Hindu religion, we are paying for the losses we have inflicted in past lives. In this sense, all that is present is perfect—the suffering, pain, poverty, and illness—because it is our retribution and our way beyond. We endure the rack to be saved from the wheel.

Religion as a form of transcendence is as old as the primitive man who, when he first looked on the body of his dead brother, noted not merely lifelessness or inertness but also something gone, indefinable by sight or touch, but definitely missing; he solved the mystery by assuming that in his world of space, it (whatever it was) must have gone some *where*—beyond, which is the religious and philosophical meaning of the word "transcendence." Everything apparent to our limited senses is always changing; the building is no longer solid, or even visible, but simply densely packed particles in motion, and there are sounds unheard, rays of light unseen, and a host of parapsychological experiences that cannot be explained (see Koestler, 1972). Therefore, the "small leap of faith" in other things unseen, unheard, unfelt seems not unlogical, as Bishop James Pike, rational lawyer as well as cleric, often observed (1951, personal communication; 1968).

Religion as transcendence helps us concentrate on positive emotions, love, acceptance, and joy, rather than the negative ones that losses call forth. It takes us out of the anguish of the moment, returning us to it with new strength. Most important, it helps us integrate a meaning from our sorrows when we cannot do so otherwise. It may even be healing. We may pray with such fervor that we actually begin to experience whatever it is we pray for; emotions of love in prayer transcend the feelings of loss, and they are supplemented by the beautiful ritual music that has outlasted centuries of services, the flowers, symbols, comforting words of those who have gone before, blessings of those invested with a special holy gift; the lastingness of all these symbols seems to confirm their power. We are exhorted to have faith or to behave as if we had faith—faith and belief in what we cannot apprehend with our senses, in the permanence of objects and persons who have disappeared from view, the basis of which we learned in early childhood. If only we believe, all we wish for will come to pass; and this is partly true in that, if we want our child to survive a mortal illness, our prayer focuses us on religiously carrying out every detail of her prescribed care so that she may indeed survive.

The goal of meditation is to achieve satori or nirvana, the enlightenment of all or of nothingness. Becker (1973) brilliantly perceives the man in meditation as "embracing the nothingness he dreads"; if he embraces it, he can no longer fear it.

Religious fanaticism is the exaggerated claim for transcendence of loss far beyond the actual loss transcended. For the fanatic, a selected form of transcendence is unlimited, encompassing all other forms. This permits the fanatic to exaggerate, or at least deny to a lesser extent, the loss to be transcended. The religious fanatic does not simply achieve a faith in God that makes the real losses of life easier to bear; she avoids hellfire and brimstone everlasting for the unspeakable evils of the carnal world in an immortal life under a God-sun of infinite glory. This transcendence is of such obviously supreme value that no action in its name can be tyranny.

Religious fanaticism could be considered delusional were it not that such a large number of individuals experience it to some degree. However, the matter is not that simple. The literal content may indeed be delusional or fictional, but there is often more "truth" in metaphor than in the tangible. The tangible cannot express adequately what is otherwise "known," felt, believed, intuited, desired. That the symbol for "book" is not the book does not mean the book does not exist in some form (although, if we were all to get together and examine the book in exhaustive detail, we would find that we do not agree on the form). The book may be between covers, or in the author's mind, or in the minds of thousands who have read it—and taken each from it according to her cognitive and L/T structures. The success of the fanatic lies in the truthful death to be transcended, of which her particular loss and mode of transcendence are only a fraction, or a part-metaphor, or synecdoche.

Each of the above general transcendence mechanisms requires a set of material objects to complete it, a knowledge of brands, a preoccupation with the quality and value of the paraphernalia associated with it (see Triandis, 1980). These symbolize and concretize the transcendence in which we seek to believe, which gives our life meaning.

These paraphernalia also form part of the trivia with which we fill our lives, as demonstrated in the "true fable" of cookies, knitting, and dying with which this chapter began. According to Becker (1973), trivia represent our attempts to distract ourselves from the overwhelming issues of life, death, and meaning. Just as we give a child a cracker, the car keys, or anything at hand to pacify his cries, we fill our lives with trivia to escape having to deal with questions of meaningfulness. Trivia are our pacifiers.

The importance of general transcendence mechanisms as sanctioned by, and manifested in, the culture is nowhere more salient than in the integration provided by the culture's myths, fantasies, and fairy tales. Campbell (1961) sees myths as having the underlying theme of "separation, initiation and return," which he terms the "monomyth," and a single myth may either incorporate all of these components or emphasize a single one. Of course, separation, initiation, and return are the most prominent themes of the life cycle; we see them in the activities of the locomoting 2-year-old, who can separate from his mother for a few minutes and initiate new activities, but always remains in proximity to her, periodically returning (Bowlby, 1969). We also see them in the mergence-individuation conflict that pervades our relationships. Campbell sees the happy endings to the myth as the "transcendence of [the] universal tragedy of man," which is man's "attachment to forms." In L/T terms, this attachment to form is to the form of self as it is constituted at any one point in time, as well as to the form of other L/T structures in individuals and to the form of society as it is constituted, the bodies, personalities, relationships, life circumstances, objects, and so forth. According to Campbell, the meaning of all religious practices is to teach the individual that through "prolonged psychological discipline" she gives up attachment and accepts self-annihilation as a condition of rebirth. The "hero" sets off on the adventure through life, on a "road of trials," often getting magical or supernatural assistance, slays his dragons, wins his battles, and is able to return and grant boons to his society, redeem his world, perhaps. Rites "disclose him" to himself as archetypal "warrior, bride, widow, priest, chieftain." For Campbell, rites are all forms of dying and rebirth, and for the L/T structure they really are small deaths and small births. He quotes Ovid's *Metamorphoses*: "All things are changing. Nothing dies."

With the decline of the myth, Campbell observes a rise in neuroticism, because there is nothing to take the place of the myth's transcending function, its promises, its assistance, and its assurance of meaning and integration in our lives. We would argue that this is the function of the other general transcendence mechanisms as well, the cultural metaphors of loss and transcendence. Further, as myth declines, we mythologize our own existence with the rise of individualism. We move from cultural myth to personal myth.

There are secular myths as well, embodied in aphorisms and adages: justice is its own reward, as is hard work; good will always triumph over evil; and all the legacy of Benjamin Franklin. Unfortunately, real life turns out to be different.

Finally, a set of specific transcendence mechanisms may join with dispositional mechanisms to become general. Most notable of these are love and work. There is much disagreement as to whether love and work may be carried to extremes. Karen Horney (1937, 1950) believed that they could be overdone, so much so that they became what she termed "neurotic solutions." The "workaholic" may become so buried in her work that she escapes dealing with family problems, and this may result in the loss of her family and the loss to her children of her presence and guidance, ultimately eventuating in her guilt. Schaef and Fassel (1988) are concerned that there is a rise in the number of "addictive organizations" that foster, even demand, workaholism as a condition of success, making family and personal life increasingly difficult to maintain. Solomon and Corbit (1974) have turned up some persuasive evidence that love may become "addiction," comparing their opponent processes model of addiction to morphine with addiction to romantic love. Two people may become so involved with each other that they feel they literally cannot act or live without each other, and while they are wrapped up in each other they may undergo loss in other areas of their lives through lack of autonomy and other specific transcendence mechanisms. The transcendent me of the workaholic, the love-addicted, the alcoholic, or the drug-addicted may take up so much space that the transcendent I is defined almost exclusively in those terms, resulting in a concept of self distorted from wholeness. When other me's are forced on the individual, the mate must go away, or the job must be lost, the individual feels she is nothing without them, there is so little left of self with which to integrate meaning and go on.

Maslow (Chiang & Maslow, 1977), on the other hand, believes that identification of the individual with his work is a hallmark of the self-actualized person; if he is asked what he would be if he were not a lawyer, he responds that he would not be himself. Rollo May, representing the existentialist position (Chiang & Maslow, 1977), disagrees; May finds that the individual who identifies himself by his occupation is experiencing "loss of the sense of being"; he sees himself in terms of his social role only, corresponding to the transcendent me in the L/T structure, and ignores the lost me, lost I, and transcendent I. The answer to this dilemma lies in the motivation of the individual. If he does his work out of love or transcendence motivation, rather than out of escape or loss motivation, and if his work does not exclude him from other forms of transcendence (leading him to loss), then more of his self is involved than just one role-related me, and he is probably self actualizing.

Some of the dispositional transcendence mechanisms may become general transcendence mechanisms as well, in that they are culturally affirmed and supported. The mature defense mechanisms of humor and altruism, for example, are expressed culturally in giving through the World Hunger Society, Live Aid, and Hands Across America concerts; those who participate experience loss in giving, which represents transcendence, in that they overcome the deaths of others. (See Chapter 12, on death as transcendence.)

There are many metaphors of loss and transcendence in the general transcendence mechanisms of our culture. These metaphors are common to art, literature, religion, and music. The turning of the seasons ("September song," Shelley's "Ode to the west wind") indicates the passing of time, a sense of beauty in the transcendence of this turning, because spring will always come again, and there is the fundamental illusion that spring is always the same. All that dies in winter is reborn in spring, and we do not differentiate one leaf from another; we maintain the illusion that the same leaf reappears because we cannot detect the change, and that the same tree is greening because we detect no changes there, either. And yet, it is not the same. There have been minute changes in the tree, a loss of cells and a birth of others, just as there have been in ourselves if we live until spring. We speak of the spring of our lives, the heated passion of summer, the brisk forboding winds of fall, "when the storms begin, and the blasts denote I am nearing the place" (Browning's "Prospice," 1922), heralding endings in riotous color, and the dead of winter, when leaves and capacities are lost. Beyond these, we speak of the promise of spring, in the hope of not ending, as the seasons do not.

The journey is another metaphor of L/T. Life is a journey, and death is a continuation of it. Journey by train, bus, plane, or ship—each has its myths of endings and transcendence of these; each is a metaphor of travel through life until a destination is reached. In this country, there is the myth of the eternal wanderer who never reaches a destination because his journey is without end. In this way he lives in the present, having no future in which death must be included. His "going," his "leaving," his "passing through" are all symbols of his living and dying, and yet he goes on, finality is impossible, as long as he refuses to remain in a town, a job, a love, as long as he stays uncommitted to the constrictions of one way of life. His giving up of these is premature; he gives them up before they are wrested from him. There is a related myth of the search, except that there is supposedly a purpose to the search. This is a metaphor of the searching phase of mourning; it may be for a love, for gold, or for oneself, and it is almost never found, for that would be an ending, a death. Songs of searching arouse feelings of nostalgia in us, perhaps because we have become a replacement society, but this reminds us of our previous stage of development while we recognize the search as an inappropriate life style. A related metaphor is that of the dream, the pot of gold at the end of the rainbow, whose constant revision Levinson (1978) finds so necessary in periods of transition if we are to survive healthily.

Each generation of youth seems to have its counterculture of young men and women who have discovered death and who therefore live in the present, transcending generally, because in specific transcendence they have found there is no permanent escape. There were the bohemians in the 1940s, the beatniks in the 1950s, the hippies in the 1960s, the ecologically minded in the 1970s, who transcended prospective disaster by natural foods and child-birth, homespun clothing, and nearness to the land. In the 1980s they are "punks" and "rockers" (somewhat counteracted by yuppies). It is characteristic of these groups that they eschew the planning and living for the future that characterize their parents, the establishment. They see the folly of it, having newly discovered that they will end, and they seek to live in the present, to transcend death by eliminating the future in which death must occur, tran-scending through drugs, alcohol, nature, music, dropping out, alienation, sex, revolution against the social ordering of life and its directionality, of which death is the ultimate aim. All are forms of being in the present or of trying to hold back the future. In their twenties, or usually by thirty, they return as did the prodigal son, because they have rediscovered the lack of escape and they seek safety in the parental arms of the established order. This stage is followed by another one beginning at about forty (Levinson, 1978), the mid-life transition, when it is apparent in L/T terms that even the established order is not a refuge, that even doing as one ought cannot hold back the inevitable, and values once again turn to living as one wants to live (Rubin, 1979).

All of the above general transcendence mechanisms assist in the inte-gration phase of transcendence and in the creation of meaning, although they will be differentially salient in different individuals, and their absence or abuse may be related to pathology, as we have seen.

The above modes are also aspects of the supreme mode of overcoming death and re-creating the self, and that mode is love. Acts of prayer, artistry, sport, history, embracing different ways of being in different worlds, and mythmaking are acts of love by both the creator and the experiencer. Each act we perform in life can be an act of indifference, of malignance, or of love, and nowhere is the love more evident that in the modes of being in this chapter. As death robs us of the sight of that which we love, and of the hearing, and eventually of all we are, it takes away the lovingness that is our transcendent self and replaces it with loss. Our only recourse is to do all that we do in love, because it is the objects of our love that survive, carrying that love, which is our self.

LIFE HISTORY

Tori's history illuminates the influences of many of the above general tran-scendence modes, showing how they overcome loss and re-create the life and the self.

Tori

"There were three identities I had, [those of] academic, artist, and activist."

"We had always wanted life to be the way it should be and been disappointed in that."

Tori is a petite, raven-haired anthropology professor in her late twenties. She has been a professor for only a few years, is married to a successful businessman, and has a baby daughter. We are conducting the interview in a multilevel A-frame on a wooded lot not far from a major city.

Tori's parents, both traveling actors and both alcoholics, were divorced after a stormy marriage, and Tori was raised by her mother and grandmother. Many of Tori's memories are happy ones, but "I do have memories of when she was drunk. I remember when we lived alone, the two of us. I remember eating a whole box of soda crackers for dinner one night, which was fine with me, I loved soda crackers, still do, but it's one of those things that my mother will never get over feeling guilty about, being a bad mother for those years . . . and which some people would pity me for. I remember that dual reality of it, it's fine for me but not to the outside world." She also remembers "my mother passing out on the floor, I must have been 5 or 6, and her date driving away, and my grandmother wasn't home . . . and I ran outside and yelled at him to please come back in, and help me get her up, and he wouldn't, he just left, and I have to go back in and try to figure out what to do." When Tori was 7, her mother "turned herself in to the state mental hospital, saying she could no longer control her life. There was an AA person there who directed her to AA, and she never took another drink. . . . I spent my childhood going to AA meetings, so I heard everything about life, and I heard my mom give her story over and over again, at which she'd always break down and thank me at the end, because I was the only thing that kept her going, and made her life worth living. . . . So I was always made to feel like the center of the universe, and that I was responsible for my mother's happiness because it was only because of me that she recovered from alcoholism. . . . She's a very vivacious person, and there's a tremendous amount of love that I experienced in my childhood."

Tori sees her father as a tragic figure, once a talented actor, now an alcoholic, doing odd jobs. Her mother raised her "with all the horror stories about him, and so I was never raised with the feeling that I was created out of love. . . . I would love to regress into all of the stress of the first seven years, and how I just always learned to hold it all together. Never break down. Everybody depends on you. Be strong." Her stepfather was also an alcoholic with a number of children, one of whom started a Hate Tori club and then forced her to join! Her mother began the long siege of illness that is still with her.

Some of Tori's happiest childhood memories are of helping out in the restaurant her mother and grandmother owned. "I was always doing adult things." She also learned to read when she was three; people would take her on to their laps and have her read the newspaper to them. "I didn't have any negative responses to that at the time. It's only now, tracing back as an adult how I became who I am, that I see how early the equation was made between being exceptional, being excellent, being intellectual and being loved. I got those confused very early. . . . I was always at the top . . . I kept thinking with every new level that this would be the one where I would just be ordinary, and it's never been." This was something Tori had to come to terms with, to realize that she was not an "imposter." [The loss of a national scholarship, with concomitant outpourings of support from friends and relatives, convinced her that she was loved not for her intellectual ability, but for herself.] She attributes her superiority to an innate love of learning as well as high expectations of her. Tori is aware that she may be encouraging her toddler daughter in just the same path, by applauding each word she speaks. She feels she must be careful about this.

"So my mind was always a big thing in growing up and being ostracized. I skipped second grade, so I was always the youngest, and I was still the best . . . and had to tolerate all the taunts and name-calling, and wearing glasses. My solution in eighth grade was to get [for] my boyfriend the dumbest boy in class." In high school she downplayed academics, paid attention to boys, and became more popular. Another major lesson of her childhood was that she had to take care of those who were supposed to take care of her. This has extended into her adult life—"Tori, the earth mother, taking on responsibility for everybody." In some ways, this has intimidated others, because she presents to the world as a "strong, superperson." Interestingly enough, her husband does too, and they recognized this in each other.

The major regret of Tori's life was that she did not have a childhood environment that promoted intellectual development. "Who knows what I could have done had I been . . . the child of professors . . . had I gone to special schools, been taken to museums?" As it was, debate "gave me more intellectual stimulation than any of my classes did. It saved me from total boredom in high school, and developed my intellectual skills that have stood me all the way since then. . . . And I always fell in love with boys' minds . . . I was attracted to that witty repartee." As she reads her adolescent journals, she feels she should have been "reading great works of literature, thinking about them, writing things that were more substantive. I missed a classical education. I would have loved to have studied Greek and Latin. . . . There was nobody giving me guidance. . . . This contributes to my sense of so much to do." Another regret is of having had no musical training as a child. "I would love to be able to know much more about classical music." She also regrets "the decision I made to go for popularity, rather than to really stretch my talents. This is another thing Garth and I share, having decided to hold ourselves back so that we would be liked, because if people already were intimidated by us, if they saw how powerful we really were, then nobody would like us, nobody could keep up with us." Her friends in high school were always the lonely people, "the kind of faithful puppy dogs who followed you around, who just idolized me, and I could boss them around." Another regret was too much TV. She views her grandmother as "progressively killing herself by not being involved in anything, by sitting home all day and watching TV," and Tori feels she watched too much as a child. She also picked up many fears when she was a child, especially a terror of water. "A lot of my fears came from observing [my mother and grandmother] as two very fearful people, and thinking there must be a lot to be afraid of." She learned to swim a few years ago. Tori had an ongoing fantasy of visiting New York City, as a cultural and intellectual mecca—a fantasy eventually realized.

At about 12 or 13 Tori and her mother began to move apart. "I remember with such tenderness all the loving things she did, and all the sacrifices she made for me," but they had stormy times during adolescence and have been creating a new relationship in the past few years. Part of the difficulty was that Tori was becoming involved in issues like civil rights and feminism ("her whole life represented the traditional role").

At about the age of 18, Tori "went into a series of existential depressions, because I can remember since 6 questioning the meaning of my life, and I always was very afraid of death, it made no sense to me, the randomness of it. And I always felt I had to handle the whole universe, and war, and it all seemed real immense, and how was I going to do that? And I definitely had to be somebody very, very famous, and very, very powerful to have that kind of power, and it was also a kind of immortality; the only way your life mattered was if you achieved immortality by being president or something." At this time, she began having some sexual experiences, got very moody, and fell in love, and there was still the underlying terror about death. She felt unsafe around men because of television and her parents "constantly cautioning me about strange men and about car accidents. . . . I had a recurring dream throughout my childhood of being pursued, and I had elaborate escape routes throughout my neighborhood. That only ended when I took a self-defense class."

Tori's first love affairs were nurturant. "I was functioning in real ignorance about sex." In college she became engaged "until I felt like my life was ending, marriage was going to be this iron gate going over the rest of my future." She started reading women's magazines and collecting recipes, and then stopped short. "But basically a series of very deep, long, intense relationships is what I had, and I loved those." She experimented in sleeping with people she didn't know well, but this was not exciting. "For me, sexuality is always tied up with a person's mind, and with a stranger it wasn't even exciting, thinking of it was exciting, but doing it [laughter]." She remains good friends with almost all of the men with whom she had serious relationships, including a well-known actor. *"Totally* made a woman out of me," because she had always been defined by others in terms of mind.

Tori comments, "There were three identities I had, [those of] academic, artist, and activist. And my whole life has been about trying to juggle all those three and make them fit. And the artist is the writer, and the poet that loves the art, that could have gone into theater, debate is really theater, and then the academic, and the activist, committed to feminism and social change."

She quit college and became a hippie, for which her mother disowned her. "So it was everything at once, leaving home, feminism, antiwar, questioning the nature of education, just being so disappointed with it, so I spent a year living alone, writing for a radical newspaper, helping to start a women's center, declared myself a writer, and tried to figure out how I was going to support myself the rest of my life." She had a year of self-examination during which she realized that "learning, teaching, reading, writing were the things I loved to do the most, and a university professor seemed to be the only place to do that."

Later, in graduate school, Tori met Al, whom she married just before he went away to travel and see the world, "so we created a fantasy relationship. The rest of our relationship was trying to live up to the fantasy." They lived together and had a good marriage. "I'm a very domestic person . . . I've always been in little mini-marriages." Al and Tori began going different ways. "He's very intense, and very deep, but he's very quiet, so *we* had this wonderful connection, but in terms of the outside world, we had different tastes in people." Just as she graduated they divorced. "It was the death of a dream."

At the point of readying herself for her new job as college professor, Tori became reacquainted with Garth. They started spending more time together. "That connection was so deep our minds worked together like hand and glove. Our senses of humor, everything about our characters was absolutely eerie, particularly in terms of our childhood development. . . . And I had had dreams about Garth the year before, erotic dreams, but I never thought of pursuing them because he seemed unattainable, and I thought he saw me as a little sister. He'd always been just as drawn to me as I was to him. We arranged to spend more time together. We would sit and talk for five hours, and that's real magic when your minds work together that way." One day he was headed for a backpacking trip, she was going on a retreat, and they planned to meditate together at a certain hour. Later they found they had received the same images. "It was a very psychic week in terms of the connection." When he returned they spoke of how much they had thought of each other, and they slept together for the first time. He had always felt he wanted to live in the city and not to have any children, but all this changed. "So it was just like walking into a universe where there was no time and no space. Garth and I both experienced this is what life—our whole lives have been about coming together . . . and from this point on, this is life as it should be. . . . He had given up [the idea of remarrying]. . . . Everything had come together at the exact right time for our lives to join. We had always wanted life to be the way it should be, and always been disappointed in that. And here was a relationship where everything was as it should be. There were no disappointments. It was like we were one person." Another eerie aspect of the experience was that they had both started on their paths of spiritual development at the same time, many years before, reading Eastern psychology, doing meditation and body work. Now "Garth and I create in our family what we never had."

A child "clearly needed to come from this union," and indeed they had a little girl who an astrologer predicted would be as Tori was, "a writer, a public speaker, a new-age person, a feminist, a leader of people, a very strong, independent woman." Further, he said that Tori and her daughter had probably been related in a previous life as colleagues, rather than as mother and daughter. "So I figure we were Susan B. Anthony and Elizabeth Cady Stanton [laughs]. But it was very wonderful, because I already sensed her as an equal being, and it was a reminder to me [that] we ended up mother and daughter this time, so don't get any trips going about that one."

Tori has kept journals since she was 12, and this is an important activity for her. Already she has about 30 journals. The journal keeping began with a nearly fatal accident and questioning why she had not been killed, "what kind of order in the universe was there." She states that "the writer aspect of me is probably the major aspect of my identity, which is still hard for me to acknowledge, because when I feel out of sync with my life is when I'm not writing, and why don't I arrange my life to write? . . . I don't know why I've got myself into a situation of not doing the thing that nurtures me the most. And that's the central question of my life." As a writer, she wants to compose essays "like Lewis Thomas and Montaigne."

Another major experience was her training in a program of self-development, which turned out to be "the most brilliant educational experience of my life. . . . I really did experience transformation . . . a shift in my world, where I was the center of my own life . . . it was not being done to me any more. . . . I was in control, not so much the externals of my life, but how I reacted. I had a choice as to how to react. . . . And I started to create miracles. I created the [university] job in a few months. . . . Everything developed on my end to make it happen," through a series of little events that converged. She realizes that not everyone gets as much out of the training as she did, which is disillusioning. But "it all converged for me in the year of coming to [the university], divorce, remarriage, pregnancy, new job, end of graduate school, first trip to Europe and my first home, a house of my own. All of those in one year, all the external signs of adulthood." In discussing the most important people in her life, Tori says: "Garth is me, so he doesn't ever come to mind in terms of other people. It's hard to think of him as another person."

One of the advantages of her current job is "being a catalyst where people can know who they are. . . . I'll always want to be teaching. I love to teach more than anything else." Yet, one of Tori's greatest worries is not getting tenure. "It's a tremendous pressure. It's the biggest stress in your life. . . . I really feel that this is my profession, and [not getting it] would be an outrage, that I'm really destined to be in this profession. The meditation for me in the last two years has been to try to do everything idealistically, the way I thought it should be done, a process of total burnout, a process of total disillusionment about the institution, about the lack of support, about nothing being the way it should be, about the isolation, about the sexism, the double burdens, trying to figure out how to do my best given all that, and to deal with the tenure pressures, coupled with parenthood." Tori finds that trying to work as much as one should is impossible when one has a new child. She compares herself with a fellow professor in another department who has no child and no husband and can devote herself completely to the tenure matters, which involve research and publication. "So the question is, does the university have room for somebody that's trying to live a whole life?"

Tori had an illness that made future pregnancy problematic; this was the reason for the decision to get pregnant immediately rather than wait until her career and the marriage were more established. Tori feels strongly that those in power in the university, mainly men, make the decisions regarding the tenure timetable, and this gives no room to a woman who is trying to establish a home and family as well; she feels that it is different for men because the responsibility for the children is ultimately the mother's.

"I totally broke down in spring, right after we got married, and I was in the nausea state of pregnancy, and moved into the new house, and had taught since I'd been there, and I had to get out of my spring course. . . . I proceeded to go into almost a catatonic state. I couldn't feel anything. This is my house, this is what I've always wanted, and I don't feel a thing. All I could feel was this tremendous exhaustion and burnout from having given to so many people, and so many changes in my life . . . plus the enormous hormonal changes of pregnancy." She retreated to her home, read novels, and wrote in her journals, a way of delving "into my spiritual life. . . . I want a year off to be home, sit, not just to be with Leila, but to be with me." So the tenure timetable "is totally unrealistic when you combine it with parenting, and teaching, and activism." She was "born a writer" and can't even get enough time for that.

With regard to her health, Tori feels she is too weak and wants to be in better shape. She has become a vegetarian but is not yet exercising. She meditates occasionally, loves to share her thoughts with friends, but feels exceptionally sad at the "injustice and sorrow in the world, particularly the way children are treated, the denial of their essences, and the impositions on them of adult will." She does feel that psychedelics contributed to her spiritual development.

Death has been a major factor in Tori's life. Her older sister died of

Hodgkin's disease when she was just in her thirties. Tori herself was present when Robert Kennedy was killed. These have strengthened her commitment to cross-cultural death education, one of her major teaching areas. When asked what she hopes for in 5 years, she responds that she hopes to have "totally handled the busyness thing," whereby she is too rushed to exercise and write. She also hopes "that I've gotten tenure, and I'm now making good choices about where to put my energies, and not be overextended." She has a recurring dream of not being prepared for something. But a special dream for her was one of something like a colored marble that was unity, "and there was a secret there, and I could figure it out." It occurred when she was in graduate school and her husband was away; the dream left her with a sense that she could handle her life. She has also had out-of-body experiences, precognitive dreams, and déjà vu. She tends to fantasize about the past, reliving places and experiences, rather than daydream about the future. When asked about small losses, Tori replied, "They mostly have to do with time, and when I plan in my mind that I'm going to be doing more things than I can do, and then it becomes clear that the day is not going to allow me to finish all this, even little things, and then I get off center, and I have to put it in perspective, and breathe deeply, and get my center back." A psychic friend tells her that her "psychic boundaries are permeable. . . . I'm so sensitive to what is going on around me with people and events, that I let in too much, and I incorporate it, and I have to learn to be less permeable, keep my sensitivity, but infuse more of my centeredness into the situation."

When asked about her life theme, two things stand out in Tori's mind. "One was that theme of incompletion," which has been with her her whole life. "The sense there's more that I want to do, and I'm not going to have time to do it, and I'm not living up to my ideals, has always been there. And it's a measure of my progress in seeing more ease in dealing with that, and having it be less of an issue. It's a standard by which I measure how I'm doing. . . . The second thing was that I really am a writer, that I always have been, and that that's still a process of owning my identity. I'm most fulfilled and satisfied when that is a part of my life." Her friends see an intensity in her "of wanting the most out of life . . . and not settling." She worries about settling now, in terms of "buying into the academic standards that I don't particularly believe in. Not letting my values be as salient." She is currently on leave to do research, but her colleagues congratulate her as being lucky to avoid the students, and she responds that she misses them; many colleagues do not appreciate and enjoy teaching as she does.

(This theme of writing and not acknowledging, and not understanding why you don't give yourself time for it—because you're a person who takes responsibility for your life—have you any insight into this?) Tori responds that this is a time issue, that her identity is divided between academic and activist with little time left for the artist. However, she could be writing in the middle of the night. "But I think the more deep thing which Garth and I talked about is the expression of our powers, both of us for different reasons, as though if people are intimidated by us as we are, and we have difficulty being liked because people see us on such a different plane and have difficulty feeling equal to us, then, if we really manifest our power [laughter] we would be ostracized." Their invitations to others are not returned; she and Garth feel increasingly deviant, because of their high standards. They are trying to ease up on themselves, Leila, and their friends. She believes her high standards for others are simply reflections of discontent with herself.

When asked about life meaning, Tori tells us, "I don't think it's out there to be discovered. I think it's within us to be created, and that we give meaning to our life in each and every moment. Meaning resides in us, not in any external things like a job or a child or a career." By living and sharing, we can deal with the insanity of the world and the "sense of overwhelm, of how can I possibly handle everything?" She has been searching for the meaning of life since she was five, searching outside herself with reading, meditation, and self-development training. "The trainer talks about the meaning of life, and people get up and say it's truth, justice." Then the trainers "crack down everybody's idols. They're trying to show that all have belief systems, so that your meaning of life will be somebody else's nonsense." Tori believes that "it's lack of love in an infant that causes evil in the world, lack of being valued." She speaks of how the human spirit survived the concentration camp, "and I think the meaning would be simply survive, to manifest the human spirit in the worst." She feels that "parenthood unlocks the mysteries of the universe," and this is connected to loving so much, as she loves Garth, that she would die to save his life. She remembers lying on her bed with Leila "in the curve of my arm about two days after she was born, and just crying and crying: 'Now I understand what this love is.' I couldn't really understand the quality of that love before. And I felt such a connection with my mother, knowing that at one point she had felt that for me, and knowing that I could never return that love in kind. A lot of her life has been about asking me to, in fact."

Tori regrets loss of time to do all she needs to do, especially writing; her disillusionment with academia, including the tenure process for women and sexism; her lack of childhood intellectual and creative environment; losses to alcoholism, particularly her father; and finally the loss of "things as they should be." Sources of transcendence for her are writing, meditation, self-development training, activism, teaching, music, nature, debate, and especially her relationship with her daughter and her husband, in which she stresses the psychic components. Her intellectual gifts were mixed blessings. Throughout her history we can see several themes, such as lack of time, how she defines herself in several different ways, the importance of intelligence, and general transcendence. Time is important as it permits her to give full expression to the several facets of her identity. She centers herself, transcends the time conflict with time-transcending activities—spiritual growth through love, psychic connection, writing, self-development training, music, nature, and meditation. The core theme is identity split by time limits versus spiritual growth (transcending the limits).

Theoretical analysis

"The writer aspect of me is probably the major aspect of my identity."

"I love to teach more than anything else. . . . I really feel that [teaching] is my profession, that I'm really destined to be in this profession."

"There were three identities I had, [those of] academic, artist, and activist . . . committed to feminism and social change."

"Who knows what I could have done?"

"I really am a writer."

"*Totally* made a woman out of me."

"I'm a very domestic person."

"A writer, a public speaker, a new-age person, a feminist, a leader of people, a very strong, independent woman."

"Now I understand what love is."

"Imposter."

Tori redefines herself throughout the interview, now seeing one aspect of herself as paramount, now another. She seems caught in the cultural necessity to define herself rather than just to be. She is passionate about teaching, writing, feminism, social injustice, her husband, her daughter; she chafes against the limitations of time that will not allow all these aspects of who she is to fully grow. She must choose among her eyes, her ears, her limbs, because time, the measure of our lives, is not eternal but limited. Interestingly, she barely mentions research, the main activity and the sine qua non of the professor at a major educational institution.

For Tori, the "central question" of her life is why she does not give herself more time for the most important facet of her identity. The answer may lie in the above quotations. Writing may be most important, but considerable time must be expended for other very important aspects. The time needed for teaching and research in order to gain tenure (and continue these) is somewhat fixed, whereas the time needed for writing is not. One can write on less time; one cannot be a professor without expending the minimum.

Tori's ideals are high and so are bound to be dashed. She speaks of how things should be, as well as how they should have been. She and Garth have a relationship in which everything is "as it should be," which they had always wanted, although they had been disappointed. She is disillusioned in academia—it is not as it should be. She did not have the early childhood she should have had. She grieves over the injustice to children. She and Garth, like other interviewees, try to give Leila the family they did not have. There is in Tori an implicit view of a world ordered as it should be, like a template against which she is always holding up reality and finding a mismatch. Where did that world view come from?

If the world were as it should be, there would be time for all aspects of her identity to flourish and she would not be compelled to split.

How did this split come about? Tori tells us of having to hold things together in her early childhood, and having more responsibility on her little shoulders than a child could reasonably bear. She made her mother's "life worthwhile," and the implication is that she saved her mother's life. If she did wrong, broke, eschewed responsibility, her mother might die, and it would be her fault. At 18 there seems to have been a posttraumatic stress reaction: "I can remember since 6 questioning the meaning of my life, and I always was very afraid of death, it made no sense to me, the randomness of it. And I always felt I had to handle the whole universe, and war, and it all seemed real immense, and how was I going to do that. And I definitely had to be somebody very, very famous, and very, very powerful to have that kind of power, and it was also a kind of immortality." For Tori, being responsible for her mother's existence must have seemed like the universe; the solution was a child's perception of immortality—power and fame. In her teaching, activism, and writing Tori finds power to combat death in its myriad forms, to hold it off for awhile. To the extent that one aspect of her self is not fully actualized, she is not fully alive. She has to be so *much* because of the immenseness and randomness of the universe, war, and death. The death against which she fought as a child has grown greater with her own cognitive development and conceptual abilities.

Tori is no longer split when she engages in general transcendence. Time does not exist, and neither does division, when one is "lost" in meditation, nature, creativity, and music. These give her unity; she overcomes the split with time and within herself. She is finally like the multicolored marble of her dream, the mysterious unity. There is a strong influence of Eastern mysticism on her outlook; indeed, she overcomes ego with pure being and caprice and chaos with Karmic destiny.

Time is the enemy, and timelessness is the friend. Time measures the distance between life and death, but then death is timeless—enemy and friend will eventually become one. General transcendence is a small death, a loss of consciousness that gives more life than does full consciousness.

Tori is influenced by her culture. There are rules for tenure, teaching, writing, and human relationships, and general transcendence is only allowed if one does not break the rules. Otherwise, as with alcoholism, general transcendence becomes loss. The more time Tori spends in general transcendence, the higher the price situationally. She must decide. Perhaps she is deciding by downgrading one facet of herself, the teacher within the tenure process.

SOCIETAL MANIFESTATIONS OF LOSS AND TRANSCENDENCE

An examination of the organization, institutions, and rituals of any society will demonstrate that a central purpose of that society is to regulate loss and prescribe methods of transcendence. Such an examination will also lay bare the ultimate values by which the individuals in that society define, judge, and create loss and transcendence.

For example, in our society loneliness is not as important as physical disease; unpaid volunteers go into the hospitals to relieve loneliness, whereas highly paid technicians relieve disease; the volunteers are, of course, paid in compliments and approval, but these are cheaper than money. (With the continuing rise of the national debt and the projected return of double-digit inflation, they may not always be.)

The contract between the individual and society involves the transcendence by society of individual losses. When society does not abide by its contract, its institutions are in jeopardy; taxes may be unpaid, programs scrapped, parties or lords or tribal chiefs removed from office. The media are the arena wherein society's success in transcendence is weighed, whether the medium be television or tribal council.

The structure of our government shows the social transcendence of individual and collective loss. Local government, mayor, city council, county services, and their various agencies must transcend local losses, threatened or actual, as seen in the battles between ecologists and supporters of housing development; people need more and better and less expensive shelter, but on another level they want their trees left standing, a wilderness in which to get away from their adequate shelter, which also stifles. The elderly and children must be fed hot lunches, and a federal program must be administered to ascertain which elderly and which children are eligible; as taxpayers complain and government debt rises, some needy are reclassified. The local fire and police departments must minimize loss of life and property.

Local schools must train the children in the elements of the social contract, particularly its myths, so that they will not be lost to succeeding generations. The needy must be provided with medical care, because they would otherwise lose their lives, and its is unacceptable to us to have people dying in the streets—they are all someone's father, and someone else's child, and they are possibly ourselves. The young must be protected from child abuse, neglect, and starvation; and because we have more services for them, it must be our value that they are worth more protection than the elderly, who should be able to accept their destruction with better grace than the young and who do not have as much to contribute ultimately to the gross national product. There are no elderly protective services, as there are children's protective services, but the elderly are frequently abused by their children (Pedrick-Cornell & Gelles, 1982). The young are still potential, the old are past. Time is the precious commodity that is protected, and the old simply have less of it. (Never mind that they are also uncomfortable reminders of our own ultimate potential loss of all we value: beauty, worth, esteem, competence, health.) Time is also a gauge of productivity, without which we would not survive; our lives would be less in both quantity and quality. Productivity must be a high societal value.

In short, if we were to enumerate every city and county service, we would find that their *raison d'être* is to transcend a loss of some kind, and individuals must accept their long lines, forms, taxes, and judgments to receive this protection. Unfortunately for many of the recipients, the integration of the me who is not beauteous, esteemed, competent, or healthy enough to make it on her own must eventually be registered in the I and be integrated into the self, and this may prove exceptionally difficult, as it is loss from the ideal. But perhaps this is intentional in that it is permitted; those who must accept our charity are taking our time from us. We feel compelled to contribute a little of our lives to extend theirs. Because charity is bestowed with ambiguous feelings, it must be reified by the society as a superior value, and those who cannot bestow it but must receive it must be inferior.

State and federal governments simply transcend losses, potential or actual, at another level; they keep us out of war or administer victory in battle (or answer for losses with explanation, rationalization, and promises, that is, with societal defense mechanisms); they offer a higher court to adjudicate the losses inflicted by a lower one, offer assistance in national disasters, and balance the losses of one segment of the population or region of the country against the losses of another (the southwestern part of our country could survive on less gasoline for their cars, but, beyond a certain point, the north cannot survive with less heating oil; in particular, the elderly are susceptible to hypothermia and death below a temperature at which most others could survive). The individual must pay the price, accepting the draft into the armed forces which the government imposes, when loss of one life may prevent loss of many. It helps a man to think of those many as his own beloved children, spouse, parents, to accept the fiction of specific transcendence, and do battle for his lady as did the knights of old.

State licenses for driving, fishing, healing, or operating a bar or a nursing home all have as their aim the transcendence of some anticipated loss.

Each individual is part of her city, county, state, and country, just as she is part of all the other groups to which she belongs. Each of these groups has an L/T structure similar to that of the smaller group, dyad, and individual that we examined in earlier chapters. We may think of this structure as consisting of the whole nation, divided into the historical we, the historical us, the transcendent national we, and the transcendent national us. The transcendent national we is especially important in this structure; it is the story we tell ourselves and each other and the world—of who we are as a country, how we justify Vietnam and have fought heroically in two world wars, why we send aid to foreign governments (which may end up spending it for their leaders' luxuries) instead of more aid to our own poor (well, they aren't as badly off as the poor in India and Africa, who never get our wheat, anyway). We send foreign aid because we are a charitable country, and we are trying to prevent war in the Middle East by sending guns, and the world looks to us as a leader. We do not send money, men, or weapons because we want oil rights, air bases, or hostages freed, or we want to allay envy of our wealth, which could result in open hostilities. Our nation relates to other nations as do individuals and groups, with myths of alliance, enmity, and cold war.

Every society has a "conservative" and a "liberal" element, with various degrees between these two divisions. The conservatives are usually concerned with saving or preserving the status quo, not losing what is already possessed, and they often have more to lose, although preservation of the status quo is an illusion much like that of romantic love. Nothing ever really stays the same. The liberals, in their concern with more equitable division of resources, have less to lose and are transcending loss of what they do not possess (votes, bread). The regulation of loss will change according to who is in power. The wealthier can afford more and better protection from loss than can the poor, that is, better lawyers, less or no punishment for crimes they commit, better neighborhoods that are more regularly patrolled for crime, vacations from stress, and so forth.

Society also regulates the loss an individual must incur in order to avoid or transcend greater loss. This is the system of taxation. In our country, people who have less to lose are supposed to lose less proportionately, but then they have less of an influence on the social contract than do the wealthy, who can buy influence, lobbies, even votes, whole sections of political parties, and, to some extent, laws. The wealthy spend this influence trying to lose less than their "fair share." There is a reason why long-recognized tax loopholes still remain unclosed (even with new tax legislation there are hundreds of legislated exceptions), why fallow tobacco fields are subsidized and the oil industry can suddenly hike its rates and end up with windfall profits at the expense of the poor. No matter what we tell ourselves and each other about our unity, L/T becomes a battleground between individuals as well as groups and nations.

When people go to the polls, they vote essentially for candidates whom they believe will act to minimize loss to themselves (fewer taxes, lower crime rates, peace). Candidates know this, of course, and promise transcendence of whatever major loss is threatening at the time; this is known as "the issue." The voter is in a paradoxical crisis of belief, which might be traumatic to her had she not been immersed in similar crises every election day, as well as through the advertising industry. She chooses to believe one candidate or another, which is wishful thinking in action, because she knows that any resemblance between campaign promises and what eventuates after the election is purely. . . . She can mock the futility of her vote with a short laugh as she emerges from the booth. Only after the election will she find out what new form her losses will take.

Any infliction of loss of life or property by one member of society on another is supposed to be punished by infliction of loss on the criminal. The criminal is a deviant who has inflicted loss on either the individual or society or himself, in the form of stealing, murder, injury, or defiance of values and rules that society has set up for its own protection in the opinion of the majority (drugs, prostitution, etc.). All laws are made with attention to the regulation of loss. Criminals are "losers." Implicit in this regulation is an underlying taxonomy of loss, reflected in the taxonomy of penalties; for example, loss of life is greater than loss of money or property, which is greater than a few lost minutes in the activity of prostitution. But loss of life is a greater loss of time than is loss of property, which takes less time to make or earn, and which is still greater than the time spent with a prostitute. (Although time spent in Hell for such activities might be excessive, according to some beliefs.)

Time is thus the crucial factor in the taxonomy of crime and punishment. Its loss is a small death; its loss is the crime of lessening the amount of time in life. Anything that brings anyone closer to death through loss of time is a crime, except for a modicum of general transcendence activities discussed above, such as art, religion, and movies; these society will permit but must control. On the other hand, "victimless" crimes are all crimes of transcendence, that is, the choice of a present over the future. By engaging in activities in which time is "lost," the criminals have erred in not "banking" their valuable time, escaping death metaphorically. Society will tolerate only so much of this because, if carried to extremes, general transcendence could herald society's dissolution; indeed, people may drink, have sex, or get stoned to the point where they are described as leading a "dissolute life." (This is not to ignore the fact that "victimless crimes" may be organized and regulated by professional criminals who also victimize.)

Society reifies certain values, which are essentially rewards to the individual for incurring loss to himself in order to protect other members of society from loss. These include honesty (he returns the bag of money and is rewarded with a small portion of it and public attention), philanthropy (she gives of her largess to those who have less and is rewarded with the esteem of, and power over, those to whom she gives, as well as those she employs as instruments of her giving), altruism (she saves the child from the burning building and is rewarded with a medal and a promotion), bravery in battle (he is rewarded with veterans' benefits, medals to display his courage to the world, brass bands, and speeches in ticker tape parades); gentleness to the weaker and infirm, a modicum of cleanliness, and so forth. When no loss to society, or the individuals who constitute it, will result from certain activities, the values regulating them change, as with changing sexual mores resulting from more effective modes of contraception and excess population growth. When other losses crop up, such as new sexually transmitted diseases like AIDS, the values change again; there is a new celibacy in the land (Brown, 1981). When loss results only conditionally, values are mixed, as with alcohol, pornography, and drug consumption. Those who would censor books or who favor temperance are always those who perceive more loss as inherent in these activities, who are not as open to them as methods of transcendence.

Society employs certain "hook" words, such as "responsibility," "community," "relevance," and "communication," to bind individuals to societal values for further regulation of L/T. To the extent that the individual executes his life in accordance with these values, he conforms, such conformity carrying its own possibilities of loss to the individual, as the existentialists have observed. There is then less possibility of individuation. To Koestler (1978) the individual was a social holon, carrying with her the polarity of whole and of part of the social group, a polarity that, in his view, may never be reconciled, except on the level of recognizing the energy that runs through all and may be grasped paranormally (Koestler, 1971; Weenolsen & Barron, 1979).

Society is also responsible for regulating transcendence of loss to some extent in the form of ritual and prescription. The most common rituals are, of course, graduations, weddings, retirements, and funerals. At the first three occasions, we are instructed to be happy at the loss of old familiar structures and relationships; discontinuity is an occasion of joy; but the tears flow, so they must be interpreted as tears of happiness to reconcile the dissonance between the rational and the irrational. Tears are more appropriate at funerals, although the effort is to see some form of continuity; because belief in afterlife is often strong, prescribed, and professed, tears are anathema or betrayal. The fact is that the individuals are in mourning on all four occasions. Birthdays and anniversaries are both ways of marking time, but the attention is focused on time elapsed rather than on time left. Some time in adulthood, this tends to break down. As the individual begins to focus on time left, she stops celebrating birthdays or lies about her age. The ignoring of birthdays in adulthood is the discreet ignoring of time left, or birthdays might become occasions of anticipatory mourning.

Prescriptions for behavior vary according to the social and cultural milieu as well as the sex, age, and socioeconomic status of the individual. They concern "proper" or normal reactions to loss, as evidenced in the concept of "age clocks" set forth by Neugarten (1968), but now considerably loosened (Neugarten, 1987). The middle-aged may be inappropriate on the disco dance floor, having lost elasticity and attractiveness; the value of their courtship and mating is certainly questionable in that children will not result—there will be no productivity.

Some behavioral prescriptions are less formal. Strauss and Glaser (1985) outline the behavior prescribed for the "good" patient who is anticipating loss of life; he must cooperate with the doctors and nurses, he must make brave attempts at asserting he will get well, such as "tottering" off to the bathroom on his own, and on no account must he verbalize what everyone knows; he must, in effect, cooperate in the denial of his impending death, so that others will feel comfortable around him. Patients who do not conform to the socially prescribed role are considered "problems" and may even suffer from delays in pain medication and increased isolation from the staff and family.

Holiday rituals arising from the religious segment of the society are peculiar mixtures of loss from previous holidays, such as Christmas, and the attempt to transcend these with the presence of relatives and gifts. Apparently, these work only variably. Christmas depression is a well-known phenomenon. It occurs because the depressed individual is reacting in the context of Christmas past, the disillusion with material things as ways of transcending, the pretense that these gifts create happiness and take the place of what is lost and will be lost, the gap between love felt and extended at this time of the year, and the problems within relationships year-round. Christmas is a massive denial that often does not work; the depression is partly over the fact that it did when we were children and loss was not boundless. Holidays celebrating rebirth, or the ultimate transcendence over the ultimate loss, such as Easter and Passover, also help denial only variably. They take place in families where those who were here last holiday are no longer present, and those who are still present are no longer as they were; Aunt Madeleine no longer remembers our names, or where she put the wine, or what we told her a moment ago, although she very well recalls that mother nearly drowned in the river when she was five, the stimulus for this sudden recollection being a mystery to us. New Year's Eve and pre-Lenten festivities such as Mardi Gras are ritual farewells to life, and particularly to past relationships, auld lang syne (old long since). We strike up the most intimate relationships with a stranger for the night, accepting the evanescence against which we struggle the rest of the year. Ritualized general transcendence in alcohol and promiscuous sexual activity is permitted by society on these occasions as rewards for our denial or restraint the rest of the year and is part of the social contract.

With each loss, the other (society) tells the self how to define itself. Excreta are to be flushed down the toilet, to disappear in water down a hole forever, as not worthy of mourning or even of close examination, unless there is something wrong. Until they are defined as a part of the self that may be safely dispensed with, their loss may be frightening. Toilet training is being trained to lose a part of the self in a certain manner and to devalue it. Devaluing what we lose is a societal defense mechanism; we are not trained the other way around. It is an L/T aspect of cognitive consistency (Festinger, 1962; Aronson, 1984). Teeth are to be put under the pillow, where their loss will be replaced with coins; parts of the body may be bought, others should not be (the sexual parts). Scratches, the appearance and extension of the heretofore unknown self to include blood, are as nothing compared to the ultimate injuries one may sustain but should be treated to keep out harm (invisible germs, evil spirits).

Society thus prescribes a taxonomy of losses and the values that attach to them, and the child learns these at the rate his cognitive structure permits. He is trained. His parents ask him where a certain possession is (where are you shoes?), and their reaction to his ignorance tells him about the value of the loss. If their reaction is severe (if they are poor, and this is the only pair he owns), he will learn to place a higher value on that part of himself, indeed to identify it as such, than if their reaction is mild. Each violation of his body and his thought is a loss, which, if it were extended, would become total and would be death. Although he does not conceive of his own death at this point, he is sensing the terror of disintegration or its possibility. At some point, he discovers death is the only loss that cannot entail recurrence of the thing lost, although it, too, can be replaced. To the extent that something is more highly valued, its replacement can only be approximate.

Society also acts to protect itself from cosmic losses. Barron (1979) demonstrates that the three great revolutions, the Copernican, the Darwinian, and the Freudian, threatened the human concept of self as being at the center of the universe, as being unique among all things including animals, and as being basically good, innocent, holy, and capable of complete control. These losses to the human concept of self were violently opposed in every instance and have, to some degree, been transcended by the rational and the intuitive. We can reason that being at the universal center is now unnecessary, as spirit transcends geography; that God could have created evolution in what for him was a timeless moment and what for us are millennia; that the human person is capable of greatly transcending the sexual and the aggressive through creativity, altered states of consciousness, love, and so forth. We can even find uniqueness in the "tragedy of man" (Campbell, 1961), who, alone of all creatures, knows his own prospect of his own change of form and whose every sorrow in life may be attributed to his attachment to forms that must inevitably be lost. (See Chapter 12, on death.) Finally, philosophy rescues us with epistemology; no form is the same to different individuals even in the same moment, because the standpoints of observation are always different, and science saves us with the equation of energy and matter, making us indestructible.

It is possible that societies may be classified as falling into one stage of the L/T process or another. Ours might be considered to be a replacement society, comparatively speaking; we dispose of a multitude of things, we have developed consumerism as an art, it is the basis of our economic structure as we use and throw out (Moos, 1977). This is supposed to save us time, and therefore life, although in actuality it does not; the number of things to be consumed rises, as the time needed for their consumption lessens. The advent of the washing machine has dictated a higher standard of cleanliness. Becker (1973) acutely perceives our preoccupation with trivia as a form of distraction from the existential issues of life and death, a necessary aid to repression. And many would argue that such minor replacement is a form of search and possibly despair, putting us in the mourning (lost) phase rather than in the resolution phase. Our resolution is too superficial and does not deal with the most important aspects of existence. The frontier societies might be thought of as in a searching stage; their focus was on the search for gold, land, and independence, in other words, heaven. Perhaps India is an example of a yearning society, with its emphasis on Karma and Nirvana or Samadhi. The ultimate goal would be an integration society. Whether societies progress in order through stages of the L/T process, what the relationship of their transcendence is to loss, and to what degree such progress might be universal and irreversible remain to be investigated.

LIFE HISTORY

In Harriet's story we see the impact of societal training in behavior and values on her life, and on the formation of her self.

Harriet

"[Life is worth living] if your child grows well and is thriving, the plants are growing well, and they're thriving, the chickens are growing well. . . . My cats . . . look like healthy cats."

Slim and gray-haired at 60, Harriet has a no-nonsense manner, but a cat plays with a ball of yarn suspended in the doorway.

Harriet recalls her father, a college professor, as passive, "a romantic dreamer. He always thought about things, but never got them done." Sickly in childhood, "he thought he was a semi-invalid [so] he never did anything physical around the house." He was also a "bookaholic," so they were always in debt to the university bookstore. Harriet also thinks of him as "sort of a parlor rebel. He liked to be in favor of things that people didn't approve of . . . free love . . . contraception. . . . He liked the shock side of things." But he tended to be quite proper and ended up with a number of children, so Harriet laughs over the thought that he didn't really know anything about contraception.

Her mother was more active—"at 86 she's still chopping wood"—and she tended to finish what her husband started. If he planned a trip, he'd never carry it out, but she'd buy the tickets. "She's also rather critical, but I don't think she was critical of my father. She was only a high school graduate, and he was a Ph.D., so she felt at a disadvantage educationally." Possessed of high ideals and standards, Harriet's mother was also a strict disciplinarian. "A good spanking set things to rights, and castor oil was a cure-all. . . . Praise was rather harmful to people. . . . My mother has absolutely no patience with fools." When Harriet and her brothers fought, she would spank them with the hairbrush or douse them with cold water. "For instance, on a rainy day when people were apt to be fractious, she'd put cold water in the bathtub and . . . they got doused [laughter]. She wasn't unpleasant about this, there was no rancor"; in fact, her discipline was preferred over their father's, who scolded until they felt "utterly awful."

Harriet and her siblings were raised on a lovely old Victorian estate in the east. She remembers it with fondness. "Because there was so much [wooded] land around us, we did a lot of constructions. We dug holes in the ground and covered them with old boards and made tunnels between them, and we used to crawl through the grass through grass tunnels, and when it rained a lot we used to have grass fights with our neighbors and come in all muddy."

The relationship between her parents was good until "he hit the dangerous age of about 55 . . . got interested in a younger woman, and finally ended up marrying her, to his surprise." Meanwhile, he had been writing a theoretical book "most of his life . . . and people that had seen individual chapters of it said it was very good, but he never felt able to finish it. He kept polishing it all the time, and as a result he really didn't publish anything . . . but he was always working on his book." After he retired he became ill, "his mental capacity kept waning . . . he could no longer function as a writer, and he kept poking around with his notes and his writing, and I think he just messed it all up. It was really sad."

Harriet feels her mother's influence on her was positive. She was likable and had a lot of ability; she made them Christmas clothes and unusually lifelike stuffed animals when they had little money. Her father influenced Harriet in his ideals of what a young woman should be like, "spirited, but sort of feminine . . . he didn't like what he called 'bluestockings'." He encouraged her to be a good student, but worried about her becoming a female professor. He was also a "reverse snob," feeling that intellectuals were "vastly overrated and were not very genuine, even though a great many of his friends were intellectuals."

Her parents "tended to have people over a lot," students or people her father knew; "he was always asking people to come home for supper, come and stay a week," which was a positive influence. This pattern has remained with Harriet. "I just have a feeling that you invite people for dinner, or overnight, and sometimes they're people you don't know at all. My father would just like the looks of someone he met and ask them home, and then get to know them better."

Like her mother, Harriet suffered from lack of self-confidence, which was particularly pronounced in childhood. She and her brothers did not go to regular public school much, because her father did not approve. Instead, they were tutored in the home. So Harriet lacked contact with people her own age. Her first year of high school she attended school until Christmas, then spent 2 or 3 months in Arizona in an attempt to get over recurrent sinus infections. She stayed with family friends, mainly reading and taking riding lessons. She notes that she was fat at that time. Her second year her parents hired tutors, who were highly variable in competence, although her mother taught the children well; her father taught them Latin, to which Harriet reacted with passive aggression. Her third year she actually spent in a school and had one or two friends by the end of the year. Her fourth year she studied at home.

Harriet entered a major university, where she met Michael, the man she would later marry, but "I was essentially a nondater because I was socially inept. I'd gotten over the fat by the time I entered college, but I had not any of either the attitudes or the skills of an ordinary teenager. I'd never fussed with my hair. . . . I had no friends, honestly, literally no friends. . . . [I was] very self-conscious, completely unused to being with people my own age. . . . When I got nervous I got too talkative, and the result was that I was constantly saying foolish things, or just chattering on in a stupid way, and then kicking myself afterwards. . . . I was having crushes on occasional fellows . . . who . . . didn't see anything in me. . . . I didn't feel I was an interesting person. . . . I didn't know how to do anything female, I was sort of an amateur, and everybody else were professionals. They all knew how to be women, and I didn't." It was a very lonely time, but Harriet feels this loneliness is universal among teenagers and college students; "I didn't belong to anything, I didn't belong. . . . I was the queer duck, I didn't fit with anybody else, and I was always the outside person." Over the years, Harriet gradually began to feel "socially a little more at ease," but her siblings had similar problems. Her oldest sister is very shy, artistic, friendless, and married to a schizophrenic. A brother she describes as "a delayed adolescent at 50," irresponsible and bright, avoids work like the plague. Other siblings are more socially adapted.

Harriet's first impression of Michael was that he also was very self-conscious. Destined to be a distinguished social scientist, at the time Michael had flunked out of one university and had to do well this time around. They became friends, and he often stayed with her family. "I was very much interested in him, but concealed this I think fairly effectively." He married a girl he had known at his previous university, but they remained friends.

As an undergraduate Harriet found herself loving bacteriology, biology, anatomy, and genetics. She went to graduate school because she received a small scholarship and wanted to get away from home for a while. She disliked graduate biology work, lost weight, and could not sleep, so she decided there was no future for her in graduate biology. She needed something leading to a job and suddenly realized that all the courses she loved were prerequisite for nursing, so she became a nurse. "I think that was my biggest breakthrough, discovering that I really enjoyed it and I liked people, and I got along well with people." She tended to be slow and was put on probation, "and then I hit the three P's that all agreed with me," pediatrics, psychiatry, and public health. In the army for a year, the only nurse at a small southern air station, with a drunken unreliable medical corpsman, Harriet was forced to assume "a lot of responsibility, and I was really wondering what my limits of competence were, and I was pushed right to the limits. And it was a wonderful exhilaration to find that I could do it." After the army she became a visiting nurse on the East Coast. Michael had meanwhile divorced and began to visit her more and more. They were married and had their first child.

Harriet feels that marrying Michael was one of the "best things that ever happened to me. . . . He is very good at encouraging people and bringing out the best things in them." She says they were very much in love. Her natal family had been undemonstrative physically. Her parents seldom touched her, and she disliked it when her father did. "I remember disliking his hands because they were too soft. I liked my mother's hands, the contrast between the two—I remember thinking that my mother's hands were strong and rough from dishwashing, and all the sorts of things she did. . . . I like touching actually . . . [I was] somewhat deprived from touching as a child." She remembers a physician who touched and got close to his patients, even though it was nonsexual, and occasionally he was misunderstood, but she liked him.

Michael was a professor at a top women's college, and they had more children. "Luckily, I've got what you could call a deaf ear. . . . The youngest would come up when he was little, grab hold of my face like this, and say: 'Now, Mummy, listen!' 'Cause I wouldn't listen, and that was a great lifesaver for me. I could be with talkative children without really being bothered by it. . . . I liked having children and raising them. It was something I'd always felt I could do well, and it turned out I could do well, 'cause our children have turned out well." By this she means that they are happy on the whole. "All the children except the oldest one, I think, are miles ahead of me socially, both Michael and me. . . . They're essentially happy, outgoing, well-liked people." Her daughter is a social worker, well liked, has made a happy marriage, and is in good shape financially.

Michael took a position at a major university in the west. Harriet did volunteer work until her children were old enough and then returned to school, with Michael's encouragement, to get her public health nurse credential. The children were attending high school, and they had foreign students living with them as well, so there was often a houseful. Harriet got work as a public health nurse half-time. There was another move to a major midwestern university as Michael became more successful. At this point he became interested in another woman, which precipitated a marital crisis, happily resolved with counseling, but it is a situation about which Harriet is reluctant to speak.

As the children began to leave home, Harriet says she did not experience the discomfort some parents feel. "We were delighted to see them growing up and developing." There were a few episodes of difficulty, but "seeing that my children were turning out okay I felt much more comfortable about myself as a parent. I was a very tentative parent for a long time. I was never sure that what I was telling them was the right thing. . . . They were none of them very difficult children particularly," although she found raising a girl a bit of a challenge because she hadn't had much contact with girls. "I wouldn't say our communication was all that wonderful . . . but we respected . . . and liked each other." Harriet and Michael were at a party one night when their son called and said, "My best girl and I are going to bed together, and she's on the pill, and her mother says it's okay, is it okay with you, too? [laughter]."

Their son was only 15; Michael was shocked that he would "ask permission. . . . I was a bit taken aback, and said: 'Well, she's awfully young, and are you sure you're adequately protected?' And they reassured me, and I said: 'Well, okay, that's the way it is. . . . It's your choice, but at least you are doing all the sensible things about it.' " Harriet says the children are cautious "sort of the way I am," but they don't let their cautiousness get in the way of things they want to do. "Two of them are mountain climbers, but one of them is a very slow mountain climber." She attributes the fact that they turned out well to their intelligence and to her and Michael's cautiousness. Harriet concludes that "my thirties and forties were some of my best years. I think things are getting progressively better."

In her fifties Harriet became active in a suicide prevention center, which "has turned out to be something very important to me. . . . I've known most of the other volunteers for quite a while now, and feel familiar and comfortable with them, and also I've learned that I can help people in crisis. [It's] satisfying. . . . People [are] mostly just lonely and feeling that everybody else is happy, but they're not." (A big illusion?) "A big illusion, right! Just by listening to them and giving a certain amount of rational encouragement—not telling them everything's going to be rosy, but that they can get through the night." Harriet talks about the people she has helped. They are important to her. "Each case I get is a new challenge. It's fascinating. . . . My children have been concerned because I don't have any really personal friends, and for a while there I was getting a bit of counseling and sort of worrying about this, and I tried for a while being more sociable, and I don't think I'm ever going to get on a very personal friend basis with people, because I don't have the background for it, and I don't have the personality." But one of Harriet's fantasies, not shared by Michael, is to become a foster parent. She tells stories about the foreign students whom they've had in their home and how she has been able to enjoy them, even one who was a "holy terror" but has developed into a pretty law-abiding and conservative person.

Harriet marvels at what it's like to be 60. "Here I am 60, and I thought I was going to be feeble and in poor shape. . . . I'm really delighted and surprised to find that at 60 I'm in excellent shape physically (I could be in better), but I do a lot of gardening involving fairly heavy digging, and I think that, generally speaking, I've been very pleased with my getting older, to get to 60 and find that 60 is a good age. You know when you're 20, you think 60 is terribly old, and here I am." She does have an ulcer, which she believes is due to being overly conscientious, feeling that she's not working hard enough or well enough. She tends to blame herself. She and Michael have been fixing up the house for their retirement, although she wants to work as long as possible.

One of the things that makes Harriet happy is "gardening—again it's raising things." If she could come back as anything she pleased "I'd come back as a mother." Her peak experience was being pushed to her limits at the southern army hospital. The death of a beloved neighbor many years ago brings tears to Harriet's eyes. Her regrets include a sexual episode of "petting on a train," when her parents were getting a divorce, and being unwittingly cruel to a retarded child when she was babysitting, for which she has blamed herself all her life. She does find herself getting more fearful of new situations as she gets older.

As for death, "I think it's a cessation of consciousness. It's like a continuous sleep, only you're dead. I also think people are more afraid of it if they've had a poor life, that the people that can manage death adequately are usually the people who feel they have gotten what was coming to them. And those who are fearful of death and really worried about it tend to be people that have not felt they have finished. They haven't got what they wanted to get. They've been cheated." (How have you developed this feeling?) "I think mostly by seeing people that were about to die. The people that fight it most tend to be the people that aren't ready for it because they haven't had a decent life." (Have you found people with rotten lives more willing to die?) "No, they may want to commit suicide, but they can't face death with any sort of equanimity. . . . A good death would be one . . . at an advanced age where preferably you have family or friends with you . . . where you feel you've accomplished something before you died. It may not be a great thing, but you can look back and feel your life has been worth living."

When asked if there is such a thing as a useless life, and how she would describe it, Harriet responds: "I sometimes wonder what the point is in some people's lives, in a lot of people's lives. That's one reason I feel rather strongly that a lot of people shouldn't have been born, because they are sort of doomed from the start to lead either miserable lives or worthless lives . . . someone who's constantly on welfare, who never can earn his own living, who really . . . doesn't have very much feeling of self-worth or self-respect, who maybe spends a lot of time in jail, or being in various kinds of programs trying to get them better. . . . They are lives which are a drag upon the rest of the world. Their lives are a burden to the rest of us, and not much satisfaction to them."

One of Harriet's current patients is a teenager who has just had her second child; her boyfriend is borderline psychotic, "he's often in mental hospitals, he can't hold a job because he gets into fights. She herself is schizophrenic, not overtly so, but she can't have a good relationship with her child. She doesn't even want to pick it up, and her children are just plain deprived, and the best thing I can see to do is to keep her and her boyfriend separated, so they don't have a third, or fourth or fifth child. People would say she ought to have a right to have her children, and lead a normal life, but I don't think, considering who she is and how she's been raised herself, that this is a reasonable expectation. I don't think she's ever going to have a normal life, and I don't think it's fair to leave the children with her, because it means depriving them of a normal life, or even the chance of it. Leaving those children with those parents I think is very unkind, and they should be, not put in foster care, but adopted as soon as possible. People say she ought to have the children, or that he ought to have the children, because he's the one that's more parental, but he can't take good care of them really, and can't raise them. It's very hard. I think adoptive parents would be so much better for these children." (Note the connection with her own childhood deprivation, her own desire to be an adoptive or foster mother.)

Harriet has a recurring dream of a big house, not always the same, "so big that there were people living up on the third and fourth floors of it, and I didn't even know they were there. And yet I'm quite sure that it was my house. . . . I think it's mostly my fantasies of having people in my house." She has a recurrent fantasy of having people of different ages living in her house, "an intergenerational household."

Generally Harriet doesn't believe in psychic phenomena; there are rational explanations for them. She sees as her life theme: "I want to take care of people or things. Another thing . . . I like to set things to rights . . . I'm someone that wants to take care of things or people." Life is worth living "if you get something out of it, if you get rewards like pats on the back. Like being a parent, if your children turn out well, if your child grows well and is thriving, the plants are growing well, and they're thriving, the chickens are growing well—I have chickens, too—that's what I say, I take care of things, it makes a great deal of difference to me. My cats, for instance, they look like healthy cats; I'm trying to get rid of their fleas, [but] they're well behaved. . . . But you get out of life what you put into it. . . . Life is meaningless if you get no response from life, if you don't see any results from your being there. . . . If you can once get a person to feel that their being alive makes a difference, even if it's a very small thing, like the kid [the "holy terror" who was living with them] raising marijuana. I didn't really come down on him hard immediately when I found out about it, because I said, my gosh, here's something at least that's constructive that he's doing. He's raising plants [laughter]."

Harriet concludes the interview with "an example of my deprived teenage years—I became friendly with two other 'social outcasts' in our community who also had no friends—one was obviously homosexual, and the other didn't know he was. They did not know each other."

Thematically, a sense of deprivation runs through Harriet's life history, a distance from others, self as "queer duck," socially incompetent, lonely, not belonging, shyness, incompetence as a female, friendlessness, outcast. This loss, felt most keenly as a child, is still with her; her own children worry about her lack of personal friends, and she even sought counseling for it until she accepted that this was her personality and her background. This distance is transcended by the closeness involved in helping others, a kind of rational parenting to children, patients, students, people contemplating suicide, even plants and animals, all of which are viewed by Harriet as "accomplishment" and making life worthwhile. Her husband has acted as her mentor as well, encouraging this aspect of herself. Thus, she generates life and closeness in those she helps, while remaining apart herself. The L/T life theme is loss through distance from people, a sense of not belonging, loneliness; this is transcended through mothering service to others—children, students, patients, suicidal individuals, even animals, although the set-apartness returns and is finally accepted. Core theme: Distance from others versus closeness through mothering service.

Harriet's personality profile shows a balance between thinking and feeling functions: introversion as one would expect; sensing over intuition, again expected, considering her answers to the questions on paranormal experiences; and judging over perceiving, for an introversion, sensing, thinking, judging profile. Such people are "serious, quiet, earn success by concentration and thoroughness. Practical, orderly, matter-of-fact, logical, realistic and dependable. See to it that everything is well organized. Take responsibility," and are not easily distracted (Myers, 1962, 1977).

The protocol as a whole is transcendence oriented, with an emphasis on the *challenge* of problems. It is rated as demonstrating high loss, high transcendence, although the loss pole is more difficult to assess as the distance from others is a serious and pervasive one, especially early in the protocol. It should be noted that Harriet is satisfyingly engaged in transcending the losses of others, which are high.

Theoretical Analysis

One way of thinking about a metaphorical system is that it is how the individual perceives that the world is ordered, the societal organization. These perceptions will then influence that order. We can begin with the smaller world of Harriet's childhood and then move through her discovery of her place in the world, her relationship to it, and her present world view.

Harriet's parents were very different from each other. Her father dreamed and talked and wrote, but took little action and carried few things to completion (outside of his teaching), or his action was inconsistent with his words. His book was a lost accomplishment, a tragedy, potential not brought to fruition. Harriet's mother accomplished; her actions brought desired results. Harriet disliked her father's "soft hands" and loved her mother's, strong with accomplishment (dishwashing, etc.). Her father was sickly and did little around the house, and died; her mother is still vigorously chopping wood at 86. They differed in the handling of money as well, her father running them into debt over books (ideas, possibilities, dreams) and her mother triumphing over this with handmade Christmas gifts, products of her considerable skill (actualities, realities). We have seen life histories in which such a split between parents resulted in a split self in the child with problematic results (Lexie and Lorellen, for example), but this does not seem to have happened with Harriet. She has identified with her mother; she raises people and plants in no-nonsense fashion.

Her father's influence shows in her full household and in the fact that she married a professor, like her father (although different in that he is world renowned for his accomplishments and has published widely). He also fell for another woman while in his fifties. However, Harriet seems to be mainly her mother's child and without the conflict of being both. Her father's romanticism, dreaming, and idealism led to nonaccomplishment and death, which seem to be metaphorically related in Harriet's system. If the undesirable death is not being "finished," what about her father's?

The split that Harriet did experience was from others, and also other. She has happy memories of her family life, brothers, and their many guests, but she did not learn to get on well with others her own age, particularly females. She did not, then, experience the normal learning and identification process which would have informed her of her identity as a female her age. On the contrary, she was a tomboy, fat, did little with her hair, did not know the art of makeup or how to flirt or behave in front of boys, and was shy and self-conscious—"a queer duck," alien, on the outside looking in, able to be friends only with other outcasts, who also were different from their own sex, being homosexuals. Otherwise, she was dateless and boring. Who Harriet was, her self, was an outsider, and in view of her later development it seems reasonable to say that some aspects of self were emerging, others not yet actualizing, a hurtful unevenness in her development. During adolescence, then, Harriet's view of the world was as more competent than herself in social areas, a kind of inner sanctum from which she was excluded.

There is a sense of distance here between Harriet and others, an inability to be with them on their terms, to be close. A different child might have retreated in the face of such persistent rejection, withdrawn possibly into her own world. Schizoid personality and schizophrenia form a latent theme in this history: the other girl with whom she shared school in her home sounds schizoid; one of her brothers married a schizophrenic; when Harriet got out of the army she stayed with and helped a schizophrenic friend; she is concerned now about the schizophrenic young mother who can't relate to her child. Instead of retreating, Harriet helps others overcome their retreat. This is a major pattern in Harriet's life; she overcomes her own loss by helping others overcome theirs, and distances close temporarily.

The distance from others has inhibited Harriet's full development of her self. She has transcended this loss by giving life to others, consistently and abundantly. She raises children, plants, and animals; she has foreign students visit for a year; she would have been willing to adopt children had she and her husband been unable to have their own; she fantasizes about being a foster parent and also about filling her house with people of different generations— an unwed mother whose child she could care for during the day while the mother worked, an old lady in the back room who couldn't manage the stairs, middle-aged people on the second floor. Even her dreams are of a full house, people she doesn't even know. She brings the dying back to life, be they physically ill or suicidal, and this work is fulfilling to her. We could also see some of this "rearing" or "raising" as closing distances between people, as well as being responsible for those who can close distances. Her strong identification with a mother who performed good works (not her tenderness) is probably central here. Her children are happily married and are much more competent socially—part of this is her creation. She has created alternate lives that, to some extent, transcend aspects of her own. Touchingly, they worry about her ability to have friends, as they have.

Harriet's siblings had difficulties in social competence, too, and they have not all fared as well as she. One is shy, friendless, married to a schizophrenic girl; another is socially adept; another is a counselor, presumably transcending distance in a fashion similar to Harriet's—ministering to the needs of others is a way of compelling closeness; another is an adolescent in his fifties, an irresponsible father. It is possible that success in transcendence stemmed from positive family influences as well as the intelligence and cautiousness to which Harriet attributes the success of their childrearing.

It would be tempting to see Harriet's mothering as "nurturing," but it doesn't quite feel this way. There still is a strange kind of distance between Harriet and her activities. Love is never mentioned. Raising anything is an accomplishment, and that is where the good feelings seem to lie. There is a sense of completion, finishing business, the same finishing her father did not experience, the completion that makes one able to face death with equanimity. However, there may be a hesitation in Harriet, New England born and bred, to express feelings. Still, one returns to her statements that her children, plants, and animals are "growing well and thriving," and it is this slightly distanced view that makes life worth living. In other words, Harriet performs many loving acts, and yet they are seen as things in need of doing because life, growth, and thriving are of value.

Harriet's world view is consistent with her development. People are seen in terms of how and whether or not they can maintain themselves, make their contributions to the world, properly raise their children, hold jobs, remain mentally healthy. If they cannot, then the worthwhileness of their lives is called into question, apparently for themselves and for the society on whom they are "a drag." They deprive their children of a normal life. This world view seems to be a direct descendant of her own view of her own childhood as "deprived" of normal human interaction and of her concern for good mothering. Some of her alternate lives, her siblings, have shown her who she might have been, not raising her children normally. She has overcome this again and again in many ways. Her view of people at the end of their lives is that they die within the context of how they've lived, and particularly if their lives have been worth living, if they have accomplished something, made a difference, not been cheated of being who they need to be; then they can accept death. They are complete, as are their lives, they "have done," in both senses of the phrase.

Harriet transcends the loneliness of her past through her work with suicidal people, who she feels are basically lonely. She transcends her outcastness by having a full house, with many foreign (alien) students; she transcends her distance from others by nursing and mothering, compelling closeness and touching; she transcends her separation and uncertainty of who she is by giving life to those who are separate and uncertain.

What are the values underlying Harriet's history, and how might they reflect and influence the societal manifestations of loss and transcendence? Clearly, productivity is one value. Harriet partially invalidates her father's existence by saying he was not who he professed to be, rather a dreamer and a "parlor rebel," a man who polished rather than published. As we have noted, productivity of goods and services leads to survival of the society; in a society where worldly survival is valued (most societies), productivity must be of high worth. It leads to life. What *good* are dreams, opinions, and ideas if they happen only within the individual or in the parlor? Competence and achievement or accomplishment, other aspects of productivity, are also values. Harriet's peak experience was being pushed to the limits of her competence as a nurse. If one does not achieve, one feels cheated, is more fearful of death. Those who lead lives that do not promote other lives, are a drag, should not have been born.

Harriet's mother chops wood, bought the tickets to her father's dreams and plans, had high standards and ideals, was a strict disciplinarian. Action is to be taken, and according to stringent rules. "A good spanking set things to rights" with a hairbrush, and "fractious" children got doused with cold water. "Castor oil was a cure-all." Here is an interesting example of societal values undergoing change. Today, spanking, especially with an implement, is often regarded as child abuse. In those days it was not. What does this say about our views of bodily injury, pain, and possibly loss, against the standards of correct behavior inculcated in the past? Clearly, the value of one rises as the other falls. Or perhaps the actions that warranted spankings in other days, such as dishonesty, are not as clear-cut today.

Another value is the notion of community with others, sharing of both meals and home. These are values that Harriet grew up with and that she holds today. Another is male-female differences and the professionalization of femininity within a societal norm, of which she felt deprived. Implicit in this is the societal value of being enough like others to "fit in." Society is a space of limited dimensions that can stretch only so far.

When Harriet speaks of her children, she reveals other values. She says they are happy, outgoing, well liked. Her daughter is happily married, financially well-off, and a social worker. Promoting life is a major value for Harriet. She prevents death by suicide, says children, cats, chickens, and plants are "thriving"—they are living strongly. Cautiousness is part of her nature, and she speaks of her children in terms of how cautious they are. This is linked to being sensible. It is sensible to be cautious, because life is preserved, as we saw in Chapter 10. Health is still another value; she is surprised at how fit she is at 60, and her mother chops wood at 80.

Harriet has told us the family myth, defining the members of her family in terms of the values she holds. If their values are different, they may tell the myth differently, possibly to preserve their own role in it. The siblings may agree that their father was a dreamer, particularly if they do not themselves tend in that direction. Certain aspects of a life are emphasized and others de-emphasized. We have no sense of what and how he taught, presumably a major aspect of his existence, but one unobserved by the children. A good part of the family myth (see Chapter 9) is the myth of the place of individuals within the family and the place of the family within the community and the broader society.

Thus we see that a number of basic values underlie Harriet's history as she relates it, that these values are part of the basic fabric of societal values, and that she and others are in pain to the extent they do not conform to them. When she was not in school, the creation of her self by society in its own image was limited, a difference keenly felt. In her daily life Harriet sows these values, broadcasting them like seeds over all with whom she comes in contact, just as she has to us, by deed and word, by vote, and by tax payments. The society reflects Harriet's values back to her, and those of others, just as it has taught her and continues to teach. Individuals and their society are in an assimilation-accommodation relationship, to apply the Piagetian (1952) notion societally, and this is how both survive. When societal accommodation would be too great, the individuals may elect revolution.

CONCLUSIONS

Society exists to regulate the transcendence of loss. Individual lives dem-onstrate the relationship of the individual to society and reflect the successes and failures with which society has dealt with individual loss, as well as the extent to which it has inflicted loss in its attempt to regulate, avert, and transcend group loss. We saw in Chapter 10 that what is pathological in one society may not be pathological in another; the therapist is often faced with a society that does not fit the individual, rather than vice versa. Therapists are in a special position to recognize where society needs changing, to conduct clinical research, and to become a political force for that change, as well as to reflect it in their therapy.

For example, the use of family systems approaches to behavioral disorders recognizes the immediate environment as affecting individual pathology and health. But it ignores the impact of the larger community, in which standards, values, behaviors, and activities such as the taking and selling of drugs affect both the family and the individual. To recognize the family system without recognizing the societal and cultural systems is as bad as the old view that ignored the family and treated the patient as an isolated entity or, even worse, simply blamed the mother.

Therapists treat those addicted to general transcendence. Addiction has physiological and psychological components. It may begin with a physiological predisposition (i.e., alcoholism) or certain behaviors may lead to a physiological problem (such as bulimia). In both cases, the problem begins with attempts to transcend loss, and eventually transcendence becomes loss, whose transcendence is pursued with the same behaviors. The challenge for the therapist is to break the cycle by recognizing the losses and recognizing the value of transcendence to that individual's identity, finally providing alternative modes of transcendence, often situational.

If the therapist could prove to his client, once and for all, that she will never die, would he effect a cure?

Time and Death

As we have observed throughout this book, time and death are intimately related to loss and transcendence. In this chapter I begin with cultural, perceptual, and biopsychological analyses of time in our daily and metaphorical lives, illustrating with the history of Elaine. In the second section I elucidate the paradox of death's ambivalent relationship to both loss and transcendence; Em's wonderful story helps to show aspects of this, as well as the influence of death on the lives of other interviewees. Finally I conclude the chapter and the book fittingly, with some "last words."

ROLE OF TIME IN LOSS AND TRANSCENDENCE

Time is the measure of our progress from birth to death. Its control is a supreme value that underlies our existence. When we control time, we control death.

In our Western culture we attempt to control time in a myriad of ways. One way is to *measure* it. We mark the seconds, minutes, and hours on our clocks and watches. We may even be obsessed with setting them to exact time; a watch too slow is a loss of the minute or two we thought we had; a watch too fast may rob us equally, threaten us with waiting or wasting, or it may be a very small gift that we give ourselves—that is, we find to our delighted surprise that we have more time, and life, than we thought we had. We mark the days, weeks, and months on calendars, each slash mark on the calendar signifying an accomplishment or a loss; with a single stroke of pen or pencil we accept our destruction, and each day as yet unmarked signifies a hope.

We mark the years with celebrations of birthdays and anniversaries by which we say, "I'm glad you were born," or "I'm glad we married," or "congratulations on the length of time you've lasted," and we flatter the individual by attributing her survival to her own efforts, implying that continuity lies within her control. We are labeling birthdays and anniversaries with numbers, but their meanings are ambiguous. At some point in adulthood, the candles on the cake abruptly dwindle from the number signifying an age "plus one to grow on" to a single candle signifying an age that is indeterminate. We say we cut their number because there are "too many." Too expensive to buy, perhaps? Too many to wish on and blow out with a single breath? Too tedious to place on a cake one by one? Too insulting, or revealing, or shameful? No cake could possibly hold them all? Who's counting? With such rationalizations, we disguise the fact that it is at this point that the number of years lived is greater than the number left—an embarrassment, a terror better left unspecified. Birthday candles come in packages of 24 and 36; they do not come in larger ones.

Wedding anniversaries are marked with gifts of increasing value, from paper to silver, gold, and diamonds for those who can afford them. These symbolize the value of a long-time marriage to the society that survives by stability.

Another way of controlling time is simply to *lie* about it. We dye our hair, advance our birthdates by a few years, fight the fat that adds years to our appearance (and takes years from our lives), struggle to keep up with a secret language that is always being reinvented by teenagers, allowing such phrases as "grody to the max" and "totally awesome" to trip awkwardly from the tongue. We pretend to greater interest and involvement in the newest fads and fashions than we may really have. Like Calvinists, to whom the mere appearance of being one of the "elect" destined for Heaven somehow metamorphosed into the feeling that they indeed might be—like them, we may be younger than we are, at least for a while. By fooling others we might succeed in fooling ourselves, particularly as we are treated as we appear. Somewhere along the way, our real ages catch up with us in a rush.

Some of us manage to control time by *ignoring* it, by addiction to general transcendence or by dropping out. Alienation is one way of rejecting how society has regulated the time of its members and seeks to regulate our own. We cannot tolerate the alienated individuals—street people, drunks, and madmen—who have no regard for their time, because they end up robbing us of ours and threaten our denial of the realities, which is a necessary facet of our acceptance of social control.

By making *plans* great and small, detailed schedules and complex organizations of activities, we may control time, extending by filling it to overflowing. Somehow, the more detailed our planning, the more we manage to squeeze in, the more living we do, then the fuller our lives (or so we think) and, by extension, the longer. Time pressures us when we feel that much is left undone, we miscalculated, we were interrupted (robbed of time), we took a break deserved or undeserved, we lost. The overfilled vacation may be exhausting, although it flies.

Social *conventions* are still another means of controlling time. They vary with the culture, the geographic area, the social class, the situation. To wait is to lose one's valuable time, a fraction of one's life. Those who are kept waiting lead lives less valuable than those who keep them waiting. A person's time is valuable to the extent that she is engaged in saving the time of others. The doctor keeps her patients waiting; her time is perceived as more valuable, because she saves lives—and time—for others. The higher the businessperson in the corporate or governmental structure, the more timesaving devices he has in the form of secretaries, chauffeurs, and others who save his valuable time by performing duties that free him for work he alone is skilled to do, work that will eventually lead to the saving of money (time), a sector of the lives of those to whom he is responsible, himself, his family, his stockholders, his employees, his voting constituency.

A most common, although unspoken, demonstration of power or dominance in the social hierarchy is to keep someone waiting, to be engaged in one's own more important affairs, a telephone call to one's stockbroker, perhaps, while the budding actress in the outer office must sit and dream—or scheme. Secretaries are experts at assigning time values to all with whom they are in contact; they do not routinely place all telephone calls on hold while they finish business with the applicant at the desk before them or vice versa. The message of whose time, or life, is more valued and whose may be frittered away for a few minutes, hours, or days is quite clear. Secretaries play amusing games with each other on the telephone: "Is Mr. Jones in, please? Mrs. Smith is calling." "Is Mrs. Smith on the line?" "No, I'll put her on as soon as Mr. Jones is on the line." "Why don't you put Mrs. Smith on the line while I put Mr. Jones on the line. Mr. Jones, Mrs. Smith is on the line." "Hello, Mrs. Smith?" "She'll be right with you, sir." Mr. Jones has been one-upped; he has been told his life is not quite as important and worthy of length as is that of Mrs. Smith. For his secretary's sake, we hope his wait is only a matter of seconds!

It is often said that "time is money" to the salesman, because the faster he sells you, the more time he has to sell someone else. Cabbies race us to our destinations not simply because we are in a hurry. But the reverse of the equation holds as well—money is time. Money is for better food, shelter, medical care, leisure, relief of stress in little and great luxuries, better neighborhoods with greater protection from crime. And money is for the distraction from thoughts of death that "things" provide. We are superior to the refrigerator, and if it will last 15 years, surely so will we! It is no accident that longevity is associated with higher socioeconomic status (Butler & Lewis, 1983). The bitterness of class and ethnic struggles is not born of envy; it is a struggle to survive in the most literal sense, to wrest a normal or extended life span from those others who would live beyond it. The rich buy the time of the poor. We pride ourselves on not being bought, but we are. The waitress waits.

Time is power, and whoever controls it is powerful. The more time a society controls, requiring military service and forms filed, the more powerful it is, and the more autocratic the government is likely to be. Feudal lords and plantation owners possessed *all* the time of their serfs and slaves.

It is a saying among clinical psychologists that patients who are early for their appointments are anxious, those who are late are hostile, and those who are on time are compulsive! Time is the dimension of their neuroses (and they're all neurotic!), expressed either in anxiety to conserve it (ultimately expended in waiting), in a hostile attempt to steal it (ultimately robbing themselves, as the clinician's hour is not elastic), or in a compulsion to save as much as possible without inflicting its loss on someone else, who would be sure to inflict some loss on them in return. When we behave within the dimension of time toward one another, we are saying something about how we feel toward that person. (I'm late because I don't want to come here, you're of no value to me, your life is worthless.) We must negate such implicit statements with apology.

We control time by the use of our *memory*. There is a double meaning in the word "immortality." First, it means to live forever; second, it means being remembered forever, either in one's children or in one's works. Because we cannot have the former, we seek the latter. We adjust our own memories. We do not "speak ill of the dead" because we would not be ill-spoken of ourselves when our time comes, and we try not to remember ill of them, either. Individuals in their twenties remember the traumas of childhood, but as they age, traumas fade, and the past takes on a more positive glow; even the worst can be remembered as camaraderie, or as pulling through; life *must* have been worth living, or our integration, meaning, and transcendence are incomplete. Jane Rhyne (personal communication, 1979) found in her art therapy research that the young think more about the past than do the middle-aged. She says the young are "in it."

The onset of such organic mental disorders as Alzheimer's, which, contrary to stereotype, is due to disease rather than to aging and is present in 2 to 4 percent of the population over 65 (American Psychiatric Association, 1987), is often characterized by remembrance of things in the distant past and forgetfulness of things in the recent past. But perhaps things in the distant past—how the children grew, vacations, old work colleagues and friends— are more worthy of remembrance than the clinician's standard test question "What did you eat for breakfast?" Past experiences could be seen as more necessary to a logical integration of self as one ends one's life, as one constructs the final meaning of it. To what extent might this influence physiological brain changes and atrophy?

All loss is ultimately loss of time, which is loss of life and of whatever we value in life—love, money, pleasure. We live by many metaphors of time, as Lakoff and Johnson (1980) pointed out. All transcendence is attempted or partial control of this loss of time. Time may hang heavy on our hands. Time kills, and we, in turn, kill time. We are at war, and time is the enemy. We kill time with general transcendence, with alcohol, drugs, TV, movies, sports, art, music, hobbies, religion, travel, and literature, and even with love and work. But past a certain point, general transcendence may kill us in return and must thus be controlled by society and by ourselves. Many forms of killing time are potentially addictive and suicidal. There may be a continuum between drugs, alcohol, some sports on the one hand, and suicide on the other. Culture approves art, music, literature, and religion more than drugs and alcohol, because the former are less potentially lethal and it is more "altruistic," "philanthropic," and "prosocial" to help others "killing time" than to simply be immersed in your own. The experience of timelessness, or escape from time, may eventually take over so great a part of the life of individuals and of society that activities that preserve life—work, proper nutrition, exercise, productivity, enforcement and passing on of society's rules—are curtailed. The experience of timelessness is the transcendence closest to the ultimate transcendence, and those addicted to any one form are metaphorically addicted to death, "half in love with easeful death" (Keats, in Quiller-Couch, 1943, p. 744).

Time is the measure, not only of our personal history over the life span but also of the world history in which our personal history is embedded. The measuring of time passes into decades, centuries, and epochs, to the history of the past and the hope of the future. Because our lives are part of these, we may find some sense of continuity in our awareness of them. Our lives are at once insignificant beside them and significant within them, depending on whether we feel ourselves as on the outside looking in or as somehow making a contribution to the flow. Immortality pervades London, the streets, squares, restaurants, buildings, institutions, drinks, and sandwiches named for royalty, nobility, and historical events. These belong to the people. The people are part of them, and so they endure.

World history is the account of losses to whole groups of people and how they were transcended; thus, it is personal history on a mass scale. It includes national we concepts, who we are, and the myths of how we got to be that way. History is the integration phase of the individual and national L/T structures, the story of their meaning in the aggregate along the dimension of overwhelming events, a myth with grains of truth but dependent on the point of view of the historian. The American Revolution happened, but the account is different in British and U.S. history texts and indeed is revised in this country as the concept of who we are and the myth of how we got to be that way require changing (the place of ethnic minorities, for example). That Britain and the United States are long-term allies accounts for less difference between mythologies than if they had been enemies.

The losses of history are often loss of life in wars or plagues, loss of freedom, of culture, of land, and of money; these losses are usually conflictual in nature, the transcendence of one group causing loss to another (as with the dysfunctional family system). Historical time may be traversed in memory, vicarious or immediate, and in imagination, but future time may be encompassed only in imagination. Both are susceptible to distortion, the past through the necessity to make sense of what has happened and the future through expectation. History helps us to know people, places, and events that we can never really know; in that sense, it represents an irretrievable loss of time to us, which can be only approximately recaptured through study and story. We say we study history to learn from the past, but historical periods bear fragile similarity to the present and, in any case, we do not seem to learn what we purport to; we have hardly erased violence from the face of the earth.

Like personal history, world history is characterized by losses that are on time, off time, or time irrelevant, although most of the larger events seem to be of the irrelevant type. This may be a matter of perspective. War has no acceptable developmental timetable (although some claim it erupts in cycles and is predictable), nor is natural disaster ever age appropriate, at least not enough for prediction. Even long periods of "growth" such as the industrial revolution, though molecularly developmental, seem to be time irrelevant as a whole, or on a molar level. We would not have expected it to come before the Stone Age, admittedly. We can trace out forces that led to the overthrow of absolute monarchy in England in 1689, but there is less of inherent necessity. Insofar as a nation may be characterized as "warlike" or "peaceful," we might speak of dispositional transcendence on the historical level, but the situational seems to predominate, with the strong personal dispositional tendencies of eminent individuals and leaders. Nonetheless, history is subject to the same psychological and metaphorical analysis, description, explanation, and cautious prediction as individuals and groups. Sometimes today's science fiction is tomorrow's history.

As has been shown, time is the measure of our development over the life span. When an aspect of the transcendent self passes into the lost self, time ceases to exist; it is a measure imposed from without by the culture from the day of birth. For the individual, the past is part of his present activity (Sherover, 1975) and his future aspiration (Heidegger, 1962). Because, what is already within the lost self is no longer active, it can grow, change, be subtracted from or added to only with difficulty; new events and relationships are added to the lost self, and these may sometimes revise the perception of the older experiences; the individual may reconstrue her past (James, 1890; Kelly, 1955) but cannot change the *fact* that her child died or her house burned to the ground. An individual event or relationship in the lost sector often becomes a frozen image, so we feel as though the lost me was active only yesterday. We try to go home again; we greet an old friend with the words "you haven't changed" not only to flatter her but also because her external image is so similar to that in our memory that we assume her internal structure is, too; it is a way of denying changed L/T structures and preserving old bonds. As James (1890) has pointed out, we strive for a "sense of sameness."

Time is differently conceived in different cultures. In the Mexican culture, lateness, informally dropping in, putting off until tomorrow are all perfectly acceptable (Campbell, 1986). In some cultures, there is no yesterday or tomorrow, no past or future, all that happens is in the present. This makes sense in that the inner lost experience converges with the outer transcendent. Some cultures use the "time to boil rice" as a basic unit (Ornstein, 1969). The culture demands culture-specific revisions of interpretations of past time. The lost self needs to assimilate and to accommodate new transformations from transcendent to lost. Both cultural revisions and the assimilation-accommodation process can lead to a revision of lost time.

We have seen that time is a basic metaphor of the arts and that one of society's ultimate purposes is the regulation, valuation, and preservation of time as life. And we have found that pathology, both physical and emotional, has time as its cultural referent, in that pathology distorts time and life in some fashion and that it also arises as a form of dealing with time and its limits. As we deal with time, our different pathologies manifest themselves. Multiple personalities are frozen at different ages. For the depressive, time is slowed, and for those afflicted with other pathologies, time is disordered, impulsive, nonexistent. It seems that when we fight time in a certain way, we are more prone to heart disease; when we despair of it, we may be more prone to cancer (Jenkins, 1971; Friedman & Rosenman, 1974).

This is not all. We can see that time is a dimension of many of the inborn temperament characteristics discovered by Thomas and Chess (1977). For example, rhythmicity is a way of regulating time, for both child and caretakers; adaptability refers to immediacy, persistence and attention span to duration of time. These are ways of binding time, preventing chaos and disorganization.

It is a social value to appear as though one is filling up one's time and to proclaim the value of others in terms of time filled. "Busy" housewives chat about and compete over how much they can cram into their time by listing what they have to do. They even lay the foundations of friendship by asking, "How do you ever get so much done?" They downplay the hiring of a cleaning woman or say it takes so much time to direct her work, and she does the least time-valued chores. As "timesaving" devices have been invented, standards have been raised to fill time; with an automatic washer and dryer, there is now time to be cleaner, so clothes should not be worn more than once, in order that housewives may fill their time and talk about how many loads of laundry *need* doing.

Elkind (1981) has shown that there is increasing pressure on the "hurried child" to do more in less time at an earlier age and to grow up quickly, by doing things characteristic of those older. I believe the hurried child then becomes the hurried adult, squeezing more and more work into the 8-hour (?) day so that another employee will not have to be hired, often holding down two jobs—those of parent and employee. Workaholism is bemoaned, but it is also demanded and fashionable among yuppies, for example. There is increasing greediness for the experiences that money can buy; stuff a life, and it makes the human enterprise meaningful. Then the worker on the tread-mill of office and child-tending, with no time for reflection, leading Ivan Illych's unexamined life (Tolstoy, 1960), wonders why life is meaningless.

I know a man whom I secretly call Tim-on-the-run. That he never walks, or has time to stop and pass the moment in idle (?) chatter, you have already guessed. You'll never see him not rushing, not taking the stairs two at a time, with a strained look on his gray face, car to office, office to meeting. You'll never see him just sitting, contemplating trees, or eating without reading and talking on the phone. I do not know what he does while he is sleeping, but I suspect he tries not to waste his time and so passes it in solving problems (he is a chemist). I often wonder what he does with the time he saves. Does he bank his time in a savings account—at the risk of lethal disinterest?

We use time as a measure of our success in our various endeavors. Neugarten (1968) has written that we have "age clocks" that tell us how far along we should be at a given age and what it is appropriate for us to do or not to do, although these age-behavior prescriptions have become more flexible and permissive in recent years (Neugarten, 1987). These clocks are social, in contrast to our biological clocks (Campbell, 1986). We are born with the biological clocks, but we internalize the social ones. Time is one measure of loss—on time, off time, time irrelevant. The man who has not married by age 30, the woman who has not borne children by 35, the dentist who returns to school at 40 consider themselves "off time" and must integrate their self-concepts accordingly. When we speak of a marriage that has lasted 30 years, we call it "successful." When it ends at 5 or 15 years in divorce, we call it "failed." Thus length of marriage is very often considered the measure of its success; that it may have been so successful it allowed the individuals within the partnership to grow into divorce, or that people who have remained in a marriage 30 years *may* have done so at considerable cost to individuation, is not considered. The same is true of time on a job. George Vaillant (1979) and Glen Elder (1974) both use such measures as time in marriage, on the job, in a single geographic location as criteria of successful (stable) or un-successful lives. As Brewster Smith points out (personal communication, 1979), criminologists use time out of jail as a measure of the success of various programs.

The subjective experience of time continues to be one of the great mys-teries of life, tackled by such philosophers as Bergson (1950), Heidegger (1962), and Sartre (1969) as well as by scientists. The new science of chrono-biology is making progress in answering traditional questions: Is time a sense, like vision or hearing? Does it have a physiological base in the brain or a single, internal, master clock comparable to the visual or auditory cortex, or are there several clocks? Is the sense of time innate, or do we learn it as we grow? Does our perception of time vary with our personalities? Do many events, stimuli, or activities within a given period of time make the time seem longer or shorter?

The greatest minds have wrestled with the subjective concept of time and disagreed (Orme, 1969). In ancient Greece, time was regarded as recurring in cycles; as an illusion or a mere numbering process invented by the mind (Aristotle); as paradoxical, for example, Zeno's problem of Achilles trying to catch the tortoise, which will have moved forward to another point by the time Achilles reaches its starting point, so that Achilles can never catch up with it; as related to spatial change (Archimedes and Zeno); as distinct from motion (Plotinus); more recently as arising from the succession of ideas (Locke, Berkeley, Hume); as dependent on memory (Mill); as related to awareness (Wundt and James); as having no reality—on the contrary, past, present, and future are merely relationships (McTaggart, Bradley, Russell); as subjective; as a universal form of intellect; as absolute, continuously flowing (Newton); as part of a four-dimensional world with a space-time continuum (Einstein), which the mathematician Minkowski pictured as an orthogonal rotation, showing that "events taking place at the same time but in different places in a moving system, will be considered by a ground observer as taking place at different times," the relationship being reciprocal (cited in Orme, 1969). All of these concepts seem to contribute to a definition of what time is, if indeed it is; but they are observations by minds within time, bounded by it, unable to think outside it, and they *all* take the individual as point of reference. We know that time has no beginning and no end but that *our* time within all time does, and this is what may be lost. If we lived forever, time would be eternal, a measure only if we aged infinitely, and Sartre believed that then life would be meaningless (1969).

We may think of contemporary concerns with time in terms of measurable immediate experience, longer subjective periods of elapsed times such as past, present, and future, internal time, and the development of a time sense.

The current scientific investigation of time has involved two major factors, those of duration, or how long events last, and succession, or the intervals between events (Fraisse, 1984). There continues to be a great amount of research on the estimation of duration and succession. Earlier, Fraisse (1963) postulated that the "watched pot never boils," that is, that expectations raised the estimate of duration. There is some evidence that numerous stimuli increase the experience of time duration (Ornstein, 1969; Fraisse, 1984), that when we fill our time, we lengthen it. James (1890) speculated that time filled with interesting stimulation would seem short while being experienced but long while looking back. However, Treisman (1963) reported lengthening more frequent in her bored subjects, who supposedly had fewer stimuli within a given time span. A vacation passes very quickly, and yet we feel as though we have been away much longer because so much has happened. Thus it appears that relatively empty time is perceived as passing slowly while experienced and quickly when looking back at it, whereas with time well filled, the reverse is true.

It was thought that a single "master clock" would be found that regulated all internal rhythms, but apparently this is not the case. There are at least two, and probably there are more (Campbell, 1986). These clocks run at different rates; perhaps this variation evolved so that the individual's biology and behaviors would be unpredictable to any who might prey on him, as is hypothesized with animals.

In his fascinating account of the new science of chronobiology, entitled *Winston Churchill's afternoon nap,* Jeremy Campbell (1986) posits that the timing of biological events is adaptive to cosmic cycles. He compares body clocks to "an orchestra, a silent orchestra made up of numerous players under more than one conductor, each contributing in special ways to the harmony and complexity of the whole" (p. 15). He points out that many of the body's various activities have rhythms that are not only circadian in nature (although they approximate 25 hours rather than 24) but also may vary over 90-minute, weekly, or monthly periods. Other activities such as speech, music, and hearing depend on rhythm; indeed, those who become deaf may lose a sense of the forward progression of time and feel that it is static. Knowledge of these body times can guide the timing of medication (e.g., for cancer) and medical procedures (e.g., kidney operations). Indeed, Ader (1981) has speculated that circadian rhythms probably influence the endocrine effects on immune processes. Diseases themselves are often rhythmic in progress. Even people who live together often synchronize bodily functions, such as menstruation. Hofer (1984) suggests that bereavement may remove a person to whom the bereaved's inner clocks were synchronized, resulting in the physical discomfort of dissynchronization.

Campbell (1986) cites evidence that light is the most important external factor in the regulation of bodily time. This might suggest that the meaning of light and dark—the equation of dark with death and evil as opposed to the equation of light with life and good, the mythology of dark forces battling the light—may have a biological basis in fact. Campbell points out that darkness dictates increased secretion of melatonin, which seems to increase depressions associated with climate and season (Arieti, 1978).

It is on the intersection of biology with psychology and philosophy that Jeremy Campbell (1986) seems most insightful. He points out that we may have inborn clocks for rhythmic biological activities, but there are no built-in clocks for the *extended* spans of subjective time, such as notions of past, present, and future. This is why we need outer clocks, calendars, and watches. Sartre (1969) has pointed out that even with these the experience of time is only partly factual; it is also partly imagined. Campbell (1986) also suggests that we are not as free as the existentialists surmised because biological clocks determine so many rhythms of our existence. He cites fascinating evidence that existentialists are right in believing that the sense of past, present, and future defines an individual's identity and belief in the meaningfulness of existence. In several experiments, individuals were hypnotized to erase past and future or to erase the present. Much of identity was also temporarily erased.

Physical pathology gives evidence of the possibility of disrupting time perception in the individual. Organic mental disorder may manifest itself in the individual's vivid memory of events in the distant past and her forgetfulness of recent events. In Korsakoff's psychosis, the individual antedates recent events (Orme, 1969); he believes that something that happened 5 minutes ago happened yesterday, and even years are underestimated, although the experience of shorter intervals is less affected. This disease is associated with diminished blood supply or with lesioning. Lesioning of the temporal lobe also produces disruption of the time experience. Lesions on the nondominant hemisphere may result in experiences of déjà vu or jamais vu. Fraisse (1984) sees more of a contradiction between biology and psychology, in that the biological rhythms continue to the end of life (albeit changing), whereas the psychological sense of time may lapse, as with Alzheimer's and Korsakoff's diseases.

These notions of past, present, and future are not innate, like biological rhythms. The time sense develops from childhood on (Piaget, 1970; Friedman, 1982). Very young children link time with daily activities, such as nap time or lunch time, until the stage of concrete operations at about age 7 or 8, when they begin to show notions of past, present, and future.

Campbell (1986) shows that personalities may differ according to their biological rhythms. "Larks" are those whose biological rhythms help them do better work in the morning, whereas "owls" do better work at night. But larks tend to be introverted and owls extroverted!

Campbell also theorizes that the mind has what he terms a "metasense of time" in that, if its intuitions about time are wrong, it can apply logical or rational corrections; for instance, we may feel as though an hour has passed in the dental chair, but we know it has only been about 15 minutes, and we have enough sense to check our watches in such circumstances. In comparing humans to primates, Premack states, "If we think of the concepts that are presupposed by a sense of our own mortality, one of those concepts would certainly be knowledge of time in the full, human meaning of the word" (cited in Campbell, 1986). However, Muggeridge (1974) sees time awareness as a lower order of consciousness when compared to experiences of transcending time, for example, the mystical experience.

From the above, we note that the perception of time is that of our own time within historical or ahistorical time. Our time is bounded, but time itself would be eternity if we did not use it to measure change. Our culture teaches us how it values time. This is modified by our personal concept of how time measures our losses and our transcendence, which are in turn dictated by our histories and our personalities. The more we move beyond time-boundedness, the greater our experience of transcendence, much as Muggeridge has observed (1974).

LIFE HISTORY

We can apply the above discussion to the story of Elaine. We can see her relationship to time as in the nature of a personality disposition. For example, we might classify her as type A. We can also see how her sense of time may have been learned because of the various metaphorical and literal death experiences she has undergone; time as the measure of her life is threatening to her, and so she fights it; however, her fight is culturally embedded, within the behavioral prescriptions and values that surround her.

Elaine

> *"I'm always a big time and motion person. . . . If you're walking from one room to the other, pick up something and take it with you. It's gotta be moved."*

Elaine is an attractive brunette in her early fifties, who is on the phone when I arrive and seems rushed. Even though she has walking pneumonia, she has kept her interview appointment with me. A successful businesswoman and a community leader, her speech is rapid-fire, and she runs her sentences together.

Elaine's mother died when she was a toddler, but she thinks of her as "no dummy," musically gifted, attractive, interested in teaching, a woman of breeding and sophistication, having entered college at 16. Elaine has two memories of her mother: one is of her older brother running away because he had been punished and her mother, distraught, took her to a wading pool, knowing he must be in the neighborhood; the other memory is of her lying in her casket. She died of a chronic disease. "I think that's where I missed my mother most—I would have had a happier home situation. I never had anybody to—like the mother-daughter things, breakfast. I couldn't participate in that sort of thing. All the things that, you know, you like to have someone to confide in, well, I never did, or someone that would take an interest in me like for proms." Elaine feels keenly the loss of what she never had, which must be idealized because the reality is beyond her.

Elaine was raised in a large midwestern city. Her father was the disciplinarian, although, being a salesman, he was gone a lot. She attributes her rapid rise in business to her father: "Dad taught me [to be] methodical and capable. . . . If you're willing to work hard, you're not a slough-off—I've always believed in a day's work for a day's pay." He was also an avid reader and lover of music.

Elaine's brother was accident prone and once fell out of a tree and lay with a back injury for 3 or 4 hours because his friends were afraid to tell. He later went into a high-risk occupation, married someone unsuitable, had an accident, and became an invalid, subsequently dying of an injury-related illness. The son of a housekeeper was also as close as a brother to Elaine, but he left when the housekeeper did. As a child, Elaine roller-skated, played with dolls, had doll tea parties, and made doll clothes. Her grandparents were also a good influence, although her mother's sister died shortly before her mother did, probably of a primitive abortion—not discussed in the family.

In her early teens Elaine and her family moved to a beautiful suburban house of their own, surrounded by wooded areas that she loved. Her father's girlfriend moved in with them and they eventually married, but she shared none of his interest in books or music, and they didn't get along. In addition, she'd told him she could not have children, but she became pregnant, and he felt she had been dishonest with him. Under her influence, they moved from their beautiful house in the midwest to California. Here her attitude changed, and Elaine became the "whipping boy" for the stepmother's frustrations. "She took after me with a pair of scissors a few times [laughter]. She got me in the leg one time. We just taped it up real tight." (What did your father say?) "I don't remember what she told him. He was upset, but she said I had been really mean and nasty, but I really wasn't, although I was confused and began to dislike her extremely. She resented me, I think. Just unhappiness, I think she felt trapped. I was becoming a teenager then. And I can remember all the things that I wanted to do. She'd always find a reason why I couldn't do them. If I wanted to go to the beach on Saturday, I couldn't because of all this work that had to be done. . . . If a friend invited me over for dinner . . . I had to stay and take care of my little half-brother. . . . I think she was just jealous of the fact that I was growing up and I was a young girl, and I had that freedom and was being asked to do these things. She would like to have been where I was."

While Elaine's father's influence was for the better, in that he set strict standards of moral conduct which she passed down to her own daughters, her stepmother's influence was not. "I can't think of one good thing, to be honest with you, that I ever got from my association with her." Elaine did learn not to demean or degrade children, to encourage people, to appreciate each day— that it was not all made for work, as her stepmother seemed to think. Her dad and her stepmother were divorced some time later.

Meanwhile, Elaine left home and put herself through some college by becoming a live-in baby-sitter, which turned out to be an ordeal. "They entertained quite a lot, and it seemed like I would be up until one or two in the morning, cleaning, serving hors d'oeuvres, and then I would be trying to study." She switched to clerical work and then joined the armed forces so that she could get her education on the GI Bill.

As a result of her difficult teens, "I became more self-reliant . . . I figured that I'd have to fight my way through. So instead of being little girlish as I was for such a long time, it seemed like I matured late, but then when I was well into it, I said: 'Hey, you're gonna have to take care of yourself, get out and move'." In the armed forces "I learned to be more open with people and to meet people easier. I learned to appreciate people . . . take direction, take orders, another form of discipline, but I learned to be independent, take charge of myself. . . . You can be whatever you want to be. . . . And you don't blame anyone else for what you're not—your circumstances, your background, your parents, your childhood or whatever—you don't blame anybody." The service also reinforced the methodical and logical approach to a job which her father had taught her. She acted as a kind of troubleshooter for personnel who were having legal problems.

Elaine met her husband in the service, a man who was "a little like my brother in that he was a happy-go-lucky sort of person, very popular . . . fun-loving. . . . He wasn't pushy. And he didn't seem to be out to get me into bed, he was more interested in me as a person." She got out of the service to be with him. She went to business school, became a housewife, and had babies.

Unfortunately, her husband had to be gone a great deal and started having problems with alcohol. Also, "he was a pathological liar. He would prefer to lie to you than to tell the truth. I've never been able to figure that out. But he will admit it himself. It's easier for him to lie than to tell the truth. He'll take the easy route every time for the simplest little things. It's ridiculous, but you live a life of being lied to, and it destroyed all confidence and respect I had eventually. . . . He would come home and immediately blow the bank account." He was also very strict with the children, whom she feels she essentially raised herself. She began to join clubs and churches and found out she had leadership qualities. "I'm always a big time-and-motion person. I always try to make everything work so you don't spend unnecessary time, kind of lump things together and plan your activities. If you're walking from one room to the other, pick up something and take it with you. It's gotta be moved. . . . People who are doers are always the ones that are asked to do, and the ones who volunteer. You learn how to manage your time. And women who don't have anything to do have never learned how to manage their time, really. Once you find out that you *can* be a leader, and you can be efficient, get things done, there's no stopping you [laughter]. You just enjoy the challenge of getting things done."

In her thirties Elaine resurrected her high school interest in the theater and took singing and dancing lessons in order to be in local community theater productions. "You know, sometimes you come up with something that you have an innate talent, which you don't realize you have, and mine was dancing. And in no time I was dancing in variety shows." There was a certain role that "I wanted . . . with all my heart," and even though she felt she didn't have a good voice, she practiced with the accompanist and auditioned. She'd had a previous run-in with the director, but not only did she get the part, she got a "standing ovation every night, got huge applause, got written up in the review. . . . That was probably my crowning achievement in the theater." Her husband hated her participation, however.

Elaine raised her children, and things went quite smoothly until recent years. She had become a part-time beauty counselor, but in her late thirties, as her husband was retired, she went into it full-time. She thrived on the challenge of this as well. "I had to go out and recruit counselors, train them, run weekly sales meetings, write weekly newsletters, help inventory, order, all of that became a business. I ran it out of my home, and [my husband] became involved" and handled the inventory.

During this time Elaine and her husband were having serious problems. He would get drunk, beat her up, and be devastated the next day. One time he "threw me against a door, which had a louvered window, and it was glass, and it cut my back all up, and I fell on the floor . . . and I really hit my shoulders and wrenched my neck, and I was pretty badly cut up. And he would hit me or wrench my arm. . . . I learned to get out [laughter]." This usually took place at night when the children were asleep; he never threatened them. Why did he abuse her? "He was jealous of what I did. A few times it was because he would insist that he was going to go somewhere, and I would hide the car keys. . . . He was just roaring drunk. . . . Or he'd always try to get an argument started, and I would always try to avoid it. . . . If I could get the car I'd take off, not too far away. I'd just go somewhere and park the car" and think about how long it might be before she could go home. This brings tears to her eyes. "I don't like to remember."

Elaine's business was growing by leaps and bounds. "I pulled sales out of those people. I showed them how to sell. I puffed them up and said 'you can do as much as you want to, but if you want to make money, you can. I'll show you how.' I went with my kit door to door and I'd never done it before in my life, loved every minute of it, sold up a storm [laughter]. Went back and said 'We can do it,' to my counselors. 'Anyone who wants to do it, come to me after this meeting and tell me, and I will go out with you, show you your area, and how to do it, and you're going to make money'," and they did. Her husband not only helped her with the inventory but also started a small business of his own. In connection with her sales job she got into radio advertising as well.

Then disaster struck. One day her bosses took her to lunch and told her that her husband had siphoned off many thousands of dollars. His response to her when she confronted him was, "You found out about it?" He skipped town, leaving her both businesses and $52.00 in the checking account with which to feed four kids. Elaine inched her way back to solvency by taking only cash on sales, instructing her people to do likewise, depositing it, and writing checks for next week's supplies plus 10 percent. Her husband came back a few weeks later, having gambled away all their money, and he moved in with another woman, at which point Elaine felt she was really through with him. Her daughter did the inventory work for a while, but this was too much for her with school, so after the debt had been paid back Elaine went into radio advertising and was then hired by a large firm and did marketing for them. They moved to another town.

Elaine found a way to combine her interest and concern for community problems with her love of the theater and of high schoolers. She wrote, directed, and staged a number of productions that were successful. Then, totally unexpectedly, she was fired after many years of work in which she had brought much money to the firm. The boss wanted a personal friend of his in the job and "he wanted me out because I was a woman and I was too strong a woman for him and in the community." She was very hurt, but she feels one must let go of the bad stuff in life; she got another job that requires more aggressive sales work than she's used to but which she'll probably stay in for a time, because she's paid on commission and this is a challenge to her.

At present, her children are generally a disappointment to her. They tend to blame her for the divorce and do not understand what it was about, and she feels they are underachieving. She doesn't think she's really marriageable, because she is too independent. She doesn't mind living alone, and she keeps busy with all kinds of community organizations, usually in a leadership capacity. "I feel my managerial talents—I can handle thousands of people at a time, picnics for 4000 . . . big-band dances for 1400 people. I can influence people, get them to do things, move them around, entertain them."

For leisure she reads *Readers' Digest Condensed Books* and collects antique glassware. "I really enjoy it, it's something I hate to lose, hate to see broken. I use it. Because it's a tie, a link with the past. It means so much to me that people had these pieces of glassware in their homes, in their possession, probably treasuring them . . . and somehow they got all the way from the early 1900s down to me . . . unbroken. Somebody cared enough to take care of these pieces of glass." When asked in what way she is a winner, she says, "I have a good attitude." A loser? "Probably because I can't relate to a man, can't sublimate my independence to be able to be marriageable." The small losses of life "that upset me are when I think of all the stupidity on my part, all the things that get in your way when you're trying to hurry to get out to an appointment, really dumb little things and nobody's fault but your own. That really makes me mad at my myself."

Finally, Elaine says, "I firmly feel that you oughta kind of forget yesterday. Tomorrow is important." She feels you shouldn't dredge up the past, nor should you rest on laurels. "Let go of things that were bad or distasteful, or mistakes you made. . . . You begin to lose your self-confidence" if you don't let go. "Don't dwell on them, 'cause there's always tomorrow, it's a continuation of endless tomorrows—there's your time—endless tomorrows."

The losses that recur throughout Elaine's story are losses within intimate, usually family, relationships. She and her father lost her mother during her early childhood; then he married a woman who caused him further loss—of his house, his independence, his trust in her (when she got pregnant), his relationship to his daughter, and his peace of mind; eventually this marriage, ill-omened from the start by conflicting values and interests, ended in divorce. Her brother similarly was married to someone unsuited to him. Elaine suffered not only a loss in the quality of her relationship with her father but also physical abuse from her stepmother, was exploited by a family with whom she lived, and suffered abuse from her husband as well, an alcoholic who nearly wrecked her career. Her relationships with her children, while smooth initially, are currently disappointing, because they are underachievers and seem to take her ex-husband's part. She is in a positive relationship with a man but seems to be repeating the situations her brother and father found themselves in; his background, interests, and values are quite different from hers. Finally, Elaine lost her job to a close friend of her boss. Relationships for Elaine have been unsuitable, damaging, and destructive.

Elaine leaves no doubt about the nature of her transcendence of loss; it is predominantly situational—her skills in this area are very strong. There are multiple achievements in business, community activities (she holds or has held office in almost every community organization in the area), theatrical triumphs, particularly in churches with high schoolers. She has worked her way out of difficult situations, particularly the debt with which her husband left her but also her escape from home to work her way through college; and she seems to thrive in situations where the odds are stacked against her, such as auditioning for theater parts when she doesn't have the requisite training and getting the part by dint of extreme effort, with subsequent ovations as well. Such achievements are relationships *at a distance,* easier to experience as successful. While people close to her tear her down, people at a distance applaud.

Dispositionally, Elaine places heavy emphasis on being methodical, logical, disciplined, well organized, ordered, on schedule, on getting things done and saving time. The armed forces were perfect for her, but she attributes many of these qualities to her father's guidance. Also, she believes in not looking back, either to losses or successes, and not blaming anyone, taking responsibility for yourself. There is very little general transcendence (which overcomes time as limiting) in her protocol, although she does jog once a week, "play at" a musical instrument, collect antique glass, and read. Her participation in theater and work in general is told from such a situational standpoint that the generality of this transcendence is questionable. She is accomplishing.

The core L/T life theme seems to be unsuitable and destructive relationships versus achievements multiplied by saving time.

Elaine's protocol would be rated as high loss, high transcendence; there is plenty of both. As might be expected, the personality profile showed one who is extroverted, somewhat intuitive, thinking, and judging. She did not have time to complete the Social Readjustment Rating Scale!

Theoretical analysis

Elaine's history sheds light on the place of time within the L/T paradigm, as well as being illuminated by it.

Her race with time predominates over much of her life. She speaks quickly, running sentences into each other (but she does not speak economically, she repeats a lot). She describes herself as a "time-and-motion person. . . . If you're walking from one room to another, pick up something and take it with you. It's gotta be moved." She reads *Reader's Digest Condensed Books,* presumably to save the time that would be expended reading the full texts. She does tap dancing and finds she has a special talent for it—an activity in which speed and timing are criteria of quality. She might be thought of as a type A personality (Friedman & Rosenman, 1974; Friedman & Ulmer, 1984) with her pressured and rapid speech, tendency to do several things at once, and achievement orientation. One can accomplish anything and as much as one wants to if one is only well enough organized. She hates to stupidly allow things to get in her way when she's racing to an appointment. Time can get away from her then, can beat her. One might even think of Elaine as a time collector—not only does she save time; her antique glassware is from another period of time, treasured enough to keep it unbroken, by people idealized as her mother is, unknown. Time is transcended by love here, apparently her only real flow activity besides reading. One can squeeze as much of life into time as possible.

Perhaps it is no wonder there is little general transcendence in Elaine's life. In general transcendence activities, simply listening to music or doing something for the fun of it, for the intrinsic reward rather than for extrinsic rewards like approval and money—in these activities time disappears, is lost, unimportant, forgotten, of no concern. But Elaine's life is geared to be aware of time always, manage it, never lose it or lose *to* it, never let it beat her. For Elaine, there will be less accomplishment, which is the stuff of life, if she loses time. Lost time translates into lost life; it is a mortal threat to Elaine and would make her extremely uneasy. Even illness is not an occasion to lose time. Thus, general transcendence would not be enjoyable for Elaine; it would be a form of dying.

Is Elaine any the worse for this virtual lack of one form of transcendence? I think she is. If having fun, hanging out, doing something for pure pleasure isn't enjoyable to Elaine, one cannot help but wonder how much fun she is to be around. The lack of general transcendence may interfere with intimate relationships, in which general transcendence activities are so common.

It is possible that work achievement is general transcendence for her in the Maslow sense, a peak experience. If she loses a sense of time and purely enjoys during these experiences, then work may be like alcohol, an addiction.

Or perhaps the mere beating of time helps her lose a sense of it—beating time as a hobby. Her demeanor seems intense for this interpretation.

How did Elaine become the person she is? There is, of course, always the possibility that she did not, that the workaholism is fairly recent, and through these spectacles she reinterprets the rest of her life. But when we look at her entire life, we do see several conceivable roots of her development. Her stepmother *kept* her from general transcendence (she mentions not going to the beach, being with friends) by saying she had too much work to do, by making time impossible to manage. One might expect her to have rebelled against this by overdoing the fun once she was out and grown. But perhaps instead she *learned* the nonessential nature of fun; perhaps self-denial became a habit, reinforced itself, to borrow from the behaviorist viewpoint for a moment. But why would this have been so with Elaine and not someone else?

Once again, we can look for special vulnerability in Elaine's past. Her mother died of a chronic illness, and her aunt died of an abortion, both within months of each other, when Elaine was very young; she learned that life could be short. With another set of life circumstances this loss might have manifested itself in a different way. But Elaine's particular set of life circumstances was that her stepmother was originally a live-in housekeeper, and Elaine must have been able to identify her both with her own mother and with the previous beloved housekeeper who left when they moved, another breakup of the family as she describes it, the housekeeper's son like a brother. Some feelings of love and expectation must have been transferred to this housekeeper who was kind until she became a stepmother, much like the wicked ones in fairy tales. Aborted or betrayed identification broke her relationship with her father as well. In the oedipal Freudian paradigm, the child of four won in the rivalry between herself and her mother for the father's affections; then her mother died, a devastating outcome; the housekeeper-stepmother took Elaine's place as primary in the affections of the father, as she took Elaine's mother's place. Was Elaine also in danger of dying? There were a number of attacks with scissors, the father accepting excuses and not protecting her; there was also a less vital life, being forced to remain at home and work, baby-sitting her new stepsib. Her father seems to have trusted his new wife's word over his daughter's.

When we look at Elaine's earlier childhood, we do not see a child at odds with time. On the contrary, she played with dolls and roller-skated. She wanted to go to the beach with her friends. Her dad taught her logical and methodical approaches to life tasks. We might think of her as overdoing the competence of the 6- to 12-year-old period. The armed forces may have confirmed this; her identity was that of one who was disciplined. To be disciplined means to do as one should, not what one wants—the essence of general transcendence.

Elaine's marriage was perhaps a watershed. She married a man who became addicted to a form of general transcendence, alcohol, and under the influence beat her to the point of threatening her life. Not only had her mother and sister died off time, her brother also died of the consequences of injuries sustained in his risk-taking, general transcendence activity (racing cars against time). The combination of all these influences helps us to understand how Elaine is as she is.

Time is the measure of a life, how much has been lived, how much is left. At the end of her interview, Elaine says, "Let go of things that were bad or distasteful, or mistakes you made . . . 'cause there's always tomorrow. It's a continuation of endless tomorrows—there's your time—endless tomorrows." The past is something to let go of, good as well as bad, and the present is never mentioned. Tomorrow is endless—but of course it isn't, and certainly not to someone in her fifties. She denies the race with time, and her entire life belies this denial. Things are denied because they are too painful to bear.

It seems as though, when Elaine is saving time, she is actually saving her life.

DEATH: THE ULTIMATE TRANSCENDENCE?

Death is at once the ultimate loss and the ultimate transcendence. For this reason, our feelings, attitudes, and behaviors around death (the state) and dying (the process) are inconsistent and ambivalent. In this section I begin by examining the ways in which we manifest our ambivalence. This is followed by a description of how death has influenced my interviewees both positively and negatively, showing some of the reasons for ambivalence from a practical standpoint. Bereavement cannot be understood until we grasp what is lost. Em's history illustrates the roots of ambivalence and the fruit they bear. A final discussion outlines our modes of handling death as well as our attraction to, and innate love of, death.

Our Ambivalence Toward Death

Everyone has dreams of the ultimate transcendence. Somewhere beyond time and space, or over the rainbow, there is a harlequin lover with whom we will attain the ultimate physical and spiritual orgasm; there is a land of no loss, gated and paved with pearls and gold, in white light far brighter than our sun, where we will all rejoin each other in eternal love (we may need to cross a river to get to it, or go on a long journey, or be reborn). "Beyond this vale of tears" "the good die young," they escape loss to transcendence. Death is eternal life, love, joy, sun, truth, beauty. Or there is a devil who will cleanse us of sin in fire, always or for a time, Hell or Purgatory. Even the less lifelike metaphors of death—the great adventure, the dreamless sleep—are images of ultimate transcendence in that they continue consciousness, during adventure, before and after sleep. Lack of consciousness is only an intellectual exercise. Hell's terror is something that is experienced. We may opt for Hell over nonexistence, at least in our imaginations. Finality and continuity are joined; time and eternity are equated. Whatever death is, we will know; bliss or agony, the images all convey the sense of the unimaginable, the ultimate. There is nothing moderate about death.

Whether God created man and woman, or primitive humans created God to protect them from the death-dealing elements; whether God died in flesh or spirit, from lack of belief or boredom, or whether He is the principle behind ongoing creation; whether he created death and time, is separate or one in soul with humans, he remains the embodiment—or enspiritment—of all transcendent qualities. He slays only to heal.

Many linguistic metaphors of death are also metaphors of transcendence, or life. In these metaphors, loss and transcendence are joined, perhaps because the urge to continued existence is so great that we create some semblance of it. It is difficult to create a metaphor of death without implicit continuity, even if that implication is simply an expression of noncontinuity. For example, death is the "good night" into which we must not "go gentle" (Thomas, 1952). But night is always followed by day—it would not be night otherwise. Death is the winter "when the snows begin, and the blasts denote I am nearing the place" (Browning, 1922), but again, we cannot conceive of winter without spring. Death is a hooded figure with a scythe—that moves and lives!

Dying is pain, isolation, mutilation, renunciation, and anguish. But death is release. We know dying, but we do not know death; we can beautify it, and romanticize it if we choose, and who is to argue?

We may view death as the ultimate transcendence, and in that sense we may be a "death-embracing society" (Dumont & Foss, 1972) rather than a death-denying society, but we do all we can to keep ourselves and our loved ones alive! We make heroic efforts to preserve lives by machines, medical tests, surgery, and drugs that often cause pain comparable to that of the disease they treat; we have suicide prevention centers and may risk the life of a police officer to save a "jumper" on the Golden Gate Bridge; abortion—death at the very beginning of life—is a topic on which normally sane people cannot even exchange views without virulent epithets and bombings; we bend over backward to avert the abuses potential in euthanasia. If an animal breaks a leg we may "put her to sleep," but we are far less merciful to our own kind, often preferring that they experience pain rather than die. We weep inconsolably at the funerals of our beloved, while the minister whom we have hired speaks of the joys of eternal life. Do our tears betray our disbelief of him? Then why do we insist he tell us fairy tales? Or do we weep at the happiness of the dead? Our own guilt or release? The temporary separation? There is a fault line down our collective psyches as potentially destructive of us as California's San Andreas; we believe in eternal life and eternal death at the same time. At funerals, the plates slip and we come apart. We look to the clouds as if we might see the face of our beloved in them, and we pay hard cash for the satin-lined coffin in which the newly dead may "slumber" in far more luxury than she did in cotton-sheeted life. This is more than ambivalence, more than double bind. It is existential schizophrenia.

Life and Death Decisions: The Issue of Possession

Our pathology is nowhere better evidenced than in our attitudes toward abortion, suicide, and euthanasia, where our deepest values, beliefs, and feelings pose in the guise of rational argument.

Underlying all the arguments for and against "unnatural" death seems to be the question of *possession*. We saw in Chapter 8 on individual development, that possessions are aspects of our identity. What we have is who we are, and we guard our possessions as we guard our roles, ideas, and relationships. *Whose life is it anyway?* asked Clark (1978). Indeed, one would think we had only been loaned to ourselves.

A life is conceived, or it is born, or it is ending? Who owns it? Does the individual own his life? Does his closest relative? The state? God? Satan? Is the newly conceived embryo "human" at conception? Nine weeks later? Thirty-six? Is it something less than human until its birth, when it miraculously attains fully human status? Was there nothing of humanity in the sperm blocked by a shield or by timing, or the egg prevented from implantation? Who is responsible for the zillions of potential lives flushed away each day? Does the fetus belong to itself, or to its mother whose body it may be killing because of heart disease or invading because of rape or incest? Does the mother have a right to drugs and alcohol, to do as she pleases, even though these may harm the fetus? Does the father have half rights, since half of the baby's chromosomes are from him? Does he then have indirect control over the mother's body? Does society have rights over all of them, in the form of beliefs of other selves? What about the five other children in the impoverished family, or the tens of thousands in the starving country? Does the infant own part of their food at birth? At conception? Or is there, perhaps, a hierarchy of possession, with the parents' rights superseding the child's (or vice versa) and society's taking precedence over those of the parents? If we believe the infant is from God, we will answer that its life is God's will and we cannot go against that. But then, its death might be His will. Death teaches. The death of a mother in childbirth, or of another baby because there are too many mouths for the food, is also of God, whose plan is perfection. If the infant is from nature, all forms of death are natural in nature, even killing.

We answer these questions from our own eschatological and teleological views of life, death, humanity, and God, of the meaning of loss and transcendence, and then we impose these views on each other, preferably by law, to secure them within ourselves, to reify them. Our deep emotional investment in these issues stems from threat of loss in chaos, purposelessness, meaninglessness, and we seek to transcend once and for all. If the individual has a purpose in life, it is wrong to keep her from accomplishing it.

We construct the meaning of our lives, express it through values such as these, and then defend them as if our lives depended on their preservation. Because they do.

Another meaning for the word "possession" is to be taken over by another entity, to be dispossessed of self. In our society, that entity can only be the Devil, whose power of death through annihilation of the soul is final. We are less ourselves when we are owned by another. Throughout life we are gradually being emancipated from the possession of others, only to fall back in the end.

Amniocentesis to determine if the infant is defective is on the increase, because of improved technology, the desire of women to have children after establishing a career, and also because of shrinking resources, increased inflation, overpopulation (see Faden, 1986). As Brewster Smith (1986) has pointed out, viability of the fetus is increasingly early with improved technology; the chorionic villus can be sampled for abnormalities in the first trimester, and either abortion or the rapidly improving techniques of fetal therapy can be applied. Our abilities to visualize the fetus and to institute fetal therapy and intensive care may make the fetus seem more "human" and increase the possession conflicts among mother, fetus, and society.

Each life must be justified, must be capable of sustaining itself, rather than being a drain on a society increasingly overburdened with lengthening survival. Eugenics is no longer simply a future possibility. Institutional inmates, criminal and retarded, have been sterilized without their knowledge. We pay the price in an occasional error—a healthy fetus aborted. Our values now are health versus handicap. As resources dwindle still further, our values may tighten; the parents or the society or the world might be willing to support only humans of a certain order, IQs over 115 perhaps, males to fight or females to breed, a preferred race, a smaller size to consume less.

What if all the human eggs ever hatched had united with a sperm and produced an infant? Our planet would have died long ago. Science fiction writers have shown us how.

After an individual is born, deliberately killing it is classified as euthanasia, murder, or war. It is motivation that most discriminates these from each other, although method also tends to be different for each. The motive for euthanasia is ostensibly to prevent pain and is justified as an act of mercy. (See Faden & Beautchamp, 1986, on the issue of informed consent.) There is no further purpose to the individual's continuing life that we can discern. The infant is horribly deformed, is anencephalic and can never lead a normal life, will be a drain on parents and state, will suffer. The accident victim will vegetate. Quantity and quality of life are pitted against the rights of the handicapped—many of whom lead lives of high quality. The old person has lived her life, has only pain and suffering to look forward to, can accomplish nothing of value, is pleading for a compassionate death. The infant cannot beg for mercy killing, so we must make the decision for him, removing him from the isolette or special life-support systems; similarly helpless, the accident victim's respirator can be turned off; the older person who requests a lethal injection is often considered incompetent merely by virtue of the request or by virtue of being one who is dying. To be dying supersedes all other features of identity, so we may accede to the request. If we do, is this euthanasia or suicide? It has been called "assisted suicide."

At what point is a death euthanasia, and at what point is it "natural"? Do we define the difference by "pulling the plug," ceasing active efforts on behalf of the patient, or actively administering an overdose? In years past, individuals died "natural" deaths far earlier in their lives because medical technology was not as advanced as it is today. Does technology define "natural" death? Or is this an unnatural death? Are those whom technology keeps alive living an "unnatural life?"

The motive for euthanasia is mercy; the motive for murder is personal gain. But relatives arguing financial hardship have been able to persuade doctors to be merciful using verbal or materialistic incentives! Euphemistically, they plead that "nothing more can be done" or the doctor must "ease her pain." What then is the motive, and is the act one of murder or euthanasia, both or neither? At this point, the patient may seem to be owned by the relatives and the physician.

Euthanasia is the big medical secret in this country. We have no idea of the extent to which it is practiced or of the proportion of dying patients, relatives, or physicians who make the final decision. Our information is strictly anecdotal, subject to denial at any time. As with abortion, the possibilities of abuse are legion, not only the termination of lives that might be saved but also the eventual extension to people who are less and less seriously afflicted, the handicapped, the retarded, those susceptible to heritable illness, the chronically ill, and finally (spectrally whispered) anyone who by reason of race, religion, sex, or other classification might be politically "suspect." We already know that trajectories are determined for patients on their admission to a hospital and that an aspect of the determinants of these trajectories and consequent medical effort is social desirability (Strauss & Glaser, 1985). The old are less worth saving than the young, and sometimes the poor less than the well-to-do, the alone less than those surrounded by concerned (and demanding) relatives. Legalization of circumstances under which euthanasia might be practiced would be cold comfort to those of us who are only too aware of the human failing to which even committees of physicians and lawyers may be heir, among which the most prominent are mistakes and bribery. (It was alleged some years ago that at least one nurse in a western hospital shortened the life of a patient in her care merely to win a money pool in which staff gambled on who would die when!) Death is seen as failure to the achievement-oriented physician (Feifel, Hanson, Jones, & Edwards, 1967), and it is not inconceivable that she is therefore likely to maximize chances of success and get failure out of the way as quickly as possible, or leave it to others.

With zero population growth and increased medical prowess, we could eventually become a nation of old people, no more inherently desirable than being a nation of young. The economic implications alone, including a bankrupt Social Security system and the support of many by the few, are overwhelming.

The motivation of war is ostensibly self-defense, of country or of interests, which means defense from threats to prosperity. The threat is interpreted by those in power who send the young off to perform "legalized murder" and who soothe their consciences with definitions of necessity, orders, praise of patriotism, and medals. In every way possible, the individual is made to feel he has no choice but to kill. It also helps to make the enemy something less than human.

Through all of these issues, something is being said about the value of human life. On the one hand we proclaim its sovereign importance, on the other we must treat it as variable. Some life is more "human" or more "living" than other life. Our ambivalence is law!

If we have the "right" to drop a bomb on a group of less than human enemies—whose humanity is quickly restored to them after the fighting is over and the peace is won—do we have the right, and the responsibility, to grant that merciful injection to the patient racked with excruciating pain, whom we believe to be terminal? (After all, there are spontaneous remissions, new treatments always around the corner.) Does not the individual have the right to decide for himself?

What constitutes an acceptable quality of life, beyond which death is more desirable, and who decides, self or other? It is the ability to *think* which distinguishes us, supposedly, from animals; if thinking stops and there is only physiological activity, should (and may) the individual be treated as less than human? How much pain should an individual endure before being allowed to die? Should we withhold drugs from the dying because they might become addicted?

It is the patient's right to determine the course of her treatment, to refuse an operation that may add 3 months of comatose existence or pain, to turn down the drugs that make her vomit incessantly, to not have to undergo another painful test. It is the patient's right to know her status; if she will not recover, how long does she have to live? It is the physician's duty to expend every effort on behalf of his patient, no matter age, sex, social status, occupation, relatives, quality of life to be gained; it is also his responsibility to withhold any news from her that might cause her to be so depressed that her health would be affected. It is the right of the relatives to refuse further payments for expensive care that are depriving their children, the patient's grandchildren, surely not what she would want. It is also their responsibility to let the doctor know that she does not want extraordinary measures taken to preserve her life; who know better than those closest to her? They have spoken of it often enough, and she has even signed a living will—in days when she was healthy and could not conceive of wanting to carry on through thick and thin. It is the right of the hospital to refuse further care to nonpaying patients; they would go bankrupt if they gave care to all the worthy indigents requesting or needing it. It is the responsibility of the hospital to give maximum care to everyone, lest they be sued. It is the responsibility of the state to care for all its citizens who might otherwise be dying on the street in full discom-fitting view of everyone, inflicting guilt on innocent passersby bent on errands and window-shopping, as is indeed the situation in other countries. Moral and legal rights and moral and legal responsibilities regarding human life seem entangled because our basic values regarding life and death are so confused. Every transcendence to one is a loss to others. At present, we muddle through.

Because death is the ultimate loss, we avoid it at all costs. Because it is the ultimate transcendence, we embrace it.

Nowhere is our ambivalence regarding life and death more salient than in the matter of suicide. The 17-year-old has failed a crucial exam and his girl has run off with his best friend. He is trying to hang himself. Does he have the right? Is it a tragedy if he succeeds? Any one of us could sit down and tell him stories of failure and lost love, followed down the road by discoveries and loves so worthwhile they justified our entire existence. He thinks his life is ended. We think he doesn't know. Is it our responsibility to stop him? Perhaps because he is so young? At what age should we not stop him, then? At 24, when he has suffered a disfiguring accident? At 57, when his wife has died? At 72, when he is in intractable pain? If we stopped him at 17, are we guilty of all else that befalls him subsequently, especially if he tells us it wasn't worth all he had to go through? Age and motive seem to increase the reasonableness, the acceptability of suicide over the life span. There seems more to lose, less to gain by continuation of life. Is this a form of ageism? When we try to talk a person out of suicide, we speak of tran-scendence to come, but there is a point at which we are insincere. How much of this loss-gain ratio is our illusion? Or even our sadism? Stopping him may be our responsibility but not our right. On the other hand, do we have the right to paint bright futures for him and condemn him to the pain he will endure? Do we egregiously violate his rights when we exercise our respon-sibility and put him on the neuropsychiatric ward? Not only does responsibility clash with right but also, to make matters worse, both are susceptible of highly subjective interpretation.

We struggle over the decision to allow a patient to die in peace; yet we allow whole nations to starve with apparently little conflict or effort. True, there have been exceptions; sporadic efforts have been mounted to combat hunger. We pay for food to send others and also for the feelings of transcendence we experience—we are bribed. Is it that rights and responsibilities have national boundaries? Or that it is all we can do to take care of our own? Is that part of the hierarchization of more or less humanity in each individual— foreigners have less? We don't seem to have this problem when a country has something we need.

The view of the life cycle in terms of loss and transcendence does not solve the question of who is ultimately the possessor of a life, the controller, decision maker, dispenser, executor, terminator. But it does help to clarify the underlying issues. Life and death in terms of loss and transcendence depend on how their meaning is construed, which in turn is a matter of values. Death itself is not a tragedy. If a man is walking down the street and a piano falls on his head, it is comic. It is only as we learn the meaning of his life, the relatives and projects he left behind, the struggles and dreams, the irony of a decision to be on that spot at that time, that his death takes on meaning and consequently absurd and/or tragic overtones.

It seems apparent from the foregoing that a philosophy of life is a necessity rather than a luxury, that it will preserve lives as much as do food and drink.

Ambivalence Reconsidered

It is difficult to believe we may never know "the answer" to the riddle of death. We will die, and then we will "find out" if it is the end or not. That death may be a secret forever is inconceivable, because then death would cease to "exist" and would be only a mental construct, having none of the reality that has been impressed on us from childhood. Our minds play games with us.

It is difficult to remain in an ambivalent position about death. It is easier to "know" *either* that we end *or* that we continue. Humanity has always sought certainty. No one has returned from the dead to say there is no life after death! In other ages (Aries, 1982) the certainty lay in religious pronouncements or visions of saints or the extension of transcendence in this life to the ultimate, love of woman to love of God. For some, this has been demonstration enough. Others find comfort in the certainty of bodily decay, perhaps because there is no pain or responsibility or punishment or accounting beyond what is in this life. They take pride in not falling prey to wishful thought, not allowing it to cloud the very solid evidence of their senses. Now that we are in a scientific period, we consider the issue scientifically and seek proof. Of course, this is impossible, because the most solid proof can always be refuted by someone on some grounds, if only philosophical, or by the historical argument that yesterday's science is today's folklore.

There has been a flurry of research studies purporting to demonstrate the possibility of life after death (cf. Kastenbaum & Aisenberg, 1972; Moody, 1975; Ring, 1984; Sabom, 1982; Osis & Haraldsson, 1977). Those pronounced clinically dead have been revived and have told of similar "near-death experiences" (NDEs), often including some of the following: a feeling of being out of body and looking down at the physical one, the sensation of whooshing through a dark tunnel with a buzzing in the ears, a brilliant white light, seeing their pasts unreel before them like a movie, life evaluation and a decision to return to life, all supervised by a being of white light, and ending with the leaden sensation of reembodiment and pain. I myself had one of these experiences, long before they became fashionable (or the term NDE was even coined), and can attest to the realism and the subsequent feeling that one will never again fear death. (One may still fear the process of dying.) But as all the individuals came back, they cannot be said to have been dead. This research may show that nature is most kind in terminal moments and demonstrate the similarity of terminal experiences across cultures, the release of endorphins, perhaps, or a final burst of electricity that lights up memory like an exploding star. Although I believe the Siegel (1981) critique can be refuted point by point, the NDE does not *prove* life after death in the scientific sense.

If we knew for a fact what some suspect, that death is not the end, who of us in our dark hours would choose to continue? Suicide might become commonplace, the eternity of life would constitute a heavy responsibility, a guilt at times intolerable, the total denial of freedom, constrained as we would be to act in the context of a far broader horizon. Thus, that death should remain a mystery is quite logical from the point of view of an intelligent creator.

We are not supposed to reveal our ambivalence. Individuals are supposed to "die the good death" or die well, dying and death confounded. The values underlying this concept of good death seem to fall into two categories. One is the ability to *appear* accepting or oblivious, in comfort rather than in pain, in other words, to give the living as little trouble as possible, so as not to breach their defense mechanisms (Glaser & Strauss, 1965, 1968; Strauss & Glaser, 1985). The other set of values views dying as the culmination of development, or the last developmental stage (Zinker & Fink, 1966; Kerr, 1974), in which the individual becomes self-actualized, rounds out her life, closes her circle, concludes that her life was worthwhile and meaningful, and can then accept death rather than uselessly fight it or regret the course of it (Saunders, 1959; Kubler-Ross, 1971).

What kind of life is more likely to lead to the good death? Possibly, as our interviewee Harriet believes, the individual who has accomplished much of what he set out to do, has had fulfilling work and human relationships, can die at greater peace than the individual who feels cheated in life, is dying incomplete (Smith has suggested this also, personal communication, 1980). On the other hand, the individual with a fuller life has more to leave behind. A friend of mine whose life was rich commented, "Death—I hate the son of a bitch." Our ambivalence toward our deaths seems grounded in our ambivalence toward our lives.

Ambivalence in Ritual

Ambivalence appears in our ritual practices as well (see Mitford, 1963; Harmer, 1963). For some mysterious reason, we have rituals for other important passages through life—birth, graduation, marriage—as well as religious rituals and rituals for death, but none for the (often long) process of dying, before the final moments at which extreme unction may be administered. The development of a ritual might ease the passage for dying and bereaving alike.

I knew a woman who was given only a few more months to live and who devised her own ritual. She began wearing long gowns that hid her bodily disfigurement and were white for mourning, because she said she preferred it to black, and the gowns felt to her so much more like herself than the conventional clothing she had worn before. Around her neck she wore a string of beads, each of a different color and design and each signifying a different year in her life; there were brown beads for the years she could not remember, and occasionally she would replace a brown with one of a different color as memory returned; there were clusters of special beads for special events. She told over these beads as one would tell a rosary, both to herself and to others, children, friends, sometimes strangers. As she had refused treatment that might keep her from actively living those last few months, that might confine or debilitate her too severely, she became a familiar sight in the town where she lived; even people who did not know her knew of her, and they furtively sought some sign of anger or sorrow or terror in her face as they passed her on the street and could not detect enough of these to match the awesome thing that was happening to her. She met any questioning eyes of those who were not dying (or so they thought) with her own quite clear ones, and when people stopped to speak to her of nothing in particular, she always had the time, as she had not had before (having been a busy mother and community worker). Strangers asked her to what sect she belonged, to which she replied that she was her own; friends and acquaintances began asking her advice on things of which she had some experience and on others of which she had none and said so; eventually they could talk to her about dying, and she taught and shared the process with them, the pain, the fear, the freedom. When she was too weak to walk, friends took her to town in a wheelchair. In devising her own ritual way of giving her life a meaning from its beginning to its end, she also helped many others, and this gave her a deep sense of fulfillment. Like Casteneda's (1976) creative concept of death, she seems to remain as an advisor.

In our society she was an exception. In other times, at least the public nature of her dying would have been seen as common and even desirable (Aries, 1982). Now, we hide our dying away and uncover it only when the process has culminated in death. Why do we not have the oratory and satin pillows and wakes when the dying are still around to enjoy them? Why not a testimony from loved ones, colleagues, and community on the value of that life while it is still being lived?

Death Influences on the Interviewees

When we look at the influence of death and dying on the lives of the interviewees, our ambivalence toward death becomes readily understandable. This is because death has positive effects as well as negative ones.

For a number of interviewees, a death resulted in a better life, in transcendent experiences of love and art. Alice tells us that the presence of her husband and herself at the death of a neighbor child drew them closer together, inculcating them with a new love and respect for one another. A number of interviewees like Harriet aver that death and other negative experiences make them stronger persons. Overcoming death is the occupation of a number of interviewees, nurses Judith, Marjorie, Britt, and Harriet at the suicide prevention center. This gives them great satisfaction. The "circle of death" that surrounded Patty and her husband led to a need to break that circle with a new life. "The world is a place where people are born to die" she tells us in her sentence completion. For Della, death is resurrection. After Babs's suicide attempt, she split into two different personalities, which has proved functional for her. Experiences of being near death themselves led to a lifetime of transcending death for some; for example, Inez, who nearly died at three, feels she became a physician as a result. The accidental killing of a motorcyclist compelled Sue and her husband to focus on how temporary relationships were and to work through them. Opal speaks of the "release" her family experienced with the death of her alcoholic husband. The deaths of Janet's children so overwhelmed her that, as she emerged from her fugue state, she began a long-term love affair that was a high point in her life. For Gwen, bodies of boarders in green body bags helped her to define for herself the value of human life. Irene's father died when she was 19, so she and her mother ended up taking in another young couple to have a family and all became close friends. When Sissy's father died, she recalls all the attention she got in school. These are, of course, the positive influences of literal deaths; there were many, many positive influences of metaphorical deaths as well, as we have seen.

Death as a negative experience was reported in many instances. Germaine seems still to be in mourning after the death of her ideal husband. However, this continued mourning serves a transcendent purpose; it helps her to preserve pictures of her husband and her marriage as ideal; were she to move toward resolution of the L/T process, it would entail a cognitive reorganization, seeing flaws in him and advantages to her present life. Gwen's beloved husband's death left her alone and grieving: "I want to die. I guess most people do," she candidly admits. Elaine similarly speaks of feeling "cheated" by her mother's death at an early age; she too has preserved an idealized notion of how their relationship might have been. Marjorie's father's death by suicide led to a stepfather who abused her over a long period. For Melanie, an abortion was a denial of all she valued—life, love, network, and community. Inez's experience of abortion was a similar denial of values. Lorellen's abortions may have so damaged her body that her current fetus is endangered. Assassination of public figures made Heather feel more vulnerable. The death of Willa's brother in an automobile accident was devastating to her family and resulted in a lawsuit. Babs lost her uncle, a father figure, in a war and grieved over him a long time. Sissy reports the death of her grandmother, an alternate self, when she was 13. Britt has had much family death. "You sorrow, and learn to accept," she tells us.

For some, the circumstances of dying were particularly important. A group of interviewees reported mothering their parents during final days and hours and the positive effects of these experiences. For Tess, it was one of the few periods in her life during which she could experience a sense of competence. Ursula gives a matter-of-fact account of how her mother died in her arms and how grateful she was that she could give her this loving care. "We came home from church and we was eating lunch and my mother started to choke." She went to the sink to put her dentures in a cup, turned on the hot water, but grabbed the faucet, the hot water running over her hand. "I said, 'Mom, that's hot water.' She said, 'I know it, but I'm losing my balance.' " Ursula tried to get her to the bathroom, but she "collapsed and slid to the floor. . . . She said, 'Can you get me to the bathroom?' But she'd already gone, so I knew she was dying then. I said, 'Mom, I can't get you to the bathroom . . . just go ahead and go, and don't worry. . . . So she said, 'Okay, and her eyes were shut, and that was the end right then." Irene cared for her mother when she died; it was a release for her mother, but hard on Irene. Annette states that other people's deaths are models to fear or emulate. Some of the interviewees spoke of this caring as a role reversal, although, interestingly enough, Fischer (1986) found that the nursed parent does not refer to the relationship this way!

Some of the circumstances of the dying were negative. Gwen nursed her husband during his long deterioration, and this was an extended grieving process for her as well. Nora and others regret the sudden dying of a relative before they can complete unfinished business. Kendall's aunt's dying was grisly and stayed with her. Sibyl's sister's twin died in the womb, and Sibyl became conforming, as if she too might have been threatened—an aspect of her L/T life theme.

Threats of death have also influenced the interviewees profoundly. Kendall's sister attempted suicide, their relationship became stronger as a result, and Kendall had a hand in the happy life outcome. Charyn's mother is suicidal, so the children conceal problems from her as much as possible, a situation reported by a number of interviewees. For Lorellen, the threatened death of her child is a retribution for her past errors. Threats of death from lovers also influenced Patty, Kara, Elaine, and others—mainly to leave. It was the threat of her mother's death that made Crista a self-sacrificing helper, beginning her L/T life theme of city versus country. Nadine and her husband have both had cancer, and this has drawn them closer together. Ronnie's husband's cancer resulted in Ronnie being accused by her mother-in-law of preparing too-rich foods; thus that relationship was breached.

Some interviewees referred to the influence of near death in themselves. Kendall, in her early teen years, nearly died of a blood disorder; ultimately she could not go into the career she wanted because of this. For Denise, who nearly died twice, the word "survival" is a major one, although this refers to psychic survival as well. A number were nearly killed in car accidents, like Greer and Jaclyn; others nearly drowned, like Melanie and Elaine. Nora is "probably dying" and feels that she can no longer indulge her love of travel, her main transcendence mode. Jaclyn and her mother were in a car that flipped over; a man walked over to them, peered at them beneath the car, and then walked away—her disillusion remains with her, and she now fears being crippled. Alice's experiences of hemorrhaging were benign in that she simply felt herself drifting away. Vera nearly starved to death in grief over her husband's betrayal, before she pulled herself together and began a new life. Marjorie almost killed herself before making a decision to live, similar to Vera's.

My data show that *high* death anxiety was significantly associated with reporting *fewer* experiences of nearly dying; those who had come near death themselves tended to be less death anxious than those who had not, as measured by the Templer (1970) Death Anxiety Scale embedded in the L/T interview ($p<.05$). They also reported less fear of death on direct questioning ($p<.002$).

A number of interviewees reported psychic phenomena around death. Faith had a good experience with her mother's death, because her mother had had an NDE and was unafraid, indeed, looking forward. Willa felt her brother's presence before she found out he was dead, and this helped her cope. Several other interviewees reported similar experiences. Janet has felt the presence of her dead children, and Gwen had several extrasensory experiences; for example, she was driving from one place to another and suddenly found she could not get there, the radio played "Take my hand, I'm a stranger in Paradise," and then her son spoke to her about his friend taking his hand when he died. Several, like Charyn and Faith, had precognitive dreams of the deaths of others. Germaine knew her father had died before she received word, and another interviewee knew her first husband had died—she saw his face on television.

Death haunts the dreams of the interviewees. Some were threatened with violent death: Paula with guns, Heather with drowning, Babs with falling, Tess with dying and leaving her son. Others dream of those who have died, Ursula of her mother, Janet of her two dead children, Irene and Winnie of their fathers. Nora dreamed she was dead and heard "weird music"; the experience included "coming back" and being scared, and it was "horrible."

Della tries to escape and cannot. Inez sees animals being hunted. Charyn is chased.

Lastly, the epitaphs that the interviewees would choose for themselves shed light on the influence of death in their lives. One group chooses to be remembered in a positive manner; others refer to struggle, and still others to faith. Positive judgments include Lexie's "of help to others," Heather's "was loved," Patty's "happy, lucky," Robin's "kind," Gwen's "The world is better [for her having lived]," Annette's "liked people," Inez's "loved, cared." Janet would like to see "She had the good sense to keep her mouth shut." Yves wants "good mother, wife, and humanitarian." Vicki and Harriet want "R.I.P." and Opal "She served a purpose." Oona wants "She was a good mother," and Judith "She was a happy lady."

Struggle is reflected in Marjorie's "Life, you can do it like a dancer, or carry it like a load," Elaine's "I tried," Jaclyn's "She could have done a lot more," Vera's "I feel sorry for all humanity," Germaine's "She tried," and Kendall's "I tried." Greer wants "Free at last," Nora "Here was a woman who loved and who would have loved to have been loved," Tess "We all try to make a mark, but we're just dust."

Expressions of faith are shown in Lorellen's epitaph "Life everlasting," Kara's "functioning on a better, humane level," and Faith's "I'm going up there to paint the sunset."

Bereavement: What is Lost

When we lose a beloved spouse, why is it so painful? We can answer that question by applying the five levels of loss: primary, secondary, holistic, self-conceptual, and metaphorical. What is it that is lost?

First, we lose all the loving companionship, the touching, the words, the tiny daily interactions, silences, ways of being, and the sense of presence in the one we love.

Second, we lose our role in relationship to the loved one—all the things we did for him or her, cooking eggs a special way, arranging pillows or flowers, shopping for joke cards. Many of these activities are necessary to our daily lives, but they also serve the purpose of distraction from death, just as do all our daily trivia. They are death-postponing. We also lose the freedom from the responsibilities that the other took.

Third, we lose our sense of purpose. So much of our daily lives has been lived for the other or in the context of the other. We take purpose for granted until we do not have it.

Fourth, we lose our future. There were possibilities, hopes, and plans—for selling the house and moving to a condominium, taking a trip in a camper to Yellowstone, welcoming the grandchildren, starting a little business. When we lose a spouse, we lose much of that future, including the many possibilities of a future that we had, alternative futures. Now nothing seems worth doing.

Fifth, when we lose a spouse, we also lose part of our past. Until now, although past events could not be changed, we shared in recollecting them, and in those recollections we could revise our perceptions as well, together, confirming each other. Now those revisions must take place alone.

Sixth, we lose the world view that the other had. We were two people, seeing the world through our own eyes but also through the eyes of the other, construing the world together, living alternate lives. Now that world view is foreclosed.

Seventh, we lose the validation that the other gave us of our thoughts and feelings, as worthy of response and also of heeding. Now there are no responses, even arguments, to make us alive and worthy of life. It was as if a third entity had been created: the self, the other, and the relationship. Now that relationship must move into the lost sector of who we are and who we might have been.

Eighth, we lose the freedom from uncertainty that we were able to create, at least for a while. A pregnant mother feels somehow invulnerable; because the life she carries is so important, how could death dare? Unaware, we carry a little of this "invulnerability" over to other relationships; he needs me—I cannot die. We have been temporarily free, at home with the fundamental illusion. But now we are vulnerable, not only in feeling but also in fact. As we have seen, our body rhythms may desynchronize and our immune systems may be depressed (Hofer, 1984). We may die of a broken heart.

Ninth, death ends all possibility of resolving interpersonal problems, of asking long unasked questions. The daughter can no longer ask her father if he realized what he was doing to her, or her mother if she knew. Until the parent, spouse, or child died, there was always hope for conflict resolution. Now there is none. The conflict becomes a granite memorial.

Finally, when we lose a loved one, we lose part of our life and self structures, our identity, who we are. It is common to say, "I feel as though part of myself has died." This is true. It has. We are bereft not only of the other but also of who we are.

It is helpful for us to be aware of all these aspects of our loss because, when we break our loss into these various components, we can see that *some* of them can be replaced and how this can be done. After the shock, numbness, and yearning, we must move on to searching for replacement of some of these aspects, perhaps with the help of friends, relatives, or counselors, and then to replacement and integration, when we can tell the story of what the loss meant to us, a tribute to what has passed.

Judy Tatelbaum, in her book *The courage to grieve* (1977), helps us understand and move through the process of grieving, the physical and mental difficulties, the guilt (there was always more I could have done), and the anger (how could he leave me with all these problems?), envy, horror, the outrage at the injustice of death. Death is rarely fair. Indeed, we can apply this process to other life losses as well.

But what of chronic bereavement, the loss that is almost as acute today as it was 10 years ago? "Complicated grief," as it is called, serves its purpose and thus is a form of pathological transcendence. The continuation of grief is a way of preserving the relationship. If I continue to grieve over him, some aspect of his presence continues with me, I can *feel* him as I grieve, whereas if I move beyond grief, I will lose him again. Further, I can even make our relationship better, far more ideal than it really was, by remembering and reworking the good, forgetting the bad. In fact, now I can have the relationship with him I never had. Further still, by remaining in a past relationship, I can escape the responsibility for creating present ones and all the attendant losses these will eventually incur. Finally, my identity includes my widowhood now, and I would not kill off that aspect of myself—I cannot spare it.

We know that parents who have lost their baby at birth create an idealized picture of how the child would have been. One of my students wrote a letter to his dead baby in which the baby was a perfect child, all the things they did together were ideal, he grew to be a perfect man; by implication, such perfection could not die—it was too perfect to do so. That father had lost not only his child but also his ideal—a double bereavement. Usually parents of children who live are bereaved only once!

Continued grief re-creates identity. I am the one who has lost; that defines who I am and how I am to be treated. Perhaps I am now even more than I was; perhaps before I was nothing, and now I am somebody. If you take away my grief, you take away who I am. I will hang on to it as surely as I cling to my life!

People who continue grieving may also avoid responsibility for their own futures, particularly the part of the responsibility that was shared by the other.

Thus, they are preserving the past and even enriching it, while escaping the future. On the life-death continuum, they move toward death.

At the end of this chapter, I will make some suggestions for L/T therapeutic approaches.

LIFE HISTORY

The story of Em illustrates the loss and transcendence influences of death on the individual, thereby explaining how some of our ambivalence comes into existence.

Em

"[I] felt how important it was for me as a woman to become a voice. . . . The problem with women is they don't take themselves seriously, their life and their art."

An attractive woman in her mid-forties, Em lives with her two daughters and Charles, the man she will later marry, in a rural home with lots of land. They are both ceramic artists, and they are building a large studio in back, but currently there is an enormous shed housing long tables laden with their projects. On the floor are hundreds of cans of paint, each with a colored tile on top to identify it, because when the covers are off the paints themselves all look the same. Posters and samples of their exquisite work are everywhere, although their styles and topics are very different. But the route for Em as an artist, and also for Charles, has been a convoluted one.

Em started drawing when she was very young. She made dolls by turning flowers upside down. The only girl in a houseful of boys, she remembers competing for her father's attention by being a good athlete, but her relationship with him was not a close one. He was a disciplinarian, gone a lot, but could also laugh. Her mother was outgoing, also a disciplinarian, and "ran the show" while taking pains to see to it that her husband thought he was in charge. Em was never close to her brothers because of the competition, but all in all she had a happy, normal childhood in the midwest.

Em took piano lessons when she was very young. "I would get up early in the morning and practice an hour" at about 6:30. She accompanied her high school choir and was a singer, cheerleader, and class secretary, but she did no art work after junior high. She was going through a painful time, and besides, she thinks of art in the broad sense and includes music in her definition. She did work for her county recreation department from the age of 14 on and was head of all the arts and crafts for many parks by the age of 18. She also played the organ, was a Sunday school accompanist, and later bought a guitar.

Em's teen years were happy until the age of 17, when "the shit hit the fan." She wanted to go away to art school, but her parents "gave me a lot of static around that. I started drinking, and some smoking and hanging around with musicians, and all of this rebellion, I think." She started going with a musician who was also rebellious and had dropped out of school. They were talking marriage. Her parents were Latter-day Saints, and Mormons "push a lot of education, but . . . like the young people to go into early marriages, and the women are to be taken care of, and to have children, propagate." In spite of this, her parents wanted her to have a university education, but to get her away from the musician they packed her off to art school. He joined her at art school, but without the pressures of her parents she found "all sorts of things I didn't like" about him. She was sure he was going out with other women, and she got so sick from the gonorrhea he gave her that she had to go home, have an operation, and recuperate.

After this she did office work, which she hated, and then started college. It was here she met her first husband, Adam, who was handsome, outgoing, but a heavy drinker and therefore disliked by her parents. "We were very much in love. . . . I remember him asking me: 'Do you want to be my wife, or do you want to be an artist? You ought to make that choice.' And I said: 'No, I want to be a wife.' Although that was just a play on words, because

I don't think that either he or I understood what a husband-wife relationship was."

Em got pregnant right after their marriage, and they fought a lot, partly because of their financial struggles. However, her baby daughter gave her joy. "I was needed, you know, very responsible with this baby. And it was a job to make her clothes, and take her places." Her mother tried to take control, but Adam also was happy with the baby. Em's only regrets around this period were missing out on things like travel. She feels she was raised too conservatively. She graduated from college with a teaching credential and had another baby. "And again I was very creative. I made a lot of drapes for the house, and quilts for the children's beds, and I upholstered the furniture, 'cause we didn't have a lot of money. So I was happy to be able to have the talents to do those things. And paneling walls and building fences and gardening . . . crewel work, making children's . . . and my clothes . . . paper flowers. I did some printmaking and oil painting, [and] watercolor. I think, after going through therapy, I found out that if I gave my children watercolors while I was watercoloring, I was able to accomplish what I wanted to."

The relationship between Em and Adam was a rocky one, but it improved with counseling, and he was beginning to experience success. She was going for counseling to deal with some of her own problems. "You marry because one fits the other, and when one changes, then the other one sort of gets lost and can't figure out what it's all about. So I had some maturing to do to understand." Her therapist described her as "being like a little bird in the nest, and if you pushed too fast" she'd "back up and, I wouldn't be able to handle it. . . . I was going back through all those painful teens," particularly her relationship with her father. "I found out there was no way that I could please my mother, and so I quit trying to please her."

Em took a class to explore careers and get back into the job field. "I just discovered all of a sudden that there must be something important about my life besides raising these children and my husband." She renewed her teaching certificate and began doing art projects within the schools. Adam sanctioned this as long as it didn't interfere with dinner, and since it sometimes did, they had problems with it. "I wanted to experience something, I wanted to accomplish something." It was around this time that they discovered Adam's real problem to be manic depression. He went through years of counseling, but he could be very destructive and violent during his "highs." (Did he ever abuse you?) "I'd duck [laughter]. At one time he did hurt the oldest, but I was always there to save. I was an in-between. I knew when he was drinking not to bring up subjects that should not be discussed."

In one year Em lost her best friend, her father, and her husband. Her friend died of cancer. Then her father became ill. "Father regressed. . . . The family, over a period of 24 hours—we each took a four-hour shift in order to be with him. And we spent maybe three months—Adam was in one hospital in the psychiatric unit, and dad was in the other hospital, and I had to manage

all the children. . . . Then I'd go up and see Adam, and then I'd go up and
stay with my dad . . . and I'd have to take a bedpan and hold his penis. I
don't think it was as much of a father-daughter relationship, because there
never had been that close relationship, but it was a very humanistic kind of
relationship in watching the parent turn around and need to be taken care of,
instead of caring for—and feeling very capable about doing that—I did—
and being with him the night he died." He waited for a brother to come, but
meanwhile "I remember for three hours singing to him some of the very old
Mormon folk songs that I learned as a girl, and I think that really helped him
to carry him through his passages."

Adam continued drinking, which threw off his medication (lithium). "And
the last year of our marriage he was in and out of psychiatric wards. . . . So
in the end what he did was take a gun and kill himself." The experience was
a devastating one, but several close friends helped Em over this difficult period
in her life—three deaths in one year. "I'm still here," she laughs. Em feels
she now prizes her women friends especially, and she speaks frequently of
the need for women to support each other. There is a sense of "sisterhood"
in Em's words. Her brother also helped her "pick up the pieces" during this
time.

Meanwhile, Em had met Charles shortly before Adam died. She had to
take a trip with an artist friend to another city, and there they were introduced.
The attraction was immediate, partly because Charles, a profoundly intuitive
artist who dreams his works before he creates them, had had a dream of Em
a few months before!

After Adam's death, Em took some time to sort out her life and decided
she wanted to become a professional artist, with the encouragement of Charles.
Charles himself had quit his job at 50 and become extremely successful within
5 years. "I felt how important it was for me as a woman to become a voice,
not only for myself as a person, but how I feel, and how women feel about
the world around them. . . . The process is actually more important to me
than the end result. Because I'm not interested in fame and a lot of money.
I'm interested in finding out who I am . . . and sharing. . . . I traded a painting
for a teepee. . . . I own [many] acres of ground, and I will put my teepee
up there. It will be mainly so I have solitude. Every woman that I talk to
needs time to be by themselves. Because we are so spaced out with so many
things around us, that we don't ever have time to really complete ourselves
in an area, and if you don't complete yourself, then you always feel fragmented. And women have a way of being very fragmented, if you just go
through a whole day, and write down everything you've done that day. . . .
A man can get up, breakfast is fixed for him, he leaves in the car and he
goes, and all of his time in the office is put forth taking himself very seriously.
And the problem with women is that they don't take themselves seriously,
their life and their art."

As an artist spends so much time alone, Em finds she must make a special effort to get out, and she gardens and enjoys a class at the Y. After Adam's death, Em succeeded in getting jobs teaching arts in federally and locally funded school programs, and this launched her career. She had done similar work on a volunteer basis during her marriage and had the teaching credential besides. She was particularly successful in art therapy with adolescents in juvenile halls and detention centers because of the problems she had had with her own adolescent children.

The problems with her children are the losses Em feels most keenly. They have included drug abuse, sexual promiscuity, and other difficulties that became worse after her husband's death. She "tried to keep life balanced with no major changes, and help them work out guilt, anger, fears, frustration, sorrow, loss. But it was hard." One of her daughters tried to commit suicide and seemed to be without identity and motivation. Another has been and in and out of detention centers. Em feels she is partly to blame, for not insisting on "more out of life than just to be, in quotes, a mother, wife, homemaker, then maybe the children would have seen some of this." She feels very sad to see her children having such a struggle and also that they are such a distance away from her. "They can't seem to get their shit together [laughs]. . . . No matter how much help, or how much love is around, or how much understanding. For me as a woman that's quite painful." She regrets that they don't have college degrees and speculates that perhaps they don't do art because they are afraid to compete with her, and "I'm a hell of a competitor, because I do everything." She wants them to be responsible for their lives and has tried to give them the tools.

Currently Em has a number of her artworks on display at various galleries around the country. Her topic is variations on the theme of birth and motherhood. (Her work and that of her husband, Charles, is so beautiful that I wish it were possible to display it in this book.) Em works 7 days a week from 8 in the morning until 10 or 11 at night, although there are days when she doesn't "do much." "I hope to accomplish things like Georgia O'Keefe," she says, and when she speaks of hopes for the future: "I'd be doing very large murals around women, women's feeling." Charles supports her to the extent of being a mentor. When asked how the decision to be an artist changed her life, she replies, "I really had to take myself seriously." She feels a need for solitude and a need "to be out touching the earth, to ground ourselves again. . . . Art is the only form of saying who we are, what we are, and how we perceive the world." She feels people don't understand that "the artists have enough guts, drive, and motivation in order to go out and be the historian of what is left of what people are. You know, Mozart, go back through the ages, Picasso—these are the men who have transcribed what people are."

"I paint a lot of women and children. I also paint Indian figures. And the reason that I paint the Indian is that I think that they're a very special, spiritual people that have not abused the land or their culture, and they're highly sensitive and creative, the bowls that they eat from, they make their own pottery, they weave their own clothes and blankets, they make their own teepees . . . in Mexico . . . their own candelabras. They have a real close feeling for how they live," different from our own way of life, which she sees as fast, filled with suicide, mental illness, and depression.

In recent years Em sees herself as having developed to the point where "I'm not as naive about life in general. Even my children don't see me today as I was, for instance, five years ago. I was the mother that was always so loving and so giving, and now the most important person in my life . . . is me. And my children probably see me as selfish, and they don't understand that they can't do any growing as long as I'm a rescuer." She sees the myth of the woman getting married, having children, growing old together with her husband as "a bunch of bullshit." However, toward the end of the interview she talks about her main conflict in life: "I think it's been very difficult to resolve that thing of again, mother, to be able to let go of other people needing, filling other people's needs, and also learning to say 'No,' that's my Achilles' heel. Trying to take myself seriously and working as a serious woman artist, and on the other hand having a lot of pulls again."

Among her most precious possession, what she'd save in a fire, Em mentions her guitar and all her business papers—simply to be practical. However, "my wristband is Hopi Indian, and it means that this man spent all his time making this, and I remember where I bought it, and I was with my husband, and it has a lot of memories. . . . And I do have a . . . filigree gold ring set with pearls that my mother gave me when I graduated from high school." There is also some poetry, particularly a poem she wrote when her first grandchild was born, at the same time she was doing a mural on birth.

The topic of her husband's suicide is painful to her; she thinks of it as a loss because he was so talented, there was "much more that he could give the world. . . . I think that's a tragedy to lose not only a husband and a father, but to lose someone that's gifted." And yet "I wouldn't be sitting here today as the artist I am unless that had happened." Charles tells her there's an old Spanish proverb, "Out of everything that seems to be bad, something good will come." She feels Adam had such a hold on her and might even have killed her, that her present life might never have happened. So there was a purpose in his death, and she is now doing a large mural around death. She's in touch with a friend who is dying, as well as other women, to understand how women feel about death. Her friend said, "I'm sad that my husband is going to be left without me. I told him that I will always be with him when he sees the sunset," so Em thinks "we try and leave reminders." Em says she would be glad if she were the one who had leukemia instead of her children because she is so much stronger and would be able to "suffer it out." Her mural will register the many different feelings people have about death, the pain of sorrow, the peace of the death, the gladness some have about death. She feels her murals should show the unhappiness surrounding some births, children with birth defects, unwed mothers, mothers who don't need another child—it seems only right to show both sides. In another painting she points out the "face on an Indian woman, and she has a stomach, she's pregnant, and . . . it's not really sadness but there is a mystical feeling about the endurance, what she's going through."

Em has similar feelings about gardening. She spends an hour a day outside. "I love to garden. And I find as I read and talk with other women that that's pretty common. Women have a feeling for flowers, plants, working in the soil, a rebirth type of thing. I'm never sure that it's all going to go on, but once I see that that bulb is coming up in the ground, and I know that in a month or six weeks there's going to be a few of them, I'm pretty sure that everything's going to be okay. Just life is going on. . . . There is that rebirth. And I just finished doing a mural on birth."

Em has a recurring dream. "It's a dream of a house with a lot of rooms, and I wander through the house. The house is really my life, the rooms are the different periods in time. . . . It's very big, like a castle . . . and it has large rooms and small rooms, and I guess the large rooms are the big experiences, and the smaller ones maybe things that filter in. It's furnished with feelings." There was another dream of a house some years ago. "I believed that I knew a musician friend in a previous life, and this probably was the house. And I think that if I ever went to Europe that I would spot that house some place, maybe possibly in England or France." She believes that some day she may do a mural that will hang in the school where her father taught.

She feels divorce is just as difficult as death. "It's just a different type of separation. It's not quite as definite, permanent. Death is quite permanent. You don't have time to work a lot of that out."

The extended L/T life theme of Em's history includes losses through death—her husband, father, and friend—as well as losses involving motherhood; the major transcendence is through her art, in which she converts the losses of motherhood and death into works of beauty, thereby re-creating herself as a professional artist experiencing rebirth. Her second husband facilitates transcendence. The core theme, then, is death of relationships versus rebirth through art. Her protocol is rated as transcendence oriented, in the replacing stage. I think a few years ago she might have been seen as searching and possibly during the last years of her marriage as yearning or grieving—that is, her history would have been loss oriented. I say this because there is still so much loss in it, and the strength of her transcendence is still relatively new. Integration seems far away, because her losses of her children are still raw.

Em's Myers-Briggs Type Indicator (Myers, 1962, 1977) personality profile shows her to be "warmly enthusiastic, high-spirited, ingenious [and] imaginative"—a good description of her.

Theoretical analysis

Em's story is a beautiful example of someone living quite explicitly on the birth-death or loss-transcendence continuum.

Her losses included difficult relationships with her parents and brothers and a conservative family background through which she felt she missed a lot of living. She felt she had to compete with her brothers for attention; this may have been the root of her becoming "a hell of a competitor," to which she attributes some of her children's difficulties. She experienced a traumatic adolescence, culminating in gonorrhea from her lover-musician, which could have made her incapable of giving birth but fortunately did not. Her relationship with Adam was difficult; he was alcoholic and manic-depressive and could be violent and destructive, all of this eventuating in his suicide. Her friend's and father's deaths also hit her hard; she points out that after death you can't work out any problems. In addition, there was the loss of the art she might have been doing during her marriage—setting a better example for her children, even rescuing them by being who she really was. Her losses of her children's happiness, adjustment, and presence she feels most keenly. By trying to take herself seriously as an artist, she is trying to overcome a past in which she was mother first. Motherhood has brought her the needed endurance of childbirth, sorrow over her adolescent children, but also the joy of raising them during early childhood!

Art as transcendence pervades Em's history from early childhood to the present in the form of music, poetry, many crafts, instruction, and painting. Art, the American Indian culture, and gardening are interrelated under the overarching value of being and becoming who one really is, a type of rebirth. Em's works are American Indian in flavor, depicting Indian birth, because she feels Indians are closer to the land, which represents their physical and spiritual essence. By gardening, living in a teepee, traveling through the southwest and Mexico, and then expressing all in art, Em experiences her own rebirth. She extends this experience to women collectively.

Em has become aware that she has painted birth and motherhood in idealized form, thus converting her own mixed experiences into the dream she once had of them. She now feels the responsibility to paint the other, more negative side, to give full voice to the truth of mothers' experiences (to which she may have been sensitized by her own difficulties). Similarly, with death she will show that not all is sorrow and grieving. She is moving from the idealized to the realized, from aspects of a false self to a true one.

Additional modes of transcendence for Em have been the class in career exploration; therapy to work out her family relationships; mothering her dying father and singing to him; subsequently becoming closer to her brother; women's support groups and networks, particularly identification with women in her relationships and her art; the relationship between Em and Charles, the man and the mentor; and the realization that she would not be experiencing the transcendence now without the tragedy of Adam's death, the view of purpose (an example of integration). She will make of his death an artwork, and then perhaps finally it will be finished. Were she to make of her children works of art as well, that is, her daughter's suicide attempt, the group in detention—this also might help her overcome losses in this area.

For Em, birth is not simply the literal experience of a mother producing a child, nor is death simply the end of life. Both are metaphorically much more. Birth is a mystical experience, the ability to endure, being close to the earth—flowers signify rebirth; it is also the birth of the spirit and the self. Death is separation; Em feels the loss of her children keenly because this is a form of death for her; there is death not only in that one child attempted suicide but also the death of dreams, ideals, their alternative futures, and what they might have been, as well as the heretofore idealized mother-daughter relationship. There is, of course, much self-blame in Em, probably not warranted to such a degree. The children possibly inherited some of their negative tendencies and predispositions to depression from their father (see Arieti, 1978), reinforced by some of his contribution to their childhood environment. Finally, the loss of Adam seems most tragic in the death of talents and gifts, of potential transcendence that could not come to fruition. Talent unfulfilled, in Adam, in her children, and heretofore in herself, is the tragedy for Em—a kind of death of transcendence.

Em is integrating loss with her art. She is as yet unsure of herself. She declares herself to be a professional because, in the past, women were not taken seriously, by themselves or others; their daily lives were fragmented, and, as Tillie Olsen (1978) would say, filled with distractions from their art. The exciting aspect of Em's story is that in mid-life, and through much sorrow, she has declared herself to be who she feels she is becoming. She has bought the supplies, set up a studio, acquired a loving mentor, joined the proper organizations, and now works full-time and overtime at her craft. Success in the form of exhibitions and commissions is coming to her. Em is indeed in the act of re-creation and rebirth.

TRANSCENDING DEATH BY DYING

To survive as individuals, we must eat, eliminate, sleep, and be protected from the elements by clothing and shelter. To survive as a race, we must also procreate and care for the young. According to some beliefs, to the extent that we minimize the necessary conditions of bodily survival, we win spiritual survival. That is, we embrace temporary losses, intensifying our recognition of their temporariness and of the transitory nature of life in general in order to transcend time. We live less when we eat less. We die as much as is humanly possible while we are "in the midst of life." Psychologically, there is much wisdom in this. The less we have, the less we have to lose or leave behind. If we commit ourselves to loss and spiritual transcendence in every waking moment, we become habituated to both. We fight the fundamental illusion with its opposite, the fundamental disillusion. This is, perhaps the core meaning of the biblical injunction, "Whosoever will save his life shall lose it; but whosoever will lose his life for my sake, the same shall save it" (Luke 9:24). Not only commitment to what we cannot see, not only martyrdom.

. . . We are only partly in this life, we are also partly in the next. I knew a young nun once who was dying of a neurological disease, and she expressed this kind of existence very clearly. She had "a foot in both worlds," and it was a source of joy to herself and inspiration to others.

TRANSCENDENCE THROUGH FAITH

We have seen developmental paradigms of faith, such as the early games of peekaboo, the acquisition of object constancy, hide-and-seek, magic, and religion, that makes it seem as though faith in the overcoming of separation, the reappearance of what is lost, may be an inherent biological trait in the human organism. The dead cat will return at sunset down her customary garden path. All the dead will rise on judgment day. Faith that life has meaning seems inseparable from the imputation of some dimension of immortality. Faith is the expression of the ultimate fundamental illusion—there is no death, there are no metaphors of it. Loss is not loss. Loss will not happen.

TRANSFERENCE OF ATTACHMENT

Habituation to loss is another way of viewing the problem of attachment, an Eastern concept on which Campbell (1961), among others, has expounded beautifully. According to this concept, we are attached to the forms of all things, but because all things change form, we are continuously experiencing a sense of loss. Attachment to form is attachment not only to shape, color, and movement of physical objects but also to the forms of relationships, concepts, meanings, and illusions. Possessions will be marred, lost, or broken, but so will marriages, friendships, careers, social orders, and the world as it is.

The first attachment bond that the infant forms is the prototype for other attachments she will make in life (Bowlby, 1969). If she does not form such an attachment, there may be pathology, autism, or schizophrenia, according to our Western way of thinking. Indeed, our attachment behaviors, crying, clinging, grasping, smiling, promote our very survival, but consequently they seed our loss. We will lose that to which we cling, for which we cry.

Nonattachment to forms will protect us against their loss. The problem with nonattachment, or disattachment, is that it precludes the joys of passion and desire as well as the heartbreak. We become less human if indeed we are becoming more "divine." The root of evil is desire, and as the ego desires less, it becomes less itself, and more one with whatever other there may be— or with nothing. The weaning away from attachment to form is also a weaning away from living, a way of dying. Diggory and Rothman (1961) found that people's greatest fears of death lay in the end of plans and projects. They were much attached to these! Disattachment is a form of anticipatory rehearsal for these endings without the final loss of consciousness. The euphoria that may accompany this rehearsal is necessarily perceived within this very consciousness, which sets up a particularly insidious illusion. After all is given up (or almost all) and the inner life reigns supreme, there is still something left!

The denial of life becomes the denial of death.

We have a tradition of nonattachment in our own country, referred to in Chapter 11 on cultural modes of transcendence. This is the wanderer, the individual who never stays long enough in one place to become committed to an individual, a job, a location. He tends to be regarded negatively or enviously by different segments of his society. It is also the teenager postponing identity, the dropout, the alienated (see Bret Easton Ellis's *Less than zero*, 1985, and Sartre's *Nausea,* 1964). Attachment protects and kills. Its goal is mergence, or death by suffocation. The nonattached die of exposure.

The supreme discipline of Eastern religions and the asceticism of some Christian sects are founded on the promise of continuation in some guise; some part of us—our personality, our Karma, our relationships—goes on. The promise of immortality is nothing less than the promise that the attachment to the form of self will not be completely and irrevocably broken. Something of the self will endure, or rather something of the myth of self.

The guarantor of immortality has many guises. She is the parent, teacher, lover, therapist, boss, God. Just as small losses are metaphors of death, small transcendences are metaphors of birth, life, or immortality. Metaphors are forms of transference, but throughout the myriad transmutations of life-death symbolization, it is the self, myth, and myth's meaning that we struggle to preserve.

In the original Freudian concept of transference, the patient transfers anxieties, hostilities, or sexual feelings from a previous problem relationship to the therapist and then proceeds to work out a solution that he could not achieve originally. Freud (1910, reprinted 1957; 1912, reprinted 1958; DeWald, 1972) himself saw much wider application of the concept to relationships other than those between therapist and patient—to parents and lovers, for example. In an explication of the forces underlying this mechanism, Becker (1973) sees transference as a crucial way of handling fear of life and fear of death; we transfer our anxiety to an omnipotent other, a hero of some kind, a president, an actress, a rock star, and she becomes the shield from death. It is the transference of the idealized from previous relationships that were not ideal.

If the hero dies, the repression of our awareness of mortality temporarily breaks down, and it is this for which we really grieve. Within the L/T paradigm, we may see that all the attachments in an individual's life, attachments to people, situations, and ideas, can be viewed as transferences from previous people, situations, and ideas representing loss and transcendence. They therefore represent attachment to form. The self in the present is always working out the past to create a meaningful myth of itself. As we saw in Chapter 8, the first attachment to parents continues because they are omnipotent. They control our environment in a myriad of ways, when we are helpless. Thus, our subsequent attachments to individuals represent transference of omnipotence (power over death) from parents and therefore continuity or immortality for the self. Self's losses continue to be transcended. Terror over our mortality is once again repressed by attachment to others, who are illusorily omnipotent and will preserve the various forms of our life. Attachment to form is attachment to life.

To restate the thesis in Campbell's terms (1961), transference to other relationships, objects, or ideas represents a transformation, a change from one form to another, but because these forms are metaphors of one another, the attachment remains. An illustration is the transformation of one's own insubstantiality into substance, a child, a poem, or transubstantiation (to extend the old religious concept) from flesh to spirit. All of these can be seen as forms of the replacement stage of the L/T process.

Transcendence thus becomes the transference of meaning to a work of art, a love, a deed of charity, or the transformation of this work into meaning, or the transubstantiation of the self into the work. The lifework, or "project" as the existentialists call it (Sartre, 1969), is like a mirror, reflecting immortality on a mortal being. In our lifework, we create our own substance, which is now so much more than the substance of ourselves. When we are creating, we are not dying irrevocably with no hope of return, at least that is the illusion.

IMMORTALITY OVER THE LIFE SPAN

Transference throughout the life cycle begins with the prototypical attachment of the infant to the caretaker, with the attachment behaviors of clinging, grasping, sucking, and so forth. The infant learns that the fulfillment of needs necessary to survival is in the hands of an omnipotent other. There is no limit to the power of this other, who can overcome all, including death. At this point, threat is discomfort in the belly, homeostatic disequilibrium; the cycle of discomfort and relief is gradually comprehended cognitively. Threat and its obviation develop in tandem. The caretaker is able to provide all the infant's needs. There is a catch, however; the same omnipotent other who can provide relief can also withhold it or even inflict pain, which the infant's resources are too limited to combat. If the pain is considerable and frequent, as in cases of abuse, the infant may experience feelings of catastrophic anxiety. The seeds of dependence-independence and internal-external locus of control, among other personality traits, are sown in this period, or fertilized if there is genetic predisposition. The most doting of parents will withhold, if only for the few minutes it takes to heat the bottle or unbutton the blouse. Thus, the omnipotent one has the power to inflict either death or life eternal, a God who can be loving or vengeful, for reasons unknown and therefore capricious.

As the infant grows to childhood she controls more of her environment, but the number of those who exercise control over her needs increases as well. Siblings, playmates, other parents, teachers, schoolmates may confer or deny. The felt emotional intensity of their power will be transferred from the primary caretaker; however, within the L/T paradigm, this will always be undergoing revision, depending on the actual interactions between child and environment. If her needs are met with a modicum of delay, she is learning a balance between her own resources and the power of others. As an adolescent, she transfers power over life and death metaphors from parents to the peer group, then the community, the state, the nation, acts of God (which are always disasters!). As the omnipotence of each is found to be illusory, lacking in some newly perceived area of need, the circle of transference widens. Each object of attachment and transference is outgrown, but the relationship, conflicts, and needs are transferred from old to new, always, of course, undergoing modification.

Meanwhile, the form of old attachments changes. Parents may still provide food, but they cannot provide sex and usually not employment. Even their ability or willingness to provide food is no longer unlimited or unending. The relationship itself is continually undergoing revision, with aspects moving into the lost us and we. Gratitude is behaving as if less had moved into the lost than actually has. There is a pretense and an attempt to hold parts of the relationship from loss. Gratitude is transcendence over lost relating. It has the virtue of becoming a transcendent aspect of the relationship, however, encouraging the me's in a relationship to intersect out of desire instead of necessity. It also is a form of guilt, thanks for losses incurred to parent that the child may transcend. The child is guilty over these losses but even guiltier if she does not recognize and give thanks.

As life goes on, the transference of the power to overcome annihilation is made to still others. The husband can earn and purchase housing and food. The wife can nurse to health. The children protect their parents from death, not only because they bestow immortality by carrying genetic material (see Wilson, 1975), seeds of body and mind, values and feelings, but also because parents are able to overcome death for their children, godlike, each victory over a child's loss filling them with love, the antithesis of death fear! The pregnant woman is holy; that any ill could befall her, while rationally possible, seems irrationally improbable. The physician overcomes death by healing; he may be the parent figure on whom body-loss anxieties are transferred. The company also overcomes by bestowing security; it is easier to repress death awareness when our company lines the nest with activity for one's hours, colleagues, salary, pension, stockholding plans, insurance; the company is a protective womb—until it expels us.

Lastly, we transfer the power of immortality to ideas and values, often assumed in mottos: "An apple a day keeps the doctor away," "Early to bed, early to rise, makes a man healthy, wealthy, and wise"; the saws of Ben Franklin and Confucius, the aphorisms of the great and forgotten, common sense on how to survive—all are words to follow if we would be immortal. The existentialists would observe that the above transferences require conformity, that it is easy to lose one's identity and authenticity, to desert the life project by becoming too dependent on husband, wife, children, physician, and company for illusory power over death. Loss of identity is a form of death. This transference from one relationship to another is the transference of power to save our lives; we are angry as we perceive this power threatening, loving as we may be saved.

Transference of immortality power takes place within the structure of self, as well as without. There are relationships among the various parts of self, but these may form a reasonably tight-knit whole, especially in the integrated self. These various parts are accorded omnipotence, depending on the situation of the moment. The me of the self who smiles, cajoles, and manipulates can sell anyone anything—until a different skill is required. The attempt to use this me inappropriately, say with a lover, may meet with disaster. Dialogues take place between different aspects of the self; many of the internal relationships are analogues of relationships between self and other. Transcendent I may ask a transcendent me why she performed in such a manner; a relationship analogous to that between patient and therapist may exist, a gestalt therapeutic approach of me to I. Transference of omnipotence within the self is perhaps best illustrated by examples from the clinical literature. For example, Billy Milligan was a multiple personality (Keyes, 1981) who had aspects of himself that he called on to "take the pain" (David), perform deeds of great strength (Ragen), or escape handcuffs and straitjackets (Tommy). Parts of self are sometimes resurrected from the lost, given new life, raised like Lazarus from the dead. The responsibility for survival is in a very literal sense transferred from one part of self to another.

ILLUSION AND DELUSION

Because we cannot transcend death literally, we spend our lives transcending it metaphorically, as I have shown. We accomplish this by creating illusions, the myth of self, the interpretation of other selves, the "finding" of meaning that we have ourselves created. Illusion has its uses and abuses. We know these by their fruits. Abuse of illusion becomes delusion, variably defined by different cultures. It is perfectly all right for a woman to see herself as a committed housewife, a paragon of wifely virtue, a mother who sacrifices much for the welfare of her children—as near to the ideal as she can be. She transcends loss for others at considerable loss to herself. (There may not be many people who can stand to be around her, but her attempt to live up to the cultural standard is admirable.) When she becomes a little holier, mother of God, she has moved from illusion, which society will countenance and applaud, to delusion, which others will deny and on which society will not permit her to act. Becker (1973) makes the point that illusions are necessary, the positive side of repression. We see delusions of grandeur as partly a failure in illusion; the mother cannot weave the illusion of greatness sufficiently and must transcend as a greater me. The delusion of persecution is, to recast Laing (1976), a split between the false, conforming me and the transcendent I; the false me threatens the I and the very myth and meaning of self as integrated whole, also a failure of illusion.

THE LONGING FOR DEATH

As we grow older, and sometimes when we are very young, we lose more of that which we love. Grandparents and parents, a child perhaps, friends and lovers, homes, abilities, dreams, wedding rings and gardens, alternative futures and possibilities, places we will not visit again, the world as it was and might have been, self-concepts and family myths, even life meaning perhaps—all move into the lost sectors of our selves, making of these a storehouse richer by far than the transcendent I and me. We may grow in love for all that we have lost, as it remains frozen in a memory illuminated by a light we have never seen on earth. This is a nostalgia, the present love for what is lost. Within ourselves we clasp the past that we have called "dead," feeling it often more vital than anything presently alive. In this sense, we are in love with what is dead, newly recommitted like the regenerated idealist to his ideals. Life is not as it *should* be, and these people, these loves, these beautiful things should not have died. Something is wrong with the order, the very nature of things.

So we move within a love for what is dead to a longing to shed the less meaningful transcendent I and me's and to become fully reunited with what is truly, authentically ourselves, the lost sector, to be one with that dead love and beauty. This is the secret that psychiatry, psychology, philosophy, religion, and all the rest of us try to keep from ourselves.

We deny death in order that we not be tempted to embrace it. We envy and are furious with the suicide who rips the veil. We are mystified by teenage suicide epidemics. Gwen blurts out the truth when she says, "I want to die. I guess we all do." When anthropologists ask if we are a death-denying or death-embracing society, they assume we cannot be both—but we are.

Death, the ultimate loss, becomes the ultimate transcendence. What is more, we knew it all along. We knew it when we took unnecessary risks, created heroism and heroes, devised metaphorical losses to repeat previous ones, called warmongers "insane," labeled suicide a sin, condemned abortion and euthanasia, and tentatively suggested the heresy of a "death instinct"— then snatched it back.

CLINICAL APPLICATIONS

Life and self-development involve loss and transcendence, microscopic and macroscopic, at every second of our existence. Therefore, the clinician with an L/T view will recognize that all clients come to her in mourning for what is lost. Because of this, all therapy can be viewed as grief therapy. The client is in nothing less than a metaphorical (or literal) struggle between life and death. This view should assist the counselor in a number of ways.

First, the therapist can identify what represents death to her client and what represents life, the metaphorical system. She can diagram this system, as I have done in Kara's case history. She and her client will be in far better communication, as the client will feel he has conveyed what even he only dimly understood, and the therapist will be wholly responding to real issues at the deepest level, not simply vague signifiers or distractors from the truth.

Second, the therapist can help the client identify the L/T life theme or patterns of loss and transcendence that pervade his life. With guidance and work on both sides, the loss patterns can be changed to something more benign or converted into transcendence, as Marjorie and Faith have done.

Third, the therapist can assist the client in understanding the relationship of the life to the self, of behavior or external experience to inner experience, and especially the nature of the self. The self structure, lost and transcendent me's and I's, can actually be diagrammed, using the basic model structure outlined in Chapter 6, the better to help the client understand what is happening to him. The client's stage of self-development can be recognized and the next stage encouraged.

Fourth, the dimensions of loss should be far better understood by both therapist and client; often the bereavement seems to exceed the loss, but when the various levels of loss are recognized—not only primary but also secondary, holistic, self-conceptual, and metaphorical levels—the understanding of what is really lost becomes clearer, and search, replacement, and integration are more feasible. One does not replace what one does not know is lost.

Fifth, it will be helpful to the clinician to recognize the client's major modes of transcendence, to recognize any deficiency of situational, dispositional, or general transcendence (the latter in nonaddicted depressives, for example), and to work toward the balance that seems to characterize the more transcendent individuals.

Sixth, it should be helpful to the clinician to recognize the stages of the client's transcendence of loss as well as his orientation to loss or transcendence, the better to work with him.

Seventh, reconceptualization of personality and psychopathology in the L/T framework casts a different explanatory light on much that was dark before. Some personality difficulties and pathologies should respond to the positive transcendence approach and should help with various types of pathology, although clinical experience with this approach is as yet very limited. However, some good results have been reported. Clinicians have found the L/T interview helpful in a number of settings; it makes salient some of the most important aspects of the person and thus serves as a guide to therapy.

Eighth, recognition of the societal and cultural context of L/T should assist in guiding the client toward appropriate cultural and social transcendence, once the losses have been identified.

Ninth, the relationship of time and death to L/T should be of invaluable assistance in recognizing the existence and roots of pathology, the motivations and transcendent approaches that must be taken.

Tenth, the L/T approach leads to a reconceptualization of the "boundary issues" so basic to the training of therapists. Although much pathology (and countertransference) is involved in not recognizing the boundaries between mother and child, therapist and client, and so forth, where one leaves off and another begins, I believe that therapists are also trained in the *illusions* of boundaries where they do not exist, where they must created, or artificially constructed, but not denied. As shown in Chapter 6, all our relationships are part of who we are; it is just that we are so much more than any one of these. If I am abused, the abusing parent is within me; it is for this reason that I am also an abuser. I become what is done to me—thus, the ultimate horror of the victim. Fortunately, there is much more within me than one event or relationship. The area of boundary issues needs reexamination.

Eleventh, from an L/T perspective, it is important not only to work through previous losses but also to strengthen transcendence. In many instances this can be done closer to the beginning of therapy, rather than working through losses first. For example, one way is to ask, "What do you love?" or "What have you loved in the past?—to probe and remind and then to prescribe these loving, transcending behaviors for the client. Then the transcendence aspect of the self will begin to grow again.

It is especially important that clients not be allowed to sink into such a deep well of grief that they can never climb out again. Grief therapy must have an end point. Carol Tavris (1982) found that the expression of anger could actually constitute the *rehearsal* of it, rather than its release, making the angry person feel angrier still. I believe that the same may be true of grieving. It may become the rehearsal of grief, rather than its release. Therefore, the therapist must assist the client in re-creating more of the transcendent thoughts, feelings, and behaviors *before* the grief is "worked through," not after. The self is not a vacuum; more loss will fill it if transcendence is not marshaled and moved into the self structure.

Twelfth, as this volume goes to press, I have begun investigating what I term the "life dream," using exploratory data from this research (Weenolsen, 1988). This preliminary evidence suggests that most individuals report a life dream in childhood or adolescence, that is, something they especially wanted to do in life; that this dream usually centers on occupation, just as is true of the men in Levinson's (1978) study; that half fulfill the dream, at least to some extent, and half do not; that those who fulfill their life dream report positive experiences, and those who do not fulfill it ultimately regret this; that the life dream is the "path with heart" (Casteneda, 1976) rather than a head decision; that all five interviewees who did not report a life dream also reported very severe abuse as children, so that it seems very much related to identity formation. I conclude that inquiries into life dreams might prove diagnostic of emotional disorder, its roots, and also possible avenues of therapy. Identity formation might have been interrupted, and there is additional evidence for life dreams formed in adulthood. Therapeutic possibilities might include assistance with the resurrection of the life dream, its modification, or its initial formation.

With these aspects of the L/T framework in mind, grief counseling can proceed with the tasks of mourning as outlined by Worden (1982), Tatelbaum (1977), and McKitrick (1981) on working with dying clients. One may also proceed with the resolution of pathological grief (newly reinterpreted) and with a greatly expanded list of special types of losses that need specific resolution. Obviously, a family systems approach to dealing with the family L/T myth would be helpful (see Hoffman, 1981; Satir, 1967; Worden, 1982). Awareness of the fundamental illusion can be a kind of inoculation for the future.

Both avoidance and embrace of death form the root motivations for much of our existence. We try to avoid what it would be lethal to embrace, but ultimately sex and aggression, love and death, become unity and, as to the white light, we are drawn. It is this "heretical" knowledge we seek to escape.

LAST WORDS

Death is the basic fact of our existence and our development—physical, mental, emotional, social, cultural, and spiritual. It is the context of our decisions, beliefs, regrets, and commitments. It pervades our lives through symbol and metaphor; the great variety of its possibilities is represented by the themes and metaphorical systems of our lives. We are always in a metaphorical struggle between life and death, at any one point moving toward life or death on the life-death continuum. We live the metaphorical life. Nothing is irrelevant.

Many of our relationships are fights to the death; we feel this, although often we do not understand the great intensity of our feelings. We are always dying and being reborn, killing each other, or giving birth.

Death is represented in our lives by the many limitations of our humanity and our finitude. These are the limits to our possibilities that death imposes, and yet death itself has no limits, is eternal. Limitlessness to us is pure life, and in that sense we are drawn to the limitless, the pure life that is death. This is the source of our dread, our double bind, our denial, and our embrace. It is the nature of life to limit us. As one chooses one's life, one chooses one's death also, by exposure through growth and individuation, by smothering or asphyxiation through mergence with other and with all that is beyond. We spend most of our lives oscillating between these two forms of death.

We love, we lose, we love what we have lost, we love the dead who are gone and remain within us, we love what is dead in us, preserved in the ideal. It remains seductively deep within us, ready to betray.

What is the meaning, the significance, of acknowledging the truth of the human condition?

Consciousness leads us to understanding. We understand that we will kill or create with each act of our lives. We may commit to life or to death. We may murder with envy as our weapon, but then our envy burgeons within us because we are so drawn to the death we have inflicted on the other. Killing becomes an act of kindness we cannot tolerate within ourselves. We had intended murder. The hatred we have thereby turned toward ourselves is far worse than anything we could inflict on another. We have created ourselves as murderers, for which we can never forgive the victim, the scapegoat, the one who gained this ultimate power over us.

We understand that suffering serves a purpose, even if it was not created for that purpose, if it simply *is*. All loss is transcended in some manner, to some degree. Our suffering gives another the opportunity to overcome it and re-create himself, if not us, just as Tess grew more competent caring for her dying mother. This was her mother's last act of service for her daughter. Thus, suffering becomes an act of love, albeit one we could do without! When we give another the chance to care, to love, to effect the supreme transcendence, our lives and even our deaths have meaning.

We have followed the course of loss and transcendence over large portions of the life span in many women. In gratitude, let us wish them well. Beneath the boundaries between them and us, there is unity. They are also ourselves.

Appendix A

Sample

SAMPLE DESCRIPTION

This study is cross-sectional, because only one interview has been conducted and no systematic follow-ups are planned. It is open to the criticism of historicity; there will be no way to tease out the influence of environmental effects in comparing 50-year-olds with 40-year-olds; we can only make suggestions.

Of the sample, 30 were married, 9 divorced, 3 separated, 3 widowed, and 3 single. (For statistical purposes, two women were classified as married and employed, although one was single and living with a long-time boyfriend and the other was separated from her husband but living with a boyfriend.)

By occupation, 11 were not employed and 9 were employed part-time; for 5 of the part-timers, their employment was considered only casual, a few hours a week, and they were put into the MU category. Four of them earned their living through part-time employment, or contributed substantially to the family income, and were placed in the ME or UE category. Of those employed full-time or part-time, 1 fell into the unskilled category, 1 into skilled/service, 11 into clerical/secretarial, 23 into junior executive, arts, nurse, or teacher categories, and 1 (a physician) into the professional-executive category.

Educationally, 2 had not completed high school, 3 were high school graduates, 21 had either completed some college or held certificates from technical/vocational schools, 10 were college graduates, and 12 held graduate or professional degrees.

With regard to children, 9 had no living children, 9 had one, 12 had two, 12 had three, 5 had four, and 1 had seven children. Two of the women were pregnant at the time of the interview, one with her first child. Women who had given up a child for adoption at birth were not counted as having a living child, a difficult decision in one instance, because the mother thought of her child often, remembers his birthday, and hopes to be reunited with him when he turns 18.

Socioeconomic status was derived by combining occupation or husband's occupation, education, and income. (Information on housing was taken as an additional criterion if needed but was not used, partly because some interviewees chose to be interviewed in the university offices or the researcher's home rather than their own.) By this measure, 10 were working class, 28 were middle class, 10 were upper-middle class and 2 were upper class. The upper-middle class and upper class were collapsed for statistical analyses. This classification has an inherent bias favoring the two- or more-income family and against the single individual and is submitted only for rough comparison purposes. (See Table 1 in Chapter 1.)

Appendix B

Interrater Reliability

To determine interrater agreement, four new undergraduate research assistants were trained in the L/T paradigm as well as in rating the protocols using this paradigm. Their training consisted of reading the theoretical literature, group discussions with me, and reading and discussing several protocols. This training was congruent with the training sessions of other studies (cf. Block, 1971). Then eight (nontraining) protocols were randomly selected.

The research assistants were asked to make separate lists of the losses and the transcendences in each protocol they evaluated and then to look for common denominators or patterns in each list. For example, Nora's protocol was interpreted by the raters as transcendence through leaving, or "turning away" from bitter relationships to fantasy (about travel and remembered kindness). Core theme: Bitter relationships versus getting away. The polar core theme was thus supported by the specific major events of the life; Nora's expanded theme supported her core theme. When approached in this fashion, no protocol seemed diffuse, senseless, or themeless. Whenever a number of themes were found, they were always seen as being encompassed by an overall life theme, as shown in Chapter 4, on life themes.

To assess the amount of interjudge agreement on the content of the L/T life themes, a matching procedure was employed. Eight protocols were randomly selected from the 48. These protocols included the typed life histories, the L/T Life History form, the Myers-Briggs Type Indicator, and the Social Readjustment Rating Scale. In the *first* phase of the check, they were submitted to the four raters. On each protocol, each rater typed up a 3 × 5 card with an L/T life theme as she or he saw it, expanded and core versions. I also typed up my theme, which I dubbed the "key theme." The raters' 3 × 5 cards for the eight protocols were all randomly numbered. In the *second* phase of the check, each of the four raters was asked to judge which 4 of the 32 randomly numbered themes matched each key theme. For example, for key theme A, theme cards numbered 7, 11, 19, and 26 (one from each rater) would be the match.

After all the ratings had been turned in, the ratio of correct numbers to total numbers (32) was calculated. Two raters had 27 out of 32 correct and two had 28 out of 32 correct, for percentages of .88 and .84. Thus, the average was .85. This is moderately high evidence of interjudge reliability. It suggests that the L/T life themes were not merely imposed on the protocols by me but can also been seen by others. However, the task and procedure were susceptible to a number of problems, the main one being that each rater could recognize his or her own ratings. This would have been a more serious drawback had they been matching their themes to *protocols*. Because they were matching the 32 themes to *my 8 key themes*, it does not seem a major concern. However, a better method would be to submit the ratings to a fresh panel of trained judges.

Measures of interjudge agreement were sought on the following: (1) the loss orientation of each protocol, (2) the transcendence orientation, (3) placement of the protocol on the loss-transcendence dimension, and (4) categorization by loss-transcendence stage.

For assessments 1 and 2, the loss and transcendence orientations, the raters were asked to rate each of the eight protocols using the following orthogonal dimensions:

TRANSCENDENCE
High
1
2

LOSS Low   1   2   3   4   5   High LOSS

4
5
Low
TRANSCENDENCE

A rater might rate a certain protocol as low loss, moderately high transcendence using this instrument; the rating would be 1 and 4. (The numbers represent 1, low; 2, moderately low; 3, moderate; 4, moderately high; 5, high.) An attempt to have the raters also rate each protocol in a fourfold manner, as HLHT (high loss, high transcendence), for example, unfortunately did not work out, because training time was short. However, judgments of interviewees using this fourfold approach may still be viable.

For assessment 3, the raters placed each of the eight protocols on the following dimension:

LOSS 1———2———3———4 ———5 TRANSCENDENCE

This is different from the first set of dimensions, in that it forces L/T into a bipolar dimension. One cannot be both high loss and high transcendence.

For assessment 4, the raters placed each of the eight protocols in one of the following stages of the L/T process (see Chapter 3, "Transcendence"), which were treated as a dimension, ranging from loss to transcendence, but were verbal rather than numerical.

1. Grieving   2. Searching   3. Replacing   4. Integrating

Thus, there were four interjudge agreement scores to be calculated. Intraclass correlations were computed for each of the four sets of ratings. The results for each set of ratings are as follows.

Interjudge agreement on the loss orientation of the ratees was represented by an intraclass correlation of .49; transcendence orientation yielded an intraclass correlation of .52; employment of the dimensional loss to transcendence rating system yielded an intraclass correlation of .56; finally, an intraclass correlation of .62 was achieved using the L/T stage method, confirming the impression of the raters that this was the easiest system to use.

Intraclass correlations of the *sum*, reducing the importance of measurement error and enhancing the relationships (Guilford & Fruchter, 1973), resulted in the following: an intraclass correlation of .83 was obtained for ratings of loss orientation; transcendence orientation showed an intraclass correlation of .85; an intraclass correlation of .87 was achieved using the dimensional rating system; and the highest intraclass correlation of .89 was obtained with the L/T stage rating. Thus, the correlations were very high, confirming judgments of orientation. Most important, neither age nor marital-employment status discriminated one from another, showing that orientation is not dependent on marital status or occupation.

Some problems occurred during the actual rating procedure. First and foremost, a natural disaster cut our training period virtually in half, from 5 weeks (a few hours a week) to 3 weeks. Related to this were problems within the training. It requires some practice to divest one's own judgment of loss from the report of the interviewee, particularly considering that our own judgments vary. A typical example was the divergence on a protocol in which the interviewee said, "I have lost myself." A number of us felt that the loss of self is the highest loss one can experience and rated her protocol a 5 on loss. However, some thought her protocol was not that highly loss oriented as a whole. Expectations regarding socioeconomic status, culture, relationships—attitudes that each of us brings to the rating situation—also interfered.

There was also contamination from other protocols; if we had just read a very highly loss-oriented protocol, it could affect our judgment of the present protocol. It is most desirable to consider the proportion of loss to transcendence reported by the individual within his or her protocol rather than try to compare it to others.

Finally, the entire concept of loss and transcendence has unexpected complexities and can be ambiguous when one is rating a protocol. There is a tendency on the part of some raters to want to rate an individual who has had a lot of loss as very highly transcendent simply because she has survived, and even though the protocol shows virtually no transcendence. In a way this is understandable; someone with a lot of loss has had a lot to overcome. However, when she reports a great deal of loss and very little of what she did to overcome it, how she changed, few transcendence activities, her protocol should be rated loss oriented. She has endured her losses in some fashion, to be sure, but does not report overcoming and re-creation.

Also, simply listing the losses and transcendences and determining whether they were balanced is a good idea *only* if the rater remembers that the interviewee spent most of the protocol on the few transcendence aspects, art and major relationships, for example, and very little on the more numerous small losses; a simple numerical list gives a false picture of some protocols and to some raters. This problem, unfortunately, did not become apparent until the end of the rating sessions.

However, despite the training and conceptualization problems, good solid reliability ratings in the .80s were achieved using all four methods of rating the protocols on loss and transcendence. Therefore, the conclusion is that employing a loss and transcendence approach to life span development is feasible.

Appendix C

Loss and Transcendence Life History

The following people and organizations have given their permission to use questions from their material in the L/T life history. The author expresses gratitude for that permission. Question 56, Dr. Mihalyi Csikzentmihalyi, University of Chicago. Questions 91–105, Templer, D. I. (1970). The construction and validation of a death anxiety scale, *Journal of General Psychology*, 82(2), 165–177. Copyright © 1970 by Heldref Publications. Reprinted with permission of the Helen Dwight Reid Educational Foundation. Questions 106–113, Shneidman, E. (1970). You and death. *Psychology Today* questionnaire, *Psychology Today*, 8, 67–72. Copyright © 1970 by American Psychological Association. Reprinted with permission from *Psychology Today*, 4(3).

LOSS AND TRANSCENDENCE LIFE HISTORY*
(Form B)

Name: (see consent form in separate file)   S#_____

Code: ME   MU   UE

Age: Marital: M   D   Se   W   Si   Religion: P   C   J   O   N

Live with: _____   # in household:
                    (relationship)

Home: Own?   Apt./Condo   # rooms:
           Rent?   House
                          Other

Occupation: Are you currently employed full-time?   Part-time?

If so, what is your occupation? _____

Previous employment (if any) _____

(If married) What is your husband's occupation? _____

Education?   Years in School?   HS Grad?

             Years in College?   College Grad?

             Graduate/Professional Degrees?   _____

             Technical/Vocational Training?   _____

Mother living?   Where? _____

Father living?   Where? _____

Siblings living?   How many?   Where?_____

Children living?   How many?   Names and Ages: _____

What are your major sources of income? _____

Into what range would you say your yearly income falls (for entire household)?
Under $8,000 $17,500–$25,000   Over $40,000
$8,000–$17,500 $25,000–$40,000

    1. CHILDHOOD: Tell me about your childhood? What incidents come
       to your mind? (Write on separate sheets of paper.) Did they affect
       you for better or worse?

    2. Who were the most important people in your life at that time? Why
       were they important? Did they influence you for better or worse?

3. Did you change during your childhood? If so, do you think you changed a lot, somewhat, or very little?

4. How did you change?

5. Do you wish anything had been different about your childhood? If so, what?

6. ADOLESCENCE: Tell me about your adolescence. What incidents come to your mind? Did they affect you for better or worse?

7. Who were the most important people in your life at that time? Why were they important? Did they influence you for better or worse?

8. Did you have any special things you wanted to do in your life?

9. Did you change during your adolescence? If so, do you think you changed a lot, somewhat, or very little?

10. How did you change?

11. Do you wish anything had been different about your adolescence? If so, what?

12. TWENTIES: Tell me about your twenties. What incidents come to your mind? Did they affect you for better or worse?

13. Who were the most important people in your life at that time? Why were they important? Did they influence you for better or worse?

14. Did you change during your twenties? If so, do you think you changed a lot, somewhat, or very little?

15. How did you change?

16. Do you wish anything had been different about your twenties? If so, what?

17. THIRTIES: Tell me about your thirties. What incidents come to your mind? Did they affect you for better or worse?

18. Who were the most important people in your life at that time? Why were they important? Did they influence you for better or worse?

19. Did you change during your thirties? If so, do you think you changed a lot, somewhat, or very little?

20. How did you change?

21. Do you wish anything had been different about your thirties? If so, what?

22. FORTIES: Tell me about your forties. What incidents come to your mind? Did they affect you for better or worse?

23. Who were the most important people in your life at that time? Why were they important? Did they influence you for better or worse?

24. Did you change during your forties? If so, do you think you changed a lot, somewhat, or very little?

25. How did you change?

26. Do you wish anything had been different about your forties? If so, what?

27. FIFTIES: Tell me about your fifties. What incidents come to your mind? Did they affect you for better or worse?

28. Who were the most important people in your life at that time? Why were they important? Did they influence you for better or worse?

29. Did you change during your fifties? If so, do you think you changed a lot, somewhat, or very little?

30. How did you change?

31. Do you wish anything had been different about your fifties? If so, what?

32. SIXTIES: Tell me about your sixties. What incidents come to your mind? Did they affect you for better or worse?

33. Who were the most important people in your life at that time? Why were they important? Did they influence you for better or worse?

34. Did you change during your sixties? If so, do you think you changed a lot, somewhat or very little?

35. How did you change?

36. Do you wish anything had been different about your sixties? If so, what?

37. EXPERIENCE: What has been your most difficult experience?

38. How did you handle it?

39. What has been your best experience?

40. OCCUPATION: How did you come to choose your present (or if unemployed, previous) occupation or line of work? Why did you choose it?

41. Do you wish you'd chosen a different occupation or line of work? Why or why not? What work would you have chosen? Why?

42. Do you hope to change occupations? To what? Why? What are the chances?

43. What are the advantages of your present (previous) occupation?

44. What are the disadvantages of your present (previous) occupation?

45. Have you ever been employed in a different line of work? Why did you leave? Would you go back to it?

(Note: The above questions will be asked of all women who are currently employed full-time, all who are currently employed part-time, but who therefore fall into the category of married-unemployed, and the wording will be adjusted to accommodate those who have been employed but are not currently. The object is to get at attitudes toward occupation/ working.)

46. MOTHERHOOD: Have you ever had children? Was having, or not having, children a matter of luck, or was it a conscious decision on your part?

47. What are the advantages of motherhood?

48. What are the disadvantages of motherhood?

49. If you had this decision to make again, would you say you would definitely have children, definitely not have children, or have mixed feelings?

50. SUPPORT NETWORK: When you have a problem, what people can you turn to for support or help?

51. FRIENDS: What do you like to do with friends? How often do you do something with a friend? Would you say you do something 2–3 times a week, once a week, or once a month or less?

52. DECISIONS: What were the most important decisions you made during your life? How did they change your life? Do you think they were the right decisions, the wrong decisions, or somewhat in between?

53. Have you ever made a seemingly minor decision that changed your life?

54. Do you feel mostly responsible for these decisions, somewhat responsible, or were they a matter of luck?

55. Have there been important decisions made by others that affected your life?

56. POSSESSIONS: What is your most private and personal possession? Why? What does it mean to you?

57. Have you ever lost something very important to you? What did it mean to you?

58. PLACES: What places have you been that you especially love? Why do you love them?

59. Is there any place you especially hate?

60. GENERAL TRANSCENDENCE: I am going to show you a list of activities. Would you please check off the activities you engage in once a day, once a week, or once a month or less.

	Once a day	*Once a week*	*Once a month*
TV			
Movies			
Drugs			
Religious			
Music/play an instrument			
Music/listen			
Arts/crafts			
Read			
Garden			
Athletic sports/participate			
Athletic sports/watch			
Board or card games			
Alcohol			
Collection			
Clubs/organization meetings			
Volunteer			
Other (Specify)			

61. I note that you engage in (specific activities) often? Could you please tell me why you like to do them?

62. HEALTH: Do you have any health problems? What are they? Would you say they are very distressing to you, somewhat distressing, or not very distressing?

Health Problem   *Very*   *Somewhat*   *Not*

63. Do you have any trouble sleeping, either getting to sleep or early waking?

64. Have you had any recent weight gain or loss in excess of five pounds?

65. When last did you visit a physician? Are you under regular medical care?

66. When last did you visit a counselor, psychologist, psychiatrist, or therapist?

67. Are you on any regular medication at present?

68. AFFECT: Can you tell me some of the things that make you happy, such as activities, thoughts, people? Why do they make you happy?

69. Can you tell me some of the things that make you sad? Why?

70. HISTORY: Would you say there have been any historical events, or movements, or things happening in your community, country, or world that have influenced how you lived your life? What are they, and how have they influenced you? (Probe women's movement?) For the better or the worse?

71. APPEARANCE TO WORLD: How would you describe the way you dress?

72. Why do you dress as you do rather than in some other ways?

73. What do you think your appearance says to others about you? What would you like it to say?

74. Are you generally satisfied or dissatisfied with your appearance?

75. How would you describe your home—its smells, feelings, etc.?

76. What do you think your home says to others about you? What would you like it to say?

77. Are you generally satisfied or dissatisfied with your home?

78. DESPAIR: Would you rate the following statement as True or False: "Most people lead lives of quiet desperation."

79. CONTROL: How much control do you feel you have over your life? Would you say you have a lot of control, a moderate amount, or not very much?

80. In what ways would you say you have not had much control?

81. Do you think of yourself as a winner, a loser, or something in between?

82. In what ways do you think of yourself as a winner? A loser?

83. REGRETS: Do you regret some things that you did not do? What were they? Why do you regret them? Why didn't you do them?

84. Do you regret some things that you did? What were they? Why do you regret them? Why did you do them?

85. DISAPPOINTMENTS: Are there any disappointments in life that have bothered you over an extended period of time? What are they?

86. Was there ever a time that you were very fearful? When was that? Why were you fearful?

87. DEATH AND DYING: How do you feel about death (your own)? What do you think it's going to be like?

88. What do you think is the appropriate or good death?

89. What have been your experiences with death? What were they like?

90. If you could write your own epitaph, how would it read? (How would you like to be remembered?)

91–105. TEMPLER: I'm going to read and show you 15 statements. Would you please tell me if they are True or False about your own feelings.

91. I am very much afraid to die.

92. The thought of death seldom enters my mind.

93. It doesn't make me nervous when people talk about death.

94. I dread to think about having to have an operation.

95. I am not at all afraid to die.

96. I am not particularly afraid of (getting) cancer.

97. The thought of death never bothers me.

98. I am often distressed by the way time flies so very rapidly.

99. I fear dying a painful death.

100. The subject of life after death troubles me greatly.

101. I am really scared of having a heart attack.

102. I often think about how short life really is.

103. I shudder when I hear people talking about World War III.

104. The sight of a dead body is horrifying to me.

105. I feel that the future holds nothing for me to fear.

106–113. SHNEIDMAN: I am going to show you some groups of
statements on cards. Would you please tell me the statement with
which you most agree.

106. To what extent do you believe in life after death?
   A. Strongly believe in it.
   B. Tend to believe in it.
   C. Uncertain.
   D. Tend to doubt it.
   E. Convinced it does not exist.

107. Regardless of your belief about life after death, what is your wish
   about it?
   A. I strongly wish there were a life after death.

   B. I am indifferent as to whether there is a life after death.
   C. I definitely prefer that there not be a life after death.

108. What does death mean to you?
   A. The end: the final process of life.
   B. The beginning of a life after death: a transition, a new beginning.
   C. A joining of the spirit with a universal cosmic consciousness.
   D. A kind of endless sleep, rest, and peace.
   E. Termination of this life but with survival of the spirit.
   F. Don't know.
   G. Other (specify) _____

109. What aspect of your own death is most distasteful to you?
   A. I could no longer have any experiences.
   B. I am afraid of what might happen to my body after death.
   C. I am uncertain as to what might happen to me if there is a life
   after death.
   D. I could no longer provide for my dependents.
   E. It would cause grief to my relatives and friends.
   F. All my plans and projects would come to an end.
   G. The process of dying might be painful.
   H. Other (specify) _____

110. If you were told that you had a terminal disease and a limited time to
   live, how would you want to spend your time until you died?
   A. I would make a marked change in my life style; satisfy hedonistic
   needs (travel, sex, drugs, other experiences).
   B. I would become more withdrawn; reading, contemplating,

praying.

C. I would shift from my own needs to a concern for others (family, friends).

D. I would attempt to complete projects; tie up loose ends.

E. I would make little or no change in my life style.

F. I would try to do one very important thing.

G. I might consider committing suicide.

H. I would do none of these.

111. How do you estimate your lifetime probability of committing suicide?
    A. I plan to do it some day.
    B. I hope that I do not, but I am afraid that I might.
    C. In certain circumstances I might very well do it.
    D. I doubt that I would do it in any circumstances.
    E. I am sure that I would never do it.

112. What efforts do you believe ought to be made to keep a seriously ill person alive?
    A. All possible efforts; transplantations, kidney dialysis, etc.
    B. Efforts that are reasonable for that person's age, physical condition, mental condition, and pain.
    C. After reasonable care has been given, a person ought to be permitted to die a natural death.
    D. A senile person should not be kept alive by elaborate or artificial means.

113. What are your thoughts about leaving a will?
    A. I have already made one.
    B. I have not made a will but intend to do so some day.
    C. I am uncertain or undecided.
    D. I probably will not make one.
    E. I definitely won't leave a will.

114. CONTRIBUTION: In reviewing your life, what contributions do you feel you've made? What are the most important things you've done?

115. HOPES: When you look back on your life five years from now, what do you hope to be able to say about it?

116. When you look back on your life at the end of it, what do you hope to be able to say about it?

117. HISTORICAL PERIOD: Is there any historical period when you would have liked to have lived? Why?

118. ALLPORT: What would you rather have than anything else in the world?

119. RETURN: If you could come back as anything you pleased, what would you come back as? (Person, Thing, Animal, Idea?) Why?

120. DEMOGRAPHICS: Do you feel being a woman has been mainly an advantage for you, a disadvantage, or neither?

121. Is it better to be a man or a woman? Why?

122. Do you feel your present age is an advantage, a disadvantage, or neither?

123. What is the best age to be and why?

124. What is the worst age to be and why?

125. ALONE: Do you need time to be alone? What do you need time alone for?

126. Do you get as much time as you need?

127. SECRETS: If you were to say you had a secret, what would it be about? Would you be willing to share it?

128. TIME: Are you usually early for an appointment, late, or on time? Why?

129. Do you feel time is very valuable, somewhat valuable, not that valuable? Why?

130. On what occasions does time seem to pass quickly for you?

131. On what occasions does time seem to pass slowly for you?

132. TIME AND MONEY: If you had all the money and time in the world, what would you do?

133. TEACH: If you could teach us a lesson about life, what would you teach us?

134. SENTENCE COMPLETION: How would you finish the following sentences?

134. Time is like a _____

135. The world seems like a place where _____

136. I have lost _____

137. Life is like a _____

138. My highest peak experience has been _____

139. PARANORMAL: Do you dream very much?

140. Some people have the same dream over and over. Do you? Could you tell me about it?

141. Have you ever had a very special dream that meant a lot to you? Could you tell me about it?

142. Have you ever had a near-death experience? What was it like? Would you say you are more afraid of death as a result of it, less afraid, or equally afraid?

143. Do you believe people can foretell the future?
Move things with their minds?
Have déjà-vu experiences?
Dream something about the future?
Have out-of-body experiences?
Communicate with the dead?

144. Have you ever had any experiences like these? What was it like? What did you make of it?

145. SONG: Do you have some song or a piece of music that you associate with something important in your life?

146. FANTASY: Many of us have secret fantasies or daydreams. (Offer: I love to think about going to another planet.) Do you have any like that that you would be willing to share?

147. SMALL LOSSES: Many little things often upset a person, such as missing a bus, or breaking a pencil. Could you name any little things that upset you, and tell me why they do?

148. LIFE THEME: When you think about your life, do you see some sort of theme(s) to it? If so, what do you feel it is? (Suggest "pattern" if they're stuck.)

149. If you were another person looking at yourself, would you see any theme(s) in it? (Or pattern.)

150. CONFLICT: Do you think there has been a central conflict or group of conflicts in your life which you have found hard to resolve?

151. LIFE MEANING: Do you believe life has a meaning? If so, what do you think that meaning is? (Why are you here in this world? What's the whole point of everything?)

152. When we talk about "meaning of life," how would you define it?

153. What makes life worth living?

154. Is there anything without which life would be meaningless to you? What?

155. LIFE REVIEW: Would you say you think about the above questions often, occasionally, or rarely or never?

156. How important is it to think about these things? Would you say it is not important, somewhat important, or very important?

157. What matters do you think about most?

158. Have you always thought about these things? If not, at what age did you start?

159. Do you think about these things more often as you grow older, less often, or about the same?

160. Do you think this interview will make you think about these matters more than you have in the past, less, or about the same? Do you feel that is a good thing or not? Why?

161. How do you feel about this interview? Are there questions you wish I had asked? What would they be? Were there questions you didn't like? Would you like to add something?

162. OFFER: After the interview, some people think of things they wish they had mentioned. Would you like me to phone you in a week or so to check on anything important you may have forgotten? In any case, you have my work telephone number in case you want to reach me.

Appendix D

Stressful Life Events Schedule

Below is a list of life events which have been rated as more or less stressful by many people. With a pencil, on a scale of 0–100, would you please rate how stressful you think they are, 0 being not at all stressful and 100 being most stressful. Do not use any number more than once. (For example, if you think two events are worth 100 points, give one 100 points and the other one a 99. A few events from your own life have been added in.) After you have rated these, would you please check off the events that have happened to you in the past year, or longer ago than that, noting the age, in the appropriate column.

Event	Rating	Experienced in last year	Longer ago Age
Death of spouse			
Divorce			
Marital separation			
Jail term			
Death of close family member			
Personal injury or illness			
Marriage			

Event	Rating	Experienced in last year	Longer ago Age
Fired at work			
Marital reconciliation			
Retirement			
Change in health of family member			
Pregnancy			
Sexual difficulties			
Gain of new family member			
Business readjustment			
Change in financial state			
Death of close friend			
Change to different line of work			
Change in number of arguments with spouse			
Mortgage over $50,000			
Foreclosure of mortgage or loan			
Change in responsibilities at work			
Son or daughter leaving home			
Trouble with in-laws			
Outstanding personal achievement			
Spouse begins or stops work			
Begin or end school			
Change in living conditions			
Revision of personal habits			
Trouble with boss			
Change in work hours or conditions			
Change in residence			
Change in schools			
Change in recreation			
Change in church activities			

Event	Rating	Experienced in last year	Longer ago Age
Change in social activities			
Mortgage or loan less than $50,000			
Change in sleeping habits			
Change in number of family get-togethers			
Change in eating habits			
Vacation			
Christmas			
Minor violations of the law			

Source: Adapted from The social readjustment rating scale, T. H. Holmes & R. H. Rahe, 1967, *Journal of Psychosomatic Research, 11,* 216, table 3. Copyright © by Pergamon Journals, Ltd. Permission to reproduce is gratefully acknowledged.

References

Ader, R. (Ed.). (1981). *Psychoneuroimmunology*. New York: Academic Press.

Ader, R., & Cohen, N. (1981). Conditioned immunopharmacologic responses. In Ader, R. (Ed.), *Psychoneuroimmunology*. New York: Academic Press.

Alexander, F. (1950). *Psychosomatic medicine*. New York: Norton.

Allport, F. (1937). Teleonomic description in the study of personality. *Character and Personality, 6*, 202–214.

Allport, G. (1962). The general and the unique in psychological issues. *Journal of Personality, 30*, 405–421.

American Psychiatric Association. (1987). *Diagnostic and statistical manual of mental disorders* (3rd ed., revised). Washington, DC: Author.

Anderson, G. (1982). How the mind heals. *Psychology Today, 16* (12), 51–56.

Ansbacher, H., & Ansbacher, R. (Eds.) (1959). *The individual psychology of Alfred Adler*. New York: Basic Books.

Applegath, J. (1982). *Working free: Practical alternatives to the 9 to 5 job*. New York: Amacom.

Aries, P. (1962). *Centuries of childhood*. New York: Vintage.

Aries, P. (1982). *The hour of our death*. New York: Vintage.

Arieti, S. (1974). *Interpretation of schizophrenia* (2d ed.). New York: Basic Books.

Arieti, S. (1978). *Severe and mild depression*. New York: Basic Books.

Aron, A., & Aron, E. (1986). *Love and the expansion of self: Understanding attraction and satisfaction*. Washington, DC: Hemisphere.

Aronson, E. (1984). *The social animal* (4th ed.). New York: Freeman.

Bandura, A. & Walters, R. (1963). *Social learning and personality development*. New York: Holt, Rinehart & Winston.

Bank, S., & Kahn, M. (1982). *The sibling bond*. New York: Basic Books.

Barnett, R., & Baruch, G. (1978). *The competent woman: Perspectives on development*. New York: Irving, Halsted, division of Wiley.

Barron, F. (1972). *Artists in the making*. New York: Seminar Press.

Barron, F. (1979). *The shaping of personality*. New York: Harper & Row.

Bartrop, R., Luckhurst, E., Lazarus, L., Kiloh, L., & Penny, R. (1977). Depressed lymphocyte function after bereavement. *Lancet, 1*, 834–836.

Baruch, G., Barnett, R., & Rivers, C. (1983). *Lifeprints: New patterns of love and work for today's women*. New York: McGraw-Hill.

Bass, E., & Thornton, L. (Eds.). (1983). *I never told anyone*. New York: Harper & Row.

Bateson, G. (1972). *Steps to an ecology of mind*. New York: Ballantine.

Beck, A., Rush, A.S., Shaw, B.F., & Emery, G. (1980). *Cognitive therapy of depression*. New York: Guilford.

Becker, E. (1973). *The denial of death*. New York: Free Press.

Belenky, M., Clinchy, B., Goldberger, N., & Tarule, J. (1986). *Women's ways of knowing: The development of self, voice and mind*. New York: Basic Books.

Bellah, R., Madsen, R., Sullivan, W., Swidler, A., & Tipton, S. (1985). *Habits of the heart: Individualism and commitment in American life*. New York: Harper & Row.

Bem, D. (1972). Self-perception theory. In L. Berkowitz (Ed.), *Advances in experimental social psychology* (Vol. 6). New York: Academic Press.

Benedict, R. (1934). *Patterns of culture*. New York: New American Library.

Berger, P. (1969). *The human shape of work*. New York: Macmillan.

Bergson, H. (1950). Time and free will: An essay on the immediate data of consciousness. New York: Macmillan. (Originally published in 1913)

Bermann, E. (1973). *Scapegoat: The impact of death-fear on the American family*. Ann Arbor, MI: University of Michigan Press.

Binswanger, L. (1958). The case of Ellen West. In R. May, E. Angel, & H. Ellenberger, (Eds.) *Existence: A new dimension in psychiatry and psychology*. New York: Basic Books.

Birren, J., & Sloane, R. (Eds.). (1980). *Handbook of mental health and aging*. Englewood Cliffs, NJ: Prentice-Hall.

Blasi, A. (1983). The self and cognition: The roles of the self in the acquisition of knowledge, and the role of cognition in the development of the self. In B. Lee & G. Noam (Eds.), *Developmental approaches to the self*. New York: Plenum.

Block, J. (1971). *Lives through time*. Berkeley, CA: Bancroft Books.

Bluebond-Langner, M. (1978). *The private worlds of dying children*. Princeton, NJ: Princeton University Press.

Book of common prayer. (1789). Burial of the dead, p. 332.

Boss, M. (1957). *Analysis of dreams*. London: Rider.

Bowen, M. (1978). *Family therapy and clinical practice*. New York: Jason Aronson.

Bowlby, J. (1969). *Attachment*. New York: Basic Books.

Braun, J., & Domino, G. (1978). The purpose in life test (review). In O.K. Buros (Ed.), *The seventh mental measurements yearbook*. Highland Park, NM: Gryphon.

Brim, O., & Kagan, J. (1980). *Constancy and change in human development*. Cambridge, MA: Harvard University Press.

Brislin, R. (1983). Cross-cultural research in psychology. In M. Rosenzweig & L. Porter (Eds.), *Annual review of psychology*. Palo Alto, CA: Annual Reviews.

Broughton, J. (1983). The cognitive-developmental theory of adolescent self and identity. In B. Lee & G. Noam (Eds.), *Developmental approaches to the self*. New York: Plenum.

Brown, G. (1981) *New celibacy*. New York: Ballantine.

Browning, R. (1922). "Prospice." In *Poems and Plays*. New York: Scribner's. (Originally published in 1864)

Buber, M. (1961). The way of man according to the teachings of Hassidism. In W. Kaufman (Ed.), *Religion from Tolstoy to Camus*. New York: Harper Torchbooks.

Buhler, C., & Massarik, F. (1968). *The course of human life*. New York: Springer.

Butler, R. (1968). The life review: An interpretation of reminiscence. In B. Neugarten (Ed.), *Middle age and aging*. Chicago: University of Chicago Press.

Butler, R. N., & Lewis, M. I. (1983). *Aging and mental health* (3d ed.). St. Louis, MO: Mosby.

Byrne, D. (1969). Attitudes and attraction. In L. Berkowitz (Ed.), *Advances in experimental social psychology* (Vol. 4). New York: Academic Press.

Campbell, Jeremy. (1986). *Winston Churchill's afternoon nap: A wide-awake inquiry into the human nature of time*. New York: Simon & Schuster.

Campbell, Joseph. (1961). *Hero with a thousand faces*. New York: Pantheon Books.

Camus, A. (1946). *The stranger*. New York: Knopf.

Camus, A. (1948). *The plague*. New York: Modern Library.

Casteneda, C. (1976). *The teachings of Don Juan*. New York: Pocket Books.

Chagnon, N. (1977). *Yanomamo: The fierce people*. New York: Holt, Rinehart & Winston.

Chapman, W. (1967). *The golden dream*. New York: Bobbs-Merrill.

Cherlin, A., & Furstenberg, F., Jr. (1986). *The new American grandparent: A place in the family*. New York: Basic Books.

Chesler, P. (1972). *Women and madness*. Garden City, NY: Doubleday.

Chiang, H., & Maslow, A. (1977). *The healthy personality*. New York: Van Nostrand.

Chiriboga, D. A., & Thurnher, M. (1975). Concept of self. In M. F. Lowenthal, M. Thurnher, D. A. Chiriboga, & Associates (Eds.), *Four stages of life: A comparative study of women and men facing transitions*. San Francisco: Jossey-Bass.

Clanton, G., & Smith, L. (1977). *Jealousy*. Englewood Cliffs, NJ: Prentice-Hall.

Clark, B. (1978). *Whose life is it anyway?* New York: Bard/Avon.

Cobb, S. (1974). A model for life events and their consequences. In B. Dohrenwend & B. Dohrenwend (Eds.), *Stressful life events: Their nature and effects*. New York: Wiley.

Cooley, C. (1902). *Human nature and the social order*. New York: Scribner's.

Crumbaugh, J., & Maholick, L. (1964). An experimental study in existentialism; The psychometric approach to Frankl's concept of noogenic neurosis. *Journal of Clinical Psychology, 20*, 200–207.

Csikszentmihalyi, M. (1975a). *Beyond boredom and anxiety*. San Francisco: Jossey-Bass.

Csikszentmihalyi, M. (1975b). Play and intrinsic rewards. *Journal of Humanistic Psychology, 15*(3), 41–63.

Csikszentmihalyi, M., & Beattie, O. (1979). Life themes: A theoretical and empirical exploration of their origins and effects. *Journal of Humanistic Psychology, 19*(1), 45–52.

Csikszentmihalyi, M., & Rochberg-Halton, E. (1981). *The meaning of things: Symbols in the development of self.* Boston: Cambridge University Press.

Cytrynbaum, S., Bluum, L., Patrick., R., Stein, J., Wadner, D., & Wilk, C. (1980). Midlife developments: A personality and social systems perspective. In L. Poon (Ed.), *Aging in the 1980's.* Washington, DC: American Psychological Association.

Datan, N., Rodeheaver, D., & Hughes, F. (1987). Adult development and aging. In M. Rosenweig, & L. Porter (Eds.), *Annual Review of Psychology, 38,* 153–180.

Davidson, G. (1978). *The hospice: Development and administration.* Washington, DC: Hemisphere.

Davis, L., & Cherns, A. (Eds.). (1975). *The quality of working life.* New York: Free Press.

DeBeauvoir, S. (1972). *The coming of age.* New York: Putnam's Sons.

De Ropp, R. (1960). *Drugs and the mind.* New York: Grove.

Deutsch, D. (1987). Reported in *The Seattle Times,* Science Digest, January 5.

Dewald, P. (1972). *The psychoanalytic process: A case illustration.* New York: Basic Books.

Diggory, J., & Rothman, D. (1961). Values destroyed in death. *Journal of Abnormal and Social Psychology, 63,* 205–209.

Dohrenwend, B., & Dohrenwend, B. (1974). *Stressful life events: Their nature and effects.* New York: Wiley.

Domino, G. (1978). The purpose in life test (review). In O.K. Buros (Ed.), *The seventh mental measurements yearbook.* Highland Park, NM: Gryphon.

Dumont, R., & Foss, D. (1972). *The American view of death: Acceptance or denial?* Cambridge, MA: Schenkman.

Elder, G. (1974). *Children of the great depression.* Chicago: University of Chicago Press.

Elkind, D. (1981). *The hurried child: Growing up too fast too soon.* Reading, MA: Addison-Wesley.

Ellis, B. (1985). *Less than zero.* New York: Penguin

Erikson, E. (1950). *Childhood and society.* New York: Norton.

Faden, R. R. (1986, August). *Presymptomatic screening in fetuses and adults: Moral and psychological issues.* Paper presented to the American Psychological Association, Washington, DC.

Faden, R. R., & Beautchamp, T. L., with King, H. M. P. (1986). *A history and theory of informed consent.* New York: Oxford University Press.

Farnsworth, P. (1969). *The social psychology of music.* Ames, IA: Iowa State University Press.

Farrell, M. P., & Rosenberg, S. D. (1981). *Men at midlife.* Boston: Auburn House.

Feifel, H., Hanson, S., Jones, R,. & Edwards L. (1967). Physicians consider death. *Proceedings of the American Psychiatric Association, 2,* 201–202.

Festinger, L. (1962). *A theory of cognitive dissonance.* Stanford, CA: Stanford University Press.

Finkelhor, D. (1984). *Child sexual abuse: Theory and research*. New York: Free Press.

Finkelhor, D. (1986). *A sourcebook on child sexual abuse*. Beverly Hills, CA: Sage.

Fischer, L. (1986). *Linked lives*. New York: Harper & Row.

Fischman, J. (1987). Type A on trial. In *Psychology Today, 21*(2), 42–50.

Flavell, J. (1963). *The developmental psychology of Jean Piaget*. New York: Van Nostrand.

Fox, B. (1981). Psychosocial factors and the immune system in human cancer. In Ader, R. (Ed.), *Psychoneuroimmunology* (pp. 103–157). New York: Academic Press.

Fraisse, P. (1963). *Psychology of time*. New York: Harper & Row.

Fraisse, P. (1963). Perception and estimation of time. In M. Rosenzweig, & L. Porter, (Eds.), *Annual Review of Psychology*. Palo Alto, CA: Annual Reviews.

Frankl, V. (1963). *Man's search for meaning: An introduction to logotherapy*. New York: Pocket Books.

Freud, S. (1901, reprinted 1960). The psychopathology of everyday life. In J. Strachey (Ed.), with A. Freud, *The standard edition of the complete psychology works of Sigmund Freud* (Vol. 6). London: Hogarth.

Freud, S. (1905, reprinted 1953). Three essays on the theory of sexuality. In J. Strachey (Ed.), with A. Freud, *The standard edition of the complete psychology works of Sigmund Freud* (Vol. 7). London: Hogarth.

Freud, S. (1910, reprinted 1957). Five lectures on psychoanalysis. In J. Strachey (Ed.), with A. Freud, *The standard edition of the complete psychology works of Sigmund Freud* (Vol. 11). London: Hogarth.

Freud, S. (1912, reprinted 1958). The dynamics of transference. In J. Strachey (Ed.), with A. Freud, *The standard edition of the complete psychology works of Sigmund Freud* (Vol. 14). London: Hogarth.

Freud, S. (1916–1917, reprinted 1963). On psychoanalysis: Introductory lectures. In J. Strachey (Ed.), with A. Freud, *The standard edition of the complete psychology works of Sigmund Freud* (Vol. 15). London: Hogarth.

Freud, S. (1917, reprinted 1957). Mourning and melancholia. In J. Strachey (Ed.), Freud, *The standard edition of the complete psychology works of Sigmund Freud* (Vol. 19). London: Hogarth.

Freud, S. (1920, reprinted 1955). Beyond the pleasure principle. In J. Strachey (Ed.), with A. Freud, *The standard edition of the complete psychology works of Sigmund Freud* (Vol. 18). London: Hogarth.

Freud, S. (1923, reprinted 1955). Totem and taboo. In J. Strachey (Ed.), with A. Freud, *The standard edition of the complete psychology works of Sigmund Freud* (Vol. 13). London: Hogarth.

Freud, S. (1923, reprinted 1961). The ego and the id. In J. Strachey (Ed.), with A. Freud, *the standard edition of the complete psychology works of Sigmund Freud* (Vol. 19). London: Hogarth.

Freud, S. (1925). Our attitude toward death. In *Collected Papers*. London: Hogarth.

Freud, S. (1926, reprinted 1959). Inhibitions, symptoms and anxiety. In J. Strachey (Ed.), with A. Freud, *The standard edition of the complete psychology works of Sigmund Freud* (Vol. 20). London: Hogarth.

Freud, S. (1930, reprinted 1961). Civilization and its discontents. In J. Strachey (Ed.), with A. Freud, *The standard edition of the complete psychology works of Sigmund Freud* (Vol. 21). London: Hogarth.

Freud, A. (1946). *The ego and its mechanisms of defense*. New York: International Universities Press.

Freud, S. (1953–1964). *The standard edition of the complete psychology works of Sigmund Freud,* James Strachey (Ed.), with Anna Freud. London: Hogarth.

Friedan, B. (1963). *The feminine mystique*. New York: Norton.

Friedman, M., & Rosenman, R. (1974). *Type A behavior and your heart*. New York: Knopf.

Friedman, M., & Ulmer, D. (1984). *Treating type A behavior and your heart*. New York: Knopf.

Friedman, W. (1982). *The developmental psychology of time*. New York: Academic Press.

Fromm, E. (1967). *Escape from freedom*. New York: Holt, Rinehart & Winston.

Garraty, J. (1957). *The nature of biography*. New York: Knopf.

Gendlin, E. (1962). *Experiencing and the creation of meaning: A philosophical and psychological approach to the objective*. New York: Free Press of Glencoe.

Gergen, K., & Davis, K. (1985). *The social construction of the person*. New York: Springer-Verlag.

Gilligan, C. (1977). In a different voice: Women's conception of self and morality. *Harvard Educational Review, 47*(40), 481–517.

Gilligan, C. (1979). Women's place in man's life cycle. *Harvard Educational Review, 49*(4), 431–446.

Gilligan, C. (1982). *In a different voice*. Cambridge, MA: Harvard University Press.

Glaser, B., & Strauss, A. (1965). *Awareness of dying*. Chicago: Aldine.

Glaser, B., & Strauss, A. (1968). *Time for dying*. Chicago: Aldine.

Goffman, E. (1959). *The presentation of self in everyday life*. New York: Anchor Books.

Goleman, D. (1987). Who are you kidding? *Psychology Today, 21*(3), 24–30.

Goodkin, K., Antoni, M.H., & Blaney, P.H. (1986). Stress and hopelessness in the promotion of cervical intraepithelial neoplasia to invasive squamous cell carcinoma of the cervix. *Journal of Psychosomatic Research, 30*(1), 67–76.

Gough, H. (1952) *The adjective check list*. Palo Alto, CA: Consulting Psychologists Press.

Guilford, J., & Fruchter, B. (1973). *Fundamental statistics in psychology and education*. New York: McGraw-Hill.

Guttman, D. (1968). Aging among the Highland Maya: A comparative study. In B. Neugarten (Ed.), *Middle age and aging*. Chicago: University of Chicago Press.

Haan, N. (1977). *Coping and defending: Processes of self-environment and organization*. New York: Academic Press.

Haley, J. (1978). *Problem-solving therapy: New strategies for effective family therapy*. San Francisco: Jossey-Bass.

Harmer, R. (1963). *The high cost of dying*. New York: Collier-Macmillan.

Heidegger, M. (1962). *Being and time*. New York: Harper & Row.

Henry, J. (1971). *Pathways to madness*. New York: Random House.

Hess, R., & Handel, G. (1959). *Family worlds*. Chicago: University of Chicago Press.

Hofer, M. (1984). Psychobiological perspective on bereavement. *Psychosomatic Medicine, 46*(3), 183–197.

Hoffman, L. (1981). *Foundations of family therapy.* New York: Basic Books.

Holland, N. (1985). *The I.* New Haven, CT: Yale University Press.

Holmes, T., & Masuda, M. (1974). Life change and illness susceptibility. In B. Dohrenwend & B. Dohrenwend, *Stressful life events: Their nature and effects.* New York: Wiley.

Holmes, T., & Rahe, R. (1967). The social readjustment rating scale. *Journal of Psychosomatic Research, 11,* 216, table 3

Horne, A., & Ohlsen, M. (1982). *Family counseling and therapy.* Itasca, IL: F. E. Peacock.

Horney, K. (1937). *The neurotic personality of our time.* New York: Norton.

Horney, K. (1950). *Neurosis and human growth: The struggle toward self-realization.* New York: Norton.

Hunt, M. (1974). *Secual behavior in the 1970's.* New York: Dell.

Huston-Stein, A., & Higgins-Trenk, A. (1978). Development of females from childhood through adulthood: Career and feminism role orientation. In P. Baltes (Ed.), *Life span development and behavior* (Vol. 1). New York: Academic Press.

James, W. (1890). *Principles of psychology* (Vol. 1). New York: Holt. (Reprinted 1983, Cambridge, MA: Harvard University Press)

Jenkins, C. (1971). Psychologic and social precursors of coronary disease. *New England Journal of Medicine, 284,* 244–255, 307–317.

Jenkins, C. (1976). Recent evidence supporting psychologic and social risk factors for coronary disease. *New England Journal of Medicine, 294,* 987–994, 1033–1038.

Jones, E. E., & Nisbett, R. E. (1972). The actor and the observer: Divergent perceptions of the causes of behavior. In E. E. Jones, D. E. Kanouse, H. A. Kelley, R. E. Nisbett, S. Valius, et al. (Eds.), *Attribution: Perceiving the causes of behavior* (pp. 79–94). Morristown, NJ: General Learning Press.

Jones, M., & Bayley, N. (1971). *The course of human development.* Waltham, MA: Xerox College Publishers.

Jowett, B. See Plato.

Jung, C. (1971). *The stages of life.* In J. Campbell (Ed.), *The portable Jung.* New York: Viking.

Kagan, J., & Moss, E. (1962). *From birth to maturity.* New York: Wiley.

Kahn, E. (1985). Heinz Kohut and Carl Rogers: A timely comparison. *American Psychologist, 40*(8), 893–904.

Kane, R., Wales, J., Bernstein, L., Leibowitz, A., & Kaplan, S. (1984). A randomized controlled trial of hospice care. *Lancet, 21,* 890–894.

Kanner, L. (1976). Parents' feelings about retarded children. In S. Harrison & J. McDermott (Eds.), *Childhood psychopathology.* New York: International Universities Press.

Kaplan, L. (1978). *Oneness and separateness.* New York: Touchstone/Simon & Schuster.

Kasl, S., Evans, A., & Niederman, J. (1979). Psychosocial risk factors in the development of infectious mononucleosis. *Psychosomatic Medicine, 41,* 445–466.

Kastenbaum, R., & Aisenberg, R. (1972). *The psychology of death.* New York: Springer.

Keats, J. (1943). Ode to a nightingale. In Sir Arthur Quiller-Couch (Ed.), *The Oxford Book of English Verse.* New York: Oxford University Press.

Kegan, R. (1982). *The evolving self: Problem and process in human development.* Cambridge, MA: Harvard University Press.

Kegan, R. (1983). A neo-Piagettian approach to object relations. In B. Lee & G. Noam (Eds.), *Developmental approaches to the self.* New York: Plenum.

Kelly, G. A. (1955). *The psychology of personal constructs.* New York: Norton.

Kerr, K. W. (1974). Death and grief counseling. Presented at the conference of the Association for Humanistic Psychology, Santa Barbara, CA.

Keyes, D. (1981). *The minds of Billy Milligan.* New York: Random House.

Kierkegaard, S. (1946). In R. Bretall (Ed.), *A Kierkegaard anthology.* Princeton, NJ: Princeton University Press.

Kimmel, D. (1974). *Adulthood and aging.* New York: Wiley.

Klinger, S. (1977). *Meaning and void: Inner experience and the incentive in people's lives.* Minneapolis, MN: University of Minnesota Press.

Koestenbaum, P. (1976). *Is there an answer to death?* Englewood Cliffs, NJ: Prentice-Hall.

Koestler, A. (1949). *The god that failed.* New York: Harper & Row.

Koestler, A. (1971). *The ghost in the machine.* New York: Henry Regnery.

Koestler, A. (1972). *The roots of coincidence: An excursion into parapsychology.* New York: Vintage Books/Random House.

Koestler, A. (1976). *The act of creation.* London: Hutchinson.

Kohlberg, L. (1973). Continuities in childhood and adult moral development revisited. In P. Baltes & K. Schaie (Eds.), *Life span developmental psychology: Personality and socialization.* New York: Academic Press.

Kohn, A. (1987). Shattered innocence. *Psychology Today, 21*(2) February, 54–58.

Kohut, H. (1977). *The restoration of the self.* New York: International Universities Press.

Kohut, H. (1984). In A. Goldberg (Ed.), *How does analysis cure?* Chicago: University of Chicago Press.

Kreilkamp, T. (1976). *The corrosion of self: Society's effects on people.* New York: New York University Press.

Kubler-Ross, E. (1971). *On death and dying.* New York: Macmillan.

Kuhn, T. (1962). *The structure of scientific revolutions.* Chicago: University of Chicago Press.

Laing, R. (1976). *The divided self.* New York: Penguin. (Original work published 1959)

Lakoff, G., & Johnson, M. (1980). *Metaphors we live by.* Chicago: University of Chicago Press.

Lazarus, R. (1966). *Psychological stress and the coping process.* New York: McGraw-Hill.

Lea, H. (1906). *A history of the inquisition of Spain.* New York: Macmillan.

Lee, B., & Noam, G. (1983). *Developmental approaches to the self.* New York: Plenum.

Leonard, G. (1968). *Education and ecstacy.* New York: Dell.

Levinson, D., with C. N. Darrow, E. B. Klein, M. H. Levinson, & B. McKee (1978). *The seasons of a man's life.* New York: Knopf.

Lewis, M., & Brooks-Gunn, J. (1979). *Social cognition and the acquisition of self.* New York: Plenum.

Livson, F. (1977). Patterns of personality development in middle-aged women: A longitudinal study. *International Journal of Aging and Human Development, 7*(2), 107–115.

Lonetto, R. (1980). *Children and death*. New York: Springer.

Machotka, P. (1967). Incest as a family affair. *Family Process, 6,* 98–116.

Maclean, D., & Reichlin, S. (1981). Neuroendocrinology and the immune process. In R. Ader (Ed.), *Psychoneuroimmunology* (pp. 475–520). New York: Academic Press.

Maddi, S. (1976). Developmental value of fear of death: Courage, creativity and enhancement of life. *University of Chicago Magazine*, Spring, 20–23.

Mahler, M. S. (1968). *On human symbiosis and the vicissitudes of individuation*. New York: International Universities Press.

Maier, S., & Laudenslager, M. (1985). Stress and health: Exploring the links. *Psychology Today, 19*(8), 44–49.

Malraux, A. (1949). *The psychology of art*. New York: Pantheon (Bollingen).

Markus, H., & Nurius, P. (1986). Possible selves. *American Psychologist, 41*(9), September, 954–969.

Marris, P. (1975). *Loss and change*. New York: Doubleday/Anchor.

Marsella, A., De Vos, G., & Hsu, F. (1985). *Culture and self: Asian and Western perspectives*. New York: Tavistock.

Maslow, A. (1968). *Toward a psychology of being*. New York: Van Nostrand.

Maslow, A. (1971). *The farther reaches of human nature*. New York: Viking.

Masters, W., & Johnson, V. (1966). *Human sexual response*. Boston: Little, Brown.

Masters, W., & Johnson, V. (1970). *Human sexual inadequacy*. Boston: Little, Brown.

Masters, W., & Johnson, V. (1981). Sex and the aging process. *Journal of the American Geriatrics Society, 29,* 385–390.

May, R. (1977). *The meaning of anxiety*. New York: Norton.

May, R., Angel, E., & Ellenberger, H. (Eds.), (1958). *Existence. A new dimension in psychiatry and psychology*. New York: Basic Books.

McClelland, D. C. (1961). *The achieving society*. Princeton, NJ: Van Nostrand.

McClelland, D., & Jemmot, J. (1980). Power motivation, stress and physical illness. *Journal of Human Stress, 6,* 6–15.

McKitrick, D. (1981). Counseling dying clients. In *Omega: The Journal of Death and Dying, 12*(2), 165–186.

Mead, G. (1934). *Mind, self and society*. Chicago: University of Chicago Press.

Menaker, E. (1982). *Otto Rank: A rediscovered legacy*. New York: Columbia University Press.

Meyer, L. (1956) *Emotion and meaning in music*. Chicago: University of Chicago Press.

Minuchin, S. (1974). *Families and family therapy*. Cambridge, MA: Harvard University Press.

Mitford, J. (1973). *The American way of death*. London: Hutchinson.

Moody, R. (1975). *Life after life*. New York: Bantam.

Moos, R. (1976). *Human adaptation*. Lexington, MA: Heath.

Moos, R. (1977). *Coping with physical illness*. New York: Plenum Medical Book Co.

Morris, W. (1975). *The American heritage dictionary of the English language*. New York: Houghton-Mifflin.

Mosak, A. (1979). Adlerian psychotherapy. In D. Corsini (Ed.), *Current psychotherapies*. Itasca, IL: Peacock.

Moustakas, C. (1958). *Loneliness*. New York: Prentice-Hall.

Muggeridge, M. (1974). *The infernal grove, chronicles of wasted time number 2*. New York: William Morrow.

Munroe, R., & Munroe, R. (1975). *Cross-cultural human development*. Monterey, CA: Brooks/Cole.

Munroe, R., Munroe, R., & Whiting, B. (Eds.). (1981). *Handbook of cross-cultural human development*. New York: Garland.

Murray, H. (1938). *Explorations in personality*. New York: Oxford University Press.

Myers, I. (1962). *Manual: The Myers-Briggs Type Indicator*. Palo Alto, CA: Consulting Psychologists Press.

Myers, I. (1977). *Supplementary manual: The Myers-Briggs Type Indicator*. Palo Alto, CA: Consulting Psychologists Press.

Neugarten, B. (Ed.). (1968). *Middle age and aging*. Chicago: University of Chicago Press.

Neugarten, B. (1987). *Acting one's age: New rules for old*. In E. Hall (Ed.), *Growing and changing: What the experts say*. New York: Random House. (Interviewed for *Psychology Today*, 1980.)

Nolen-Hoeksma, S. (1986). Cited in *The Chronicle of Higher Education*, January 28, 1987, p.7.

Ollman, B. (1971). Alienation: Marx's conception of man in capitalist society. London: Cambridge University Press.

Olsen, T. (1961). *Tell me a riddle*. New York: Dell.

Olsen, T. (1978). *Silences*. New York: Delacorte/Seymour Lawrence.

Orme, J. (1969). *Time, experience and behavior*. London: Ilifte Books.

Ornstein, R. (1969). *On the experience of time*. Baltimore, MD: Penguin.

Ornstein, R., & Sobel, D. (1987). *The healing brain: A new perspective on the brain and health*. New York: Simon & Schuster. (Cited in *Psychology Today*)

Osis, K., & Haraldsson, E. (1977). *At the hour of death*. New York: Avon.

Palmore, E. (Ed.). (1970). Normal aging: Reports from the Duke longitudinal study, 1955–1969. Durham, NC: Duke University Press.

Palmore, E. (Ed.). (1974). *Normal aging II*. Durham, NC: Duke University Press.

Papalia, D., & Olds, S. (1986). *Human development* (3d ed.). New York: McGraw-Hill.

Parke, R., & Asher, S. (1983). Social and personality development. In M. Rosenzweig & L. Porter (Eds.), *Annual review of psychology* (pp. 465–509). Palo Alto, CA: Annual Reviews.

Parkes, C. (1972). *Bereavement: Studies of grief in adult life*. New York: International Universities Press.

Paykel, E. (1974). Life stress and psychiatric disorder. In B. Dohrenwend & B. Dohrenwend (Eds.), *Stressful life events: Their nature and effects*. New York: Wiley.

Pedrick-Cornell, C., & Gelles, R. (1982). Elder abuse: The status of current knowledge. *Family Relations, 31*, 457–465.

Pelletier, K. (1977). *Mind as healer, mind as slayer*. New York: Delta.

Piaget, J. (1952a). *The child's conception of the world*. Totowa, NJ: Littlefield, Adams.

Piaget, J. (1952b). *The origins of intelligence in children*. New York: International Universities Press.

Piaget, J. (1970). *The child's conception of time*. New York: Basic Books.

Piaget, J. (1974). *The construction of reality in the child*. New York: Ballantine.

Pike, J. (1968). *The other side*. New York: Doubleday.

Plaidy, J. (1967). *The Spanish Inquisition: Its rise, growth and end*. New York: Citadel.

Plato. (1956). *Symposium*. B. Jowett (Trans.). New York: Branden.

Plaut, S. M., & Friedman, S. (1981). Psychosocial factors in infectious disease. In R. Ader (Ed.) *Psychoneuroimmunology* (pp. 3–30). New York: Academic Press.

Pogorolich, I. (1986). Interview on "The Today Show," April 8.

Rank, O. (1973). *The trauma of birth*. New York: Harper & Row. (Originally published in 1929)

Read, H. (1967). *Art and alienation*. London: Thames & Hudson.

Reich, W. (1951). *Selected writings*. New York: Noonday Press.

Ring, K. (1984). *Heading toward Omega*. New York: Morrow.

Rogers, C. (1961). *On becoming a person*. Boston: Houghton Mifflin.

Rogers, C. (1972). *Becoming partners: Marriage and its alternatives*. New York: Dell.

Rokeach, M. (1968). *Beliefs, attitudes and values*. San Francisco: Jossey-Bass.

Rorer, L., & Widiger, M. (1983). Personality structure and assessment. In M. Rosenzweig & L. Porter (Eds.), *Annual review of psychology* (pp. 431–463). Palo Alto, CA: Annual Reviews.

Rosenthal, R., & Jacobson, L. (1968). *Pygmalion in the classroom: Teacher expectation and pupils' intellectual development*. New York: Holt, Rinehart & Winston.

Rossi, A. (1980). Life span theories and women's lives. *Signs: Journal of Women in Culture and Society, 6*(1), 4–32.

Rossman, P. (1977). *Hospice: Creating new models of care for the terminally ill*. New York: Association Press.

Royce, J. (1981). *Alcohol problems and alcoholism: A comprehensive survey*. New York: Free Press.

Rubin, L. (1979). *Women of a certain age: The midlife search for self*. New York: Harper & Row.

Sabom, M. (1982). *Recollections of death*. New York: Harper & Row.

Sarbin, T. (1968). Role theory. In R. Lindzey & E. Aronson (Eds.), *Handbook of social psychology*. Palo Alto, CA: Addison-Wesley.

Sarbin, T. (1986). *Narrative psychology: The storied nature of human conduct*. New York: Praeger.

Sartre, J. (1964). *Nausea*. New York: New Directions.

Sartre, J. (1969). *Being and nothingness*. New York: Washington Square Press.

Satir, V. (1972). *Peoplemaking*. Palo Alto, CA: Science and Behavior Books.

Satir, V. (Ed.). (1967). *Conjoint family therapy*. Palo Alto, CA: Science and Behavior Books.

Saunders, C. (1959). *Care of the dying*. London: Macmillan.

Scarf, M. (1980). *Unfinished business: Pressure points in the lives of women*. Garden City, NJ: Doubleday.

Scarf, M. (1987). *Intimate partners: Patterns in love and marriage*. New York: Random House.

Schaef, A. W., & Fassel, D. (1988). *The addictive organization*. New York: Harper & Row.

Schoeck, H. (1966). *Envy: A theory of social behavior*. New York: Harcourt, Brace & World.

Schreiber, F. (1974). *Sybil*. New York: Warner.

Seashore, C. (1947). *In search of beauty in music*. New York: Ronald Press.

Seligman, M. (1975). *Helplessness: On depression, development and death*. San Francisco: Freeman.

Sellitz, C., Jahoda, M., Deutsch, M., & Cook, S. (1959). *Methods in social relations*. New York: Holt.

Serinus, J. (Ed.). (1986). Psychoimmunity and the healing process. Berkeley, CA: Celestial Arts.

Shakespeare, W. (1936). *The complete works of William Shakespeare*, William A. Wright (Ed.). Garden City, NY: Garden City.

Sherif, M., O. J. Harvey, B. J. White & C. Sherif. (1961). *Intergroup conflict and cooperation: The robber's cave experiment*. Norman, OK: University of Oklahoma Book Exchange.

Sherover, C. (1975). *The human experience of time: The development of its philosophic meaning*. New York: New York University Press.

Shneidman, E. (1970). You and death. *Psychology Today* questionnaire. *Psychology Today, 4*(3), 67–72.

Siegel, R. (1981) Accounting for "Afterlife" experiences. *Psychology Today, 15*(1), 65–75.

Silberman, A. (1963). *The sociology of music*. London: Routledge & Kegan Paul.

Siskind, J. (1975). *To hunt in the morning*. London: Oxford University Press.

Skinner, B. F. (1938). *The behavior of organisms: An experimental approach*. New York: Appleton-Century.

Skinner, B. F. (1971). *Beyond freedom and dignity*. New York: Bantam.

Slater, P. (1976). *The pursuit of loneliness*. Boston: Beacon.

Smith, M. B. (1978). Perspectives on selfhood. *American Psychologist, 33*(12), 1053–1063.

Smith, M. B. (1986, October 8). Value dilemmas and public health: A psychologist's perspective. Andie L. Knutson Memorial Lecture, School of Public Health, University of California at Berkeley.

Smith, M. B. (1985). The metaphorical basis of selfhood. In A. Marsella, G. DeVos, & F. Hsu (Eds.), *Culture and self: Asian and Western perspectives*. New York: Tavistock.

Solomon, G. F. (1981). Emotional and personality factors in the onset and course of autoimmune disease, particularly rheumatoid arthritis. In R. Ader (Ed.), *Psychoneuroimmunology* (pp. 159–182). New York: Academic Press.

Solomon, R., & Corbit, J. (1974). An opponent process theory of motivation. I: Temporal dynamics of affect. *Psychology Review, 8*, 119–145.

Sontag, S. (1972). The double standard of aging. *The Saturday Review, 55*, September, 29–38.

Sontag, S. (1979). *Illness as metaphor*. New York: Random House.

Stoddard, S. (1978). *The hospice movement: A better way of caring for the dying*. New York: Stein & Day.

Stokes, A. (1961). *Three essays on the painting of our time*. London: Tavistock.

Stokes, A. (1965) *The invitation to art*. New York: Chilmark.

Strauss, A., & Glaser, B. (1985). Awareness of dying. In S. Wilcox, & M. Sutton (Eds.), *Understanding death and dying*. Palo Alto, CA: Mayfield.

Stryker, S. (1984). Identity theory: Developments and extention. (Chair), *Self and social structure, conference on self and identity*. Symposium conducted at meeting of the British Psychological Society, University College, Cardiff, Wales. (Cited in Markus & Nurius, 1986)

Szasz, T. (1964). *The myth of mental illness*. New York: Secker & Warburg.

Tatelbaum, J. (1977). *The courage to grieve*. New York: Harper & Row.

Tavris, C. (1982). *Anger: The misunderstood emotion*. New York: Simon & Schuster.

Templer, D. (1970). The construction and validation of a death anxiety scale. *Journal of General Psychology, 82*(2), 165–177.

Templer, D., & Ruff, F. (1971). Death anxiety scale means, standard deviations and embedding. *Psychological Reports, 29*, 173.

Thomas, A., & Chess, S. (1977). *Temperament and development*. New York: Brunner/ Mazel.

Thomas, D. (1952). Do not go gentle into that good night. In *The poems of Dylan Thomas*. New York: New Directions.

Tillich, P. (1952). *The courage to be*. New Haven, CT: Yale University Press.

Tolstoy, L. (1960). *The death of Ivan Illych and other stories*. New York: Signet Classics. (Originally published in 1884)

Tomkins, S. (1978). Script theory. In E. Howe (Ed.), *Nebraska symposium on motivation* (Vol. 26). Lincoln, NE: University of Nebraska Press.

Traphagan, J., & Traphagan, W. (1986). The nature of meaning in music. *ReVision, 9*(1) 99–104.

Treisman, A. (1963). Temporal discrimination and the indifference interval: Implications for a model of the internal clock. Psychological Monographs, 77(573).

Triandis, H. (1980). *Handbook of cross-cultural psychology*. Boston, MA: Allyn & Bacon.

Turkel, S. (1975). *Working*. New York: Avon.

Ueland, B. (1987). *If you want to write*. St. Paul, MN: Graywolf. (Originally published in 1938).

U.S. Bureau of the Census. (1986). Statistical Abstract of the United States. (1987). (107th ed.). Washington, DC.

Vaillant, G. (1977). *Adaptation to life*. Boston: Little, Brown.

Vaillant, G. (1979). Natural history of male psychological health: Effects of mental health on physical health. *New England Journal of Medicine, 301*, 1249–1254.

Villon, F, (1960). Ballades des dames du temps jadis. In A. Legarde & L. Michard (Eds.), *Moyen age*. Paris: Bordes.

Vogt, E. (1970). *The Zinacantecos of Mexico: A modern Maya way of life*. New York: Holt, Rinehart & Winston.

Walster, E., & Walster, G. (1978). *A new look at love*. Reading, MA: Addison-Wesley.

Wass, H., & Corr, C. (Eds.). (1984a). *Childhood and death*. Washington, DC: Hemisphere.

Wass, H., & Corr, C. (Eds.). (1984b). *Helping children cope with death: Guidelines and resources*. Washington, DC: Hemisphere.

Weenolsen, P. (1977, 1981). *Loss and transcendence life history interview*. Forms A, B and C.

Weenolsen, P. (1978). *The road not taken: A study in life themes*. Unpublished manuscript, University of California, Santa Cruz.

Weenolsen, P. (1982). *The creation of meaning over the life span: A new theoretical approach to life span development*. Ann Arbor, MI: Xerox Publishing Corporation. (Dissertation completed at University of California, Santa Cruz)

Weenolsen, P. (1985a, April). *The creation of meaning over the life span*. Presented at the Western Psychological Association Convention, San Jose, CA.

Weenolsen, P. (1985b, August). *Loss and transcendence life themes*. Presented at the 93d annual convention of the American Psychological Association, Los Angeles, CA.

Weenolsen, P. (1986a). *Loss and transcendence life themes*. Los Angeles: American Psychological Association (ERIC Document Reproduction Service No. ED 262 354).

Weenolsen, P. (1986b, April). *An exploration of loss as a metaphor of death*. Presented to the annual convention of the Association for Death Education and Counseling, Atlanta, GA.

Weenolsen, P. (1986c, May). *The origins of loss and transcendence life themes*. Presented to the Western Psychological Association at the annual convention, Seattle, WA.

Weenolsen, P. (1986d, June). *Women's loss and transcendence life themes*. Presented with Drs. Patricia Sullivan of Seattle University and Kathy Steckline of Loras College, Dubuque, IA, to the National Women's Studies Association as part of a symposium entitled *Life themes*, Champaign-Urbana, IL.

Weenolsen, P. (1986e, August). *Life and self meaning: The process of their creation*. Presented to the American Psychological Association at the annual convention, Washington, DC.

Weenolsen, P. (1987a, August). *The representation of life and death: Individual "metaphorical systems."* Presented at the annual convention of the American Psychological Association, New York, NY.

Weenolsen, P. (1987b, May). *The extent, nature and purpose of the life review*. Presented at the annual convention of the Western Psychological Association, Long Beach, CA.

Weenolsen, P. (1987c). *Life and self meaning: The process of their creation*. Washington, DC: American Psychological Association (ERIC Document Reproduction Service No. ED 274 913).

Weenolsen, P. (1988, May). *Life dreams in childhood and adolescence: How they turned out*. Presented at the annual convention of the Western Psychological Association, Burlingame, CA.

Weenolsen, P. (in press). The influence of parental death on identity formation: An existential analysis of *The neverending story*. In *Proceedings of the Children's Literature Association*. (Part of a two-paper presentation on Grieving in Children's Literature, with Dr. Hamida Bosmajian, Seattle University. Presented at the Annual Children's Literation Association Convention, June 1986, Kansas City, MO)

Weenolsen, P., & Barron, F. (1979). *The roots of dualism: A split in the grammatical fiction. Psychobiography of Arthur Koestler*. Unpublished manuscript, University of California, Santa Cruz.

Wegner, D., & Vallacher, R. (1980). *The self in social psychology*. New York: Oxford University Press.

Weil, A. (1972). *The natural mind*. Boston: Houghton Mifflin.

White, G., & Kirkpatrick, J. (1985). *Person, self and experience: Exploring Pacific ethnopsychologies*. Berkeley, CA: University of California Press.

White, R. (1975). *Lives in progress*. New York: Holt, Reinhart & Winston.

Whiting, J., & Child, I. (1973). *Child training and personality*. New Haven, CT: Yale University Press.

Whiting, B., & Whiting, B. (1975) *Children of six cultures*. Cambridge, MA: Harvard University Press.

Wilcox, S., & Sutton, M. (Eds.). (1985). *Understanding death and dying* (3d ed.). Palo Alto, CA: Mayfield.

Wilson, E. O. (1975). *Sociobiology*. Cambridge, MA: Harvard University Press.

Wolff, C., Friedman, S., Hofer, M., & Mason, J. (1964). Relationship between psychological defenses and mean urinary 17-hydroxycorticosteroid excretion rates: A predictive study of parents of fatally ill children. *Psychosomatic Medicine, 64*, 576–591.

Wood, C. (1986). The hostile heart. *Psychology Today, 20*(9), 10–12.

Worden, W. (1982). *Grief counseling and grief therapy: A handbook for the mental health practitioner*. New York: Springer.

Wylie, R. (1979). *The self concept: A critical survey of pertinent research literature*. Lincoln, NE: University of Nebraska Press.

Yalom, I. (1981). *Existential psychotherapy*. New York: Basic Books.

Yalom, I. (1985). *The theory and practice of group psychotherapy*. New York: Basic Books.

Yankelovich, D. (1981). *New rules: Searching for self-fulfillment in a world turned upside down*. New York: Random House.

Zimbardo, P. (1984). *Shyness*. New York: Jove.

Zinker, J., & Fink, S. (1966). The possibility for psychological growth in a dying person. *Journal of General Psychology, 74*, April, 185–199.

Index